JAPANESE MAPLES

JAPANESE

MAPLES

THE COMPLETE GUIDE TO SELECTION AND CULTIVATION

FOURTH EDITION

J. D. VERTREES & PETER GREGORY

TIMBER PRESS
Portland · London

Photographs and paper records created and assembled by J. D. Vertrees were donated by his family to the Oregon State University Archives in 1993 and are maintained by the Archives as the J. D. Vertrees Papers. These materials include correspondence, reports, published materials, and photographs pertaining to Japanese maples as well as other subjects of interest to Vertrees, including weeds and insects. The bulk of the Vertrees Papers pertains to his authorship of *Japanese Maples*; photographs published in that volume as well as numerous other photographs are part of the collection. For more information about this or other horticultural collections, please contact the OSU Archives, 94 Kerr Administration Building, Corvallis, Oregon 97331, or visit the OSU Archives Web site at http://osu.orst.edu/dept/archives.

Previously published as *Japanese Maples: Momiji and Kaede* in 1978 (first edition), 1987 (second edition), and 2001 (third edition).

Published in 2009 by Timber Press, Inc.

The Haseltine Building
133 S.W. Second Avenue, Suite 450
Portland, Oregon 97204-3527
www.timberpress.com

2 The Quadrant
135 Salusbury Road
London NW6 6RJ
www.timberpress.co.uk

Printed in China
Text designed by Susan Applegate

Library of Congress
Cataloging-in-Publication Data

Vertrees, J. D.
    Japanese maples: the complete guide to selection and cultivation/J. D. Vertrees, Peter Gregory—4th ed.
        p. cm.
    Includes bibliographical references and index.
    ISBN 978-0-88192-932-4
    1. Japanese maple. 2. Maple—Japan.
I. Gregory, Peter, 1929– II. Title.
    SB413.J34V47 2009
    635.9′77378—dc22   2008050300

A catalog record for this book is also available from the British Library.

To Roseann
Without her unselfish encouragement,
wisdom, and devotion,
none of this
would have been possible.

—J.D.V.

To my close friends,
the late Harry Olsen
and his wonderful wife, Suzanne,
who have encouraged me
and arranged meetings
with numerous knowledgeable
North American maple growers
and enthusiasts.

—P.G.

CONTENTS

9 Foreword *by Hideo Suzuki*
11 Preface to the First Edition
by J. D. Vertrees
15 Preface to the Fourth Edition
by Peter Gregory

19 **Chapter 1: Character & History**
19 What Is a Japanese Maple?
20 *Kaede* and *Momiji*
20 The Character of Japanese Maples
23 Variegation
24 In Regard to *Fu*
25 History of Japanese Cultivars
27 Old Literature on Japanese Maples

29 **Chapter 2: Taxonomy & Nomenclature**
29 The Taxonomy of Maples
30 Systematic Treatment of the Genus *Acer*
31 Taxonomy of *Acer palmatum*
32 Nomenclature Difficulties and Confusion
34 The Naming of Plants Originating in the Wild
35 The Naming of Cultivars

39 **Chapter 3: Culture**
39 Culture in the Garden
51 Growing Japanese Maples in Containers
56 Pests and Diseases

65 **Chapter 4: Propagation**
65 Seedling Production
70 Grafting
77 Cuttings
78 Layering

81 **Chapter 5: *Acer palmatum* and Cultivars**

283 **Chapter 6: Other *Acer* Species from Japan and Their Cultivars**

333 Appendix A: Japanese Words and Their Meanings
336 Appendix B: Guide to Uses and Characteristics
349 Appendix C: Cultivars Not Yet Assessed
365 Appendix D: Cultivar Names Not Elsewhere Described
374 Appendix E: The Maple Society
375 Appendix F: Nursery Sources
378 Glossary
379 Bibliography
382 General Index
387 Index of Japanese Maples

FOREWORD

The history of horticulture in Japan cannot be told without mentioning maples. For hundreds of years, the maple has penetrated into the hearts and gardens of the Japanese people from all walks of life. As far back as the seventh century they admired and appreciated its beauty in a romantic way, as shown by a book of poems, *Man-Yoshu*, published in 614 A.D.

During the peaceful Edo era (1603–1867), the zeal and enthusiasm for cultivating this beautiful plant reached its height. People not only went out into the wild to enjoy it, holding maple-viewing parties, but also brought it into their places as a garden plant or as a bonsai. New varieties and new forms were especially sought after and poetic names given them as cultivars. A record shows that as many as two hundred named cultivars existed in those days.

However, to our regret, many of these cultivars were lost or disappeared during two world wars. As peace was restored both to the country and to the minds of the people, interest has revived and the popularity of the plant increased. Today our nursery owners are trying to select new cultivars to compensate for what we have lost, although it seems that the number of cultivars is still far from reaching that of old days. Growers now propagate them on a larger scale, and with the increasing popularity overseas, also ship them to other countries.

A maple is a must in every Japanese garden, large or small—planted in the ground or potted as bonsai. Maples are cherished in the gardens because of their brilliant crimson new spring growth, bright green leaves in summer, red or gold foliage in autumn, or the shapely appearance of branches in the winter. A maple never fails to grasp the hearts of people when they recognize the ever-changing beauty. Thus, for hundreds of years in Japan the maple has been the subject of poems, novels, dramas, paintings, and other art forms. It has played an important role in developing the culture of the country.

An old writing, *Chikinshō Foroku*, published by Ibei Itō in 1733, illustrates 36 cultivars. Associated with the name of each cultivar is an old, famous poem. For instance, beside the precise drawing of the leaf of an old cultivar called 'Shigitatsu sawa' is a poem printed in artistic calligraphy:

> *Kokoronaki minimo*
> *Aware wa shirarekeri*
> *Shigitatsu sawa no*
> *Akino yūgure*

Shigitatsu sawa means "snipes, or woodcocks, flying up from a swamp in winter." In the poem, the name of a place where

Facing: 'Eddisbury', fall color. Photo by Peter Gregory

snipes often stay is called Shigitatsu sawa. The gist of the poem is that even an insensitive person will deeply appreciate the charm of the scenery when standing by the maple cultivar 'Shigitatsu sawa' in the dusk of an autumn evening, as when standing by the Shigitatsu sawa swamp at the close of the day.

I have known the author of this book for many years. He was so fascinated with the beauty of these plants that he has devoted all his effort to intensive study of *Acer palmatum* and other maple species and their cultivars for more than 10 years. He also accumulated one of the most complete collections of cultivars to be grown in one place. Although all of them have been grown in Japan at one time, some of them have become extremely rare and others no longer exist in Japan to my knowledge.

I recognize that not a few cultivars are in the trade under mistaken names in countries where Kanji characters are not used but are supposed to be intriguing poetic names in Japanese. Also, many synonyms seem to be confused. The author of this book is dedicated to clarifying the nomenclature and describing all the cultivars, based on careful examination of his extensive collection.

This is the first book to be published on the subject in the English language. It will certainly be found useful around the world by gardeners, nursery professionals, arboreta, and horticulturists.

HIDEO SUZUKI

PREFACE to the First Edition

For more than 300 years Japanese maples have been developed and selected for their beauty and variation of form and color. Japanese horticulturists have contributed to the world a heritage of beauty from this group of plants which are indigenous to their country.

The native Japanese maple has the tendency to produce great variations within the species. By selection and cross-pollination, more than 250 cultivars have been developed. Plants to fit every need in landscaping can be found, from the extremely dwarf forms with minute leaves to the bold, upright types with large leaves. There are variations of foliage color in spring growth which are not found in other types of trees. Fall coloration among these cultivars becomes a second period of color explosion. There are variations of leaf shape, from tiny, crinkled, straplike, and lacelike to the bold, broad, large leaves of 'Ō sakazuki'. As time has passed, these beautiful ornamental plants have found their way around the world in horticulture. Discerning plant enthusiasts in many countries have recognized the beauty available in the use of these plants. They fit well with other genera as companion plants or make outstanding specimen plants.

A great many people associate the name "Japanese maple" principally with the dissected form known in horticulture as "red laceleaf maple" but desire information about other forms. Further confusion exists because other *Acer* species growing in Japan are included with the *A. palmatum* in commerce. Nursery owners, collectors, propagators, and maple enthusiasts have indicated a need for a guide to the determination of the numerous forms of these maples.

There are small books, now in print in Japan, which give good descriptions of many of the cultivars presently grown. Because they are printed in Japanese, they are largely inaccessible to English-speaking horticulturists. In the English-speaking world, there have been occasional writings in horticultural publications and magazines, together with annotated lists and taxonomic arrangements. Early nursery catalogs have given descriptions of some of the major cultivars. There has not been, however, a comprehensive work on Japanese maples which provides the English-speaking world a reference tool by which these maples may be understood.

This book has therefore been prepared to provide such a comprehensive source of information on, and description of, this general group of plants. "Typical" color leaf identification prints of most cultivars are presented to aid in determination of the cultivars. The difference between some cultivars is so slight that verbal descriptions may not be clear. Therefore, this is in part a book intended for identification.

The second purpose of the book is to clarify and simplify the nomenclature of these plants. Over many decades these plants spread from Japan to all parts of the world. In the course of this dispersion names have been confused, duplicated, lost, or new names substituted. The differences in languages, dialects, writing, spelling, and pronunciation, and the neglect of detail in many countries have created nomenclature difficulties and confusion.

I have spent many years collecting information, having documents translated, viewing cultivars in several countries, and collecting specimen plant material. In many cases by growing plants of various names side by side I have been able to demonstrate and clarify synonyms or misnomers. In other cases I have studied original descriptions in the literature or received propagating material from verified stock plants for comparisons. The generous assistance of arboreta, collectors, nurseries, propagators, and research stations from many countries has added greatly to the availability of plant material and information for these comparative studies.

My third purpose in writing this book has been to provide guidance to gardeners, landscapers, nursery owners, and others with an authoritative guide to propagation, cultivation, and horticultural characteristics of this extraordinarily useful group of plants.

This book is designed to meet the needs of four types of readers: the amateur gardener, the avid plant enthusiast, the commercial nursery professional, and the serious dendrologist. I hope that it will assist all readers in enjoying and understanding Japanese maples.

Acknowledgments

There will perhaps be some surprise that a comprehensive book on Japanese maples should come out of the little town of Roseburg, Oregon, in the United States. It is the result of a desire to learn as much as possible about these maples and to grow in one location for comparative purposes as many cultivars as we could find.

During the early years the progress in getting information and plant material was extremely slow. There were the readily available 8 or 10 cultivars produced commercially throughout the United States. There were also a very few short and general-subject articles and references in the English language. The only books which dealt in any depth with the subject were written in kanji (mainly illustrated with black-and-white pictures) and were of little use to me since I could not read Japanese.

Gradually, through correspondence and personal visits, we became acquainted with people who had segments of information on the subject. With the complete cooperation of an understanding wife, the collection of cultivars began to grow in numbers—slowly at first, but more rapidly in later years. We obtained plant material from cooperative people around the world. Also, the collection of information began to grow: old books, publications in Japanese and Chinese, descriptive material from other countries, paintings in rare publications, copies of old Japanese nursery catalogs, and a few rare Japanese horticultural publications. In addition, the files of helpful, friendly and informative correspondence grew rapidly.

It is to all the people who have helped in so many ways that I wish to express my sincere appreciation. In listing those who have been so helpful I do so with the fear that I may inadvertently omit someone who should be remembered. If I commit this error, I beg to be forgiven, it is not intentional.

Hideo Suzuki has been of immeasurable assistance in the entire production of this book. He is an outstanding authority in horticulture, particularly in azaleas and rhododendrons of Japan. As a life member of the American Rhododendron Society, President of the Japanese Rhododendron Society, and a frequent writer of horticulture articles, his authoritative assistance has been valuable. Hideo searched out obscure cultivars in the many islands of Japan and supplied descriptions and history of rare types. He also obtained books (some very rare) for my nomenclature and descriptive work. His ability and willingness to translate great amounts of Japanese writings into English gave authenticity to many cultivar descriptions and nomenclature. The countless hours and his tireless efforts on my behalf are gratefully acknowledged. This volume would have been less authentic without his assistance

D. M. van Gelderen has also contributed greatly to this book. His unselfish assistance in obtaining plant material and furnishing information has made the descriptions of cultivars and species much more complete. Dick and his wife, Hildi, devoted several days' time personally conducting us around the Netherlands, giving us an opportunity to see old plants of many cultivars which we do not see in the United States. The van Gelderens have an excellent nursery at Boskoop, Netherlands—Firma C. Esveld—where they specialize in rhododendrons, conifers, Japanese maples, and other high-quality plant material. Dick supplied a large amount of information in several years of correspondence with me. This included information on descriptions, nomenclature, and history. His article in *Dendroflora* (1969) was one of the more descriptive articles to come from Europe

in recent years. I am indeed indebted to the van Gelderens.

J. G. S. Harris of Wiveliscombe, England, contributed greatly to the interest in other species of *Acer* (besides *A. palmatum* and *A. japonicum*), particularly those from Japan. Gordon is a well-recognized authority on the genus, widely traveled, and an excellent writer of many articles on maples and their propagation. Following his visit to Maplewood Nursery, we have had the pleasure of spending a few days at The Cottage, in Somerset, England. Many obscure Asiatic species have been grown and added to the Maplewood collection from seed supplied by him. His assistance rounded out my entire study of maples, and I am grateful to him.

I would also like to express my gratitude to Harold G. Hillier for the several hours he spent with us "talking maples." Going with him through Hillier Gardens and Arboretum at Jermyns (Romsey, Hampshire) was most educational. This aided greatly in my search for clarification and verification of many cultivars, descriptions and nomenclature.

Many individuals in arboreta have contributed greatly to this study. Plant material, information, and encouragement have all been unselfishly given over the years. At times, I well imagine I might have been of considerable bother to some of them. It would take many pages to list in detail all the assistance given me, and my gratitude is no less as I list them in a group: Academie Scientarium Hortus Botanicus Principalis (P. Lapin), Russia; Arnold Arboretum (Alfred J. Fordham, Richard E. Weaver Jr., Gary L. Koller, Stephen A. Spongberg and Jack Alexander), Jamaica Plain, Massachusetts; Botanischer Garten and Botanisches Museum (Herr Kraft), Berlin-Dahlem, Germany; Knightshayes Garden Trust, The Cottage Garden (Michael Hickson),

Tiverton, Devon, England; Loth Lorien (Dan E. Mayers), Wadhurst, Sussex, England; Morton Arboretum (Walter E. Eickhorst), Lisle, Illinois; New York Botanical Garden (Thomas Delendick), Bronx, New York; Proefstation voor de Boomkwekerij, Boskoop, Netherlands; Trompenburg Arboretum (J. R. P. Van Hoey Smith), Rotterdam, Netherlands; United States National Arboretum (Sylvester G. March and Judith Shirley), Washington, D.C.; University of Washington Arboretum (Joe Witt and Brian O. Mulligan), Seattle, Washington; Willowwood Arboretum (Benjamin Blackburn), Gladstone, New Jersey; and Zuiderpark, The Hague, Netherlands.

Many people in nurseries as well as other horticultural enthusiasts have been cooperative in supplying information, history and plant material. I would like to thank the following friends: Fred W. Bergman, Raraflora, Feasterville, Pennsylvania; William Curtis, Wil-Chris Acres, Sherwood, Oregon; Toichi Domoto, Domoto's Nursery, Hayward, California; Herman J. Grootendorst, F. J. Grootendorst and Sons, Boskoop, Netherlands; Mrs. John Henny, Henny and Wennekamp, Salem, Oregon; the late Henry Hohman, Kingsville Nursery, Kingsville, Maryland; Boyd Kline, Siskiyou Rare Plant Nursery, Medford, Oregon; Jiro Kobayashi, Kobayashi Nursery, Japan; Michael Kristick, Wellsville, Pennsylvania; Roy Lancaster, Hillier Arboretum at Jermyns, Hampshire, England; John Mitsch, Mitsch Nursery, Aurora, Oregon; Ken Ogata, Forest Experiment Station, Meguro, Tokyo; the Don Smiths, Watnong Nursery, Morris Plains, New Jersey; Joel Spingarn, Dwarf and Rare Plants, Baldwin, New York; Arnold Teese, Yamina Rare Plants, Monbulk, Victoria, Australia; Robert Ticknor, North Willamette Experimental Station, Oregon State University, Aurora, Oregon; Y. Tsukamoto, College of Agriculture, Kyōto University, Kyōto, Japan; Richard P. Wolff, Red Maple Nursery, Media, Pennsylvania; and Arthur Wright Jr., Wright's Nursery, Canby, Oregon.

In every large undertaking there is one outstanding factor that makes the entire procedure possible. In my case, it is my wife, Roseann. Her contribution was of prime importance and consisted of grammatical reconstruction, editing, guidance, encouragement, patience, and countless hours of typing and retyping.

My eternal gratitude!

J. D. VERTREES

PREFACE to the Fourth Edition

WHEN J. D. VERTREES PUBLISHED *JAPA-nese Maples* in 1978, he wanted to provide a comprehensive source of information on the culture, identification, and nomenclature of Japanese maple cultivars. He also intended to reduce confusion and bring stability to the naming of these cultivars. That his volume has become an invaluable reference book, the bible for maple growers and enthusiasts worldwide, is a measure of its success in achieving these objectives.

Since the last revision of this work in 2001, communications and the exchange of plants and materials between maple growers worldwide has mushroomed, resulting in almost a doubling of the Japanese maple cultivars now grown and collected by enthusiasts. Hence the time is appropriate for a larger, expanded 4th edition incorporating many of the newer cultivars and any changes in the growing techniques, taxonomy and nomenclature which have occurred in recent years—thus making it a more comprehensive up-to-date reference or encyclopedia of Japanese maples. And, as in the previous edition, to avoid endless repetition, cultivars of *Acer palmatum* are cited without a species name (for example, 'Red Pygmy'), while cultivars of other species are always cited with the appropriate species name (for example, *A. japonicum* 'Green Cascade').

The introductory chapters remain essentially unchanged, although some topics are given more or less attention to reflect current trends. Chapter 2 places more emphasis on how to avoid and correct illegitimate cultivar names, chapter 3 has an expanded section on growing maples in containers, and chapter 4 moves away from commercial propagation methods toward those for garden and amateur enthusiasts.

Clearly, the main revision occurs in the plant description chapters with the inclusion of more than 100 additional cultivars which have proven their worth or become readily available since 2001. A total of some 420 *A. palmatum* cultivars are described in chapter 5, while 80 cultivars of other Japanese maple species, including those of *A. japonicum*, are described in chapter 6. Between them, chapters 5 and 6 cover the majority of the Japanese maples in cultivation. The remaining cultivars are briefly described or listed in appendices C and D. The descriptions of cultivars known in the late 1970s are primarily derived from specimens growing in the Maplewood collections, augmented by written material from early literature. The descriptions of the newer cultivars are based on specimens seen in various collections and nurseries, material received, and information provided by the originators or other knowledgeable collectors and growers. It has been difficult to describe adequately all the subtle differences occurring between cultivars.

The plant descriptions indicate the likely mature size of a plant grown under normal garden conditions and care. The detailed leaf measurements have been replaced with general terms for size—small, medium, large—which are more useful to most gardeners. Where it has been possible to accurately determine the meaning of Japanese cultivar names, that information has been added. Since most Japanese maples can grow in normal garden conditions in USDA hardiness zones 5 through 9, that information is omitted from the individual plant descriptions. Plants noted as being "tender" are only cold-hardy to zone 6. The color illustrations of the foliage were planned to assist in identification and not to present landscape situations. Where practical, an attempt has been made to include photographs which show the plant's main attractive feature, whether spring or autumn color, winter stems, unusual foliage, or so forth.

The appendices have been updated. An additional appendix includes a list of plant suppliers who stock a good range of Japanese maples. The index, with nearly 2300 plant names, serves as the definitive list of all published Japanese cultivar names. Included in the index are all the Japanese maple cultivar names published in books, journals, and major catalogs of growers, including synonyms, and the names of cultivars no longer in cultivation—so that *Japanese Maples* will continue to be the foremost reference book for this wonderfully versatile collection of ornamental plants.

This revision could not have been accomplished without the cooperation, help, advice, and encouragement of numerous friends, colleagues, and correspondents.

Conscientious attempts have been made to check the correctness of the cultivar names, origins, and descriptions acquired from my own knowledge and experience or from information and material received, to maintain the standards set by J. D. Vertrees. Whenever possible, samples from two or more different sources were compared. Hence, any errors or weaknesses that may have crept in are mine and mine alone.

It is hoped that these additions and changes will help to foster and strengthen J. D. Vertrees' principal aim of introducing stability in the naming of Japanese maple cultivars while, at the same time, preserving his ideas, research, and unique style of writing.

Acknowledgments

For their willingness to provide information and encouragement I would like to thank Brendan Gallagher, Plantiles Plant and Garden Centre, Chertsey, Surrey, England; Nello and Giordano Gilardelli, Fratelli Gilardelli Nursery, near Milan, Italy; Jan Kelley, Kelleygreen Nursery, Drain, Oregon; David Morrey, F. Morrey and Sons, Tarporly, Cheshire, England; Kerin Owen, Otter Nurseries, Ottery St. Mary, Devon, England; and Alan Trott, Trott's Nursery and Garden, Ashburton, New Zealand.

I would like to express my appreciation to the following, who made available plant material for the descriptions of particular plants, and provided valuable information and encouragement: Allen Coombes, Sir Harold Hillier Gardens and Arboretum, Romsey, Hampshire, England; John Emery, Raraflora Nursery, Berry, New South Wales, Australia; Harold Greer, Greer Gardens, Eugene, Oregon; Harold Johnston, Johnnie's Pleasure Plants Nursery, Tallassee, Alabama; Jim Rumbald, Duncan and Davies Nursery, New Plymouth, New Zealand; Billy Schwartz, Green

Mansions Nursery, Downington, Pennsylvania; and Don Teese, Yamina Rare Plants, Monbulk, Victoria, Australia.

In addition to help and encouragement, I am especially grateful to the following who gave me a warm welcome and generously allowed me to enjoy their plant collections and nurseries: Talon Buchholz, Buchholz and Buchholz Nursery, Gaston, Oregon; Judy and Frank Byles, F. W. Byles Company Nursery, Olympia, Washington; Don and the late Nancy Fiers, Mountain Maples Nursery, Laytonville, California; Primrose and Gordon Harris, Mallet Court Nursery, Taunton, Somerset, England; Dan Hinckley, Heronswood Nursery, Kingston, Washington; the late Howard Hughes, Montesano, Washington; Andre Iseli, Iseli Nursery, Boring, Oregon; Karen and Nick Junker, PMA Plant Specialities, Taunton, Somerset, England; Del Loucks, Del's Japanese Maple Nursery, Eugene, Oregon; Dick van der Maat, Nursery Laag, Boskoop, Netherlands; Baldassare Mineo, Siskiyou Rare Plant Nursery, Medford, Oregon; Tom Robuck and Larry Brooks, Mimaye Maple Nursery, Laytonville, California; Don Schmidt, Don Schmidt Nursery, Boring, Oregon; John and Matthew Skinner, Bartholemy and Company, Wimborne, Dorset, England; Clare and Ed Smith, Credale Nursery, Herefordshire, England; John Weir and Hugh Angus, Westonbirt Arboretum, Tetbury, Gloucestershire, England; and Ned and Wendy Wells, Wells Medina Nursery, Medina, Washington.

The generosity and helpfulness of everyone I have contacted has been impressive, but none more so than Haruko and Talon Buchholz, Ellen and Cor van Gelderen, plus Suzanne and the late Harry Olsen. My sincerest thanks go to these dear friends for the unstinting support, advice, encouragement, and warm hospitality.

Many thanks to Nicky Whelan, Gillian Truslove, Rosemary and Maurice Foster, and especially to my fiancée, Helen Jameson, for their help in preparing this manuscript. My thanks also to the staff of Timber Press, Neal Maillet and Anna Mumford for their patience and guidance, and my editor, Linda Willms, for her expert assistance in eliminating errors and in improving the readability of the text. Finally, my appreciation to Stewart and Sharon Wilson for the warm welcome during my visit to J. D. Vertrees' world-famous nursery, Maplewood, now a private garden. The Wilsons also graciously provided me with the opportunity and pleasure of meeting the sprightly Roseann Vertrees, whose kind permission to revise *Japanese Maples* made this exciting and worthwhile project possible.

Many photographs from earlier editions of *Japanese Maples* have been retained. New illustrations have come from my own collection and the picture libraries of Cor van Gelderen and the late Harry Olsen. Other photographs were generously loaned to me by Hugh Angus, Talon Buchholz, Harold Greer, Robert Jamgochian, Andrea Jones, Carl Munn, Daniel Otis, Ray Prag, Bernard Pye, Francis Schroeder, and Bill Schwartz.

PETER GREGORY

CHARACTER & HISTORY

What Is a Japanese Maple?

The term "Japanese maple" has two meanings. One is applied by the nursery industry which has often grouped all the cultivars of several *Acer* species under the general term "Japanese maples." Most often included in this group are all the cultivars and forms of *Acer palmatum*. Sometimes the cultivars of *A. japonicum*, *A. pseudosieboldianum*, *A. shirasawanum*, and *A. sieboldianum* are listed and, in some cases, forms of *A. buergerianum*, *A. crataegifolium*, *A. pictum*, *A. rufinerve*, and *A. truncatum*, even though several of these species, such as *A. buergerianum* and *A. pseudosieboldianum*, are not endemic to Japan.

The second meaning of the term "Japanese maple" is used by the serious dendrologist to indicate all 23 *Acer* species that are endemic to the islands of Japan and nearby territories. In some instances, writers group these plants with other Asiatic species. Central and eastern Asia include 106 of the 124 species recognized by P. C. de Jong, whose system of classification is followed here.

The horticultural group centers on several hundred cultivars of *Acer palmatum* plus those of *A. japonicum*. These cultivars have been bred, selected, and propagated since the early seventeenth century by the Japanese who, in their love of beauty and their infinite patience, have been most discerning in their selection. Like many other aspects of their horticulture, the selection of maple cultivars forms a great part of their heritage and has been shared with horticulturists around the world. Since the late eighteenth century, these cultivars have found their way into horticultural collections, arboreta, and the nursery industry.

In this book, I use the term "Japanese maples" to refer to the cultivars of *Acer palmatum* and *A. japonicum*. All of the other species from Japan with their cultivars I refer to as "maples from Japan." Many of these other species have interesting forms, horticultural cultivars, and varieties, which are becoming popular in ornamental horticulture. Though long neglected, these magnificent forms should be more widely used in the garden landscape.

The close relationship between *Acer palmatum* and *A. japonicum* (the "Japanese maples" of horticulture) and certain other *Acer* species (the "maples from Japan") is supported by taxonomy. More discussion of this topic is given in chapter 2. Here it is sufficient to simply note the species assigned to series *Palmata* in genus *Acer*: *A. ceriferum*, *A. circinatum*, *A. duplicato-*

Facing: The brilliant red and yellow foliage of Japanese maples brightens the otherwise dull fall garden.
Photo by Peter Gregory

serratum, *A. japonicum*, *A. palmatum*, *A. pauciflorum*, *A. pseudosieboldianum*, *A. pubipalmatum*, *A. robustum*, *A. shirasawanum*, and *A. sieboldianum*. Note that the only non-Asian species among them is the North American *A. circinatum*, the vine maple of the Pacific Northwest.

Kaede and Momiji

The Japanese language has two words for *Acer* species and cultivars: *kaede* and *momiji*. In academic contexts, *kaede* is more correctly applied; in horticultural contexts, both *kaede* and *momiji* are used. There seems to be no distinct separation in the use, although most often *momiji* is applied to maples such as *Acer palmatum* and its cultivars that have leaves with deeply separated lobes. Most other maples are called *kaede*.

The word *kaede* stems from the ancient word *kaerude*, composed of *kaeru*, meaning "frog," and *de*, meaning "hand." The lobed leaves of maples brought to mind the webbed hand of a frog. As the centuries passed, *kaerude* was shortened to *kaede*.

The word *momiji* may literally be translated "baby's hands," but it is not correct in this case to apply the meaning directly. Instead, one may apply it as "little baby extends its tiny hands which are like *momiji* (maple) leaves." The modern word *momiji* has a second meaning derived from the ancient verb *momizu*, meaning "becomes crimson-leaved" (Hideo Suzuki, pers. comm. to JDV).

The Character of Japanese Maples

I admit prejudice, but I feel this group of plants has one of the greatest ranges of use and beauty of any horticultural group in use today. The diversity of size, color, form, shape, and utility is so great that, when Japanese maples are selected wisely, they will fit almost any landscape need.

We do not think of them as flowering shrubs, although maples have very interesting blossoms, some quite colorful. The flowers are not a predominant characteristic. So many people do not even realize that maples flower. The blossoms of many cultivars, such as *Acer japonicum* 'Aconitifolium', are quite striking, though not large and perhaps of interest only to the more discerning gardener.

The lack of bold blossoms is more than offset by the great variation of leaf color and shape which these plants can add to the garden landscape. Spring foliage among the cultivars offers a wide choice in plant selection. The large forms display bold greens with rust or tangerine tones in the new foliage. The brilliant reds, orange-reds, and maroons of many upright forms will lend accent to plantings. Wide choices are also possible with the variegated white-pink-green leaves of maples such as 'Asahi zuru', 'Kasen nishiki', and 'Oridono nishiki'. Nothing could look more like a flowering shrub than the extraordinary shell-pink foliage of 'Corallinum', 'Karasu gawa', or 'Matsugae'. The eye can never pass lightly over the flare of color presented by the flaming foliage of 'Beni komachi', 'Chishio', 'Seigai', or 'Shin deshōjō', to name only a few. These brilliant fire-reds, crimsons, and tangerine-reds are so intense at times as to be almost fluorescent. All of these color combinations occur in the larger, more upright forms. The same choices occur in dwarf cultivars, which lend themselves to small companion plantings or container growing.

Unusual cultivars such as 'Hikasa yama' have a "flower" quality as the new buds open much like popcorn, with irregular unfolding leaves colored in yellows and reds. The new foliage of 'Tsuma gaki' also approaches a floral display. These stages last for several weeks, thus giving a long "flower" period. All the colored foliage retains its brilliance for at least one or two months, which is longer than the period during which most of our flowering shrubs will perform.

Maples with dissected leaves offer unusual brilliance and delicacy. Combinations of lacelike tracery of form, plus crimson, maroon, green-red, or variegated white-pink-green and red-pink-green tones blend in the most pleasing way with the delicate cascading of the plant form. These make breathtaking specimen plants. They are even more striking when planted in groups in the proper setting.

A second color display occurs each fall, which is surely an added bonus when comparing maples to most other flowering shrubs. This show of fall foliage color is absolutely spectacular. The bold color of 'Ō sakazuki', for example, adds a strong green accent all season, but then, in the fall, it bursts forth with the most vivid crimson flame display imaginable. Even in the early morning light or late evening dusk, the tones carry a fluorescent quality that demands attention. Equally vivid, but of a different crimson tonality, is the display of *Acer japonicum* 'Aconitifolium', the fernleaf japonicum. I hesitate to list specific cultivars, fearing readers will limit their thinking to just these few when the possibilities are almost limitless. Many of the *A. palmatum* cultivars present vivid yellow, orange, and red foliage. Most of the selections of *A. japonicum* are outstanding for fall color. The delicate, golden fullmoon maple, *A. shirasawanum* 'Aureum', follows the spring display of chartreuse, yellow, and green with a fall display of gold, crimson, and orange, blended at times with purple overtones. One must see to believe.

Fall colors are an inherent characteristic of *Acer* species and cultivars, but they can be suppressed or enhanced somewhat by growing conditions. The gardener who is aware of this malleability can aid nature in bringing about an excellent fall display. As late summer approaches and the late season growth is hardening off, it is best, when possible, to reduce the supply of moisture. Hardening a tree for fall will intensify the leaf coloration as the season advances and the colder temperatures begin to occur. A plant that has a continuous supply of water will retain the leaves in greenish condition well into the fall and may never color brilliantly. Eventually the leaves will just turn brown with the early winter temperatures and fall off. Slight stress, and I emphasize *slight*, will intensify the coloration of most maples. Too much stress (or neglect, as I mention elsewhere) and the leaves will rapidly turn brown and fall off. Discerning gardeners will find the best level of culture under their own conditions.

In addition to having two "flower" periods or seasons of striking coloration every year, maples come in such a wide range of sizes that there is a plant for every occasion. Some cultivars and selections of *Acer palmatum* subsp. *palmatum* form upright-growing trees. These can be expected to

Like colorful kernels of popcorn, new buds of 'Hikasa yama' open and leaves unfurl, creating a sensational kaleidoscope of red, pink, yellow, and cream. Photo by Peter Gregory

become trees up to 14 m (42 ft.) or more tall. They fit in a landscape in many ways—as accent plants, as shade for understory plants, in outline plantings along driveways and walks, interplanted with other similarly sized plants for naturalizing landscapes, or as outstanding specimen plants holding forth with their own importance.

Then there are the endless possibilities of the medium-sized selections. These include all the uses listed for previously plus others. Medium-sized maples can be interplanted with rhododendrons and other flowering shrubs to provide variety and color. The magnificent cascading maples, which would include all the laceleaf (or dissectum) cultivars, work well in

mixed plantings. Also available are numerous forms of lower-growing plants with great interest, such as 'Katsura', 'Shishigashira', 'Tsuchigumo', and linearilobums such as 'Red Pygmy'. These smaller maples naturally shape themselves into room-conserving plants and, with additional shaping and pruning, can be established in limited spaces.

Again, it is worth pointing out that the beautiful fall colors of these plants will brighten the otherwise dull fall garden. Even the red forms of the laceleaf and linear-leaved cultivars take on an entirely different appearance in the fall. Changing from their normal red, maroon, or greenish red tones of summer, they flame out in a glory of crimson or gold tones which dominate a planting in late fall and early winter.

Dwarf maples constitute another group that offers endless possibilities for use. Tucked in among alpine plants they will develop a blend of textures that cannot be attained with other plant groups. Dwarf maples are splendid companion plants with some of the smaller rhododendrons and other low-growing shrubs and perennials. They excel as accent plants in secluded nooks or in bold sites in an informal landscape. A wide range of dwarf cultivars is available: 'Goshiki kotohime' with magnificent miniature growth and foliage, 'Kotohime' with tiny leaves, and 'Koto ito komachi' with delicate foliage. All of these small plants are suitable for small landscape plantings as well as for containers ranging from large patio-sized pots down to small bonsai pots. By using the dwarf forms for bonsai, some of the problems of early training and establishment are overcome, but I hasten to say that any form of *Acer palmatum* and *A. japonicum* adapts quite well to bonsai. All of the cultivars and species have been used for this purpose. Because they respond so well to

The delicate lacelike leaves of 'Red Pygmy' turn from red-maroon in summer to a bright orange in late fall.
Photo by J. D. Vertrees

pruning and shaping, Japanese maples are an excellent choice for bonsai.

Variegation

The Japanese people have long been attracted to plants with variegated foliage. They have selected and bred such plants for centuries and still regard these plants with special fondness. The following story was told to me to illustrate the Japanese love of variegation. A variegated *Rhododendron degronianum* exhibited in the 1970s at an ornamental plant fair was priced at 20 million yen, which at the time was equal to 66 thousand U.S. dollars. (I wonder if business was booming!)

Variegation ranges from the extremes of a total lack of chlorophyll to a very subtle marking on a few leaves. *Acer buergerianum* 'Nusatori yama' has no green, the leaves emerging with a pink tone, soon changing to almost a pure white. Not quite so lacking in chlorophyll, 'Karasu gawa' has predominantly pink and white foliage, irregularly marked with small amounts of green. White and pink variegations also occur in a few of the laceleaf cultivars. At the other extreme is 'Iijima sunago' with strong red-green foliage minutely flecked with darker spots. 'Kasen nishiki' has very subtle minute white flecks almost overshadowed by the basic green leaf color.

Technically, these variegated maples belong in a physiological group called *chimeras*. The term indicates that on a single plant, a structure, in this case the leaf, may have two or more distinctly different types of tissue growing adjacent to each other. The white and pink variegations are totally devoid of chloroplasts in those cells and so lack the capacity to produce chlorophyll. The normal cells have chloroplasts producing chlorophyll and so are green in color. The mixture of these two types of cells within the leaf produces the pattern of variegation. (For a more thorough description of the genetic and cellular origin of chimeras, see any of a number of technical books on the topic such as the one by Hartmann et al. 2001.)

Some maple cultivars were named and selected because of color variation that occurs only in fall with the changing of seasons. I consider this a different source of "variegation" than that described above. Quite often the young stems producing variegated foliage also have a streaking of color tones in the bark. Some, like 'Oridono nishiki', have pink stripes in the green bark, often rather subdued.

It is sometimes claimed that maples grow out of their variegation. Perhaps as trees reach maturity their variegated character tends to become suppressed. I have taken wood from old plants of 'Versicolor' that had "lost" the variegation. By selecting young terminals from healthy side branches, I was able to produce grafted plants with variegated leaves.

I have observed in the nursery, and in older plantings, that culture may have a large influence on the retention of variegation. Plants that are overfed and that produce exceptionally long shoots of new growth may have the variegation suppressed in that wood. Markings may also be masked, or overcome, with excessive nitrogen feeding in the absence of sufficient phosphate and potash. This can be observed in container growing of young grafts.

Conversely, trees grown in totally unfavorable conditions may produce wood so lacking in vigor that the tendency toward variegation is masked. I have received scions from such types of plants and grafted well-marked plants. Summer foliage of the parent plant showed an almost total lack of marking.

Occasionally, a variegated cultivar of mine has produced a shoot that lacked all markings of the cultivar. I intentionally grafted from these shoots. The majority of these grafts resumed the characteristic variegation, while the remainder developed typical foliage. In view of this, I usually try to mark the best-variegated young growth on a cultivar during the growing season. Then, when collecting scions for grafting during the dormant season, I am able to cut the best-marked wood. This rule does not apply to all cultivars but only those that produce strong, unmarked shoots.

Other causes of variation in leaf markings include certain viruses, excessive soil pH, or a lack of one of the minor elements necessary for total nutrition. Such variations are all so different in appearance from true leaf variegation that they are immediately apparent. If in doubt, check with a plant disease expert; these individuals can usually give a prompt determination.

Variegated cultivars can only be perpetuated true to form through vegetative propagation. The seed from variegated cultivars will not produce the true form of the parent tree. There are a few exceptions. I have planted large amounts of seed, for example, from 'Shigitatsu sawa'. Most of the seed will produce the normal green-leaved seedlings. Occasionally, a seedling

will show the characteristic yellow leaf with green veining of the parent. One must not distribute these as the cultivar 'Shigitatsu sawa' but only as "seedlings from 'Shigitatsu sawa'." This principle holds true with seedlings from all other named cultivars of any type when the seedling is similar to the parent. Named cultivars must be propagated vegetatively to prevent dilution of the true cultivar.

In Regard to *Fu*

The variegated group of Japanese maple cultivars is increasing due to selection and crossbreeding. New and beautiful cultivars continue to arise from these efforts. The Japanese word for variegation is *fu*. A Japanese-English dictionary might list at least 20 interpretations for this word, and undoubtedly there are more. When applied to horticultural usage, the word refers to dots, mottles, specks, and marks on a leaf of different background. Several Japanese terms and names are used to identify the various forms of variegation:

Fukurin fu (*fuku*, "cover," and *rin*, "ring" or "circle"): Denotes the type of variegation that appears as a different color or tone along the outer margin of the leaf lobe. Usually used for rather uniform marking as exemplified by the very popular 'Butterfly'.

Fukurin kuzure (*kuzure*, "irregular"): Indicates an irregular margin of variegation around the edge of the lobe, as occurs with 'Beni shichihenge'.

Goma fu (*goma*, "sesame seed"): Indicates green blotching when it appears on pure white leaves (*ubu fu*) usually as quite small markings. An excellent example is 'Ukigumo'.

'Harusame' occasionally throws out a white variegation in the leaf during the early growing season. It is so infrequent that it could not be called a characteristic. In some years there have been only two leaves on the whole tree so variegated.
Photo by J. D. Vertrees

Haki homi fu (*haki homi*, "brushed in"): Describes variegation that appears to be created by brushing in white or yellow on the base tone of the leaf. 'Nishiki gasane' is an example.

Hoshi fu (*hoshi*, "star" or "stars"): Denotes the delicate "star-dust" variegations that appear on the background of green. *Acer pictum* 'Hoshi yadori' derives its name from this term.

Hoso fukurin fu (*hoso*, "slender"): Contrasts with *shin fukurin fu* to describe a very narrow margin around the lobe. Also known as *ito fukurin fu* (*ito*, "thread"). 'Matsugae' is an example.

Kiri fu (*kiri*, "cut"): Describes leaves that are variegated to the center vein on one half while the other half is normal, as exemplified by *Acer truncatum* 'Akikaze nishiki'.

Shimo furi fu (*shimo*, "frost," and *furi*, "scattered"): Similar to *sunago fu* variegation. The yellow flecks in the leaves of *Acer buergerianum* 'Inazuma nishiki' exhibit this type of variegation.

Shin fukurin fu (*shin*, "deep"): Indicates a deep variegated marking around the edge of the lobe, as in 'Hikasa yama'. Contrasts with *hoso fukurin fu*.

Sunago fu (*sunago*, "sand"): Indicates dots or tiny markings (smaller than *hoshi* variegation), which cover most or all the surface of the leaf, often indistinctly. 'Tama nishiki' shows this kind of variegation.

Sunago fukurin (*sunago*, "sand"): Refers to a fine speckling or dotting in the margins only.

Tsuma fukurin fu (*tsuma*, "nail"): Describes variegation on a margin that is stronger near the point of the lobe and not even all around the lobe. Leaves with white tips on the lobes are referred to as *tsuma jirō*, meaning "white nail," while leaves with red nails are referred to as *tsuma beni*. 'Tsuma beni' has a light green leaf with the tip of the sharp lobe contrasting red.

Ubu fu (*ubu*, "naive" or "virgin"): Denotes variegation that covers almost the entire leaf, or a pure white leaf, such as that of *Acer buergerianum* 'Nusatori yama'.

History of Japanese Cultivars

The Japanese have long been famous and admired for their intense and sensitive work in horticultural science. Their work with azaleas, bonsai, flowering cherries, chrysanthemums, and maples has contributed much to the pleasure of the rest of the world. A native species, *Acer palmatum*, was found to adapt to the specialized types of horticulture which became a significant part of the Japanese heritage. From very early times the Japanese people revered, selected, propagated, and increased the number of different forms of this species.

Acer palmatum and its natural varieties are endemic almost wholly to Japan. A few geographic forms occur in Korea and in parts of China. The species occurs in a wide range of soil conditions, on most islands of Japan, and in a variety of exposures. It is found from 100 to 1300 m (330–4290 ft.) above sea level. In its wide range it is like the North American native *A. circinatum*, vine maple, a close relative. *Acer palmatum* displays many variations in its native habitat, and these are designated subspecies, varieties, and forms. "New" types, mostly developed in the confines of domestic horticulture, give rise to the term "cultivar" in its present-day sense, that is, "a cultivated variety."

I have to conclude that *Acer palmatum* has a strong genetic tendency to proliferate into many variations, mutations, and sports. In the early days of horticulture, the Japanese collected the outstanding and beautiful forms of the species from the native stands. These consisted of seedling sports and variants. In addition, as bud mutations were discovered, they were propagated vegetatively and introduced into cultivation. As the number of these plants increased, they were planted in close proximity and cross-pollination occurred. The various parents of unusual form, therefore, gave rise to additional hybrid variants. This process expanded, and the genetic potential for new and interesting seedlings and sports proliferated. Over 300 years of intensive culture this process has yielded a great number of selections and cultivars.

During the Edo era (1603–1867), horticulture flourished and reached a high level of development in selection, breeding, culture, and specialization. Many cultivars of native Japanese trees and shrubs were brought into intensive development—notably azaleas and maples. Japanese maples reached a peak of popularity from the middle of the seventeenth century to the late eighteenth century. It became fashionable to select, cultivate, and nurture as many different types as possible. Collectors and gardeners searched for mutations and sports among the native stands as well as through gardens and large landscape plantings.

A standard garden book, *Zōho Chikinshō*, published in 1710 by Ibei Itō, mentioned 36 named varieties of *Acer palmatum*. By 1733 an additional 28 names were listed in the supplement to that list. And in 1882, Seigorō Oka and colleagues compiled a list of 202 varieties or cultivars in *Kaede Bin-*

ran. This rapid increase in the number of maples is spectacular, and yet undoubtedly did not include all the named types due to the extent of cultivation, lack of communication, and the large number of gardeners pursuing the vogue. Combining lists from older literature, we can safely assume that there were more than 250 cultivars at the height of this period.

In the early twentieth century interest waned and some of the less-spectacular cultivars were dropped from wide propagation. Even during this period, outstanding new cultivars were being named. As late as 1930, the Angyo Maple Nursery in Tokyo listed 219 named cultivars and types in propagation.

A sad period occurred in the 1940s. During the war years economic conditions caused many cultivars to be destroyed and lost to cultivation. Areas previously devoted to ornamental horticulture were used for food production. Old maples were cut to alleviate shortages of fuel and wood. One nurseryman tells of his ancestors having put together a very large collection of cultivars over the generations, only to have many of the trees burned as firewood.

In the 1960s, interest in Japanese maples was rekindled. Once again observant selection and careful development of additional cultivars went forward. Increased propagation of some of the older cultivars allowed the wider distribution of many choice types to the rest of the world.

While the number of names referred to in the present volume totals many, many hundreds, the presence of synonyms, alternative names, misnomers, and misapplications reduces the valid number of cultivars. As interest spreads and observant fanciers work with this group of plants, we can expect more outstanding cultivars to be "discovered" and introduced. The recently introduced 'Fall's Fire', with its magnificently colored fall foliage, exemplifies this point, as does the spectacular 'Red Dragon'.

Old Literature on Japanese Maples

One of the earliest known Japanese books with descriptions of maples was published in 1695. Titled *Kadan Chikinshō* and written by San-nojō Hanado, it must have been a major work on horticulture, as it extended to six volumes and covered the entire range of ornamental trees and shrubs.

In 1710 Ibei Itō, who is said to have been the son of San-nojō Hanado, although their family names are different, published *Zōho Chikinshō*. This revision of *Kadan Chikinshō* covered the range of ornamental trees and shrubs of Japan and comprised eight volumes. The fourth volume dealt with maples.

Kōeki Chikinshō was another revision by Ibei Itō done in 1719 as an eight volume set, with maples described in the third volume. In 1733 Itō put out *Chikinshō Furoku*. "Furoku" means "supplement."

In 1882 *Kaede Binran* ("Maple List") was published by Seigorō Oka, Isaburō Itō, and Gosaburō Itō. Probably the latter two authors were descendants of Ibei Itō who wrote the earlier publications.

The last book I mention is *Kaede Rui Zuko* ("Maples with Illustrations"), which was a rather complete work of three volumes. This set described most of the maple cultivars existing at that time, many of which have since been lost to cultivation.

In 1898, the Yokohama Nursery issued a catalog of Japanese maples for export. Illustrations were included and created much early interest in the United States. Subsequent issues of the Yokohama Nursery catalogs included additional descriptions and illustrations,

These Japanese publications, plus a very extensive bibliography of books and articles on maples published from 1688 to the present day and compiled by Hisao Nakajima, are listed in Masayoshi Yano's beautifully illustrated *Book for Maples*. Published in 2003, with the text in Japanese and English, *Book for Maples* illustrates 24 maple species plus some 475 cultivars currently grown in Japan.

Acer palmatum in the native forests of Japan.
Photo by J. D. Vertrees

2 TAXONOMY & NOMENCLATURE

The Taxonomy of Maples

Plant taxonomy is concerned with the classification of plants. Modern classification systems are based on the reconstruction of the evolution of plants which, in turn, reflects their relationship to each other. Presented here in tabulated form are the genetic and taxonomic relationships between the maple species dealt with in this book and other species closely related to them.

This book, written for the horticulturist and gardener, has not been designed as a definitive technical reference or key for identification by the serious dendrologist. The means of determining the relationships of maples continue to change as research progresses. In addition to examining plant chemistry, floral morphology, and wood anatomy, taxonomists are turning to the comparison of DNA from different species of plants for better determination of their relationships. These newer taxonomic methods are being applied to *Acer*, to refine our understanding of the delimitation of species and the relationships of the sections and series of the genus. In the meantime, P. C. de Jong's classification is followed here.

The interrelationship of species within sections and series, though interesting in its own right, is also important in propagation. Greater success in grafting and cross-hybridizing is usually achieved when species within the same series are selected and used. Notable exceptions to this rule exist, but in most cases knowledge of plant relationships is a useful guide in choosing a more common or easily obtained rootstock on which to graft a rare specimen. An obvious example from my own work is using *Acer palmatum* (smooth Japanese maple) as an understock on which to graft an unusual form of *A. circinatum* (vine maple). Although they are natives of two different continents, the species are closely related to each other in the same series *Palmata* and so are more likely to be compatible. (The reverse graft is possible but has been less successful in my own work.) It is worth pointing out that more than 85 percent of the maples described in this book belong to species in series *Palmata*. Because *A. palmatum* seedlings are the most readily available, they are often used as rootstock for the cultivars of the other species in the series.

In contrast, propagators would not normally choose *Acer platanoides* as an understock for a variegated form of *A. rufinerve*. The two species are from different sections of the genus, hence more distantly related and less likely to be compatible. Using an understock from another species in

Facing: The fiery foliage of *Acer palmatum* accents a large landscape.
Photo by Peter Gregory

the section to which *A. rufinerve* belongs, namely, section *Macrantha*, would be more likely to be successful. A notable exception is *A. pentaphyllum* which I successfully grafted onto such unrelated understock as *A. davidii*, *A. pseudoplatanus*, *A. rubrum*, and *A. saccharinum*. *Acer pseudoplatanus* has, perversely, been successfully used elsewhere as understock for a number of maple species from other sections. These two species, *A. pentaphyllum* and *A. pseudoplatanus*, can be looked on as the exceptions that prove the rule!

In spite of these anomalies, the closer the relationship between two species, the more likely their compatibility, and so the greater the chance of a successful union. With that in mind, the classification that follows may be useful in helping growers to choose which understock to use when grafting new maples. It is based on P. C. de Jong's biosystematic study, originally published in 1976, modified since, and used in *Maples of the World* (van Gelderen et al. 1994). Species in bold type are described in this book (see chapters 5 and 6). Other species are closely related and possible sources of rootstock.

Systematic Treatment of the Genus *Acer*

Section *Parviflora*
  Series *Parviflora*
    A. nipponicum Hara (1938)
  Series *Distyla*
    A. distylum Siebold & Zuccarini (1845)
  Series *Caudata*
    A. caudatum Wallich (1830)
    A. spicatum Lamarck (1786)

Section *Palmata*
  Series *Palmata*
    A. ceriferum Rehder (1911)
    A. circinatum Pursh (1814)

    A. duplicato-serratum Hayata (1911)
    A. japonicum Thunberg (1784)
    A. palmatum Thunberg ex Murray (1784)
    A. pauciflorum Fang (1932)
    A. pseudosieboldianum (Pax) Komarov (1904)
    A. pubipalmatum Fang (1932)
    A. robustum Pax (1902)
    A. shirasawanum Koidzumi (1911)
    A. sieboldianum Miquel (1865)

Section *Macrantha*
  A. capillipes Maximowicz (1867)
  A. caudatifolium Hayata (1911)
  A. crataegifolium Siebold & Zuccarini (1845)
  A. davidii Franchet (1885)
  A. micranthum Siebold & Zuccarini (1845)
  A. morifolium Koidzumi (1914)
  A. pectinatum Wallich ex G. Nicholson (1881)
  A. pensylvanicum Linnaeus (1753)
  A. rubescens Hayata (1911)
  A. rufinerve Siebold & Zuccarini (1845)
  A. tegmentosum Maximowicz (1857)
  A. tschonoskii Maximowicz (1886)

Section *Glabra*
  Series *Arguta*
    A. acuminatum Wallich ex D. Don (1825)
    A. argutum Maximowicz (1867)
    A. barbinerve Maximowicz (1867)
    A. stachyophyllum Hiern (1875)

Section *Negundo*
  Series *Cissifolia*
    A. cissifolium (Siebold & Zuccarini) Koch (1864)
    A. henryi Pax (1889)

Section *Indivisa*
  A. carpinifolium Siebold & Zuccarini (1845)

Section *Pentaphylla*
  Series *Trifida*
    A. buergerianum Miquel (1865)

Section *Trifoliata*
  Series *Grisea*
    A. griseum (Franchet) Pax (1902)
    A. mandshuricum Maximowicz (1867)
    A. maximowiczianum Miquel (1867)
    A. triflorum Komarov (1901)

Section *Lithocarpa*
  Series *Lithocarpa*
    A. diabolicum Blume ex Koch (1864)
    A. sinopurpurascens Cheng (1931)
    A. sterculiaceum Wallich (1830)

Section *Platanoidea*
    A. campestre Linnaeus (1753)
    A. cappadocicum Gleditsch (1785)
    A. longipes Franchet ex Rehder (1905)
    A. miyabei Maximowicz (1888)
    A. pictum Thunberg ex Murray (1784)
    A. platanoides Linnaeus (1753)
    A. tenellum Pax (1889)
    A. truncatum Bunge (1833)

Section *Ginnala*
    A. tataricum Linnaeus (1753)

Section *Rubra*
    A. pycnanthum Koch (1864)
    A. rubrum Linnaeus (1753)
    A. saccharinum Linnaeus (1753)

Taxonomy of *Acer palmatum*

Of all the maple species, by far the most variable is *Acer palmatum*. This variability has caused considerable confusion in the past and has resulted in numerous species being described, such as *A. amoenum, A. dissectum, A. formosanum, A. matsumurae, A. nambuana, A. ornatum, A. polymorphum, A. sanguineum*, and *A. septemlobum*, to name just a few! The confusion has extended into the splitting of *A. palmatum* and several of the above taxa into numerous subspecies, varieties, and forms, such as *A. palmatum* var. *heptalobum, A. palmatum* f. *atropurpureum*, and *A. palmatum* f. *linearilobum*.

Because taxonomists are attempting to show evolutionary relationships between the different taxa, as reflected in the variations between natural populations, it added to the confusion to name species and infraspecific forms from cultivated plants. For instance, *Acer dissectum, A. ornatum*, and *A. palmatum* var. *heptalobum* were based on Japanese garden plants.

Modern taxonomic techniques, including chemical analysis, have indicated that all these plants, in spite of large, visible, morphological differences, have the same fundamental characters and can be placed under the one species, *Acer palmatum*. The numerous subspecies, varieties, and forms of the past have been simplified even further in P. C. de Jong's system, which recognizes only three subspecies—*A. palmatum* subsp. *amoenum, A. palmatum* subsp. *matsumurae*, and *A. palmatum* subsp. *palmatum*. These subspecies are identified on the basis of leaf size, number and depth of lobes and teeth, flower and fruit size, chemical constituents, and geographic location.

Acer palmatum subsp. *palmatum* has small leaves 3–6 cm (1⅛–2⅜ in.) long with five to seven lobes and with coarsely toothed margins. The tiny fruits are about 1.5 cm (⅝ in.) long. This is the type from which the original species was described. *Acer palmatum* subsp. *amoenum* and *A. palmatum* subsp. *matsumurae* have much larger leaves (7–10 cm or 2¾–4 in.) and fruits (2.5–3.5 cm or 1–1⅜ in.). The mainly seven-lobed leaves of subsp. *amoenum* are moderately divided, up to two thirds of the way to the leaf base, and the margins are regularly and finely toothed. The seven-to nine-lobed leaves of subsp. *matsumurae* are usually deeply divided to near the leaf base and usually have coarsely toothed margins. These three subspecies are more fully described in chapter 5.

Nomenclature Difficulties and Confusion

Nomenclature (from the Latin *nomen*, meaning "name" or "noun") is the man-made system of naming plants. There has been much confusion in the naming of Japanese maple cultivars caused by name variations of older cultivars in Japan; alternative transliterations and translations; localized names in Europe and America; differing trade, selling, and registered names; and lack of any agreed guidelines for naming maples in the early years. Add to these causes the mistakes, misspellings, and changes that inevitably creep in during the hundreds of years that Japanese maples have been in cultivation, and it is not surprising that some cultivars have several names and some names have been used for several different cultivars. The result is that the naming of Japanese maple cultivars has been confusing and complicated, often inconsistent and sometimes quite wrong.

Prior to the mid-eighteenth century, no uniform guide or set of rules existed for naming "new" plants. Many Japanese plant names arose from common usage in a limited and perhaps isolated area. Furthermore, linguistic dialects resulted in spelling and pronunciation variations. For example, a particular plant name may be spelled or pronounced differently in the northern islands than in other parts of Japan.

Serious study of the old literature reveals, in some instances, that the same Japanese name has been applied to several different cultivars. Japanese and Chinese horticulturists of several centuries ago were located throughout a widespread territory, including many islands, and lacked adequate communication. Therefore, similar names could be applied to entirely different species or selections without the duplications being realized.

The Japanese word *itaya* illustrates this problem. It has been used both as the name of a popular cultivar (*Acer japonicum* 'Itaya') and as a common name for three species—*A. japonicum*, *A. pictum*, and *A. shirasawanum*. "Itaya kaede" has been used as the common name for *A. japonicum*, *A. pictum*, and *A. truncatum*, while "itaya meigetsu" has been used for *A. japonicum* and *A. sieboldianum*.

The system of transliterating Japanese characters to the Roman alphabet has been changed several times by the Japanese government. To promote literacy following World War II, the government reduced the number of Japanese characters from tens of thousands to about two thousand. Hence, many Japanese cannot read a large number of characters used prior to that time.

A further difficulty occurs when changing certain Japanese sounds into English. Very few Japanese pronunciations have a direct English equivalent. For example, the sound "ch" (like a sneeze) may be spelled in a name as "chi," "shi," "tsu," and so forth. Thus 'Chikushi gata', 'Shikishigata', and 'Tsukushi gata' were all valid ways to write the name of a single plant, as were 'Chishio' and 'Shishio'. When used in names, the letters *g* and *k* were often interchanged. Some Japanese vowels are interpreted in different ways when they are carried over to the English name equivalent. Thus one can find "o," "oo," and "oh." The name of the Japanese cultivar 'Shōjō' has been spelled many ways in the publications of other languages.

Difficulties of translation from one language to another may produce more than one valid name for a given plant. Most Japanese names for maples are written in kanji characters, which were adapted from Chinese characters several centuries ago. In addition, minute differences in the structure of some Japanese characters contributed to the variation in naming when transliterated into English. Furthermore, there are different ways of transliterating the same kanji character into English. For example, 'Ō sakazuki' and 'Taihai' are read from the same characters. 'Daimyō nishiki' and 'Taimin nishiki' are valid interpretations of the same characters, and 'Aka shigitatsu sawa' and 'Beni shigitatsu sawa' are fitting renderings of the same characters. The kanji characters for "tsuma" and "uri" are so similar that 'Beni tsuma' can easily be confused with 'Beni uri', though, in fact, the former is the name of a cultivar of *Acer palmatum* while the latter is the name of a cultivar of *A. rufinerve*.

The circuitous route some plants have traveled as they were dispersed around the world is another consideration. Transliterating the name of a cultivar going from Japan to Europe is difficult no matter what the language. If the plant was then introduced into an English collection, it might receive a further transliteration. And when that same cultivar was sent to a nursery in the United States, the spelling of its name could possibly change again. Several maple names have been traced through these many "sea" changes.

Another problem arises from the unwillingness of some nurseries to cope with Japanese names, especially in the United States. There have been cases where cultivars from Europe or Japan were given popular names in the United States to promote sales or to save the trouble of learning to spell the correct name. 'Ever Red' in place of 'Dissectum Nigrum' and 'Roscoe Red', possibly in place of 'Novum,' are thought to be examples of this practice.

The difficulties that can arise when plant names are not adhered to meticulously is demonstrated by the following example. 'Okushimo' is found in older taxonomic texts as *Acer palmatum* subsp. *genuinum* subvar. *crispum* and *A. palmatum* subvar. *eupalmatum* f. *crispum*. In the United States this plant is called 'Crispa', presumably because it is easier to write this name on a nursery label than to write 'Okushimo' (also occasionally written 'Okishima'). But the name 'Crispa' has been applied to four cultivars. Some nurseries designate the entirely different cultivar 'Shishigashira' as 'Crispum'. A second example is 'Hikasa yama' (also spelled 'Higasa yama'), which is sold in the United States under several names, depending on whether it originates on the East Coast or the West Coast. It can be found in collections and nurseries under the names 'Aureovariegatum', 'Cristatum Variegatum', 'Roseomarginatum', and 'Roseovariegatum'. Unfortunately, some of these popular names rightly belong to other cultivars, leading to more confusion. The true *Acer palmatum* subsp. *matsumurae* f. *roseomarginatum* bears the Japanese name 'Kagiri nishiki' and is quite different from 'Hikasa yama'. A third example is 'Shishigashira', which has been found under at least five different names around the world: 'Crispa', 'Crispum', 'Cristata', 'Minus', and 'Ribescifolium'.

Finally, we must consider penmanship, haste in writing labels or (later) hitting the wrong key on a typewriter or computer. The letter *u* can become an *o*, and an *r* can become an *n*. These mistakes undoubtedly happen. Transposing letters also causes name differences which, when repeated often enough, result in the wrong name becoming established. One such example is the cultivar 'Hōgyoku', which is sometimes found under the (incorrect) name 'Hōgyuko'.

Although these issues may not be considered important by readers who want a few maples in their landscapes, they are vital to nurseries and serious collectors. If someone requested a plant under the name 'Crispa' or 'Roseomarginatum', I would not be sure which of several cultivars is desired.

I strongly prefer to adhere to the Japanese names of maple cultivars wherever possible and valid. Since this plant group

originated in and was developed primarily by discerning and devoted Japanese horticulturists, and is an important part of their horticultural heritage, I consider such practice both courteous and appropriate. This is not to say that the new cultivars from Europe, the United States, or Australasia should not carry non-Japanese names. I am referring mainly to the cultivars that originated in Japan and have suffered name changes in other countries. Throughout this text I have attempted to list all the nomenclature variances under each cultivar and, therefore, will not list them here.

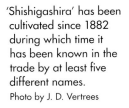

'Shishigashira' has been cultivated since 1882 during which time it has been known in the trade by at least five different names.
Photo by J. D. Vertrees

The Naming of Plants Originating in the Wild

Since ancient times plant names have consisted of descriptive phrases. The era of plant hunters from the mid-eighteenth century until the early twentieth century brought in many, many thousands of species not previously seen. Giving these plants names in unwieldy phrases and in many languages created chaos, so it became necessary to establish an international set of rules. The great Swedish naturalist Carl Linnaeus attempted to fill the gap with the publication of his binomial system of nomenclature in 1753. It was not universally accepted until the International Botanical Congress (IBC) was set up in 1862. The Linnaean system gives every species a unique name of paired words; the first word is the genus and the second the species within that genus.

In 1905 the IBC decreed that plant names should be written in Latin as it was the most widely used language in Europe. All educated Europeans could read, write, and converse in Latin at that time. But the American Society of Taxonomists produced its own set of rules in 1947, which did not include the use of Latin. Agreement between the two organizations was not reached until 1959. The first *International Code of Botanical Nomenclature* (the *Botanical Code*) was published before this, in 1952, and has been revised by the IBC every five to six years since. Today the "Latin" permitted in botanical names is often highly imaginative and would not necessarily be understood by a classic Latin scholar! Botanical names can more accurately be described as Latinized or scientific names. Thanks to the *Botanical Code*, botanical names represent a more stable system of nomenclature, usable by people of all nationalities. It sets out the rules for the formation, publication, and use of all scientific names for plants originating in the wild.

The Naming of Cultivars

Guidelines for the naming of plants in horticulture (that is, cultivars) are contained in the *International Code of Nomenclature for Cultivated Plants* (the *Cultivated Plant Code*). Since the *Cultivated Plant Code* was first published in 1953, the rules have been adapted and developed to meet the needs of users—growers, collectors, and gardeners—and to promote uniformity, consistency, and stability in the naming of cultivars.

The *Cultivated Plant Code* introduced the term *cultivar* (a cultivated variety) for any plant maintained solely by cultivation. It defines a cultivar as a plant that has been selected for a particular attribute or group of attributes that is clearly distinct, uniform, and stable in its characteristics and, when propagated by appropriate means, retains these characteristics. Some cultivars arise as sports (mutants) in the wild or as natural hybrids which are then taken into cultivation. The vast majority arise in cultivation as chance or induced sports, or as chance or deliberate hybrids.

In the case of Japanese maples, most cultivars arise from a keen-eyed grower or collector spotting an unusual form among a group of seedlings. 'Ariadne', 'Eddisbury', 'Red Filigree Lace', and 'Sharp's Pygmy' are examples. Other plants, such as 'Shaina' and many dwarf cultivars, arise from witches'-brooms on existing plants, while atypical shoots on a tree have been noticed and given rise to new cultivars. Several of the variegated forms arose by this means. Finally, but rarely, new cultivars may be the result of deliberate cross-pollination, as in the case of *Acer* 'Autumn Flame' from New Zealand.

To distinguish cultivar names from botanical names, which refer to plants growing in the wild, cultivar names are written in roman type, begin with a capital letter, and are enclosed in single quote marks. These names are normally preceded by the botanical name of the genus and species to which they belong, for example, *Acer palmatum* 'Shishigashira'. In this book, to avoid endless repetition, cultivars of *A. palmatum* are cited without the species name—as, for example, 'Red Pygmy'—while cultivars of other species are always cited with the appropriate species name—for example, *A. japonicum* 'Green Cascade'.

Cultivar names can be in any modern language, but Latinized cultivar names have been illegitimate since 1959—again to distinguish them from botanical names. Latinized names in use prior to 1959 are still valid. To avoid mistranslations, varying translations in different languages, and alternative translations, it is recommended that cultivar names should remain in the language in which they were first published. Translated names should not be used, though it is perfectly acceptable to include a translation of the foreign name, in parenthesis following the accepted cultivar

Although 'Reticulatum Como' is very desirable in the landscape for its large variegated leaves, it needs to be renamed as its Latinized name has been illegal since 1959. Photo by Peter Gregory

name. Cultivar names should be used only once in the maple genus; if a name has been used with one species, it should not be used to name a second cultivar even when the species name is different.

It is obviously desirable and less confusing for each cultivar to have a unique, constant, correctly spelled name. Growers and collectors could not be blamed for incorrect naming or for duplication of names when no up-to-date, authoritative source existed to guide them. One of the main purposes of this book is to identify errors and try to rectify them for the purpose of bringing clarity and stability to Japanese maple cultivar names. This purpose has been aided considerably by the rules of the *Cultivated Plant Code* and, also, the appointment of the International Cultivar Registration Authority (ICRA) for Maples.

To be accepted a cultivar name must be published in an appropriate place (trade catalogs do not count) with a description and date, and be available to the public. It is recommended that cultivar names be registered with a registration authority as a precaution against the duplication of names, misuse, fraudulent use, and misspelling. For details on registering maple names, see the section titled "Registering New Cultivars" in chapter 4.

The names of all cultivars described in this book conform to the rules of the latest *Cultivated Plant Code* as far as is practicable, particularly in respect to the use of the modified Hepburn system of transliteration from Japanese characters. The Hepburn system has been approved by the Japanese government, taught in Japanese schools, and widely accepted in the West.

Three upright dwarf
cultivars growing in
containers: 'Beni kawa'
(center), 'Tsukomo' (left),
'Oto hime' (right).
Photo by Harry Olsen

3 CULTURE

Culture in the Garden

Japanese maples are remarkably adaptable to soil and climatic conditions. In their native habitats, *Acer palmatum* and its natural varieties have adapted to a wide range of environments on the islands of Japan. In North America, these plants thrive in soils and climates ranging from the rainforest conditions of the Pacific Northwest to the very warm climate of southern California, and from upstate New York down the Atlantic seaboard to the humid southeastern states and through the Midwest. In Europe, they grow in the warm Mediterranean conditions of Italy, in the almost pure peat soils of Boskoop, Netherlands, and in the varied soils in Britain. They also thrive in many parts of Australasia. Thus we begin to understand the versatility of these plants as ornamentals throughout the world.

Locations

Japanese maples are widely used as specimen plants and companion plants. Since they rarely attain great heights, they are not classed as shade trees. A magnificent specimen of *Acer palmatum* at The Ford, Wiveliscombe, near Taunton, Somerset, England, was planted about 1850 or before and still thrives, more than 155 years later, at about 12 m (40 ft.) tall. There are taller examples in cultivation, such as the 18-m (59-ft.) tree at Westonbirt Arboretum in Gloucestershire, England.

Most upright cultivars of *Acer palmatum* and *A. japonicum* attain a height of 8–9 m (26–30 ft.) in 50 years, depending upon site and conditions. Many cultivars, especially from the Dissectum Group, mature at 5 m (16 ft.) or less, which places them in the large shrub category. Mature cultivars in the Dwarf Group are even smaller; they rarely exceed 2 m (6 ft.) and may be less than 1 m (3 ft.) tall.

The green varieties and cultivars take full sun very well. In extremely hot situations they may sunburn slightly under late-summer conditions. Afternoon shade aids in preventing this, as does an adequate supply of water. Forms with variegated leaves need semishade, or at least protection from the blistering afternoon sun. 'Nishiki gasane', for example, does best with afternoon protection to keep the golden variegation in the leaves from crisping brown. Other white-and-pink variegated forms should also have afternoon shade. Variegates such as 'Versicolor' and 'Waka momiji' are more tolerant and can often be grown in full sun without serious sunburn. Such extreme forms as the variegated dissectum 'Toyama nishiki' must have ample shade or they will be seriously sunburned.

Facing: A lakeside planting of maples and other large trees and shrubs doubles the fall color at Sheffield Park Garden in southern England.
Photo by Laura Jones

39

The red-leaved dissectums appreciate some shade, but cannot develop their typical deep red colors without the benefit of full sunlight for at least part of the day. A fine specimen of 'Garnet' grown under *Calocedrus decurrens* (incense cedar) at Maplewood doesn't develop the true color for which it is known. Instead of turning a strong orange-red, it remains a greenish red, although in fine condition and leaf form. In general, the color of most red cultivars is greatly enhanced in full sun, and in some forms, such as 'Fior d'Arancio', leaf color readily reverts to green in too much shade.

Sunlight filtering through foliage creates a backlighting effect that results in brilliant coloring.
Photo by Peter Gregory

Use in the Garden Landscape

The use of many Japanese maples in the garden landscape is a challenge because there are so many types, colors, shapes, and rates of growth from which to choose. Of course, this very fact makes it easy to establish a variety of moods or effects in the garden. Homeowners should create a personal landscape, design, or mood and should not slavishly try to match a rigid book outline or a landscape concept better suited to a different site or sense of taste. A garden should reflect the owner's personal preferences not those dictated by someone else. To this end, Japanese maples offer unlimited choices.

DISSECTUMS

The most familiar and widespread form of the Japanese maple is the dissectum, or laceleaf, of the nursery trade, *Acer palmatum* f. *dissectum*. This form occurs naturally with red or green foliage, as well as in various named cultivars. It is commonly offered in nearly every retail nursery of any size.

Dissectums have been propagated and sold for many decades and have found uses in a wide variety of situations and garden landscapes. They are outstanding as individual specimen plants, container trees for the patio, accent plants in lawns, companion plants in a mixed border, or in a special spot in the rock garden. Dissectums are particularly showy when used as an accent plant beside a pool or overhanging running water, or as a feature plant in a prominent spot along a winding path.

Properly cared for 75- to 100-year-old specimen plants possess a magnificent stateliness. Once the autumn foliage is off, the characteristic shapely, twisting branch scaffolding carries the featured beauty on through the dormant season, especially if the dead leaves and debris are cleared out of the interior.

Young plants can grow rapidly at first, during which time they can be trained in shape and structure to make good accent plants. They have a natural tendency not to become too large too soon. But, the "cute little plant" purchased as a starter should be allowed plenty of room to spread, so that it can make the typical cascading shape which is so desirable.

Choice red-leaved dissectums are 'Baldsmith', 'Crimson Queen', 'Garnet', 'Inaba shidare', 'Red Dragon', 'Red Filigree Lace', and 'Tamuke yama'. Among the green-leaved forms are 'Ellen', 'Emerald Lace', 'Green Mist', 'Palmatifidum', 'Seiryū', and 'Waterfall'. Variegated dissectums include 'Filigree' (green with gold or cream flecks), 'Pink Ballerina' (deep red with pink and greenish streaks), and 'Toyama nishiki' (purple or green-red with pink or white marks).

UPRIGHT GROWERS

The upright-growing forms present the greatest number of choices and landscaping possibilities. First, there are the colors with many shades of yellow, green, or red, including fascinating variegations, sometimes their brightest in spring, other times predominant in fall. Next, there is the plant shape ranging from tall to spreading, sometimes cascading, but all offering easy acceptance of pruning to guide them to the desired shape. Some cultivars, such as *Acer japonicum* 'Ō isami', develop unusual limb structures for winter enjoyment, while other cultivars, such as 'Aoyagi', 'Bi hŏ', and 'Sango kaku', offer bright-colored shoots and branches in winter, and still others, such as 'Arakawa' and 'Ibo nishiki', have a unique, corky bark.

An individual large accent plant placed in a prominent place attracts attention from every part of the garden. Red-leaved cultivars, such as 'Bloodgood', 'Emperor 1', 'Glowing Embers', and 'Trompenburg',

A mixed planting of *Acer palmatum* f. *dissectum* creates a dramatic border.
Photo by J. D. Vertrees

stand out boldly in the landscape, as do green-leaved selections, such as 'Aoyagi', 'Autumn Glory', 'Katsura', and 'Summer Gold', and even variegated plants, such as 'Asahi zuru' (white and green), 'Butterfly' (cream and blue-green), and 'Uncle Ghost' (green, white, pink). For larger plantings a blending of several color types forms an ever-changing canopy throughout the seasons.

The large, upright forms of *Acer palmatum* and closely related species are useful in several ways—as overstory plants for alpine, rock garden, or flower borders; as solid plantings employing several types to make a "woodsy" grove; as a border for the background edge of a garden landscape by adding various colors and textures; or as a corner or end specimen to emphasize a change in landscape design or use.

These maples have the additional advantage of ready adaptability to a wide range of cultural situations. This tolerance allows them to adjust to the needs of various companion plants. Acid-loving plants such as rhododendrons, azaleas, kalmias, and dwarf conifers, plus a great variety

The warty bark of 'Ibo nishiki' adds interest to the garden long after the leaves are gone.
Photo by J. D. Vertrees

'Hōgyoku', 'Ichigyō ji', and 'Ō sakazuki', to maintain the interest in this season as well. Cultivars of *Acer japonicum* also always display bright fall colors, plus they show interesting limb scaffolding in winter. To complete the year-round special interest, include cultivars with unique bark texture and color, such as 'Aoyagi', 'Kogane sakae', 'Nishiki gawa', 'Red Wood', 'Sango kaku'.

Boldness in locating the plants for a special effect and contrast is an especially satisfying device. At Maplewood Nursery a planting of 'Yezo nishiki' near *Sequoiadendron giganteum* (giant sequoia, redwood) creates a striking effect in spring as the sun highlights the contrasting color and texture of the two very different plants.

In large plantings, another opportunity presents itself in planning for lighting effects. Highly colored red cultivars, such as 'Bloodgood', can be planted so that the viewer is looking through the foliage at the sun with the light filtering through the foliage. The results are spectacular and may be enjoyed during a major portion of the season. Weeping dissectums, when blended with dwarf maples of various heights and shapes, visually tie the whole planting to the ground. A "hedge" of dissectums makes a unique and extremely distinctive planting for the edge of a landscape. A planting of green or red maples in a row, covering a range of autumn colors, spaced so that they will merge in a few years, presents an unusual and distinguished planting not often seen. Those who like color patterns may choose to alternate plants with green and red foliage.

It is not usually wise to make a mass planting of only one type of plant, however. Even though many cultivars have an interesting limb structure, the overall effect of bare limbs becomes monotonous. Interplanting larger dwarf conifers with rhododendrons, azaleas, kalmias, camellias, and other low-growing evergreen shrubs

of perennials and bulbs, all make excellent companion plants. Maples also blend well with shrubs and perennials that prefer slightly alkaline to medium alkaline soils. Where soils are very alkaline, maples are best grown in raised beds or containers. Finally, maples do not have a strongly invasive root system which might damage borders or ornamental walks. Root competition is not vicious, so Japanese maples are compatible with most plants.

MASS PLANTINGS

For larger gardens or sites with sufficient space, mass plantings offer tremendous possibilities through all seasons. In some settings, it may be advisable to include two or more cultivars or species possessing outstanding features to insure a bold effect through each season. For example, the brightly colored spring foliage of 'Katsura', 'Orange Dream', 'Seigai', 'Shin deshōjō', and 'Ueno homare' would highlight a mass planting. Blending taller-growing red-leaved cultivars with upright green-leaved forms makes a dramatic color pattern throughout spring and summer months. Plan to emphasize cultivars with especially bright fall foliage, such as helps break the tedium of purely deciduous plantings.

DWARF CULTIVARS

The large variety of dwarf cultivars opens other endless possibilities, the first of which, of course, is bonsai culture. Those who practice bonsai either know, or have access to, the literature about the uses of *Acer palmatum* and its cultivars and related species for this purpose. There is no need here to expand on the vast potential of this very old art. Both the type species from seedlings and many selected cultivars, such as 'Deshōjō', have made some of the most spectacular and famous bonsai in various parts of the world. Three newer cultivars with potential for bonsai are 'Diana', 'Taro yama', and 'Tiny Leaf.'

Dwarf forms are especially well suited for inclusion in shrub borders and among alpine plantings. They blend with nearly all the border perennials, annuals, bulbs, and shrubs. In the northwestern United States, common plant choices include most ericaceous shrubs and conifers. In the eastern United States the choice is nearly as wide, but more attention must be paid to the winter hardiness of many shrubs. Japanese maples can withstand temperatures well below 0°F (−18°C) once well established, if well mulched and given adequate root protection. In mixed plantings in more arid climates, Japanese maples will survive in a fairly low-moisture situation, although the growth rate is slowed considerably.

Dwarf Japanese maples adapt well to the art of alpine gardening. They like the conditions of such gardens—well-drained soil, minimal water and fertility, and a mid-range soil pH. They do not grow in an overpowering manner, and they blend well with most alpine plants. The range of dwarf, dissectum, and smaller-sized maples offers many chances for imaginative companion planting in rock garden and alpine cul-

ture. A few outstanding dwarf cultivars are 'Baby Lace', 'Shidava Gold', 'Pixie', 'Wilson's Pink Dwarf', and the newer selection 'Japanese Princess'. 'Groundcover' is a dense, twiggy plant that hugs the ground, as its name suggests.

Short-statured, with a spreading growth habit and dense branching, 'Garyū' is the perfect covering for a large rock in the garden. Photo by J. D. Vertrees

Planting

Japanese maples are easy to plant. Their root system is not a deep taproot-type of structure but is predominantly a fibrous root network that will stay mostly in the upper level of the soil. Naturally, with age the roots will be found rather deep, but they do not go to an excessive depth. This is especially true in irrigated soils where the roots do not need to search for moisture. Regular irrigation maintains the roots in the upper levels of the soil.

This fact, however, does not make Japanese maples serious competitors with companion shrubs. The trees coexist well with practically all landscape plantings. A surprisingly large number of Japanese maple enthusiasts also have fine plantings of rhododendrons and azaleas, because the culture of all three plant groups is similar.

The manner in which maples root in the upper surface allows them to be planted in soils which may have a hard stratum or bedrock close to the surface. With adequate root coverage and attention to uniform moisture supply, these plants do an excellent job of beautifying difficult areas. This reason is also why they do so well in containers of all sizes. The fibrous roots will utilize the limited area without root binding and choking themselves too easily. The requirement for a uniform level of moisture supply, whether great or small, must be emphasized. I cannot stress the importance of the uniformity of watering too much. I do not imply the need for large amounts, but rather, constant amounts.

PLANTING STOCK

The newly purchased plant may come from the grower in one of several ways. Young plants, whether produced from grafts or seeds, will probably be in containers. Medium-sized and very old plants can also be purchased in containers. In modern nursery production, maples of any size are successfully produced as "containerized stock." This allows for successful transplanting into the permanent position with very little transplant shock. Hence, the planting season can be extended to any month of the year.

Young plants up to four years of age, when purchased in the dormant season, may be bare-rooted. These trees are dug up or taken out of containers and transported without soil on the roots to save the expense of shipping heavy growing medium. Bare-rooted plants can be moved safely only during the dormant season and usually only when less than four years old.

Field-grown material several years of age is usually dug up with an earthen ball intact around the roots. It comes from the nursery with the root ball often wrapped in burlap or similar material to prevent the root ball from drying out. Ball-and-burlap plants are usually only safe to transport during the dormant season.

When moving a plant to a different location within a garden, the plant must be dug with an earthen ball intact around the roots. If the plant is of any size or age, this root protection is important. It is also desirable that the planting hole be prepared in advance, so that it can receive the plant with its root ball as soon as the plant is dug up. Having the new planting hole ready minimizes the risk of the fine feeding roots drying out. For this reason it is imperative that, whatever method, material, or season is used when planting a Japanese maple, the roots are not exposed to air or to direct sunlight for any length of time. Such care will help prevent them from becoming desiccated, which would cause too much transplant shock and the possible loss of the tree.

PLANTING METHOD

The planting hole should be dug slightly larger than the root mass of the plant. To encourage the root system to establish itself quickly, the soil can be mixed with organic materials, such as composted conifer bark mulch, rhododendron or azalea planting mix, or rose compost. In tight, heavy clay soils the compost helps condition the soil, while in light, sandy soils the compost assists in water retention. Sawdust, wood chippings, or uncomposted bark should never be used as, during their breakdown, they use up the available soil nitrogen, rendering it unavailable to the newly planted tree.

The planting hole should be deep enough so that the root collar of the plant, the ground line at which the young plant was grown, is level with the ground surface. The exception to this rule applies to tight, heavy soils, like clay, where success will be greater if the hole is rather shallow so that the root system is partly above ground level. When filling in the hole, the soil should then be mounded up to the root collar to protect the roots from drying out. Setting a tree in a deep hole in heavy soil is like planting it in a big iron kettle with no drainage. The plant will soon drown and die.

Whatever the soil conditions, the tree should never be planted deeper than the root collar. After the first season or two, the tree will find the level of root activity at which it can exist in the particular soil conditions. I have observed maples growing in some surprisingly dry, shallow, and exposed conditions.

MULCHING

Mulching serves several useful purposes. It maintains weed-free conditions. It minimizes water loss in dry spells. And it provides winter protection for the roots in prolonged freezing conditions.

A newly planted Japanese maple needs several years before its relatively shallow root system is established enough to successfully compete with other vegetation for moisture and nutrients. The competition from grass roots is especially intense. Hence, the area around a newly planted maple should be kept weed-free for the first two to three years. After that the root system will be strong enough to hold its own in most conditions. Of course, once the area is weed-free, the right mulching can keep it that way.

The aerial parts of most Japanese maple cultivars, once established, can withstand winter freezing and air temperatures down to 0°F (–18°C), and below. The roots can only survive to 14°F (–10°C). When planted normally in the soil, the plants can withstand extreme temperatures because the roots are protected sufficiently in the deeper soil. The roots of newly planted trees are not necessarily protected sufficiently, hence the importance of correct mulching.

If the mulch material is too fine or matted, as in compost or farmyard manure, it provides a perfect seedbed for weeds and prevents the free exchange of air and gases between the soil and the atmosphere— the maple roots and the lower stem must breathe. If the mulch material is too absorbent, as in sawdust and wood chippings, it allows water loss through capillary action and, as mentioned previously, uses up nitrogen needed by the plant. In addition, the breakdown of the woody material can cause too much heat to be generated and thus scorch the bark above the root collar.

The ideal mulch is a 5-cm (2-in.) layer of coarse bark with an average chip size of about 2 cm (¾ in.). Such a mulch allows

Commerical production of 'Pendulum Julian' as containerized stock. Photo by Harold Greer

moisture downward but not upward. It encourages the free exchange of gases, it deters weeds from developing because of the lack of moisture in the upper mulch layers, and it acts as a protective, insulating layer during cold winters. There are other suitable mulch materials and compromises, including mulch mats, but bear in mind the absorbency, porosity, weeding, and insulating requirements.

Microclimates

Microclimates are small areas where conditions differ slightly from those in most of the garden and landscape. These spots may be hotter, colder, windier, drier, or wetter. Japanese maples do not differ from other garden plants in adverse responses to such conditions. For example, a spot with a constant strong wind will misshape the plant and may burn the leaves. In winter, the wind-chill factor may cause bark and cambium damage.

When a tree is planted close to a pure white wall, its foliage may be burned by the intense reflected light. In foundation plantings around a building, people tend to plant too closely to walls. Plant positioning should allow for at least 10 years of growth and this should be envisaged when planting.

In areas of strong marine breezes, leaf damage from salt deposits may occasionally occur. Anyone growing plants under such conditions should be familiar with the necessary protection and the need for periodic washing of the foliage with fresh water. Many maples are successfully grown on seashore sites.

Drought and waterlogged sites are discussed in the next section on soils. If these problems are recognized, corrective measures can be taken at planting time. Given some additional care in the first year or two of establishment, Japanese maples will adapt to most conditions, even though somewhat adverse.

Soils

The ideal soil for Japanese maples is a slightly acid, sandy loam with a low to medium amount of organic matter. Such soil is hard to find in many places. Fortunately, Japanese maples adapt well on less-than-perfect soils of most types. In very sandy or tight, heavy soils, their growth rate will be reduced somewhat. Sometimes simple procedures in planting or moisture management will compensate for poor soils. The richer the soil, the more rapid the growth. But, rich soil can also be a drawback. Some upright cultivars become too "leggy" when forced by rich soils or high fertility, and many variegated cultivars lose their variegations when growing vigorously.

The site must be reasonably well drained. Japanese maples do not do well in a wet or swampy location, but they may be grown beside pools and little streams provided the root zones have sufficient drainage and aeration. I have seen these plants growing on dry hillside locations in clay soil and under a hot sun. Although their annual growth was limited and certainly could not be called lush, at least the plants were fine, small trees, fulfilling a particular need.

Japanese maple trees also require mulching when planted in tight, heavy soils. Since the shallow roots cannot easily penetrate the heavy soil, a layer of mulch over the roots helps them retain moisture and keep cool in the heat of summer. Extremes in alkaline conditions prevent maples from performing well. Soils with a very high pH should be adjusted with acid fertilizers or neutralizing soil additions.

Growing Japanese maples in containers or raised beds offers alternative choices where impossible soil conditions exist.

The acid or neutral soils in which rhododendrons do well seem to be equally suitable for maples. Soils of an extremely sandy nature will need considerable organic matter incorporated, plus mulching, to help with water retention.

Moisture

Japanese maples do not have any unusual moisture requirements. The average amount of water supplied to the normal range of garden shrubs is usually adequate, so when maples are grown as companion plants with most other shrubs and perennials, they are carried along nicely with the normal irrigation.

The principal water requirement is a uniform supply. By this I mean that if the plant is in a fairly dry situation, it should not be flooded with water at irregular intervals, and if it is grown where moisture is plentiful, it should not be left to dry out during dry spells, but should be watered during such times. The water supply whether little or much should be constant.

Maples will grow with limited water but will produce a shrubbier plant. This can be an advantage with the taller-growing cultivars and species if larger trees are not desired but, remember, even though the water supply is limited, it should still be constant.

The main danger to guard against is very wet periods followed by very dry periods or vice versa. This pattern will surely cause summer leaf drop or leaf scorch. One of the most common causes of leaf scorch is an excessively dry period, even if only a few days, in a normally watered situation. In fact, the leaves may fall off as if it were the

Japanese maples grow best in the slightly acid soils also preferred by rhododendrons and conifers. Here 'Crimson Queen' thrives in a mixed planting with rhododendrons and cedar.
Photo by J. D. Vertrees

beginning of winter, completely defoliating the tree. I have seen this occur in midsummer. A thorough soaking into the deepest part of the root zone will possibly save the tree and perhaps even cause a new crop of leaves to grow in late summer and early fall, if the tree has not been damaged too badly. Watering the leaves in full sun during the hot summer months causes another leaf scorch problem, especially with container-grown specimens. Watering in early morning or early evening during the hottest weather prevents this type of scorch.

Containers must not be allowed to get waterlogged as overwatering can be worse than underwatering. Aeration is as important as irrigation, because the roots must be able to breathe. The grower should determine the water requirement of a particular medium and adjust watering accordingly. Proper water management is even more important than the type of soil or fertilizer.

Feeding

Japanese maples do not demand large amounts of nutrients. If the soils are generally fertile for most garden plants, maples will do well with little or no additional attention. It is not possible to generalize here about the nutrient needs in all the locations in which maples grow around the world.

In soils of the northwestern United States, *Acer palmatum* seems to resent ammonium sources of nitrogen. I have found that calcium nitrate works best, with other non-ammonium sources also working well. A balanced garden fertilizer, such as that recommended for roses, applied lightly not more than once a year, will provide for these nongreedy plants. If very rapid growth is required for some purpose, then calcium nitrate should be applied to the landscape plant in early spring and again in early summer. Both times it must be watered well into the soil.

On very poor soils and problem areas, a balanced complete fertilizer for shrubs and trees may be used. A once-a-year, early spring application before the leaves emerge is generally best. Slow-release fertilizers work well as they reduce the risk of chemical burn, but the cost is higher. Old barnyard manure is rich in many nutrients but may need the addition of nitrates and tends to introduce weed seeds. Because of capillary action, it will also lose moisture to the atmosphere in hot, dry spells.

A word of warning—never apply fertilizers containing nitrogen (such as nitrates) after early summer (July in the Northern Hemisphere), as this tends to delay hardening off of the shoots in the autumn, leaving them prone to frost and cold-wind damage.

Pruning

A major sin in landscaping and gardening is the frequent neglect of pruning and shaping of plants. So homeowners get busy and let their plants become too high, too wide, or too floppy. Plants subject to this neglect include rhododendrons, flowering shrubs, dwarf conifers, and even perennials in most gardens. At Maplewood Nursery we, too, have been guilty of such treatment. In far too many cases we let a fine plant go unchecked for a few years and then suddenly realized that it was too big to continue to live in its allotted space. Hence, we either had to tear it out or prune it back drastically and start all over again. Severe pruning leads to several years of unsightliness or, even worse, a tree that cannot recover from such treatment.

Thoughtful pruning and shaping should be done each year. Better still, limited but constant pruning to shape a plant every season of the year is desirable. The smaller the pruning wound, the quicker it will callus over and heal. Shaping should start once the young plant is established, about two to three years after planting. These detailed remarks are given to emphasize the need to prune all Japanese maples.

Where large plants and great expanses allow, it is magnificent to permit these trees to grow unhindered. But unless a very tall, upright-growing Japanese maple is wanted, top shaping and pruning should be started early in the life of the tree.

Major pruning should be done during the dormant season after the leaves have fallen, from late autumn to midwinter (November to early January in the Northern Hemisphere), well before the sap starts rising prior to leaf production in the spring. Corrective pruning and training can be done at any time of the year except from late midwinter to late spring (January to May) when the sap is rising and all the plant's energy is devoted to the emergence and development of the young leaves.

Cuts should be made just beyond a pair of buds on the twig. Usually this will then produce two side shoots. When removing a larger limb, like any other pruning, the cut should be made just above the branch collar—the ridge or line where the branch joins an older branch or stem. Never cut below this natural barrier against the ingress of disease from a pruning wound. Cutting beyond this point not only gets behind the plant's last line of defense but it also creates an even bigger wound surface for disease to attack. At the same time an unnecessarily long stub should not be left, as it provides a greater food source for any disease to build up its strength before attempting to penetrate the tree's natural defense system.

The need for sharp pruning tools cannot be overemphasized. A clean pruning wound heals much more quickly than a jagged, torn wound created by blunt tools, and the wound calluses over more effectively. To prevent spreading disease from tree to tree, it is good practice to clean and sterilize pruning tools regularly. The use of tree-wound paint on cut surfaces is not recommended. Studies and trials in the 1980s and 1990s showed clearly that allowing the wound to dry out discourages the germination of disease spores on the open wood surfaces. Painting the pruned wood prevents drying out, and the spores, which are inevitably already on the wood surface, can live like lords, well protected from the elements and with ample moisture and food to thrive.

The fine, twiggy growth in some larger maples must be removed, especially from the laceleaf cultivars (*Acer palmatum* Dissectum Group). A tree that is too bushy inside invites insect and disease problems. Perhaps, even more important, is the proper display of the plant's structure. The cascading, undulating, and twisting branches of dissectums can be as beautiful and interesting as the foliage. Part of the beauty of this group of maples is the trunk and limb structure and texture. Periodically removing the inside growth of the trees enhances the display of the graceful trunk and branches during the winter months when the foliage is absent. In the case of 'Sango kaku', which has coral-red shoots, and 'Aoyagi', which has bright green shoots, the bark and shoot color is the outstanding feature and should be exposed.

The planting area at Maplewood was quite limited. It was necessary to plant hundreds of stock plants of numerous cultivars in a small area. Therefore, they were put much too close to each other to allow them to mature to the size which they would have reached had they been left unchecked. With judicious pruning

Magnificent fall foliage gives way to strong limb structures for winter enjoyment.
Photo by Peter Gregory

and shaping, these plants still fulfill their purpose and make good specimen plants. It would be nice to own unlimited areas, but not all of us are that fortunate. Pruning and shaping is the answer.

Plant Appearance and Cultural Conditions

It is important to consider several factors if one is seeing a cultivar for the first time—especially a young plant or a new graft. Different cultural conditions can alter the immediate appearance of many cultivars. This factor should be taken into consideration when comparing written descriptions with a plant growing in the landscape.

Sunlight is one factor affecting plant appearance. Extremely hot, direct sun will cause red-leaved cultivars, particularly in the Dissectum Group, to bronze more severely. Most variegated forms also need afternoon relief in areas of hot sun.

Excessive shade, like too much sun, also changes the leaf color of dissectum, variegated, and red-leaved cultivars so that they do not show their individual character to the fullest extent. The leaves of 'Garnet', for example, will display green tones rather than the garnet color for which the cultivar was named. Other red dissectums will have predominantly green leaves with subdued red. When newly propagated plants are grown under shadecloth (55 percent), they do not develop red colors or variegations in true color tones. Lighter colored leaves, such as those of 'Aureum', do not show the gold undertones for which they are so desired. Variegated leaves may be more predominantly green in deep shade.

Another factor in plant appearance is

soil fertility. Plants grown in very fertile conditions may mask the characteristics for which they were originally selected, particularly if they are variegated forms. Odd-leaved forms may produce normal leaf shapes and sizes. Good health is important, but overfertilizing can cause several difficulties.

Variegated cultivars are most often suspected of reverting (losing the color for which they were named). In some cases reverting is undoubtedly linked to overfertility on certain soil types or growing composts. Plants that have lost their variegation have been observed in later seasons to return to the variegated form as they matured and had less nitrogen available. This may not be applicable in all areas due to varying soil types. I have repeatedly made grafts of "non-cultivar" tips of 'Hikasa yama' and 'Hagoromo' (as well as some variegates). In every case, the second season after grafting produced the type foliage of the cultivar. If strong, nontypical shoots, which occasionally appear, become disturbing to the plant owner, they can easily be removed at any season of the year. When such shoots appear on very young plants, they should not be removed in the first year or so as this might weaken the plant too much.

Age also has some bearing on a plant's appearance. A cultivar should be judged only by the foliage produced on older wood. Leaves on vigorous new growth are quite often nontypical for the cultivar; instead, they are more typical for the species. This rule is especially true in the Linearilobum Group and with variegates, as well as the odd-leaved types, such as 'Hikasa yama'. Particularly in the linearilobums, the new foliage may have rather coarse lobes, even on two-year-old wood. This is an important consideration when judging the future quality of a seedling. Any special feature that may make a cultivar a possible candidate for naming may not appear until the third or fourth year. I have found several unusual forms in two- to three-year-old plants, which were not apparent for the first year. It is best to make a final judgment of a new seedling from the fifth year onward.

Growing Japanese Maples in Containers

Growing Japanese maples in containers has greatly increased in popularity in recent years. Many of the cultivars are ideal subjects for pots because of their tolerance, adaptability, shallow fibrous root systems, minimal feeding needs, and enormous choice of shapes, sizes, and colors. The adaptability, tolerance, and variation of Japanese maples for container growing is illustrated by their favored place in the ancient Japanese tradition of bonsai—plants on plates—an extreme example of how even the more vigorous forms can be grown as miniature trees.

Small gardens and landscapes, as well as patio gardens, fit the nature of these plants very well. Containers give Japanese maples even greater flexibility on where they can be placed for maximum impact: at entrances, in dark courtyards or sunny patios, on rooftops, against walls, among groups of other plants for added dimension and contrast, among flower beds and borders, and so forth. The effects of storms, high winds, or prolonged hot sun can be minimized by moving the containers into more sheltered conditions. In cold-exposed areas, they can winter in the garage, conservatory, or greenhouse and be placed outside for the summer. The container plant can be moved from place to place, according to the effect to be achieved, or the needs of the maple, thus thwarting the elements.

With proper but not overdemanding care, Japanese maples may be grown in

Most Japanese maples can be successfully grown in containers.
Photo by Harry Olsen

containers for several years without needing to be repotted or to have their roots pruned. Dwarf maples in ornamental urns are well suited to small patios and can be used singly or in small groupings. Where larger containers can be utilized, the range of choices increases greatly; the larger-growing dissectums and the upright cultivars do extremely well. The choice of form, color, leaf texture, and winter branching is wide-ranging.

The full-sized species and cultivars are easily grown well in tubs or large, permanent containers. Occasional directive shaping or pruning is not a demanding chore, attention possibly once or twice in a season being all that is required.

Two important requirements must be met in all container planting. First, the planting mixture must be open enough to allow good drainage and aeration and thus avoid becoming waterlogged. Second, the containers must be given faithful attention and not neglected for long periods of time during the growing season, such as a vacation or some other absence. Minimal fertilization is necessary to maintain good color, and moderate watering is required. Overwatering can be detrimental, but so can lack of watering during long dry spells. Unlike the roots of plants grown in open ground, the roots of container plants cannot search further afield for moisture. In areas subject to very cold spells during the winter, the containers should be wrapped in insulating material, such as straw, bracken, burlap, or bubble polyethylene, to prevent frost damage to the roots.

The gardener chooses not only the plant, but also the container, compost, position, aspect, timing of feeding and watering, so that the plant's well-being is completely in the gardener's hands. From the maple's viewpoint, this is potential luxury hotel treatment, receiving the full attention of the gardener, food and water tailored to its needs, no competition with few or no weeds, plus nursing, sun, shelter, or shade as needed.

Types of Containers

Containers can be any size, shape, or material. Generally, natural materials such as stone, terracotta, and wood are the most suitable for maples. They weather well and their appearance can improve with age. The traditional flower pot is a versatile shape which fits in with almost anything, as is the wide-mouthed deep bowl. These are often available in attractively colored glazed ceramics, such as deep blue, light turquoise, blue-green, and warm brown. Terracotta pots provide weight for stability and ideally should be frostproof or protected in extreme cold. The plain solid wood half-barrels suit most of the larger cultivars and can be very attractive, but can rot unless treated with non-toxic preservatives.

Light plastic containers allow the plants to be moved more easily, but tend to be unstable and, like glazed ceramics, restrict the movement of air between the roots and atmosphere. They can also get too hot in summer and need frost-protection in winter. Avoid pots that are too light or top heavy, and thus susceptible to being blown over even in moderate winds. Look in garden centers after gusty winds. Think twice about fat-bellied, globular, or small-necked containers—when the plant will need to be repotted in a couple of years, the only way to remove it will be by breaking the container.

The graceful and individual shapes of Japanese maples cry out for their own matching container. Ideally, the container should complement the plant and vice versa, but in practice the most suitable container available is generally used. Where possible, try to match the container with the maple and its surroundings and use natural materials.

Planting

Good drainage and an open friable planting medium which allows water and air movement through the soil is all-important. The rooting medium has to provide the initial nutrients for the tree roots to take up, remain open and porous enough to allow air and gases to pass through, have sufficient drainage to avoid waterlogging, and be free of weeds, diseases, and pests. Avoid the temptation to use garden soil or garden compost which rarely fulfils all these criteria, especially the last.

Japanese maples will grow in most commercial and loam composts, but they thrive best in slightly acid ones. An ericaceous, rhododendron, rose, or multipurpose compost is suitable, as is a loam-based compost such as John Innes No. 3 or John Innes ericaceous mix (both available in the United Kingdom). Loam-based composts have the added advantage of weight for stability. For adequate air and water movement, I find a mixture of three parts ericaceous compost and one part sharp sand the most successful. Avoid the temptation to use the readily obtainable builder's sand. It usually has a high proportion of fine particles which will soon clog up the compost and inhibit water and air movement.

Give the maple the best possible start by planting it properly. Ensure the container is clean by scrubbing it with a mild disinfectant and then thoroughly rinsing it. Place a 2.5- to 5.0-cm (1- to 2-in.) layer of drainage material, such as broken pot fragments, in the bottom. If the container is lightweight or top heavy, include some heavy stones or large pebbles to help stability. Cover with about 2.5 cm (1 in.) of stone chippings, and then a few inches of compost.

Gently loosen some of the outer young roots. If the roots are congested, tease out as many of the slender roots as possible. Place the maple upright in the center of the pot. Fill the pot with the rest of the compost up to about 5 cm (2 in.) from the container rim, to allow for watering. Only slightly firm the compost in stages. Avoid compacting the compost as watering will tend to do that. Apply a 13-mm (½-in.) layer of sharp granite chippings on the surface to help aerate medium, discourage weeds, and prevent water from clogging the surface layers. Granite chippings are ideal as their sharp edges are the perfect defense against slugs, snails, and creepy crawlies, and also discourage birds and small animals from foraging.

Immediately after planting is completed, soak the container and place it in position, preferably with the base off the ground. Propping it off the ground has several benefits: it helps air circulation and drainage, avoids waterlogged roots, discourages insects congregating underneath, and air prunes roots attempting to grow into the ground below.

Aftercare

Once in position, containerized maples are not demanding and do not entail much work, but frequent observation is essential. Conditions can change rapidly. The potted maple can be soaking wet one day and bone dry the next, looking great one day and covered with aphids a few days later. Container plants need regular attention during the growing season, including during holidays and other absences. Watering is necessary to keep the compost moist but not saturated during hot or dry spells, early in the morning or late evening on hot sunny days. Minimal but regular fortnightly feeding with a general purpose fertilizer from late spring to midsummer (May to July) is sufficient. If feeding starts too early, it encourages soft growth which is susceptible to late frosts and cold winds. If fertilizing continues later than midsummer, the soft lush growth does not ripen and harden before the autumn frosts. Weeding is rarely needed; the few weeds which do appear are easily plucked out.

By itself, growing maples in containers restricts plant size, so any pruning required is mostly simple and commonsense. Remove dead, diseased, weak, or straggly shoots as they appear. Also remove any shoots as necessary to maintain an attractive plant shape. Pruning can be done at any time of the year except when the sap may be flowing like a mountain stream and the first flush of leaves is appearing and developing. Ideally, prune young shoots during the growing season (from late spring) onward when the plant can quickly heal, thus sealing the pruning wounds.

Pests and Diseases

Keep an eye open for damage to container-grown plants by pests, disease, and the elements. Aphids, the horrid little green and black flies that may appear as early as late spring, should be treated with an insecticide as soon as they are spotted. Several products are available, including those for aphids on roses.

The roots of even the hardiest maples in tubs and containers are vulnerable to extreme frost damage from midautumn to early spring (October to March), as the frost can reach the roots via the container sides and bottom, which it is less able to do when the tree is planted in the ground.

Many terracotta and similar pots are also vulnerable to frost damage. Sleeves of straw, bracken, burlap, or several layers of bubble plastic can be wrapped round the container during this period to act as insulating cylinders.

In areas of extreme winters, the maple top can also be protected from freezing winds with bracken or straw wrapped loosely around the trunk. Young plants and tender maples can be moved into more sheltered areas such as the garage, conservatory, porch, or cool greenhouse.

Repotting

Young Japanese maple plants need to be repotted every year for their first couple of years. When planted in a suitable open medium and fed, watered, and looked after regularly, a well-established maple can grow for several years in the same container. Even with regular attention and pruning, the compost eventually becomes spent and the roots congested in the pot. Hence, the plant needs transferring into a larger pot with fresh compost. This can be done at almost any time, but is probably best during mild spells in late winter or early spring (February to March), so that the roots become immediately active in the new compost. Avoid transplanting in late summer and autumn, as the surrounding compost can become stale and sour while the roots are inactive through the long winter.

It is generally best to increase pot size gradually, from small to not-so-small, to medium, to larger, and eventually large, unless planting in a trough or sink with other companion plants. Replanting follows the same procedure as the original planting of the maple into a container, but it is even more essential to tease out the finer roots and to prune damaged or encircling older roots. It also is important that the surface of the compost in the new container is at the same level with the junction of the shoots and roots as in the previous container.

Conclusions

Japanese maple cultivars adapt well and make excellent subjects for container culture. The enormous diversity of shapes, sizes, leaves, and colors make them invaluable and easy to fit into any planting scheme as single specimens, complementing other container plants, among bedding and border plants, in dark courtyards or sunny patios. Always try to make the container the best you can afford, and the selection and care of the plant, planting medium, and situation of the highest standard you can provide.

The joys of container gardening are the way the plants work with you, improving all the time, arranging themselves in better ways and shapes, covering blank walls, and lightening dark corners. All they ask is to be fed and watered, sheltered from the cold winds and hot midday sun, and planted in adequate-sized pots. Perhaps, most exciting of all, container growing can extend the range of gardens in which beautiful tender maples, such as *Acer pentaphyllum* and *A. fabri* can be grown, and even allow other maples not yet in cultivation to be introduced.

However much thought and time is spent choosing the container, the maple, planting and selecting the perfect setting, it will all be for nothing without regular inspection and attention—feeding, watering, weeding, pruning, pest and disease control and protection. As mentioned in the introduction, from a maple's viewpoint, being grown in a container can be potentially the equivalent of luxury hotel living, receiving the full attention of the gardener to its needs, no competition, and with sun, shelter, shade, and protection as needed. In contrast, the container is a potential death trap if neglected. Maples are our friends, they give us a lot of pleasure, so we should not begrudge them the little but frequent attention necessary for their well-being.

Pests and Diseases

It should be emphasized that no attempt has been made here to present specific chemical controls. With the wide range of chemicals in use today, the constant change in control measures growing out of research, the fluctuating status of chemical residues and safety, and the varying regulations in different countries, it would be unwise to include specific recommendations for specific controls. If serious problems arise, contact the local authorities in plant disease and insect control or the nearest agricultural and horticultural research station. For the individual gardener, the experienced commercial nursery owner is usually a dependable source of advice.

Mass planting of *Acer palmatum* cultivars in the large landscape.
Photo by J. D. Vertrees

Insect Problems

Japanese maples are not often subject to serious insect infestations. No specific insects are major predators of these plants other than the range of insects normally found in any garden landscape. These include various aphids, mites, and worms (caterpillars). Thrips, leaf hoppers, scale insects, leaf miner flies, and leaf cutter bees are occasional pests. All can spoil the appearance of the leaves—significantly so in the case of an aphid explosion—but the general health and vigor of the trees are barely affected. Root weevils, such as the strawberry root weevil or vine weevil, kill off the roots of young trees with the subsequent death of the plants. They are mainly a problem in propagation and nurseries, but can also affect container-grown plants.

APHIDS

Aphids (plant lice of the family Aphididae) are small sap-sucking insects that feed along the veins on the undersides of leaves and on soft, newly emerged young shoot tips. Occasionally, they occur in great numbers in mid or late spring following a relatively mild winter. More rarely, sporadic infestation will be serious again in early summer or early fall. The excretion of the feeding aphids is the "honeydew" causing unsightly but harmless black sooty molds to develop in these areas. Usually the mold is barely noticeable. In serious infestations the appearance of choice maples can be ruined by the leaves becoming shriveled and stunted, but the harmful effect on the tree's future health and growth is minimal.

An aphid spray for the garden, such as that used for roses (which are especially susceptible to aphid attack), is usually an adequate control when applied from below to coat the undersides of the leaves. The treatment is especially effective if the infestation is anticipated and the spraying is carried out as soon as the first aphids are spotted.

MITES

Even more unusual are the occasional infestations of spider mites (from the family Tetranychidae). A hand lens is needed to see these minute "spiders" which, like aphids, also suck the sap from leaves. They cause speckled, yellowish areas along the leaf veins and, if a plant is badly infested, it can become defoliated as the leaves dry up, shrivel, turn brown, and drop off. Generally, spider mites can only successfully attack already sick trees, those under stress through growing in unsuitable conditions or in times of insufficient moisture. An experienced eye will detect the difference between mite damage and lack of water.

Sometimes, spraying the leaves with streams of water several times daily plus increased irrigation may offer some relief. Although several mite-control chemicals are available, the only effective control is to plant and maintain maples in suitable growing conditions, provide an adequate watering routine, and keep plants in good health.

Various gall mites and midges cause occasional disfigurement on maple leaves. Usually the damage is so slight on Japanese maples that no treatment is necessary.

WORMS (CATERPILLARS)

Leaves are again the target of several groups of other insects, including "worms," wasps, bees, and beetles (such as the Japanese beetle), which chew holes in the leaves and around the edges. The larvae of certain moths and butterflies—the "worms" or caterpillars (order Lepidoptera)—do most of this kind of damage. Examples are the fall cankerworm, the green-striped maple worm, and the maple-leaf cutter.

Usually these pests do only scattered damage on Japanese maples and are not a sufficient problem to cause concern. In areas where a serious outbreak does occur, mass-feeding larvae will sweep across the garden, consuming maple leaves along with those of other garden plants.

Some of the leaf-chewing larvae belong to the leaf-roller moth. The larva spins a web which rolls the leaf together, so that it can feed in the protective enclosure. These pests are difficult to control with sprays unless a wetting agent (surfactant) is added. For small areas handpicking is effective.

Gardeners experiencing serious or repeated problems with leaf-eating larvae may need to use chemical sprays which cover the insect or leave a deposit on the foliage which the insect takes in as it feeds. In most instances, the damage is minor and scattered, and controls are unnecessary.

BARK BEETLES

Bark beetles (from the family Scolytidae) occasionally attack stems and small limbs of Japanese maples, particularly in large concentrations of young trees and, often, when the trees are in poor health. Except in very unusual circumstances the damage is confined to a small limb or two. These tiny beetles, less than 1–2 mm long, attack a wide range of woody plants. In almost every instance the plant is in poor condition prior to the attack. The beetles are attracted to sick trees. The eggs are laid in the bark crevices, and the resulting larvae penetrate the bark and cambium and create a series of characteristic tunnels and "galleries" on the wood surface. They carry fungal spores in with them which develop along the tunnel walls and provide food for the larvae and resulting young beetles.

In this symbiotic relationship, the beetles take the fungi into a protective home with abundant food and moisture, while the fungi provide the beetles with a never-ending supply of mycelium as food. Only the tree suffers. The fungi block the cambium and cut off the sap flow to the leaves. In the spring, the fully grown beetles emerge to lay more eggs. The damage is done during the summer and autumn and may not be noticed until the following spring when the buds fail to develop because the limb or stem is dead. It is then that the numerous exit holes can be seen giving rise to the common name for these insects of shot-hole borers.

Cutting and burning infected material before the beetles emerge will help reduce further spread of the infestation. The chemical control methods needed are too exacting for the average gardener. Maintaining plants in good vigor is the best protection against this type of injury.

ROOT WEEVILS
Root weevils are occasional but specialized pests. Several species (usually genus *Otiorhynchus*, synonym *Brachyrhinus*) cause root damage to a host of plants, such as rhododendrons, maples, strawberries, and vines. Two popular names refer to these pests: strawberry weevil (*Otiorhynchus ovatus*) and vine weevil (*Otiorhynchus sulcatus*).

Vine weevil damage is rarely a problem for maples growing in open ground, but can be a problem for container-grown plants, especially in the nursery or greenhouse. Both the adult weevil and its grubs cause damage, although the adults are rarely a problem. The adult beetles are about 1 cm long and have dark brown, pear-shaped bodies with a black head and long snout. During the growing season the weevils emerge at night and chew irregular patches from the leaf margins, which can look unsightly but are rarely serious.

Weevil eggs are laid in midautumn (October). On hatching the resulting plump, creamy white, 1-cm (½-in.) long grubs with tiny brown heads burrow into the soil and start feeding on the plant roots. They do this through the winter, and the damage is not noticed until the spring when either the buds fail to develop or, because of insufficient sap reaching them, the emerging leaves wilt and die.

Pesticides available to gardeners are not usually strong enough to deal with vine weevil grubs. The grubs can be controlled by manually removing them when repotting the plant into fresh new compost in the autumn, or by watering nematodes, such as *Heterorhabditis megidis*, into the containers in the autumn, while the compost is still warm and moist.

WOOLLY SCALES
Woolly scales and horse chestnut scales (all in the genus *Pulvinaria*) are small, usually about 1 cm (½-in.) long, oval, and brownish scale insects that lay their eggs in mid to late spring (April to May) in conspicuous protective, white, woolly mounds on the stems and branches of maple, lime, and horse chestnut trees. They then lie on the mound surface and die. Their eggs hatch in midsummer and the tiny, yellowish nymphs migrate to the leaf undersides, along the veins where, like aphids, they feed on the sap, creating honeydew and encouraging sooty molds. The damage to the tree is very minor, but the white woolly mounds are unsightly and can spoil the tree's appearance.

Infestations are commonest after mild winters and in urban areas with mild microclimates. If these woolly lumps are considered too unsightly, they can be gently rubbed off throughout the summer using a mild detergent. In heavy infestations an additional control is to spray the leaf undersides with a garden insecticide from midsummer onward, thus reducing the chances of reinfestation the following spring.

Diseases and Other Problems

One of the most talked about and least understood problems of Japanese maples is twig dieback. Any one of a number of fungal diseases, insects, climatic conditions, cultural practices, and soil chemistry can cause this symptom. Disease should not be confused with a certain amount of "natural pruning" that takes place as the plant matures.

VERTICILLIUM WILT

One of the main causes of shoot or twig dieback in maples is *Verticillium* wilt. This fungus and its various strains affect an extremely large range of host plants, including maples. The effects of the disease are apparent in the native forests across the United States where wilt is a threat in arboreta and large-scale landscape plantings in all parts of North America—if not the whole Northern Hemisphere.

The early signs are wilting and dying back from the margins of the leaves. Then the shoots and branches die back and, occasionally, the whole tree. At this stage in most cases, bluish green to brown or black streaks can be seen in the sapwood when the branch is split. The tree may die in one year or over several years, with branch after branch dying back.

The spores of *Verticillium* wilt occur in the soil, and they enter the tree via damaged roots and root hairs. The fungus then travels up the tree via the cambium layers, blocking the sap and water movement upward. For this reason, the first sign of trouble is the wilting of the leaves and dieback of young shoots. Leaf blight, leaf scorch, and root damage cause similar early symptoms and are sometimes mistaken for *Verticillium* wilt.

A common means of transmitting the disease is by carrying it from plant to plant on contaminated grafting or pruning tools—cutting into healthy wood after cutting into infected material. It can thus be spread in the propagation house while cutting scions if the knives are not frequently sterilized.

Wilt is widespread and can be serious. Not enough is understood about its life history and there does not appear to be a dependable cure. Meticulous sanitation during propagation, careful attention to the maintenance of plant vigor and health, and the removal and burning of infected material help to limit further spread. If the tree dies, remove and burn all parts,

Mixed cultivars of *Acer palmatum* line a pathway.
Photo by J. D. Vertrees

including as much of the root as possible. In the garden it is a wise practice to clean pruning tools frequently with sterilants as a matter of routine, whether the disease is known to be present or not.

FUSARIUM AND BOTRYTIS

Verticillium is only one of many soil-borne fungi causing root rot in young plants. Root rot, or damping-off, presents a potentially serious problem in the propagating process, especially in nursery seedling production. Seed flats or concentrated seed beds may be attacked by the damping-off process, which often results in heavy losses. *Botrytis* and *Fusarium* species are two other culprits.

Fusarium, a fungus involved in dieback or loss of young plants, affects older plants also. Damage may occur at ground level, destroying the cambium at the base, or it may occur on twigs and limbs, destroying new buds and shoots.

Botrytis, also a serious threat, manifests as twig dieback, destruction of unfolding buds, or a breakdown of tissue at the base of young plants. During propagation in a warm, humid greenhouse, new shoots and leaves can be totally destroyed by this fungus. And in the field, overfeeding young plants, particularly with nitrogen, can increase losses. The danger escalates in warm, humid conditions without sufficient air circulation. *Botrytis* also invades dead, dying, and sick twigs and shoots. It can be seen as a gray mold on dead twigs. This fungus is secondary, invading only after the twigs and branches have been weakened or killed by other agents.

At Maplewood we experienced losses in one instance following frost damage. With a warm, humid, long fall, growth of new shoots continued to be very soft and sensitive into late autumn (November). Then a sharp frost occurred, "burning" back these unseasonably soft shoots. Once the shoots were killed, the remaining tissue was left susceptible to the entrance of *Botrytis*. The normal hardening-off process eliminates some of this vulnerability. As is true for many other problems, the best control for *Botrytis* is to keep the plants healthy, remove any diseased or damaged shoots and branches, and to grow the more susceptible cultivars, such as 'Beni hime' and 'Kiyohime', in conditions with good air circulation and not too much shade. Excessive shade and humidity around the young plants in the nursery can increase the risk of these diseases.

Like many very small-leaved dwarf maples, 'Beni hime' tends to suffer early spring damage from fungi on the new growth. This can happen as early as the breaking-bud stage and on fully developed new leaves. Diseases, such as *Botrytis*, can seriously affect the new leaves and terminal development. Good air circulation and full sun aid in prevention. Some fungicides help to suppress the disease.

ROOT ROTS

Two of the major causative agents of root rot in young Japanese maples are *Pythium* and *Pseudomonas* species. Like *Botrytis*, these fungi also invade dead, dying, and diseased twigs and shoots wherever high levels of soil moisture or of humidity prevail. In addition, *Pseudomonas* may cause sudden dieback in very small twigs, small branches or, in some cases, the loss of large branches and a major part of the tree.

Pythium and *Pseudomonas* attack and penetrate the fresh, unprotected tissue of the young emerging seedlings at ground level or below. The tissue at the base of the infected shoots darkens and withers, and the seedlings collapse onto their sides and die. The disease can swiftly sweep through nursery beds, causing quick death to very young seedlings. The danger in seedbeds is greatest in warm, moist springs and sum-

mers, and in alkaline and neutral conditions, especially if the soil is too heavy or rich in nitrogen. It is much less likely to affect seedlings on light, acid soils.

These fungi can also damage older seedlings and transplants, particularly during propagation in warm, humid greenhouses with poor air circulation. Losses can occur with these older plants but are rare. In these cases it is usually only parts of the cambium which are damaged. If excessive water is applied to container-grown plants or to plants growing in poorly drained soils, the danger is ever present. Excessive irrigation or poor drainage is ideal for fungal attack.

Culture testing in plant pathology laboratories is the only sure way of determining which fungus is responsible for the damping-off. Commercial growers should check local recommendations with the professional pathologist in their region. It is enough for amateur gardeners and landscapers simply to assume the problem exists if the above symptoms occur.

Soil drenches with fungal sterilants obtained from local garden stores for this purpose may be applied to seedlings, young transplants, and containers to provide some protection and to minimize spreading of the disease. Other control methods include coating the seed with fungicide, sowing seed less densely, and sowing early to get the seedlings through the most vulnerable stage before the warm weather arrives. The best remedy is to correct the adverse conditions which support the disease—usually overwatering, poor drainage, poor air circulation, and perhaps insufficient light. Giving special attention to the watering regime, growing medium, air circulation, and control equipment can help to prevent excessive moisture and enable the young plants to grow out of the susceptible stage as quickly as possible.

ANTHRACNOSE

Anthracnose (leaf blight) is a fungus that overwinters on dead shoots and attacks leaves the following spring, especially during wet, cool conditions. It causes reddish brown to purplish brown spots to appear on the leaves, which in turn become irregular dead patches. These spots may engulf entire young leaves of Japanese maples, causing them to shrivel and die. The fungus then moves down the leaf stalk into the shoot, eventually killing the infected shoot. By this stage there is no remedy that will save the plant. It is too late.

Preventing anthracnose is more effective than curing it. Where an attack has been known to occur, all dead shoots should be pruned, removed, and burned, and preventative chemical sprays applied just before bud-break the following spring, then twice more 10–14 days apart. By the end of treatment, the leaves and shoots should have passed out of the vulnerable phase and, combined with warm weather, be strong enough to resist any further attacks.

Good air circulation and full sun help protect 'Beni hime' and other small-leaved dwarf cultivars from fungal diseases which can damage new growth in early spring.
Photo by Peter Gregory

LEAF SCORCH

Leaves are also damaged by leaf scorch. Brown, dead patches spread from the leaf tip and margin inward between the veins. Defoliation and dieback of shoot tips follow prolonged droughts and heat.

Leaf scorch occurs whenever water is lost from the leaves faster than the roots can take it up. A wide range of untoward environmental factors, such as drought, drying winds, and hot sun, can cause it. Salt-laden winds, excessive alkalinity or nitrogen in the soil, and spring frosts can all have similar effects. Likewise, watering foliage during the sunniest and hottest part of the day results in leaf burning of container-grown stock and many maple cultivars, especially the red dissectums.

Usually, the plant is not lost, but appearance and vigor, for at least that growing season, are damaged. Watering and mulching can help to reduce the problem during drought and heat spells, but again, prevention is better than cure. Plant maples in less-exposed conditions, partially sheltered from prevailing or cold winds and from afternoon sun in the hotter areas. The availability of water should be regular and consistent to avoid prolonged drying from whatever cause, and good mulching helps reduce moisture loss from the soil. Most maples can cope with periods of hot, sunny spells, provided the roots have access to sufficient moisture to ensure that whatever is lost from the leaves is replaced immediately.

CHLOROSIS

Chlorosis, a gradual or general yellowing of the leaves, is a nutrient deficiency. It is most commonly associated with soils that are too acid or too alkaline, preventing the plants from taking up the nutrients concerned, usually one or a combination of essential micronutrients (trace elements). For instance, lime-induced chlorosis, occurring in soils of high pH, begins as a yellowing between the greener veins. It is due to a lack of iron available to the plant because of the presence of excessive calcium.

Strong, healthy Japanese maples can tolerate a wide soil pH range from acid to alkaline (pH 6.0–7.6), provided they are introduced into new conditions gradually—by mixing the appropriate compost with the soil at planting (that is, a rose compost for acid soils, and a rhododendron compost for alkaline soils). Like most plants, Japanese maples have limits. Very acid or very alkaline soils should be avoided by growing the trees in raised beds or in containers. Remedies involving the application of proprietary iron solutions provide only temporary relief in high pH conditions.

POWDERY MILDEWS

Powdery mildews are patches of whitish powder on the leaf surface which may sometimes cover entire leaves. Scattered tiny black spherical specks may develop later in these patches. These specks are the fruiting bodies of the fungi, which overwinter in the spore stage. The powdered areas are colonies of the summer spores of the fungi, which live on the surface, but penetrate and feed from the contents of the leaf cells. The leaves are not killed, but their appearance is spoiled.

Because powdery mildew becomes a nuisance only in very moist localities and seasons, preventative chemical spraying is rarely necessary, but can be successfully used if desired. Mildew is only a sporadic and not a general threat. In certain years some dwarf maple cultivars, such as 'Kiyohime', seem to be more susceptible than most Japanese maples for reasons not fully understood.

CANKERS

Cankers, or discolored, cracked, and often swollen patches on branches and stems, are a problem in some areas but generally are not major threats to Japanese maples. Dead spots occur on the bark, then increase in size annually to cause the dead tissue to discolor and split and, in some cases, exude reddish brown sap down the bark. Callusing around the canker creates a swollen, distorted appearance. If the growing canker encircles the branch, the branch above the canker dies. Small reddish or black pustules, fungal fruiting bodies, may occur on the dead areas in the summer, and a "fuzz" of small tendrils may extrude from these.

Many different fungi cause canker, including *Nectria* and *Phytophthora* species. They nearly always need damaged areas or pruning wounds to gain entry. Hence, the most effective treatment is to keep the trees healthy and vigorous and to carry out good pruning techniques, thereby helping to prevent the canker spores from gaining a foothold. If canker does occur, remove and burn all infected material, remembering to sterilize pruning tools in between cuts.

In conclusion, Japanese maples generally have fewer pathological problems than many other groups of woody ornamentals. When grown under normal conditions and with good culture, maples are remarkably free of disease and insect problems. The most serious dangers occur in the mass production of young plants, with possible infestations of root weevils and fungal attacks causing damping-off. Reasonable soil conditions, good positioning and planting techniques, regular watering, and sound cultural practices, especially regarding pruning and sanitation, will encourage healthy and vigorous growth, thus eliminating or minimizing most problems that can occur with Japanese maples in the garden landscape.

Acer palmatum and *Cedrus atlantica* 'Glauca' at Westonbirt Arboretum, Gloucestershire, England.
Photo by Peter Gregory

4 PROPAGATION

PROPAGATION METHODS VARY GREATLY from one part of the world to the next. Each propagator has developed his or her own technique, adapting procedures to suit the locality, climate, facilities, and personal abilities. I am convinced that Japanese maples can be propagated by almost any method used for other woody plants. Propagators should choose the method that gives them the best plants consistently and economically under the conditions in which they work. Today most Japanese maple plants are produced from seed or by grafting. Other methods of propagation used in a limited way include budding, rooted cuttings, and layering. Several excellent books on propagation are listed in the bibliography at the end of this book.

In the commercial production of maple trees, variables such as light, temperature, moisture, and air circulation are automatically controlled electronically. The widely used mist system of maintaining and controlling a moist atmosphere, and the newer "fogging" technique continue to be improved. Considerable progress has been made in the use of tissue culture techniques for propagating many woody plant clones, although no cases are known of its use for the large-scale propagation of Japanese maples. Nonetheless, serious propagators need to continue to monitor the prog-

ress of these and other improved propagation methods.

Seedling Production

The primary purpose of seedling production in nurseries is to obtain large quantities of understock for propagation by grafting. Of importance also, at least in the United States, is the production of strong, seedling-grown planting stock of *Acer palmatum* for garden landscape material. Such plants are much less expensive than grafted plants of named cultivars. They also make excellent trees, some even better than certain named cultivars.

In a few cases, a particular parent seed will yield a very uniform strain of red-leaved seedlings which lend themselves to growing-on for landscape material. These seedlings are usually sold as *Acer palmatum* f. *atropurpureum*. Good red-leaved strains of the upright forms are often grown to larger sizes, making excellent nursery plants for larger scale plantings. Also for large-scale plants, the green-leaved trees of the species can be impressive.

Most propagators prefer the green-leaved species for grafting understock. Some individuals even claim that grafting cannot be done on the red-leaved varieties. I find this to be completely untrue. Under like conditions I find grafting as success-

Facing: Japanese maple cultivars in a woodland setting at Westonbirt Arboretum, Gloucestershire, England.
Photo by Peter Gregory

ful, and the plants grown out to five-year tests perform equally well, whether on red- or green-leaved understock. Because the green-leaved understock is more plentiful, it is only logical to save the red-leaved seedlings for growing-on purposes.

Germinating Seed

The importance of stratification and the desirability of fresh seed cannot be overstressed. Since early times plant propagators have known that seeds of certain trees and shrubs must be chilled prior to germination. This rule is especially true for species of the temperate zone. In nature the seeds drop on moist ground in the fall and usually freeze prior to germination in the spring. Sometimes it takes two years or more for this process to occur in the wild. This knowledge led to the nursery practice of stratification.

Originally, stratification meant that seeds were layered in moist sand or soil and kept in cold storage near freezing temperature until it was time to sow them in the spring. A more accurate term might be "moist chilling." Maple seeds are mixed with moist peat or sand (a mixture of equal parts peat and sharp sand works well), enclosed in light, *breathable* plastic bags (which must be clearly labeled with the name and origin of the seed), and stored in the refrigerator.

I have had excellent results with both imported and domestic seed, which has been allowed to dry thoroughly in storage or transit, by pre-soaking it before stratification. Whether the seed comes with or without the wings attached, it is immediately soaked in warm water at 104–122°F (40–50°C), covered completely, and then held for 24–48 hours while the water is allowed to cool gradually. After cooling, the seed is drained and placed in a mixture of equal parts peat moss and sharp sand for stratification and immediately

treated with a fungicide. The seed is mixed about 50 percent by volume with the peat-sand and enclosed tightly in well labeled, breathable, polythene bags. The bags are stored at 33–39°F (1–4°C), the normal temperature of a domestic refrigerator, for no less than 60 days and no more than 120 days. The cooler temperature is desirable to minimize germination in the bag prior to preparation for sowing.

Seedling production from fresh-picked seed is preferred over dry seed and is almost identical to the procedure described above. The only difference is that pre-soaking should *not* be done if the seed was collected properly. At Maplewood, seed picked fairly early in the fall germinated at a rate of 75–90 percent. The best collecting period in Oregon was early autumn (September). Stock seed was gathered when the wings had become brown and dried, but the seed itself retained its original color, whether green, red, or yellow. Dewinging the seed would have not only created extra labor, but also the process could have allowed the seed to dry out to an unacceptable degree and, worse still, provided a possible access to disease. The seed was then immediately dusted with a fungicide, stratified, bagged, and labeled as previously described, until the following late winter or early spring (February–March).

The freshly harvested seed can also be sown immediately into pots, seed trays, or outside seedbeds to allow natural processes to stratify the seed. Unfortunately, all the enemies of the seeds are at work as well, so precautions against natural predators, such as mice and birds, must be taken.

Sowing

Seed trays and pots are usually used by amateur enthusiasts or when only small quantities of seeds are being sown. Each nursery will have its own method of preparing seedbeds, sowing seed, and protecting it to suit local conditions. Seedbeds can be raised flats or ground beds.

A suitable medium for amateur gardeners planting Japanese maple seed in trays or pots is the normal seed compost obtainable from garden centers. It already has a balanced fertilizer mix. The seed should be covered to twice the depth of the seed, preferably with a sharp, small grit to deter slugs and other pests as well as moss growth, and to help prevent excessive moisture around the root collar of the seedlings. No further nutrient applications are necessary as the seedlings, when large enough to handle, are "pricked out" into individual pots. Pricking out should be done with care and tenderness. It is best to handle only the leaves as the stems and roots are easily bruised and damaged at this stage.

Young seedlings require some shade, at least during the first growing season, commonly provided by lath shelters or netting. Watering should be done carefully to assure a constant supply of moisture, but the seedlings should never be allowed to become waterlogged. In early fall it is important to withdraw water gradually and to begin to harden-off the seedlings so they will be prepared for the first frost. They should not be in "soft-tip" condition at that time.

Constant attention to pests is necessary. Small leaf-eating caterpillars, aphids, spider mites, slugs, root weevils, birds, and squirrels all present a threat. Disease can quickly damage a concentrated planting of seedling maples. Damping-off fungi and gray-mold *Botrytis* are particular threats at this time.

Although I have grown seed both in seed flats in a shade house and in ground beds, I prefer raised seed flats to help prevent infection from soil bacteria, fungi, and other pathogens, as well as attacks by soil-inhabiting insects and other soil pests. Planting directly into well-prepared soil beds with the proper protection from soil pests and external pests, such as squirrels, cats, and other digging animals, is equally effective.

The seedlings should make a good growth from germination and go through a brief summer rest period. In late summer a second growth will occur. If prepared for this second growth period, the grower can obtain surprisingly large one-year-old seedlings with proper fertilization and moisture. At Maplewood, one-year-old Japanese maple seedlings reached up to 1 m (3 ft.) tall in seed flats.

Even though it is among the older Japanese maples, 'Tamuke yama' surpasses many of the newer hybrids because of its ability to hold its color through the summer. Photo by Peter Gregory

Usually one-year-old seedlings are separated during dormancy and potted-up in grafting pots for the following year, or transferred to larger pots, or lined out in ground beds for the second-year growth. Handling of understock is discussed in the section on grafting.

Much variation will be seen in seedling crops of *Acer palmatum*, depending on the parent trees. Some seed lots will produce quite uniform seedlings; others will show variations in almost every seedling. The latter is especially true with seed gathered from some forms and cultivars of *A. palmatum* subsp. *matsumurae*. Some of the most beautiful individual plants will be found among these seedlings.

Naming Seedlings

It is an enormous temptation for enthusiasts and commercial growers to name seedlings with great enthusiasm. Witness the past naming of rhododendrons and azaleas, certain dwarf conifers, and cultivars of many other plant genera. In his book titled *Azaleas* (1987), Fred Galle addressed very well the manifold problems arising from hasty and heedless naming. He noted that the only sound reason for registering a new cultivar name should be readily evident in one or more of the plant's characteristics—flower, habit, leaf, and so forth. He also pointed out the frequent confusion arising from the duplication of names for different selections.

The attraction to name almost every red-leaved Japanese maple seedling that appears is apparently a strong one. These seedling variations occur with great frequency when seed from certain red-leaved cultivars of *Acer palmatum* is sown. For example, sowing seed of 'Bloodgood' produces hundreds of red-leaved seedlings. With more than 60 red-leaved, upright cultivars already named, it is difficult to imagine the need for many more in this group.

It should be clearly evident that any new selection suitable for naming as a new cultivar must have such outstandingly desirable and distinctive features that it can easily be distinguished from any other existing cultivar. Discerning judgment must be exercised in selecting and naming a new form. This dictum applies with equal force in the case of dissectums and variegated maples.

Another valid reason for caution in selecting and naming new cultivars is that of misnomers or incorrect names. For instance, if enough seed of 'Sango kaku' is sown, several seedlings will undoubtedly appear that have the same kind of red bark as the parent. The rules of the *Cultivated Plant Code* (see discussion in chapter 2) do not allow any of the seedlings to carry the same name as the parent. They may well be look-alikes, but there will be differences in other characteristics which may or may not be immediately noticeable. This is just one example of a naming rule that growers should follow. Unfortunately, since this rule has been breached in a few cases, confusion already exists. 'Atropurpureum' is a prime example.

Experience has shown that selecting and naming a seedling too early may lead to disappointing results. Sometimes an outstanding feature may not persist into later years. A first-year seedling may show a particular characteristic. In the second, third, and fourth years, the seedling will settle down to show if that characteristic increases in desirability or if it tends to disappear. In some cases, the desirable features of a seedling remain for the first four to five years, but then gradually disappear by the eighth year. These disappointments are better discovered prior to naming and distributing new cultivars. Conversely, another seedling may show much better traits after the fifth year.

None of this should discourage the close

inspection of seedling populations and the picking out of outstanding seedlings. It is great fun to watch a seedling bed and, in some cases, see diverging types develop. Of course, most of the seedlings will be fairly uniform and similar to the species parent. Certain cultivars will produce variants much more readily. The seedlings not selected as particularly special are not a loss, of course. They can be used as understock or, particularly if the leaves are red or dissected, they can be grown to larger size for landscape and for large-scale plantings at reasonable cost.

Hybridizing

At Maplewood I have been doing a limited amount of controlled hybridization with hand pollination of selected male and female blossoms from various named cultivars of interest. Also, open-pollinated seed between interesting named cultivars has been sown and observed. This has resulted in tremendous variation in the seedbeds.

Very vigorous selection of seedlings is made after the second year, when leaf form and color are best judged. Usually the true character of a seedling does not show until leaves develop from two-year-old wood. Many outstanding red forms and other worthwhile seedlings have resulted, but only the truly outstanding clones should be retained. It is unnecessary to add to the already confusing abundance of red upright forms of named *Acer palmatum* cultivars.

From tens of thousands of seedlings produced at Maplewood over the years, I have found only two or three so outstandingly different as to warrant named cultivar status. One, a dwarf with divided and recurved leaves, was named 'Kamagata'. A second, with extremely fine and delicate linear separations of the leaf—almost hairlike—is a very dwarf form named 'Koto ito komachi'. These are well adapted for container, patio, or alpine gardens, but not

large landscapes. There was also an entirely different, deep crimson-maroon variegate named 'Yūbae', and another very different form of green-white variegate that showed considerable promise.

Cross hybridization within *Acer japonicum* clones produces some extreme forms. These range from very finely dissected leaves, approaching the delicacy of many of the *A. palmatum* Dissectum Group, to very large leaves, exceeding even those of the popular cultivar *A. japonicum* 'Vitifolium'.

Leaf pairs from selected *Acer palmatum* cultivars demonstrate visible differences between leaves growing on new, vigorous shoots (bottom row) and on older wood (top row). From left to right, 'Shinobuga oka', 'Trompenburg', 'Okushimo', 'Hikasa yama', and 'Red Pygmy'.
Photo by J. D. Vertrees

Leaf variation in *Acer japonicum* hybrids.
Photo by J. D. Vertrees

Distinct opportunities to develop worthwhile plants by crossing cultivars of *Acer palmatum* with other species in the series *Palmata* are available to anyone interested. Hybrids between *A. palmatum* and *A. circinatum*, *A. pseudosieboldianum*, *A. shirasawanum*, or *A. sieboldianum* offer possibilities for the serious propagator or hobbyist willing to spend the time and informed effort. Chance crosses such as the one that resulted in 'Trompenburg' indicate the possibilities, as do deliberate crossings, such as that of *A. palmatum* with *A. circinatum*, both in the series *Palmata*, to produce the outstanding *A.* 'Autumn Flame'.

Registering New Cultivars

Any new selection that has proven its worthiness and stability over a period of time should be registered to establish its name and its unique features. The registration of maple cultivars costs nothing except the effort of completing the registration form. The International Cultivar Registration Authority (ICRA) then publishes the details and history of newly named cultivars at regular intervals.

The advantages of registering the names of new maple seedlings are to minimize the risk of duplicating cultivar names, to aid in the recognition of new cultivars by publishing their description and history, and to help answer the problems arising from the use of local names. Many fine specimens are not known or properly registered outside their immediate area.

At present the registration of maples is done by The Registrar, ICRA for Maples, Westonbirt Arboretum, Tetbury, Gloucestershire, GL8 8QS, England. The ICRA for Maples maintains a comprehensive checklist of maple cultivar names which are in use or have been used or published in the past. It is updated annually and can also be used as a reference for the correct spelling of each name. Previously, such a fully comprehensive list of correctly spelled names has not been available to growers and enthusiasts, resulting in the duplication and misspelling of some names.

How easy is it to register a new cultivar name? Once a name has been selected, it can be sent to the registration authority together with at least a brief description highlighting the main features of the new cultivar, especially why it has been selected and how it differs from a similar existing cultivar(s) if any, and if it has been published, the name and date of the publication should be included. If possible, include a copy of the published account and, ideally, shoot/leaf samples.

It should be noted that registering a plant is not the same as patenting a plant. Plant patents are pursued through quite different channels.

Grafting

Grafting is the principal method of propagating Japanese maple cultivars both in commercial production and for the hobbyist. In collecting data from commercial operations in the United States, Japan, and Europe, I found that the timing and methods of grafting vary considerably. I also found that each propagator introduces his or her own variant of the basic operation to suit local conditions and purposes. It should be emphasized that, because there are wide variations in the same basic principles, it does not follow that some are right and some wrong. Each variation is appropriate for that particular propagator.

Timing varies widely. Most grafting is done during late winter (January–February), especially in the United States and Japan. Summer grafting (mid-June to early July), when the tips of the current shoots are just beginning to firm up, is popular with many propagators in Europe and with some in the United States. A few propagators in the United States do successful grafting in mid to late autumn (October–November).

Understock

The understock used varies from one- to three-year-old stock in grafting pots varying from 5 cm (2 in.) "rose-pots" to 4-liter (1-gallon) containers, as for *Acer palmatum* Dissectum Group standards. Most grafting is done using two-year-old seedlings of *A. palmatum* as understock. Some propagators prepare the understock by potting-up one-year seedlings and growing them on for the second year in their grafting pots. Others grow the understock in the ground until the fall of the second year, and then pot them up and transfer them to the greenhouse or grafting house for winter. Summer grafting requires potting the understock in the fall prior to grafting.

Carrying the potted understock during the second growing season demands extra care. Water stress must be avoided to produce good growth and full root systems. The potted understock must be protected against soil insects and disease, for the grafting effort will have been wasted if the understock has had unknown insect or disease damage. Potting-up the understock just before the grafting period automatically sorts out stock with poor root systems or weevil damage.

In an old Japanese method used at Maplewood, grafting was done on potted understock freshly dug up from the growing beds. In late autumn or early winter (November–December) the understock was dug up and potted, then watered and left to drain thoroughly outside or in the unheated greenhouse. The growing medium was allowed to dry but not to the point of stress or desiccation, because a medium that is too wet permitted the understock to "bleed" exces-

sively during and immediately after grafting, thus inhibiting the healing of the graft union. The potted understock for winter grafting was placed in the unheated greenhouse in late fall or early winter, and the shoots trimmed back to about 15 cm (6 in.) tall. About two weeks prior to grafting, the greenhouse temperature was raised to 60°F (15°C) to bring the understock into active growth. The stock was ready to graft when the buds began to swell but before leaves were produced.

One good way to determine if the stock is ready for grafting is to gently turn out a pot or two and observe whether white roots are starting to show in the root ball. If there is good root activity, grafting

Newly cut graft of 'Aratama' with the understock trimmed.
Photo by J. D. Vertrees

should begin. It is important not to have the understock too advanced as the sap flow in maples could be strong enough to "bleed" at the cut surface and drown the graft, thus preventing the healing of the cut surfaces.

When the grafting was done, the night temperature in the greenhouse was increased to 65°F (18°C) and the day temperature was maintained, as much as possible, below 80°F (27°C) when the grafts were producing leaves. Shading and ventilation were used to protect the young growth from excessive heat and sunlight, which would burn the new tips.

Propagators in other areas, and thus employing different time schedules, must make adjustments to meet their own needs.

Scions

For winter grafting, scions are collected from dormant plants. The scion is the short piece of shoot that is inserted into the understock to form the graft. Ideally, scions should be collected immediately prior to grafting, when the understock is ready. In commercial nurseries, large quantities have to be collected in advance. In this case, they should be trimmed to the proper length and stored slightly moist (not saturated) in a plastic wrap or polyethylene bag in a refrigerator at a temperature very close to freezing—33–36°F (1–3°C). The scions should never be allowed to dry out, even when handling during the grafting operation.

I prefer a scion of one-year-old shoots or, if not available, then a scion from wood not older than two years. Young wood heals more quickly. For extremely dwarf cultivars, with only 6–12 mm growth per year, I have used four-year-old wood. The scion should have at least three pairs of buds. The length will vary from 2.5 to 20 cm (1–8 in.), depending upon the cultivar and its vigor. Terminal shoots are often selected and are usually excellent wood for grafting. Very special care should be taken when selecting the scion wood. Winter damage, hidden disease, and other weakness might be present. Each scion should be carefully inspected again prior to grafting. Wood damage caused by low winter temperatures may not show the weakness at time of collection.

Cambium

The single most important aspect of grafting is the successful union of the cambium layers of the scion and the understock. It is important to understand what this layer is and how it can be matched and united so that the resulting graft will heal.

In woody plants the structure of roots and stems is formed of three basic parts. The bark is the outer covering, mainly for protection. The central core is the wood, which mainly provides structural strength to support the plant. It is the major part of the plant. Between these two parts is the relatively thin circle of tissue called the cambium layer. In this layer most of the life functions take place. The cambium contains growth production cells, tubes conducting moisture and nutrients up and down the plant, and the cells responsible for the growth and regeneration of tissue.

The following oversimplified explanation may help readers visualize the important plant structures involved. Imagine a broomstick with a tight-fitting pipe slipped over it which, in turn, is wrapped up in strong burlap. The broomstick represents the wood structure, the pipe represents the cambium layer, and the burlap is the bark. It is the "pipe," or cambium, with which we are most concerned in grafting. The cambium is composed of cells involved with growth and with regeneration when damage occurs. Grafting cuts are a form of damage that the plant tries to heal via the cambium. If the cambium layers of the scion and the understock fit closely, the cells will unite and repair the "damage," resulting in a graft union.

All other aspects of grafting are essentially either culture or mechanics, such as the growth and care of the understock, grafting methods, and post-grafting care. Each is variable. The one constant item is that the cambium layer of the scion must match, or join at some point, that of the understock to start regeneration of the cells, which results in the union of the graft.

It is true that a graft can succeed when only a few cells are joined, but the more that do, the quicker the damage will be repaired and the better and stronger the graft. The ideal graft is one where the cambium diameter of the scion exactly matches the cambium diameter of the understock. Such a scenario is usually not possible. Therefore, specific attention must be given to matching at least one side of the scion cambium to one side of the understock cambium. The older the understock, the thicker its cambium layer under a deeper bark cover. Conversely, in young scions, the cambium is a very thin layer under very thin bark. Matching these can be very difficult, especially with tiny, dwarf cultivar scions. It is often impossible to place these on understock of equal diameter, as this size base would be too weak.

Grafting Techniques

Japanese maples are normally propagated by the side graft method, also called the veneer graft. Detailed descriptions and step-by-step illustrations of this method and others can be found in any good publication on plant propagation, including those listed in the bibliography.

'Ki hachijō' and 'Nuresagi' are excellent companions for fall color.
Photo by J. D. Vertrees

I cannot emphasize too strongly the necessity of having an extremely sharp knife for graft cuts. It is not possible to have it too sharp. The cambium layer is so thin and soft that it is easily bruised. The smaller cultivars with tiny scions have an unbelievably thin cambium—only a few layers of tiny cells in thickness. A knife that may be thought sharp may, in fact, be comparatively dull. All cuts must be very clean. Bruised cambium tissue does not heal or, at best, heals weakly. It can cause up to 50 percent loss in grafting. A new, single-edged razor blade does an excellent job as a grafting knife and is easily replaced when it loses its sharpness.

With a very sharp knife, a long, slanting slice is removed from the base of the scion. The cut will be 12–25 mm (½–1 in.) long. The thickness of the cut varies with the diameter of the scion. On the opposite side, a very short cut is made to form a point at the scion base.

A corresponding cut is made, angled downward, into the side of the understock. The cut should be slightly longer than that on the scion to assure a closely matched placement of the graft. The cut should be very low on the plant, toward the shoot base, and should never penetrate more than one third of the shoot diameter. The resulting flap should have the upper two thirds of the end removed.

The scion is then slipped into the matching cut of the understock, pressing the point firmly into the notch to unite as much of the two cambium rings as possible. Next, the flap is brought up over the short cut on the outside of the scion base. The graft should be tied firmly. I have used strips of budding rubber pulled firmly tight but not tight enough to choke the cambium layer. Holding the scion in place, the tie is spirally wrapped around the graft to immobilize the scion until the cuts are healed

(callused over) and a good union has been achieved. Some propagators tie with plastic strips, cotton thread, grafting tape, and so forth. The important point is to keep the scion firm in the understock, with both cambium layers in contact, until healing is completed.

After tying, it is usual to coat the graft with a good grafting wax or compound to protect the vulnerable cut surfaces from disease entry, minimize moisture loss, and keep the tape in position. Some grafters paint with beeswax mixtures or paraffin. Others dip the entire graft, understock and scion, into melted wax. I prefer the grafting wax emulsions, only coating the cut and joined surfaces on both sides of the understock. Some of the new plastic-based pruning paints are too constrictive on the very small grafts of some cultivars. As growth starts, these preparations will constrict and choke the growth. The ties are usually cut later in the season when the grafts are planted out of the greenhouse.

There are as many variations to this method of grafting as there are propagators. In Europe many grafters will make a short, tapered cut in the scion, rarely over 1 cm (⅜ in.) long, with a rather stubby point. In Japan, grafting is sometimes done with the top of the understock removed, grafting directly onto the stub with the entire union wrapped to keep out the air. One variation on this is saddle grafting where the top of the understock is removed with two shallowly angled cuts to leave a "blunt screwdriver" cut surface, and two corresponding cuts are made in the scion base to form an angled channel to fit closely over this. A cleft graft is the exact reverse. My feeling is that neither a cleft graft nor a saddle graft results in as smooth a union as a side or veneer graft.

In commercial grafting with unpotted understock, a dormant scion on a bare-root is attached to a dormant understock with a short side graft into the top of the stub. The entire graft is then plunged into moist peat beds in the greenhouse to cover the union. This technique is known as a bench graft. As growth develops, these grafts are then potted up and kept in the greenhouse for the rest of the growing season.

As mentioned earlier, grafting is done very low on the understock, especially for the upright cultivar forms. This makes a nice trunk when planted out and the tree matures. With cultivars of the Dissectum Group, low grafting is also done, but in this case the pendulous new growth is staked and trained upward for a few years.

Many dissectums are grafted onto a standard, in which case the scion is grafted near the top of a 30- to 90-cm (1- to 3-ft.) tall understock. This gives a good, strong, straight understock from which the cascading varieties can arch down. I have seen and have made a few grafts on good, straight, three-year-old understock which was 1.5–2.0 m (5–6 ft.) tall. With a few years of training, these special grafts form spectacular specimens of dissectum cultivars.

Summer Grafting

Summer grafting follows the same process as winter grafting but with variations in handling and, of course, timing. The understock is potted up during dormancy the previous late fall or early winter. After the active spring growth period, the understock is allowed to dry out in the pots until the leaves approach wilting point. The understock is then cut back to 15 cm (6 in.) and the leaves carefully removed. Mean-

Interest in this large landscape is achieved in part through the skillful combining of Japanese maples with a variety of foliage textures.
Photo by J. D. Vertrees

while, the new growth on stock plants has gone into the summer rest period. The scions are collected from those new shoots and protected from drying out. They are cut and inserted into the prepared understock using the side-graft method, and tied together with grafting tape.

Except for the terminal pair of leaves, most leaves are removed to reduce water loss by transpiration. Waxing is not necessary when the newly grafted young trees are placed immediately under an automatic mist system. The frequency of misting is timed to keep the grafts moist but not waterlogged. There must be no delay in getting the grafted plants under the mist system. The graft will heal within days (temperature also determines the length of time), and the union will be complete, allowing the misting to be reduced over a week or so until it ceases altogether. Summer grafts do not always put out new shoot growth.

Budding

I have been successful with T-budding, chip-budding, bud sticks, and patch budding. I have even seen good grafts made with short bud sticks inserted at right angles to the understock. This method of using limited material assures that more cambium cells are in contact with the understock. The final graft may not be as smooth, but it is a method which will allow more successful grafts to increase the stock plants of a very rare and limited cultivar.

Chip-budding is popular with some propagators and is an excellent adaptation of a long-used procedure involving an individual lateral bud with its thin backing of wood. A chip is made with a short downward cut below the chosen bud. A longer, slightly curved, slanting cut is made starting above the bud, going down behind the bud, and joining the back of the chip.

An identically shaped cut is made in the understock and removed. The new bud is then inserted and secured in this position. Minute variations in cutting, inserting, and securing the bud depend on the individual propagator and his or her experience, but seem to yield equally good results.

One advantage of chip-budding is that it can be done successfully at almost any time of the year, thus extending the grafting period. Also, because it utilizes only a single bud, more grafts can be made from limited material of scarce or rare cultivars or species. Some propagators like it because they can make two, three, four, or even more chip-bud grafts on a single understock. This can save a lot of time to produce saleable plants when top-working dissectums on tall standards. Other ornamental variations are sometimes made, such as inserting one bud from each of two or three different cultivars into the same understock. Chip-budding also gives something larger to work with than the small single bud used in regular budding.

Of course, all these objectives can be achieved by T-budding, bud sticks, and patch budding, but chip-budding seems particularly adaptable for use with Japanese maples. T-budding and patch budding work well for cultivars with larger buds but not for dwarf forms such as the many yat-subusas. The extremely small buds are difficult to place properly. Any good reference book on propagation will show these basic procedures.

Budding, patch buds, and bud sticks may be used in the summer grafting method as outlined above. It is also possible to bud on the understock lined out in the field, if necessary. Likewise, various types of budding are successful when done in the greenhouse in winter. None of these methods is widely used because the size of the material is quite small and thus hard to handle properly.

Post-Graft Care

Post-graft handling, also known as weaning, must be given close attention. After the scion produces new growth in the greenhouse, the understock should be clipped off immediately above the graft. Care should be taken that the new graft is not pressed or put under strain or else the union of the newly healed scar tissue will be broken. The newly trimmed grafts should be shaded from hot sun and given adequate water and fertilizer. The temperature should be controlled to prevent excessive chilling or overheating. The scions will go through a period of new growth and, within two months, newly formed buds will become apparent. This is the time to start hardening-off the grafts, preparing them for winter by reducing the feeding and watering, eliminating nitrogen feed altogether, and increasing air circulation. It is very important that grafted plants be well hardened-off as fall approaches, ready for overwintering.

Cuttings

Propagation of Japanese maple cultivars is usually by grafting, but the rooting of cuttings has been successfully used in some cases. Most propagators feel that many cultivars are better grafted than on their own roots from cuttings. Japanese maple cultivars, in general, have not proven to be as strong or as reliable on their own roots as when grafted onto good seedling understock. Some plant failures in rooted cuttings, as they get older, is attributed to their being on their own roots, but I have observed very satisfactory plants from two nurseries where rooted cuttings of several cultivars were made.

I have made cuttings of many cultivars of *Acer palmatum* and *A. japonicum* and demonstrated to my satisfaction that some root very poorly, if at all. Other cultivars, such as 'Bloodgood', root very well and seem to make very strong older plants. The dissectums in general and most dwarf cultivars are not readily rooted, although certain cultivars do fairly well.

Propagation by cuttings can be done in several ways. Most cultivars can be propagated by using either softwood cuttings in summer or dormant, hardwood cuttings.

Summer Cuttings

Summer cuttings of semihard wood are one method used. As soon as the spring shoot has hardened or stiffened up in early summer, the selected shoots can be cut into pieces 8–15 cm (3–6 in.) long. Care must be taken to protect the cuttings from drying out and wilting. The cutting is prepared by carefully removing all but the top pair of leaves to reduce water loss by transpiration. With a very sharp, clean blade, a 2-cm (¾-in.) long slanting cut is made in the base of the cutting. This cut should not extend into the center of the cutting. It is usually necessary to dip the base of the cutting into a proprietary rooting powder or solution.

The prepared cuttings are then inserted into a peat-sand, perlite-sand, or other suitable mixture in cutting beds or pots. Good drainage is essential so that the cuttings do not become waterlogged. Many commercial nurseries provide bottom heat set at 71–75°F (22–24°C), as well as an automatic mist system to prevent any drying out. For the amateur, humidity can be maintained by placing the pot in an upturned, thin, breathable plastic bag, sealing the base round the pot with an elastic band. The pots must be sheltered from any sun, at least until the roots are firmly established. In propagating houses or in pots, some shading is necessary for new growth on *Acer palmatum* cuttings.

Winter Cuttings

Some propagators have equal success with dormant (winter) cuttings of hardwood. The material is gathered in midwinter (January), prepared and inserted in the same way as the summer cuttings. Bottom heat is held fairly low, at 65°F (18°C) for the first 7–10 days until callusing occurs. Heat is then increased to 72°F (21°C). As new growth develops, close attention must be given to moisture supply and shade.

Layering

Layering is a method of obtaining a few larger plants in a short time, or of expanding the supply of a choice plant. Hobbyists who do not have grafting or other propaga-

tion facilities sometimes find this method easier.

Air Layering

Air layering can be successful for *Acer palmatum* cultivars using the same technique described in any good propagation book for other plants. At Maplewood, midspring (April and very early May) is the most desirable time as active cambium cells and some leaf production appear to speed up the callusing. With a clean, sharp knife, a slanting cut to about one third of the stem diameter is made at the point chosen for the new base of the plant-to-be. The cut is dusted with a hormone powder just before wrapping. The cut area is then packed with damp sphagnum moss and enclosed with polyethylene sheeting. The covering must be tightly sealed at both ends to prevent

Japanese maple cultivars in a woodland setting at Westonbirt Arboretum, Gloucestershire, England.
Photo by Peter Gregory

drying out and to prevent rain from entering and wetting the enclosed area excessively. The plastic enclosure must then be wrapped in aluminum foil or some other material to protect the enclosed area from excessive heat from the sun's rays.

New roots will have formed and can be observed in the fall or the following spring. The shoot is then cut off just before the rooted area. The new roots are very brittle, and so planting must be done with great care. Shade and shelter should be given the new plant for the first season following planting.

Normal Layering

Normal layering or "stooling" into the ground works well for special conditions. It can give several good plants from a single stock plant at any one time. The stock plant is cut back or "coppiced" the previous year to induce bottom sprouting the following spring. A small slice or wound is made near the base of each new young shoot. A mix of peat moss, bark, and open loam or any good, friable material with good drainage is mounded up around the bases of the new shoots. This arrangement should be left for two seasons to ensure that a new strong root system develops. The rooted shoots are then removed from the parent plant (the "stool") during the following dormant season and transplanted for growing-on. This method is very hard on the stock plant, which should be rested for a year or two before repeating the layering.

Alternatively, layering can be done by carefully bending one or two low current-year shoots to the ground, wounding the underside of the bend, and pegging them down on the already prepared ground patch. The ground preparation will be the same as for the mound mentioned above. The vertical end of the shoot will need to be staked to hold it upright and to prevent disturbance of the rooting area. This technique would be more suitable for the amateur grower than the "stooling" form of layering.

5 *Acer palmatum* and Cultivars

Acer palmatum Thunberg ex Murray (1784)

COMMON NAME: Smooth Japanese maple

JAPANESE COMMON NAMES: Iroha momiji, Iwato beni, Kaede noki, Momiji, Tako kaede

Acer palmatum is a variable, complex species with numerous varieties and forms. It is the species to which most Japanese maple cultivars belong. Three subspecies are currently recognized.

Acer palmatum subsp. palmatum has bright green small to medium-sized leaves. The five to seven lobes are palmately arranged, usually divided moderately deeply, but sometimes almost entirely to the leaf base. The lobes are ovate-lanceolate and acuminate, and terminate in a sharp tip. The margins are coarsely double-toothed. The small red and cream flowers appear in late spring to early summer (May to June) and develop into small winged fruit (samaras), which ripen in early to mid autumn (late September to early October). The samara wing plus nutlet is one of the smallest in the genus, about 1.5 cm long, and has a small, smooth, rounded nutlet.

This subspecies forms an upright-growing tree, usually with a domed or broad canopy. In its natural habitat, the tree reaches a height of up to 12 m (40 ft.), although trees this tall are not often seen in cultivation. Some plant explorers have reported trees of 25 m (83 ft.) in native stands. Trees of this subspecies are thrifty and hardy, and in cultivation seem to adapt to a wide variety of growing conditions. Subspecies *palmatum* is confined to Japan, on the islands of Honshu, Shikoku, and Kyushu, and to southwestern Korea. It grows in moist valleys and along streams up to an elevation of 1100 m (3630 ft.).

Acer palmatum subsp. amoenum (Ō momiji) has much larger leaves with usually seven shallowly to moderately deeply divided lobes. The margins are evenly and finely toothed. The flowers and fruits are much larger than those of subspecies *palmatum*, and each samara measures 2.5–3.0 cm long. This subspecies is found as an understory tree in and on the edge of mountain forests throughout Japan, and in the southwestern coastal areas of China and Korea.

Acer palmatum subsp. matsumurae (Yama momiji), like *A. palmatum* subsp *amoenum*, has larger leaves, flowers, and fruits, but the seven- to nine-lobed leaves are very deeply divided—more than three quarters of the way to the leaf base—and

Facing: 'Westonbirt Red'.
Photo by Peter Gregory

the margins are often coarsely double-toothed. This subspecies is more shrub-like than either of the other two subspecies and, if it forms a small tree, is rarely more than 10 m (33 ft.) in height. It is native to the mountain forests of Japan at elevations up to 1300 m (4290 ft.) and is mainly part of the understory.

The cultivars of *Acer palmatum* are described in the following pages in alphabetical order. Included are most of the plants that are in cultivation. The descriptions of cultivars known in the late 1970s are primarily derived from specimens growing in the Maplewood collections, augmented by written material from early literature. The descriptions of newer cultivars are based on specimens seen in various collections and nurseries, material received, and information provided by the origina-

tors or other knowledgeable collectors and growers. It has been difficult to describe adequately all the subtle differences occurring between cultivars. The color illustrations of the foliage were planned to assist in identification and not to present landscape situations. The cultivar are described under seven groups, based mainly on the division of the leaf lobes or, in the case of the dwarf group, the ultimate height of the cultivar. These groups are as follows:

Amoenum Group
Leaf lobes shallowly to moderately divided, usually up to two thirds of the way to the leaf base.

Palmatum Group
Leaf lobes moderately to deeply divided two thirds to three quarters of the way to the leaf base and, in some cases, almost to the base.

Acer palmatum in fall at Westonbirt Arboretum, Gloucestershire, England.
Photo by Andrea Jones, Garden Exposures Photo Library

Matsumurae Group

Leaf lobes mostly very deeply divided more than three quarters of the way to the leaf base.

Linearilobum Group

Leaf lobes narrow, straplike, divided to the leaf base.

Dissectum Group

Leaf lobes very deeply divided and deeply dissected into sublobes.

Dwarf Group

Cultivars whose mature height does not usually exceed 2 m (6 ft.).

Other Group

Cultivars that cannot be placed in any of the above groups.

The names of the first three groups (Amoenum, Palmatum, and Matsumurae) follow the terms used in earlier editions of this book and in recent literature. Although they imply that each member of the group has all the characteristics of the natural subspecies associated with these group names, that is not necessarily true and can be very confusing. Splitting up the hundreds of cultivars into these artificial groups has been done for convenience and as an aid to identification. Many cultivars are hybrids between the subspecies or between *Acer palmatum* and other related species. As a result, the various characteristics distinguishing the subspecies are mixed up. Hence, there are a few cultivars, which could equally well be placed in either of two groups.

'Abigail Rose'

DWARF GROUP
VARIEGATED

This eye-catching plant is like a small form of the well-known and unmistakable popcorn maple 'Hikasa yama'. It was selected by Harold Johnston, Alabama, and named

The five basic leaf shapes of *Acer palmatum* (clockwise, from top left): Amoenum Group, Dissectum Group, Matsumurae Group, Palmatum Group ×2, Linearilobum Group. Photo by Andrea Jones, Garden Exposures Photo Library

'Abigail Rose'. Photo by Talon Buchholz

after his granddaughter. Like 'Hikasa yama', the buds of 'Abigail Rose' open up in spring to create a burst of red, pink, and cream color. The small five- to seven-lobed palmatum-type leaves have a dominant center lobe and become bright pink and cream, then a cream and green network for the summer. Fall color is orange-pink to red. 'Abigail Rose' grows slowly to 2 m (6 ft.) tall and about 1.5 m (5 ft.) wide in 10 or so years and is ideal for small gardens, raised beds, and containers.

'Aka kawa hime'

PALMATUM GROUP
GREEN

A semidwarf form of 'Sango kaku', this outstanding cultivar was selected and named by Del Loucks of Del's Japanese Maple Nursery. It retains all the desirable attributes of 'Sango kaku'—fresh yellow-green spring foliage, bright red shoots and leaf stalks, eye-catching yellow, gold, and red fall colors, culminating in attractive coral-red winter stems. The typical palmatum-type leaves are identical in shape, size, and seasonal coloring to those of 'Sango kaku',

'Aka kawa hime'.
Photo by Francis Schroeder

'Akane'.
Photo by Cor van Gelderen

but this cultivar is unlikely to exceed 3 m (10 ft.) in height, making it ideal for container culture and small gardens. The name means "small red bark."

'Akane'

PALMATUM GROUP
GREEN

This small cultivar is one of several valuable for their bright spring foliage. As the leaves of 'Akane' emerge, they are a striking orange-gold with margins shading into deep pink. The orange is more intense than that of the well-known 'Katsura', another member of this group, and the color contrasts well with the bright, coral-red leaf stalks and shoots. The spring colors last for almost a month and turn a deep, clear yellow, gradually becoming a light green. The fall colors are shades of orange and yellow with reddish blushing, but not outstanding.

The small to medium-sized mainly five-lobed leaves are usually longer than broad and deeply divided. The lobes are ovate-triangular with pointed tips and are broadest in the lower third and narrowing toward the lobe junctions. The margins are clearly toothed. The straight, slender leaf stalks are shorter than the leaves.

Firma C. Esveld imported this delightful, compact, semidwarf tree into the Netherlands from Japan in 1991. It is proving to be slower growing than 'Katsura', but the spring coloring is more intense and longer lasting. Plant height at maturity is unlikely to be more than 3 m (10 ft.) with a crown spread of about 1.5 m (5 ft.). The short, thin shoots make this cultivar difficult to cultivate. The name means "the madder plant." Because of the color of the dye obtained from the madder plant, the name has also come to mean "glowing evening sky," which describes perfectly the foliage color in spring.

'Akegarasu'

MATSUMURAE GROUP
RED

This very old cultivar from Japan has large red leaves with five to seven lobes divided nearly to the leaf base. The broadly ovate-elliptic leaves come to a very sharp point and have toothed edges. The early season color is a very deep purple-red or black-red, depending on the light. Later in the summer, the leaves bronze somewhat, showing more green. As is true for other red-leaved Japanese maples, the red of 'Akegarasu' is not as intense in early summer when the plant is grown in shady conditions. The deep red leaf stalks are shorter than the leaves. The branches are green.

This upright, strong maple reaches at least 5 m (16 ft.) tall at maturity and tends to widen into a broad-topped, short tree. It is a hardy cultivar for landscape use, the color contrasting slightly with other red forms. It is a good choice among the larger-leaved cultivars, reliable and easy to propagate. The name means "the crows at dawn."

'Akita yatsubusa'

DWARF GROUP
GREEN

This robust dwarf is similar in leaf and form to 'Sharp's Pygmy', with the small, deeply divided palmatum-type leaves. Unlike 'Sharp's Pygmy', it has dark brown shoots. The small leaves are deeply divided into mainly five long, ovate-triangular lobes. The margins are clearly but shallowly toothed. When they first appear, the young leaves are a pinkish red, turning yellow-green before becoming a medium to dark green for the summer. The fall color is a vivid orange-red. 'Akita yatsubusa' is a reliable, hardy cultivar that forms a dense round shrub 1–2 m (3–6 ft.) tall. It is ideally suited for the small garden, container culture, or bonsai. It was reared and introduced by T. C. Plants of Oregon. The name means "unusual autumn dwarf."

'Alpenweiss'

PALMATUM GROUP
VARIEGATED

This attractive variegate, selected and named by Baltzer Nursery, Oregon, is similar to, but smaller than, the outstanding old Japanese cultivar, 'Hikasa yama', and is considered to be even more colorful as the buds open in spring. The small five-lobed leaves are deeply divided to about three quarters of the way to the leaf base and are about the same size as the leaves of the

'Akegarasu'.
Photo by Peter Gregory

'Akita yatsubusa'.
Photo by Harry Olsen

popular variegate 'Butterfly'. Like 'Hikasa yama', the summer leaves have light green main veins bordered by mid to dark green and with creamy white borders, which themselves are pink-tinged earlier in the summer. Fall color is orange to scarlet.

'Alpenweiss', the name means "white alpine," forms a vase-shaped tree and is estimated to reach 3 m (10 ft.) or so in 10 years. It is ideal for small gardens and container growing. It was originally known by the code name "Baltzer-Hig."

'Alpenweiss'.
Photo by Peter Gregory

'Amber Ghost'.
Photo by Peter Gregory

'Amagi shigure'

MATSUMURAE GROUP
GREEN

This dense, low-growing cultivar has rather small leaves considering the type of plant, and they are fairly closely spaced on short twigs. The bright green medium-sized leaves have five to seven lobes that radiate outward in the star shape typical of subspecies *palmatum*. Each lobe is ovate and terminates in a short, sharp point, and has an evenly toothed margin which tends to be attractively crinkled. In general the middle three lobes are much longer than the two or more lateral lobes. The leaf stalks and small twigs are dark red. Fall color is yellow-orange. This semidwarf tree grows broadly as well as upright. It tends to be dense and twiggy and forms a low-growing background for landscaping. The name means "soft drizzle."

'Amber Ghost'

MATSUMURAE GROUP
VARIEGATED

The spring leaves are a delightful amber with a network of dark veins, the colors becoming darker through the summer. The large deeply divided leaves have five to seven lobes with long pointed tips and fairly evenly toothed but slightly crumpled margins. This cultivar forms a semiupright tree to about 3 m (10 ft.) tall and 2.5 m (8 ft.) wide. It adds another attractive color to the garden landscape. 'Amber Ghost is one of the Ghost Series selected and named by Talon Buchholz of Oregon.

'Aoba jō'

DWARF GROUP
GREEN

This good, strong, dwarf shrub has large seven-lobed leaves. In fact, the leaves are surprisingly large for a dwarf. The long lobes radiate out well, with the leaf base somewhat flat. The lobes are strongly ovate-lanceolate with long tapering pointed tips, moderately deeply separated, and with well-toothed margins. The color of the foliage is a strong green with bronzed edges and tips. Fall color is yellow with reddish hues, but not outstanding. The mounded shrub stays less than 1 m (3 ft.) tall. This cultivar enjoys some popularity with bonsai enthusiasts and has been widely used for this purpose. It is also attractive in the right place as a dwarf in the landscape. 'Aoba jo' has been known under the names 'Aoba bo' and 'Aoba cho'.

'Aoba nishiki'

AMOENUM GROUP
VARIEGATED

This cultivar seems to be rather shy in its display of variegation. The stock plant at Maplewood has been reticent in producing markedly variegated leaves. Older plants seen in Europe were not strong in variegation either. The medium-sized leaves are of a pale green tone and are slightly longer than wide. The five to seven lobes graduate to a sharp point and separate about halfway to the leaf base. The variegations are creamy yellow and in small sections of the leaf. Occasionally, the light areas occupy almost the entire leaf. Nonetheless, most leaves are not variegated.

This plant eventually forms a short, broad tree of up to 3 m (10 ft.) in height. It is not a strong, vigorous grower or a bold plant in a garden landscape. The name means "yellow-green brocade" and is possibly a synonym of 'Aocha nishiki'. 'Siecha' and 'Siecha nishiki' (misspelled 'Seika nishiki') are so similar that they are treated as synonymous. There are, though, much better similar variegated cultivars, such as the reliable 'Asahi zuru'.

'Ao kanzashi'

PALMATUM GROUP
VARIEGATED

This small to medium-sized tree or shrub has variegated leaves, which are very like 'Tennyo-no-hoshi' in leaf shape and variegation. Habit also is similar. Although the two plants are suspected of being synonymous, 'Ao kanzashi' originated from Japan and has slightly smaller leaves and more compact growth. The light cream-green variegation around the leaf edges does not turn pink in the sun as readily as that of 'Tennyo-no-hoshi'. This cultivar forms a densely branched, upright tree up to 4 m (13 ft.) tall, with the crown spreading out at the top in a similar fashion to

'Aoba jō'.
Photo by Cor van Gelderen

'Ao kanzashi'.
Photo by Peter Gregory

'Butterfly'. 'Ao kanzashi' has been known as 'Oa hanzashi'.

'Ao shidare'

DISSECTUM GROUP
GREEN

Differing slightly in leaf form from many of the other green dissectums, 'Ao shidare' is similar to 'Kiri nishiki' and 'Sekimori'. The color of the leaves is a slight blue-green, not the sharp green of 'Viridis'. Fall color is yellow. The seven-lobed leaves are of medium size and doubly dissected as in the typical dissectum. The secondary cuts are not as deep, nor are the lobes as long as in the better known forms of green dissectum. The many points of each leaf seem not as sharp, giving the whole leaf a more blunt appearance in outline. Each lobe, from halfway to the leaf base downward, is quite narrow, almost just the width of the midvein. The stems and branches are a pleasing green with a whitish overtone at times.

This cascading cultivar grows up to 5 m (16 ft.) in height and 3 m (10 ft.) in width. When planted near other dissectums the difference in color is apparent. The name means "green cascading." 'Aoba shidare' is a synonym.

'Ao shime-no-uchi shidare'

LINEARILOBUM GROUP
GREEN

This plant is quite similar to 'Shinobuga oka', except that its branches are more pendulous in habit, and it rarely grows taller than 2.5 m (8 ft.). The branches tend to droop and give a round bush effect in contrast to the other members of the Linearilobum Group, whose branches tend to be more upright. The deep green leaves are mostly seven-lobed. The lobes are long and narrow, like a blade of grass, about 3–5 mm wide and up to 8 cm long. They turn yellow in the fall, sometimes to a deep gold.

There are many cultivars in the Linearilobum Group that are quite similar but show slight differences. All are finely separated in their characteristics but overlap in description. A single leaf from one plant could appear to belong to another cultivar. It is necessary to see the entire plant to see the differences. 'Meshime-no-uchi shidare' is a synonym.

'Aoyagi'

PALMATUM GROUP
GREEN

The bright pea green bark on twigs, small branches, and limbs is the outstanding feature of this cultivar and gives it its name, literally "green coral." 'Aoyagi' is sometimes referred to as the green counterpart

'Ao shidare'.
Photo by Peter Gregory

'Ao shime-no-uchi shidare'.
Photo by Peter Gregory

of 'Sango kaku'. The typically palmatum-type leaves have five to seven lobes and are medium-sized. The moderately deeply divided lobes radiate outward and taper gradually to a long, sharp point. The margins are toothed. The bright green is of a light tone and becomes a pleasing yellow in the fall. The green leaf stalks are very short, making the leaves rather compact along the shoots.

While this is an upright-growing tree, it is not quite as vigorous as 'Sango kaku'. It becomes a wide-topped tree reaching 8 m (26 ft.) tall. The brilliance of the bark is surprising for a green tone and, when planted near the contrasting 'Sango kaku', makes a pleasing effect. The stem and shoot colors are most intense during the winter season. A snowfall enhances the beauty of this cultivar by emphasizing the bark color.

'Ukon' appears to be similar in leaf, color, habit, and size. Although it originated from a different clone than the one from which 'Aoyagi' originated—both names are found in old Japanese literature—no differences between the two cultivars have been observed, so it seems reasonable to include it under 'Aoyagi'. 'Aoyagi' can also be found misspelled 'Ao gaki'. 'Ukon' is sometimes called 'Ukon nishiki' or misspelled 'Yukon'.

'Arakawa'

PALMATUM GROUP
GREEN

Generally, cultivars of *Acer palmatum* are chosen for some outstanding feature of the foliage. In this case, it is the interesting bark. The Japanese name means "rough bark" and the plant's common name in English is, logically enough, rough bark maple. Young plants do not show this feature for three to five years, at which time the roughening begins. It develops more rapidly each year until the bark is quite roughened and corky, with longitudinal

creases and also short cracks and irregularities across the surface. It is not as deeply fissured as 'Nishiki gawa'. Other names for 'Arakawa' are 'Ganseki momiji' and 'Nishiki sho'. The word "nishiki" usually indicates variegated foliage but, in this case, refers to the rough bark feature.

The small to medium-sized green leaves are of the typical palmatum type. The five to seven lobes are narrowly ovate, tapering gradually to a long slender pointed

'Aoyagi'.
Photo by Cor van Gelderen

'Arakawa'.
Photo by Robert Jamgochian

tip. They radiate outward and are deeply divided. The margins are clearly toothed. The fall color is yellow-gold. The red leaf stalks are short and slender. This vigorous, upright plant matures at over 8 m (26 ft.). It will dwarf well for bonsai use and make a very interesting plant. The rough bark is prominent even when the plant is dwarfed.

'Aratama'

DWARF GROUP
RED

The bright foliage of this extremely desirable dwarf shrub varies from brick red to light purple-red. It is difficult to describe except that it is a pleasant color and is showy. The larger, older leaves carry the darkest tones, while the new foliage is more bright red during growth. Under these colors is a base of strong green, which often shows through along the midribs of the lobes and adds an interesting two-tone effect. As the plant goes into the heat of midsummer, more and more green shows through as bronze-green.

The small to medium-sized leaves have five to seven moderately deeply divided lobes. These are long-ovate with long, tapering pointed tips and well-toothed margins. The leaf base is almost straight across. The leaf stalks are short. In the majority of leaves, the center lobe (usually the largest) is often shortened, a characteristic of cultivars derived from witches'-brooms. 'Aratama' was originally derived from a witches'-broom on 'Ko murasaki'.

The growth is fairly short, even under intense culture, and produces a round, dense, twiggy, shrubby plant. The leaves lie rather flat along the twigs. This shrub slowly reaches up to 1.5 m (5 ft.) tall in 10 years. 'Aratama' is among the most desirable shrubs for the garden landscape. It takes on full sunlight very well, and, because it is dense, short, and branching, this dwarf cultivar makes a very good container plant. The name means "uncut gem."

'Aratama'.
Photo by Peter Gregory

'Ariadne'.
Photo by Peter Gregory

'Ariadne'

MATSUMURAE GROUP
VARIEGATED

'Ariadne' is an introduction of Firma C. Esveld, Boskoop, Netherlands, in the 'Shigitatsu sawa' group of conspicuously marbled leaves in contrasting colors to the network of veins. The new young growth is especially attractive and noticeable, with yellow-green veining on pastel shades of light orange-pink-red marbled background. This gradually changes through the summer to become red-veined on a purplish red background by late summer, with the undersides becoming purplish green. In the fall the colors of the leaves return to the orange-pink-red marbling with a deeper pink-red spreading inward from the margins, while the network of veins remain yellow-green. This cultivar also has attractive green young stems with fine, closely packed grayish striations and lovely red fruits.

The large five- to seven-lobed variegated leaves are very deeply cut. The lobes are narrowly ovate with narrow tail-like tips and with the broadest point about one third to halfway, narrowing toward the lobe junctions, which are less than 1 cm from the leaf base. The central lobe occasionally has a short, truncated tip, similar to that found in many dwarf cultivars propagated from witches'-brooms. The lobes are widely spread, with the small basal lobes angled backward and outward. The margins are coarsely double-toothed, the teeth having very sharp-pointed tips. The strong pink to red leaf stalks are shorter than the leaves and have swollen bases.

'Ariadne' matures to a 3-m (10-ft.) tall, spreading shrub and is at least as wide. It was a chance seedling discovered among a large batch of open-pollinated seedlings and, after lengthy observation, was named after one of D. M. van Gelderen's granddaughters.

'Ariake nomura'

AMOENUM GROUP
RED

This upright form is reported to be a seedling from the well-known 'Musashino' (syn. 'Nomura'). Its leaf shape is more or less identical, which makes it very difficult to distinguish from 'Musashino', except 'Musashino' leaves have coarser toothed margins. The medium to large five- to seven-lobed leaves are moderately deeply divided and have finely toothed margins.

The distinguishing feature is a slightly different tone of red. 'Ariake nomura' is a little more brown-red in its spring color, a lighter purplish red-bronze in late summer, and a bright crimson in the fall. The very slender leaf stalks and young shoots are red. This cultivar is not widely found in collections or nurseries.

'Asahi zuru'

PALMATUM GROUP
VARIEGATED

'Asahi zuru' is among the dependable cultivars with sharply defined and clear variegation. The white portions have distinct and sharp margins, and the green portions are a rich color. The leaves vary considerably

'Ariake nomura'.
Photo by Peter Gregory

'Asahi zuru'.
Photo by Cor van Gelderen

in markings on each plant. Some, especially the smaller leaves, are almost entirely white, while others are almost completely green with only one small patch of white. Some leaves have only minute flecks of white or pink. Solid green leaves occur and are usually larger in size than the variegated ones. Quite often the new growth in the spring is a light to bright pink, which later turns white.

The typically shaped small to large palmatum-type leaves are usually five-lobed and symmetrical, but a percentage have sickle-shaped lobes when containing white sections. The leaf stalks vary from pink on some leaves to green on the normal-colored leaves. Shoots and small branches are dark green and do not have the pink striping often present in the similar 'Oridono nishiki'.

This upright but spreading, round-headed tree grows rather fast as a young plant. As it becomes older, growth slows down and becomes more compact. The tree can reach 8 m (26 ft.) in height and 4 m (13 ft.) in spread. Multistemmed trees are quite striking in appearance. New growth occasionally is totally green but the variegation develops well in the second and subsequent years.

'Asahi zuru' is desirable in many landscape situations. Afternoon shade helps prevent excessive leaf burn, as it does for all variegates. This cultivar has been known under the alternative names of 'Asahi nomura' and 'Asahi beni zuru'. It has also been misspelled and misnamed 'Asahi juru', 'Asahi kaede', and 'Asaji'. The name means "dawn swan."

'Atrolineare'

LINEARILOBUM GROUP
RED

This maple has dark, black-red foliage when in its prime in the early season. It may bronze out with greenish undertones later in the season, especially in full sun. The leaf has five to seven widely separated, very narrow lobes, which are divided completely to the base. The midrib of each lobe is green. The lobes are long and fairly narrow but coarser on vigorous young shoots and may even be semipalmate. As the season progresses, the leaves develop the characteristic stringlike lobe shape.

The upright-growing small form is quite dense. The plant might be classed as a tall shrub rather than a small tree, reaching a height of 4 m (13 ft.). It is a very desirable form, contrasting with the more round-headed linearilobums, such as 'Red Pygmy' and 'Villa Taranto'.

'Atrolineare' has been known under the names 'Aka-no-hichi gosan', 'Blood Vein', 'Filifera Purpureum', 'Linearilobum Purpureum', 'Linearilobum Rubrum', 'Pendulum Angustilobum Atropurpureum', 'Pendulum Atropurpureum', 'Purpureum Angustilobum', 'Scolopendrifolium Purpureum', and 'Scolopendrifolium Rubrum'. Several slightly different red linearilobum clones are named as 'Angustilobum' and 'Angustilobum Purpureum' in a few Dutch nurseries. This practice is confusing and misleading so, as there are alternative named cultivars as good or better, such

'Atrolineare'.
Photo by Harold Greer

as 'Atrolineare', these names should be dropped.

'Atropurpureum'

AMOENUM
RED

The leaves have five to seven medium to large, moderately deeply divided lobes. The lobes are ovate to ovate-lanceolate with pointed tips and finely toothed margins The leaves are a rich purple in the spring, becoming deeper in early summer, and turning to a brilliant scarlet in the fall.

This name is universally used for different clones and seedling plants with red leaves. These should more properly be named *Acer palmatum* f. *atropurpureum*. The original plant of this name was an excellent clone originating from the old nursery of Constant Wattez in Woudenberg, Netherlands (van Gelderen et al. 1994). It forms a vigorous upright tree up to 10 m (33 ft.) tall. Because many nurseries have used this name for any red-leaved seedling selection, it has become so diluted as to be meaningless. It is from such red seedlings that many outstanding cultivars have been selected, such as 'Shōjō', 'Nuresagi', and later 'Bloodgood' and 'Moonfire'. 'Atropurpureum' has also been known under the name 'Blood Leaf'.

'Atsu gama'

AMOENUM GROUP
GREEN

Noted for its brilliant fall color, 'Atsu gama' has large leaves that are green with pink edging in spring, becoming a darker green for summer, before turning an eye-catching bright pink-red in the fall. The leaves are moderately to deeply divided into seven lobes whose sides and tips tend to curve downward, giving each leaf the appearance of a down-turned bowl. The margins are very finely toothed. The leaf stalks and shoots are bright red. 'Atsu gama' is a rela-

tively fast growing, spreading tree reaching about 5 m (16 ft.) tall with a broad crown up to 3 m (10 ft.) wide.

'Attraction'

PALMATUM GROUP
RED

This cultivar was imported into the Netherlands from Japan in 1970 and, a few years later, from there into the United States via Maplewood Nursery as 'Atropurpureum Superbum'. Because Latin names after 1959 became illegitimate under the international nomenclature rules, the name was changed to 'Attraction'. This cultivar is a seedling selection. Its color is deeper and

'Atropurpureum'.
Photo by Cor van Gelderen

'Atsu gama'.
Photo by Peter Gregory

'Attraction'.
Photo by Harold Greer

markings of yellow or gold appear on the green background. The variegation is discernible but not brilliant. The medium-sized leaves are five-lobed with a straight leaf base. Each lobe is oblong-ovate gradually terminating in a slender pointed tip. The lobes are deeply divided. The margins are finely toothed on the outer half of each lobe. The firm, short leaf stalks are reddish. This upright-growing tree does not get as tall as the species. Older trees are broadened at the top, not overly twiggy, and about 4 m (13 ft.) in height, but trees can reach 8 m (26 ft.).

According to the literature, the name 'Aureovariegatum', which means "golden yellow variegation," has been applied to more than one cultivar. One source considers it synonymous with 'Komon nishiki' (van Gelderen et al. 1994). Because 'Aureovariegatum' is much larger and has deeper lobing, while 'Komon nishiki' grows to only 3 m (10 ft.), has lobes only moderately deeply divided, and its variegation is more evident, these two are treated as separate cultivars here. 'Aureovariegatum' has been known under the name 'Aureomaculatum' and misspelled 'Aureumvariegatum'.

holds better than the usual seedlings of *Acer palmatum* f. *atropurpureum*.

The large five- to seven-lobed leaves are divided almost to the leaf base. The lobes are long-ovate and the outer ends gradually taper to a sharply pointed tip. The inner third of the margin is rather smooth, while the outer two thirds is sharply and regularly toothed. The red leaf stalks are short and stiff. Leaf color is a deep purple-red or maroon. Tones are brightest on new leaves and then become deeper in summer. The color, though not quite as deep as that of 'Bloodgood', holds almost as well, but burns in hot locations. The leaves turn a bright crimson in the fall.

As a young plant, 'Attraction' is a vigorous and sturdy grower, and is perfectly hardy. It becomes a tall, upright round-headed tree of 7 m (23 ft.) or more. It is a good landscape plant, often marketed in the United States under its synonym 'Superbum'.

'Aureovariegatum'

MATSUMURAE GROUP
VARIEGATED

The new foliage in spring is not strongly variegated, being a rather uniform light green. The stronger variegation comes later in the summer. Small and indefinite

'Aureum'

PALMATUM GROUP
GREEN

The distinctive yellow of the leaves is quite dominant, although an undertone of light green becomes more noticeable when the plant is grown in shade. When the new foliage appears, the margins of the lobes have a slight tinge of rust-pink color, which soon disappears. As the season progresses, the leaves turn into a purer light green, the golden tone softening. In plants grown at Maplewood, the yellow tones are even more pronounced as the second growth occurs in early August. This seasonal flush is also more vigorous.

This cultivar does not have the same type of golden cast as the more familiar golden fullmoon maple, *Acer shirasawanum* 'Aureum', with which it must not be confused. In shady conditions the yellow is rather masked and assumes a light green tone. In full sun the color develops into golden shades. Fall coloration produces a display of bright yellow.

The small to medium-sized palmatum-type leaves have five to seven lobes and are moderately deeply divided. The lobes extend outward, forming an almost circular leaf. The shoots are bright red. The form of this plant is upright and bushy, reaching a maximum of 8 m (26 ft.) tall. This cultivar has also been known under the name 'Sunrise'.

'Autumn Fire'

DISSECTUM GROUP
GREEN

Originating as a chance seedling in 1979, this cultivar was propagated and introduced by Del's Japanese Maple Nursery, and registered in 1996. It differs from most green dissectums in having a semierect habit, not the usual dome shape. Its outstanding feature, as the name suggests, is that the medium green leaves turn an intense, brilliant red in the fall. New growth is a light yellow-green with pink edging, and makes a very attractive contrast with the older, darker green foliage.

The large, very coarse, seven- to nine-lobed leaves are deeply divided, but not as deeply divided as most laceleaf maples, and so border on those of the Matsumurae Group. They have surprisingly small, narrow, sharply pointed teeth compared to the leaf size. The leaf stalks are relatively short. 'Autumn Fire' forms a vigorous, semierect, wide-spreading bush, reaching only about 2 m (6 ft.) high in 10 years, but spreading even wider.

'Aureum'.
Photo by Peter Gregory

'Autumn Fire'.
Photo Peter Gregory

'Autumn Flame'

PALMATUM GROUP
GREEN

The outstanding feature of this interesting hybrid (*A. palmatum* × *A. circinatum*) introduced by Duncan and Davies Nursery of New Zealand is that the deep green summer foliage turns vivid shades of gold, orange, and red in the fall, even in New Zealand's mild climate. 'Autumn Flame' was originally named 'Autumn Fire', but, as there is a green dissectum already registered in that name, the name was changed to 'Autumn Flame'. The seven- to nine-lobed medium-sized leaves are moderately to deeply divided. The broad oblong-ovate lobes have large coarsely toothed margins. The pink-red leaf stalks are short. This vigorous, upright grower has an estimated mature height of up to 8 m (26 ft.).

'Autumn Glory'
MATSUMURAE GROUP
GREEN

This cultivar name was applied to a few seedlings that were notable for their beautiful coloration patterns—mostly crimson. These maples were selected and introduced by Robert de Belder of Arboretum Kalmthout, Belgium, about 1958, and commercially distributed out of the Netherlands. The fall coloring has proven to be

'Autumn Glory'.
Photo by Peter Gregory

'Azuma murasaki'.
Photo by J. D. Vertrees

inconsistent in different places, raising the question of whether this form deserves cultivar status. The leaves are broad, five- to seven-lobed, with the lobes deeply divided and with coarsely toothed margins. These upright small trees of up to 6 m (20 ft.) form a broad canopy.

'Autumn Red'
MATSUMURAE GROUP
GREEN

'Autumn Red' was selected at Fratelli Gilardelli Nursery, Italy, for its spectacular fall color. It forms a medium-sized shrub or small tree, reaching 5 m (16 ft.) tall, and has an upright form with an open crown. The newly emerged pink-red leaves quickly turn a light greenish yellow with rose edging, and become a bright green through the summer. Then, as the name suggests, they turn a fiery red in the fall. The foliage can withstand full sun without damage. The large five- to seven-lobed leaves are deeply divided almost to the leaf base. The margins are coarsely but fairly evenly toothed. The leaf stalks are bright red and shorter than the leaves.

'Azuma murasaki'
MATSUMURAE GROUP
RED

The unusual red tone of the leaves distinguishes this cultivar. It has a slight purple hue to it, but the entire leaf has an undertone of green showing through. New foliage is a yellow-orange that has a "dusty" appearance due to a covering of fine pubescence which soon disappears. As midsummer arrives, the leaves alter to a deep green with a reddish cast to the surface. The large leaves are seven-lobed; the fall color of each lobe being a beautiful deep red. Each lobe is separated from the rest and is long, ovate-lanceolate with definite toothed margins. The leaf stalks are a bright red for most of the season.

'Azuma murasaki' is not a tall-growing cultivar. Early growth is fairly rapid but slows down as the years pass. This tree reaches 6 m (20 ft.) in height and becomes rather round-topped and about 5 m (16 ft.) wide. Outside shoots take on a cascading form in time. The color tones of this choice tree contrast well with other red-leaved forms in the landscape. This old Japanese cultivar was listed in the 1882 *Sekihin Binran*. 'Toshi' has been used as an alternative name for this cultivar, but the descriptions in the Japanese literature do not seem to agree.

'Baby Lace'

DWARF GROUP
GREEN

This very desirable and interesting cultivar was the first dissectum witches'-broom to be discovered. It was found by Rick Rey of the Delaware Valley Agricultural School in the early 1980s and named by Edward Rodd of Raraflora Nursery, Kinterfield, Pennsylvania.

The finely dissected leaves are half the size of normal dissectum leaves in the first year, becoming smaller with age until reduced to the size of a thumbnail. The leaves emerge a reddish orange in the spring, quickly becoming a bronze-green for the summer, and turning a brilliant orange-red to pink-red in the fall. During the summer, the orange-red new growth makes a very attractive color contrast to the darker, older growth.

Like most witches'-brooms, this one produces relatively vigorous shoots from the graft, but slows down in subsequent years, attaining a little over 1 m (3 ft.) in height and spread after 10 years. It eventually forms a small, round, densely twigged shrub. It is very sensitive to the wind and needs protection for at least the first three years.

'Baldsmith'

DISSECTUM GROUP
RED

'Baldsmith' is among the best of the newer dissectum introductions, bearing light, bright orange-red spring foliage. The leaves become paler and green-tinged in the center with pink-tinged margins as they develop. The combination of mature and new leaves through the summer gives a multicolored appearance of greens, pinks, and orange-reds. In the fall the leaves turn a bright yellow with orange hues.

The lower end of the large, finely dissected five- to seven-lobed leaves narrows to the width of the midrib. The division of the sublobes, unlike that of many other dis-

'Baby Lace'.
Photo by Peter Gregory

'Baldsmith'.
Photo Peter Gregory

sectums, does not quite reach the midrib. The sublobes have conspicuous large, narrow, sharply pointed teeth. 'Baldsmith' has the usual mounded habit and vigor of most dissectums but has a distinctive appearance because of the very pendulous, finely dissected, light orange-red foliage, which contrasts markedly with the deeper reds of 'Crimson Queen' and 'Dissectum Nigrum'.

'Beni chidori'
PALMATUM GROUP
GREEN

'Beni chidori'.
Photo by Cor van Gelderen

'Beni fushigi'.
Photo by Cor van Gelderen

This small-leaved Japanese cultivar has typical palmatum-type leaves that are deeply divided into mainly five lobes. It is one of the bright pink-red spring color maples, similar to 'Beni tsukasa'. The new leaves emerge a deep pink, gradually changing to orange-red with conspicuous yellow main veins and margins. The leaves become medium green for the summer before turning scarlet for the fall. The leaf stalks and shoots are red. The tree grows slowly to about 3 m (10 ft.) and is ideal for growing in containers. It is also valued in Japan for bonsai culture.

'Beni fushigi'
PALMATUM GROUP
RED

Similar to 'Beni komachi', this small-leaved slow-growing cultivar is easier to grow, has deeper bright red foliage, and is not as dwarf a shrub at maturity. Unlike 'Beni komachi', it does not tend to revert. Like 'Corallinum', it looks its best in the spring and early summer, with intense pink-red young leaves that become a deeper red. Thus, the summer color is an unusual mixture with the mature leaves a green-bronzed red with dark red margins, and the new leaves bright pink. The downward-curving lobe tips add extra character to the tree.

The very deeply divided, narrow leaves have five long, narrow lobes, almost straplike with long, narrow tips. The center lobe is usually appreciably longer than the other lobes and often has a curved tip. The margins are irregularly and coarsely toothed. The purple-red leaf stalks are slender and shorter than the leaves.

This unusual, and very desirable cultivar matures at about 3 m (10 ft.) in height after 10–12 years, and is usually wider than tall. It is ideal for small to medium-sized gardens.

'Beni gasa'
MATSUMURAE GROUP
RED

This attractive slow growing cultivar is similar in growth and leaf to the better known

'Kinran'. The medium to large seven-lobed leaves are very deeply divided, almost to the base. The lobes are narrowly ovate with long, sharply pointed tips and conspicuous very sharply pointed teeth on the margins. The spring leaves emerge bright red, becoming purple-red for the summer, before turning scarlet in the fall. The leaf stalks are short and red. The cultivar name, which means "red umbrella," is derived from the bright red spring leaves which are closely overlapping like an umbrella. The plant is relatively slow growing and forms a broad, round-topped small tree about 4 m (13 ft.) tall. It is suitable for small gardens and container culture.

'Beni hime'

DWARF GROUP
RED

'Beni hime' is among the smallest red-leaved dwarf shrubs. The palmatum-type leaves are star-shaped, short, and deeply divided. They end with acute sharply pointed tips. The very small leaves are clustered on short leaf stalks. Twigs are very thin, and annual growth is quite limited. Shoots are very short and slender, and often come out in an angular manner that eventually creates a rather dense, compact bush. New leaves are predominantly an attractive, rather pale, pink to rusty red tone. Full sun increases the intensity of color. A greenish shade spreads from the center in midsummer. Fall colors are a vibrant red.

Like many very small-leaved dwarf maples and some of the smaller cultivars with reddish foliage, this cultivar produces new growth susceptible to early spring damage from fungi. The damage can happen as early as the breaking-bud stage and on fully developed new leaves. Diseases, such as *Botrytis*, can seriously affect the new leaves and terminal development. Good air circulation and full sun aid in prevention, while some fungicides help to suppress the disease.

'Beni gasa'.
Photo by Peter Gregory

'Beni hime'.
Photo by Peter Gregory

This small dwarf, while very delicate in overall appearance, is not as tender as one would assume. It does better in open situations with plenty of light and tends to weaken in strong shade. Some plants attain a height and width of 1 m (3 ft.) or so in eight to ten years. 'Beni hime' is ideally suited to container culture and bonsai. The name means "red dwarf." 'Chishio yatsubusa' is a synonym.

'Beni hoshi'

DWARF GROUP
GREEN

Originating as a chance seedling in 1979, this cultivar was introduced by Del's Japanese Maple Nursery in 1992. The leaves

This page:
'Beni hoshi'.
Photo by Peter Gregory

'Beni kagami'.
Photo by J. D. Vertrees

'Beni kawa'.
Photo by Harry Olsen

Page 101:
'Beni komachi', spring color accenting a mixed border.
Photo by J. D. Vertrees

'Beni komachi', foliage detail.
Photo by Harold Greer

emerge a bright red in the spring and turn green during the summer. A second growth of new red leaves creates splashes of red on a green background, which persists until the leaves turn yellow to orange in the fall. The small seven-lobed wide-spreading palmatum-type leaves are moderately deeply divided. Each fairly broad lobe is broadest in the middle, narrowing toward the lobe junctions, and tapering to a short, tail-like tip. There are numerous, fine teeth on the margins. The leaf stalks are short and stiff.

'Beni hoshi' forms a compact dwarf tree, reaching almost 2 m (6 ft.) in height in 15 years. It is suitable for the small garden, container culture, and bonsai. The name means "red star." Various comparisons suggest 'Ruby Star' is a synonym.

'Beni kagami'
MATSUMURAE GROUP
RED

This cultivar is a seedling selection from 'Fukagire o momiji'. In spring the leaves are orange-red to purple-red, depending on location and shade cover, not the deep black-red of many other red cultivars. The leaves have a green undertone when grown in deep shade. The fall color is a bright crimson. The medium-sized leaves are divided almost to the leaf base into seven long, narrowly ovate lobes. The margins are clearly toothed. The short leaf stalks are bright red. This fairly strong grower forms a spreading medium-sized tree and reaches a mature height of 8 m (26 ft.). It is quite graceful. The name means "red mirror."

'Beni kawa'
PALMATUM GROUP
GREEN

The effect of the winter shoot color of this cultivar has been described as spectacular. Like the ever-popular 'Sango kaku', the color of the current winter shoots is a bright but deep, salmon-red. The color persists on the second-year shoots. The plant comes into leaf two weeks later than 'Sango kaku' and has a slightly slower growth.

The medium-sized five- to seven-lobed fresh green leaves, often with red-tinged edges, are moderately to deeply divided. The lobes are broadly ovate with tail-like pointed tips and regular, double-toothed margins. The broadest point is in the lower third, narrowing toward the lobe junctions. The short, slender leaf stalks are pink to red.

This cultivar becomes a large upright shrub or small tree, reaching about 5 m (16 ft.) tall in 10 years. Though a plant for winter color and for use as a focal point in the landscape, its foliage turns a lovely golden yellow in the fall, made even more attractive by the contrasting red shoots in the background. The name means "red bark."

'Beni komachi'

PALMATUM GROUP
RED

This semidwarf plant has very unusual leaves of brilliant red. Each small to medium-sized leaf has five lobes that are separated almost entirely to the leaf base. The lobes extend widely and openly with the basal two extending obliquely backward. Each lobe is long and narrow, lanceolate but not parallel-sided. The outer half gradually narrows to a very sharply pointed tip. The margins are irregularly but markedly toothed. The lobes curl sideways, or down, or both. The sides of the lobes bend slightly upward, almost forming a shallow trough at times.

The new foliage, which appears delicate at first, is a bright crimson. The intense color begins to darken as the leaf matures, and older foliage is a greenish red. The margins remain edged in crimson. In the fall the colors again become a scarlet tone.

The total growth is short and lacy. Mature plants form small bushes up to 3 m (10 ft.) tall.

This very choice cultivar is not widely known and is rather difficult to propagate. Occasional reversions occur when the leaves are very like those of 'Shin deshōjō', which suggests it may be a sport from that cultivar. The name means "beautiful red-haired little girl."

'Beni kumo-no-su'
DISSECTUM GROUP
RED

'Beni kumo-no-su'.
Photo by Harry Olsen

'Beni maiko'.
Photo by Peter Gregory

Small enough to be in the Dwarf Group, 'Beni kumo-no-su' has unusually small leaves that are very finely cut. This lovely cultivar originated as a chance seedling in 1979 and was named and introduced by Del's Japanese Maple Nursery in 1992. The new foliage is a bright red, which gradually changes to bronze-red in the summer, later becoming bronze-green before returning to a bright red in the fall. The seven-lobed widespread leaves have slender, cut lobes, making them appear even smaller than they are. Each finely dissected sublobe is only 1–2 mm wide and the lobe narrows to the width of the midrib for up to half its length. The short, slender leaf stalks are red.

'Beni kumo-no-su' forms a low, dense, broad bush, with outwardly spreading pendulous branches, probably not reaching more than 1.5 m (5 ft.) in height in 12 years, but spreading even wider. It is ideal for the small garden, rock garden, patio, and container culture. The name means "red spider's web." It is often misspelled 'Beni komo-no-su'.

'Beni maiko'
PALMATUM GROUP
RED

'Beni maiko' produces fire-red or scarlet leaves in early spring. As they mature, their color fades into a pinkish red with a very slight green undertone. During the summer the foliage becomes greenish red with the main veins remaining red, as do the leaf stalks. In the fall, an edging of deep pink appears at the leaf margins, spreading into the center until the whole leaf is ablaze.

The leaves are five-lobed, irregular, and slightly wrinkled. Each lobe separates about halfway to the leaf base and tapers to a bluntish tip. The lobes tend to curve sideways. The margins of the lobes are toothed. The smaller leaves on the plant tend to be even more irregular and more intense in color. The leaf stalks are very short.

Mature plants are not expected to

exceed 3 m (10 ft.) in height. Compared with bright scarlet cultivars, such as 'Shin deshōjō', this one is not quite as brilliant. Nonetheless, the irregular leaf shape adds to the interest. In Japan, 'Beni maiko' is considered more colorful than such cultivars as 'Seigai'. It is an exciting plant, especially when positioned with contrasting foliage plants. It is very adaptable to container culture. The name means "red-haired dancing girl."

'Beni ōtake'

LINEARILOBUM GROUP
RED

This attractive, vigorous, upright cultivar has straplike leaves and a distinctive bamboo-like appearance and shape. The deep purple-red foliage is outstanding in the spring, holds the color throughout the summer, and then changes to a vivid crimson in the fall. The large leaves are divided into five to seven widely spread lobes. Each straplike lobe is long and narrow, but broader than most linearilobums, with long, tail-like pointed tips and sharply pointed teeth along most margins. The more vigorous juvenile shoots carry broad matsumurae-like leaves with the lobes up to 2 cm wide.

'Beni ōtake' may form a vigorous, upright tree, which may reach 8 m (26 ft.) in height, but usually grows into a tall spreading bush. It was first noticed as a chance seedling by Edward Wood and was introduced by T. C. Plants company of Hillsboro, Oregon. The name means "big red bamboo."

'Beni shichihenge'

PALMATUM GROUP
VARIEGATED

The outstanding feature of this cultivar is the color in the variegated medium-sized leaves, which is similar to 'Kagiri nishiki' and 'Butterfly', but the spring markings are pink-orange rather than pink and are

irregular (*fukurin kuzure* type). The basic leaf color is green or bluish green with strong white margins. The white is overlaid or blushed with pink-orange, a distinct color that becomes orange-brown later in the summer. Occasionally, the entire lobe is orange. Each five- to seven-lobed leaf varies in shape. Some of the lobes are very slender and uniform, while others are contorted and of different widths. The short leaf stalks are crimson.

This slow-growing plant forms an upright shrub up to 5 m (16 ft.) tall with a spread of 2 m (6 ft.). It is greatly desirable

'Beni ōtake'.
Photo by Peter Gregory

'Beni shichihenge'.
Photo by Peter Gregory

and attracts much attention, especially in the spring, but is rather difficult to propagate. The name means "red and changeful." This cultivar has been known under the names 'Beni schishihenge' and 'Beni shishihenge'.

'Beni shidare'

DISSECTUM GROUP
RED

This cultivar has the typical form and color of the red dissectums. The name, which means "red and cascading," appears to be the common name in Japan for the red dissectum. This usage would compare to the English usage of "dissectum atropurpureum." It is felt that a superior clone was originally selected, and the material received from original sources is of excellent quality and color. Therefore, the cultivar status should be retained for this particular clone.

Each medium to large leaf is divided into seven to nine lobes, each lobe multi-dissected into sublobes. The leaf stalks are slender. The leaf color is a very uniform deep red. It does not stay a deep red, but assumes a bronze color in midsummer, as contrasted with such cultivars as 'Crimson Queen'.

Old specimens may form a mound at least 5 m (16 ft.) in height and 6 m (20 ft.) in width. Some very old specimens in Japan are more than 7 m (23 ft.) in height and spread. 'Dissectum Atropurpureum' was cited as a synonym of 'Beni shidare', but so many seedlings with red dissectum leaves had been used under the former name that it has become meaningless and misleading.

'Beni shi en'

PALMATUM GROUP
VARIEGATED

'Beni shi en' is an unusual cultivar whose almost straplike, deeply divided leaves change color throughout the growing season. The foliage holds its colors well

'Beni shidare'.
Photo by Peter Gregory

'Beni shi en'.
Photo by Peter Gregory

without burning, even in full sun in the southern United States. The young, feathery leaves emerge a rosy red color, which changes to purple as the leaves develop, and then to medium green for the summer with conspicuous light green midribs. Many lobes develop an interesting creamy yellow to light green edging, which sometimes broadens downward from the tips, often causing the lobes to become sickle-shaped. The leaves take on a pinkish hue in late summer and turn golden in the fall, the fall color lasting later than with most cultivars.

The five- to seven-lobed, medium-sized leaves are mostly longer than wide. The lobes are long, narrow oblong-ovate, coarsely toothed, widest in the middle, and with long tail-like tips. Each leaf is divided almost to the leaf base. Oddly, the distance between the lobe divisions to the leaf stalk on the same leaf can vary. Most leaves fit the above description, but some leaves are much longer and coarser with broader lobes. Occasionally, some leaves are distorted. The short slender leaf stalks are green.

This moderately vigorous cultivar forms a small, upright tree up to 6 m (20 ft.) tall. It requires full sun or partial shade and a reasonably well-drained soil. The plant makes an excellent and unusual specimen tree, with changing seasonal interest. 'Beni shi en' was discovered and propagated by Johnnie's Pleasure Plants Nursery from a witches'-broom on *Acer palmatum* f. *atropurpureum*. The name means "red smoke."

'Beni shigitatsu sawa'
MATSUMURAE GROUP
VARIEGATED

The red-tinged form of 'Shigitatsu sawa', 'Beni shigitatsu sawa' has leaf lobes that are slightly longer and more deeply divided. The medium-sized leaves have seven to nine lobes and are moderately deeply divided. The lobes are elongated and taper to sharply pointed tips. The clearance between the lobes is rather wide, probably because the lobe edges are partially and irregularly curled downward. The margins are wavy and have large, coarse, sharp teeth.

As the buds first open, the inner bud scales and new leaves are maroon. When fully opened the typical leaf has quite dark veins on a light yellow-green background. The entire leaf has strong overtones of pink and red, which is the striking feature of this cultivar. This color holds very well into the summer, when the whole leaf darkens somewhat and develops a strong green tone within. This triple variegation of green, yellow, and pink is quite striking. The patterning can persist all summer when the tree is partly shaded, but is lost in full sunlight, as the leaves become light green.

'Beni shigitatsu sawa' is not as strong growing as its green counterpart. It becomes a somewhat bushy, tall plant up to 4 m (13 ft.) in height and 5 m (16 ft.) or so in spread. It is hardy, but not easy to propagate and is rather rare in nurseries and collections. It makes a very interesting specimen plant because of the unusual combi-

'Beni shigitatsu sawa'.
Photo by Peter Gregory

nation of colors. This cultivar has also been known under the names 'Aka shigitatsu sawa', 'Samari', and 'Samurai'. The Japanese characters for 'Beni shigitatsu sawa' have been applied to one or two plants which differ from the above description.

'Beni tsukasa'
PALMATUM GROUP
RED

The remarkable color tones of this plant make it a very noticeable cultivar. In spring, the small leaves are a bright orange-red or peach tone. As they mature, the color changes to delicate shades of pink and red with greenish undertones. Some leaves have strong yellow-green veins showing through the blend of red-pink. In early summer the leaves turn green with light mottling, becoming a medium green. Fall color is a deep red. The leaves are five- to seven-lobed and, when seven-lobed, the basal lobes overlap the leaf stalk. The lobes are moderately to deeply divided and are ovate-lanceolate with distinctly toothed margins. The lobes taper quickly to a slender, pointed tip. The leaf stalks are short and slender.

This willowy, slender-twigged plant is not cascading. It makes a medium-sized shrubby plant, up to 5 m (16 ft.) tall, but is usually smaller. It makes a fine accent plant in small landscapes and lends itself to container culture. 'Beni-no-tsukasa' is another name under which this cultivar has been known.

'Beni yatsubusa'
PALMATUM GROUP
GREEN

In spite of its name, which means "red dwarf," this cultivar grows too tall for that category, to 3 m (10 ft.) or more in height. It is best described as a strong-growing small shrub with medium to large leaves.

The bright green leaves hold their color well throughout the growing season. They are mostly five-lobed, with lobes radiating outward in a strong manner. The long-ovate lobes have short tail-like tips and are moderately deeply divided. The margins are strongly toothed. The leaf stalks are long and thin, allowing the leaves to hang rather loosely on the plant. Fall colors are an attractive feature and are bright crimson to deep maroon-red.

A good cultivar for contrast in smaller landscapes, this small shrub blends quite well and provides variety in larger plantings. It has a tendency to throw out strong, vigorous new shoots when growing in highly fertile soil.

'Beni yubi gohon'
LINEARILOBUM GROUP
RED

This unique cultivar has the typical characteristic of most red linearilobums, except that it is the smallest member of this group, both in leaf dimensions and ultimate size. It attains only a little over 2 m (6 ft.) in height. The small five-lobed, straplike leaves hold the basal lobes at right angles or pointing slightly forward. Each lobe is broadest in the center with a sharp-pointed tip and fine-toothed inner margins. The red leaf

'Beni tsukasa'.
Photo by J. D. Vertrees

stalks are slender and short. The young leaves are a light bronze-red with green-tinged bases, rapidly becoming purple-red. The red color holds well throughout the summer in full sun. This cultivar makes an unusual and attractive container plant and may be well suited to bonsai culture. The name means "five long red fingers." It has often been misspelled 'Beni ubi gohon'. 'Beni ubi ocha' may be a synonym.

'Beni zuru'

PALMATUM GROUP
GREEN

This Japanese cultivar with colorful orange-yellow spring foliage is similar to 'Akane' in leaf shape, size, and spring color. The small typically palmatum-type leaves are mainly five-lobed and deeply divided, and have coarsely toothed margins. The new leaves emerge a bright pink-orange with yellow main veins, changing slowly to orange-yellow then, from the main veins turning light green for the rest of the summer. Fall color is bright red. This small cultivar is ideally suited to container and bonsai culture. The name has been misspelled 'Beni tsuri'.

'Berrima Bridge'

DISSECTUM GROUP
GREEN

The main feature of this robust green dissectum is the unusual sequence of color changes throughout the growing season. The leaves emerge green in the spring, change slowly to reddish green, then bronze-green through the summer, and turn a fiery red in the fall. It grows vigorously at first, eventually forming a 4 m (13 ft.) tall domed mound. It originated from a seedling selected in the Berrima Bridge Nursery, Australia.

'Beni yubi gohon'.
Photo by Peter Gregory

'Beni zuru'.
Photo by Peter Gregory

'Berrima Bridge'.
Photo by Cor van Gelderen

'Berry Dwarf'

DWARF GROUP
GREEN

This cultivar forms a wide-spreading, low, dwarf shrub and has distinctly shaped, relatively large, bronze leaves. It arose from a seedling selected in the early 1980s and was propagated by Raraflora Nursery in Australia, and named after the town where the nursery is located. The attractive leaves emerge a light apple green, becoming a bronze-green for the summer. They are carried on olive-green leaf stalks and shoots.

The unusually (for a dwarf) large five-lobed leaves are borderline between the Palmatum and Matsumurae groups as defined here. The lobes are spread outward so that they are distinctly separated right to the lobe junctions. Each lobe is broadly ovate with a pointed tip and the sides of the lower quarter angle inward. The lobes are broadest in the middle, narrowing toward the lobe junctions. There are about three pairs of irregular lobules along the lobe margins which, themselves, are coarsely toothed. Some of the leaves display the stubby center lobe characteristic of cultivars arising from a witches'-broom.

'Berry Dwarf' is a surprisingly strong and busy grower for a dwarf, at least for the first few years. It forms a wide-spreading, dense, twiggy, low bush with a spread of 3 m (10 ft.) in 10 years, but a height of only a little over 1 m (3 ft.).

'Berry Dwarf'.
Photo by Francis Schroeder

'Bewley's Red'

DISSECTUM GROUP
RED

This Australian red laceleaf, which originated at the Bewley's Nursery in the Blue Mountains, Australia, has an unusual upright habit, not the normal pendulous mushroom shape of most dissectums. This excellent plant thrives best in full sun, but is a slow grower, eventually reaching about 3 m (10 ft.) tall.

The medium to large leaves have mainly seven lobes divided right to the base. Each lobe is subdivided but not as deeply, each ending in a sharply pointed, slightly hooked tip. The spring leaves are deep red with a slight sheen, bronzed red for the summer and often suffused with green from the midveins, especially if shaded. Fall colors are bright orange-red. The reddish leaf stalks are much shorter than the leaves.

'Bewley's Red'.
Photo by Peter Gregory

'Bi hō'

PALMATUM GROUP
GREEN

This delightful small tree was introduced into Europe from Japan by Guy Maillot of France. It is a maple for all seasons with pink-flushed light yellow-green new leaves in the spring, becoming light to mid green for the summer, then turning a very bright yellow, often reddish tinged, in the fall. The pink-flushed orange-brown shoots become an eye-catching orange to apricot-yellow for the winter. This color lasts for several years. The small mainly five-lobed typically palmatum-type leaves are similar to those of the popular 'Sango kaku'. The shoots and young branches of 'Bi hō' provide a novel new color to the winter scene and contrast well with the red shoots of 'Sango kaku' and its cultivar subgroup and the bright green of 'Aoyagi' shoots. The name means "beautiful mountain range."

'Bloodgood'

AMOENUM GROUP
RED

'Bloodgood' is one of the most popular large-leaved, upright-growing tree forms of red palmatum in the United States and Europe, and has become a standard by which all newer cultivars like it are judged. It is a very deep red or purple-red and holds its color into late summer better than most red-leaved forms. It does not "bronze-out" as many do.

The five- to seven-lobed leaves are deeply divided and finely and evenly toothed. The underside is usually a shiny, dark green. Light transmitted through the leaves on a bright day gives a beautiful red effect. The fall coloring is usually bright crimson. The dark red leaf stalks are shorter than the leaves. The prominent fruits are a bright red and add to the overall beauty of the plant.

This strong-growing cultivar makes an upright tree maturing at up to 10 m (33 ft.) or so. Strong branches form a broad-topped tree with the spread about equal to the height. 'Bloodgood' was about the only cultivar being grown from cuttings on a large scale in Dutch nurseries. It is also grafted there. In the United States there are thousands being grafted onto strong understock. These make vigorous trees in a short time.

It is hoped that this cultivar is kept pure as it has very good qualities not found in some other red-leaved cultivars. Carville (1975) suggested it was a selection from *Acer palmatum* f. *atropurpureum* seedlings by the Bloodgood Nursery, Long Island, New York. Vrugtman (1970) suggested the pos-

'Bi hō'.
Photo by Peter Gregory

'Bloodgood'.
Photo by J. D. Vertrees

sibility that this cultivar had its origin in Boskoop, Netherlands, and was propagated by the now discontinued nursery Ebbinge and Groos. It was subsequently exported to the United States where it was named, and the propagation expanded. Whatever its origins, it appears to have been cultivated in the United States since well before World War II. Received the RHS Award of Garden Merit.

'Boskoop Glory'

'Boskoop Glory'.
Photo by Cor van Gelderen

'Brandt's Dwarf'.
Photo by Harry Olsen

AMOENUM GROUP
RED

The origins of this cultivar are uncertain except that, contrary to its name, it did not originate directly from Boskoop in the Netherlands. It is possible it was selected and named at Wright's Nursery in Canby, Oregon, now no longer operating. Its principal claim to recognition among the many red cultivars seems to be that it grows into a dependable robust, vigorous, medium-sized tree, with large deep red leaves that hold their color well throughout the summer. Its ultimate height is up to 8 m (26 ft.).

The large leaves have five to seven neatly spread out lobes with the smaller basal lobes pointing outward or angled slightly backward. Each lobe is broadly ovate with a long tail-like tip and the broadest point in the middle. The lobe junctions are about two thirds of the way to the leaf base. There are numerous sharp, fine teeth on the leaf margins. The short, stout leaf stalks are red.

The young leaves emerge a bright pink-red. As they develop and fill out, their color changes to a deep plum red in early summer. This color remains through the summer if the plant is not shaded, changing to purple-red with green undertones in early fall. The tree tolerates full sun very well and is a very reliable grower.

'Brandt's Dwarf'

DWARF GROUP
RED

This cultivar is one of the best known and oldest of the many witches'-brooms arising from *Acer palmatum* f. *atropurpureum*. The foliage emerges a bright plum red, quickly changing to a good dark red, and then slowly fading to a rusty green later in the season. It turns a brilliant crimson in the fall. The small five- to seven-lobed leaves are deeply divided with the lobes well spread out. Each lobe is ovate with a long, tapering tip and the broadest point in the middle. The margins are finely toothed. In common with many witches'-brooms, the center lobe is often shortened with a rounded top. The slender

red leaf stalks are short and slender. Like several other witches'-brooms, 'Brandt's Dwarf' produces vigorous shoots in the season or so after grafting, but this soon slows down with age to a few centimeters a year. At maturity it forms a dense rounded bush, up to about 1 m (3 ft.) in height and spread.

'Brocade'
DISSECTUM GROUP
RED

'Brocade' is another of the very fine red dissectums and is similar to 'Ornatum'. The differences between many of the red dissectums are hard to describe and must be seen to be appreciated. Not as dark as some of the other cultivars, this red is a soft but deep color, lacking the blood-red quality of 'Crimson Queen' or 'Dissectum Nigrum'. 'Brocade' holds its color well, but gradually turns to a green-red and bronze later in the summer. It is a pleasant bronzing, not as harsh as some other cultivars. Fall color is usually bright red to crimson, blended softly with orange. The multidissected seven- to nine-lobed leaves are of medium size. This form cascades and eventually makes a large, rounded bush 3 m (10 ft.) high and a little wider.

'Bronzewing'
DISSECTUM GROUP
RED

This old Australian laceleaf of unknown origin has bronze-red to -green foliage all summer, hence the name. In fall, leaf color turns orange to gold. The mainly seven-lobed medium-sized leaves are divided to the leaf base. The lobes themselves are coarsely cut to create sublobes with large sharply pointed hooked teeth. Moderately vigorous, 'Bronzewing' forms the characteristic broad mushroom shape of most dissectums, eventually reaching 3 m (10 ft.) in height. The bronze foliage is quite

distinct and makes an excellent contrast with other maples.

'Brocade'.
Photo by Harry Olsen

'Bronzewing'.
Photo by Peter Gregory

'Burgundy Lace'
MATSUMURAE GROUP
RED

This striking American cultivar has almost ribbonlike lobes and burgundy wine colored foliage. The medium to large leaves are deeply divided with the seven lobes separated virtually to the leaf base. The lobes hold closely together, making the leaf appear longer than broad. Each lobe is long ovate-lanceolate, coming to a very gradual sharp point. The lobes are broadest in the middle and narrow to a tiny 1 mm at the base. They are sharply toothed along the

'Burgundy Lace'.
Photo by Cor van Gelderen

entire margin. Spring and early summer color is the typical burgundy red, but as the season progresses, leaf color turns bronzy or greenish. The leaves burn in full sun.

This spreading, small tree, up to 6 m (20 ft.) in height and spread, develops a wide canopy when given room. Although upright, it is classed in the smaller tree group. Hardy and beautiful, it makes an excellent contrast with other upright cultivars. With judicious pruning, it fits into smaller landscapes. Received the RHS Award of Garden Merit.

'Butterfly'

PALMATUM GROUP
VARIEGATED

'Butterfly' is a very spectacular small-leaved variegate. The leaves are variable in shape—rarely are any two alike—and they are mostly five-lobed. Each small lobe is different—some short, some long, and most of them irregularly shaped. The leaves on new growth have lobes that are more uniform. The slender lobes are long and narrow, and

are separated almost to the leaf base. The leaf stalks are short.

The *fukurin fu* type of variegation is basically a cream or whitish color on a bluish to grayish green or pale green. Sometimes an entire leaf is cream-colored, but most often this color appears on the edges of lobes or on an entire lobe. Quite often the cream portion of the lobe is sickle-shaped. Noticeable in the spring are the light pink markings that border the white or cream portions. In the fall, the white areas become a striking magenta, lending an entirely new quality to the appearance.

Growth is normally short and twiggy, making a dense, large shrub or very small tree of up to 6 m (20 ft.) tall. It is stiffly upright. New shoots and twigs appear very delicate and slender. The plant is difficult to graft because of the very small diameter of the scions.

One of the most reliable and desirable cultivars of the variegated group, this dainty and attractive tree always brings comments from visitors. It differs from the similar 'Beni shichihenge' in its taller, narrower growth and the lack of pink variegation except along the edges of the cream in spring. Also, the variegation of 'Beni shichihenge' is pink-orange in the spring, becoming white-brown. 'Butterfly' has deeper cut lobes than the similar-shaped 'Kagiri nishiki'. The Japanese name is thought to be 'Kochō nishiki', which translates as "variegated butterfly," or 'Kochō-no-mai'. The plant has also been known under the names 'Cho cho' and 'Choco-no-mai'.

'Calico'

PALMATUM GROUP
GREEN

Orange-yellow spring leaves hold their bright color longer than most, before changing to yellow-green then lighter green for the rest of the summer, eventually turning orange in the fall. The small leaves have five to seven lobes. 'Calico' forms a small shrubby tree up to 2.5 m (8 ft.) tall and is very suitable for the small garden or for container culture.

'Caperci Dwarf'

DWARF GROUP
GREEN

This lovely shrub probably originated in the 1970s with the late Jim Caperci, a nurseryman in Seattle, Washington. It is like a dwarf 'Corallinum', with small coral or light pink leaves becoming medium to light green for the summer and then turning a golden color in the fall. The small five- to seven-lobed typically palmatum-type leaves have fairly deeply divided, ovate lobes. The center lobe is dominant with the broadest point in the lower third. The pretty, very slender leaf stalks are shorter than the leaves.

When young, 'Caperci Dwarf' has a long, slender leader and horizontal branching pattern. As it matures it becomes a neat,

upright, rounded shrub, reaching about 1.5 m (5 ft.) tall. The cultivar name is sometimes misspelled 'Capersi Dwarf' or 'Capersian Dwarf'.

'Carlis Corner'

DWARF GROUP
RED

Originating in New Jersey from a witches'-broom, this neat, attractive dwarf has small palmatum-type five-lobed leaves, very deeply divided almost to the base. It is very like a red-leaved version of the green-leaved 'Tiny Tim', and is similar in size and shape. The spring leaves emerge a bright pink-red, gradually changing to a rich purple-red and holding this color well

'Butterfly'.
Photo by Peter Gregory

'Calico'.
Photo by Cor van Gelderen

throughout the summer, whether in shade or sun, then turning scarlet in the fall. The leaf lobes are narrowly ovate with coarsely toothed margins and sharply pointed tips, though the central lobe is sometimes shortened and bluntly rounded. 'Carlis Corner' forms a dense, round shrub up to 1.5 m (5 ft.) tall and is ideally suited to container culture.

'Chantilly Lace'
DISSECTUM GROUP
GREEN

This attractive laceleaf from Pennsylvania, introduced by Bill Schwartz, has medium-sized, finely cut leaves which emerge orange-red in the spring, changing to a pleasant medium green for summer, and turning golden yellow in the fall. A second flush of coppery red leaves in midsummer gradually becomes bronzed green. The plant is quite hardy and fairly vigorous, and forms a mushroom-shaped mound about 2.5 m (8 ft.) tall.

'Chikumano'
AMOENUM GROUP
RED

This tree of unusual quality and leaf size has a broad, upright growth habit. The large, strong, bold leaves are fairly deeply divided. The lobes taper to a long point and have double-toothed margins. Vigorous spring growth produces very large leaves, while older wood carries leaves that are slightly smaller. Spring foliage is a deep, rich, dark purple-red. During summer, green undertones appear in the purple-red. Fall colors are a rich, burnt orange and yellow-orange. This cultivar matures into a medium-sized tree of spreading habit, and makes a strong color contrast with the brighter red- or green-leaved cultivars.

'Chirimen nishiki'
PALMATUM GROUP
VARIEGATED

Basic foliage color is deep green. Irregular markings of yellow are predominant. These are often light areas involving an entire lobe. Other markings are indistinct little areas of a subdued white-green. There are occasional flecks of light yellow. It is a very delicate variegation on a very delicate type leaf. Many of the leaves are entirely green. In the spring the leaves emerge with very striking, bright pink variegation.

These small, unusual leaves are five-lobed and are separated to within 1 cm of the leaf base. Each lobe is very elongated, almost linear, and has a short tail-like tip. The margins are very irregular, wavy, and toothed; sometimes with small short round lobules. The leaf stalks are short and slender.

This plant is not strong growing. It is a small, shrubby type of plant reaching about 3 m (10 ft.) tall, rather delicate, and not easily propagated. The name means "colorful crepe paper." This very choice cultivar from Japan is not very well known nor is it found in many collections. It is better known as 'Kochō nishiki' in Japan and is mentioned in the *Sekihin Binran* in 1882.

'Chishio'
PALMATUM GROUP
GREEN

The brilliant crimson spring foliage turns a normal green in summer, before developing orange-red tones of varying intensity in fall. The small five- to seven-lobed leaves are divided fairly deeply. Each lobe is ovate-lanceolate and has slightly toothed margins. The slender leaf stalk is shorter than the leaf. 'Chishio' is slow growing and does not exceed 4 m (13 ft.) in height and spread.

The intense crimson new growth and new leaves make this plant as colorful as a flowering shrub. Compared to 'Coralli-num' and 'Shin deshōjō', the color can be described as having a tinge of orange in the scarlet, rather than being red-scarlet.

Since it is among the hardier cultivars, 'Chishio' is a desirable garden plant where a small tree is needed. The name means "blood red." This cultivar is also known under the names 'Sanguineum Chishio' and 'Shishio', and has been misspelled 'Chisio'. The name 'Chishio' has often been misused for the cultivar 'Okushimo'.

'Chitose yama'
MATSUMURAE GROUP
RED

This deeply divided red form has medium to large leaves with long, narrow lobes sep-

Page 114:
'Carlis Corner'.
Photo by Peter Gregory

'Chantilly Lace'.
Photo by Harold Greer

'Chikumano'.
Photo by Cor van Gelderen

This page:
'Chirimen nishiki'.
Photo by J. D. Vertrees

'Chishio'.
Photo by J. D. Vertrees

arating almost to the leaf base. The margins are double-toothed with many sharp teeth. New leaves are often pale crimson, but open to a rich purple-red. They do not color well in deep shade. As the season progresses, a bronze-green to dark green color appears. Fall color is a bright crimson. This cascading maple makes a mound-like tall shrub, 3 m (10 ft.) tall and as wide. It is an excellent cultivar, often used as a specimen in containers and occasionally for bonsai. Received the RHS Award of Garden Merit.

'Chitose yama'.
Photo by J. D. Vertrees

'Coonara Pygmy'.
Photo by Peter Gregory

'Coonara Pygmy'

DWARF GROUP
GREEN

Arnold Teese of Victoria, Australia, selected and named this excellent little form which he propagated from a witches'-broom. It forms a dense bush, up to 1.5 m (5 ft.) tall and broad, and is very reliable. A fine addition to the dwarf group, this beautiful maple has small, bright green leaves that pass through beautiful pastel yellow-orange-pink stages in the fall before turning a bright, deep pink, perfectly matching the deep, coral pink shoots. The twigs and branches are thin but stiff. The leaf is five-lobed and typically palmate. Each lobe is broad-ovate and acuminate, with a sharp tip. The margins are toothed, sometimes bluntly so.

'Coonara Pygmy' performs extremely well in the landscape, being a natural globe shape without much pruning. It is vigorous without being unruly and has attractive foliage in all seasons. It is also valuable as a bonsai plant.

'Corallinum'

PALMATUM GROUP
GREEN

The deep shrimp-pink spring foliage is the most outstanding feature of this very distinctive cultivar that attracts much attention. It is a thrill to see this plant in its spring and early summer glory. During the summer, the leaves turns green, and some leaves have minute flecks or speckles of light tones. The new growth in late summer or early fall is scarlet. The small leaves have five to seven lobes and are divided moderately deeply. The lobes are ovate, tapered, and very slightly toothed. Many leaves develop a slight crinkling, not lying in a perfectly flat plane. The short leaf stalks are slender and reddish pink.

I had the pleasure of seeing Sir Harold

Hillier's fine specimen plant at the Hillier Gardens and Arboretum in Hampshire, England. Viewed during the first week in June, it was in its glory of rich pink tones. In my opinion, it rivaled many flowering shrubs. It grows slowly and makes a dense, compact plant.

Unfortunately, the name 'Corallinum' has also been applied to the coral-bark maple 'Sango kaku'. 'Corallinum' has also been known under the names 'Beni seigen', 'Carmineum', and 'Spring Fire'.

'Coral Pink'

DWARF GROUP
GREEN

This lovely, small, slow-growing cultivar is outstanding in the spring with its eye-catching light coral-pink young foliage and slender pink-red shoots. The leaves become yellowish with pink edging before turning light green, often with lighter gray-green mottled variegation in early summer. The plant is similar to 'Wilson's Pink Dwarf' and has a much lighter and softer pink color than 'Corallinum'.

The mainly five-lobed small to medium-sized palmatum-type leaves are fairly deeply cut. The lobes are ovate-triangular to oblong-ovate with long, tail-like tips, the broadest point being about half-way along. The margins are irregularly and very coarsely toothed. The short, slender leaf stalks are pink to yellow-green.

'Coral Pink' is a slow-growing, upright shrub that reaches 2 m (6 ft.) tall. It merits a place in any landscape, however small, but prefers some shade. It was first noticed by Jelena de Belder at the Arboretum Kalmthout in Belgium about 1965, was kept under observation for many years, and eventually was named and propagated by Cor van Gelderen of Firma C. Esveld, Boskoop, Netherlands, in 1985.

'Crimson Carol'

MATSUMURAE GROUP
RED

This promising cultivar originated from a seedling collected in the early 1990s. The large seven-lobed leaves are quite distinctive and are very deeply divided right to the junction of the leaf base and stalk. Each lobe is long-ovate, broadest in the middle, and narrowing to little more than the width of the midvein at the junction with the leaf stalk. The lobe tips are tail-like and sharply pointed. The margins are distinctly

'Corallinum'.
Photo by Peter Gregory

'Coral Pink'.
Photo by Peter Gregory

'Crimson Carol'.
Photo by Peter Gregory

'Crimson Queen', habit.
Photo by Harold Greer

'Crimson Queen',
foliage detail.
Photo by Harold Greer

and, unusually for a Matsumurae, evenly toothed, each tooth itself with one or two tiny teeth, giving the foliage a feathery appearance. The leaves are a dark purple-red until late summer, turning a reddish orange in the fall. The plant prefers full sun and will grow into an upright tree with an estimated height of up to 5 m (16 ft.) or so.

'Crimson Queen'

DISSECTUM GROUP
RED

The outstanding feature of this very popular cultivar is the persistent, good, deep red color of the foliage. Most dissectum cultivars with excellent red color during spring and early summer turn green or bronze. In contrast, 'Crimson Queen' carries the deep red color throughout the entire growing season. It has endured periods of 100°F (38°C) temperatures in full sun with practically no sunburn, but under these conditions the deep red became orange-red. Fall color is a very bright scarlet.

The medium to large seven- to nine-lobed leaves are finely dissected. Each narrow lobe is deeply divided and notched. The scarlet leaf stalks are short. This strong-growing cultivar originated in the United States and ages into a beautiful, cascading tree 3 m (10 ft.) in height and 4 m (13 ft.) in spread. Among the many known red dissectum cultivars, 'Crimson Queen' has become a favorite in the United States. Received the RHS Award of Garden Merit.

'Curtis Strapleaf'

LINEARILOBUM GROUP
RED

William Curtis of Wil-Chris Acres in Sherwood, Oregon, selected this robust cultivar. The young straplike leaves emerge a bright red, quickly changing to plum red on top with a bronzy gray-green underside. The plum red color is held well into late summer and lasts longer than that of the popular 'Atrolineare'. Fall color is orange. The large five-lobed leaves are well spread out. Each straplike lobe is slightly broader in the middle. Irregular, shallow-pointed teeth are scattered along the margins. The short, slender leaf stalks are dark red. 'Curtis Strapleaf' forms a vigorous, upright tree with open crown and foliage, and eventually attains a height of 3 m (10 ft.) or so.

'Demi Sec'

DISSECTUM GROUP
GREEN

This slow-growing green laceleaf originated as a chance seedling and was selected and named by Cor van Gelderen of Firma C. Esveld in the Netherlands. In shape, it is very similar to 'Green Globe', having a ball-shaped, upright habit rather than the mushroom shape of most dissectums, and it eventually forms a medium-sized shrub. The finely cut dissected foliage is also similar to that of 'Green Globe', but differs in having slightly orange-tinted margins on the young leaves.

The medium-sized, emerald green leaves have a faint orange tinge on the margins and lobe tips when they emerge in the spring and on the young leaves as they appear through the summer. The leaves become medium green for the summer, before turning a bright yellow to gold in the fall. The mainly seven-lobed leaves are deeply divided to the base with the lower lobe ends narrowing to the width of the midveins. The lobes themselves are coarsely divided into sublobes with hooked teeth on the margins. The leaf stalks and young shoots are bright red.

'Deshōjō'

PALMATUM GROUP
RED

The spring foliage is a very bright carmine red, but the color does not hold as long as it does on other, similar cultivars. For the rest of the year it is a lighter green, often with reddish bronze edges, turning scarlet in the fall. The small to medium-sized palmate leaves usually have five lobes. The lobes are moderately divided two thirds of the distance to the base, radiate from the center, and are strongly tapered to a point. The margins are finely toothed. The thin leaf stalks are shorter than the leaves.

The *shōjō* part of this cultivar's name, meaning red-faced monkey, can become confusing. 'Shōjō' is an old standard form of the red palmatum. 'Deshōjō', as described here, is the base for other selected cultivars. 'Shin deshōjō' is a newer selection (*shin* means "new" or "newer"). 'Konde

'Demi Sec'.
Photo by Cor van Gelderen

'Deshōjō'.
Photo by Peter Gregory

shōjō' and 'Ima deshōjō' are other forms of varying red shades.

The upright-growing 'Deshōjō' makes a rather tall shrub of 3 m (10 ft.) and is as wide as it is tall. It is an outstanding ornamental companion plant for smaller gardens and bonsai, and is quite desirable in the group of Japanese maples with brilliant new growth. The name is sometimes misspelled 'Desyōjō'.

'Deshōjō nishiki'.
Photo by Cor van Gelderen

'Diana'.
Photo by Peter Gregory

'Deshōjō nishiki'
PALMATUM GROUP
VARIEGATED

This Japanese cultivar arose from a variegated sport on the well-known and popular 'Deshōjō'. In the spring, the young leaves are bright red with brownish variegation. They change to a light, reddish green with red margins, before turning a deep green with creamy yellow variegation for the summer. The variegation is in mottled patches which occupy parts of the leaves, and sometime whole leaves. 'Deshōjō nishiki' is similar in leaf and habit to its parent, but is slower growing.

'Diana'
DWARF GROUP
GREEN

This neat dwarf cultivar, selected by Dick van der Maat of the Netherlands and named after his daughter, has small palmatum-type leaves which, very unusually for *Acer palmatum*, have small tufts of brown hairs in the vein-axils on the leaf undersurface. The five-lobed leaves are very deeply divided almost to the leaf base, and are long-ovate with triangular, pointed tips and very coarsely toothed margins. The new leaves are light yellow-green with pink-bronzed margins and with a slight sheen. Fall colors are orange-red to crimson. The leaf stalks are quite short and pinkish. The young shoots are bright red, contrasting sharply with the leaves. 'Diana' forms a compact dense shrub up to 1.5 m (5 ft.) in height and would be ideal in an alpine garden or for bonsai culture.

'Dissectum Nigrum'
DISSECTUM GROUP
RED

The new spring growth of 'Dissectum Nigrum' is this cultivar's distinguishing characteristic. The new shoots and foliage are noticeably covered in fine, silvery hairs that make the unfolding new growth look almost gray. It soon loses the pubescence and attains the rich, deep red color so typical of this cultivar. Unfortunately, there are many plants labeled 'Dissectum Nigrum' which are not this cultivar. These plant do not have the silvery pubescence on the newly developing leaves, nor do they retain the deep red for which this cultivar is known.

The large leaves have seven long, finely dissected lobes, each lobe deeply divided to the midrib. The lobes tend to hang down, giving the whole plant a feathery, cascading appearance, so desirable in the Dissectum Group. As the name implies, this maple holds a deep red color much longer into midsummer than many other red dissectum cultivars; but not as long as 'Crimson Queen'.

Planting in full sun or in partial shade affects the length of color retention. Partial shade prolongs the deep colors. In late summer, bronze or bronze-green colors take over. In the fall, rich, bright red tones become prominent. 'Dissectum Nigrum' is a vigorous dissectum with the typical mushroom growth habit. Large, old specimens are 5 m (16 ft.) high and at least as wide.

This plant was one of the better red dissectums of the nursery trade, but has probably been overtaken by 'Crimson Queen'. It was originally imported from Japan into Europe and named 'Dissectum Nigrum', but renamed 'Ever Red' by Cascio when imported into the United States in 1965. Hence it is better known there as 'Ever Red'. Nonetheless, keeping the earlier name of 'Dissectum Nigrum' has priority and so this is the legitimate name. It has also been known under the names 'Dissectum Atrosanguineum', 'Dissectum Ever Red', 'Nigrum Dissectum', and 'Pendulum Nigrum'. Although it has also been grown under the name 'Nigrum', it should not be

'Dissectum Nigrum', habit.
Photo by J. D. Vertrees

'Dissectum Nigrum', silvery pubescence of spring growth.
Photo by J. D. Vertrees

confused with the true 'Nigrum', which is not a dissectum cultivar.

'Dr Tilt'

PALMATUM GROUP
GREEN

This attractive small tree was propagated by Harold Johnston of Alabama and named by him after its discoverer, Ken Tilt, who picked it out because of its outstanding fall color. The small to medium palmatum-type leaves have five to seven lobes and are fairly deeply divided. The lobes are ovate with triangular, pointed tips and have relatively fine, evenly toothed margins for a Palmatum Group cultivar. The spring leaves are light yellow-green with light pink-blushed margins, slowly turning light to mid green often with bronze-red lobe tips. 'Dr Tilt' is hardy and has withstood temperatures of 105°F (41°C) in full sun without burning. It forms an upright tree up to about 5.5 m (18 ft.) in height and would earn a place in most gardens.

'Eagle's Claw'
DISSECTUM GROUP
GREEN

This very attractive laceleaf resembles a smaller version of the well-known 'Palmatifidum' in leaf shape, color, and habit. It differs in its slower growth, the lobe tips of the seven-lobed leaves curving downward and sideways "like an eagle's claw," and the striking fall colors. In early fall, the leaves become multicolored in greens, yellows, oranges, and golds before finally turning yellow to gold with red-tinged margins. 'Eagle's Claw' forms a slow-growing small mound a little over 2 m (6 ft.) tall and is very well suited to container and bonsai culture.

'Eddisbury'
PALMATUM GROUP
GREEN

'Eddisbury' is a reliable and desirable coral-bark maple, rather like the popular 'Sango kaku', with similar medium-sized palmatum-type leaves. It does not grow as tall as 'Sango kaku' and its deeper, bright red shoots and leaf stalks contrast markedly with the green leaves throughout the growing season.

The leaves have five to seven ovate lobes that taper to a fine pointed tip. The leaf margins are regularly and evenly toothed. The slender, bright red leaf stalks are shorter than the leaves. In the spring, the young leaves are a lighter yellow-green with red-tinged tips and edges. As summer approaches, the foliage becomes a more uniform green, but the red tinge persists on some leaves. Fall colors are yellow to gold with light red overtones.

This sturdy, upright plant grows vigorously when young, but rarely exceeds 4 m (13 ft.) in height. Its outstanding feature

This page:
'Dr Tilt'.
Photo by Peter Gregory

'Eagle's Claw'.
Photo by Daniel Otis

Page 123:
'Eddisbury', fall color.
Photo by Peter Gregory

'Eddisbury', summer color.
Photo by Peter Gregory

'Edna Bergman'.
Photo by Peter Gregory

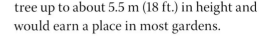

is the coral-red winter shoots, the color persisting into the second and third year. 'Eddisbury' was a chance seedling spotted by a keen-eyed employee at the F. Morrey and Son Nursery in Cheshire, England, who was attracted by its brilliant red stems. It is named after the district in which the nursery is situated.

'Edna Bergman'

MATSUMURAE GROUP
RED

This excellent, strong-growing, reliable cultivar was selected by Fred Bergman of North Carolina. The medium-sized, deeply divided leaves are a rusty red color in spring, but have a tendency to turn a bronzed green later, then change to orange and bright red in the fall. The leaf stalks are a bright red throughout. 'Edna Bergman' forms a vigorous, well-balanced, open-crowned, upright tree, reaching 6 m (20 ft.)

in height. It has a reputation of being very easy to propagate.

'Eimini'

DWARF GROUP
GREEN

This lovely bushy dwarf has very small, perfectly shaped palmatum-type green leaves that are divided into five lobes. The short, stiff leaf stalks and the shoots are reddish. The cultivar was found in the gardens of Villa Taranto in Italy and named, in about 1985, by Otto Eisenhut, a Swiss collector and magnolia specialist living nearby. 'Eimini' is densely branched, forming a 1.5-m (5-ft.) round bush, with a spread of 2 m (6 ft.). It is among the smallest of all *Acer*

palmatum cultivars and is highly suitable for bonsai.

'Elegans'

MATSUMURAE GROUP
GREEN

The glory of this cultivar is displayed in the fall with a burst of bright orange and red. The season starts in the spring with the new leaves a yellowish green color, then turning a darker green as they finally develop. The medium to large leaves have five to seven deeply divided and widely separated ovate lobes with distinctly toothed margins. The leaves are divided almost entirely to the leaf base, with the lobes very narrow at the base. The short leaf stalks are strong and stiff.

This stocky, low-growing tree tends to become as wide as it is tall, reaching a height of 3 m (10 ft.) or more. It is a good, hardy, trouble-free plant and is useful when a short tree is desired for background planting. Other names under which this cultivar has been known are 'Heptalobum Elegans', 'Pinnatum', and 'Septemlobum Elegans'.

'Elizabeth'

DWARF GROUP
RED

This small plant is similar to 'Kandy Kitchen' and, like that cultivar, originates from a witches'-broom. It was found and named in 1988 by Edward Rodd of Raraflora Nursery, Kinterfield, Pennsylvania. The small, mainly five-lobed palmatum-type leaves are deeply divided. The lobes are ovate with tail-like tips, though the center lobe may be short and rounded in some leaves. The margins are toothed. Young leaves emerge a bright pink-red and become purple-red, holding their color well all summer until changing to a vivid crimson in the fall. The bright pink-red young leaves, produced throughout the

summer, are attractive against the darker red older foliage. 'Elizabeth' forms a dense, upright, rounded shrub up to 2 m (6 ft.) tall and almost as wide.

'Ellen

DISSECTUM GROUP
GREEN

This vigorous, fresh, green laceleaf is characterized by its very low, wide spreading growth habit. The young leaves are yellow-green when first emerging. They turn a clear yellow in the fall. The large seven- to nine-lobed, deeply dissected leaves are very variable in size. Each lobe is itself coarsely and deeply incised, narrowing to the width of the main vein for the lower 1 cm or so to the junction with the leaf base. The margins of the lobules are, in turn, very coarsely toothed with hooked, sharply pointed teeth. The strong leaf stalks, swollen and hooked at the base, are quite short.

The plant grows to about 1 m (3 ft.) high in 10 years; with a spread of 2.5 m (8 ft.). This lovely, graceful cultivar was first noticed at Firma C. Esveld in Boskoop, Netherlands, in a batch of open-pollinated seedlings. After years of observation and propagation, it was named in 1992 after Ellen van Gelderen, the owner's daughter-in-law.

'Emerald Lace'

DISSECTUM GROUP
GREEN

This interesting cultivar was a chance seedling that David Sabo of North Carolina grew and liked. He sent scion material to Del Loucks of Del's Japanese Maple Nursery, who propagated and named it. It is a much deeper green than most green dissectums, has lacy foliage, and is a fast grower with very pendulous branches. The foliage is yellow-green when it first appears in the spring, darkening by midsummer,

and then unexpectedly turning a bright burgundy red in the fall.

The medium-sized five- to seven-lobed leaves are deeply dissected to the leaf base where the lobes narrow to the width of the midrib, less than 1 mm. The lobes and sublobes are well spread outward. The slender green leaf stalks are short and stiff.

'Emerald Lace' is a vigorous dissectum and forms an irregular semiupright but spreading bush with long, pendulous branches. It reaches a height and spread of up to 4 m (13 ft.) in 10 years. It would make a pleasant contrast with other dissectums with its darker green foliage and different growth habit.

'Emi'.
Photo by Peter Gregory

'Emma'.
Photo by Peter Gregory

'Emi'

PALMATUM GROUP
VARIEGATED

The variegation on the small typical palmatum-type leaves of this cultivar is very rare among *Acer palmatum* cultivars and consists of light yellow mottling and patches on a dark green background. It occurs as slight mottling or, more frequently, as conspicuous patches which can occupy sections of a lobe, half a lobe, the whole lobe and even the whole leaf.

The mainly five-lobed leaves are fairly deeply divided, each lobe long-ovate with a pointed tip and lightly toothed margins. The leaf stalks are short and pink, and the shoots a pink-red. Fall color is orange. 'Emi' grows into an upright small shrub up to 3 m (10 ft.) tall, and was selected and named by Dick van der Maat of the Netherlands. The name means "smile."

'Emma'

DISSECTUM GROUP
RED

This Dutch introduction is similar to the popular 'Ornatum' in growth habit and early color, but the leaves remain a deeper purple-red throughout the summer when 'Emma' is grown in full sun. When grown in shade, the foliage greens up easily and is an interesting mixture of light purple-red and green. The leaves turn a rich orange-red in the fall. The medium to large finely cut leaves have seven to nine lobes and are divided right to the base with the lower third or so of each lobe barely more than the width of the midrib. Each lobe is further divided almost to the midrib into sublobes with bluntish hooked teeth, giving an attractive lacy effect.

'Emma' grows into a spreading mushroom-shaped mound up to about 3 m (10 ft.) high and slightly wider. It was selected by Fritz van der Horst at the Firma C.

Esveld Nursery and named in 1990 after his daughter.

'Emperor 1'

AMOENUM GROUP
RED

This outstanding cultivar of exceptional vigor was discovered and developed by Richard P. Wolff of Red Maple Nursery, Pennsylvania. It is comparable with 'Bloodgood', the reliable standard with which all newer red upright palmatums are compared. 'Emperor 1' exceeds even 'Bloodgood' in leaf retention and growth rate, and has the additional advantage of coming into leaf two weeks later—thus reducing the risk of damage by spring frosts and cold, drying winds. It also holds its color well in shade and is more versatile.

Foliage color is a deep purple-red, retained throughout the growing season until changing to a beautiful dark crimson in the fall. Because the leaves are thinner textured than those of 'Bloodgood', they are more translucent and glow in the sunlight. They are large and deeply divided into five to seven lobes. Each lobe is ovate with a long, pointed tip and is broadest in the middle, narrowing to about 1 cm at the lobe junction. There are numerous fine, small teeth along the margins. The strong, dark red leaf stalks are shorter than the leaves.

'Emperor 1' is a hardy, upright wide-crowned tree and makes a good focal point for a large landscape. 'Red Emperor', which also originates from Red Maple Nursery, fits the above description and may be the same cultivar.

'Englishtown'

DWARF GROUP
RED

This unusual red dwarf, from a witches'-broom, was discovered by Stephen Krist-off of New Jersey, who named it after the city in which he found it. Its small, purple-red, palmatum-type leaves have five to seven lobes divided almost to the base. The lobes are long-ovate with clearly toothed margins and pointed tips. Like most cultivars from witches'-brooms, this one too has a center lobe that is sometimes shortened. 'Englishtown' looks intermediate between 'Shaina' and 'Pixie', but differs from both and many similar red dwarfs in its narrow, upright fastigiate habit. It is very slow-growing, barely reaching 20 in. (0.5 m) in 10 years under normal garden conditions.

'Emperor 1'.
Photo by Harry Olsen

'Englishtown'.
Photo by Peter Gregory

'Enkan'

LINEARILOBUM GROUP
RED

'Enkan' is a dwarf, red, strap-leaved maple from Japan, brought back to Europe in 1991 by Cor van Gelderen of Firma C. Esveld, Netherlands. It is very similar to another outstanding strap-leaved cultivar, 'Red Pygmy', also introduced by Firma C. Esveld, but holds its deep, wine-red coloring even better in all conditions, even in the hottest climates. It is the darkest red of the linearilobums. The medium-sized five-lobed leaves are very deeply divided almost to the base and are slightly broader than long. The smaller basal lobes are almost at right angles to the leaf stalks. The lobes have bluntly pointed or rounded tips and untoothed or barely toothed margins. The purple-red leaf stalks are quite short. 'Enkan' forms an upright tree of up to 3 m (10 ft.), but not so wide, and is similar in habit to the green-leaved 'Koto-no-ito'.

'Enkan'.
Photo by Peter Gregory

'Ever Autumn'.
Photo by Francis Schroeder

'Ever Autumn'

PALMATUM GROUP
GREEN

The outstanding feature of this strong, upright cultivar is the flush of autumn colors, gold through orange-red, in the otherwise rich green leaves throughout the growing season, hence the name. Fall coloring is quite exceptional. The almost rounded seven- to nine-lobed leaves are fairly deeply divided. Each lobe is broadly ovate with a short, tail-like, pointed tip and has coarsely toothed margins. The leaf stalks are short. 'Ever Autumn' was selected from a seedling in his garden in the mid-1980s and named by Dan Heims, Terra Nova Nurseries, Oregon. It appears to be a cross between a matsumurae and a palmatum and could justifiably be placed in either group. 'Omure yama' is a possible parent among other *Acer palmatum* cultivars.

'Fairy Hair'

LINEARILOBUM GROUP
GREEN

This remarkable, deceptively fragile-looking dwarf, green strapleaf arose as a seedling of 'Scolopendrifolium', selected by Talon Buchholz of Oregon in 1985. As the name implies, this cultivar has very narrow, stringlike leaves. These tend to be branched together and hang down to give a fragile appearance. 'Fairy Hair' is similar to the well-known but somewhat delicate 'Koto ito komachi' and, like that cultivar, none of its foliage reverts to the broader, more palmate-shaped leaves that occur with many other strap-leaved cultivars. 'Fairy Hair' is proving to be sturdier and more versatile than 'Koto ito komachi', and can be grown in the open, without shade, where it can reach up to 1 m (3 ft.) tall in 10 years.

'Fall's Fire'

PALMATUM GROUP
GREEN

Noted for its spectacular fall color, this vigorous cultivar forms an upright, medium-sized tree. It has small to medium palmatum-type leaves which are light yellow-green in spring with faint pink leaf tips and margins, becoming midgreen for the summer. The foliage turns brilliant yellow, orange, and red in the fall. The five- to seven-lobed leaves are deeply divided almost to the leaf base. Each lobe is broadly ovate, widest in the middle, and ending in a triangular, pointed tip. The margins are very conspicuously and coarsely toothed. The slender leaf stalks are red and the young shoots green. 'Fall's Fire' reaches up to 6 m (20 ft.) in height. It is particularly desirable for its stunning autumn display.

'Fascination'

MATSUMURAE GROUP
GREEN

This fast-growing, vigorous cultivar, introduced by Frank Mossman, has large leaves that are deeply divided into mainly seven lobes. The lobes tend to curve sideways. The leaves are similar to those of the long-established 'Omure yama', but with coarser, very conspicuous teeth on the leaf margins. The plant vigor and leaf shape and size suggest *A. japonicum* 'Aconitifolium' as a possible parent.

When the leaves first appear in the spring, they are an attractive yellow-orange, becoming a darkish green for the

'Fairy Hair'.
Photo by Talon Buchholz

'Fall's Fire'.
Photo Peter Gregory

'Fascination'.
Photo by Harold Greer

summer and then turning an eye-catching orange-scarlet in the fall. The leaf stalks are short and tinged red, especially on the external upper side. The shoots and stems are green with numerous white striations, giving a very attractive, gray-green appearance. 'Fascination' forms an upright, large tree, and grows to at least 8 m (26 ft.) tall.

'Felice'

DISSECTUM GROUP
RED

This outstanding red dissectum has two unusual features. First, the leaves bunch up at intervals along the shoots, causing the yellowish young leaves to look like brush tips. Second, the seven-lobed, deeply dissected red leaves are of two kinds. One has the lobes narrowing near the leaf base to little more than the width of the midrib, with the lobes themselves deeply incised. The other has broader, much less deeply divided lobules, sometimes little more than large teeth. The margins have coarsely sharp-pointed teeth. The broader-lobed leaves hold their purple-red color on the upper surface into the fall, with the undersurface becoming a dark green suffused with purple. The strong, short leaf stalks are red and have swollen bases.

The young leaves emerge a light yellow with pink edging, becoming a bronze-green with purple edging later in the season. At this stage, depending on the season and the amount off shading, it is sometimes debatable whether to put this cultivar into the red or the green category! The bunches of young yellow leaves against the darker, bronze-green older foliage have a pleasant, multicolored effect.

'Felice' forms a bushy mound, estimated to reach a height and spread of about 3 m (10 ft.). It arose as a chance seedling which was named and introduced by Firma C. Esveld, Netherlands.

'Filigree'

DISSECTUM GROUP
VARIEGATED

The delicate texture and interesting color changes of this laceleaf make it a conversation piece. The basic color is light green, almost yellow-green in the spring, darkening as the season progresses. Overlaid on the basic color is a profusion of minute dots, specks, or flecks of pale gold or cream, which creates a lighter green leaf with a network of slightly darker green veins. In the fall the medium to large leaves attain a rich gold color. The bark of the shoots and branches is a silvery green with definite white striping or elongated flecking.

The leaves are dissected entirely to the

'Felice'.
Photo by Cor van Gelderen

'Filigree'.
Photo by J. D. Vertrees

leaf base. Each of the seven lobes is delicately and deeply dissected almost to the midrib. In turn, each lobule is again toothed, making a double-dissected and very lacy leaf. Each dissected tooth is quite sharp.

The growth habit of this compact cultivar is pendulous like that of most dissectums, making a well-rounded, cascading plant 4 m (13 ft.) in height and 3 m (10 ft.) in spread. Tall staking during early growth of the plant or high grafting on a standard is desirable. The plant will then cascade as it matures. It is one of the more desirable cultivars for garden landscapes and also for collectors, but it is not easy to propagate. The original plant was named by Joel Spingarn of New York. It was a chance purchase by him of a young green dissectum that developed these characteristics. It has been called 'Green Filigree' and 'Silver Lace'.

'Filigree Rouge'
DISSECTUM GROUP
RED

The summer coloring of this distinctive laceleaf can vary between purple-red and bronze-green. The spring leaves are red, becoming bronze-red to purple-red. In full sun, the purple-red is retained through most of the summer, with the leaf undersurface green to gray-green. The leaves become bronze-green in late summer. Depending on the degree of shading, the bright red young leaves change to bronze-red, then bronze-green for the rest of the summer. Fall color is a bright orange-red. The medium-sized mainly seven-lobed leaves are deeply divided and each lobe is also deeply divided with the margins of the resulting sublobes sharply toothed. The short leaf stalks are red. 'Filigree Rouge' forms a spreading mound, much wider than tall.

'Fior d'Arancio'
MATSUMURAE GROUP
RED

The leaves are similar in shape and size to those of 'Wakehurst Pink', without the variegation, and with broader, less hooked teeth on the margins. The leaves emerge a bright orange-red, becoming bronze and copper-red as they develop. They tend to green up easily when shaded. The contrast of orange-red young leaves on a background of copper-green older leaves and possibly green shaded leaves can produce an attractive multicolor effect.

The large seven-lobed leaves are deeply divided to within 1 cm of the leaf base. Each lobe is ovate with a long, pointed tip

'Filigree Rouge'.
Photo by Peter Gregory

'Fior d'Arancio'.
Photo by Peter Gregory

and is broadest in the middle, narrowing to 3–6 mm at the lobe junctions. The outer margins tend to curve downward and are conspicuously toothed. The coarse, sharp teeth are angular and very prominent in young leaves. The short, stiff leaf stalks are reddish bronze. The sturdy shoots are green with whitish stripes and with a slight gray bloom when first appearing.

This cultivar forms an upright, rounded tree up to 6 m (20 ft.) in height. It originated at Fratelli Gilardelli Nursery in Italy. The name has been misspelled 'Fior d'Arangio'.

'Fireglow'

AMOENUM GROUP
RED

This impressive and reliable cultivar is a vigorous, upright, well-branched shrub or small tree, similar to the popular, tried-and-tested 'Bloodgood', but the leaves are not as deeply divided. It has a deeper, more intense red color, which stays throughout the summer, even in very hot, sunny conditions. The new leaves emerge a very bright pink-red in the spring before turning a deep red. The upper surface retains its color well into late summer and does not burn in hot sun. The foliage becomes purple-red suffused with green by early fall.

The seven-lobed, medium to large leaves are moderately deeply divided with the small basal lobes at right angles to the short, purple leaf stalks. The leaf margins are evenly and sharply toothed.

This cultivar forms an upright shrub with many slender, dark red shoots, eventually reaching up to 5 m (16 ft.) in height. Although vigorous, it does not become as tall and widespread as 'Bloodgood' and thus makes an excellent garden or container plant.

'Fireglow' was first selected and developed in Italy by Fratelli Gilardelli Nursery under the code 'FG1'. The name 'Fireglow' aptly describes the eye-catching effect when the leaves are backlit by the sun. A Dutch nursery later sold this same cultivar under the name 'Effigi', which became 'Effigy'.

'First Ghost'

MATSUMURAE GROUP
VARIEGATED

A distinctive variegate in the Ghost Series which was selected and named by Talon

'Fireglow'.
Photo by Peter Gregory

'First Ghost'.
Photo by Talon Buchholz

Buchholz in Oregon, this cultivar arose from a branch mutation on the old-established 'Beni shigitatsu sawa'. The large seven-lobed, deeply divided leaves are similar to those of its parent, the lobes having irregular, wavy margins and coarse, sharp teeth. They differ in the creamy white color of the leaves with a contrasting, dark network of veins. Young leaves are lightly tinged pink around the margins. These ghostlike leaves are supported by the distinctive gray-white bloom on the young shoots. 'First Ghost' forms a small to medium-sized tree up to 4 m (13 ft.) tall, but needs some shade and protection from the afternoon sun and cold winds.

'Fjellheim'

PALMATUM GROUP
GREEN

Arising from a witches'-broom growing on the ever-popular 'Sango kaku', this cultivar was discovered by the late Ilo Sorenson from the Blue Mountains near Sydney, Australia. It has retained all the characteristics of its famous parent—the beautiful coral-red shoots and the five-lobed palmatum-type leaf shape, size, and coloring. The notable difference is that 'Fjellheim' is much bushier and shorter; it forms a much more compact bush than 'Sango kaku'. For this reason, it was known under the illegitimate name 'Sango kaku Dwarf'. With spectacular bark, beautiful spring and fall leaf coloring, and compact growth, this introduction is ideally suited for the small garden and as a container plant.

'Flavescens'

DISSECTUM GROUP
GREEN

The distinctive yellow-green of this cultivar makes it a worthwhile addition. Although the leaf is quite typical of the dissectums, its distinct color phase in spring and early summer makes the tree quite different.

The green tones of the large leaves darken as summer progresses. The fall color is usually a bright yellow, occasionally tinged with orange. There are five to seven lobes, which are divided entirely to the leaf base. Each lobe is cut and toothed along the margins. The individual lobes are not as deeply pinnatifid as in most typical dissectums.

'Flavescens' is very vigorous and has the characteristic, pendulous, dome-shaped habit of the Dissectum Group. It is desirable to train the young plant into an

'Fjellheim'.
Photo by Harry Olsen

'Flavescens'.
Photo by Peter Gregory

upright stem so that the cascading form may develop. The tree can eventually reach 2.5 m (8 ft.) in height and slightly wider in spread. Other names by which this cultivar has been known are 'Dissectum Aureum', 'Dissectum Flavescens', 'Dissectum Unicolor', and 'Sulphureum'.

'Fujinami nishiki'

MATSUMURAE GROUP
VARIEGATED

This very distinct variegate from a seedling of the long-established 'Musashino' (syn. 'Nomura') was selected and named in 1998 by Yoshimichi Hirose in Japan. The medium-sized, mainly five-lobed leaves with clearly toothed margins are almost intermediate between the matsumurae-type and the amoenum-type leaves, and are fairly deeply divided. They emerge a bright, coppery red, soon showing the bright pink-red variegation on a darker purple-red background for the summer. The variegation occurs in flashes and patches and often occupies whole lobes and sometimes the whole leaf.

'Fujinami nishiki' is very similar in appearance to the American 'Yūbae', but has more frequent and reliable variegation. It is said to be susceptible in damp, humid conditions, but is otherwise a very colorful and attractive bushy tree.

'Garnet'

DISSECTUM GROUP
RED

The outstanding features of this cultivar are its color and vigor. The leaf color is the rich red-orange of the gemstone garnet. When this maple is grown in shade, the leaves retain a greenish cast, but in a sunny location the garnet color develops well. This vigorous-growing form eventually attains a height of 4 m (13 ft.) or more. It has the pendulous, spreading habit of dissectums and, as it matures, forms a beautiful, cascading, mound-shaped specimen.

The leaves are large for a dissectum, and the deep color holds well into the summer season. The seven lobes separate entirely to the leaf base. The side incisions on each lobe are neither as deeply cut as in most other dissectums nor as delicate. The whole leaf appears a little coarser than most red dissectums.

'Garnet' originated with Guldemond of the Netherlands. It has become a popular cultivar with nursery propagators and

'Fujinami nishiki'.
Photo by Peter Gregory

'Garnet'.
Photo by J. D. Vertrees

makes a good quality plant of saleable size in a short time. It retains its color well and is a durable landscape plant. It has also been known under the name 'Dissectum Garnet'. Received the RHS Award of Garden Merit.

'Garyū'

DWARF GROUP
GREEN

The small to medium-sized leaves are very distinctive and delicate in appearance. Each leaf has three to five lobes, which divide almost entirely to the leaf base roughly forming a T. They are narrow at the base, tapering to a narrow tip, with the center lobe being long and slender but not nearly as parallel-sided as are cultivars of the Linearilobum Group. The margins are complex, deeply toothed or lobulate, or combinations of both. They do not lie flat but twist sideways, curl up or down, or become slightly sickle-shaped. This variation occurs between leaves or even on the same leaf. The overall appearance of the foliage is disorganized but attractive.

The colors also vary. Basically the foliage is medium to light green. Spring foliage has a definite red-brown overtone, which may persist around the margins. Some older foliage also assumes a red tone in full light. The leaves turn a deep red in the autumn.

This compact, densely branched dwarf tends to produce indefinite directions of the twigs, much as with the foliage. It is semiprostrate in habit, but also has some shoots growing erect. It eventually only reaches 1 m (3 ft.) or so in height and spread after many years. The name means "sleeping dragon."

'Gasshō'

AMOENUM GROUP
GREEN

This interesting Japanese introduction has medium to large five- to seven-lobed leaves with the outer half of the lobes tending to curve downward and sometimes to overlap. Spring leaves emerge a light yellow-green with bronzed lobe tips, soon becoming mid to dark green for the summer. Fall colors are orange and red.

The fairly deeply divided lobes are long-ovate, broadest in the lower third, and end with long triangular tips. The margins are finely toothed. The reddish leaf stalks are shorter than the leaves. The pairs of leaves are spread out along the very slender red young shoots, so that the branches tend to hang down slightly, giving a graceful cascading appearance.

It is estimated that 'Gasshō' will grow into a rounded spreading tree or shrub up to about 5 m (16 ft.) tall. The name, which means "clasp one's hands together" and refers to the leaf shape, has also been spelled 'Gassyo'.

'Geisha'

DWARF GROUP
VARIEGATED

Duncan and Davies Nursery of New Zealand raised this amazing and attractive dwarf cultivar. In spring, the deeply divided leaves are delicate shades of pink to light cream, sparsely flecked with dark and

'Garyū'.
Photo by Peter Gregory

medium green spots and small patches. The creamy areas turn pale yellow-green and the main veins become green in summer, but the attractive pink tone often persists. The fall colors pass from green through orange, pink, and finally crimson.

The five- to seven-lobed leaves are divided almost to the leaf base and are surprisingly large for such a dwarf plant.

'Geisha'.
Photo by Peter Gregory

'Geisha Gone Wild'.
Photo by Talon Buchholz

The lobes are narrowly ovate with narrow, tail-like pointed tips. The margins have large, coarse teeth. The pink leaf stalks are slender.

'Geisha' is a slow-growing, bushy dwarf, eventually reaching 1 m (3 ft.) or so high and about as wide. It is a distinct and very unusual cultivar and, as the pastel colors suggest, is somewhat delicate and in need of protection and semishade. It makes a fine patio plant and is ideal for containers. The name means "a lady singer and entertainer."

'Geisha Gone Wild'
PALMATUM GROUP
VARIEGATED

This unusual variegate arose as a seedling of 'Geisha' and has similarly shaped foliage but, instead of the spotted variegation of its parent, it is more like that of 'Tennyo-no-hoshi', with varying pink and cream sections along the margins of the greenish light purple leaves. The variegated patches distort the lobes causing them to twist and curve in any direction, rather like a jester's cap. The "typical" leaf has five long narrow lobes divided almost to the leaf base. Each lobe is ovate with a thin pointed tail-like tip and irregularly toothed margins. The short leaf stalks are reddish. Fall color is purple-orange.

'Geisha Gone Wild' prefers sun or light shade and a well-drained soil, and has withstood temperatures down to –10°F (–23°C). This small tree has only grown to 2 m (6 ft.) tall and about half as wide in 10 years. It was selected and named by Buchholz and Buchholz Nursery, Oregon, for their Flora Wonder Collection. By a strange coincidence, a similar seedling of 'Geisha' with similar variegated leaves was selected and named 'Shirazz' in New Zealand, but the leaves tend to be a stronger purple-gray-green color and the plant is more vigorous.

'Germaine's Gyration'

DISSECTUM GROUP
GREEN

This laceleaf grows more vigorously than most dissectums, so the cascading branches twist and undulate, giving rise to the "gyration" half of the name. The plant arose from a seedling selected by Bob Vandermoss, Oregon, and was named by him after his neighbor and friend Germaine Iseli. The large coarsely dissected leaves have seven to nine lobes that are divided into sublobes, but not as deeply as in most dissectums. The sublobes are little more than large teeth reaching about halfway to the midrib and are themselves coarsely toothed. The dark green summer foliage changes to beautiful tones of yellow, orange, and red in the fall. Like most dissectums, this plant forms a cascading, mushroom-shaped mound, but is much wider than tall.

'Globosum'

DWARF GROUP
GREEN

As the name implies, this dwarf forms a round ball. The thick, brown shoots have very short internodes so the fully grown tree is only up to about 1.5 m (5 ft.) tall and wide. The medium-sized, typically palmatum-type, mainly five-lobed leaves are moderately deeply divided. The broad lobes are angled downward and outward. Each lobe is ovate-triangular with a tail-like tip. The large, angular teeth, uniformly arranged around the margins, give the leaves an attractive, feathery look. The leaves are the same shape and green color as those of 'Ō jishi' and turn yellow in the fall. 'Globosum' is thought to have been imported from Japan and introduced into Europe by the Dutch nursery of K. Wezelenburg and Son.

'Glowing Embers'

PALMATUM GROUP
RED

A small dense, vigorous, upright cultivar with characteristic palmatum-type small to medium-sized leaves, 'Glowing Embers' can be grown in hot, sunny conditions and will eventually reach a height of 3 m (10 ft.). It produces bright red new shoots and leaves in the spring. The leaves become plum red as they mature and form a contrasting background for the fiery red new growth produced all summer. The cultivar is named for this new growth. It contrasts

'Germaine's Gyration'.
Photo by Harry Olsen

'Globosum'.
Photo by Peter Gregory

'Glowing Embers'.
Photo by Peter Gregory

'Golden Pond'.
Photo by Peter Gregory

'Goshiki kotohime'.
Photo by J. D. Vertrees

well with the more frequent darker purple-red cultivars.

'Golden Pond'

AMOENUM GROUP
GREEN

Sharing the same stunning deep yellow-orange fall color of 'Hōgyoku', the leaves of 'Golden Pond' are similar in shape but smaller in size, more like the leaves of 'Shigure zome'. The summer color is a medium green. The growth habit is exactly opposite to that of 'Hōgyoku', but about one and a half times as wide as tall—4.5 m (15 ft.) wide and 3 m (10 ft.) tall. 'Golden Pond' has been growing at Firma C. Esveld in Boskoop, Netherlands, for 25 years and was named in 1996.

'Goshiki kotohime'

DWARF GROUP
VARIEGATED

This beautiful little plant is the variegated form of the excellent dwarf 'Kotohime'. The basic color of the foliage is a rich green with each leaf varying in the amount of variegation. Some are completely marked with tiny flecks and speckles, others are solid green. The markings are always minute, often overlapping, and are white, cream, light yellow, pink, and red. The individual tones are subdued, but the total effect is quite brilliant in the spring. The newest growth tips are often quite pink as they develop, but soon assume the normal variegation. As the summer approaches the leaves take on a darker green color.

The leaves are quite small, each one having five lobes radiating outward and fairly deeply divided toward the leaf base. The lobes narrow slightly toward the lobe junctions, being widest about one third of the way from the base, and taper to a long, sharp point. The margins are toothed. The leaves are not flat but are irregular, hooked or slightly crinkled.

The growth of the plant is very slow and stubby. Side branching is often profuse, thus making a very dense, compact small plant. It is, indeed, a true dwarf selection of less than 1 m (3 ft.) tall. This variegated cultivar is quite rare, even less well known than its green counterpart 'Kotohime'. It is quite difficult to propagate because of the lack of vegetative growth. Scions for grafting are extremely short, offering less than 1 cm to work with. The name means "small multicolored old harp."

'Grandma Ghost'

MATSUMURAE GROUP
VARIEGATED

A small to medium-sized tree, this cultivar is one of the Ghost Series of netted variegates from the Buchholz and Buchholz Nursery, Oregon. The yellowish leaves tinged pink around the margins and "throat" and superimposed with a green network of veins give this plant a distinctive look in the spring. The large broad-lobed, deeply divided leaves change to creamy white and amber with the green network for the summer, turning to gold and orange in the fall. The tree grows to about 2.5 m (8 ft.) high and about half as wide in 10 years. It needs protection from afternoon sun.

'Green Globe'

DISSECTUM GROUP
GREEN

As its name implies, this selection from Fratelli Gilardelli Nursery in Italy tends to form a rounded ball shape. It does not have the pendulous habit characteristic of most dissectums, but has a more upright rounded form.

The spring coloring of the emerging young leaves is attractive, the initial rose color turning to shades of creamy white, and quickly becoming a fresh emerald green. This color is held throughout the summer until turning yellow in the fall. The shoots and leaf stalks are an attractive medium green. The large seven-lobed, deeply dissected leaves narrow to the width of the midvein for approximately 1 cm to the base. The lobes themselves are fairly deeply cut. The sublobes have narrow toothed margins. The leaf stalks are short and have swollen bases.

This vigorous, rounded cultivar is estimated to reach a height of up to 5 m (16 ft.), with a spread of up to 4 m (13 ft.). Because the plant has a rounded rather than cas-

'Grandma Ghost'.
Photo by Peter Gregory

'Green Globe'.
Photo by Cor van Gelderen

cading habit, the graft is low down on the understock, not as high as is usual with dissectum cultivars. Another name for this plant is 'Viridis Olandese'.

'Green Hornet'

DISSECTUM GROUP
GREEN

This finely cut laceleaf has the distinction of being the only green dissectum whose leaves produce an outstanding, brilliant red fall color. The spring leaves are green tinged orange, changing to a fresh green for summer, before turning a beautiful bright red in the fall. The green summer foliage contrasts attractively with green-flecked orange new growth which appears throughout the summer. The tree is very vigorous in its early years, with long sweeping shoots, eventually forming a wide-spreading, mushroom-shaped mound up to 3 m (10 ft.) high.

'Green Lace'

DISSECTUM GROUP
GREEN

This desirable green dissectum has a fine leaf texture, graceful pendulous shape, and outstanding fall colors. It was selected and named by Fratelli Gilardelli Nursery of Italy. The seven-lobed leaves are deeply dissected to the leaf stalk, the lobes themselves divided to the midrib. These are, in turn, strongly toothed. The new leaves emerge a light creamy green, becoming a light emerald green for the summer. In the fall, their color changes to a beautiful clear golden yellow. This cultivar grows into a wide, mushroom-shaped mound up to 4 m (13 ft.) tall and at least as broad. It can be planted in full sun or partial shade.

'Green Mist'

DISSECTUM GROUP
GREEN

This excellent, medium green laceleaf maple is similar to 'Waterfall' in leaf and habit, but with orange-red, not yellow, fall color, and is considered to be hardier. The medium to large deeply dissected leaves have seven lobes that narrow sharply to the width of the midrib for up to 2 cm from the leaf base. The lobes themselves are divided into sublobes almost to the midrib and have narrow, sharp-pointed, curved teeth. The slender leaf stalks are quite short. 'Green Mist' is vigorous grow-

'Green Hornet'.
Photo by Francis Schroeder

'Green Lace'.
Photo by Cor van Gelderen

ing and, like most dissectums, forms a cascading mound up to 3 m (10 ft.) in height. The color and delicate appearance of the pendulous foliage give the tree the soft, misty look that gave rise to the cultivar name. The plant was introduced by Red Maple Nursery, Pennsylvania.

'Green Star'

AMOENUM GROUP
GREEN

This large, vigorous cultivar is very similar in leaf, habit, and size to the ever-popular 'Ō sakazuki' but, instead of turning scarlet, it turns a brilliant orange in the fall. Its medium to large bold leaves are star-shaped, with the lobes often slightly folded at the midvein to form a shallow trough. The five moderately deeply divided, broadly ovate lobes have sharply pointed tail-like tips, and finely and evenly toothed margins. The spring leaves are light green with slightly pink tips and margins, becoming mid to dark green for the summer, and turning burnt pink then vivid orange and gold in the fall. The leaf stalks are reddish and the young shoots brown. 'Green Star' is a fast-growing upright tree which reaches about 8 m (26 ft.) in height. It makes a stunning contrast to the scarlet 'Ō sakazuki' and yellow 'Aoyagi' in the larger landscape.

'Green Trompenburg'

MATSUMURAE GROUP
GREEN

This tall-growing tree has distinctive green foliage. The large leaves are almost identical to the well-known, red-leaved 'Trompenburg'. The difference is in the color. The leaves are a dark, rich green, with no lighter undertones. The dark green carries well into the summer and does not appear to show sunburn. The early spring foliage carries a shading of rusty red on the tips and edges, which disappears in the summer. Fall colors are orange and yellow tones.

'Green Mist'.
Photo by Peter Gregory

'Green Star',
spring foliage.
Photo by Peter Gregory

'Green Star', fall foliage.
Photo by Peter Gregory

The seven to nine lobes radiate outward in almost a completely circular manner, and are separated most of the way to the leaf base. Each lobe is long and slender, which is further accentuated by the curved or slightly rolled-down edges, making a long semitube. The edges of the lobes are coarsely toothed but partly hidden by being rolled down. Strong leaf stalks hold the leaf outward.

This interesting, very vigorous tree reaches a full size of about 8 m (26 ft.) tall. As with the red 'Trompenburg', the foliage texture and form of tree are quite desirable. The green form gives an added choice for the landscape. This cultivar originated in a large batch of seedlings grown from open-pollinated seed, harvested at Firma C. Esveld, Netherlands. It was propagated at Maplewood Nursery, named and registered in 1988. Its alternative name is 'Groene Trompenburg'.

'Green Trompenburg'.
Photo by Cor van Gelderen

'Groundcover'.
Photo by Peter Gregory

'Groundcover'
DWARF GROUP
GREEN

The leaves of this useful, small-leaved dwarf are deeply divided and have five narrow-ovate lobes with long, pointed tips. The margins have relatively large, coarse teeth. The short leaf stalks are threadlike. The foliage is a medium green with the leaf tips and outer margins often tinged pink to red-bronze. This cultivar is aptly named, growing into a very dense, twiggy plant which hugs the ground. It reaches 60 cm (2 ft.) tall and twice as wide.

'Hagoromo'
OTHER GROUP
GREEN

The distinctive leaf of this very unusual form of *Acer palmatum* can be described in common terms as having "five feather-type divisions joined to a stem." More specifically, the leaf is divided completely to the base, and the lobes attached directly onto the shoot without a leaf stalk. Each leaf lobe is broadly lanceolate with the base quickly tapering to a leaf stalklike attachment, and with coarsely toothed margins. Each portion has a different plane of attitude, twist, and curve as does each leaf on the shoot, thus forming an overall very feathery and nonuniform foliage cover.

Leaf color is dark green with emerging young leaves tinged pink. Fall colors are a blend of light yellows and oranges. This cultivar has a narrow, dense, upright form, slowly reaching about 6 m (20 ft.) in height. Plants growing in the Maplewood collection do not grow as vigorously as do those of 'Koshimino'. Perhaps this is the main distinction between these two cultivars. Japanese authorities state that 'Hagoromo' does not grow very vigorously. Nonetheless, several authorities consider 'Hagoromo' and 'Koshimino' to be synonymous.

The cultivar name, which means "Japanese angel's dress," has been misspelled as 'Hagaromo'. The lack of leaf stalks probably gave rise to the names 'Sessilifolium' and 'Stalkless' which have been applied to this cultivar in the past. Other names under which it has been known are 'Decompositum', 'Dissectum Sessilifolium', 'Fischergeraete', and 'Kakure mino'.

'Hama otome'

AMOENUM GROUP
GREEN

This Japanese cultivar has been classed as a variegated form because new foliage is light colored, but it becomes almost completely green for the summer. New leaves are a very pale yellow-green or whitish green the lightest tones in the center of the leaf, gradually becoming darker toward the lobe margins. The division of color is not a sharp one but rather a soft blending of tones. As the leaves mature they gradually darken to a light green, while still retaining the undertone of whitish yellow. The foliage turns yellow with reddish variegation in the fall.

The medium-sized leaves have five to seven lobes with the pair of basal lobes extremely small when the leaf is seven-lobed. The lobes separate almost to the leaf base. Each is ovate-lanceolate with a long, slender tip. The margins are finely toothed.

This cultivar is a small-sized shrub up to about 3 m (10 ft.) in height. It is hardy, not fast growing, and relatively easy to propagate. The name has been misspelled 'Hana otome'.

'Hanami nishiki'

DWARF GROUP
GREEN

One of the rare dwarf forms, 'Hanami nishiki' is also one of the smallest leaved forms. The five- to seven-lobed, light yellow-green leaves have lightly bronzed edges and tips in the spring. The five lobes radiate out and are moderately deeply divided. Each lobe tapers sharply to a point and has lightly toothed margins. The leaf stalks are very thin, delicate, and short.

'Hagoromo'.
Photo by J. D. Vertrees

'Hanami nishiki'.
Photo by J. D. Vertrees

The small palmatum-type leaves appear in the spring with an orange-red tint, particularly along the margins, becoming a uniform light to yellowish green, changing to orange-red in the fall. Occasionally, the leaves on older wood show minute pinpointing of light variegations, but the markings are so light and the leaves so tiny that this does not become a major feature. The leaves are closely placed along the tiny twigs which branch frequently, making a tight-growing dwarf form.

The plant can eventually reach 2 m (6 ft.) in height and spread. When grown in containers or as a bonsai, plants can be expected to make just a few centimeters of growth per year. Although this maple is slightly delicate to grow and is difficult to propagate, it is one of the real gems of the dwarf group. The name means "flower-viewing tapestry."

'Hanazono nishiki'

PALMATUM GROUP
VARIEGATED

This shy variegate is beautiful when carefully grown. The small to medium-sized, usually five-lobed leaves have a pale green base color. Variegations are mostly of the *kiri fu* (cut in) type, with some additional irregular marking. Colors range from pink to cream, the pink being predominant when the leaves first develop in the spring. Shoots also have faint pink markings in the young bark. The pink 'Karasu gawa' is more widely known. This lesser-known cultivar is not strong growing and rarely exceeds much more than 2 m (6 ft.) in height. The name means "variegated flower garden."

'Harusame'

PALMATUM GROUP
GREEN

'Harusame' is best known for its fall color, when the red color is dusted with yellowish brown markings of the *sunago fu* (sand-dusted) type of variegation. The newly emerging leaves are red, changing to yellow-green from the veins and becoming light green for the summer. This cultivar is an example of the type of plant worth waiting for to see its fall display. Occasionally, 'Harusame' has the amusing quirk of throwing out a white variegation in the leaf during the early growing season. It is so infrequent that it could not be called a characteristic. In some years there have been only two leaves on the whole tree so variegated.

The small to medium-sized leaves are lanceolate ovate on coarsely toothed leaf stalks. The leaf stalks are almost as long as the leaves. This plant makes an upright,

'Harusame'.
Photo by Peter Gregory

bushy, small tree up to 3 m (10 ft.) in height and spread, and that after a considerable age. The name, which means "spring rain," is sometimes misspelled 'Harusume' or 'Marusame'. It was first mentioned in the *Sekihin Binran* in 1882.

'Hazeroino'

OTHER GROUP
VARIEGATED

The stalkless leaf shape of this cultivar is almost identical to that of 'Hagoromo'. The primary difference is in the variegation. The leaf is green, occasionally white-flecked with cream-colored irregular spots. The variegation is not strong nor does it appear on all the leaves. In the spring the variegation is pinky brown tinged, and in the fall the foliage turns red. If the plant is too vigorous-growing or too highly fertilized, the variegations are masked for a growth period or two. Every effort should be made to keep the plant in good vigor but not overstimulated.

'Hazeroino' is not as strong growing as the nonvariegated forms 'Hagoromo' and 'Koshimino'. It eventually reaches a height of 3 m (10 ft.) or so. 'Hazeroino' was selected and named in 1930. The name has been misspelled as 'Hageriono'. 'Ama-no-hagoromo' is a synonym.

'Heartbeat'

DISSECTUM GROUP
RED

'Heartbeat' is a very attractive Australian laceleaf with bright red spring growth, gradually changing to bronze-red with red margins in the summer, then turning a glowing crimson in the fall. The seven-lobed medium-sized leaves are divided right to the leaf base, where the lobe is no wider than the width of the midvein. Each lobe is itself cut into feathery sublobes with narrow, sharply pointed teeth. The lobes have the additional attraction of being held

apart like the spokes of a wheel. The plant forms a low-spreading mushroom-shaped mound and would fill a niche in almost any garden.

'Helena'

PALMATUM GROUP
GREEN

This small shrubby tree is notable for its eye-catching bright fall colors of yellow to-red. The young leaves emerge a bronzed coppery pink and orange in the spring, changing to light green with bronzed margins and tips, gradually turning a darker green for the summer. Fall color is yellow then orange to bright red. The young shoots are pink-orange. The small leaves have five to

'Hazeroino'.
Photo by J. D. Vertrees

'Heartbeat'.
Photo by Peter Gregory

'Helena'.
  Photo by Peter Gregory

'Herbstfeuer'.
  Photo by Cor van Gelderen

ful bark and shoots with a red-gray pattern. The young leaves emerge a deep purple-red with deeply divided lobes, gradually changing to a nondescript bronze-purple for the summer and becoming a brilliant orange-red to scarlet in the fall. The large five-lobed leaves are divided deeply almost to the leaf base. Each broad lobe is ovate with a pointed tip. The margins have numerous, fine-pointed double teeth. The stout, dark red leaf stalks are quite short. The plant forms an upright bushy tree, reaching about 6 m (20 ft.) in height and spread at maturity.

'Herbstfeuer'
PALMATUM GROUP
GREEN

This rather special cultivar is possibly a cross between *Acer palmatum* and *A. circinatum*. It was a chance seedling, spotted among his maple collection and named by German nurseryman Andreas Bartel. The Dutch Firma C. Esveld, Boskoop, propagated it in the mid-1980s before the original plant died.

'Herbstfeuer' has medium to large, seven- to nine-lobed, almost circular leaves. The lobes are divided about halfway to the leaf base and are broadly ovate with pointed tips. The stout, short red leaf stalks have swollen bases. The leaves are dark green during the summer, becoming green with bronze and purple tones in late summer. The tree comes into its own in the fall with its outstanding orange and red colors. It is very vigorous, densely branched, upright but wide spreading, reaching up to 6 m (20 ft.) tall and almost as wide. The name means "autumn fire."

seven lobes and are deeply divided. Each lobe is narrowly long-ovate with tail-like tips and clearly toothed margins. 'Helena' forms a compact upright tree to 3 m (10 ft.) in height. It was selected and named by Dick van der Maat, Netherlands.

'Heptalobum Rubrum'
AMOENUM GROUP
RED

This old Dutch cultivar comes into its own with its sensational fall color and beauti-

'Hessei'
MATSUMURAE GROUP
RED

The large leaves are deeply divided almost to the leaf base into usually seven long,

'Hessei'.
Photo by Peter Gregory

'Hikasa yama',
tricolored leaf.
Photo by J. D. Vertrees

'Hikasa yama',
spring buds.
Photo by J. D. Vertrees

narrow lobes with toothed margins. The lobes are held closely together, thus making the leaf appear longer than wide. The leaves droop slightly and give the plant a ribbonlike effect. Leaf color from spring to early summer is a rich purple-red. Later, in the heat of summer, it changes to greenish bronze. Fall color is a quite brilliant crimson. Although the plant is not tall, it tends to spread, growing to about 5 m (16 ft.) in height and 4 m (13 ft.) in spread.

'Hessei' is a hardy cultivar with sturdy twigs and branches. It is not easy to propagate because it heals slowly after grafting. Other names it has been known under—all illegitimate—are 'Atropurpureum Laciniatum', 'Elegans Atropurpureum', 'Elegans Purpureum', 'Heptalobum Elegans', and 'Laciniatum Purpureum'.

'Hikasa yama'

PALMATUM GROUP
VARIEGATED

As the buds open and leaves unfurl, 'Hikasa yama' can be sensational, with a kaleidoscope of reds, pinks, yellows, and cream.

It is one of the variegated forms that has unusually shaped leaves, as its name, which means "umbrella mountain," indicates.

This cultivar has been found in maple lists from Japan since the early 1880s. Many different names were applied as it worked its way around the world, probably because of the variation in foliage traits at different times of the year. One widely used name in the United States is 'Roseomarginatum'. This confusion is unfortunate because the name has also been used for 'Kagiri nishiki', a cultivar both outstanding and beautiful in its own right. Other names, such as 'Cristatum Variegatum', have been applied to depict certain traits. I saw large specimen trees of 'Hikasa yama' in the Netherlands and England. These mature (several decades old) plants strengthened my opinion on the veracity of this nomenclature.

Leaf color is so changeable it is difficult to describe. In early spring, the buds unfold with pale cream, tightly curled leaflets, and with the elongated bud sheath a brilliant crimson, giving the effect of two-toned popcorn. The combination of colors equals the flowering effect of some shrubs and remains until the unique leaves unfold. The light green veins are bordered in dark green, especially the broad band along each midrib. The borders of each of the seven lobes are cream-colored, and the striping continues down toward the leaf base. This color is quite pale early in the season and changes to a light creamy green as the season advances. For the first month or so the leaves also have strong pink tones on the margins, overlying the cream color and lightly bordering the edges of the lobes (*shin fukurin fu* type variegation). This undoubtedly gives rise to the confusing misnomer of 'Roseomarginatum'. The pink color fades and disappears as the season progresses. In the fall, the cream-colored portions take on an orange to dark yellow, and occasionally red, tone.

The small to medium leaves are moderately to deeply divided into seven lobes. Slender and elongate, each lobe tapers to a sharp point and has strongly toothed margins. Usually the leaves are crinkly and curl downward, making the overall appearance unique. The twigs are closely spaced, and the nodes are close together, so that when the plant is suppressed in a pot, it becomes dense and lends itself to shaping. It is popular for bonsai and in California is sold for that purpose under the name "Shinn's #2."

The tree, which can be quite vigorous, and have a narrow, upright habit, reaches 8 m (26 ft.) in height. It is a hardy plant which lends itself well to landscape use. The unique growth habit and foliage make it most attractive. Light shining through the variegated leaves gives a very unusual and pleasing effect. This cultivar is more widely known as 'Higasa yama' and has been misspelled 'Hisaga yama'.

'Hinata yama'

AMOENUM GROUP
RED

Grown since 1923, 'Hinata yama' is reportedly a seedling selection of 'Musashino' (syn. 'Nomura'), one of the oldest known cultivars. The leaf lobes are longer and more slender than those of its parent. The spring color is a deep purple-red with a silvery hue, which becomes less intense as the season progresses. By late summer it is greenish bronze-purple, turning bright red in the autumn. The medium-sized leaves are five-lobed. The lobes radiate outward and are widely open. Each lobe is long, ovate-elliptical, and the margins are finely toothed. The leaf stalks are short. The branches are green and slender, and the growth habit rather erect.

This cultivar is not widely grown, probably because it has no outstandingly dif-

'Hinata yama'.
Photo by Peter Gregory

ferent features from many other red cultivars. This cultivar has also been known as
'Hiūga yama', a name that has been misspelled 'Higūga yama' and 'Hyuga yama'.

'Hiryū'
PALMATUM GROUP
VARIEGATED

This unusual Japanese variegate is characterized by the irregularly shaped leaves
that are distorted by the varying amount
and distribution of the gray-green variegated patterns. Each medium-sized leaf
is deeply divided almost to the base into
mainly five narrow, irregular, almost straplike lobes and has crumpled erratically
notched margins. The leaf base is angled so
that all lobes point forward. Occasionally,
scattered among these leaves is a larger leaf
with some or all lobes longer and broader
and with finer-toothed margins, indicating
some amoenum parentage. The light green
spring leaves become midgreen for the
summer, with light green and gray-green
variegation, often as a thin band round the
margin. Fall color is orange to red. This
distinctive cultivar forms an upright, vase-
shaped tree up to 4 m (13 ft.) in height.

'Hōgyoku'
AMOENUM GROUP
GREEN

This cultivar was selected for its rich, deep
orange fall color. At Maplewood the stock
plant usually turned a bright pumpkin
orange. The spring and summer color is a
deep, rich, green. The medium-sized leaves
have seven lobes which radiate out and
are divided up to halfway to the leaf base.
The lobes are ovate-triangular with very
finely toothed margins. The leaf stalks are
shorter than the leaves. This sturdy, hardy
tree has thick and sometimes stubby new
growth. It reaches 6 m (20 ft.) high with
age and responds well to pruning and
shaping. Although not widely distributed,

it is a very worthwhile plant as, for most of
the year, it is an attractive, rich green, followed by the unique orange fall color. The
name, which means "a jewel," has been
misspelled 'Hōgyuko'. The cultivar has also
been known under the name 'Yog saku'.

'Hondoshi'
AMOENUM GROUP
GREEN

Introduced into Europe from the Milim
Botanic Garden, Korea, 'Hondoshi' has
very large five-lobed leaves that are moderately deeply divided. The ovate lobes are

'Hiryū'.
Photo by Peter Gregory

'Hōgyoku'.
Photo by Peter Gregory

'Hondoshi'.
Photo by Peter Gregory

'Hoshi kuzu'.
Photo by Cor van Gelderen

according to the degree of variegation. The leaves generally lie in a flat plane, although the lobe tips tend to curve downward. The lobes are mostly long and slender, slightly broader in the middle and gradually tapering to a fine point. The margins are faintly toothed.

The general foliage color is a pleasant light green. Each leaf has variegated breaks of varying size and shape. Some leaves are totally colored with the pale cream-green variegation, while others may only have a portion of one lobe colored on the edge. The markings vary between these two extremes. The cream-green variegation is quite subtle, not garish, and may even have a faint tinge of pink on the borders in early spring.

This neat-growing, upright, nonspreading shrub usually has short terminal shoots. It blends well with many types of companions and makes a good patio plant. The cultivar was spotted at Maplewood Nursery as a chance seedling from 'Kamagata' and named in 1987. The name means "star-studded sky."

'Hupp's Dwarf'
DWARF GROUP
GREEN

This choice green dwarf was a chance seedling first noticed by Barbara Hupp, Oregon, in a seedling bed before its was moved to Maplewood Nursery in 1976. It seems similar in growth type to some of the other compact dwarfs, such as 'Kotohime', 'Mikawa yatsubusa', and 'Tsukomo', but appears more compact in habit than these cultivars and more vigorous than 'Tsukomo'. It is distinct enough to warrant its place in the range of dwarf cultivars.

The foliage is a deep, rich green which holds well into the season. The small leaf has five long, slender lobes separated almost entirely to the leaf base. The lobes have sharp, slender points, and the mar-

broadest in the middle and have short tail-like tips and finely, evenly toothed margins. The spring leaves are a light green with pinkish bronzing, becoming mid to dark green for the summer, before turning golden yellow in the fall. The short leaf stalks are pink-red and the young shoots are bluish green. This cultivar forms a vigorous, spreading tree estimated to reach up to 10 m (33 ft.) in height.

'Hoshi kuzu'
DWARF GROUP
VARIEGATED

This dwarf shrub has small, unusual leaves that are star-shaped and predominantly five-lobed, with each lobe varying in shape gins are strongly toothed. The very stubby shoots branch out and form a dense, compact, upright tree. The original seedling at Maplewood measured 45 cm (1.5 ft.) tall and 35 cm (14 in.) wide after 10 years. The very few young plants grafted onto strong rootstocks show no greater growth rate. The very brittle twigs and the minimal annual growth make this cultivar difficult to propagate. It is ideal for bonsai.

'Ibo nishiki'

PALMATUM GROUP
GREEN

This tall-growing plant is one of the rough-bark cultivars. *Ibo*, one of the Japanese words for "warty," indicates the interesting character of the bark. The wartiness is shaped like an oblong lens and is slow to develop, appearing on third-year (or older) wood. It is very slow to join up, remaining separated for a few years, finally joining into larger, roughened areas. Although 'Ibo nishiki' is not as showy as some of the other cultivars with rough bark, the intermediate bark color is a good green.

The small to medium palmatum-type leaves are fairly deeply divided into five to seven long-ovate lobes. The margins are heavily toothed. Spring color is a light yellow-green with bronze-tinged margins, becoming a fresh green in summer. Fall colors range from yellow-orange to deep crimson. This fairly strong grower has the typical upright palmatum habit. The warty bark makes an interesting point for the collector of unusual forms. The name has been misspelled 'Ebo nishiki' and 'Iibo nishiki'.

'Ichigyō ji'

AMOENUM GROUP
GREEN

This plant is almost identical to 'Ō sakazuki' except for the fall color, which is an intense, brilliant yellow or orange-yellow, while 'Ō sakazuki' is crimson. It is reported that

'Hupp's Dwarf".
Photo by Cor van Gelderen

'Ibo nishiki'.
Photo by Peter Gregory

'Ichigyō ji'.
Photo by J. D. Vertrees

they may have been sister seedlings when selected in the 1880s. 'Ichigyō ji' stands out from all other maples for its brilliance. Because of its large leaves, the colors are flamboyant. During the summer the leaves are a pleasant green. The seven lobes are broadly ovate, shaping to a sharply pointed tip, and with the edges slightly toothed. The lobes are joined about halfway to the base. The leaf stalks are about the length of the leaves.

The upright, broad tree becomes round headed and can attain a height of about 7 m (23 ft.), although it is not usually seen this tall. With pruning, the tree shapes well and there need be no fear of keeping it within bounds in smaller plantings. Japanese writ-

ers wisely suggest planting 'Ichigyō ji' and 'Ō sakazuki' near each other on a rise or hillside, or near a pond, to allow the full glory of the fall brilliance to be appreciated. The name 'Ichigyō ji' has been misspelled 'Ichijoji' and 'Ighigyoji'. The cultivar is named after the Ichigyō ji temple.

'Iijima sunago'

MATSUMURAE GROUP
VARIEGATED

The colors of this dark-leaved variegate make it an unusual addition to the garden landscape. The large leaves have seven broadly ovate, deeply divided lobes with pointed tips and with finely toothed edges. The leaf stalks are shorter than the leaves.

The spring foliage is a rich red, slightly on the orange side, and lasts into early summer. At this time, the feature for which this cultivar is named develops. The leaves become a rich purplish brown— a rather unique color—with tiny and irregular green spots, sometimes rather obscure, but resembling sprinkled sand. It is for this type of variegation, known as *sunago fu* (sand-dusted), that the cultivar has been named. These colors intensify in late summer and fall. The midrib of each lobe remains a distinctly contrasting yellow-green, while the leaves turn to yellows, oranges and reds in the fall.

This strong-growing tree remains upright but does not reach great heights. It probably matures at up to 8 m (26 ft.) in height and forms a round-headed tree. The branches are sturdy and not willowy. 'Iijima sunago' was recorded in the *Sekihin Binran* in 1882.

'Inaba shidare'

DISSECTUM GROUP
RED

This outstanding cultivar differs from other dissectums in its deeper color. The seven-lobed leaves are very large with the

'Iijima sunago'.
Photo by J. D. Vertrees

'Inaba shidare'.
Photo by J. D. Vertrees

basal lobes pointing backward. Each lobe ends in a fine tip. The lobes measure less than 1 mm at the tip, broadening to 3 cm in the middle, and tapering to 1 mm at the leaf base where all the lobes join. The lobes are dissected toward each midrib, but the many separations are not as fine as in the more common dissectums. Thus, each lobe appears to be sturdier, and the leaves appear to have more substance than those of most other dissectums. The bright red leaf stalks are very short.

The leaves become deep purple-red as they develop in the spring and retain that color all season. They do not bronze out in late season, as do other reds. In the fall they turn from purple-red to a brilliant crimson. 'Inaba shidare' is the red counterpart of 'Palmatifidum'. For a dissectum, 'Inaba shidare' is a rather upright-growing form. Although it does cascade, it tends to be a little more erect in appearance. It is vigorous and sturdy. Although not widely found in cultivation, it should become a popular garden landscape item. It has been listed in Japan since 1882. Received the RHS Award of Garden Merit.

This cultivar presents an interesting example of Japanese nomenclature. The Japanese observed that in the rain this plant looks a little like *ine* ("a rice plant"), an old form of which turned crimson in the fall. Thus, *inaba* is "leaf like a rice plant." 'Red Select' and 'Select Red' are reported to be the same as 'Inaba shidare', but there is some doubt about this. The name, which means "a cascading, ricelike leaf," has been misspelled 'Anaba shidare' and 'Inabe shidare'. Another name by which this cultivar has been known is 'Holland Select'.

'Inazuma'

MATSUMURAE GROUP
RED

The large leaves are of a rich, deep, purple-red in the spring and early summer. As they mature they turn a dark purple tinged green. The veins are green when the leaves carry the purple colors. Bright red-crimson tones appear in the fall. This is one of the outstanding cultivars for fall color. The seven lobes are long, ovate-lanceolate, separated widely, and divided almost entirely to the leaf base. The edges are strongly toothed. The short leaf stalks are reddish.

This hardy cultivar is vigorous without being leggy. The result is a tall, rounded shrub or tree, up to 10 m (33 ft.) in height and 6 m (20 ft.) in spread. The foliage is somewhat pendulous, but not with the cascading habit of the dissectums. This cultivar has been known under the names 'Dissectum Inazuma' and 'Pendulum Inazuma'. 'Inazuma' has been recorded in Japan since 1882. The name means "the thunderer."

'Iso chidori'

DWARF GROUP
GREEN

The small leaves have five to seven lobes. On many leaves, the two very small basal lobes clasp the top of the leaf stalk. Usually these are very small or absent. The middle three lobes are quite large for the leaf, and the two basal lobes (when five-lobed) are small, giving the leaf almost a three-lobed appearance. The margins are strongly toothed. The

'Inazuma'.
Photo by Peter Gregory

lobes are oblong and fairly deeply divided. They gradually taper to a sharp, pointed tip. As the leaves mature, the margins often become wavy and the points of the lobes curl downward slightly. Some leaves are quite convoluted. The leaf stalks are slender but stiff, and are often almost as long as the leaf. The leaf color is a light to medium green, sometimes a yellowish green. Fall colors are yellows and golds.

This stubby-growing plant matures into a shrubby cultivar up to 2 m (6 ft.) in height. It has long been in cultivation but is not widely known. There are references to it in K. Uehara's book (1961), and in the 1882 maple list of Oka et al. The name means "a beach plover with a zigzag walk."

This page:
'Iso chidori'.
Photo by J. D. Vertrees

'Issai nishiki momiji'.
Photo by Peter Gregory

Page 155:
'Japanese Princess'.
Photo by Talon Buchholz

'Japanese Sunrise'.
Photo by Harold Greer

'Jerre Schwartz'.
Photo by Peter Gregory

'Issai nishiki momiji'
DWARF GROUP
GREEN

This dwarf form of 'Nishiki gawa' has extremely rough bark. Unlike 'Nishiki gawa', it develops the bark characteristics within a year or so of propagation, becoming rougher with each season. The bark and leaf characteristics are described under 'Nishiki gawa'. Contrary to previous assumptions, this maple is a cultivar, and it can be found listed in Japan, together with its Japanese characters. The name means "early developing rough bark maple" and refers to the short period of time required for the rough bark to develop. This cultivar is also known under the names 'Issai nishiki' and 'Amime nishiki'.

'Italy Red'
AMOENUM GROUP
RED

This plant is very similar to 'Bloodgood' in leaf and habit. It differs in being slower growing and reaches only half the size of that popular palmatum. 'Italy Red' is very sturdy, tolerates wind and sun, and eventually forms a small, upright tree up to 3 m (10 ft.) in height. It is worth considering for gardens in which 'Bloodgood' would be too large. The original is growing at Mountain Maples Nursery, California, which obtained it from Maplewood Nursery. It is thought to have been received from an Italian source, hence its name. The name has been misspelled 'Haly Red'.

'Japanese Princess'
DWARF GROUP
GREEN

This neat little dwarf was discovered and named by Talon Buchholz of Oregon and is like a smaller version of the well-known 'Mikawa yatsubusa', with similar dense habit but even more compact, and with similarly shaped but smaller leaves. The new young leaves emerge an eye-catching bright shiny orange-pink with yellow-green midribs and slightly rolled-down margins. They become light green for the summer before turning bright orange in the fall. 'Japanese Princess' grows to about 60 cm (2 ft.) tall and wide in 10 years. It is ideal for the rock garden and container culture.

'Japanese Sunrise'

PALMATUM GROUP
GREEN

This cultivar, selected and named by Bill Schwartz, Pennsylvania, is very similar to 'Sango kaku' and is possibly a seedling from it. Its characteristic is the colorful winter shoots, which are a lighter red than 'Sango kaku' on the upper, exposed side, and yellow-orange on the lower, sheltered side. Its leaves are typical of the Palmatum Group and, like those of the probable parent, emerge yellow-green, becoming a light, fresh green for the summer. The fall colors are said to be even better than those of 'Sango kaku', with yellow, gold, and crimson tones. 'Japanese Sunrise' is very tolerant of full sun and grows into a narrow, upright, vase-shaped, flat-topped tree, up to 7 m (23 ft.) tall at maturity.

'Jerre Schwartz'

DWARF GROUP
RED

Bill Schwartz of Green Mansions Nursery, Pennsylvania, named this robust and reliable dwarf after his mother. It originated from a witches'-broom. The small, five to seven narrowly lobed leaves are divided almost to the base, each lobe with a sharply pointed tip and conspicuously toothed margins. The center lobe sometimes differs in having a shortened, rounded tip, characteristic of most witches'-brooms. The new young leaves are bright pinky red, becoming darker, purplish red in the summer, and often bronzed green later. Fall color is

bright scarlet. The short, slender leaf stalks are bright red. This cultivar forms a dense, upright shrub up to about 1.3 m (4.5 ft.) in height.

'Jirō shidare'
PALMATUM GROUP
GREEN

Unlike most cascading cultivars, this one does not belong to the Dissectum Group. The small, bright green leaves are deeply divided into seven to nine ovate-elliptic leaves. The margins are clearly toothed. The leaf stalks are very short. The emerging leaves are yellow-green with bronzed tips, becoming green for the summer, and brilliant orange to crimson in the fall.

As the young plant develops, the shoots are somewhat erect. Then, as the plant ages, the long, slender branches tend to droop, weeping back to the ground in some cases. This characteristic results in a round-headed bush up to 3 m (10 ft.) tall and at least as wide. The leaf nodes, which are spread far apart on the slender, pendulous shoots, form the cascading growth and give a very lacy appearance. This maple is suitable for the small garden and the larger rock garden. It was imported from Japan.

'Johnnie's Pink'
PALMATUM GROUP
RED

The unusual but attractive semiglossy, hawthornlike leaves make this cultivar highly desirable. It was selected and named by H. Johnston, Alabama. The spring leaves are bright pink, hence the name, becoming bronzed red for the summer and fading to bronzed green late in the season. The small leaves have five broad lobes divided about halfway to the leaf base. The central lobe is dominant. The margins have relatively large double teeth, like hawthorn leaves. 'Johnnie's Pink' forms a small round shrub and is ideal for small gardens and for patio and container culture.

'Kaba'
DWARF GROUP
GREEN

This strange-leaved, small, compact, erect, green dwarf shrub was named by Firma C. Esveld, Netherlands, after its discoverer, John Gibbon's Hippopoterring Nursery in northeast England. The word *kaba*, meaning "hippopotamus," is a play on the nursery's name. The tiny leaves are deeply divided almost to the leaf base into five very narrow, almost straplike lobes. The margins, which are sometimes red-tinged, are unevenly toothed and crinkled. 'Kaba' resembles a miniature 'Wabi bito', with

'Jirō shidare'.
Photo by Peter Gregory

'Johnnie's Pink'.
Photo by Harry Olsen

similar distorted, dark green leaves, but only growing to about 60 cm (2 ft.) tall in five years.

'Kagerō'

AMOENUM GROUP
VARIEGATED

This outstanding form is distinguished by having predominantly yellow variegations instead of the usual white. The small to medium leaves have five to seven lobes and are deeply divided. The lobes radiate openly. Each lobe is elongate-ovate with a long, tapering tip. The margins are finely and regularly toothed. The two small basal lobes point backward toward the short, stiff leaf stalk.

The variegation blends in various patterns with the rich green basic color. The light markings may be only a few irregular specks on a leaf, or concentrations of small, light blotches, or a coalescing of larger markings into solid areas. Sometimes the colors occupy only half the lobe, separated sharply from the solid green by the midrib. Entirely green leaves occur and occasionally solid yellow leaves. The variegations are quite variable and irregular from leaf to leaf. Fall color is red to orange.

This fairly strong, but slow-growing upright cultivar forms a short tree of up to 4 m (13 ft.) in height. It is hardy and not too difficult to propagate. The name means "gossamer." This cultivar has been known under the name 'Yoen'.

'Kagiri nishiki'

PALMATUM GROUP
VARIEGATED

The smallish leaves have five to seven lobes, each lobe a different shape, and each leaf a different shape. The typical lobe is elongate-ovate, tapering to a sharp point. Edges are slightly and inconsistently toothed, while some are lightly notched. The lobes are sickle-shaped to varying degrees, depend-

ing upon the amount of variegation in that segment. On some leaves the lobes are minute, while on other leaves they are completely absent. There is no uniformity in leaf shape. The short leaf stalks are slender and pinkish in color.

Basic leaf color is deep green with a bluish cast, never bright green. White margins on all the lobes are present in varying widths, up to and including one-half the width of the lobe. Blended with, or suf-

'Kaba'.
Photo by Peter Gregory

'Kagerō'.
Photo by J. D. Vertrees

fused over all this, are markings of pink or rose colors. In the spring the rose markings are quite distinct, as the summer advances, the rose becomes indistinct and the markings remain cream. The rose and cream areas change into a vivid rose-crimson in the fall.

The plant is somewhat open growing, but upright, and can reach 8 m (26 ft.) or more in height. It does not grow as twiggy as 'Butterfly'. 'Kagiri nishiki' has a more upright growth habit, more rose in the leaf markings, and less deeply toothed leaf margins.

Other names that have been used for this cultivar are 'Pinkedge', 'Rosamarginalis', 'Rosavariegata, 'Roseopictum', 'Roseotricolor', and 'Roseovariegatum'. The name has also been misspelled 'Kagari nishiki'. According to Yano (2003), 'Kagiri nishiki' was originally named just 'Kagiri' in 1688 and 'Shōjō' in 1695. 'Roseomarginatum' is a synonym of 'Kagiri nishiki'. Unfortunately, confusion exists because the name 'Roseomarginatum' has been applied to other quite different cultivars, especially 'Hikasa yama'.

'Kamagata'
DWARF GROUP
GREEN

This very delicate appearing dwarf has been very durable and hardy, tolerating winters of 0°F (−18°C). Even in exposed positions with full sun and on very dry sites, it has performed excellently.

The small leaves are mainly five-lobed. Often some leaves have only three lobes, widely separated, with side lobes almost at right angles. The lobes are hooked or downward-curved at the tip, and the margins turned slightly upward to form a trough shape, and tend to twist slightly, giving the entire plant a lacy, delicate look. Each lobe is long and narrow, tapering gradu-

ally to a sharply pointed tip. The margins are toothed. The lobes separate outward like extended fingers and join only about 1 cm from the base of the leaf. The short leaf stalks are very thin but stiff, and are green with the exposed side red.

As the leaves unfold in the spring, the edges are strongly tinted with red to rusty red. The early summer foliage becomes a bright, light green. The fall colors are brilliant in shades of yellow, orange, and scarlet. The leaves remain on the plant well into late fall and thus extend the color period. The bright green shoots are thin and delicate looking but quite durable. The second period of growth forms much side branching, which is quite lacy and makes the plant denser. 'Kamagata' forms a small, round bush. After eight years, a plant at Maplewood was a little over 1 m (3 ft.) in height.

'Kamagata' is one of two cultivars I have chosen to name. Out of many thousands of seedlings grown at Maplewood Nursery, quite a few were selected to grow on and observe. Many of these are rather choice plants but resemble other valid cultivars much too closely to name. This dwarf type 'Kamagata', performs and appears quite differently from any other cultivar with which I am familiar, or can find in the literature.

'Kandy Kitchen'

DWARF GROUP
RED

Arising from a witches'-broom of *Acer palmatum* f. *atropurpureum*, 'Kandy Kitchen' was discovered and named by Joseph Stupka, Pennsylvania. It forms a compact, rounded shrub reaching up to 2 m (6 ft.) in height and spread. This cultivar is ideal for containers. It is similar in growth habit and in leaf shape, color, and size to 'Elizabeth', another witches'-broom. The lobes appear to be slightly narrower with longer, tail-like tips. The new leaves form a bright

Page 158:
'Kagiri nishiki'.
Photo by J. D. Vertrees

'Kamagata', spring color.
Photo by J. D. Vertrees

This page:
'Kamagata', fall color.
Photo by J. D. Vertrees

'Kandy Kitchen'.
Photo by Harry Olsen

pink bunch at the end of the shoots, contrasting with the purple-red of the mature leaves throughout the summer. When shaded, the leaves become a bronze-green. The fall color is a very bright scarlet-red.

'Kara ori nishiki'.
Photo by Peter Gregory

'Kara ori nishiki'

PALMATUM GROUP
VARIEGATED

The medium-sized, variegated leaves have five to seven lobes. Each lobe is oblong-ovate and fairly deeply divided. The margins of the lobes are finely toothed and sometimes irregularly but slightly curled. The short leaf stalks are dark in color. Spring foliage is reddish, changing to a greenish red in midsummer. The whitish variegations range from indistinct to very bold and sometimes have a pink overtone. When distinct, the light markings will cut in and occupy a large section of the lobe. These variegations are yellowish in midseason. Fall color changes to yellow and then predominantly crimson in tone.

'Kara ori nishiki' is neither a large-growing plant nor a fast-grower; rather it slowly matures as a tall bush up to 4 m (13 ft.) in height. The cultivar name refers to a type of brocade used for dancers' garments. The plant grown in the West under this name appears to differ from that grown in Japan which has longer, more amoenum-type leaves, and very little variegation. This very old cultivar (1745) is also known under the name 'Kara ori'.

'Karasu gawa'

PALMATUM GROUP
VARIEGATED

The most outstanding feature is the bright pink new growth. Most of the new foliage is a bright, light pink. Some leaves are entirely white with pink shading. Others are almost completely pink, but with tiny flecks of bright green or white, or both. The leaf stalks and shoots are also pink. While 'Karasu gawa' compares to 'Oridono nishiki' and 'Asahi zuru', the new growth is more spectacular. Older foliage also has streaks or flecks of pink in the white areas. Sometimes the mottling consists only of pale green areas on the base of darker green. Other leaves have rather large, bold inserts of light colors. In the fall, the white and light green areas become bright rose, in contrast with the base color of dark red.

The small to medium-sized leaves are basically five-lobed. The lobes are elongate-ovate, terminating in a slender, tapered tip. When a deep variegation occurs, that portion is sickle-shaped, while the rest of the lobe is normal. The margins are clearly toothed. 'Karasu gawa' has a narrow and upright growth habit that broadens with age. Older plants rarely exceed 4 m (13 ft.) in height. This maple is not a vigorous grower and is somewhat tender. It should have a protected spot in the garden and also have protection from strong sun. Although the pale sections of the foliage sunburn in the hottest weather, this tree is well worth the extra care. 'Kagon nishiki' appears to be a synonym of this cultivar.

'Kasagi yama'

MATSUMURAE GROUP
VARIEGATED

The foliage of this reticulated cultivar has one of the most unusual color combinations found in the group. The principal color is brick red, but it varies some-

what, whether in full sun or shade, and depending on the age of the leaf. The tone is very distinctive from other red-leaved cultivars. This unique red is shaded into an undertone of green on the sides of the lobes, blending the two colors. In addition, the main veins are dark red, almost black, while the side veins are distinct but lighter in tone. This contrast diminishes during the course of the season. Fall color is bright to deep red.

The medium-sized leaves have seven lobes which radiate outward, with the two basal lobes almost closing over the leaf stalks. The middle three lobes are larger than the other four. Each lobe is openly separated almost to the leaf base, and is elongate-ovate with a long, tapering, sharp tip. The margins are wavy and very finely but sharply toothed. The leaf stalks are red, stiff, and very short. The bright red fruits

complement the foliage. The plant grows into an open shrub or small tree, up to 7 m (23 ft.) or so tall. It is a rare, very unusual cultivar, and quite exciting to watch as the new foliage develops in the spring.

'Karasu gawa'.
Photo by J. D. Vertrees

'Kasagi yama'.
Photo by Peter Gregory

'Kasen nishiki'

PALMATUM GROUP
VARIEGATED

New foliage in the spring is often a surprising pink-red or light orange-red which soon matures into variegated greens. The variegation is quite subtle, not bright or conspicuous as in 'Oridono nishiki'. There are irregular and indiscriminate sections of white or cream on many leaves, and these portions are usually sickle-shaped. Most leaves have a very light or pastel shading. Speckling and dotting of white, cream, or occasionally whitish green make up the variegation. The color is a very soft tone, shading throughout the foliage. It differs considerably from most variegated cultivars. Fall colors are yellow to red.

The medium-sized leaves have mainly seven lobes, which are fairly deeply divided. Each lobe is ovate-acuminate, with clearly toothed edges. The lobes are often quite irregular in shape, especially where the variegation is present in strength. This small, bushy tree may eventually reach about 6 m (20 ft.) in height. It is hardy and well worth its place in the garden landscape. 'Kasen nishiki' has been known since 1882. It has also been known under the name 'Hana izumi nishiki'.

'Kashima'

DWARF GROUP
GREEN

Widely used for bonsai, this very different dwarf has tiny rich green five-lobed leaves. The center lobe is the longest. Each lobe is elongate-ovate, terminating in a sharp, pointed tip. The margins are coarsely toothed. The lobes are moderately deeply divided. The leaf stalks are short and slender. The basal lobes are spread at roughly right angles to the leaf base. As they open, the new leaves are a very light yellow-green, which margins a brick or rust color, thus making the new growth very noticeable. Fall colors are mostly in the yellow tones.

This plant is a very shrubby grower and can reach up to 2 m (6 ft.) in height and spread. It can be forced in the landscape or retarded in container culture or bonsai. 'Kashima' lends itself very well to rock garden culture. It takes well to shaping and pruning, as do other dwarf forms. It is hardy and sturdy, and tolerates some drought when reduced growth is desired. 'Chiba' is a synonym of 'Kashima'. 'Chiba yatsubusa' and 'Kashima yatsubusa' are very similar plants.

'Kasen nishiki'.
Photo by Peter Gregory

'Kashima'.
Photo by Peter Gregory

'Katja'

PALMATUM GROUP
GREEN

The new foliage is pinkish to coppery bronze as the buds open in the spring, becoming light yellow with pink margins and tips, before changing to midgreen with slight bronze-red tips for the summer, then turning reddish orange in the fall. The small to medium leaves have seven lobes and are of the typical palmatum type. The moderately deeply divided lobes are broad ovate with tail-like tips and lightly toothed margins. The leaf stalks are bright red and up to as long as the leaves. 'Katja' is vigorous in the early years and forms an upright-spreading tree or bush, reaching up to about 4 m (13 ft.) in height. It was selected and named by Dick van der Maat, Netherlands.

'Katsura'

PALMATUM GROUP
GREEN

This delightful form is quite striking in its spring growth. As the leaves develop, they are a pale yellow-orange. The margins shade into a brighter orange. As the season progresses, the leaves turn into a light to yellowish green for the summer. Fall colors are bright yellow and orange. The small leaves are moderately deeply divided into five ovate-lanceolate lobes that taper to a long point. The sides of the lobes are shallowly toothed. The center lobe is always longer, and the leaves tend to turn downward, giving the plant a distinctive appearance. The leaf stalks are quite short.

'Katsura' seems to be a smaller-growing tree in North America, with the leaf nodes and twigs quite close together so that the foliage is dense. The upright growth quickly broadens with side branching. In Europe, this cultivar seems to grow taller, reaching more than 8 m (26 ft.) in height. It adapts well to bonsai culture. The name means "wig." The plant has also been known as 'Katsura yatsubusa'. Received the RHS Award of Garden Merit.

'Katja'.
Photo by Peter Gregory

'Katsura'.
Photo by Peter Gregory

'Keiser'
LINEARILOBUM GROUP
RED

This very vigorous cultivar resembles 'Atrolineare' in leaf color, size, and shape, and in growth habit. The five-lobed medium-sized straplike leaves are divided almost to the base. Possibly because of the plant's vigor, it is very unstable and tends to revert to palmatum-type leaves rather more easily than most other linearilobums. It was propagated and named by Art Wright, an Oregon nurseryman, who originally used the code name "Keiser-Wanabee," possibly indicating the original source in Wanabee, Washington State.

'Ki hachijō'
MATSUMURAE GROUP
GREEN

The sturdy, medium to large seven- to nine-lobed leaves are a bright, dark green. The lobes are long-ovate with short tail-like tips and with very conspicuous, deep, feathery teeth on the margins. The very narrow tip of each lobe gives a distinctive effect. The leaves lie flat and are attached with short leaf stalks. The unique fall color is a distinct yellow gold with rose, becoming blended with light oranges and reds.

This cultivar develops into a well-rounded,

'Ki hachijō'.
Photo by Peter Gregory

short tree or tall bush up to 6 m (20 ft.) in height. The bark is a strong green with an overtone of bluish gray. White streaking is prominent, especially as the bark ages. 'Ki hachijō' is a good, hardy, sturdy cultivar that adds a "different" appearance for landscaping. The name, which means "from Hachijō Island," has also been spelled 'Kihatsijo'.

'Killarney'
MATSUMURAE GROUP
GREEN

Unlike most cultivars of the Matsumurae Group, 'Killarney' is a vigorous-growing small to medium-sized tree with a flat top. Bill Schwartz of Pennsylvania has compared it to the flat-topped *Acacia* trees of the African desert. 'Killarney' has seven-lobed leaves which are very deeply divided. The lobes are long-ovate with tail-like tips and fairly evenly toothed margins. The slender leaf stalks are bright red. The spring leaves are a soft green, becoming mid green for summer. Then in the fall the foliage changes to a very attractive orangey pink-red before turning a fiery red. This upright tree is hardy and sun-tolerant, and makes an attractive contrast among other maples in the garden landscape.

'Kingsville Red'
PALMATUM GROUP
RED

This cultivar of *Acer palmatum* f. *atropurpureum* was selected by Henry Hohman of Kingsville, Maryland. It is vigorous, hardy, and upright, and grows to about 8 m (26 ft.). The bright red-purple tone holds well into late summer in the Pacific Northwest climate. It does not seem to sunburn, as do most other reds. The large leaves are seven-lobed and deeply divided. The lobes are oblong, tapering to a slender tip. The smaller basal lobes of the palmatum-type leaves tend to cup slightly upward. The margins are finely toothed, most prominently on the outer half of the lobe. The leaf stalks are short and stiff.

'Kingsville Variegated'

PALMATUM GROUP
VARIEGATED

'Kingsville Variegated' is another of Henry Hohman's selections that is worthy of a place in Japanese maple collections. It is assumed that this could be a seedling selection of 'Kagiri nishiki' or 'Butterfly', both of which Hohman had as stock plants. The character is somewhere between the two. The basic leaf color is a deep green or blue-green. Variations of color patterns are irregular, and the variegation is mostly white. There is a noticeable amount of pink, and occasionally on young leaves the pink markings are almost entire. Fall color changes the white portions to a brilliant rose.

The small leaves are five-lobed and irregular. Each lobe is long and narrow with very irregular, dentate margins. The leaf margins are quite different from those of either 'Butterfly' or 'Kagiri nishiki'. The growth rate is like 'Kagiri nishiki', but the variegation is pinker and white-dusted, whereas 'Kagiri nishiki' has more cream. 'Kingsville Variegated' is a delightful companion to some of the other variegated forms. It would seem possible that 'Hohman's Variegated' is the same cultivar.

'Kinky Krinkle'

PALMATUM GROUP
GREEN

A seedling selection from Talon Buchholz of Oregon, 'Kinky Krinkle' can be described as intermediate between the palmatum-type 'Tsuchigumo' and the matsumurae-type 'Shigure bato'. Like 'Tsuchigumo', it has very deeply divided spring leaves with coarsely toothed margins. The lobe tips display the same downward curl as 'Tsuchigumo', giving the leaf

'Killarney'.
Photo by Peter Gregory

'Kingsville Variegated'.
Photo by Cor van Gelderen

'Kinky Krinkle'.
Photo by Talon Buchholz

the same spidery stance. This cultivar is quite vigorous and can reach 4 m (13 ft.) tall and 1.5 m (5 ft.) wide in 15 years.

'Kinran'
MATSUMURAE GROUP
RED

The medium-sized leaves are divided very deeply, with the seven lobes separated almost to the flat leaf base. Each lobe is long-ovate, broadest in the middle, and narrowing to the lobe junctions. The tip comes to a long, narrow point. The leaves have an open, lacy appearance. The margins are deeply and clearly toothed. The spring and early summer coloration is a deep, rich bronze-red. The midvein in each lobe is a contrasting yellow-green and is very noticeable. In late summer, the color changes to a deep green shaded with dark red. In the fall it develops the beautiful gold color, with overtones of crimson, for which it is famous, hence the name, which means "woven with golden strings."

The plant is not large-growing, only reaching 3 m (10 ft.) in five years. It does broaden out and form more of a round-topped, large bush. It is sturdy and quite hardy, and responds very well to pruning and shaping. It is quite satisfactorily grown as a container plant. It can be slowed in its growth to a fine specimen or adapted to a larger, bonsai type."

'Kinran'.
Photo by Peter Gregory

'Kinshi'
LINEARILOBUM GROUP
GREEN

This semidwarf, strap-leaved cultivar comes from Japan. Its name, which means "with golden threads," aptly describes the wonderful orange-yellow color of the leaves in the fall. The medium-sized five- to seven-lobed, medium to dark green leaves have pointed tips and sparsely shallow-toothed margins when the leaves are fully developed. The leaves are divided right up to the leaf base. Vigorous, juvenile leaves are long-ovate, up to 1 cm wide, and more conspicuously toothed. The short, slender leaf stalks are green.

'Kinshi' forms a tidy, compact, upright, semidwarf tree, attaining a height of almost 2.5 m (8 ft.). It would be at home in most landscapes whatever their size and is perfectly suited for containers. The name has been misspelled 'Ginshi'.

'Kiri nishiki'
DISSECTUM GROUP
GREEN

Most dissectums appear delicate in foliage. 'Kiri nishiki' looks more substantial, yet not coarse. Each of the seven to nine lobes is more deeply cut into sublobes, and each sublobe is less delicately cut. The medium-sized leaves have short, slender, red leaf stalks. The basic leaf color is a bright, light green. This strong color stands full sun rather well. In the fall, the intense gold color is excellent and occasionally it is suffused with crimson and scarlet on the tips.

This full, cascading cultivar is fairly strong growing and hardy. Like many cascading dissectums, it should be planted on a bank or grafted high to realize the full

effect of the beautifully cascading display. It reaches 3 m (10 ft.) in height and spread. 'Kiri nishiki' is listed in Japanese maple reference books as far back as the early eighteenth century. The name means "misty silk."

'Kiyohime'

DWARF GROUP
GREEN

Although its leaves are quite small, they are slightly larger than some of the others in the Dwarf Group. Each leaf is five-lobed, with the center lobe noticeably longer. The deeply divided lobes are ovate-lanceolate, tapering back from the widest point toward the leaf base. The lobes have sharply pointed tips which tend to turn downward, making a slightly hooked form. The margins are toothed. The short leaf stalks are a rich green tinged pink. Early spring leaves are beautiful. The edges are tinged with an orange-red, which is lightly and delicately

'Kinshi', foliage.
Photo by Peter Gregory

'Kinshi', habit.
Photo by Peter Gregory

'Kiri nishiki'.
Photo by Peter Gregory

shaded into the center of the light green leaf. Rich green leaves dominate the summer season. Fall colors are yellow-orange.

'Kiyohime' is a sturdy, vigorous plant. Of the several dwarf types, it probably grows more vigorously than other forms. Yet in containers and bonsai culture, it dwarfs down as well as the others. For landscaping, it is valuable as a dwarf with a little more size and vigor than some others. It is possible to obtain a bush 2 m (6 ft.) high in about 10 years. The plant grows densely and forms a roundish bush. 'Kiyohime' is relatively easy to propagate from cuttings. It has also been known as 'Kiyohime yatsubusa'.

'Kiyohime'.
Photo by Peter Gregory

'Kogane nishiki'.
Photo by Harold Greer

'Koba shōjō'
MATSUMURAE GROUP
RED

This interesting cultivar was apparently imported into Japan without a name and has since been imported into Europe. The leaves are similar to but narrower and smaller than those of the well-known green-leaved 'Chitose yama', with five to seven very narrow, spreading lobes divided almost to the leaf base. The young leaves emerge a burgundy red, becoming purple-red with bright red midribs through the summer, and turning a vivid scarlet-red in the fall. The short, slender leaf stalks and stems are red.

'Kogane nishiki'
PALMATUM GROUP
GREEN

'Kogane nishiki' is a full-sized cultivar for background or overstory planting. The medium-sized five- to seven-lobed leaves are a deep, rich green. The fairly deeply divided lobes are long-ovate with short tail-like tips. The margins are very lightly toothed. The early spring foliage tends to have yellow tips as the leaves emerge and then changes to a strong green for the summer. Fall colors are a bright golden display, hence the name which means "golden brocade."

This strongly growing tree probably reaches about 10 m (33 ft.) tall. It makes a good base plant for landscapes, and the golden fall color can work well as a contrast to other plantings. Full sunlight is best. This cultivar has been known as 'Kogane sunago'.

'Kogane sakae'
AMOENUM GROUP
GREEN

'Kogane sakae' is an unusual tree, notable for its bark color. The young shoots and older branches are light green with definite areas of a yellowish tone. These are in striations and irregular streaks running lengthwise on the branches. It is quite different from other bark colors of *Acer palmatum* cultivars.

The medium-sized to large leaves are seven-lobed and divided halfway to the leaf base, with the ovate lobes widest at the mid point. Toothing is very fine and occurs on the outer third of the lobe margins. The leaves are bright green in spring, with reddish tips on the lobes. Fall colors range from pale orange to yellow. This strong, upright tree is of good stature, reaching 13 m (41 ft.) tall. The name means "golden prosperity."

'Koko'

MATSUMURAE GROUP
RED

The origin of this promising cultivar, seen in the beautiful Villa Taranto garden in Italy, is unknown. It has been propagated and re-introduced by Firma C. Esveld, Netherlands. The leaf and color are similar to 'Kinran'. The plant is also like a red form of the green-leaved 'Tobiosho', with similar leaves and habit.

The leaf shape, with the forward-pointing lobes, is very attractive. In spring the young leaves emerge a bright pink-red with narrow drooping lobes, becoming purpled-red for the summer, and turning crimson in the fall. The short leaf stalks are purpled-red and the young shoots are green. The medium-sized to large, mainly seven-lobed leaves are divided at different levels, with the central lobes divided higher up the leaf than the deeply divided outer lobes. Each lobe is ovate, widest in the middle, with a long, sharply pointed tip. The margins are distinctly toothed, but not as coarsely as most Matsumurae cultivars.

This very distinct cultivar forms a densely branched, round-headed tree up to 5 m (16 ft.) in height. The name has been misspelled 'Kokko'.

'Kokobunji nishiki'

DWARF GROUP
VARIEGATED

This slow-growing, variegated dwarf from Japan is a real gem, but is extremely difficult to propagate. Its creamy yellow to white leaf margins are unusual in *Acer palmatum* and give it a very attractive appearance. The variegation is mainly in bands of varying widths along the margins, but occasionally covers the whole lobe.

The small palmatum-type, mainly five-lobed leaves are deeply divided. The lobes are long-ovate with pointed tips and

'Kogane sakae'.
Photo by J. D. Vertrees

'Koko'.
Photo by Peter Gregory

toothed margins. Because of the uneven variegation, the lobes can be uneven, curved, and slightly crinkled. The leaves are similar in shape to those of the more vigorous, green-leaved 'Tsuchigumo' but, because of the variegation, are more irregular. The leaf stalks and shoots are also green. Though unusual and attractive, the difficulty in propagating 'Kokobunji nishiki' makes it quite rare and very much a collector's item.

'Kokobunji nishiki'.
Photo by Peter Gregory

'Kokyo'.
Photo by Talon Buchholz

'Kokyo'
AMOENUM GROUP
GREEN

This selection originated from seed collected in the Japanese emperor's garden in Tokyo and was named by Talon Buchholz of Oregon. It is similar in growth and summer leaf color to 'Oshio beni', which is a striking bronzed green. Fall color is a glorious orange-red. The seven-lobed leaves are divided to almost halfway to the leaf base. Each lobe is broadly ovate with a tail-like tip and finely toothed margins. The lobe tips have a tendency to curve downward. The leaf stalks are red. This cultivar forms a compact upright tree up to about 9 m (30 ft.) tall and is very hardy, tolerating temperatures up to −20°F (−29°C). It prefers a sunny or partially shaded well-drained spot in the garden. The name means "imperial palace," referring to the location of the garden in which seed was first collected.

'Komachi hime'
DWARF GROUP
GREEN

This lovely, slow-growing palmatum-type cultivar is similar in leaf and habit to the popular 'Kotohime', but with even brighter red leaf tips. The small five-lobed, deeply divided leaves are a light yellow-green with red tips and margins in the spring, becoming medium green with darker red tips through the summer. The leaf margins are toothed, and the lobes sharply pointed and radiating outward to give a starlike appearance. 'Komachi hime' forms a small, dense, rounded bush up to about 1 m (3 ft.) or so in height and is ideal for the alpine garden or for container culture. The name means "beautiful little girl."

'Komon nishiki'
PALMATUM GROUP
VARIEGATED

The smallish leaves have five to seven

moderately deeply divided lobes. These are ovate with tail-like tips, widest in the lower third, and gradually tapering to a point. The margins are toothed. The leaf stalks are short and thin. The basic color of the foliage is a bright, pale green, but in the spring, the new leaves have a rose-tinted edging which blends almost to the center of the lobes. Occasionally, the new tones are almost pink.

As the leaves expand fully in late spring, they take on the variegated character of *sunago fu* (sand-dusted) type of variegation, in which very tiny yellow or white specks or spots are dusted onto the leaf. The specks rarely join together to make a larger yellow or white area. This maple has a very subtle and beautiful form of variegation. as reflected in the name, which means "small figures on brocade." The leaves are bright crimson in the fall.

Neither a large-growing plant nor a dwarf, 'Komon nishiki' can attain up to 3 m (10 ft.) in height when planted in a good location in a rock garden. When grown in a container, it makes a fine-leaved small plant and also lends itself to bonsai culture. 'Aureovariegatum' has been considered a synonym of 'Komon nishiki' (van Gelderen et al. 1994) but is here considered separate. 'Komon nishiki' has been grown since 1882.

'Ko murasaki'

MATSUMURAE GROUP
RED

One of many red-leaved forms of the Matsumurae Group, 'Ko murasaki' has very deeply divided medium-sized leaves with the points of the lobes radiating outward. The lobes are ovate and each ends in a sharply pointed tip. The margins are clearly and deeply toothed. The leaf color is a deep purplish red, which holds well in the summer heat. Along the center of the lobes, the color shades into a deep green-

ish red. The fall color is a strong crimson. This hardy, small tree grows about as broad as tall. It probably attains 4 m (13 ft.) in height and spread. It has been known under the names 'Koi murasaki' and 'Noshi'. 'Ko murasaki' means "deep purple."

'Korean Gem'

AMOENUM GROUP
GREEN

This maple was described in early editions of this book under the natural variety *Acer palmatum* var. *koreanum*, and in *Maples of the World* (van Gelderen et al. 1994) under 'Koreanum'. *Acer palmatum* var. *coreanum* was the name given by Takenoshin Nakai in 1914 to this natural form, indigenous

'Komachi hime'.
Photo by Cor van Gelderen

'Komon nishiki'.
Photo by J. D. Vertrees

to South Korea and adjacent islands. This name was based on an abnormal specimen with petal-less flowers. Thus the name was illegitimate under the 1959 *Botanical Code* and was later absorbed into *A. palmatum* subsp. *palmatum* by C. S. Chang in 1986.

Despite this history, there is a well-established form, both in cultivation and in the nursery trade. The best-known example of it is probably the tree growing in Sir Harold Hillier's Gardens and Arboretum at Jermyns, Hampshire, England. Because of the confusion that results from using the Latin name 'Koreanum' or 'Coreanum' for a variable, naturally occurring population with the same name, the Hillier clone has been renamed 'Korean Gem'.

'Korean Gem'.
Photo by J. D. Vertrees

'Koriba'.
Photo by Peter Gregory

This excellent green tree has brilliant fall colors ranging from yellows to oranges, often blended with red. The shoots are dark red, especially noticeable in the fall and winter. The leaf margins have a very narrow and faint red marking in the spring. The medium-sized seven- to nine-lobed leaves are fairly deeply divided and radiate outward. The ovate lobes taper to sharply pointed tips and have finely toothed margins. The leaf stalks are red and about half the leaf length. 'Korean Gem' is strong growing and hardy, and forms an upright, round-headed, medium-sized tree up to about 7 m (23 ft.) in height.

'Koriba'
PALMATUM GROUP
GREEN

This promising Japanese cultivar is particularly prominent in the fall with its lovely color display. The spring leaves are an attractive purple-red with yellow veins, becoming green in the summer and tending to bronze somewhat when not shaded. In the fall, the leaves turn a brilliant yellow-orange. The leaf stalks are bright red. The small five- to seven-lobed leaves are moderately deeply divided. Each lobe is ovate with a triangular, pointed tip and clearly toothed margins. 'Koriba' forms an erect slow-growing tree or shrub, eventually reaching up to 5 m (16 ft.) in height.

'Koshibori nishiki'
PALMATUM GROUP
VARIEGATED

The basic color of the small leaves is light, bright green. The new leaves are edged with orange and red. The *sunago fu* (sand-dusted) variegation consists of extremely fine dots and flecks of yellow on the green. These minute dots are irregularly, indiscriminately, and often thickly scattered all over the surface.

The five lobes are long-ovate with pointed tips and toothed margins. The lobes radiate out from the center, giving a definite palmate appearance. Occasionally, they are irregularly curved. Shoots are crimson. Fall colors are yellow to orange. This short shrub has a slightly cascading habit and makes a dense but lacy plant about 2.5 m (8 ft.) tall. It is a desirable small landscape plant and also adapts very well to container culture.

'Koshimino'

OTHER GROUP
GREEN

The foliage, fall coloration, and bunched habit, among other features, are very similar to 'Hagoromo'. The leaf shape and coloring are basically the same (see 'Hagoromo' for a full description). Japanese nurseries list 'Hagoromo' as slow-growing, rarely reaching 1 m (3 ft.) or so in height and 'Koshimino' as vigorously growing to about 6 m (20 ft.) tall in 10 years. Another 10-year-old plant is only about 3 m (10 ft.) in height but multistemmed and quite broad. Another name that has been used for 'Koshimino' is 'Decompositum'.

'Kotohime'

DWARF GROUP
GREEN

This dwarf has one of the smallest leaves of *Acer palmatum* cultivars. These tiny leaves have five lobes, although much of the time they appear to have only three, as the two basal lobes almost disappear. The center lobe is always prominent, with the two side lobes angling outward. The lobes are ovate, with short tail-like tips and bluntly, deeply toothed margins. The leaf stalks are very short. The new leaves often emerge a bright rose or orange-red. This color is heaviest on the edges of the leaves and shades into the light green of the center. Summer foli-age is bright, light green. Fall color is light yellow blended with orange and becoming red.

'Kotohime' is a sturdy little plant. It tends to grow upright with much side branching which rounds out the shape. It is useful planted with other dwarf forms in special places such as alpine gardens. It is also popular with bonsai specialists and can be trained into a very tight bun shape. The name means "little harp." Other names that have been used for this cultivar

'Koshibori nishiki'.
Photo by Harry Olsen

'Koshimino'.
Photo by J. D. Vertrees

are 'Kotohime yatsubusa' and 'Tokyo yatsubusa'. 'Chichibu' and 'Chichibu yatsubusa' are similar to 'Kotohime' if not the same.

'Koto ito komachi'

DWARF GROUP
GREEN

Of the many thousands of seedlings produced at Maplewood Nursery, including those created by hand hybridization, 'Koto ito komachi' is one of the most unusual. It is an extremely dwarf strapleaf maple. The original was a chance seedling which remained very tiny for the first three years. It was not until the tiny tips were grafted onto vigorous understock that it began to get any size at all. And even then the most growth that has been possible to force on any one graft in a season was about 15 cm. (That is considerable as most grafted maples make an annual growth of only 5–6 cm.) The shoots are sturdy and the leaf nodes are very close together, thus making the foliage quite dense.

The leaves usually have five extremely long, narrow lobes, but many have only three lobes. The margins are not toothed but slightly wavy. Each threadlike lobe is only 1 mm at the widest point and narrows to half that at the base, little more than the width of the midrib. The lobes join at the leaf base. The leaves do not lie in the same plane, and each one has a different curl to the lobes. The leaf stalk is quite short.

This cultivar seems hardy and also takes full sun. It is a marvel that it grows at all since the leaf surface is so small that it can manufacture very little food. The plant is extremely difficult to propagate since any scion wood is measured in millimeters or at the most 2 cm. I was pleased to have Hideo Suzuki of Japan view this plant at Maplewood Nursery, where he proposed the name 'Koto ito komachi', which can be interpreted as "small, five-stringed old harp" or "beautiful little girl." The leaves are like harp strings, and this cultivar is Maplewood's beautiful little girl. The word *komachi* is also a horticultural term for "dwarf."

'Koto maru'

DWARF GROUP
GREEN

This lovely dwarf is the green equivalent of 'Beni hime', being similar in leaf shape and size and in growth rate. New foliage is yellow-green, with bronzed edges and tips, before turning dark green. The yellow-bronze new growth overlying the dark green older foliage continues throughout the growing season. Fall color is yellow to orange.

The small five-lobed leaves are divided fairly deeply toward the leaf bases. Each lobe is broadly ovate, irregular with a triangular or bluntly pointed tip, and with toothed margins. As is typical of witches'-brooms, the center lobe is often shortened and occasionally absent. The very short leaf stalks are about 1 cm long.

'Koto maru' forms a dense, compact, slow-growing bush. An old plant in Savill Gardens, Windsor, England, is only about 1.5 m (5 ft.) tall and 2 m (6 ft.) wide. The name, which means "round harp," has been misspelled 'Koto mura'.

'Koto-no-ito'

LINEARILOBUM GROUP
GREEN

The lobes of this cultivar are slightly broader than those of the usual linearilobum. The medium-sized leaves have five to seven narrow, straplike lobes of a rich green color. They are lanceolate, gradually tapering to an elongate, sharp point, with margins almost smooth, but irregularly toothed in the broader lobes. The leaf base is almost flat, with the lower lobes extending straight out. New leaves unfold with crimson tones but soon turn green. Fall colors are various shades of yellow and red. The red leaf stalks are fairly short.

'Koto-no-ito' usually makes a dense tall shrub of 2 m (6 ft.) in 10–15 years. Although an upright-growing form, it does not exceed 3 m (10 ft.) in very old plants.

Page 174:
'Kotohime'.
Photo by Peter Gregory

'Koto ito komachi'.
Photo by Peter Gregory

This page:
'Koto maru'.
Photo by Cor van Gelderen

'Koto-no-ito'.
Photo by Peter Gregory

The bark is a good, bright green and the plant is hardy. The name means "golden old harp." Another name under which this cultivar has been known is 'Latilobatum'.

'Kōya san'
DWARF GROUP
GREEN

The small, glossy, bronze-green palmatum-type leaves of this attractive Dutch cultivar selected and named by Dick van der Maat are quite distinctive. They are deeply divided into mainly five lobes, each lobe narrowly ovate with a somewhat elongated tip and relatively large, coarse, irregularly toothed margins. The newly emerging leaves are a bright bronze-red with sunken, yellow midveins and are produced all summer to make an attractive contrast to the bronze-green background of older leaves. The plant forms a small dense mound. It was named after a Japanese mountain, *Koyasan*, which means "wild hill."

'Kurabu yama'
MATSUMURAE GROUP
GREEN

This little known cultivar is worthy of more attention. The medium-sized leaves are seven-lobed and separated to the leaf base. Each lobe is long-ovate with the side lobes noticeably narrower. The margins are toothed. Spring growth has a reddish brown or deep rusty appearance. In early summer, the color changes to a deep, rich green with red main veins and brown tinged tips. Fall colors are yellow, orange, and crimson, making this a very conspicuous plant in the garden. Although it is not a tall tree, only reaching 4 m (13 ft.) in height and spread, it is a vigorous grower which broadens with age. It is hardy and useful in the landscape for its good fall color. The name has been misspelled 'Kurabeyama'.

'Kuro hime'
DWARF GROUP
GREEN

This attractive dwarf cultivar from Japan goes through a kaleidoscope of colors in the spring. The small, mainly five-lobed palmatum-type leaves emerge a bright pink-red, becoming green with brown-red flushed margins, before changing to mid to dark green for the summer. Fall color is bright red. The oval lobes are deeply divided and have long, triangular, pointed tips and toothed margins. The dominant center lobe is usually appreciably larger. The slender, stiff leaf stalks and shoots are red. 'Kuro hime' forms a dense, compact, small shrub well suited for smaller gardens and containers.

'Kurui jishi'

DWARF GROUP
GREEN

This delightful cultivar has small, deep green leaves, with the edge of each lobe rolled upward and inward. The undersides are gray-green. The leaf almost appears star-shaped. There are seven, deeply divided lobes, but the two tiny basal lobes cup upward, making the leaf appear five-lobed. Each lobe is long and gradually pointed, and gives the appearance of a pointed tube as the rolled edges almost meet in the center. Edges of the lobes are toothed, but this feature is lost because they roll inward. The lobe tips are extremely sharp and often hooked.

The deep, rich green leaves turn a delightful yellow to orange in the fall and are very similar to those of 'Okushimo', but usually smaller. The short leaf stalks and shoots are red, differing from the green stems of 'Okushimo'.

'Kurui jishi' is smaller than 'Okushimo'. It is a slow, dense, upright grower to 2 m (6 ft.) in height. The leaf nodes are quite close together to give a dense cover of leaves. This cultivar is a delightful plant for alpine gardens or areas in gardens calling for small to medium-sized upright plants. Japanese gardeners report it as slightly tender. The name, which means "confused lion," has been misspelled 'Korui jishi'.

'Lemon Lime Lace'

DISSECTUM GROUP
GREEN

This interesting two-toned dissectum named by Del Loucks, Oregon, has an apt name that describes the changing leaf colors. The leaves emerge a very light lemon yellow, becoming lime green in summer, creating a lovely two tone effect from early summer onward. The fall color is orange. The size and shape of the leaves is similar to 'Green Mist'. The five- to seven-lobed,

This page:
'Lionheart'.
Photo by Peter Gregory

'Long Man'.
Photo by Peter Gregory

Page 179:
'Lozita'.
Photo by Harold Greer

'Lutescens'.
Photo by Cor van Gelderen

'Maiko'.
Photo by J. D. Vertrees

deeply dissected leaves have the lobes themselves dissected almost to the midrib. The margins are edged with coarse but narrow, sharply pointed teeth. This cultivar forms a compact, irregular mound with semipendulous branches.

'Lionheart'

DISSECTUM GROUP
RED

This unique, semiupright red-purple dissectum, introduced by Duncan and Davies Nursery of New Zealand, can be described as the red counterpart to the ever-popular, upright, green dissectum 'Seiryū'. In spring its foliage is similar in color to that of 'Crimson Queen', and it retains this purple-red well into the summer, becoming bronzed with green undertones in early fall, and turning a deep crimson in the fall.

The medium to large seven-lobed leaves are dissected to the leaf base, the lobes themselves being deeply cut and narrowing sharply in the lower quarter to no more than the width of the midribs. The margins have coarse but narrow, finely pointed teeth. The short red leaf stalks have expanded bases. When young, the attractive deep red bark is covered in very close-packed vertical glaucous striations.

'Lionheart' is a vigorous small tree, reaching a height of 4 m (13 ft.) at maturity. In habit it is similar to 'Seiryū' when young, growing upright at first. It becomes more spreading with age, the branches growing horizontally with pendulous tips to give an attractive layered and arching effect. The name has been misspelled 'Lion's Heart'.

'Long Man'

MATSUMURAE GROUP
RED

This very vigorous Dutch cultivar has large very deeply divided leaves and is similar in habit to the true 'Atropurpureum'. It is reputed to have the largest central lobe of any *Acer palmatum* cultivar. The spring leaves are a bright pink-red, becoming purple-red with red midveins for the summer. Fall color is yellow-orange to red. The leaf stalks and shoots are red. The leaves have five to seven broadly ovate lobes with tail-like tips and toothed margins, but are not as coarsely toothed as the leaves of most cultivars in the Matsumurae Group. 'Long Man' is very vigorous in its early years and estimated to reach about 4 m (13 ft.) in height. It was selected and named by Dick van der Maat, Netherlands.

'Lozita'

PALMATUM GROUP
RED

The main features of this cultivar are the bright rosy red new leaves produced all summer on the background of mahogany-red older leaves, and the stunning scarlet fall color. The leaves tend to become bronze-green in shade. They are medium-sized with five to seven very deeply divided, ovate-triangular lobes. Each lobe has a tail-like tip and distinctly toothed margins. The short leaf stalks are reddish to purple. 'Lozita' forms a bushy, upright tree, eventually reaching 5 m (16 ft.) in height. It is ideal for container culture, which tends to keep it nice and compact.

'Lutescens'

AMOENUM GROUP
GREEN

The leaves of this cultivar are among the largest of the Amoenum Group and are seven-lobed. They are divided about halfway to the leaf base. The ovate lobes taper to sharply pointed tips and have finely toothed margins. The new spring growth is yellowish green, which soon changes to a rich green. The real glory is the fall coloration, which becomes a very rich yellow or gold. This medium-sized, upright tree matures at 7 m (23 ft.) or more. It is a good companion for other orange to crimson forms in a larger planting. The name means "yellowish." The cultivar has been known under the name 'Luteum'.

'Maiko'

PALMATUM GROUP
GREEN

The foliage of this interesting small cultivar is a yellowish green to bright green. Fall colors are pleasing yellows of different intensities. The small to medium-sized leaves are five-lobed but are decidedly not

uniform in shape. Some lobes are quite narrow, with margins deeply and irregularly toothed, even lobulate. Several leaves have this type of lobe combined with the more typically triangular-ovate shaped lobe which tapers to an elongate, blunt tip. A few leaves have the typical palmatum shape but with very deeply toothed margins. All these variations can occur on the same plant. 'Maiko' is similar to 'Mama', but the foliage is smaller and even more irregular. The red leaf stalks are stiff and short.

The plant makes an upright shrub up to 3 m (10 ft.) in height. After vigorous early growth it will broaden as it matures. The name means "dancing girl." Propagating material labeled 'Maoka' and 'Maioka' from different sources was grown side-by-side with 'Maiko' for comparison, and the three appear identical. The names are examples of how misnomers can be created by carelessness in writing labels.

'Mai mori'
PALMATUM GROUP
VARIEGATED

Imported from Japan, this cultivar is an interesting addition to the 'Butterfly' group of variegated palmatums. The leaves are similar in shape to 'Butterfly' but slightly larger with broader lobes. The variegation is light cream to yellow on medium green to dark gray-green and occurs in patches of various sizes and in flecks. The patches sometimes occupy one side of a lobe, causing the lobe to become sickle-shaped. Fall color is red. The small five- to seven-lobed leaves vary in size. The leaf base is usually more or less straight at least when five-lobed. The lobes are ovate with tapered tips and are deeply divided. The margins are distinctly and regularly toothed. The leaf stalks are slender and short.

This plant forms a compact, densely branched, small tree, more or less as wide as tall. If the soil is too fertile, 'Mai mori' loses its variegation, as do several other variegates. The name means "the dancing forest."

'Mama'
PALMATUM GROUP
GREEN

Describing the leaf of this cultivar is very difficult because no two leaves are alike. Each leaf lives up to the cultivar's name, which means "doing as one pleases," and does its own thing.

The small to medium-sized, bright green leaves are mainly five-lobed. There the uniformity stops. Some leaves have seven lobes, some as few as three. The leaves may have five long, narrow lobes separated entirely

'Mai mori'.
Photo by Peter Gregory

'Mama'.
Photo by Peter Gregory

to the leaf base with margins irregularly toothed, and appearing wind-tattered, or they may have three broad lobes separated shallowly combined with two long narrow lobes, completely separated, and with very tattered margins. Other leaves have all these combinations or any variation conceivable. Each leaf is slightly and interestingly different. The overall effect is a rather lacy appearance.

The leaf stalks are bright red. The bright green of the summer foliage turns to a beautiful blend of yellow-orange in the fall. The plant matures at 4 m (13 ft.) as a tall bush. It is rather rare in nurseries.

'Manyō-no-sato'

PALMATUM
VARIEGATED

A small upright but broad shrub, with the leaf variegation pattern similar to that of 'Beni shi en', but light yellow variegation on a purple-brown base color. Fall color is orange to red. The leaves have five to seven very deeply divided narrow lobes, with long curved tail-like tips and irregular coarsely toothed margins. The name means "the wonderful place of nature."

'Mapi-no-machi hime'

DWARF GROUP
GREEN

This desirable green dwarf is very like the popular 'Kiyohime', with similar growth habit, leaves, and coloring. It is considered to be synonymous with 'Little Princess', a dwarf introduction attributed to the late Jim Russell at Castle Howard in England. The small palmatum-type leaves are a lovely light yellow-green, edged with pink-orange in the spring, becoming light to medium green with a darker bronze-red edging which sometimes persists throughout the summer. The color changes to orange-red in the fall. The small five-lobed leaves are deeply divided, with the lobes spread out

like a star. Each lobe is ovate with a tail-like tip and with clearly toothed margins. The short, slender leaf stalks are pink-red.

This plant forms a small, round, densely branched shrub, estimated to reach about 2 m (6 ft.) high and wide when fully grown. It is becoming popular in Europe and is readily available in the trade. Unfortunately, it has not yet been possible to trace its origins, or the true relationships, if any, between 'Chiyo hime', 'Kiyohime', and 'Mapi-no-machi hime'. Curiously all three names mean "little princess."

'Manyō-no-sato'.
Photo by Peter Gregory

'Mapi-no-machi hime'.
Photo by Peter Gregory

'Marakumo'

PALMATUM GROUP
VARIEGATED

The new leaves of this very desirable variegated form are a bright pinkish or light orange, shading from the margins toward the center of the lobes. The basic leaf color is pale green. It is made even lighter by the great profusion of extremely fine dots of white or cream which are sometimes so thick that they merge, forming an almost solid area. A translucent effect results from the very dense, fine stippling of the thin leaves. Fall colors range into yellows and light gold. The medium-sized leaves are moderately deeply divided into five to seven oblong-ovate lobes. Each lobe tapers to a slender, pointed tip, thus forming a palmate-shaped leaf. The margins are toothed.

'Marakumo' forms an upright bush of 3 m (10 ft.). It is somewhat tender and needs at least afternoon shade. It is not easily propagated or widely known. The name has been misspelled 'Maragumo'.

'Margaret Bee'

AMOENUM GROUP
RED

This purple-red cultivar is considered an improvement on 'Bloodgood'. It is similar in leaf and growth to 'Fireglow' but not as outstanding. The leaves are slightly larger than those of 'Fireglow', with the lower ends of each lobe narrower, like the neck of a bottle. The large five- to seven-lobed, wide-spreading, bright purple-red leaves are deeply divided. The broadly ovate lobes with long, slender, pointed tips narrow markedly toward the lobe junctions. The margins are finely toothed, and the slender leaf stalks are purple. This plant forms a narrow, upright tree, eventually attaining a height of up to 6 m (20 ft.). It is sometimes found in catalogs as 'Margaret B'.

'Marjan'

MATSUMURAE GROUP
RED

The new leaves of this Dutch cultivar are a bright pink-red in the spring before turning a purple-red for the summer, then yellow-orange and red in the fall. The summer color is the same as that of 'Bloodgood'. The medium-sized mainly five-lobed leaves are deeply divided. Each lobe is ovate with a long, pointed tip and fairly evenly toothed margins but not as coarsely toothed as in most cultivars in the Matsumurae Group. The growth and shape are similar to that of the true 'Atropurpureum', vigorous and upright. It is estimated that 'Marjan' will probably reach up to 4 m (13 ft.) or so at

'Marakumo'.
Photo by J. D. Vertrees

'Margaret Bee'.
Photo by Harry Olsen

maturity. It was propagated by Dick van der Maat and named after his wife.

'Masu kagami'

PALMATUM GROUP
VARIEGATED

Although it is not widely known, this cultivar is one of the most interesting among those which are subtly marked. The medium-sized leaves are mainly five-lobed, separated openly and deeply, almost to the leaf base. Each lobe is elongate-ovate with the tip extended to a very sharp point. The margins are prominently toothed.

The new foliage is crimson when first appearing, occasionally showing strong pink tones. These colors lessen, but the reddish shades persist along the margins into late spring. The summer leaves are a basic green color but often so heavily marked as to appear almost whitish green. The extremely fine dots of white and yellow often merge to form more solid areas of light color. The stippling effect is almost lacking in some leaves, but most leaves are very strongly marked, making them appear pale. Fall color is red to scarlet.

This cultivar does best with light shade protection. It is a hardy, medium-growing shrub which eventually reaches 4 m (13 ft.) in height. The name is sometimes misspelled 'Musa kagami'. This cultivar has also been known as 'Masukaga'.

'Masu murasaki'

MATSUMURAE GROUP
RED

This very intense red cultivar shows best when in full sun. The red does not have the green undertone of many similar red cultivars, but shades more toward purple. When grown close to similar cultivars, its unique color is apparent. In full shade, the leaves have an almost black-red tone with deep green shading in the center of the lobes. Fall color is an outstand-

'Marjan'.
Photo by Peter Gregory

'Masu kagami'.
Photo by J. D. Vertrees

'Masu murasaki'.
Photo by Peter Gregory

ing red. The short leaf stalks and veins are bright red.

The medium-sized leaves have seven deeply divided lobes. Each lobe is ovate-acuminate with an elongated tip. The margins are toothed. This vigorous, upright plant eventually grows to about 7 m (23 ft.) in height. The name is sometimes misspelled 'Matsumura saki' and 'Musa murasaki'.

'Matsugae'

PALMATUM GROUP
VARIEGATED

'Matsugae'.
Photo by Harry Olsen

'Matsu kaze'.
Photo by J. D. Vertrees

This variegate is one of the oldest cultivars. It arose as a sport of 'Kagiri nishiki' and is a very satisfactory landscape plant. Basic leaf

color is deep green, almost a bluish green. The variegation is of several types—*fukurin fu* (along the edges of the lobes), *fukurin kuzure* (irregular), or *hoso fukurin* (shallow margins). The markings are white or cream, but, in the spring, are overlaid or blended with a deep rose. The colors lessen somewhat in the late summer, but the fall intensifies the deep rose color in all the variegated areas.

The small leaves are very irregular, each leaf being slightly different from the next. They are basically five-lobed, the long, narrow lobes deeply divided, slightly wider halfway to the apex, and terminating in a slender pointed tip. The lobes are sometimes sickle-shaped, especially where there is heavy variegation. Occasionally, individual lobes are broad, almost elongate-ovate. The edges are deeply and irregularly notched, toothed, or a combination of the two. The two basal lobes tend to point at right angles to the short, slender leaf stalk.

The general appearance is similar to 'Kagiri nishiki', but there is a greater depth of color in 'Matsugae'. It is a little more open than 'Butterfly'. 'Matsugae' grows up to 4 m (13 ft.) in height. It is a hardy plant and can take full sun. The name means "pine branch." This cultivar has also been known under the names 'Albomarginatum', 'Argenteomarginatum', and 'Fichtenast'.

'Matsu kaze'

MATSUMURAE GROUP
GREEN

This cultivar with deeply cut leaves makes a handsome landscape plant. The spring color is a spectacular bronze-red to purple-red. The bright green veins add a special effect. The leaves develop a rich green in summer and then turn rich carmine and crimson in the fall. They are medium-sized with seven long, narrow, elliptic-ovate lobes that taper to long, slender pointed tips. The lobes tend to remain together rather than radiate outward and are divided almost to the leaf base. The margins are toothed and the leaf stalks are slender.

'Matsu kaze' is vigorous growing but not upright and soon becomes a broad shrub up to 4 m (13 ft.) or so tall, with graceful, cascading branches. This striking addition to the landscape needs space to spread in order to display its unique weeping look. The name, which means "wind in the pine trees," refers to the title of one of the famous Noh plays of Japan that dates from the twelfth and thirteenth centuries. Because of its dissectum-like habit and its very narrow, deep cut leaves, 'Matsu kaze' has also been known under the names 'Dissectum Matsu kaze', 'Machi kaze' and 'Pendulum Matsu kaze'. It has been misspelled 'Matsu kase'.

'Matsuyoi'

AMOENUM GROUP
GREEN

This medium-sized tree has unusual foliage. The large leaves emerge a pale, yellowish green, turning to a light, bright green as they mature. They do not form a flat plane as most forms do, but the lobes bend up or down slightly or sometimes twist slightly. Some leaves hang down, some flat, some on edge, creating a foliage cover much like a wind-blown coiffure. The total foliage appearance is rather feathery. The fall color is bright yellow-orange to deep orange. The seven lobes are long-ovate, separated about halfway to the leaf base. The edges are notched, with fine toothing between the notches.

This unique cultivar tends to grow rather broad and not strongly upright, reaching 4 m (13 ft.) in height. It makes an unusual contrast in the landscape and an excellent bonsai plant. The name means "waiting for the early evening." Another name by which this cultivar has been known is 'Machiyou'. It has also been sold as 'Myoi' by mistake.

'Matthew'

DWARF GROUP
GREEN

Originating from a witches'-broom and named by Bill Schwartz after his third child, this excellent cultivar is like the

'Matsuyoi'.
Photo by Cor van Gelderen

'Matthew'.
Photo by Harry Olsen

better-known 'Coonara Pygmy' in leaf size and shape and in growth habit. The small five-lobed palmatum-type leaves emerge a light yellow-green, soon becoming a light green for summer, before turning a delightful yellow to deep orange and fiery red in the fall. The leaves are deeply divided, long-ovate, with long, pointed tips and distinctly toothed margins. The central lobe is sometimes short and rounded. This hardy cultivar forms a dense, round, small bush up to 45 cm (1.5 ft.) tall and wide. It is superb for the rock garden, patio, and containers.

'Mei hō'.
Photo by Peter Gregory

'Midori-no-teiboku'.
Photo by Peter Gregory

'Mei hō'

AMOENUM GROUP
VARIEGATED

An old Japanese variegate mentioned in the 1882 *Sekihin Binran*, 'Mei hō' has creamy white patches and some mottling on a green base. The leaves vary from having no variegation at all, to having various sized variegations, to the whole leaf being creamy white. Young leaves emerge bronze-green with yellow variegation, becoming green with creamy white variegation, then turning various attractive pastel shades of yellow, orange, and pinkish red in the fall. The medium-sized leaves are deeply divided into seven ovate lobes and have finely toothed margins. 'Mei hō' forms a medium-sized upright tree with a spreading crown.

'Midori-no-teiboku'

DWARF GROUP
GREEN

This unusual, dwarf laceleaf, discovered by Dr. Corbin, Oregon, is a seedling from the well-known 'Viridis', hence the V in its original code name 'V Corbin'. Attractive and low-growing, this maple stands out with its combination of dark green dissected foliage and prostrate growth. The medium to large leaves are divided to the leaf base into mainly seven very narrow lobes. The sublobes are short and more like broad saw teeth. The short leaf stalks are red-tinged.

Because of its low-spreading growth, it only reaches about 1 m (3 ft.) tall, but spreads up to three times as wide. It can survive under snow in colder climates when many other cultivars that are exposed above the snow die back. It forms an attractive ground cover or carpet between other taller contrasting plants. The name means "green spreading."

'Mikawa yatsubusa'

DWARF GROUP
GREEN

Overlapping each other like shingles on a roof, the leaves are a light yellow-green when first unfolding and are bunched up at the shoot tips when new. They become a medium green for the summer. The outer leaves have very bright red tips on the fine toothing of the margins. Fall color is a beautiful yellow to deep red.

The small leaves are slightly longer than those of other dwarf forms and have five to seven moderately deeply divided lobes. Each lobe is oblong-ovate, with a long, triangular, tapered tip. The leaf base is flattish, making all the lobes point forward. The leaf nodes are very close together, and the new shoots very short and stubby. This makes for a very dense compact little plant, ideally suited for bonsai culture.

'Mikawa kotohime' is very like this cultivar, closely fitting the above description. 'Mikawa yatsubusa', which means "a small cluster of three rivers," has also been known under the name 'Shishi yatsubusa'.

'Mikazuki'

MATSUMURAE GROUP
VARIEGATED

This very attractive cultivar selected and named by Talon Buchholz of Oregon has probably the deepest divided and narrowest-looking lobes of any of the network-veined variegates. The large mainly seven-lobed leaves are divided almost to the leaf base. Each lobe is undulated and has rolled down margins, so that it appears narrow and long. The spring leaves emerge with a bright pink background and a green network of veins. The lobe centers each side of the midrib slowly change to creamy white which spreads toward the pink margins. The slender leaf stalk is light green. Fall color is an unusually deep bright orange with green veins.

'Mikawa yatsubusa'.
Photo by J. D. Vertrees

'Mikazuki', spring color.
Photo by Peter Gregory

'Mikazuki', fall color.
Photo by Talon Buchholz

This hardy, bushy, upright cultivar has coped with temperatures down to −20°F (−29°C), prefers some sun and partial shade in a well-drained soil, and has grown to 2.5 m (8 ft.) tall and about half as wide in 10 years. The name means "crescent moon."

'Mini Mondo'

PALMATUM GROUP
GREEN

'Mini Mondo'.
Photo by Harold Greer

'Mirte'.
Photo by Cor van Gelderen

This semidwarf small-leaved cultivar arose from a witches'-broom of 'Littleleaf', and was named by Richard P. Wolff, Pennsylvania. He originally named it 'Tiny Leaf', but years later changed it to 'Mini Mondo', meaning "small world." The change of name may be because there seems to be a quite different cultivar named 'Tiny Leaf', whose shape is similar to that of 'Ogi nagashi'. The origins of this latter 'Tiny Leaf' have not yet been traced.

The tiny green five- to seven-lobed leaves of 'Mini Mondo' turn a deep red in the fall. Like most cultivars originating from brooms, it has central lobes that are often short and rounded. While the leaves are similar in shape and size to those of the dwarf 'Hanami nishiki', the growth habit is twice as tall. 'Mini Mondo' reaches 2 m (6 ft.) high in 10 years, forming a small, round, compact but upright shrub.

'Mirte'

MATSUMURAE GROUP
GREEN

This rather special cultivar has large, deeply lobed leaves. When they first emerge, the leaves are mid chocolate-brown in color, with light green veining, and are covered with a soft pubescence. They become an unusual dark olive green by early summer and turn bronze-green in late summer and early fall, with lighter green undersides. Fall color is orange-yellow. The current shoots are covered in a gray bloom for most of the summer.

The seven to nine lobes are deeply divided and are ovate with tail-like pointed tips. Each lobe is broadest in the middle, narrowing slightly to the lobe junction. The margins have conspicuous, sharply pointed, hooked teeth. The two small basal lobes are almost at right angles to the short, stiff leaf stalk.

This strong-growing, upright cultivar reaches up to 8 m (26 ft.) tall and becomes about as wide. It was noticed in a group of seedlings at Firma C. Esveld, Netherlands, and was named after one of D. M. van Gelderen's granddaughters.

'Miyagino'

MATSUMURAE GROUP
GREEN

Fall color is the outstanding feature of this cultivar. It turns crimson flecked with gold or orange. The green leaf holds good color all summer and is pleasing in the landscape. The medium-sized seven-lobed leaves have two very small and narrow basal lobes. Each lobe is narrowly oblong, with the base gradually tapering to just the width of the midrib, and the outer end gradually tapering to a long, narrow tip. The lobes are widely divided right to the leaf base and radiate outward. The leaf stalks are slender and short. This medium-strong growing plant becomes a wide-spreading tall bush up to 4 m (13 ft.) in height.

'Mizuho beni'

PALMATUM GROUP
GREEN

This very attractive form has colorful orange-yellow spring foliage. The leaves have dark pink edging which merges into the orange-yellow background, gradually turning green from the main veins.

The small to medium, five- to seven-lobed leaves are fairly uniform in shape and color. They are characterized by the large, coarse, almost sublobate, triangular, pointed teeth around the margins. Each leaf is deeply divided with the lobes well separated. Each lobe is broadly ovate, with a pointed tip, and is broadest in the middle. The light yellow-green midribs are very slender, as is the leaf stalk. Fall color is a deep red.

'Mizuho beni' is similar to 'Katsura' in leaf shape, size, and color, and in growth habit and vigor, except for the much more conspicuous toothing. The important difference is that it comes into leaf at the normal time, some two to three weeks after 'Katsura', and so is less likely to be damaged by early spring frosts and cold winds.

This introduction has sometimes been misspelled 'Mitsuho beni'. The name means "red Mizuho," Mizuho being a Japanese girl's name.

'Mizū kiguri'

AMOENUM GROUP
GREEN

The spring color of this old Japanese cultivar is unusual for a form of *Acer palmatum*. The leaf undersurface is light green, but the entire leaf has a pinkish rose to light brick red overshading, with red lobe tips in the spring. The effect is a gentle overall brushing of color. Later in the season the leaf tones become a deeper green. Fall color is yellow to red. The typical, medium-

'Mizuho beni'.
Photo by Peter Gregory

'Mizū kiguri'.
Photo by Cor van Gelderen

sized leaves are seven-lobed and regular in shape, with a flat leaf base. The lobes are ovate, but taper to elongated, narrow tips, and have fine, sharp-toothed margins. The leaf stalks are short. This cultivar becomes a bushy plant rather than a tall tree, reaching 3 m (10 ft.) in height. The name means "passing under a waterfall."

'Momenshide'

OTHER GROUP
GREEN

The leaves of this cultivar look very much like 'Hagoromo', but the lobes are not as deeply cut, and 'Momenshide' is a smaller plant. The leaves have practically no leaf stalks and are attached almost directly to

'Momenshide'.
Photo by J. D. Vertrees

'Momiji gawa'.
Photo by Peter Gregory

the shoot. They are mainly five-lobed, with each lobe oblong-ovate, tapering to a blunt tip. The lobe base tapers abruptly for the last 1 cm to the width of the main vein, so that it appears to have its own leaf stalk. The lobes do not lie flat but twist slightly on different planes. The entire effect is of feathery foliage. The margins are only slightly and irregularly toothed.

The foliage is reddish in the spring, but soon changes to a deep, rich green. The veins are somewhat prominent and give a slightly textured look to the surface. In the fall, the bright yellow colors add to its beauty in the garden.

This cultivar assumes an upright bush shape and will probably not reach more than 4 m (13 ft.) tall. The Japanese have found this cultivar rather tender, and it is regarded as a bud sport from 'Hagoromo'. It is difficult to propagate. Another name by which this cultivar has been known is 'Yūshide'.

'Momiji gawa'

MATSUMURAE GROUP
RED

This old Japanese cultivar mentioned in the 1882 *Sekihin Binran* has leaves similar to the better-known 'Ō kagami'. The spring foliage is an attractive orange-red as it first appears, becoming darker red-maroon and then reddish purple for the summer, and turning a deep bright gold to red in the fall. The medium-sized leaves have mainly seven fairly deeply divided lobes, with the small basal lobes pointing outward to form a flat base. Each lobe is long-ovate, with a long, pointed tip and evenly toothed margins; the teeth are unusually small and even for the Matsumurae Group. The short leaf stalks and the young shoots are slender and red. 'Momiji gawa' grows into a sturdy tree with a broad, rounded crown, reaching 5 m (16 ft.) tall and 3 m (10 ft.) across.

'Momoiro kōya san'

DWARF GROUP
GREEN

This small-leaved, compact dwarf selected and named by Dick van der Maat, Netherlands, is notable for the attractive kaleidoscope of changing colors all through the growing season. The emerging leaves are brightly peach-colored, quickly changing to orange-red, then red and pink, before becoming green with bronze-red margins. Some leaves may have light, creamy, speckled variegation. Fall color is a bright red.

The mainly five-lobed leaves are fairly deeply divided. The short, ovate lobes have sharply pointed tips and coarse, irregularly toothed margins. The developing leaves are unevenly crumpled and rounded, giving an attractive disheveled appearance.

'Momoiro kōya san' forms a dense bush up to 2 m (6 ft.) in height. It is very similar in size and shape to the well-known 'Seigen'. It is somewhat delicate and needs some shade, but is ideal for bonsai and container culture. The name means "peach-colored wild mountain."

'Mon Papa'

MATSUMURAE GROUP
RED

This purple-red cultivar from Belgium is similar to the popular 'Nicholsonii', but with sharper, more pronounced teeth around the leaf margins, giving it an attractive feathery appearance, and with an outstanding fall color. The medium to large, mainly seven-lobed leaves are divided almost to the base. Each lobe is long-ovate, broadest in the outer third, and has a sharply pointed tip. The conspicuous teeth are also sharply pointed. The deep purple-maroon leaves become bronze-green in late summer before turning brilliant oranges and red in the fall. The red leaf stalks are very slender.

'Mon Papa' becomes a wide-spreading tree, up to 4 m (13 ft.) tall and almost as wide. Its deep purple-red coloring and feathery foliage make it a conspicuous feature in the garden landscape.

'Mon zukushi'

AMOENUM GROUP
GREEN

This old Japanese cultivar has bright, pleasant green leaves. Early in the season they

'Momoiro kōya san'.
Photo by Peter Gregory

'Mon Papa'.
Photo by Peter Gregory

are a light yellow-green with reddish hues and reddish tips, and sometimes the veins show a faint red. This soon changes to a solid green. Fall colors are brilliant orange-reds. The medium-sized leaf is an open palmate shape with five radiating, moderately deeply divided lobes. Occasionally, the basal lobe produces a small spur lobe. Each lobe is ovate, tapering to an elongated tip. The margins are very finely toothed. The leaf stalks are stiff and short. This rather vigorous, hardy plant reaches a height of 5 m (16 ft.). The name means "one of the sacred treasures." The cultivar has also been known under the name 'Yama hime'.

'Mon zukushi'.
Photo by Talon Buchholz

'Moonfire'.
Photo by J. D. Vertrees

'Moonfire'

MATSUMURAE GROUP
RED

The excellent purple-red, almost black-red color of this cultivar is almost opalescent. Diffused sun gives it a faint blue overtone similar to 'Nuresagi'. The good, deep colors last very well throughout the summer and do not bronze out as do many of the red cultivars. The center vein of each lobe is also a deep purple-red, and the underside of the leaf is a very deep, rich reddish green. Later the leaves turn crimson for a delightful fall display. The medium to large leaves are mainly seven-lobed and are deeply divided. Each lobe is elongate-ovate, gradually tapering to a fine pointed tip, and with clearly toothed margins. The red leaf stalks are rather short.

'Moonfire' is a strong, upright-growing form of *Acer palmatum* f. *atropurpureum*. Fast-growing when young, it broadens and slows down as it matures. Older trees assume an upright, rounded crown and reach 7 m (23 ft.) or so in height. 'Moonfire' was selected from seedlings by Richard P. Wolff, Pennsylvania, and is a very worthwhile cultivar. It is durable and its long-lasting season of color rivals that of the well-known 'Bloodgood'.

'Murakumo'

MATSUMURAE GROUP
RED

This outstanding red form has medium-sized leaves that are usually seven-lobed and are very deeply divided. Each ovate-elongate lobe ends in a long, pointed tip. The basal lobes are quite small. The margins are coarsely toothed. The short leaf stalks are reddish. The spring color as the leaves unfold is almost crimson and soon becomes a very good, deep purple-red. The leaf veins are also red and are noticeable. Fall colors range into crimson shades.

This upright cultivar is quite hardy and

reaches about 6 m (20 ft.) tall. It is valuable in the landscape because it retains the red colors well into late summer. The name, which means "village in the clouds," is often spelled 'Muragumo' and has been misspelled 'Muraguma', 'Murakama', and 'Murakuma'. 'Ō shidare' is a synonym.

'Murasaki hime'

DWARF GROUP
RED

This purple-leaved dwarf grows into a rounded shrub not exceeding 2 m (6 ft.) in height. The small to medium-sized leaves have five to seven lobes and are divided almost to the leaf base. Each lobe is oblong-lanceolate, terminating in a long, slender tip. The inner margins are smooth, while the outer margins are sharply toothed. The color of deep purple shades to a green-red inside the plant where the leaves are shaded. This cultivar seems a little delicate and not vigorous. The name, which means "purple dwarf," has been misspelled 'Murasaka hime'.

'Murasaki kiyohime'

DWARF GROUP
GREEN

Another of the dwarf cultivars, this plant is most desirable but not widely known. The small leaves have five deeply divided lobes, which radiate openly from the center. The leaf base is almost flat. Each lobe is ovate-lanceolate, tapering to an elongated, sharp tip. The center lobe is broad and very prominent, especially in the new leaves where it is often dominant. The margins are coarsely toothed on the upper half and smooth on the lower half. The red leaf stalks are short and slender.

New foliage is a light yellow-green, but is heavily marked around the margins with a broad area of bright purple-red, shading gradually into the leaf blade. As the leaves mature, they become a solid green. Often there is very light speckling of minute white markings within the green. Fall colors become gold or blends of orange and pink flushed, with the veins a contrasting red. This maple is excellent for alpine

'Murasaki kiyohime'.
Photo by Daniel Otis

plantings, container culture, and bonsai. It tends to be upright, reaching heights of about 1 m (3 ft.).

'Mure hibari'

MATSUMURAE GROUP
GREEN

The medium-sized leaves of this old Japanese cultivar are deeply divided into seven narrow, elongate-lanceolate lobes that taper to long, slender pointed tips. These lobes separate almost to the leaf base and radiate sharply outward. The edges of each lobe are slightly curved up or trough-shaped and prominently toothed. The short leaf stalks are reddish. The basic leaf color is light green. Margins of new leaves

'Mure hibari'.
Photo by J. D. Vertrees

'Muro gawa'.
Photo by Cor van Gelderen

are tinted with a bright brick red. In the fall, yellow to crimson blends appear.

This medium-strong grower forms an upright plant up to 5 m (16 ft.) tall. It is quite vigorous and hardy. One Japanese writer described the leaf shape as "like a crystal of snow" and unique. 'Mure hibari' is indeed a beautiful cultivar but is little-known. The name means "flock of skylarks."

'Muro gawa'

AMOENUM GROUP
RED

This strong cultivar brings a lot of color to the landscape. In spring and early summer the leaves are a striking light to dark orange-red and the contrasting green veins show the tracery of their design for several weeks. As the season progresses, the tones change to a rusty green and then into a deep bronze-green by late summer. Fall colors range from orange-red to crimson. The large seven- to nine-lobed leaves are long-ovate, tapering to slender, pointed tips, and moderately deeply divided. The margins are toothed. The green leaf stalks are long and slender.

'Muro gawa' is a hardy and fairly vigorous grower, but is not totally upright. With age, the side branches become somewhat pendulous, and the top slows its rate of growth. The mature tree is round-topped with pendulous outer branches, growing to 6 m (20 ft.) tall and to 4 m (13 ft.) across. The cultivar is named after the river Muro.

'Musashino'

MATSUMURAE GROUP
RED

The rich color of this cultivar is a deep purple-red. As the new leaves appear in the spring, the surfaces are covered with a minute, light-colored pubescence, which brings out the rich tones of purple. This pubescence soon disappears, but the basic leaf color persists well until the end of the summer. The underside of the leaf is purple-red with strong green undertones. In the fall, the foliage takes on a brilliant crimson hue. The large, bold leaves have mainly seven lobes, well separated to within 1 cm of the leaf base. The lobes are elongate-ovate, terminating in long, narrow, tapering pointed tips. The margins are sharply toothed. The deep red leaf stalks are quite short.

'Musashino' is strongly upright with a rounded crown, maturing at 8 m (26 ft.) and is fast-growing. This very famous cultivar has been grown in Japan since the early seventeenth century and was listed in 1688 as an old cultivar. It is still quite popular in Japan and is reported to be particularly beautiful in the fall. It is hardy and suitable for cooler areas of the United States. It is also known under the synonyms 'Nomura', 'Nomura kaede', and 'Nomura nishiki'.

'Nanase gawa'

AMOENUM GROUP
GREEN

The medium-sized leaves are deeply divided into five to seven lobes, which, when young, are very deeply divided, filling out as they develop. The lobes are ovate and terminate in long, narrow, sharp tips. The basal lobes point outward, forming a flat leaf base. The margins are finely toothed. This cultivar reaches 4 m (13 ft.) at maturity and becomes nearly as wide, growing into a tall, spreading bush. The spring leaves are crimson, soon changing to purplish red. In early summer, the leaves begin to turn green and the veins are a contrasting green. By midsummer the entire leaf is bronze-green. Fall color is bright crimson. This cultivar is believed to have been named after the river Nanase, whose location remains a mystery.

'Naruo nishiki'

PALMATUM GROUP
VARIEGATED

While 'Naruo nishiki' is classed as a variegated cultivar, plants from two sources have shown very little tendency to color. Admittedly, the plant were only a few seasons old, which may account for the lack of variegation. In one of the earlier descriptions, the palmate leaves are described as

'Musashino'.
Photo by Peter Gregory

'Nanase gawa'.
Photo by J. D. Vertrees

first unfolding with a light green color. As they mature, a faint creamy white shading or variegation appears. This upright-growing plant is not vigorous. It tends to form a round-headed tree or shrub up to 3 m (10 ft.) tall. The name has been misspelled 'Narvo nishiki'.

'Nicholsonii'

MATSUMURAE GROUP
GREEN

The best feature of this cultivar is its fall color. Spring foliage is a good red, slightly purplish. A deep, rich green color devel-ops during the summer and is followed by the beautiful golden yellow to crimson of the fall. The very deeply divided, medium-sized leaves are seven-lobed but appear longer because the middle three lobes are especially narrow. Each lobe is long, elongate-ovate, has a fine tip, and is narrowed at the base. The margins are clearly toothed. The leaf stalks are red. 'Nicholsonii' is a medium-strong grower, which reaches 5 m (16 ft.) in height and spread. Fritz K. A. von Schwerin first described this fairly hardy cultivar in 1893. It has been known under the names 'Atrodissectum' and 'Digitatum Atropurpureum'.

'Nigrum'

AMOENUM GROUP
RED

This selection from Hillier's Arboretum, England, is a very dark purple-red which can be almost black-red. Normally, it is a rich purple reminiscent of 'Nuresagi'. There is a characteristic fine, silvery white pubescence on the very young leaves as they unfold. Late summer tones change into brown-green mixed with dull yellow or bronze. Fall colors are bright red and crim-

'Nicholsonii'.
Photo by J. D. Vertrees

'Nigrum'.
Photo by Cor van Gelderen

son. The seven-lobed leaves are medium-sized but smaller than most amoenums. Each lobe is ovate-acuminate, ending in a sharp tip, and has finely toothed margins. The leaf stalks are short and sturdy.

This cultivar is a moderate grower and does not become as large as 'Bloodgood'. It reaches 5 m (16 ft.) in height and up to 3 m (10 ft.) in spread. It flowers and fruits readily. The winged fruits are green at first, contrasting with the deep purple-red of the foliage. Received the RHS Award of Garden Merit.

'Nishiki gasane'

PALMATUM GROUP
VARIEGATED

The pattern of variegation is very different from that found in other variegated cultivars. It is the *haki homi fu* type. The deep green leaf is speckled and flecked with yellow-gold. In most cases, the spots occur in varying amounts and concentrate along the margins. Some markings are tiny and separate, while others merge to form blotches. Occasionally, the variegation occupies almost the entire leaf. When they first unfold, the variegated new leaves have an apricot color shading from the edges into the center. This tone soon fades into the clear green and yellow-gold of the mature leaf. Fall color is a bright red.

The medium-sized leaves have five to seven ovate lobes, terminating in a long slender tip. The broad, moderately deeply divided lobes radiate openly. The two basal lobes are very small. The margins are coarsely toothed.

This upright-growing tall shrub or small tree matures up to 3 m (10 ft.) in height. As with many variegated cultivars, 'Nishiki gasane', which means "overlapping variegations," especially needs protection from hot afternoon sun to prevent severe burning of the yellow-gold variegations. 'Sagara nishiki' and 'Saintpaulianum' are synonyms.

'Nishiki gawa'

PALMATUM GROUP
GREEN

The rough pinelike bark is the outstanding feature of this maple, which is also known by the name pine bark maple. It has been likened to the bark of the Japanese black pine, *Pinus thunbergii*. The older the plant, the rougher the bark. It becomes quite corky, with coarse, longitudinal, irregular creases. This feature begins to develop in about three years. In an old plant the bark becomes very thick and convoluted.

'Nishiki gasane'.
Photo by J. D. Vertrees

'Nishiki gawa'.
Photo by Peter Gregory

This rough bark is much more pronounced in 'Nishiki gawa' than in 'Arakawa' (rough bark maple).

The small palmate leaf usually has seven lobes. The two basal lobes are very small. The elongate-ovate lobes taper to a long point and are moderately deeply divided. The margins are strongly toothed. Spring colors are light green edged with a light shading of red. Summer leaves assume a bright green color and turn to a strong yellow, then red, in the fall.

This plant is currently the only vigorous pine-bark cultivar and matures as an upright, bushy tree up to 6 m (20 ft.) tall. It is popular in Japan for bonsai and lends itself well to frequent pruning and shaping.

'Nishiki momiji'.
Photo by Ray Prag

'Novum'.
Photo by J. D. Vertrees

'Nishiki momiji'
PALMATUM GROUP
GREEN

This small-leaved cultivar develops strong, rich fall colors which are usually associated with the larger-leaved forms. The early spring leaves unfold with a pinkish or orange tone which persists along the margins as the leaves mature and turn to light green for the summer. Fall color is an especially brilliant display of crimson to fire-red. The leaves are typically five- to seven-lobed and moderately deeply divided. The long, slender, lanceolate lobes gradually taper to very sharp points. The margins are clearly toothed. The thin leaf stalks are shorter than the leaves. This upright maple forms a spreading crown and reaches a height of up to 5 m (16 ft.) at maturity.

'Novum'
AMOENUM GROUP
RED

'Novum' has medium to large leaves with five to seven lobes. The ovate lobes taper to slender, sharp points, radiate outward, and are separated at least halfway to the leaf base. The short leaf stalks are red. The spring and early summer coloration is a light purple-red. The color, which is lighter than that of 'Bloodgood' and 'Nuresagi', ranges into bright, almost orange-red tones as summer progresses. In late summer these tones blend with green-red. Fall color is an intense scarlet. This strong, upright-growing maple can reach more than 7 m (23 ft.) in height. It forms a round-topped small tree, which is hardy and vigorous.

'Novum' is widely propagated commercially because it quickly forms a good-sized saleable plant. It is probably better known in Europe under the name 'Atropurpureum Novum' and has also been known under the name 'Roscoe Red'.

'Nuresagi'

MATSUMURAE GROUP
RED

This excellent purple cultivar has large leaves with five to seven lobes which radiate strongly outward, like widely spreading fingers. Each lobe is oblong-ovate, terminating in a long, slender tip. The lobes separate almost to the leaf base. The foliage appears quite lacy. The bright red leaf stalks are short and stiff.

The deep, rich, black-purple-red is unusual. In spring and early summer the leaves appear to have an opalescence, even a bluish overtone, in a certain light. They retain the dark purple-red tones into late summer, but occasionally become suffused with a slight, deep green mottling. The veins are a strong red at this time and are a noticeable feature.

The twigs and branches are a deep maroon color, but quite overshadowed with a grayish tone. There are fine whitish vertical striations along the bark, which are a pleasant addition. This very hardy cultivar is upright and vigorous. It should not be crowded in the landscape but allowed space for full development. It may reach 6 m (20 ft.) at maturity. The name means "wet heron."

This description applies to the Western cultivar, which is very different from the green amoenum-type Japanese cultivar described in Masayoshi Yano's excellent *Book for Maples* (2003).

'Octopus'

DISSECTUM GROUP
RED

The vigorous long new shoots or "tentacles" of this attractive red dissectum arch outward and give it the name 'Octopus'. The spring leaves are pink-red with a narrow greenish midrib, becoming a darker, plum red, then coppery red with a greenish tinge along the midribs as the leaf develops in early summer. The color turns a bright crimson-red in the fall.

The deeply dissected leaves are medium to large in size. The seven lobes are themselves deeply dissected and conspicuously toothed. The teeth have many sharply pointed, hooked tips. The short, slender leaf stalks are orange-red.

This strong-growing plant grows into a broad dome with pendulous shoots and foliage, reaching up to 3 m (10 ft.) in height and 3.5 m (11 ft.) in spread. Because of the uneven growth of the current shoots, which vary between 1 m (3 ft.) and almost 2 m (6 ft.) long, the outer circumference is more irregular.

'Nuresagi'.
Photo by Peter Gregory

'Octopus'.
Photo by Peter Gregory

'Ogi nagashi'

PALMATUM GROUP
VARIEGATED

This rare cultivar has very deeply divided, five-lobed leaves which are light green with a scattering of indistinct flecks of lighter green. All markings are subdued. Occasionally, pale spots of cream or white appear, but these too are subdued. New leaves unfold a light yellow with a tint of rose along the margins, but this tint soon disappears. The fall colors are yellow and deep gold, turning to red.

The smallish leaves have mainly five ovate-acuminate, moderately deeply divided, narrow lobes which radiate outward. The margins are coarsely and conspicuously toothed, alternating deep and shallow, making a feathery edge. The slender leaf stalks and the shoots are pink to red. This strong-growing, small tree is delicate in appearance but hardy. It may reach 5 m (16 ft.) or more in height.

'Ogi-no-nagare'

PALMATUM GROUP
VARIEGATED

The light green foliage has indistinct flecks of lighter green scattered over the leaves. Occasionally, small spots of cream or white appear but these too are suppressed. New leaves unfold a light yellow with a tint of rose along the margins, but the tint soon disappears. The fall colors become a little more prominent in shades of yellow and deep gold. The small to medium-sized leaves are five-lobed and deeply divided. The ovate lobes hold their tail-like tips well apart. The margins are conspicuously toothed with the teeth alternately deep and shallow, making a feathery edge.

This strong-growing small tree is delicate in appearance but hardy and may reach 5 m (16 ft.) or more in height. The name means "stream of fans" and refers to Kyoto's famous festival where members of the ruling class tossed beautiful fans into the water, which were then collected by commoners further down the river. This cultivar has been known under the name 'Ogi nagare'. According to Yano (2003), 'Ogi-no-nagare' is a synonym of 'Ogi nagashi', but the cultivar grown in the West as 'Ogi-no-nagare' is quite different from 'Ogi nagashi'.

'Ōgon sarasa'

AMOENUM GROUP
RED

The color combination and leaf shape identify this interesting plant. Spring leaves are a brick-red brushed over the deep green base color. Each leaf varies in intensity. Also, the light green midveins are in sharp contrast to the darker lobe color. In summer, the leaves become a bronze-green. The fall colors are bright shades of orange and crimson.

The medium-sized seven-lobed leaves have a flat base and look larger because the three central lobes are large and long and the two basal lobes much smaller. The elongate-ovate lobes gradually taper to narrow points, are very deeply divided, and have sides that curve upward, forming a rounded trough. The plant forms a tall shrub, up to 7 m (23 ft.) tall and 3 m

This page:
'Ogi-no-nagare'.
Photo by J. D. Vertrees

Page 201:
'Ōgon sarasa'.
Photo by Cor van Gelderen

'Ō jishi'.
Photo by J. D. Vertrees

'Ō kagami'.
Photo by Cor van Gelderen

(10 ft.) broad. The name means "gold cal-ico cloth." This plant has also been known under the name 'Ōgona sarasa'.

'Ō jishi'

DWARF GROUP
GREEN

The well-known cultivar 'Shishigashira' refers to the mythical lion of Japanese drama and is separated into two types by the Japanese, 'Ō jishi' and 'Mejishi'. The rare 'Ō jishi', meaning "male lion," is smaller and more compact than 'Meji-shi', meaning "female lion," which is bet-ter known as the popular 'Shishigashira'. It has similar, but larger, bright green, less crinkly and more open leaves.

The green leaves are brown-tipped in the spring, becoming deep green for the summer, and turning orange to red in the fall. They are more closely arranged on the stem. The rate of growth is slow, making a very dwarf, multibranched little shrub, which grows up to 2 m (6 ft.) in height. The name has also been spelled 'Yū jishi'.

'Ō kagami'

PALMATUM GROUP
RED

The beautiful, purplish red of the new foli-age deepen into a shiny blackish red in sum-mer. It is probably this shiny, dark color that gives the cultivar its name. The strong color lasts until late summer when green tones blend in. Fall color is a bright scarlet.

The medium-sized leaves have five to seven lobes that radiate markedly, with the two basal lobes overlapping the leaf stalk like a fully extended fan. The lobes are broadly ovate, moderately deeply divided, and 1 cm wide where they join. The mar-gins are uniformly toothed. The short leaf stalks are reddish. This very desirable color form makes a delightful upright, small tree which grows to about 5 m (16 ft.) tall at maturity. The name means "mirror."

'Okukuji nishiki'
PALMATUM GROUP
VARIEGATED

This semidwarf shrub with highly variegated foliage resembles a smaller, compact form of the better-known 'Butterfly'. The leaves are quite variable in shape and strongly variegated. The whitish or cream portions are often curved or smaller than the rest of the lobe. Colors are white to cream on a powdery green background.

'Okukuji nishiki'.
Photo by Peter Gregory

'Okushimo'.
Photo by Peter Gregory

The new, small leaves may have a tinge of pink on the edges. Often entire leaves are white or cream. Fall color is red with rose pink on the whitish areas. The small leaves are mainly five-lobed with very thin stalks.

This dense, upright, tall shrub has thin, but not brittle, branches. It is not a strong-growing plant or aggressive, and blends in nicely as a companion plant, since the overall color of the foliage is light, contrasting with the dark green foliage of evergreen plants. The plant has been known under the name 'Okikoji nishiki'. 'Chirimen' is a synonym.

'Okushimo'
PALMATUM GROUP
GREEN

This very desirable cultivar has three outstanding features: odd-shaped leaves, sweeping upright growth habit, and beautiful gold fall color. The foliage is a rich green color. The small leaves are deeply divided into five to seven lobes which radiate stiffly outward. Each lobe is lanceolate and tapers to a sharp, stiff point. The most noticeable feature is that the lobe margins roll upward, almost forming a tapering tube. The margins of the inrolled lobes are slightly and bluntly notched. The ends of each lobe bend inward and upward. The stiff leaf stalks are pink-red and the shoots are green.

The shape of the tree is unusual—stiffly upright and vase-shaped. The tree is sturdy, erect, vigorous, and often reaches 8 m (26 ft.) or more tall. It forms compact bunches of leaves and fine twigs; this quality makes it adaptable to bonsai. Another feature of this cultivar is its fall color. The intense yellow and gold foliage seems almost fluorescent at times. The cultivar is very desirable for landscaping and is popular in the United States. While it can become a larger sized plant if given adequate space, it can also be kept confined to smaller plantings with pruning and shaping. The name means "pepper-and-salt-leaf maple."

It is unfortunate that some confusion has been created in the nursery trade by applying alternative names. This beautiful tree has been recorded since 1704. As it was introduced into other countries, the Japanese name was not always used. The old taxonomic descriptions placed it as *Acer palmatum* subvar. *crispum* and included the Japanese name 'Okushimo'. Unfortunately, the names 'Crispum' and 'Crispa' were used indiscriminately for this and other cultivars. 'Chirimen', 'Crested', 'Cristata', 'Cristatum', 'Frost in der Erste', 'Involutum', and 'Okustanea' are other names which have been used for this plant. 'Okushimo' has also been misspelled 'Okishima'.

'Omato'

AMOENUM GROUP
GREEN

This large-leaved maple is similar to 'Ō sakazuki'. Each of the five to seven lobes is ovate-acuminate and gradually tapers to a sharp point. The margins are sharply double-toothed. Spring foliage may have a tinge of orange-red, but the large leaves soon take on a rich green color which is fairly resistant to sunburn. Fall colors are brilliant tones of rich red, but not as intense as Ō sakazuki'. This strong-growing, round-headed tree reaches up to 8 m (26 ft.) tall and almost as wide.

'Omure yama'

MATSUMURAE GROUP
GREEN

'Omure yama' is an excellent example of the cascading or weeping type of cultivar. With increasing height the pendulous branches become willowy and form a long curtain around the perimeter of the plant. This habit is not to be confused with the cascad-

ing form of the Dissectum Group, which is almost always a low, spreading shrub.

The medium-sized leaves consist of seven long, slender lobes which are held closely together. The closed lobes along

'Omato'.
Photo by Harold Greer

'Omure yama', habit.
Photo by J. D. Vertrees

with the tendency of the leaves to hang down emphasize the pendulous effect of the branches. Each lanceolate or elongate-elliptic lobe tapers to a slender point and is separate almost to the leaf base. The lobes are less than 1 cm wide at the lobe junctions, which makes the leaf appear open near the base. The margins are deeply and finely toothed. The leaf stalks are long and slender.

The new, unfolding foliage has a bright orange cast to the leaf edges, but soon becomes a uniform, brilliant green. Fall colors are a spectacular gold and crimson. Young plants are vigorous and upright. Later they show the true pendulous character. The long, willowy shoots start upward, then bend out and down. At the same time, enough shoots continue upward to give more height. A mature tree becomes quite rounded with long, cascading side branches. In 20 years the tree reaches up to 5 m (16 ft.) with a similar spread. This cultivar is named after Mount Omure and has been known under the name 'Pendulum Omure yama'. The name has been misspelled 'Omara yama' and 'Omura yama'.

'Omure yama', fall color
Photo by J. D. Vertrees

'Orange Dream'.
Photo by Peter Gregory

'Orange Dream'

PALMATUM GROUP
GREEN

This lovely cultivar, introduced in the late 1980s by Fratelli Gilardelli Nursery, Italy, is one of the growing band of palmatums selected for their refreshing spring-colored foliage. New leaves emerge a fresh orange, quickly becoming a lemon-yellow with orange-tinged margins and tips. The plant is similar to the popular 'Katsura', but the leaves do not appear as early, so are less likely to be damaged by cold spells in early spring. Also, the leaves retain their bright yellow color for much longer, changing slowly to yellow-green, then light green later in the summer, often still with a slight reddish edging to the leaves. They become a bright yellow-gold in the fall. The slender shoots are an attractive red to light green, with only faint striations.

The medium-sized seven-lobed leaves are slightly broader than long and are deeply divided. The ovate lobes, with short, tail-like, pointed tips, narrow slightly at the lobe junctions. The margins are coarsely toothed. The short, stiff, red-tinged leaf stalks have swollen bases.

This desirable cultivar becomes an upright, bushy shrub, growing slowly at first, eventually reaching 4 m (13 ft.) in height. Like most cultivars with light-colored leaves, it is best in partial shade. It has proven to be less susceptible to drought than 'Katsura', but seems more difficult to propagate.

'Orangeola'

DISSECTUM GROUP
RED

One of the most outstanding cascading dissectums to be introduced in the 1980s, 'Orangeola' is noted for the bright, orange-red new foliage in spring. It manages to keep an orange flush on the leaves as they turn a rich red-green through the summer. This coloration is boosted by a second flush of orange leaves in midsummer, and the two-tone summer color ends with the leaves becoming dark red before turning fiery orange-red in the fall, and holding this colorful display later than most.

The large leaves have five to seven lobes which are deeply divided to the leaf base, where they are barely wider than the midribs. Each lobe is itself deeply divided into broader toothed sublobes. The lobes are wide-spreading. The short, slender red leaf stalks have hooked, swollen bases.

'Orangeola', although vigorous, is one of the smaller dissectums, barely more than 3 m (10 ft.) in height when fully grown. It is more upright and less spreading than most dissectums, forming an attractive cascading mound, usually taller than wide.

'Oregon Sunset'

MATSUMURAE GROUP
RED

This small, neat, compact, rounded bush with graceful and colorful red foliage is very suitable for the smaller landscape and container culture. It has outstanding spring and fall colors. The leaves emerge a soft red, quickly becoming plum red, and in the fall turning a vivid sunset-red.

The medium-sized leaves are deeply divided into five to seven lobes which radiate outward and forward. The elongate-ovate lobes have long, slender, tail-like

tips with lobe junctions within 1 cm of the leaf base. The margins have numerous narrowly pointed teeth. The short leaf stalks are red. The lobe tips tend to curve downward slightly like, as the Greer Gardens (Eugene, Oregon) catalog so aptly puts it, "a relaxed hand." It is a good small tree for a limited space.

'Orangeola'.
Photo by Peter Gregory

'Oregon Sunset'.
Photo by Peter Gregory

'Oridono nishiki'

PALMATUM GROUP
VARIEGATED

'Oridono nishiki' is one of the best variegates in the Palmatum Group. The medium-sized leaves have five to seven lobes and are moderately deeply divided with the lobes radiating outward. Each lobe is ovate with a long, tapering point. The margins are clearly toothed, and the leaf stalks are pink and slender.

The basic leaf color is a rich, deep, shiny green which holds very well throughout the summer. The variegations are extremely diverse. The new spring variegation is bright pink, white, cream-colored, or any combination of these, and may include various sized areas of green. Sometimes new leaves are entirely white or pink. The main impression of spring growth is pink. The pink, white, or cream markings vary from a single white spot to irregular flecks, small areas, blends, half lobes, or any combination in between. Leaf portions which are strongly variegated will curve or be sickle-shaped.

The bark of new shoots is sometimes pink or pink-striped, which distinguishes this cultivar from the similar 'Asahi zuru'. 'Oridono nishiki' is sturdy and vigorous, and forms an upright, round-topped tree of 6 m (20 ft.). The name means "rich-colored fabric of the master." This cultivar was originally introduced from Japan with the alternative name 'Versicolor', and has been misspelled 'Orido nishiki', 'Oridomo nishiki', and 'Orono nishiki'.

'Ornatum'

DISSECTUM GROUP
RED

The spring foliage is an interesting red. It is more of a bronze-red when compared with other red dissectums such as 'Crimson Queen', 'Dissectum Nigrum', or 'Inaba shidare'. The brilliant tone stands out well in the landscape. In late summer the foliage turns bronze-greenish and assumes a prominent crimson-red in the fall.

The medium-sized leaves have seven very long, thin lobes, each divided into deeply dissected side lobes, and each side lobe in turn deeply toothed. Many of the leaves do not spread widely as in 'Inaba shidare' and 'Palmatifidum'. The greenish leaf stalks are short.

Very old plants may reach 3 m (10 ft.) or more in height, creating a mounded

'Oridono nishiki'.
Photo by Peter Gregory

'Ornatum'.
Photo by J. D. Vertrees

shape with a crown spread up to 4 m (13 ft.). This very old cultivar from Europe has been popular because of its reliability and the rather distinctive foliage color. As other selections of deeper tones were made that retained their color better, its popularity waned somewhat. It still makes a good color contrast in the landscape and is hardy. It has been known under various names, such as 'Aka washi-no-o' (in part), 'Amatum', 'Dissectum Atropurpureum', 'Dissectum Ornatum', 'Ornatum Purpureum', and 'Spiderleaf'.

'Ō sakazuki'

AMOENUM GROUP
GREEN

This very famous cultivar is best known for its intense crimson fall color. Some claim it has the most intense color of all the maples. In addition, it has medium to large seven-lobed leaves and is a hardy, sturdy grower. It has been listed in catalogs since the late nineteenth century. The large leaves do not make the tree coarse-looking, but instead lend an air of orderliness. Each lobe is broadly ovate, terminating in a narrow tip. The lobes are divided about halfway to the leaf base. The two small, basal lobes cover the leaf stalk. The margins are uniformly toothed.

For most of the growing season the leaf color is a good rich green. The leaves do not burn easily. Fall coloration has been likened to a burning bush. More aptly, though, it is described as intense crimson. Even at dusk, the color seems to glow. This cultivar forms a round-topped, small tree that does not exceed 8 m (26 ft.) in height. The leaves sometimes "cup" at the base, hence the name which means "leaf like a saki cup." Received the RHS Award of Garden Merit.

There are two ways to write the kanji form for this name. "Taihai" is the other form and thus 'Taihai' is considered a syn-

onym of 'Ō sakazuki'. 'Ō sakazuki' is sometimes called 'Septemlobum Sakazuki'. 'Ō sakazuki midorime' is a synonym.

A companion cultivar, sometimes called a sister seedling, is 'Ichigyō ji'. It is just as intense a yellow or gold in the fall as 'Ō sakazuki' is crimson. These two cultivars planted together make a brilliant fall display.

'Oshio beni'

AMOENUM GROUP
RED

The color is more of an orange-red than the purple-red of similar red cultivars. The new growth is very bright, but as the

'Ō sakazuki'.
Photo by Peter Gregory

'Oshio beni'.
Photo by Peter Gregory

season advances, it becomes bronze and then a dull, reddish green. It does not retain the bright colors as well as 'Bloodgood', 'Moonfire', and 'Nuresagi', and it also tends to burn in hot sun. The fall color becomes a bright scarlet.

The medium to large leaves are seven-lobed, the lobes broadly ovate, terminating in long, sharp points, and fairly deeply divided. The margins are finely toothed. The leaf stalks are red. This sturdy, upright grower matures at up to 8 m (26 ft.) in height and has a spreading canopy. It makes a good companion tree with other cultivars for color contrast.

'Oshio beni' has been popular in the United States for many decades during which time there may have been some dilution of this cultivar name. The name is very similar to 'Oshū beni', which has an entirely different leaf shape and is widely recorded in early literature. 'Oshio beni' is mentioned in the 1898 catalog of Yokohama Nursery in Kanagawa, Japan. The name means "large red tide."

'Oshū beni'
MATSUMURAE GROUP
RED

The medium-sized leaves are separated into mainly seven lobes which are very deeply divided, almost to the leaf base. The lobes radiate forward, with the leaf base almost flat. Each lobe is elongate-ovate, almost lanceolate, and terminates in a slender, sharp tip. The margins are only faintly toothed, slightly more so toward the tip. The slender leaf stalks are greenish and are shorter than the leaves.

Spring foliage is a bright red, soon changing to maroon-red. In shade, the foliage tends to be greenish. In midsummer, the leaves become bronze or a green-red. Fall color is a bright red. This cultivar forms a short, round-topped, small tree 4 m (13 ft.) tall. It is hardy and not difficult to propagate. Ōshū beni' is very different from 'Oshio beni'. Other spellings of 'Oshū beni' are 'Oshiu beni', 'Oshyu beni', and 'Ō syu beni'.

'Oshū shidare'
MATSUMURAE GROUP
RED

This old and famous cultivar has long been a favorite in Japan. It is attractive as a small, round-headed tree with cascading form. Pendulous branches form on the outside of the plant and descend gracefully to the ground. Mature trees reach up to 5 m (16 ft.) in height and spread.

The medium-sized leaves are a strong purple-red or maroon, with a greenish cast to the undersides in summer. Fall color is a deep crimson. The lobes radiate markedly and are separated almost entirely to the base. Each is elongate-lanceolate, narrow at the base and tapering to a long, slender tip. The margins are evenly toothed.

This interestingly shaped cultivar is comparable to other pendulous forms such as the green 'Omure yama'. It does not have the type of cascading growth found in the Dissectum Group. Other spellings of this name are 'Oshiu shidare', 'Ō siu shidare', and 'Ō syu shidare'. The cultivar known in America as 'Oshū shidare' is very different

'Oshū shidare'.
Photo by J. D. Vertrees

from the plant of that name in Japan and illustrated in Masayoshi Yano's beautiful *Book for Maples* (2003). This is clearly a red dissectum.

'Oto hime'
DWARF GROUP
GREEN

This strong, dwarf cultivar has a vigorous and desirable nature. There is a fable about a queen named Otohime who reigned at the bottom of an ocean kingdom. This plant seems to be a queen of the Dwarf Group. The leaves emerge in the spring as a bright, lively yellow-green with narrow reddish edging and tips, a color maintained through the summer. Fall colors are a pleasant range of yellow through to orange and red.

The small leaves are of the typical five-lobed palmatum-type. The lobes are deeply divided and radiate out in a star-shaped manner. Each lobe is ovate-triangular, broadest at the bottom, and tapering to a sharp point. The margins are uniformly and finely toothed. The slender leaf stalks are about as long as the leaf.

This dwarf shrub is tight and dense, becoming flat-topped and much broader than high. A 10-year-old plant at Maplewood reached almost 60 cm (2 ft.) tall. 'Oto hime' lends itself to bonsai work admirably and its growth habit seems denser than the bonsai favorite 'Kiyohime'. The name means "little queen of the undersea world."

'Otome zakura'
PALMATUM GROUP
RED

This semidwarf tree has two kinds of brilliant spring leaves on the same tree. The large five- to seven-lobed leaves sometimes form on new, vigorous shoots. The lobes radiate strongly outward and are moderately deeply divided. The center lobes are rather large with the side lobes much smaller. Each lobe is generally ovate with an accentuated long, sharp point. The margins are lightly toothed.

The small leaves on older wood and less vigorous shoots are entirely different, having long, narrow lobes with almost parallel sides, only slightly broader in the middle. The margins are shallowly but strongly notched. The leaf stalks are as long as the leaves. The leaf color is a striking bright pink flame in the spring. This color holds well for several weeks, then changes to a

'Oto hime'.
Photo by Peter Gregory

'Otome zakura'.
Photo by Cor van Gelderen

maroon-red. As summer progresses, or if the leaves are shaded, green tones appear. Fall colors return to bright pink.

This cultivar is most unusual and attractive. The name has been misspelled 'Otome zakure'. According to Masayoshi Yano, 'Otome zakura' is a synonym of 'Beni komachi'.

'Palmatifidum'.
Photo by Peter Gregory

'Peaches and Cream'.
Photo by Peter Gregory

'Palmatifidum'

DISSECTUM GROUP
GREEN

The shape of the leaf lobes differs from that of other green dissectums: the lobes are just as long and narrow, but are not as deeply dissected into sublobes. The effect is a leaf which appears a little sturdier and broader, but which is just as beautiful. The large, rich, emerald green leaves have seven long, narrow, incised lobes, separated almost entirely to the leaf base. The lobes splay outward, giving a cascading effect. The foliage is green in spring and summer. Yellow, gold, and orange blend together for a very colorful fall display.

The growth is sturdy, durable, hardy, and strongly cascading. 'Palmatifidum' makes a beautiful mound-shaped plant. Older plants are often wider than tall, up to 3 m (10 ft.) in height and more than 4 m (13 ft.) in spread. Early nineteenth-century literature refers to 'Palmatifidum', but its Japanese name, 'Washi-no-o', which means "eagle's tail," can be found in the literature prior to this. There was a magnificent old plant of this cultivar at the Trompenburg Arboretum, Netherlands.

The name has been wrongly spelled 'Palmatifidium'. Other names for this cultivar are 'Dissectum Palmatifidum', 'Dissectum Paucum', and 'Paucum'.

'Peaches and Cream'

MATSUMURAE GROUP
VARIEGATED

The spring foliage of this very pretty but delicate selection emerges with a cream to greenish cream color over most of each leaf. Blended into this is a soft rose-red from the lobe tips and margins. The leaf remains pink-edged throughout the summer. The veins are conspicuous with a contrasting deep green color. In the fall, the color ranges from yellow to buff with darker tips.

The five- to seven-lobed medium-sized leaves are deeply divided. The lobes are ovate with tapered, sharply pointed tips, broadest in the middle, narrowing 5 mm at the lobe junctions. The margins are very coarsely toothed. The teeth have sharply pointed tips and point in various directions, causing the margins to be wavy and slightly crinkled, like a prickly holly leaf. The short, stout leaf stalks are green. The slender shoots are a light green.

The color patterns of this cultivar are reminiscent of 'Shigitatsu sawa', which was the seed parent, with the red form 'Beni shigitatsu sawa' as the pollen source. The lobes are more deeply divided than those of either parent and the margins more crinkled, with sharper, more pointed teeth. 'Peaches and Cream' forms a small tree or shrub about 3 m (10 ft.) in height and spread. Arnold Teese of Monbulk, Victoria, Australia, selected this cultivar in 1976, then evaluated and registered it after several years of observation.

'Pendulum Julian'

DISSECTUM GROUP
RED

The medium to large seven-lobed leaves are not quite as finely toothed on the deeply cut lobes as some other dissectums. In fact, some of the older wood produces leaves with lobes which are almost lanceolate, and with deeply cut margins, making this cultivar approach the green 'Palmatifidum'. The spring leaves are bronze-green with green veining, becoming deep purple-red in the summer. This color holds well. Gradually it changes to rusty green with a reddish undertone. In the fall, the yellow to crimson-orange combinations are quite vivid. The leaf stalks are firm and short.

This very hardy, wide-spreading plant cascades outward and then downward. Henry Hohman may have bought it from Yokohama Nursery of Kanagawa, Japan, in the early 1930s. The name has been incorrectly spelled 'Pendula Julian'. The plant has also been known under the names 'Dissectum Pendulum Julian' and 'Julian shidare'.

'Phoenix'

PALMATUM GROUP
GREEN

This outstanding Dutch spring-flowering cultivar is described as a cross between

'Pendulum Julian'.
Photo by Peter Gregory

'Phoenix'.
Photo by Peter Gregory

'Shin deshōjō' and 'Beni fushigi'. The small to medium-sized leaves emerge a bright pink-red with yellow veins, the yellow slowly expanding toward the red margins to give a long spring–early summer color display. As the yellow spreads toward the pink-red margins, the veins become greener which spreads outward until the whole leaf is a shiny green but still with traces of bronze-red margins in late summer. This forms a contrasting background to the bright pink-red new leaves emerging through the summer. The foliage then turns bright orange to red in the fall.

The five- to seven-lobed leaves are moderately deeply divided. Each lobe is ovate with a tail-like tip and toothed margins. The leaves tend to bunch together. The leaf stalks are red and the young shoots become dark red.

'Phoenix' forms a compact broad shrub, estimated to grow up to 5 m (16 ft.) tall and 2.5 m (8 ft.) wide. It was selected and named by Dick van der Maat, Netherlands.

'Pink Ballerina'
DISSECTUM GROUP
VARIEGATED

This new and very unusual variegated English dissectum arose as a sport from 'Nigrum Select'. The spring leaves emerge a dark, rich purple-red, scattered among which are whole leaves of a bright pink. These become a mixture of purple, red, and pink for the summer, with an occasional streak of green along some of the leaf lobes. Fall colors are bright red and pink. The medium to large leaves are deeply divided to the base and into coarsely cut sublobes with conspicuously hooked and sharply pointed teeth. The foliage tends to hang down, giving a cascading effect.

'Pink Ballerina' forms a tall, rounded shrub, estimated to reach up to 2.5 m (8 ft.) or so in height but not as wide-spreading as most dissectums. It makes a very attractive contrast in the garden landscape, but it is best to provide some shade during the hottest part of the day.

'Pink Filigree'
DISSECTUM GROUP
RED

This cross between 'Ornatum' and 'Stella Rossa' originated in Italy at Fratelli Gilardelli Nursery and has an unusual spring and delightful summer foliage color. The leaves emerge a unique rose pink with

'Pink Ballerina'.
Photo by Peter Gregory

'Pink Filigree'.
Photo by Cor van Gelderen

conspicuous yellow veins. In summer they become purple, making a pleasing background to the bright rose new foliage appearing throughout the summer. The leaf color is at its best in full sun and is not damaged by it. Fall color is orange-red, but not as brilliant as that of 'Ornatum'.

The medium to large leaves are similar in shape and size to those of 'Stella Rossa'. Each leaf is five- to seven-lobed and deeply divided to the leaf base. Each lobe is itself divided into deeply toothed sublobes, the base of the main lobe narrowing to little more than 1 mm. The short leaf stalks are reddish. The new vigorous shoots grow upward and outward at first, becoming pendulous to produce a cascading mound. 'Pink Filigree' assumes the same shape and size as 'Ornatum', reaching 3 m (10 ft.) or so in height.

'Pixie'

DWARF GROUP
RED

Reputed to be from a witches'-broom on 'Bloodgood', 'Pixie' has more deeply cut lobes and does not grow taller than 2 m (6 ft.). The leaves emerge a bright pink-red, becoming deep red on the upper surface, which lasts well into late summer, while the undersurface is a contrasting bronze-green. Like 'Bloodgood', the foliage turns a fiery scarlet in the fall.

The medium-sized, deeply cut five- to seven-lobed leaves have widely spreading lobes. The broadly ovate lobes are widest about the middle, with long, pointed tips, and are very deeply divided to within 5 mm of the leaf base. The small basal lobes are angled backward and outward. The margins are coarsely but regularly toothed. The short, slender, stiff leaf stalk is pink. The shoots and bark are dark red.

'Pixie' is quite vigorous when young, but slows down to form a dense many-branched, round-topped bush up to 2 m

(6 ft.) tall and no wider. It is ideal as a container plant and in the smaller garden landscape.

'Purple Ghost'

MATSUMURAE GROUP
VARIEGATED

This exciting variegate is one of the Ghost Series selected and named by Talon Buchholz, Oregon. All have leaves with a strongly contrasting network of veins against a different color background.

'Pixie'.
Photo by Peter Gregory

'Purple Ghost'.
Photo by Talon Buchholz

'Purple Ghost' is a seedling of 'Shigitatsu sawa', with the probable pollen parent of 'Kasagi yama'. The dramatic spring leaves have a deep red background to the network of contrasting, almost black veins. The summer color is a semishiny red-purple with a dark purple-red vein network and margins. The foliage turns a fiery orange to scarlet in the fall. The large, broad seven-lobed leaves are moderately deeply divided and have conspicuously sharp-toothed, attractively crumpled margins.

This semiupright, well-branched, rounded tree will reach about 4 m (13 ft.) tall and 2 m (6 ft.) or so wide. It makes a dramatic contrast or focal plant in the garden landscape.

'Purple Mask'

LINEARILOBUM GROUP
GREEN

This cultivar has straplike seven-lobed leaves which border on the Matsumurae and Linearilobum Groups and could be placed in either. It originated from a sport on the same *Acer palmatum* f. *atropurpureum* plant that yielded 'Beni shi en'. Harold Johnston, Alabama, discovered it.

The relatively small leaves (for a strapleaf) have seven deeply divided lobes. Each lobe is lanceolate to long-ovate and up to 5 mm at the broadest point in the middle or outer third of the lobe, narrowing to 1 mm at the lobe junction. The odd lobe is often curved inward or outward from the base to cross one or two others. The margins are irregularly toothed, mostly on the outer half of the lobes.

The leaves emerge purple and revert to dark green in the summer, changing back to purple in late summer before becoming yellow-orange in the fall. The short, slender leaf stalks are green and are attached to green shoots. This moderately vigorous plant forms an upright, rounded bush or tree up to 3 m (10 ft.) tall and 2 m (6 ft.) wide.

'Purpureum'

PALMATUM GROUP
RED

This old British cultivar has medium-sized leaves that are a deep purple-red when first appearing. They hold their color well into the summer, becoming a bronze-green in late summer through to fall, and then turning a bright scarlet in the fall.

The seven-lobed leaves are moderately deeply divided. The lobes are ovate with pointed tips, being broadest in the middle and narrowing slightly to about 1 cm at the lobe junctions. The distance of the lobe junctions is uneven, with the side lobe junctions nearer the leaf base than those of the central lobes. The leaf margins are evenly toothed. The small basal lobes are held more or less at right angles to the short, strong, red leaf stalks.

'Purpureum' is a slow-growing, upright cultivar, with a dense, round-headed crown, reaching 5 m (16 ft.) in height and about that in spread. It has been known under the name 'Purpureum Superbum'.

'Raraflora'

DISSECTUM GROUP
GREEN

This attractive American laceleaf has very

'Purpureum'.
Photo by Cor van Gelderen

finely and deeply cut foliage. The emerging, medium-sized leaves are a bright orange to shrimp-pink, changing to yellow-green centers with pink edging, then becoming forest green for the summer. The leaves turn a day-glow red in the fall. The leaf stalks are pink. 'Raraflora' is typically mushroom-shaped, eventually reaching 3 m (10 ft.) tall and spreading somewhat wider.

'Red Autumn Lace'
DISSECTUM GROUP
GREEN

This outstanding dissectum from Fratelli Gilardelli Nursery, Italy, is noted for the varying tones of green of the summer foliage with bronze- and red-tinged new leaves at the shoot tips. The spring leaves emerge a reddish bronze, quickly changing to a bright green for the summer. The fall color is rather special as the green leaves change through yellow to orange to vivid red.

The large, deeply divided leaves have seven lobes divided into coarsely toothed sublobes and narrowing to about 1 mm at the leaf base. The short leaf stalks are green. This cultivar forms a broad, cascading mound up to 4 m (13 ft.) tall with a spread of 5 m (16 ft.). It is very similar to 'Green Lace', but differs in its dazzling, red autumn color.

'Red Baron'
AMOENUM GROUP
RED

A small to medium-sized, broad, upright tree, 'Red Baron' was selected and named by Richard Wolff, Pennsylvania. It has medium-sized, five- to seven-lobed, moderately deeply divided leaves. The broadly ovate lobes have finely toothed margins and pointed tips. The spring leaves are red and bright pink-red, quickly changing to purple-red for the summer. Fall color is bright red. The leaves are similar in shape and color to 'Shōjō nomura'. 'Red Baron' is a reliable shorter and broader tree for the smaller garden, barely reaching 5 m (16 ft.) in height.

'Red Cloud'
LINEARILOBUM GROUP
RED

This red strapleaf, named by Talon Buchholz, Oregon, originated as a seedling from the green 'Scolopendrifolium'. It grows

'Red Autumn Lace'.
Photo by Peter Gregory

'Red Baron'.
Photo by Peter Gregory

faster than 'Red Pygmy', but is not as vigorous as 'Beni ōtake', and the medium-sized leaves are intermediate between the two.

The five to seven lobes, divided almost to the base and with slightly but distinctly toothed margins, are bright red in the spring with yellow-green midveins, changing to a purple-red which lasts all summer. Fall color is an eye-catching orange-red.

'Red Cloud' eventually forms a rounded tree up to about 4 m (13 ft.) in height, more open and wider spreading than most strapleaf cultivars. This habit combined with the long, narrow leaves gives a cloudlike effect, hence the name.

'Red Cloud'.
Photo by Peter Gregory

'Red Dragon'.
Photo by Peter Gregory

'Red Dragon'

DISSECTUM GROUP
RED

This deep purple-red dissectum, selected in 1991 at Duncan and Davies Nursery in New Zealand by Graham Roberts, keeps its deep color, in sun or shade, better than any other red dissectum, including 'Dissectum Nigrum', 'Inaba shidare', and even 'Crimson Queen'. Though the young foliage of 'Tamuke yama' is an even darker shade, it does not hold its color as well as 'Red Dragon'. The spring leaves are bright scarlet, becoming dark burgundy in early summer. This rich coloring is retained throughout the summer, changing to an outstanding flaming scarlet again in the fall.

The large, very deeply cut seven-lobed leaves are slightly wider than long. The broad lobes themselves are deeply incised right to the midrib and narrow to less than 1 mm toward the leaf base. The sublobe margins have coarse, sharply pointed and hooked double teeth. The stiff, short, slender leaf stalks are purple.

The growth habit is like a more dwarf form of 'Crimson Queen', a compact, well-branched, cascading mound, reaching 2.5 m (8 ft.) in height. 'Red Dragon' prefers full sun and tolerates frosts but needs protection from cold wind and summer drought. It makes an excellent small garden, rock garden, container or bonsai plant.

'Red Elf'

DWARF GROUP
RED

Harold Johnston, Alabama, discovered this interesting red dwarf cultivar as a sport on 'Skeeter's Broom'. It is notable for the irregularity of the lobes, which curve and twist and vary from relatively wide lobes to stringlike lobes similar to those of 'Koto-no-ito'. The central lobe is sometimes so stunted as to be almost vestigial and appearing dragonfly-shaped, up to three times as wide as it is long.

A further interesting characteristic is that the leaf blade is often held at an angle to the leaf stalk. The leaves have three to seven deeply divided, mainly narrow lobes, varying in shape from long-ovate to straplike, some cupped upward from the midrib. The teeth on the margins increase in coarseness with the size and width of the lobes. The leaves are red when given adequate light, the color persisting well into the fall. In shaded situation, the leaves green-up readily.

This unusually dwarf strapleaf is a bonsai enthusiast's or collector's plant due to its slow growth, curious leaves, and growth habit. Its mature height is estimated at up to about 1 m (3 ft.), with a similar spread.

'Red Filigree Lace'

DISSECTUM GROUP
RED

The leaves of this outstanding red dissectum must be seen to be appreciated: they are among the most finely cut of all laceleaf maples. The uniform color is a deep purple-red or maroon and it persists extremely well throughout the entire growing season. In the fall the foliage becomes a bright crimson.

The medium-sized leaves are seven-lobed. Each lobe is extremely lacy, being more delicately dissected than the type, the center of the lobe being no wider than the midrib and 1 mm or less. The dissected side portions are equally fine and are interspersed with sharp, toothlike divisions. With these finely double-dissected lobes lying close together, the effect is certainly filigree-like. The leaf stalks are short and stiff.

The pendulous habit is typical of most dissectums. The overall effect is one of extreme beauty. The rate of growth is not as fast as most other dissectums. This cultivar is considered one of the most beautiful and unusual introductions of the Dissectum group. 'Ruby Lace' is very similar to 'Red Filigree Lace', and it is very difficult to pick out the differences, if any, between them. 'Red Filigree Lace' has also been available as 'Red Lace'. 'Beni saihō shidare' is a synonym.

'Red Filigree Lace'.
Photo by Peter Gregory

'Red Filigree Lace' was a chance seedling grown by William Curtis, Oregon. As a yearling it was given to William Goddard, British Columbia. Goddard cultured and nurtured the plant for a number of years and finally sold it to John Mitsch, Oregon. In the late 1980s the plants and ownership were transferred to Iseli Nursery, Oregon, which built up stock and distributed it to growers and collectors. Iseli Nursery found stick budding was the best way to propagate this cultivar because of the smallness and thinness of the scion material. It was very fortunate that this plant was not lost, for it adds greatly to this magnificent series of cultivars.

'Red Flash'.
Photo by Cor van Gelderen

'Red Pygmy'.
Photo by Cor van Gelderen

'Red Flash'

AMOENUM GROUP
RED

The very vivid red spring foliage turns a dark purple-red and holds its color well throughout the summer, especially in full sun. The leaves become green-hued by late summer. All new leaves appearing during the summer have the vivid red of the spring foliage and contrast well with the darker red background of older leaves.

The large leaves are five- to seven-lobed and are deeply divided. Each lobe is ovate with a pointed tip. The margins are finely and evenly toothed. The strong, short leaf stalks are red. This moderately strong grower reaches only 5 m (16 ft.) in height and so is suitable for smaller gardens. It is often multistemmed and forms a medium-sized upright bush or tree. 'Red Flash' originated at Fratelli Gilardelli Nursery, Italy.

'Red Pygmy'

LINEARILOBUM GROUP
RED

This excellent red cultivar from the Netherlands is superior to 'Atrolineare', the standard cultivar. The large red or bright red-maroon leaves have mainly seven lobes. The long, straplike lobes separate entirely to the leaf base. The effect of these delicate leaves is lacelike. The leaf stalks are short. The spring and early summer color of red-maroon holds quite well through the hot weather. In late summer, it deepens into a more purplish tone. In direct sun it bronzes with green undertones somewhat late in the season. The color holds much better and sunburns less than the standard cultivar 'Atrolineare'. The young shoots are red.

Older plants tend to broaden and become round-topped, and are smaller and less upright or rangy than other linearilobums, such as 'Atrolineare'. They reach up to 3 m (10 ft.) high and wide.

'Red Pygmy' makes a delightful contrast in shape and tone when combined with other forms. Firma C. Esveld, Netherlands, initially recognized the value of this form, which they named, propagated, and introduced. Received the RHS Award of Garden Merit. The original material came from an unnamed plant in an old garden in northern Italy.

'Red Spider'
LINEARILOBUM GROUP
RED

This Canadian cultivar has remarkably uniform leaves in shape, size, and color. They are an even, robust red which lasts into the fall, when the color changes to a vibrant sanguine-red. The medium-sized five-lobed, straplike leaves have the basal lobes stretched outward to form a flat leaf base, or are angled slightly forward. The long-ovate lobes are chunkier than the lobes of most strapleaf maples and are unusual in having numerous, fine, sharp-tipped teeth along the entire margins. 'Red Spider' forms an upright, small tree, reaching 4 m (13 ft.) or so tall, with horizontal branches whose tips tend to curve down to give a spiderlike but graceful lacy effect.

'Red Spray'
AMOENUM GROUP
RED

Similar in leaf color and growth habit to the well-known 'Bloodgood', 'Red Spray' appears to be more vigorous than most other red-leaved *Acer palmatum* cultivars. The large spring leaves are a bright pink-red, deepening to purple-red, and holding this color well through the summer. The foliage turns a fiery orange-red in the fall. The stiff leaf stalks and shoots are bright red. The five- to seven-lobed leaves are moderately deeply divided, but lobe division may vary on individual leaves, with the division shallower on the central lobes. Each lobe is mostly broadly ovate, with a long, pointed tip and finely toothed margins. 'Red Spray' attains a height of 12 m (40 ft.) or more, so is suitable for larger gardens.

'Red Wood'
PALMATUM GROUP
GREEN

This attractive winter bark cultivar, selected by Edward Wood and named by Talon Buchholz of Oregon, has red shoots, similar to those of the popular 'Sango kaku', but holding their color for two or more years. The smallish five- to seven-lobed leaves are also the same shape and size as those of 'Sango kaku'. They are a light yellow-green in the spring, becoming a fresh green for summer, then turning a golden yellow, tinged pink and red in the fall. 'Red Wood'

'Red Spider'
Photo by Harold Greer

'Red Spray'.
Photo by Peter Gregory

forms an upright, vase-shaped tree up to 4 m (13 ft.) tall. It makes an excellent landscape and container plant.

'Reticulatum Como'
MATSUMURAE GROUP
VARIEGATED

Similar to the leaves of 'Shigitatsu sawa', the leaves of this Australia variegate have a lovely pink to cream background with a mid to dark green network of veins in the spring. As the leaves mature, the background color becomes a light cream-green. The very large seven- to nine-lobed leaves divide only a third to halfway to the leaf base and so provide a large surface for the colorful fall display of salmon-pink. The leaf stalks are red merging into the red-brown young shoots, which become light brown by the end of the year.

Like most of the 'Shigitatsu sawa' group, the tree needs some protection from hot sun and cold winds. Because Latinized cultivar names became illegal after 1959, this desirable variegate should be re-named.

'Rokugatsu en nishiki'
PALMATUM GROUP
VARIEGATED

This strongly variegated Japanese cultivar has typical palmatum-type leaves with the white patchy variegation on a midgreen background. The new leaves emerge a bright pink in the spring, becoming green with white variegation for the summer, then turning yellow and red in the fall. The variegation can occupy the whole leaf or be totally absent and every stage between.

'Rokugatsu en nishiki' is a very promising addition to the 'Asahi zuru' group, with its abundant variegation contrasting with the bright red leaf stalks and shoots. 'Hana kanzashi' and 'Ashitaka nishiki' are synonymous.

'Royle'

DWARF GROUP
RED

This striking red dwarf is thought to have come from a witches'-broom on *Acer palmatum* f. *atropurpureum*. It was found by Joseph Stupka and named by William Schwartz after his wife's family. Its main features are the irregularly shaped leaves, small globelike habit, and striking autumn color.

The small five- to seven-lobed leaves are divided almost to the base. Each long, narrow-ovate lobe has a long, pointed tip and coarsely toothed margins. Many of the lobes curve sideways or downward, and some of the center lobes are shortened and rounded, or may be irregularly shaped. The short leaf stalks are red. Spring foliage is a bright pink-red, which gradually changes to red, then purple-red for the summer. Fall color is a brilliant crimson.

'Royle' grows slowly into a small, very dense, compact, round shrub, reaching about 1.5 m (5 ft.) tall and almost as wide. It is hardy, reliable, and ideal for the small garden and container culture. The name has been misspelled 'Royal' and 'Royale'.

'Rubrifolium'

DISSECTUM GROUP
RED

The leaf color is a different red from most of the purple-reds of the Dissectum Group. It is more a brown-red or rust-red, with conspicuous green main veins. This color is retained well into the summer and then changes to a rich, dark reddish green. In the fall the leaves become a rich gold with occasional crimson edges.

The medium to large leaves are typically double pinnatifid. The leaf stalks and slender shoots are red. The tree bark is a powdery green with minute white striations. This fairly strong-growing dissectum develops the typical dome shape, reaching 3 m (10 ft.) in height. It grows fairly fast and becomes pendulous with maturity.

'Rubrifolium' is one of the lesser-known cultivars, yet it has been known under several names, including 'Adlerschwanz', 'Akashigata' (Akashi Bay), 'Dissectum Rubellum', 'Dissectum Rubrifolium', 'Dissectum Tinctum', and 'Rubellum'. The name 'Rubrifolium' is preferred to 'Akashigata' because it has been an established name in Western culture for about a century.

Page 220:
'Red Wood'.
Photo by Harold Greer

'Reticulatum Como'.
Photo by Peter Gregory

This page:
'Rokugatsu en nishiki'.
Photo by Peter Gregory

'Royle'.
Photo by Peter Gregory

'Rubrifolium' is also preferred to 'Dissectum Rubrifolium' because Friedrich A. W. Miquel was referring to a wild form when he originally named *Acer palmatum* f. *dissectum rubrifolium*, and so it seems unlikely that it could be the clone Ferdinand Pax named as 'Rubrifolium'. Furthermore, 'Dissectum Rubrifolium' is included under 'Rubrifolium' because its description is so similar that it would be difficult to differentiate the two. The only observable difference appears to be that the leaves have a greenish tinge with a light edging of red in 'Dissectum Rubrum'. Although Ferdinand Pax attributed the name 'Washi-no-o' to this red dissectum, the former is grown in Japan and described in the Japanese literature as a green dissectum.

'Rubrum'

AMOENUM GROUP
RED

The medium to large leaves are divided into seven broad, ovate lobes, separated more than halfway to the leaf base. Each lobe tapers to a sharp point and has slightly toothed margins. The leaves are a dark maroon-red. The color is lighter as they first unfold, but assumes the very rich tones in late spring and into summer. In late summer the leaves turn green-red or bronze. Fall color is a strong crimson. The short leaf stalks are a dark purple-red.

This strong-growing, upright tree has a broadly spreading crown as it matures. It reaches 4 m (13 ft.) tall and more in width. Some early references equate this cultivar with 'Sanguineum', but 'Rubrum' is consistently darker in color. It has also been known under the name 'Septemlobum Rubrum'.

'Ruby Ridge'

MATSUMURAE GROUP
RED

Introduced and named by Buchholz and Buchholz Nursery, Oregon, this cultivar has possibly the darkest red foliage of any Japanese maple. The new leaves emerge a bright pink-red which gradually darkens, becoming a dark purple-red for the summer with green midribs and a slight sheen on the upper surface. By late summer, the green tends to spread. Fall colors range through the oranges and reds.

The medium-sized leaves are seven-lobed and deeply divided. Each lobe is roughly ovate with a tail-like pointed tip and coarse, unevenly toothed margins. The lobes are undulate and partly curved in various directions, as if each is doing its own thing. The small pair of basal lobes often point back down the leaf stalk.

'Rubrum'.
Photo by J. D. Vertrees

'Ruby Ridge'.
Photo by Talon Buchholz

'Ruby Ridge' forms a compact upright tree and grows up to 2 m (6 ft.) or so tall and half as broad in 10 years. 'Crumple Leaf' is probably a synonym.

'Rufescens'

PALMATUM GROUP
RED

The color of 'Rufescens' is rather distinctive when grown near other red cultivars. The unfolding leaves are quite bright and the rufous (brownish) color becomes strong as the leaves mature. Later in the season, green tones appear. Good fall colors of orange and crimson develop.

The medium-sized leaves have mainly nine lobes which are moderately deeply divided. Each lobe is elongate-elliptic, gradually tapering to a slender, sharp point. The lobes are only 1.0–1.5 cm wide in the middle. The long center lobes tend to hold closely together. The margins are distinctly toothed. The slender leaf stalks are about as long as the leaves.

This cultivar is not vigorous, but forms a tall bush of 5 m (16 ft.). Although described by J. A. Siesmayer in 1888, it is not widely known. Unfortunately, the name 'Rufescens' has been applied to different clones at different times, so there is uncertainty about some specimens in collections.

'Rugose'

MATSUMURAE GROUP
GREEN

This somewhat peculiar, large-leaved cultivar, although it cannot be classed as beautiful, is of interest because it is unusual and because of the dramatic change from an ugly duckling in summer to an almost beautiful princess in the fall. The leaves are of a dull bronzed, army green, with somewhat rough, wrinkled (rugose) surfaces for most of the summer, but with contrasting beet-red midveins and leaf stalks. The leaves change to a stunning plum red to

bright crimson in the fall. The shoots and branches are almost black.

The shape of the medium-sized to large leaves is decidedly non-uniform. No two leaves are the same shape and size. Though mostly five- to seven-lobed, occasionally a leaf may have one full lobe plus two rudimentary basal lobes. Some lobes are almost straplike, but many are broad-ovate, with tail-like tips and coarse, uneven-toothed margins. Lobes, even on the same leaf, are irregularly incised, mostly almost to the leaf base. The sturdy leaf stalks are shorter than the leaves. Like the leaves, the shoots can also twist and do strange things.

Shrubby and upright in habit, this plant

'Rufescens'.
Photo by Peter Gregory

'Rugose'.
Photo by J. D. Vertrees

has an interesting way of twisting both the stem and branch as it grows; not enough to be called "tortuosa," but enough to be noticed. This cultivar was selected and named at Maplewood Nursery. The original seeding is growing at Mountain Maples Nursery, California. The name has been misspelled 'Rugosa'.

'Ryoku ryū'
PALMATUM GROUP
GREEN

Imported from Japan to the Netherlands in 1991, this green semidwarf has small leaves with mainly five, slightly misshapen, slender lobes. The lobes are quite distinctive, and one or two may be missing on some leaves. The spring leaves are pink-red, changing to fresh green from the center, and becoming midgreen for the summer. Fall colors range from orange to red.

The leaves are deeply divided, almost to the base, long-ovate with coarse, irregu-lar toothed margins. The small basal lobes mostly point forward to form a triangular leaf base. The long, triangular, slender leaf stalks are light green to yellow-green. 'Ryoku ryū' forms a densely upright shrub, up to 2.5 m (8 ft.) in height.

'Ryūmon nishiki'
PALMATUM GROUP
VARIEGATED

The green foliage has white or yellowish irregular areas composed of small markings. The new growth in the spring develops with reddish or pinkish tones. Sometimes the new growth (including new shoots) is quite pink, but less so than with certain other cultivars. Later the leaves tend to become dull and the variegations less pronounced. The medium-sized leaves are flat-surfaced with five to seven irregular lobes, which are not uniformly separated or divided, so that they vary somewhat in size. This upright-growing small

'Ryūmon nishiki'.
Photo by Peter Gregory

'Ryū sei'.
Photo by Talon Buchholz

tree or tall bush probably does not exceed 3 m (10 ft.) at maturity. The growth is rather twiggy and multibranched.

'Ryū sei'

PALMATUM GROUP
GREEN

Like 'Jirō shidare', this new, unusual cultivar from the famous Kobayashi Nursery in Angyo, Japan, carries the pairs of typical palmatum-type leaves spread far apart on the very slender, cascading shoots, which reach down to the ground. The new leaves emerge yellow-green, soon becoming a deeper green for the summer, then turning an attractive orange to red in the fall. The medium-sized five- to seven-lobed, deeply divided leaves are on very slender leaf stalks, contrasting with the very long green cascading shoots.

'Ryū sei' forms an upright, weeping mound estimated to reach 3 m (10 ft.) when fully grown. It makes an attractive contrast in the garden landscape with the usual-shaped maples and the wider-spreading dissectums.

'Ryūzu'

DWARF GROUP
GREEN

This delightful compact shrub is popular for bonsai as well as for the rock garden. It reaches little more than 2 m (6 ft.) at maturity. The leaves are tightly spaced, overlapping, and bunched, giving rise to the name "ornamental dragon's head."

The spring leaves have a faint shade of pink overlying the pale green. The pink soon disappears and the mature leaf is green. The margins are very prominently toothed. The tips of these teeth are often bright brick red, but the color does not come into the leaf. The foliage turns a stunning fall color of warm orange-yellow. The leaf has five to seven lobes which radiate openly. Each lobe is ovate, but gradu-

ally tapers to a long, sharp point. The edges of the lobes bend slightly upward, almost making a shallow trough. The stiff leaf stalks are only about 1 cm long.

Bill Schwartz of Green Mansions Nursery, Pennsylvania, an expert on brooms and dwarf maples, describes the leaves as ironed out 'Shishigashira' leaves and the plant shape as a flattened globe.

'Samidare'

AMOENUM GROUP
GREEN

When first unfolding in spring, the large leaves are almost pink. Quite soon they turn a rich green with margins a light reddish tone. The deep green holds well

'Ryūzu'.
Photo by Peter Gregory

'Samidare'.
Photo by Peter Gregory

without burning, even in full sun. In the fall a gold-green center develops, with the lobes turning purplish, and with gold and crimson blend in different leaves.

The leaves are mainly seven-lobed, the broadly ovate lobes radiating sharply outward and terminating in blunt tips. They are shallowly divided, making a large, palm-shaped leaf. The margins are very finely toothed, almost smooth. The leaf stalks are slender and stiff.

This hardy cultivar has thick, stiff shoots and young branches. It grows rapidly and upright at first, but soon makes a short, broad tree as it slows down. It eventually reaches up to 6 m (20 ft.) high and wide. It is a very durable garden plant which adds good color. The name means "early spring rain."

'Sandra'

DWARF GROUP
GREEN

This very low Dutch dwarf forms a dense round shrub under 1 m (3 ft.) or so in height. Its small palmatum-type five- to seven-lobed leaves are very deeply divided. The narrow lobes are long-ovate with tail-like tips and conspicuously toothed margins. The spring leaves are a bright coppery red with green midveins, the green spread-

'Sandra'.
Photo by Peter Gregory

ing outward to occupy the whole leaf by midsummer. Fall color is orange-red. 'Sandra' was selected and named by Dick van der Maat, Netherlands. It is ideally suited for alpine gardens and bonsai culture.

'Sango kaku'

PALMATUM GROUP
GREEN

The brilliant coral color of the bark is the outstanding feature of this maple and gives it its name, which means "coral tower." At times the color becomes almost fluorescent. The younger the wood, the stronger the color. The tones brighten in the fall and then intensify as winter approaches. The color is especially striking in snow.

The small typical palmatum-type leaves have five to seven ovate-acuminate lobes that taper to a sharp point. The margins are toothed. In the spring the light yellow-green leaves have strong reddish margins, giving the tree a striking appearance. As summer approaches, the foliage becomes a bright, light green. The color turns to yellow-gold in the fall, with a blend of apricot and light red.

This upright-growing tree gradually spreads at the top as it ages. It makes a fine-shaped specimen for landscaping since it attains a height of 8 m (26 ft.) or more and broadens to about 6 m (20 ft.). As an accent tree it offers size, good form, interesting seasonal foliage changes, and outstanding bark color in winter. Planted near the contrasting green-barked 'Aoyagi', the red-barked 'Sango kaku' makes a striking color combination for winter accent. Received the RHS Award of Garden Merit.

This cultivar used to be well known by the name 'Senkaki', which is now a synonym. 'Ebi-no-hige' is the Japanese synonym of this cultivar. It has also been known under the names 'Cinnabarinum', 'Cinnabar Wood Maple' and 'Coral Bark Maple'. In some areas it has been called

'Corallinum' because of the bark color. That name rightfully belongs to an entirely different cultivar, noted for its brilliant pink-red spring foliage.

'Sanguineum'
PALMATUM GROUP
RED

This name has been applied so variously by authors during the nomenclatural history that its proper use is clouded and impossible to unravel. Primarily it has been applied to a selection of *Acer palmatum* f. *purpureum* with blood-red or orange-red spring color, rather than the darker or maroon-red tones. Since Charles Lemaire described it in 1867 as a "blood-red selection," some commercial nurseries have apparently propagated different forms, for variations under the name 'Sanguineum' are found in collections. Hence, the name should no longer be used, especially as several excellent red palmatum cultivars are available. Other names by which this plant have been known are 'Latifolium Purpureum', 'Rubrolatifolium', and 'Septemlobum Sanguineum'.

'Saoshika'
AMOENUM GROUP
GREEN

The star-shaped, bright green foliage of this cultivar, when backlit by the sun, appears almost transparent. The leaves are held out horizontally, making a layered effect in older portions of the plant. The new foliage is a bright yellow-green, with the tips of the lobes tinged in red or carmine. The leaves

'Sango kaku',
winter shoots.
Photo by J. D. Vertrees

'Sango kaku', fall color.
Photo by J. D. Vertrees

then gradually change to a uniform light green. As summer advances, the tones darken. The fall color is a striking golden yellow.

The medium-sized five- to seven-lobed leaves have short leaf stalks. Each lobe radiates outward, is broadly ovate, and terminates in a sharp point. The lobes are divided up to midway toward the leaf base. The margins are lightly toothed.

This plant does not have a strongly upright habit but makes more of a bushy shrub. When mature, it reaches up to 3 m (10 ft.) high and wide. The older twigs have a bright green bark. The name means "small male Japanese deer." 'Saoshika' was also known under the name 'Ogashika'.

'Saotome'

PALMATUM GROUP
GREEN

This small-leaved cultivar forms a semi-dwarf, bush-shaped plant, maturing at 3 m (10 ft.) tall. The leaves are a pale yellow-green with a rather thin texture and a rusty red on the edges, becoming mid to dark green as summer progresses, and turning bright red in the fall. Each leaf is deeply divided into five lanceolate lobes which terminate in long, slender, sharp tips. The two basal lobes often have tiny spur lobes. The lobe edges bend slightly upward, and the margins are irregularly toothed. The name means "rice-planting girl."

'Satsuki beni'

AMOENUM GROUP
GREEN

This strong, upright tree has very good fall color. The foliage gives a sturdy appearance, the medium to large leaves being almost circular in effect. With a broader center, the seven short lobes are shallowly divided. Each lobe has a short, sharp tip. The edges have extremely fine teeth. Spring color is a light green, with reddish bronze leaf tips, becoming completely green for the summer. Fall is the significant time, when the tree turns brightly colored with flame and crimson foliage. 'Satsuki beni' makes a good background tree in the landscape. It probably reaches 8 m (26 ft.) in 20 years. The name is sometimes spelled 'Satzuki beni'.

'Sawa chidori'

MATSUMURAE GROUP
VARIEGATED

This attractive, but rather delicate Japanese introduction belongs to group of variegates with reticulated veins that includes 'Shigitatsu sawa' and the Ghost Series. The medium to large, mainly seven-lobed leaves are held stiffly outward. The very deeply divided oval lobes narrow like a bottleneck toward the base and have long, tail-like tips and crinkled, coarsely toothed margins.

Emerging with delicate blush pink shades, the early spring leaves are darkest toward the margins and tips, becoming pink, blushed amber with a green network of veins. In summer the leaves become creamy white with a darker green network and green margins, often with persisting pink traces. Fall color is bright red.

This striking cultivar develops into a small to medium-sized, bushy tree, and needs some protection from hot sun and drying winds. The name means "marsh plover."

'Sazanami'

MATSUMURAE GROUP
GREEN

The sharp-pointed leaves create the unusual impression given by this plant. They are seven-lobed and rather small. The lobes are deeply divided toward the leaf base, which is flat. The margins are distinctly and sharply toothed. The spring color is an interesting light orange-red, with the center veins a contrasting very light green. The color becomes a rich green, from the center, for summer. Fall colors are strong, gold blends.

This rather slow-growing but hardy cultivar forms a large, compact bush, eventually reaching 6 m (20 ft.) tall and half as wide. It is not common in collections, but is a charming plant because of the leaf shape. The Japanese point out that the shade pattern of the leaves on the ground is most delightful. The name means "ruffles."

Page 228:
'Saoshika', summer color.
Photo by Peter Gregory

'Saoshika', fall color.
Photo by Daniel Otis

'Satsuki beni'.
Photo by Peter Gregory

This page:
'Sawa chidori'.
Photo by Peter Gregory

'Sazanami'.
Photo by J. D. Vertrees

'Seigai'

MATSUMURAE GROUP
RED

The brilliant scarlet spring foliage is the most attractive feature of this cultivar. The smallish leaves are mainly five-lobed, each lobe narrowing rapidly to a sharp point, and with toothed margins. The lobes are fairly deeply divided. The spring leaves give a brilliant show of bright crimson with the midveins a contrasting yellow. These colors remain for about a month. In early summer the leaves change to a bronze-green and continue into the blue-green of summer. Bright colors become prominent again in the flame-red tones of the fall.

This hardy cultivar eventually makes a small upright tree or large shrub up to 4 m (13 ft.) tall. Because of its tendency to produce short, twiggy growth, it is quite popular for bonsai. It tends to be difficult to propagate. The name means "blue-green cliff."

'Seigai' is identical to 'Akaji nishiki' and is listed under both names in early literature. It was recorded as early as 1710 in *Zōho Chikinshō*. Because 'Akaji nishiki' is sometimes confused with the similarly named 'Akikaze nishiki' (it is not variegated as the word *nishiki* implies) and because Japanese nurserymen usually use 'Seigai', the latter name is to be preferred. 'Seigaiha' and 'Sekaiha' are also synonyms of this cultivar. 'Seigai' has had many, unfortunate misnomers in the United states. References can be found equating it with 'Chisio', 'Corallinum', 'Crispa', 'Crispum', 'Cristata', 'Cristatum', 'Okushimo', and 'Sanguineum Seigai'. It is better known in the United States as 'Bonfire'. The very similar name 'Seigen' represents a separate cultivar, which is more compact with daintier leaves turning yellow in the fall.

'Seigen'

DWARF GROUP
GREEN

'Seigen' is among the most popular cultivars of the group that develops crimson foliage in the spring, but it is one of the first in that group to produce leaves, and hence is susceptible to cold winds and spring frosts. The new leaves range into the bright, fire-red tones which last for several weeks and are similar to the popular 'Corallinum', but are a pinker red. They then develop a light green color for summer. Fall colors range from yellow to persimmon.

The small five-lobed leaves appear dainty and are held close together on the short branches. The lobes are fairly deeply divided, and the margins are lightly toothed. The leaf stalks are stiff and short.

'Seigai'.
Photo by Peter Gregory

'Seigen'.
Photo by Harry Olsen

This dwarf plant is similar to 'Tama hime' and 'Kiyohime'. It forms a small, rounded bush up to 2 m (6 ft.) in height. 'Seigen' is very popular for bonsai in Japan because it is dwarf and multibranched. The crimson spring foliage gives added value to the bonsai plant. This cultivar has also been known under the name 'Seika ha' and, more recently, 'Carmineum'. The name 'Seigen' means "dark blue-green."

'Seiryū'
PALMATUM GROUP
DISSECTUM GROUP
GREEN

It is unusual to see an upright-growing dissectum. Almost all other dissectums cascade or weep. Leaves are a pleasing bright green. Each leaf is yellow-green and tipped with reddish tones as it unfolds in the spring. The color soon changes to a uniform light green, though later in summer, on exposed leaves, the reddish tones reappear on the margins. Fall colors are quite spectacular and range from strong gold to light yellows with a suffusion of crimson.

The small leaves are slightly smaller and chunkier than those of most other green dissectums. The even lobes are pinnately dissected into sublobes, but are not as finely cut as typical dissectums, although more so than 'Palmatifidum'. The leaf stalks are short and stiff. The bark is a dark, brown-green.

The upright growth is quite strong but not overly vigorous. The new shoots are stiff, not willowy. This desirable plant may reach 7 m (23 ft.) in height and 4 m (13 ft.) in spread. Its upright habit makes it a delightful addition to the garden landscape and offers a pleasing contrast when planted among cascading dissectums. The name means "blue-green dragon." Received the RHS Award of Garden Merit.

'Seiun kaku'
PALMATUM GROUP
GREEN

This upright, flat-topped shrub, growing up to 3 m (10 ft.) tall, is like a vigorous form of the dwarf 'Mikawa yatsubusa'. Its smallish, very deeply divided, mainly five-lobed leaves are similar. They are long-ovate with long, pointed tips and coarsely toothed margins. The center lobe is the longest. Like 'Mikawa yatsubusa', the leaves overlap like the shingles on a roof. The spring leaves emerge a light yellowish green, quickly changing to dark green for the summer and turning a splendid red in the fall. 'Seiun kaku' makes an attractive addition to the small garden. The name means

'Seiryū'.
Photo by Peter Gregory

'Seiun kaku'.
Photo by Peter Gregory

"blue-green palace in the clouds" and has also been spelled 'Seiwen kaku'.

'Sekimori'

DISSECTUM GROUP
GREEN

The leaf shape and color set this cultivar apart. Also the bark is a delightful green, which lasts quite well on the older branches and limbs. The green has a faint whitish dusting and distinct, lengthwise, white striations. The fall color is one of the best bright yellow-gold combinations of the green dissectums.

The deep green, medium-sized leaves have seven to nine lobes. They tend to hang down slightly and fold together, so the leaf spread appears narrower. Each of the lobes is deeply but uniformly pinnatifid, but not as finely cut as the typical dissectum. This feature gives the leaf an appearance of more substance. It does not have the coarse cut of 'Palmatifidum'. The basal quarter of each lobe is little more than the width of the midrib. The lobes look more feathery, while other green dissectums look more lacy.

'Sekimori' is a strong, hardy plant. Growth on young shoots can be vigorous, forming a nicely shaped bush in a short time. The plant reaches a height of 3 m (10 ft.) and a width of 5 m (16 ft.) at maturity. The cascading branches go out and down. The top shoots can be trained to give the plant more height from which to cascade more beautifully. Planting this cultivar on a slope enhances its beauty. The name may mean "bride's escort."

'Sekka yatsubusa'

PALMATUM GROUP
GREEN

'Sekka yatsubusa' differs from the other palmatums in having narrower lobes. The five lobes are long-ovate with gradually tapering tips and are broadest in the lower third. The lobes are very deeply separated. The margins are sharply toothed and the tiny tip of each tooth turns slightly upward, giving the lobe edges a slightly crinkled appearance. Sometimes the two basal lobes are so small that the leaves appear only three-lobed. The red leaf stalks are slender and short, but the shoots are stout. The small leaves have a shiny, deep green color. The new growth is edged with a rust color.

This small plant takes full sun quite well. The fall colors range into the yellow tones. The leaf nodes are close together, and the foliage is rather bunched. The plant reaches 3 m (10 ft.) when mature. It is hardy and

'Sekimori'.
Photo by J. D. Vertrees

'Sekka yatsubusa'.
Photo by J. D. Vertrees

offers the choice of another small shrub for rock gardens, bonsai, and small plantings. It has also been known with the name reversed, 'Yatsubusa sekka'.

'Semi-no-hane'

MATSUMURAE GROUP
RED

This vigorous tree of medium size and spreading habit has large and variable foliage, but even the large leaves are not massive in appearance, due to the feathery nature of the lobes. They are separated almost entirely to the leaf base and are long-ovate with long, tapering tips. Each distinctly separated lobe is toothed on the margins to give a delicate edging.

New growth is rusty red which is quite variable, depending on the degree of exposure to full sun. By midsummer the leaves become brown-red, blushed green. Fall colors are strong and vary from yellow to burnt orange.

While it grows as an upright tree, 'Semi-no-hane' does have a tendency to spread and become a broad, medium-sized plant. It is vigorous, but not aggressive. The texture is pleasant in the landscape and gives an unusual effect. The name, which means "wing of the cicada," has also been misspelled 'Seme-no-hane'.

'Shaina'

PALMATUM GROUP
RED

This compact, upright, round-leaved cultivar concentrates its dark maroon-red leaves in dense tufts or clusters at the ends of the short shoots. Its deeply divided leaves emerge a bright red in the spring, become a dark maroon-red for the summer, and turn bright crimson in the fall. They hold the deep color well throughout the summer and early fall.

The five-lobed leaves are very deeply

'Semi-no-hane', fall color.
Photo by Peter Gregory

'Semi-no-hane', summer color.
Photo by Peter Gregory

'Shaina'.
Photo by Peter Gregory

divided into narrow, long-ovate lobes with pointed tips, except that many of the center lobes are shortened with rounded tips—a characteristic of many cultivars originating from witches'-brooms. The shoots are vigorous in young plants, but become shorter and thicker when established.

The plant forms a dense, globe-shaped shrub, eventually up to 3 m (10 ft.) or more tall, and is ideal for container culture and rock gardens. Richard P. Wolff of Red Maple Nursery, Pennsylvania, discovered a witches'-broom on a 100-year-old, 15-m (49-ft.) tall *Acer palmatum* f. *atropurpureum* in the early 1980s, propagated it, and in 1984 named it 'Shaina'. It has proved to be very reliable and popular.

'Sharp's Pygmy'.
Photo by Peter Gregory

'Sherwood Flame'.
Photo by J. D. Vertrees

'Sharp's Pygmy'

PALMATUM GROUP
GREEN

This outstanding cultivar is one of the smallest palmatum cultivars, but is not a dwarf as originally supposed. Jimmy Sharp first noticed it as a chance seedling in the early 1980s and propagated it at his nursery in Oregon.

The small five-lobed leaves have narrow lobes, almost straplike, very deeply divided, and broadest in the lower third. The margins have coarse, broad teeth. The center lobe is always much longer than the others. The three middle lobes are close together and point forward while the small basal lobes are held more or less at right angles to the leaf stalk, so that the leaf is distinctly longer than it is wide. The lobe tips tend to turn down. The short, slender leaf stalks and shoots are green. The green leaves turn a deep orange to scarlet in the fall.

'Sharp's Pygmy' forms a densely foliaged, compact, low-spreading tree, up to 3 m (10 ft.) tall. It needs no pruning or training to give it a bonsai-like appearance. It is a truly remarkable dwarf.

'Sherwood Flame'

MATSUMURAE GROUP
RED

The beautiful leaves are a rich, reddish purple color, approaching burgundy. The color remains very strong until the end of the summer, then fading slightly to red-green. This cultivar holds its color better than most similar cultivars of the Matsumurae Group.

The medium-sized leaves are seven-lobed. The lobes are divided almost to the leaf base and tend to hold together slightly so that the leaf appears longer than wide. The lobes are elongate-ovate, quite narrow at the lobe junctions, with the outer ends tapering to very long, sharp points. The margins are deeply and regularly toothed. The leaf stalks are short and red.

This vigorous, small tree makes a pleasant, round-topped form reaching 5 m (16 ft.) tall at maturity and up to 4 m (13 ft.) wide. It is an excellent specimen tree for the landscape, adding color in the spring and retaining the deep tones throughout the summer. 'Sherwood Flame' is almost identical to 'Burgundy Lace', but has slightly smaller leaves and its deep color does not fade or turn greenish brown or bronze in midsummer. William Curtis of Oregon selected and developed 'Sherwood Flame', reportedly a seedling selection of 'Burgundy Lace'. 'Sherwood Flame' has been mislabeled 'Sheerwater Flame'.

'Shichihenge'

PALMATUM GROUP
RED

This red cultivar is very similar to 'Musashino', which is propagated more often. The leaves of 'Shichihenge' are slightly smaller and tend to be borderline between the Palmatum and Matsumurae Groups.

The deep purple-red foliage is especially bright as the leaves unfold. The color keeps well into the summer, but gradually fades into a deep green-red tone. Fall colors are various shades of red. The seven lobes are strongly ovate and are very deeply separated. They are held more closely together than in 'Musashino', almost overlapping at the base, and each one terminates in a long, sharp point. The two basal lobes extend almost at right angles to the leaf stalk. The margins are toothed.

This strong-growing, upright tree matures as a round-topped specimen. It is a good maple for the large garden. A large tree in the Tosho Gu shrine in Nikko on Honshu, Japan, was about 5 m (16 ft.) high and wide in the mid-1970s. 'Nikko shichihenge' is a synonym. The alternative spellings 'Schichihenge' and 'Hichihenge' have also been used for this cultivar.

'Shidava Gold'

DWARF GROUP
GREEN

This highly desirable dwarf was discovered as a witches'-broom on the well-known 'Aoyagi' and was propagated and named by Raraflora Nursery, Australia. It is a miniature replica of its parent, with bright yellow-green leaves contrasting with the pea-green bark and turning bright yellow in the fall.

The five-lobed palmatum-type leaves are fairly deeply divided and are slightly smaller than those of 'Aoyagi'. Otherwise,

'Shichihenge'.
Photo by Peter Gregory

'Shidava Gold'.
Photo by Peter Gregory

the leaf shape, toothed margins and coloring through the seasons is the same. 'Shidava Gold' also has the same upright growth as 'Aoyagi' but is shorter and more compact.

One of the original plants reached 2 m (6 ft.) tall and 1.2 m (4 ft.) wide in seven years under Australian conditions. As John Emery of Raraflora rightly points out, the growth of Japanese maples in New South Wales is probably much faster than in many parts of Europe and North America, hence, 'Shidava Gold' is unlikely to reach 2 m (6 ft.) in height under most conditions. The name has been misspelled 'Shidaba Gold'.

'Shigarami'.
Photo by J. D. Vertrees

'Shigi-no-hoshi'.
Photo by Talon Buchholz

'Shigarami'

PALMATUM GROUP
GREEN

The spring foliage is a bright green, with the tips and upper margins of the lobes a light purple. The contrast is quite noticeable. In summer the leaf becomes solid green. Fall colors are rich yellow and orange suffused with red.

The medium-sized leaves have seven lobes which radiate stiffly outward with the two very small basal lobes angled back along the leaf stalk. Each lobe is fairly deeply separated and is long-ovate with almost parallel sides in the lower part, tapering gradually to a sharp tip. The sides of the lobes tend to turn upward from the midrib, forming a slight trough. The margins are almost smooth with only very fine toothing. The leaves are held in a horizontal plane by the stiff leaf stalks.

This small tree is upright-growing, but the side branches grow horizontally as they mature and give it a layered appearance. After many years it reaches a height of 4 m (13 ft.).

The close similarity of 'Shigarami' to 'Tana' has created a slight confusion between the two cultivars. The narrower, parallel-sided lobes and the deeper divisions in the leaves of 'Shigarami' distinguish it from 'Tana', which has broader, triangular lobes and divisions to about halfway. 'Kuchibeni' is a synonym. 'Shigarami', which means "posts in a river to which boats are tied," has also been known under the name 'Saku'.

'Shigi-no-hoshi'

MATSUMURAE GROUP
VARIEGATED

Similar in size and shape to the well-known 'Shigitatsu sawa', this cultivar has leaves that are more deeply divided and that emerge with a cream-yellow base color on which a light green network of veins is visible. The foliage becomes a light cream-green with a mid to dark green network for the summer, then turns bright yellow in the fall.

The large, mainly seven-lobed leaves are very deeply divided and have strong, coarse, uneven toothing on the margins, especially conspicuous on young leaves. This edging initially creates an uneven crumpled appearance. As they develop fully, the leaves straighten out and become star-shaped.

'Shigi-no-hoshi' grows into a small broad-crowned tree or shrub, reaching 5 m (16 ft.) tall and 3 m (10 ft.) or more in width. It is suitable for most garden landscapes.

'Shigitatsu sawa'

AMOENUM GROUP
VARIEGATED

The leaves display a network of prominently green-colored veins and light yellow to light green interspaces. For this characteristic this cultivar has been known under the names 'Greenet' and 'Reticulatum'. Other names used in the past are 'Marginatum', 'Marmoratum', 'Shigitatsu', and 'Striatum'.

In the spring and early summer the contrast is obvious. The unique marking is bright and holds well, especially when the plant has protection from the hot sun. In summer, the leaf darkens and the yellowish interspaces become greener, while the network of veins becomes an even darker green, sometimes with reddish main veins. In the fall, the leaves change to orange or rich red, which is quite different from other cultivars.

Each large leaf is inclined to cup slightly upward from the leaf base, while the lobes radiate sharply outward. The leaves have seven to nine lobes, the lobes joining about halfway to the leaf base. The lobes are broadly ovate, each one tapering to a long,

sharp point. The margins are sharply and quite regularly toothed.

This fairly hardy plant is not as tough and vigorous as some other old cultivars. It appreciates some protection from the hottest sun, which tends to burn the leaves. It is a medium-sized, upright grower, reaching 5 m (16 ft.) tall, and up to 4 m (13 ft.) in spread. The Japanese consider it tender, dwarf, and best grown in containers. In the Pacific Northwest, it is a vigorous, small tree, suitable for gardens. A magnificent plant!

The name appeared in literature for the first time in the mid-eighteenth century and has appeared many times since. It means "snipe rising from a winter swamp." The name also refers to a place in Sagama-Ōiso, where the poet Michakaze Oyodo lived during the Genroku era (1688–1704). The cultivar grown in Japan under this name, as illustrated in Yano (2003), has much deeper cut lobes than that grown in the West as 'Shigitatsu sawa'.

'Shigure bato'

MATSUMURAE GROUP
GREEN

The beautiful, relatively small leaves of this cultivar are seven-lobed, with the two basal lobes very small and angled backward toward the leaf stalks. Each lobe is

'Shigitatsu sawa'.
Photo by Peter Gregory

'Shigure bato', newly
emerging leaves.
Photo by J. D. Vertrees

'Shigure bato',
summer color.
Photo by Peter Gregory

green is lighter under shade. Fall colors range from gold to crimson. 'Shigure bato' is not a rapid-growing cultivar. Although it forms an upright bush, it only attains 3 m (10 ft.) in height, spreading its branches outward so that it may be as wide as it is tall. It is tender and not easily propagated. The name means "rain of the late fall."

'Shigure zome'

MATSUMURAE GROUP
RED

This cultivar is not widely known, even though it has been listed since 1719 and is still being propagated in Japan. The medium-sized leaves are seven-lobed and separated almost to the leaf base. Each lobe is strongly ovate but ends with a long taper to a sharp tip. The margins are faintly toothed. Leaf color in the spring is a bright, purplish red, becoming greenish with reddish tones and red veins as the summer progresses. The fall colors are reds through to oranges. The reddish brown leaf stalks are short. The small branches are a brown-red. This hardy plant forms an upright tree, reaching up to 4 m (13 ft.) tall. It has also been known under the name 'Shigure zono'.

'Shikage ori nishiki'

PALMATUM GROUP
RED

The purple-red leaves have a brownish overtone that helps distinguish this cultivar. The indistinct brown tones are often suppressed by the purple-red in new foliage, later becoming apparent, although never strong. The leaves become a dull green color in late summer, changing to orange in the fall. The large leaves are mainly seven-lobed, but the two basal lobes are very small and sometimes absent. Each lobe is oblong-ovate and terminates in a long, slender point. The lobes are deeply divided. The upper half of the lobe has

narrowly elongated, broadest in the middle, but gradually tapering to a very long tip. The lower quarter of the lobe quickly narrows as it almost reaches the leaf base. The tips of the lobes tend to curve down. The margins are deeply and irregularly toothed. The lobe shape approaches that of the green dissectum 'Palmatifidum'. Although the leaf is one of the Matsumurae Group, it aspires to be a dissectum, but does not quite make it. The leaf has a lovely feathery appearance and is borne on a short, slender stalks.

The new foliage emerges a brilliant red, which lasts into late spring. During the early summer the leaves turn green, but the tips and edges remain tinged red. The

deeply toothed margins, while the lower half is almost untoothed. The short leaf stalks are red.

This cultivar is fairly hardy and strong-growing, and matures as a broad bush up to 5 m (16 ft.) tall. It is not widely known today although it dates back to the early eighteenth century. Gen'ichi Koidzumi referred to it as 'Kageori nishiki'. That name has been confused with 'Kagiri nishiki', a quite different variegated cultivar.

'Shime-no-uchi'

LINEARILOBUM GROUP
GREEN

The long lobes of this strapleaf are green turning orange and yellow in the fall. Earlier editions of this book describe 'Shime-no-uchi' as having red leaves, but it is a very old cultivar from Japan, first mentioned in 1688 and described in Masayoshi Yano's *Book for Maples* (2003) as being green-leaved.

The leaves usually have five narrow lobes, each with slightly toothed margins. The leaf stalks are short and, like the shoots, green. The plant has an upright but twiggy growth habit. In the past the name has been spelled 'Schime no uchi'. Synonyms include 'Aka-no-hichi goshi', 'Aka-no-shichi gosan', 'Ao shichi gosan', 'Ao shimen-no-uchi', and 'Schichigosan'.

'Shin chishio'

PALMATUM GROUP
GREEN

This small-leaved cultivar has extremely brilliant spring foliage. It is considered as good as 'Shin deshōjō', but is more crimson than scarlet. The "improvement" over 'Chishio' is that the bright crimson color is thought to last two or three weeks longer.

The main veins of the leaf become yellow, then green, and the green spreads from the veins to the whole leaf for the summer, turning to a bright crimson for the fall. The five to seven, deeply divided lobes are ovate with tapering, well-defined pointed tips. The margins are coarsely and sharply toothed. The short, slender leaf stalks and the shoots are red.

This vigorous small tree grows up to 5 m (16 ft.) tall and is among the best of the red spring-flowering cultivars, with no weaknesses. It adapts well to container growing for patio display and for bonsai culture. Shoots and leaves dwarf with this type of care. 'Shin chishio', which means "new blood-red," is known and sold mainly under the name 'Chishio Improved', which is illegitimate under the *Cultivated Plant Code*, because of the mixing of languages in the name. The cultivar was also known as 'Shishio Improved'.

'Shin deshōjō

PALMATUM GROUP
GREEN

Shin means "new," indicating that this cultivar is a later, improved selection of the well-known 'Deshōjō'. In spring it is one of the most brilliant foliage plants in the Maplewood collection or anywhere else. Some refer to the leaf color as fire-engine red. Flaming scarlet or crimson-scarlet would be a better description. The leaf color is considered by many to be brighter than that found in similar plants, such as 'Chishio', 'Deshōjō', and 'Seigai'.

The new foliage retains this color during the first month or more of spring. As midsummer arrives, it turns to a pleasant reddish green. Occasionally, leaves are found with minute flecking of light cream or white. The variegation is not strongly marked. In the fall, the colors become blends of reds and oranges.

The small seven-lobed leaves have tiny basal lobes. The strongly ovate lobes are fairly deeply divided and taper to a point. The margins are toothed, the teeth having sharp tips. The short, slender leaf stalks are red-brown to purple-red. The young shoots are also reddish brown to dark purple-red.

'Shin deshōjō' forms a shrub up to 3 m (10 ft.) high and 2 m (6 ft.) wide. It is an excellent container plant for patio display and is also popular as a bonsai plant. With proper care, the rate of growth and leaf size can be reduced without harming the plant. The name has been misspelled 'Shinideshiojo'.

'Shin chishio'.
Photo by Peter Gregory

'Shin deshōjō'.
Photo by Peter Gregory

'Shinobuga oka'

LINEARILOBUM GROUP
GREEN

The medium-sized leaves are shaped in the long, slender form of the Linearilobum Group. They usually have five straplike lobes that tend to hang down, giving a cascading appearance. The margins may be smooth or lightly toothed. Juvenile leaves have ovate, broader toothed, deeply divided lobes similar to the matsumurae-type leaves. The leaf stalks are short. The bright but dark green foliage holds its color well all season. As fall approaches, the color changes to a pleasant yellow.

This upright-growing plant attains 5 m (16 ft.) in height. It is well-adapted to container growing for the patio as it is a shrub type which is easily shaped. It also provides interesting effects when used in bonsai culture.

Synonyms, alternative spellings, and misspellings are numerous and include 'Fingerlobe', 'Lineare', 'Linearifolium', 'Scolopendrifolium Viride', and 'Sinobuga oka'. 'Ao meshime-no-uchi' is so similar to 'Shinobuga oka' that it is also included here, together with its alternative and misspellings—'Aome-no-uchi', 'Ao-no-hichi gosan', 'Ao-no-shichi gosan', and 'Ao shime-no-uchi'. 'Linearilobum' might be identical to 'Shinobuga oka' (van Gelderen et al. 1994). Thus, to avoid confusion with the group name and the cultivar name, it seems best to include this cultivar under 'Shinobuga oka'. 'Scolopendrifolium' appears to be synonymous. It is the most frequently met name in North America.

'Shinonome'

MATSUMURAE GROUP
RED

The spring foliage is a bright orange-red and turns a deeper red in summer. These are very noticeable color tones when compared with other red cultivars. Late in the summer, the leaves become green with a deep red overtone. This pattern accentuates the green of the midribs. The pink to orange-red second growth contrasts well with the reddish green of late summer.

The medium-sized seven-lobed leaves are very deeply divided. The lobes are elongate-ovate, broadest in the middle, narrowing drastically toward the lobe junctions and with the outer ends tapering to elongated, sharp points. The inner third of the lobes has smooth margins, while the outer two thirds are markedly toothed. The short, slender leaf stalks are deep red.

'Shinonome' has an open habit of growth and reaches up to 4 m (13 ft.) in height. It is not well-known but offers a nice contrast

'Shinobuga oka'.
Photo by Peter Gregory

'Shinonome'.
Photo by J. D. Vertrees

when used in large plantings. Well-grown container plants make a fine display. The name, which means "eastern cloud in the early morning," has been misspelled 'Shioname'.

'Shiraname'

MATSUMURAE GROUP
GREEN

Although this cultivar is mentioned as far back as 1710, it is not well known or widely distributed. The medium-sized five- to seven-lobed leaves are deeply divided, almost to the leaf base, with the lobes radiating outward. Each lobe is elongate-ovate, narrowing at the base, and with the outer end tapering to an elongated point. The margin in the lower half of each lobe is almost smooth, while the upper half is sharply toothed. Each lobe has a slight longitudinal upward roll from the midrib. The leaf stalks are short.

Spring foliage is bright red with green undertones, gradually changing to green during the summer. The fall colors are tones of yellow. 'Shiraname' forms a tall

bush, to a height of 4 m (13 ft.). This cultivar has also been known under the name 'Shiranami'.

'Shirazz'

PALMATUM GROUP
VARIEGATED

New and unusual, 'Shirazz' is the red equivalent of the green 'Beni shi en'. It was selected and named by Duncan and Davies Nursery, New Zealand.

The variegated leaves are colored pink-cream, maroon, and dark green, and are perfectly happy in full sun. The small to medium, irregular leaves have mainly five deeply divided almost straplike lobes with long pointed tips and sparsely toothed margins. The lobes can be very irregular, curved and twisted, depending upon the degree of variegation. The spring leaves emerge a bright pink-purple with light pink variegation, mainly along the lobe margins. In summer the background changes to a gray-purple and the variegation turns cream, often with pink toward the tips and margins, plus occasional green streaks. Fall color is a bright purple-red.

'Shirazz' is a strong, vigorous grower when young, establishing itself quickly. It is estimated to form an upright tree with a spreading crown, and would make an excellent and unusual specimen tree.

'Shishigashira'

PALMATUM GROUP
GREEN

The name refers to the mane of a mythical female lion of Japanese drama and was given to this cultivar because of the shape of the bunched-up, heavily curled leaves at the end of short, stout shoots. There are two forms of *shishigashira* in Japanese horticulture. 'Mejishi', which means "female lion," is the designation of the more widely distributed form, better known as 'Shishi-

'Shirazz'.
Photo by Peter Gregory

gashira'. 'Ō jishi', meaning "male lion," is a more compact cultivar with slightly larger leaves.

The compact, stubby growth makes this cultivar very popular for small gardens, container culture, and bonsai. The outstanding feature is the close-packed arrangement of the leaves on the twigs and the close arrangement of the twigs, giving the compact, shrubby character of this cultivar. The bright green foliage is quite crinkled, which adds to the effect.

The small leaf has five to seven lobes, the two basal lobes being much smaller. The lobes are very deeply divided. Each lobe is ovate and tapers to a point. The sides are curled upward, occasionally convoluted, and in most cases form a V-shaped trough. In addition, most leaves are further crinkled along the edges of the lobes. The margins are coarsely but irregularly toothed. Most of the crinkled leaves display the veins prominently, providing an almost rugose-appearing surface, but some leaves do retain a smooth appearance. The leaf stalks are short and stiff. Color is maintained very well during summer, even in hot sun. There is very little sunburn on vigorous plants. The fall color is a striking combination of gold suffused with rose and crimson tones.

Usually a slow-growing plant, 'Shishigashira' can eventually reach 6 m (20 ft.) or more in height. Training and pruning this cultivar to accentuate the shrubby tufts of growth on the branches can emphasize the plant's character; the effect is outstanding. This unique cultivar always attracts attention. It has been in cultivation since 1882 and is popular around the world. Japanese literature indicates its wide use both in the landscape and in bonsai. Other names under which it has been known are 'Mejishi', as explained above, 'Cristatum', 'Minus', 'Ribescifolium', and 'Ribesifolium'.

'Shishio hime'

DWARF GROUP
GREEN

This dwarf shrub has small green leaves of the palmatum type which have red edges and tips when young, becoming an even, medium green for the summer and changing to a bright yellow to gold in the fall. The five-lobed leaves radiate outward and are fairly deeply divided. Each lobe is ovate with a sharp tip. The margins are deeply and evenly toothed. The short leaf stalks are very slender.

The growth habit is very similar to that of 'Murasaki kiyohime', but smaller, forming a low, round, spreading shrub. The cultivar is densely foliaged and slow-growing

'Shishigashira'.
Photo by Peter Gregory

'Shishio hime'.
Photo by Peter Gregory

at first, reaching 80 cm (2.5 ft.) tall and 1.2 m (4 ft.) wide in 10 years. It eventually becomes one of the more vigorous dwarfs. It is an excellent plant for container culture and bonsai.

There is some doubt about the correctness of the name 'Shishio hime' and whether it should be spelled 'Shishi hime' or 'Chishio hime'. It does not appear to be of Japanese origin. This maple is widely available in northwestern North America as 'Shishio hime'.

'Shōjō'.
Photo by J. D. Vertrees

'Shōjō-no-mai'.
Photo by Peter Gregory

'Shōjō'

AMOENUM GROUP
RED

The very deep purple-red foliage is almost

black-red and holds its color well into late summer, especially if the plant is given afternoon shade. In the fall, crimson tones dominate.

The medium-sized leaves have five to seven elongate-ovate lobes that spread openly. The lobes terminate in slender points and are divided almost to the leaf base. The margins are regularly and lightly toothed. The slender, short leaf stalks are red-brown. The leaves are spaced openly along the shoots, giving the appearance of less foliage than normal. The growth is upright and vigorous when the plant is young. It branches laterally and at maturity becomes a wide, tall tree, at least 4 m (13 ft.) in height.

'Shōjō' is the name of the red-faced orangutan character in many Japanese dramas and is used in the names of several cultivars. This cultivar has also been known under the names 'Syoiou' and 'Syojo'.

'Shōjō-no-mai'

PALMATUM GROUP
VARIEGATED

'Shōjō-no-mai' is one of the best of the 'Beni shichihenge' spring-color group of variegated palmatums. The basic leaf color is medium green to gray-green, with attractive, deep-pink edging and tips, sometimes extending more than halfway toward the leaf base. The variegation causes the lobe tips to bend outward, creating a delightfully windblown effect.

The mainly five-lobed, irregularly shaped, small leaves are deeply divided. The long-ovate lobes often have curved, sharply pointed tips. The margins are distinctly coarse-toothed. The leaf stalks are short and slender.

'Shōjō-no-mai' is very similar to 'Beni shichihenge' in all aspects of growth, habit, and leaf. 'Beni shichihenge' differs in having brownish tones in the pink variegation, whereas 'Shōjō-no-mai' is a pure pink, even deeper and more intense than 'Beni shichi-henge', especially in the spring. This culti-var was found and named by Edward Rodd of Raraflora Nursery, Pennsylvania. The name means "dancing red-faced monkey."

'Shōjō nomura'

AMOENUM GROUP
RED

This little-known cultivar is a distinct color form. In early spring, its foliage is a good light bronze-red to purple-red. As the leaves mature in the summer, there is an undertone of green, but it is strongly over-shadowed with a bright orange-red. These tones are both solid and mottled and give the plant a distinctive appearance. The fall color is bright scarlet.

The leaf is divided almost entirely to the leaf base into seven lobes which radiate strongly. Each narrow lobe is oblong-ovate, constricted at the base, and tapering to an elongated, sharp tip. The margins are finely toothed. The leaf stalks are red.

The name means "beautiful red-faced monkey." This cultivar has been known under the names 'Sioiou nomura' (misspelled 'Soiou nomura') and 'Syoiou noumura'.

'Shōjō shidare'

DISSECTUM GROUP
RED

The basic color of the leaf is a deep maroon, brightest in the new foliage and darkening as the leaf matures. A dark, rich green tone is suffused down the center of each lobe and sublobe. The two-tone color combina-tion gives this plant a unique appearance. The leaf stalks are deep maroon, as are the young shoots and branches. Fall color is a dark red.

The medium-sized leaves are seven- to nine-lobed, pinnately dissected, and with irregular toothing on the sublobes. Some sublobes are long and slender. The leaf

stalks are slender but firm and are short.

This cultivar has forms a tall dome, up to 3 m (10 ft.) in height. To see the beauty of the cascading form, the plant should be grafted high or staked up for a few years. It is very beautiful but little known, possi-bly because it is a little tender and not eas-ily propagated. The name means "cascad-ing red-faced monkey." 'Shōjō shidare' has also been known under the name 'Nomura shidare', which may be synonymous. The name has been misspelled 'Syojo shidare'.

'Shū shidare'

DISSECTUM GROUP
GREEN

This weeping dissectum, selected and

'Shōjō' nomura'.
Photo by Harold Greer

'Shōjō shidare'.
Photo by Cor van Gelderen

named by Buchholz and Buchholz Nursery, Oregon, has yellow-orange spring leaves that change to orange-green, then green with purple-red tips, before turning a brilliant orange-red in the fall. The lobes are deeply divided right to the leaf base, the lower third no thicker than the midvein. The lobes themselves are not as deeply cut into clearly toothed sublobes.

'Shū shidare' forms a broad, weeping mushroom-shaped dome twice as broad as tall. It reaches about 1 m (3 ft.) tall in 10 years. It is vigorous and very hardy—to –20°F (–29°C)—and prefers sun or partial shade in a well-drained soil. The name means "orange weeping."

'Sister Ghost'
MATSUMURAE GROUP
VARIEGATED

Like other members of the Ghost Series, this worthwhile selection from Buchholz and Buchholz Nursery, Oregon, has a dark network of veins on a light-colored background. The medium-sized to large leaves have seven deeply divided lobes, almost to the leaf base. Each lobe is narrow-ovate, with a long, curved, tail-like tip and with large, conspicuous, sharply hooked teeth on the margins. The cream-green leaves with their conspicuous green veins can look quite ghostly in the shade. It is estimated that this small, bushy tree will reach 4 m (13 ft.) in height. It needs some protection from the afternoon sun.

'Skeeter's Broom'
DWARF GROUP
RED

Originating from a witches'-broom on 'Bloodgood', this selection was found and named by Edward Rodd of Raraflora Nursery, Pennsylvania. It is similar to several other dwarf red cultivars derived from witches'-brooms on 'Bloodgood', but has longer leaves than most. Whereas the other witches'-brooms often have the central lobe truncated, 'Skeeter's Broom' may have any of the other lobes short and rounded. Occasionally, the central lobe can be almost absent.

The small, five- to seven-lobed leaves are deeply divided, nearly to the leaf base, well separated, and spread out. Each lobe is ovate with a long, pointed tip. The margins are strongly toothed. The maroon leaf stalks are slender and short. The spring leaves are a bright red, becoming a deep purple-red for the summer. Like its parent, 'Skeeter's Broom' holds its color very well. It forms a narrow, upright shrub, reaching about 2 m (6 ft.) in height.

'Sode nishiki'

PALMATUM GROUP
GREEN

This very attractive Japanese cultivar is in the 'Katsura' group of bright yellow-orange spring-flowering maples. The small to medium leaves emerge a bright yellow with pink edging, changing to orange with red margins and tips, before becoming light green, then midgreen for the summer. The beautiful spring color lasts for at least a month. Fall color is deep orange and scarlet.

The mainly five-lobed leaves are deeply divided. Each ovate lobe ends in a strong, pointed tip and has coarsely toothed margins. The slender leaf stalks and shoots are red.

'Sode nishiki' forms an upright, bushy tree to about 3 m (10 ft.) tall. It is a colorful addition for the smaller garden landscape and for container culture.

'Spring Delight'

DISSECTUM GROUP
GREEN

A chance seedling with 'Viridis' as a possible parent, this vigorous cultivar is very pretty in the spring. The emerging, light green leaves are attractively edged in red, a color which lasts through spring and into early summer. The leaves turn from yellow to scarlet in the fall. In all other respects, 'Spring Delight' is very similar to 'Viridis' in leaf appearance, vigor, and growth habit. It was selected, named, and propagated by Talon Buchholz of Buchholz and Buchholz Nursery, Oregon.

'Squitty'

DWARF GROUP
VARIEGATED

Very similar to but even smaller than 'Abigail Rose', this attractive spring-flowering dwarf was raised and named by Talon Buchholz of Oregon. The original seedling came from Harold Johnston, Alabama, who raised and named 'Abigail Rose'. In spring, the tiny leaves emerge in a colorful display of rose, pink, and orange, becoming pink and cream, then light creamy green with a darker green network of veins for the summer. Fall colors are yellow, orange, and pink-red.

This delightful cultivar is very slow-growing and forms a small very dense upright shrub, reaching about 1 m (3 ft.) or so high in seven to ten years. In spite of the small size of scion material, 'Squitty' is

Page 246:
'Shū shidare'.
Photo by Talon Buchholz

'Sister Ghost'.
Photo by Peter Gregory

'Skeeter's Broom'.
Photo by Harry Olsen

This page:
'Spring Delight'.
Photo by Harry Olsen

considered not too difficult to propagate, but is susceptible to powdery mildew. It prefers some shade from the afternoon sun in well-drained soil and has proven hardy up to –10°F (–23°C). This shrub is very suitable for the alpine garden, raised bed, and container culture.

'Squitty', spring color.
Photo by Talon Buchholz

'Squitty', fall color.
Photo by Talon Buchholz

'Stella Rossa'

DISSECTUM GROUP
RED

'Stella Rossa' is one of the earliest selections of Fratelli Gilardelli Nursery, Italy, from the late 1960s. It has very attractive pink-red spring foliage, becoming a dark purple-red which lasts very well throughout the summer and early fall, before turning a bright red in the fall. The foliage coloring is similar to that of 'Dissectum Nigrum', but tends to change to bronze-green in shade.

The seven-lobed, deeply and finely dissected leaves are relatively large. Each lobe narrows markedly to the base, the lower 1.0–1.5 cm consisting only of the midrib. The upper three quarters of the lobes are deeply divided into tentatively broad, flat sublobes with delicate, fine, saw-toothed margins. The short leaf stalks are red and have swollen bases. This vigorous, pendulous dissectum forms a mushroom-shaped shrub up to 3 m (10 ft.) tall and 4 m (13 ft.) wide.

'Sumi nagashi'

MATSUMURAE GROUP
RED

This large-leaved cultivar is one of the best of the red-leaved matsumuraes. The seven-lobed leaves (two extra, very tiny lobes sometimes appear on the largest leaves) are deeply divided, almost to the leaf base. The elongate-ovate lobes taper gradually to a thin, sharp point. The lobes are well separated. The margins are toothed, the teeth having sharp, hooked tips. The short leaf stalks are red.

The spring color is a bright purple-red. In early summer, the leaves darken to become almost black-red or very deep maroon. From midsummer to fall, the color gradually changes to a deep green-red or brown-red. The leaves hold the early color better when given afternoon shade. Fall color is crimson. This vigorous, strong-growing, semiupright tree reaches up to 6 m (20 ft.) tall. It is excellent for the landscape.

'Summer Gold'

PALMATUM GROUP
GREEN

This new cultivar comes from Fratelli Gilardelli Nursery, Italy, which produced the popular 'Orange Dream'. The two plants are similar, except that the yellow leaf color of 'Summer Gold' lasts all summer and changes with the season. Its new leaves are orange-yellow, becoming light yellow, then brightening up to become yellow-gold changing to light yellow-green in late summer, and finally bright golden yellow in the fall. The medium-sized leaves have five to seven moderately divided, broad, oval lobes with short, pointed tips and clearly toothed margins.

It is estimated that 'Summer Gold' will become an upright tree to about 4 m (13 ft.) tall with a broad, rounded crown. Unlike most yellow-leaved maples, it can be grown in the open in the hotter, summer landscapes. It is proving to be the most resistant of the yellow-leaved forms to direct sun and heat. 'Summer Gold' makes an attractive specimen tree and contrasts well with other maples and shrubs in the garden landscape.

'Sunset'

DISSECTUM GROUP
GREEN

'Sunset' is a dissectum of typical mounded shape, but with non-typical leaves and colors. It possesses the same cascading growth habit of most dissectums, growing slowly up to about 3 m (10 ft.). The medium-sized leaves have a neat appearance since they are held on a common plane and do not twist, as in many dissectums. The lobes are distinct in that they are dissected only once, ranging both sides of each midrib, and are not doubly dissected as they are in

'Stella Rossa'.
Photo by Cor van Gelderen

'Sumi nagashi'.
Photo by Peter Gregory

'Sunset'.
Photo by Peter Gregory

more widely known dissectums. This gives a saw-toothed effect to the foliage. The leaf stalk is fairly short.

The color is the second outstanding feature, after the saw-toothed appearance. The base color is a bright green, rather light, but with an overall tinting of rust on mature leaves. Leaves in full sun show a very marked rusty to burnt orange tinting, while those in more shade have the tinting only on the edges or tips. Young foliage, and some of the full-grown leaves in full exposure, lack green and are predominantly yellow in color. This cultivar stands out in the landscape as quite different in both leaf texture and the dominant "rusty" appearance.

'Sunshine'

PALMATUM GROUP
GREEN

This 'Aureum' look-alike holds its yellow-green color much longer through the summer. The new leaves emerge a pink-red with yellow-orange centers, the yellow spreading from the base of the midveins to give an extended "spring-flower" color season. Then leaves slowly turn light yellow-green through the summer before becoming a light green. The fall color is a vivid orange-red.

'Taimin nishiki'.
Photo by Talon Buchholz

The leaves have five to seven broad, moderately deeply divided lobes that spread out. Each ovate lobe has a triangular, pointed tip and clearly toothed margins. 'Sunshine' grows into an upright tree to about 4 m (13 ft.) tall. It was selected and named by Dick van der Maat, Netherlands.

'Taimin'

AMOENUM GROUP
RED

This little-known red-leaved cultivar has been known in Japan since 1782 and is still cultivated in that country. The large leaves have seven broad lobes divided about halfway to the leaf base and with regular fine-toothed margins. Fall color is orange to scarlet. A much sought-after variegated selection, 'Taimin nishiki', originated from 'Taimin'. 'Daimyō' is an old synonym.

'Taimin nishiki'

AMOENUM GROUP
VARIEGATED

This red-variegated form has medium-sized leaves with five to seven lobes which are fairly deeply separated and are ovate-acuminate with the margins slightly toothed. The red leaf stalks are quite short. The spring foliage is bright red, then, as the leaves mature, bright pink patches and speckles become conspicuous, gradually changing to pink-red markings on a purple-red base, which has greenish hues later in the summer. Fall color is scarlet.

All references mention difficulties in propagating 'Taimin nishiki'. It is classed as a very tender plant and is rare in nurseries. It originated from an old, red-leaved cultivar 'Daimyō'. Earlier editions of this volume indicated that 'Daimyō nishiki' was a synonym of this cultivar, but different Japanese characters have been used in a list from Japan since then, and a photograph shows that the former is very different. It has the smaller, more deeply divided leaves of the Matsumurae Group. The name means "brocade of the Ming Dynasty."

'Taiyō nishiki'
PALMATUM GROUP
VARIEGATED

This promising, small Japanese import is similar in leaf to 'Tennyo-no-hoshi'. It is a sport from the popular 'Asahi zuru', but differs from its parent in having narrow-lobed leaves and eye-catching, bright pink-red leaf stalks and shoots. It differs from both 'Asahi zuru' and 'Tennyo-no-hoshi' in having yellow-variegated leaves, one of the true *Acer palmatum* cultivars with yellow variegation.

Spring leaves have bright pink to creamy yellow variegation, mainly on the margins of the very deeply divided leaves, which are larger than those of 'Tennyo-no-hoshi'. The variegation changes to yellow, cream, white, and gray-green on a midgreen background for the summer. Fall colors are spectacular oranges and reds. The mainly five-lobed, medium-sized leaves are divided almost to the base. The lobes are narrowly ovoid, almost straplike, somewhat irregular, with pointed tips and narrowly toothed margins. This slow-growing and unusual cultivar eventually forms a small tree.

'Takao'
PALMATUM GROUP
GREEN

This ancient cultivar has references going back to 1690. The species *Acer palmatum* was called "takao momiji" in Japanese. The plants with especially beautiful leaves were called "Takao." Old literature describes it as having seven lobes in medium-sized green leaves. The leaves of plants imported from Japan into the Netherlands are reported to be five-lobed. The lobes are oblong-lanceolate with the ends tapering to a long, sharp tip. The margins are toothed.

'Takao' is known for its bright yellow to gold fall colors. It forms a vigorous, upright, round-topped tree, growing up to 9 m (30 ft.) in height at maturity. It was named after Takao in Kyoto, famous for its maples. This cultivar has also been known as 'Oh momiji', 'Takao momiji', and 'Takawo momiji', and has been misspelled 'Tokao'.

'Taiyō nishiki'.
Photo by Peter Gregory

'Takao'.
Photo by Peter Gregory

'Taki-no-gawa'
MATSUMURAE GROUP
GREEN

This cultivar is mentioned in several early references, including some with clear illustrations. It is a fairly hardy plant, which makes a round-headed, tall shrub, up to 5 m (16 ft.) tall. The colors of the seven-lobed leaves are distinct, with the new foliage having light red overtones on the light green leaf. This color develops best in the sun. The foliage of heavily shaded plants remains a light green. The foliage color stands out in contrast with other cultivars. During summer the leaves are green. In the fall they become deep scarlet.

The medium-sized leaves extend horizontally instead of hanging down. The lobes separate almost entirely to the flat leaf base and are narrow long-ovate, terminating in long, narrow tips. The margins are finely toothed and the leaf stalks are short and stiff.

'Tama hime'
DWARF GROUP
GREEN

'Tama hime' is a good dwarf for fall color. The tiny leaves are light brown to light green as they unfold, soon becoming a rich,

'Tama hime'.
Photo by Peter Gregory

shiny green. This color holds well into the fall, when red, crimson, and yellow leaves appear. The tiny five-lobed leaves have ovate lobes which end in short tips and are moderately deeply divided. The margins are prominently toothed. The red leaf stalks are quite short.

This compact-growing, upright, vase-shaped dwarf is strong-growing when young, but does not exceed 2 m (6 ft.) high or wide. It is popular for bonsai as the leaves can be reduced to less than 1 cm with repeated pinching and other bonsai cultural techniques. The name means "small globe." Another name by which this cultivar has been known is 'Yatsubusa tamahime'.

'Tama nishiki'
PALMATUM GROUP
VARIEGATED

The bright green foliage is marked with white or yellow combinations in irregular and varied patterns known as the *sunago fu* (sand-dusted) type of variegation. These are not bold markings but rather subdued under most conditions. In the fall the markings become brighter, with rose tones coloring the white and yellow portions, then turning to deep red.

The small leaves are seven-lobed and deeply divided. The lobes are long, elliptic, and narrow, ending in a long, sharp point. Each lobe is irregular in shape where the variegations are strong and becomes sickle-shaped or curved in these areas. The margins are toothed and slightly wavy and the leaf stalks are short. This slightly delicate, upright shrub reaches 3 m (10 ft.) in height. It is a little known cultivar, not widely distributed, but mentioned in Japanese catalogs from the 1930s to the 1960s.

'Tamaori nishiki'
PALMATUM GROUP
VARIEGATED

The small to medium-sized, variegated

leaves have five lobes that radiate outward and are moderately deeply divided. Each lobe is ovate with a long, tapering point and toothed edges. The basic color is a clear green. When variegation occurs, it is in sectional portions of the lobe or leaf. The white or cream color predominates, with occasional pink tones occurring, never very strong. Often the portions of the leaf containing the variegated color are curved or sometimes stunted. Fall colors are orange and red, while the variegated sections turn to a pale rose. This maple is not a very strong grower, but becomes a medium-sized tree.

'Tamuke yama'

DISSECTUM GROUP
RED

The large multidissected leaves are not as deeply cut as are the leaves in such forms as 'Crimson Queen' and 'Dissectum Nigrum'. There is a little more width to the center of the lobe, making each lobe appear slightly bolder. The lobes radiate outward, each one terminating in an extremely fine tip. The stiff leaf stalks are red.

'Tamuke yama', leaf detail.
Photo by J. D. Vertrees

'Tamuke yama', habit.
Photo by J. D. Vertrees

The new foliage is a deep crimson-red in spring, but soon changes to a very dark purple-red. It is an excellent color tone that holds very well throughout the summer. In Oregon 'Tamuke yama' holds its color better than any other cultivar. Growers in the eastern United States report that it holds up extremely well in the combination of high temperatures and humidity. Fall color is a bright scarlet. The bark of the shoots and young branches is a deep maroon, overcast with a whitish tone.

This hardy plant is strongly cascading. It is an old cultivar, having been listed as early as 1710. The name means "tribute to the mountain." Japanese records refer to plants 50–100 years old reaching up to 4 m (13 ft.) tall.

The leaf shape, coloration, and growth habit of a plant in the Maplewood collection called 'Takiniyama' was identical to 'Tamuke yama'. As it matured, its characteristics indicated that it was the same as 'Tamuke yama' and no records have been found of 'Takiniyama'. Other names under which 'Tamuke yama' have been known are 'Aka shidare', 'Beni hagoromo', 'Chirimen kaede', 'Chirimen momiji', and 'Dissectum Tamuke yama'.

'Tana'.
Photo by Harry Olsen

'Tana'

AMOENUM GROUP
GREEN

The name, which means "shelves," refers to the layered effect of the branches and foliage. The beautiful foliage is light to yellowish green. Each lobe is tipped in a distinctive purplish red, similar to 'Shigarami', but not as deep a color. This color shades back from the tip and down along the margins for a short distance, gradually shading into the solid green color of the leaf. In new leaves this marking is quite bright. As the leaf ages in the summer, the purple disappears. In the fall the colors become a bright, eye-catching combination of gold and red.

The medium-sized leaves have five to seven lobes that radiate sharply outward. The lobes are separated up to halfway to the leaf base and are broadly ovate, tapering to sharp points. The margins are very lightly toothed and curl slightly upward. The stiff leaf stalks are short.

The leaves and new shoots are held horizontally, and the branches grow laterally, thus forming the characteristic layered effect of this plant. It is a strong-growing, upright cultivar which reaches 6 m (20 ft.) in height. It becomes round-topped with a broad canopy.

The similarity of the purple-tipped leaves and growth habit of 'Tana' with 'Shigarami' has caused some confusion. Although both cultivars form a single-stemmed tree, the much deeper leaf divisions easily distinguish 'Shigarami'. The similarity of the name has also caused some confusion between 'Tana' and 'Tanabata', which is a red-leaved cultivar with the leaves deeply divided, almost to the leaf base.

'Tanabata'

MATSUMURAE GROUP
RED

Because of the similarity of their names, 'Tanabata' has occasionally been confused with 'Tana'. The two plants are very different. 'Tanabata' has deeply divided red leaves of the Matsumurae Group, whereas 'Tana' has green, shallowly divided leaves of the Amoenum Group.

The medium-sized leaves are seven-lobed and almost completely divided to the leaf base. The lobes are elongate-elliptic, terminating in a long, narrow tip. The base of each lobe is extremely narrow, and the margins are toothed. The bright purpled-red leaves become redder as they mature in summer. The fall colors are strong reds.

'Tanabata' is a fairly strong grower that reaches 5 m (16 ft.) in height and width. It starts upright, but develops slightly pendulous outer branches as it ages. The name means "Festival of the Stars."

'Taro yama'

DWARF GROUP
GREEN

This small import from Japan has colorful spring foliage and new growth. It is very similar in appearance to 'Ryūzu', with the short internodes getting closer and closer toward the congested tips. The emerging spring leaves are pale yellow-green with pink-red flushed lobe tips and margins, changing to a lighter green with narrow pink edges, before turning a clear green which becomes darker through the summer, then turning scarlet in the fall.

The small five-lobed leaves are deeply divided. Each lobe is narrowly ovate-triangular with a long tail-like tip which curves down toward a toothed margin. The center lobe is the longest.

'Taro yama' has thick branches with short internodes. It forms a dense, compact dwarf and is ideal for bonsai. It is named after Mount Taro. 'Tarohi yama' is a synonym.

'Tatsuta gawa'

AMOENUM GROUP
GREEN

This old cultivar, mentioned in the literature of 1710, is valued for the beauty of its fall color. The leaves are spaced openly on the small branches and so display the scarlet fall color to good advantage. As one Japanese reference described it, "The sun shines on all the leaves and makes the foliage more beautiful." New leaves unfold as a very light yellow-green, which soon

'Taro yama', spring color.
Photo by Talon Buchholz

'Taro yama', fall color.
Photo by Talon Buchholz

changes to light green. The medium-sized seven-lobed leaves are very deeply divided. The lobes are long-elliptic with sharp tips and lightly toothed margins.

This plant grows to be a medium-sized shrub, up to 4 m (13 ft.) tall, with open branches and a rounded top. It has also been known under the names 'Tatsuta' and 'Tatsuta kaede'.

'Tatsuta gawa'.
Photo by Peter Gregory

'Tattoo'.
Photo by Peter Gregory

'Tattoo'
DWARF GROUP
GREEN

This little beauty is like a slow-growing 'Mikawa yatsubusa', with similar but smaller leaves and habit. The light yellow-green palmatum-type new leaves emerge bunched up at the short shoot tips and become mid to dark green for the summer. 'Tatoo' is another real gem, discovered and named by William Schwartz, Pennsylvania.

'Taylor'
PALMATUM GROUP
VARIEGATED

'Taylor' is a recent introduction with a unique and spectacular foliage display throughout the growing season. The spring leaves are a very bright pink-red with occasional small blotches of dark and light green, gradually becoming light pink and faintly tinged light green by mid-June. The green becomes darker as the summer progresses. In midsummer, there is a second flush of bright pink, continuing the eye-catching color display all summer. In the fall, the color reverts again to the very bright pink-red.

The small five-lobed leaves are deeply divided almost to the leaf base. Each narrow lobe is almost straplike, long oblong-ovate with a tail-like tip. The margins are slightly rolled under and are mostly untoothed except for a few sharp hooked teeth near the tip. The bright red leaf stalks are short and slender.

This unusual cultivar forms a low spreading bush, estimated to eventually reach up to 2.5 m (8 ft.) or so in height. It is delicate and difficult to keep growing healthily. It must never dry out or be waterlogged. It also needs semishade and lots of tender loving care. Yet, it is well worthwhile for the exceptional summer-long color display.

'Tendō'

PALMATUM GROUP
GREEN

This Japanese cultivar was imported into the Netherlands and was described as a strong-growing, rather small-leaved cultivar. The leaves have five to seven triangular lobes divided almost halfway to the base and spread out star-shaped at first. The margins have unusually tiny, sharp, evenly spaced teeth. Spring leaves emerge a light yellow-green with reddish edges and tips, becoming mid to dark green with lobes twisting in varying directions during summer. The teeth form a very thin red line round the margins. Fall color is a bright yellow. 'Tendō' is proving to be a vigorous grower in the early years. The name has been misspelled 'Tentou'. 'Mitsuba yama' is a synonym.

'Tennyo-no-hoshi'

PALMATUM GROUP
VARIEGATED

This medium-sized, upright shrub eventually reaches about 5 m (16 ft.) in height. Its chief attraction is the unusual, lightly variegated foliage. The small leaves have extremely narrow lobes, separated almost to the leaf base. The edges are wavy, with the outer half unevenly toothed. The base color is a strong green, with the variegation a cream or light cream-green, mostly confined to a fine edging entirely around each lobe, with light tones covering up to a quarter of the area of the lobe. With the stronger color breaks, the lobes develop a curve or twist. From a distance, the overall effect is a delicate cloudlike appearance. The fall colors, while not strong, turn to a pleasant mixture of pale reds and rose.

This cultivar is a strong grower and seems sturdy in the landscape. The overall texture makes it appear delicate, and it blends in well with a background of heavier foliage. It grows well in full sun,

when the variegation has pink tones. 'Tennyo-no-hoshi' was selected and registered by Maplewood Nursery. The name means "angel of the stars." The cultivar has been known under the names 'Tanyo-no-hoshi' and 'Teyono hoshi'. 'Ao kanzashi', a later cultivar imported from Japan, appears to be very similar in habit, leaf shape, and variegation.

'Teri ha'

MATSUMURAE GROUP
RED

This vigorous new Japanese import has attractive multicolored spring leaves and very distinctive, maroon-red summer foliage. The new leaves emerge a light yellow-

'Taylor'.
Photo by Peter Gregory

'Tennyo-no-hoshi'.
Photo by Harold Greer

green with light pink edging, becoming bright pink-red with green main veins. The foliage changes to red, then deep purple-red for the summer, turning to red then orange in the fall. The slender leaf stalks of the newly emerging leaves and shoots are light yellow-green, changing to pink as they develop in early summer.

The medium-sized leaves are deeply divided into five to seven ovate-triangular lobes with long, pointed tips and coarsely toothed margins. Curiously, the young leaves emerge like gray palmatum-type leaves before developing fully. It is estimated that 'Teri ha' will develop into a broadly upright tree. The name has already been misspelled 'Teriba' in one or two collections.

'The Bishop'
AMOENUM GROUP
RED

This maple is one of the late Henry Hohman's selections. It has medium-sized, fairly deeply divided, purple-red leaves. The lobes extend outward and are deeply divided. Each lobe is long-ovate, with the margins finely toothed. The purple-red is brightest in the spring and does not bronze until late summer. The fall color is an excellent crimson. This upright-growing tree is vigorous and hardy, and reaches 14 m (13 ft.) in height.

'Tiger Rose'
MATSUMURAE GROUP
VARIEGATED

Originating in Oregon from a colorful chance seedling of 'Azuma murasaki', this lovely cultivar was selected and named by Dr. Bump after his wife. Beside the variegated network of leaves, 'Tiger Rose' has cascading shoots and a semipendulous habit similar to 'Omure yama'.

The medium to large leaves are divided almost to the leaf base into seven long, oval lobes with coarsely toothed and slightly crumpled margins. The new leaves emerge in the spring a bright pink, gradually changing to creamy white with a green network of veins and pinky red margins and tips, before becoming light green with a dark green network of veins for the summer. Fall color is scarlet. 'Tiger Rose' forms an upright, rounded mound up to 3 m (10 ft.) tall and about 1.5 m (5 ft.) wide.

'Tiny Leaf'

DWARF GROUP
GREEN

At least two selections have been given this name. One, a European dwarf with a rounded habit and very tiny leaves, is now named 'Mini Mondo'. The second plant, a tiny jewel from a witches'-broom in Philadelphia, was named by Richard Wolff and has become popular in the United States. It is very similar in leaf and habit to 'Coonara Pygmy'. The very small, very deeply divided, green, five-lobed leaves have relatively long, thin lobes with scalloped margins. Most leaves have a stunted center lobe. The spring leaves emerge a pleasant avocado green, becoming a midgreen for the summer, before turning yellow, gold, and then red in the fall.

'Tiny Leaf' is very hardy and will form an irregular, rounded shrub up to 1.2 m (4 ft.) tall. It grows happily in the front of a shrub border or in containers, and its congested, irregular habit makes it ideal for bonsai culture.

'Tobiosho'

PALMATUM GROUP
GREEN

This otherwise normal, green cultivar comes alive in the fall with its vivid scarlet color. It was selected in 1982 by Milt Tobie, production manager at Iseli Nursery, Oregon, and was named after him. The small five-lobed, typical palmatum-type leaves are deeply divided and are slightly longer than wide. The ovate lobes, with tail-like tips, are broadest in the middle, narrowing slightly toward the lobe junctions. The margins are distinctly toothed. The stiff, slender leaf stalks are red. 'Tobiosho' grows into an upright, wide-topped, medium-sized tree.

'Toyama'

DISSECTUM GROUP
RED

This very old name in Japanese literature has 'Soayama' as a synonym. It is sometimes referred to as a synonym of 'Ornatum', but although the growth habit, leaves, and color are similar, 'Ornatum' is believed to be of European origin. 'Toyama' would seem to differ in the manner and timing of the change of color to crimson-red in the fall. The cultivar is named after the district of Toyama.

'Toyama nishiki'

DISSECTUM GROUP
VARIEGATED

The basic leaf color is purple-red to greenish red, variegated to a greater or lesser degree. Some leaves lack variegation; others are completely pink as they first open

Page 258:
'Teri ha'.
Photo by Peter Gregory

'The Bishop'.
Photo by Cor van Gelderen

'Tiger Rose'.
Photo by Peter Gregory

This page:
'Tobiosho'.
Photo by Harry Olsen

in the spring. Most markings are pink or white as portions of the lobes, or blend into the leaf in endless variation. When the plant is grown in shade, its colors are more intense and hold better in the heat of the summer. The leaves sunburn easily. In the fall the leaves turn orange to yellow. The medium-sized leaves are typical of the dissectums with seven to nine lobes, doubly dissected and lacy. These finely divided leaves appear to droop more than other dissectums, because slight distortions occur at or near the variegated areas.

This tender and not very robust maple needs considerable care and attention. It is difficult to propagate and is not common in collections. The name means "brocade of the Toyama district." The following are synonyms, alternative spellings, or misspellings of this cultivar's name: 'Beni shidare Tricolor', 'Beni shidare Variegated', 'Goshiki shidare', 'Sotoyama nishiki', 'Toya nishiki', and 'Yamato nishiki'.

'Trompenburg'

MATSUMURAE GROUP
RED

This outstanding cultivar was a chance seedling, selected by J. R. P. van Hoey-Smith at the Trompenburg Arboretum, Netherlands, and introduced by Firma C. Esveld. It is popular wherever it is grown.

The unusual leaves have seven to nine lobes, the lobes separated deeply to within 1 cm of the leaf base. They radiate laterally and evenly, giving the appearance of fingers extended from a hand. Each lobe is long-ovate, with edges which roll down for three quarters of the way, almost forming a tube. The remaining quarter flattens to display the deeply toothed margins. On mature leaves the tips of the lobes turn down slightly. This extraordinary leaf gives an unusual and pleasing effect. The stiff, short leaf stalks are red. The foliage color is also an outstanding feature, being a rich, showy, deep purple-red. It lasts exceptionally well into late summer. Even in full sun the leaves do not burn, but later change to a deep, reddish green and bronze. The fall color of crimson completes a colorful year.

This upright-growing cultivar, strong but not unruly, reaches 8 m (26 ft.) high and 5 m (16 ft.) wide. The branches begin to extend laterally, with the fingertip-like leaves reaching outward and down. This cultivar has become a favorite for land-

'Toyama nishiki'.
Photo by Peter Gregory

'Trompenburg'.
Photo by J. D. Vertrees

scaping. Received the RHS Award of Garden Merit.

'Tsuchigumo'

PALMATUM GROUP
GREEN

This delightful, semidwarf cultivar has small rust-red leaves that soon change to bright green. This color holds well all summer and does not burn in full sun. Fall color is bright gold, with crimson edging blending into the gold tones. The interesting leaves are five- to seven-lobed, with each lobe separated almost to the base. The lobes are elongate-ovate, tapering gradually to sharp points, and they radiate outward. The margins of the lobes turn upward slightly and are conspicuously toothed. The ends of some lobes turn downward slightly, while others turn under completely. These leaves compare with those of 'Shishigashira', but are not as convoluted. The leaf stalks are stiff and short.

This excellent small tree reaches up to 4 m (13 ft.) tall. It grows slightly faster than 'Shishigashira' at first but does not grow as tall and, although the stems are sturdy, they are not as stubby or thick. It appears that this cultivar was lost when horticulture was interrupted during World War II, but has now been reintroduced. The name means "ground spider."

'Tsukomo'

DWARF GROUP
GREEN

This delightful dwarf is stubby and upright. It makes a dense mound, reaching up to 1.5 m (5 ft.) high and wide. The stems are very stiff and upright. The new leaves unfold a bright, rusty red. As the leaves develop, they become a light red-green, maturing to a rich, deep green. The effect is quite beautiful as the shoots develop and all these color phases appear from the top of each shoot to the base. In the fall the yel-

low-gold is very strong. The small leaves are five-lobed, some with a tiny pair of basal lobes. The deeply divided leaf lobes are ovate and gradually taper to an elongated tip. The margins are sharply toothed and conspicuous. The entire leaf tends to stick out stiffly sideways. The stiff, short leaf stalks are green.

This very choice and delightful dwarf, unlike most of the Dwarf Group, tends to grow upright. It is extremely difficult to propagate, and new grafts grow very slowly. The name has been misspelled 'Tsukumo'.

'Tsuchigumo'.
Photo by J. D. Vertrees

'Tsukomo'.
Photo by J. D. Vertrees

'Tsukubane'
AMOENUM GROUP
GREEN

The small to medium-sized leaves have seven lobes which are deeply divided. In the center the lobes hold close together, but at the ends they radiate. The thin leaves are almost translucent, and the leaf base is mostly straight. The lobes are broadly ovate and taper to long, slender points. The edges are evenly and delicately toothed. The spring foliage is a bright red with a green cast to the center of each lobe. This color soon changes to green. By late summer the leaves are a rich green, tinged with dark red. Fall color is a brilliant orange-crimson.

A fairly vigorous, tall, upright-growing plant, 'Tsukubane' branches sideways and forms a broad-topped tree up to 7 m (23 ft.) or so. It was popular in the nineteenth century, but is not widely known today. The name means "ridge of Mount Tsukuba."

'Tsukushi gata'
AMOENUM GROUP
RED

This tree attracts attention in any garden. The rich purple-red to black-red leaves are spectacular and hold their color quite well all season, but on the shaded side and underside, a green cast develops under the dark tones. The midveins of each lobe are a noticeable green contrast. The beautiful fruits are almost a chartreuse color and seem to sparkle among the deep-toned foliage. The large leaves have seven lobes which radiate stiffly and are divided to about halfway to the leaf base. They are broadly ovate, tapering to sharp points. The appearance is almost star-shaped. The light, short leaf stalks are yellow-pink.

This strong-growing plant forms a medium-sized, round-topped, spreading tree of 4 m (13 ft.) or more tall and almost as wide. It is one of the best dark-toned cultivars despite not being widely known. The difficulty in translating the first syllable accounts for the numerous different spellings of this name: 'Chikushi gata', 'Shikishigata', 'Shikushigata', and 'Tsukishi gata'. 'Tsukushi gata' is the name of a bay on the Japanese island of Kyushu.

'Tsuma beni'
AMOENUM GROUP
GREEN

The outstanding feature of this cultivar is the lobe tip color of the beautiful spring foliage (*tsuma fukurin fu* type of variegation), a feature which gives rise to its name.

'Tsukubane'.
Photo by Peter Gregory

'Tsukushi gata'.
Photo by J. D. Vertrees

The light green lobes have purplish red tips and upper margins, the purple-red blending into the light green of the leaf center. This color combination continues well into the early summer, then gradually diminishes and matures into a shiny, darker green. Red colors dominate in the fall. The medium-sized leaves are five- to seven-lobed and are separated up to halfway to the leaf base. Each lobe is broadly ovate, terminating in a narrow tip. The margins are lightly and evenly toothed. The reddish green leaf stalks are short.

This cultivar is not a fast-growing plant, but more of a rounded bush, reaching up to 3 m (10 ft.) tall and almost as wide. It is somewhat tender and is not easy to propagate. The spring foliage always attracts attention. It makes a very pleasant companion plant for dissectums and other shrubs. The name means "red nail."

'Tsuma gaki'

AMOENUM GROUP
GREEN

As the foliage unfolds it tends to droop from the leaf stalk, adding a softness to the plant's general appearance. The color at this time is a soft yellow-green. The tips of the lobes are shaded with a blend of tones which are difficult to describe. Colors range from a persimmon red to a light purple-red combination. The summer foliage is deep green. Fall colors are crimsons and reds.

The medium-sized leaves have five to seven lobes. The lobes are ovate, but taper to slender tips, and are separated to about halfway to the leaf base. The margins are evenly and lightly toothed. Young shoots are deep red.

This maple is not tall-growing, but forms a round plant up to 3 m (10 ft.) tall and wide. Because of the similarity in name, leaf, and form, 'Tsuma gaki' may be confused with 'Tsuma beni', but they are distinct cultivars. The name has been misspelled 'Tsuma gari'.

'Tsuri nishiki'

MATSUMURAE GROUP
GREEN

The interesting, medium to large leaves are mainly seven-lobed. The lobes are widely and deeply divided. They spread slightly and are sometimes twisted at various angles. Narrow and almost lanceolate, each lobe terminates in a long, tapering, sharp point and is less than 1 cm

'Tsuma beni'.
Photo by J. D. Vertrees

'Tsuma gaki'.
Photo by Cor van Gelderen

wide. The margins are conspicuously and roughly toothed, and the teeth have fine-pointed tips.

The leaves are a deep green with a light tinge of red on the margins. They become darker green during the summer. The fall colors are quite brilliant with yellow, orange-gold, and crimson blended together. The leaves have a firm texture and are not easily sunburned. The plant is quite hardy and grows into a sturdy, medium-sized tree, up to 4 m (13 ft.) tall.

A different transliteration system from Japanese to English gives this cultivar a slightly different name—'Furu nishiki'. Other names under which this cultivar has been known are 'Amelopsifolium', 'Ampelopsifolium', 'Laciniatum', and 'Septemlobum'.

'Twisted Spider'

PALMATUM GROUP
GREEN

This intriguing and striking, unique green plant was discovered, propagated, and named by Harold Johnston as a chance seedling at Johnnie's Pleasure Plants Nursery. The name aptly describes many of the medium-sized, narrow-lobed, sometimes almost spiral leaves of this unusual plant.

The cultivar has a combination of fine, narrow and coarse, wide-lobed leaves, with most leaves having five, deeply cut, almost linear lobes with irregular teeth. These lobes are irregularly twisted and curved. The larger, coarser leaves are fewer in number but are more broadly ovate and with much coarser, irregular toothing. Though mostly five-lobed, occasionally one or three of the lobes may be absent. The slender leaf stalks are short. The foliage is a medium to dark green and turns a yellow-orange in the fall. The leaf stalks and shoots are green.

'Twisted Spider' is vigorous with an upright, slightly pendulous habit. Its estimated mature height is 4 m (13 ft.), with a spread of about 2 m (6 ft.).

'Ueno homare'

PALMATUM GROUP
GREEN

This medium-sized, upright tree has outstanding colored foliage in the spring. It is one of the 'Katsura' group of spring-flowering maples, but deeper and brighter orange than 'Katsura'.

This small-leaved bright green maple has five-lobed leaves which are fairly deeply divided. Each lobe is elongate-ovate and terminates in a long slender tip. The lobes do not extend uniformly but are on different planes, which gives an irregular appearance to the foliage. The margins are deeply double-toothed, giving the leaf a feathery appearance. The leaf stalks are short and stiff. The young leaves emerge a deep yellow with orange-red edging, changing to yellow-green or medium green for the summer. In the fall, they become a bright yellow-orange.

This little-known cultivar is hardy and forms a small tree up to 5 m (16 ft.) tall. It is an excellent accent plant for medium-tall landscape needs and for early spring color. It is better known in the West under

'Ueno homare'.
Photo by Peter Gregory

its synonym 'Ueno yama'. Other synonyms are 'Ebi nishiki' and 'Ueno-no-homare'.

'Ukigumo'

PALMATUM GROUP
VARIEGATED

The name, which means "floating clouds," refers to the subtle variegation of the leaves (*goma fu* type), which give rise to the expansion of its name to 'Ukigumo nishiki'. Among the variegated cultivars, this is one of the most outstanding forms. The pastel tones blend in subtle combinations, unlike others which are bolder.

The basic leaf color is light green. The least variegated leaves have a faint shading of pink on the edges, made up of very minute dots. Most leaves are marked in varying degrees by white or pink spots, sometimes merging into large areas. Other leaves are totally white or light pink. None of the coloration is garish; it is soft. Fall color is yellow-orange. The medium-sized leaves have five lobes which radiate openly and are very deeply divided. They are long-ovate and end in a sharp tip. The lobes that are highly variegated do not lie flat, but may curl downward or sideways and often they are twisted and undulate. The margins are finely and sparsely toothed.

This plant is not a rapid grower and needs some protection from the afternoon sun. The twigs are rather short, forming a semidense plant. It becomes a tall shrub, reaching 3 m (10 ft.). 'Ukigumo' is an example of a borderline cultivar which could arguably be placed in the Palmatum, Amoenum, or Matsumurae Group.

'Umegae'

AMOENUM GROUP
RED

This small-leaved form has a flat leaf base. The seven lobes are moderately deeply divided and radiate outward uniformly. They are ovate with tapered, slender points

and fold slightly upward from the midribs. The margins are lightly toothed. The stiff, short leaf stalks are green. Spring foliage is a bright brick red, which soon turns to bright, purplish red. The main veins are a prominent, contrasting green. Plants grown in full sun have bright red coloration, while those grown in shade have more purple with green undertones. The undersurface is very shiny. The foliage color lasts well into late summer. The yel-

'Ukigumo'.
Photo by Peter Gregory

'Umegae'.
Photo by J. D. Vertrees

low-green fruits make an attractive contrast to the purple leaves. Fall colors are good, mostly orange to crimson.

This cultivar is not fast-growing. It is upright yet spreading and forms a round-topped bush that may reach 5 m (16 ft.) tall. 'Umegae' has been around since 1882. The name has also been transliterated from Japanese to English as 'Umegai'.

'Uncle Ghost'

MATSUMURAE GROUP
VARIEGATED

Another of the Ghost Series, this desirable cultivar is similar in leaf style and size to its parent, the well-known 'Beni shigitatsu sawa', but with a network of green veins on a paler, whitish green background. It is especially colorful in the spring and early summer when the young leaves are flushed bright pink from the outer margins. Fall color is a bright red. The medium to large five- to seven-lobed leaves are mainly divided almost to the base. The typical lobe is long-ovate, widest in the outer half and narrowing to the junction, like the neck of a bottle. The depth of lobing and lobe shape can vary somewhat. The lobes have long, drawn-out, pointed tips, and the margins are conspicuously coarsely toothed and very crinkly. This attractive, broad, shrubby tree grows to 3 m (10 ft.) or so in height and needs some protection from the afternoon sun.

'Uncle Ghost'.
Photo by Peter Gregory

'Utsu semi'.
Photo by J. D. Vertrees

'Utsu semi'

AMOENUM GROUP
GREEN

The name, which means "grasshopper skin," refers to the shiny bright green of the broad bold leaves. The margins of the spring leaves are tinted purple or red. Later the green becomes darker, turning crimson and purple in the fall. The large leaves have seven lobes divided halfway to the base. The lobes are broadly ovate, tapering to a short point. The two small basal lobes are lanceolate with a sharp point and extend outward. The margins are finely toothed. This hardy cultivar forms a short round-topped tree, reaching 4 m (13 ft.) tall and wide. It makes a fine landscape tree and adds contrasting spring leaf texture and excellent fall color.

'Vandermoss Red'

MATSUMURAE GROUP
RED

This cultivar, which can also be found under its former name of 'Christy Ann', has deep purple-red foliage similar in color to 'Bloodgood', but the leaf lobes are narrower, more coarsely toothed, more deeply divided, and feathery. It holds its color very well throughout the summer, turning to deep orange and vivid red in the fall.

The medium-sized to large seven-lobed leaves are very deeply divided, almost to the leaf base. The lobes are long-ovate with long, tail-like tips, broadest in the middle and narrowing markedly to only 2 mm at the lobe junctions. The margins are distinctly toothed, with numerous, sharply pointed teeth. The short, slender leaf stalks are red. This vigorous plant forms an upright, round-headed, medium-sized tree, up to 6 m (20 ft.) in height. It is wider spreading than 'Bloodgood', but not as tall.

'Variegatum'

AMOENUM GROUP
RED

The large leaves have seven lobes well-separated to about halfway to the leaf base. They are ovate, tapering to a strong, prominent point. This upright-growing plant attains the stature of a small tree. Early sources described crimson variegation in the purple-red leaves. I have seen this cultivar in several different places and was never strongly impressed with the leaf coloration most of the year, but the fall color redeems it, with scarlet and crimson mottling. The plants in the Maplewood collection, received from two different sources, show basically a reddish green leaf during most of the year, followed by the good fall colors.

This cultivar is listed in 1882 (Oka et al.) and has been reintroduced several times. Evidence suggests that several different clones have been given this same name. This confusion, together with the poor variegation most of the time, suggest the cultivar is not worth perpetuating. It has also been known under the name 'Atropurpureum Variegatum'.

'Versicolor'

PALMATUM GROUP
VARIEGATED

This plant was one of the more widely distributed cultivars of commercial nurseries in the United States. It is a strong-growing, hard form and makes an upright tree exceeding 7 m (23 ft.) in height, with a broad crown. Young branches have a bright green bark which darkens as the tree matures.

'Vandermoss Red'.
Photo by Harold Greer

'Versicolor'.
Photo by J. D. Vertrees

The leaves are of the typical palmatum type, deep green in color, with a varied pattern and amount of marking. The white variegation consists of streaks, flecks, and blotches and is quite prominent on some leaves. Where variegations are large, that portion of the lobe is sickle-shaped and curved laterally. Occasionally, pink colors are noticeable, but not in the profusion of some other cultivars, such as 'Oridono nishiki'. The smallish leaves are five- to seven-lobed and attached to long, thin leaf stalks. The lobes are ovate-acuminate with elongated tips. The margins are toothed, in most cases, quite shallowly.

'Versicolor' has also been know under the names 'Albovariegatum', 'Aokii', 'Argenteomaculatum', 'Argenteum', 'Discolor Versicolor', 'Roseomaculatum', 'Roseovariegatum', and 'Roseum'. 'Oridono nishiki' was originally introduced into the United States at the turn of the twentieth century, by the famous Kobayashi Nursery (Angyo, Japan), under the name 'Versicolor', but the plant now available as 'Versicolor' is distinctly different from the popular 'Oridono nishiki'.

'Vic Pink'

DISSECTUM GROUP
GREEN

This interesting Australian dissectum is of unknown origin. Its characteristics suggest it may have been a seedling from 'Palmatifidum', as the leaf shape is identical, though the size is smaller. Like the lobes of 'Palmatifidum', those of 'Vic Pink' are sturdy and not deeply dissected, but are strong and coarsely toothed. The great asset of this plant is the brilliant scarlet color in the fall compared to the orange-gold of 'Palmatifidum'. It also comes into leaf several weeks later than its formidable parent and has beautiful dark red fruits. In all other respects—vigor, growth habit, and summer color—the two cultivars are very alike.

'Villa Taranto'

LINEARILOBUM GROUP
GREEN

This excellent cultivar from the Villa Taranto, Italy, was propagated and introduced by the Firma C. Esveld, Netherlands. The large leaves are usually five-lobed. Each lobe is long, narrow, and parallel-sided, as is typical of the Linearilobum Group. The lobes are rarely more than 5 mm wide, except for foliage on fast-growing new shoots. The center lobes are longest and create a lacy effect. The margins of the lobes are smooth. The leaf stalks are stiff and short.

The leaves emerge an orange-crimson, soon becoming green with a light reddish overtone, creating an unusual color effect. The older stock plants in the Netherlands were most impressive because of this coloring, which is a compromise between green and purple forms. All leaves are green when grown in shade and remain a clear red if in full sun. In the fall the leaves turn a pleasing yellow to gold.

This hardy cultivar forms a dome-shaped plant of 3 m (10 ft.) in height. Its growth habit is very similar to that of 'Red Pygmy'.

'Viridis'

DISSECTUM GROUP
GREEN

The term "viridis" has come to mean any form of green dissectum, just as "atropurpureum" encompasses all the red forms. In old literature, the original Latin description was "Folia viridia," whence came the general term 'Viridis', but now the name has been applied to many good forms of green dissectum, in the same way the name 'Dissectum' is applied.

The foliage is the "type" for dissectums, being usually seven- to nine-lobed. Each lobe separates entirely to the base. The lobes are multidissected or strongly pinnate, and

Page 268:
'Vic Pink'.
Photo by Peter Gregory

'Villa Taranto'.
Photo by Harold Greer

This page:
'Viridis'.
Photo by J. D. Vertrees

extremely narrow, with the deep cut side separations again recut. While the leaves are medium to large, the leaf is not "gross," but has the delicate tracery of the typical dissectum form. The bright green foliage holds color well through the summer. In extremely hot sun the tips of the leaves may burn. Partial shade keeps the foliage bright all season. In the fall, delightful gold colors will dominate, with occasional splashes of crimson.

This strongly cascading maple has long, drooping branches that form a dome-shaped plant. Very old trees of 75–100 years may reach a height of 4 m (13 ft.). 'Viridis' is a good choice for the patio or pondside planting. Because several outstanding, named, green dissectum cultivars are now available, this cultivar name, like the cultivar names 'Atropurpureum' and 'Dissectum', should be dropped, as it has become so diluted as to be meaningless.

'Volubile', spring color.
Photo by J. D. Vertrees

'Volubile', fall color.
Photo by J. D. Vertrees

'Volubile'

PALMATUM GROUP
GREEN

The small, palmate, seven-lobed leaves have two very small basal lobes. The leaf tends to cup upward from the short leaf stalk. Each lobe is triangular-ovate, terminating in a narrow point. The margins have light, prominent teeth. The leaf color in the spring is a bright yellow-green. The foliage darkens somewhat during the summer and withstands full sun very well. The fall colors are quite brilliant, and range from yellow into rusty rose and on to crimson. The shoot color becomes a rusty red.

'Volubile' is very similar to 'Aoyagi' in leaf shape, size, and color early in the season, but does not have the beautiful green twigs of 'Aoyagi'. It is an upright-growing tree that reaches at least 6 m (20 ft.) in height. The shoots are unusually dainty. This plant does not grow as fast as the species. It has been known under several alternative and misspelled Japanese names, such as 'Aoba fue', 'Aoba fuke', 'Aoba-no-fue', and 'Aoba-no-fuye'.

'Wabi bito'

PALMATUM GROUP
GREEN

The very unusual leaves of this cultivar have three to five lobes, each a slightly different shape. When the small leaf is three-lobed, the two rudimentary lobes remain only as tiny spurs at the leaf base. The lobes, separated almost to the leaf base, are very narrow—almost straplike—and shallowly or deeply toothed. These "teeth" are flat or twisted, slender or broad, short or elongate, or any combination of these. The pattern varies from one side of the lobe to the other, as well as between lobes and leaves. The total effect is a pleasing "tattered" appearance. The leaf stalks are quite short. The basic foliage color is green, and the margins are strongly edged with rose or rusty red, especially on new foliage. Summer color remains green, changing to a good scarlet in the fall.

This plant usually forms a small shrub up to 2 m (6 ft.) tall, but can reach a height of 3 m (10 ft.). It tends to be fastigiate. It is not a sturdy cultivar and is not easily propagated. 'Wabi bito' appeared in maple lists as long ago as 1710. The name, which means "lonely person," has been misspelled 'Wabito' in the past. It has also been known under the name 'Hō ō'.

'Waka momiji'

PALMATUM GROUP
VARIEGATED

No description of this plant can be found in the old literature. It has medium-sized leaves with five to seven very deeply divided lobes. Each lobe is oblong, terminating in a long, slender, prominent tip. The lobes radiate outward, but the middle lobes appear longer. The margins are lightly toothed. The long, slender leaf stalks are red. The foliage is yellow-green with white variegation, consisting of a few flecks to entire portions of the lobe but often entirely absent. In spring the variegated portions of the new leaves are pink. The intensity of the variegation is between that of 'Versicolor' and 'Oridono nishiki'. The shoots are red, in contrast to the green shoots of

'Versicolor' and 'Oridono nishiki'. Fall color is a clear golden yellow.

This vigorous, upright, medium-sized tree forms a tall, round-topped plant, probably reaching well over 7 m (23 ft.) tall. It has also been known by the illegitimate name 'Waka momiji Variegated'.

'Wabi bito'.
Photo by J. D. Vertrees

'Waka momiji'.
Photo by Cor van Gelderen

'Wakehurst Pink'

MATSUMURAE GROUP
VARIEGATED

The large greenish leaves are pink-flushed in the spring, becoming greenish bronze with pink dots and blotched variegation. A curious feature of the fully developed leaves is that the outer lobes are deeply divided to within 5 mm of the leaf base, whereas the central lobe is divided to 1.5–2.0 cm from the base. Each long-ovate lobe has a tail-like, pointed tip and regular, sharply pointed, hooked teeth on the margins. The basal lobes tend to spread at right angles to the leaf stalks, which are purple-red with swollen bases. The upright growth habit is similar to 'Nicholsonii', forming an open-branched tree up to 4 m (13 ft.) tall and nearly as wide. The original plant is growing at Wakehurst Place Gardens, England. It was named and propagated at Firma C. Esveld, Netherlands, in the late 1980s.

'Wakehurst Pink'.
Photo Peter Gregory

'Waterfall'.
Photo by J. D. Vertrees

'Waterfall'

DISSECTUM GROUP
GREEN

The leaves have the typical shape but are slightly larger than those of most green dissectums. The seven to nine multidissected lobes hold together closely and tend to cascade. Each lobe is narrowly pinnatifid and re-incised. The distinguishing feature of this cultivar is that the leaves have a longer, more flowing appearance as they cascade down the outside of the mature plants. The leaf stalks are short. The foliage is a good, bright green, which is retained well all season. The plant stands full sun very well. The fall colors are brilliant gold suffused with crimson. The branch development is strong and sturdy, and the side branches cascade strongly.

This cultivar is hardy and beautiful. The original plant at Willowwood Arboretum, New Jersey, was 3 m (10 ft.) high and 4 m (13 ft.) wide in the mid-1970s. This plant was a selected seedling named for it beautiful cascading habit by Henry Hohman in the 1920s. It has been known under the name 'Dissectum Waterfall'.

'Watnong'

DISSECTUM GROUP
RED

The medium-sized leaves of this attractive laceleaf from New Jersey have the same color as the well-known 'Baldsmith' and the finely cut, laceleaf appearance of 'Chantilly Lace'. Both spring and fall colors are outstanding. Spring leaves are a bright red, changing to salmon pink, then bronze-green for the summer. New leaves are produced throughout the growing season, producing a multicolored effect of the lacy, cascading foliage. Fall colors are a brilliant orange to scarlet. The five- to seven-lobed leaves are little wider than the midveins in the lower half, and the finely toothed sublobes are also deeply divided.

'Watnong' forms a broad, dense, cascading mound up to 3 m (10 ft.) tall and about twice as wide. It is very reliable and thrives in full sun, where the coloring is at its best. The leaf color combinations are similar to 'Baldsmith', but the fall color is more stunning. 'Watnong' is considered more versatile and hardier than 'Baldsmith'.

'Wendy'

PALMATUM GROUP
GREEN

This unusual semidwarf was selected and named by Dick Van der Maat, Netherlands, because of the attractive multicolored foliage. The new leaves emerge an appealing pink-red, becoming bronze-red, then bronzed purple-red, before changing to a shiny midgreen, sometimes tinged blue-green, with lighter bronzed margins and tips. As new leaves are appearing all summer, 'Wendy' produces a subtle, multicolored effect throughout the growing season. The upper leaf surfaces have a semiglossy sheen which accentuates this. Fall color is golden yellow.

The many small, mainly seven-lobed leaves are fairly deeply divided. Each broad, oval lobe has a triangular, pointed tip and relatively large, coarse teeth around the outer margins. The tiny basal lobes point backward at an acute angle to the slender, bright red leaf stalks. 'Wendy' forms a

small, wide-spreading shrub, ideal for the smaller garden and for container culture.

'Westonbirt Orange'

AMOENUM GROUP
GREEN

This newer introduction from a tree growing at Westonbirt Arboretum, England, is notable for its outstanding golden orange fall color. It was propagated and distributed by Firma C. Esveld, Netherlands. The medium-sized five- to seven-lobed leaves are divided mainly up to halfway to the leaf base. The lobes are broadly ovate with tail-

'Watnong'.
Photo by Cor van Gelderen

'Wendy'.
Photo by Cor van Gelderen

'Westonbirt Orange'.
Photo by Peter Gregory

'Westonbirt Red'.
Photo by Peter Gregory

like pointed tips and with finely and evenly toothed margins. The slender leaf stalks are red, and the shoots a glossy dark red which lasts for several years. 'Westonbirt Orange is vigorous and forms an upright 10-m (33-ft.) tree with a rounded crown. It is a very attractive companion plant in any large garden landscape.

'Westonbirt Red'

MATSUMURAE GROUP
GREEN

This is another outstanding cultivar from Westonbirt Arboretum, England, this time with stunning scarlet fall color, which is almost luminous in the evening light and which matches that of the ever popu-

lar 'Ō sakazuki'. This tree was also propagated and distributed by Firma C. Esveld, Netherlands.

The medium to large mainly seven-lobed leaves are unevenly divided: the central lobes vary from deeply divided to divided halfway, and the outer lateral lobes are very deeply divided. Each ovate lobe has a long tail-like tip and clearly toothed margins. The green to light pink leaf stalks are very slender with a central groove on the upper side. The young shoots are also slender and green but red-bronzed on the upper exposed side.

'Westonbirt Red' has abundant red fruits to complement the brilliant scarlet fall color. It grows into a small to medium-sized tree up to about 8 m (26 ft.) tall with an 11-m (36-ft.) broad crown. It makes a fine specimen tree or contrasting companion in the garden landscape.

'Whitney Red'

AMOENUM GROUP
RED

This vigorous tree is notable for its intense, deep purple-red leaves. The medium-sized deeply cut leaves emerge a deep purple-red and retain their color well into late summer, when the upper surfaces become a bronze-red, while the undersurfaces are suffused with green. Fall color is a vivid scarlet. Each five-lobed, medium to large leaf has a heart-shaped to straight base. The deeply divided lobes are ovate, with tail-like tips. The lobes narrow slightly at the lobe junctions. The margins are evenly toothed. The strong, dark red leaf stalk has a swollen base. 'Whitney Red' has a growth habit similar to 'Bloodgood', becoming up to 8 m (26 ft.) tall. It was found as a chance seedling at Whitney Gardens in Washington State.

'Wild Goose'

PALMATUM GROUP
GREEN

This Dutch cultivar was selected by Dick van der Maat because of the unusual leaf trait in which the lateral lobes overlap the central lobe when fully developed. The medium-sized leaves have five to seven broad lobes which are divided almost to the leaf base. The broad-ovate lobes are widest in the middle and narrow markedly to the lobe junctions. Each lobe is very coarsely toothed. New leaves emerge a striking orange-red in the spring and become midgreen for the summer. This cultivar is vigorous and estimated to form an upright tree up to 4 m (13 ft.) in height.

'Whitney Red'.
Photo by Cor van Gelderen

'Wild Goose'.
Photo by Peter Gregory

'Willow Leaf'

LINEARILOBUM GROUP
RED

Similar to 'Red Pygmy' in leaf shape and color, growth rate, and habit, 'Willow Leaf' has slightly shorter leaf stalks and sturdier shoots. The young leaves are bright orange-red, soon becoming a deep purple-red that lasts well throughout the summer. The medium to large straplike leaves are five-lobed. Each lobe is linear to long-ovate, with a long, tapering tip. The margins are sparsely and finely toothed. The slender leaf stalks are red. On vigorous young shoots, the leaves are more matsumurae-like, with broader lobes and with numerous shallow, fine-pointed teeth along the margins. 'Willow Leaf' forms an upright, round-headed, small tree, up to 3 m (10 ft.) in height, with graceful, semipendulous branches and foliage.

'Wilson's Pink Dwarf'.
Photo by Cor van Gelderen

'Wilson's Pink Dwarf'

DWARF GROUP
GREEN

This delightful, upright shrub is similar to 'Coral Pink' in having tiny leaves which are very colorful in the spring. They are usually five-lobed and a bright, light green in the summer. In early spring, the entire plant is a light, bright pinkish or pink-red. The coloration is brilliant, quite noticeable in the landscape, and lasts for several weeks. As the summer season advances, the base green leaf color increases with the pink to rusty red tones continuing on new leaves. Under some growing conditions there is even some mottling. The leaves turn orange to red in the fall. The new foliage is rather small with a long center lobe. The lobes are rather slender, have toothed edges, and vary in shape. Leaves on older wood are truly palmate and more uniform in shape. This fine shrub always attracts attention in the spring. It grows well, is vigorous but not rank, and is a welcome addition to the Dwarf Group. It was first selected as a seedling by James Wilson, California.

'Winter Flame'

PALMATUM GROUP
GREEN

This outstanding cultivar was introduced by Duncan and Davies Nursery, New Zealand, and is a small, compact, bushy form of 'Sango kaku'. It has small to medium-sized seven-lobed, very deeply divided leaves.

The three middle lobes are ovate-triangular, with tail-like, pointed tips. The broadest point is in the lower third of the lobe. At the lobe junctions, which are within 5 mm of the leaf base. the lobe narrows to 3–4 mm. The small, but distinctly basal lobes are angled backward and outward. The short, slender leaf stalks are red. Like 'Sango kaku', 'Winter Flame' has lovely soft, lime-green spring foliage contrasting beautifully with the pink-red shoots. The leaves become light green through the summer, taking on an attractive yellow-orange-red mottling in the fall before turning a light, crimson red. The bright coral-red winter shoots are like 'Sango kaku', but the habit is different, remaining compact and bushy, reaching no more than 3 m (10 ft.) at maturity. This cultivar is an ideal compact maple for the small garden and has colorful features all year.

'Wou nishiki'

MATSUMURAE GROUP
GREEN

The interesting, small leaves are very deeply divided into mainly seven lobes, which are widely separated almost to the base. Each lobe is elongate-ovate and tapers to a long, sharp tip. The margins are deeply toothed. The thin, short leaf stalks are reddish. The new leaves are a bright, almost yellow-green. The margins are strongly tinted with bright rose to rusty red, which shades into the green leaf. As the summer progresses, the rose tints fade and the leaves become a bright, light green. They take full sun quite well, but bronze in extreme temperatures. The fall color is a variable bright crimson. This upright-growing plant reaches about 4 m (13 ft.) in height and tends to be fastigiate, producing many small branches and twigs. It has also been known under the alternative translations 'Nou nishiki' and 'O nishiki'.

'Winter Flame'.
Photo by Peter Gregory

'Wou nishiki'.
Photo by J. D. Vertrees

'Yasemin'

MATSUMURAE GROUP
RED

This outstanding cultivar from Firma C. Esveld, Netherlands, has large, attractive, deeply cut, shiny red leaves. Like the similar 'Trompenburg', it is thought to be a cross between *Acer palmatum* and *A. shirasawanum*. It has very attractive, deep red foliage and red fruits. The leaves are a darker color and have slightly flatter and wider lobes with larger teeth than 'Trompenburg'. The deep red leaves hold their color well into the summer, slowly becoming bronze-green on the upper surface. The lower surface turns a gray-green with light purple bronzing toward the tips in late summer. The bark of the older shoots is a contrasting green.

The seven- to nine-lobed leaves are almost circular in shape as the very deeply divided lobes are well spread out. Each lobe is long-ovate with a sharply pointed tip. The broadest point of the lobe is in the outer third. There are large, coarse, saw-

'Yasemin'.
Photo by Cor van Gelderen

'Yatsubusa'.
Photo by J. D. Vertrees

teeth on the margins of the outer half of each lobe. The lobe edges have just a hint of being curved downward, but not to the extent seen in the leaves of 'Trompenburg'. The slender, red leaf stalks are short with swollen bases.

'Yasemin' is a vigorous, upright-growing tree, up to 10 m (33 ft.) high. It originated as a chance seedling and was noticed by Cor van Gelderen, Netherlands, who named it after his daughter. Interestingly, the original plant seems to display the influence of several nearby trees—the color of 'Bloodgood', the habit of 'Trompenburg', and the leaf shape of *Acer japonicum* 'Aconitifolium'.

'Yatsubusa'

DWARF GROUP
GREEN

"Yatsubusa" is a general term meaning "dwarf" in Japanese. It can be compared with the general term "dissectum," embracing all the relations and cultivars of this type. Several plants have been given the cultivar name 'Yatsubusa' in various collections and arboreta. They vary in plant size, leaf size, and growth rate. Although each is truly a "yatsubusa," this term should not be used by itself as a cultivar name. Many "yatsubusa" clones are correctly designated with cultivar status, such as 'Hime yatsubusa', 'Sekka yatsubusa', and 'Shishi yatsubusa'.

The "yatsubusas" of *Acer palmatum* may be generally described as having small leaves which are five- to seven-lobed and typically palmate. The lobes are short-ovate, usually separated more than halfway to the leaf base. Each lobe normally terminates in a short point, and the margins are usually distinctly toothed. The center lobe is usually more prominent. The leaf stalks are stiff and short. The basic leaf color is green. The new foliage unfolds with a shading of red along the margins, which is rather typical of many green palmatum seedlings. This red soon fades out into the solid green of summer. Fall colors are a mixture of yellows or reds. The yatsubusas all form small, compact, shrublike plants. Some selections grow more upright, while others tend to grow laterally. All are popular for bonsai, having the dwarf character as well as the ability to produce large numbers of tiny side branches, thus making a dense plant.

'Yezo nishiki'

AMOENUM GROUP
RED

This brilliant cultivar has a rich, bright reddish purple spring color, which becomes deeper as the summer advances. In late summer the leaves become red-bronze, except in deep shade where they become greenish. Fall colors are brilliant crimson and scarlet. The seven-lobed leaves are medium-sized, with a flattish leaf base. The lobes separate to about halfway to the leaf base. Each lobe is ovate-acuminate, with the end tapering to a sharp point. The margins are evenly and finely toothed. The red leaf stalks are slender and short. The upright, wide-spreading tree reaches 7 m (23 ft.) tall. The young plants grow rapidly, then slow and thicken to form a broad, arching top with a spread of about 4 m (13 ft.). 'Yezo nishiki' is a hardy, sturdy selection. Other names by which it has been known are 'Ezo nishiki', 'Jedo nishiki', and 'Sinuatum'.

'Yūbae'

MATSUMURAE GROUP
VARIEGATED

This tall-growing, red-leaved cultivar has occasional variegation. After observing the plant at Maplewood for six years, I named and registered it as 'Yūbae', meaning "eve-

ning glow." As the stock plant matured and young grafts were forced, it appeared to become less and less variegated, until as a 15-year old stock plant, the variegation only occurred in small amounts on twiggy wood of older growth. The main foliage is not variegated.

The lobes of the medium to large leaves are very deeply divided, almost to the leaf base, and they radiate strongly outward. Each lobe is ovate with a tapering, pointed tip. The margins are slightly and irregularly toothed. The color is a strong, bold, dark red or maroon. The more exposed

'Yezo nishiki'.
Photo by Peter Gregory

'Yubae'.
Photo by Cor van Gelderen

to full light, the darker the tones. Leaves inside the tree or shaded by other trees show a strong undertone of dark green. The variegation, where it occurs, consists of patches and blobs of a lighter pink-red on the deeper base red. Fall color is bright red. The foliage is rather pleasant and attractive, even if no variegation is present.

'Yūbae' makes a good, dependable, red cultivar, but may be a disappointment if grown as a variegated plant. It forms a sturdy, medium-sized tree reaching 6 m (20 ft.) tall.

'Yūgure', summer color.
Photo by J. D. Vertrees

'Yūgure', fall color.
Photo by Peter Gregory

'Yūgure'

MATSUMURAE GROUP
RED

'Yūgure' is an old cultivar found in the Japanese literature as early as 1710. The new foliage is crimson and later turns to a rusty tone. In summer, green tones suffuse into the reddish leaves. Fall color is a variable crimson hue. The medium to large leaves have seven lobes moderately deeply divided. Each lobe is ovate, terminating in a sharply pointed tip. The inner third of the lobe narrows fairly sharply at the junction. The margins are lightly and evenly toothed. The leaf stalks are fairly short. This hardy upright form has quite slender branches and shoots. It forms an upright round-topped tree up to 5 m (16 ft.) or so tall.

Unfortunately, there was confusion about this cultivar. A small-leaved green palmatum-type plant was sometimes wrongly sold under this name. Possibly it resulted from the rootstock overwhelming the original graft. Descriptions in old Japanese literature as well as illustrations in more recent publications leave little doubt about this reddish leaved Matsumurae-type cultivar. The name means "twilight."

'Yuri hime'

DWARF GROUP
GREEN

The foliage of this little cultivar, one of the dwarfest, is very dense, due to the short annual growth and closeness of the nodes and buds. The appearance is like a covering of feathers. The small leaves have five long and narrow, very deeply divided lobes. Each narrowly elongate-ovate lobe terminates in a long, tapering point. The margins are finely toothed. Long, thin leaf stalks, equal in length to the leaf blade, allow the leaves to layer down over one another. Leaf color is a light green which holds well during the summer, but does not produce an outstanding fall color. This tiny shrub is difficult to propagate since the amount of annual growth is quite limited. Although it is quite small, it seems very hardy and takes full sun and exposure. When available, it is a gem for miniature landscapes, such as alpine gardens.

'Yuri hime'.
Photo by Francis Schroeder

6 Other *Acer* Species from Japan and Their Cultivars

WHILE CHAPTER 5 COVERS *Acer palmatum* and its cultivars, this chapter includes all other species of *Acer* found in Japan and their cultivars. It also covers *Acer* species that have been cultivated and selected for particular characteristics by Japanese horticulturists. While the maples described in this chapter are not originally native to Japan, they have been so widely cultivated that they have been grouped with the Japanese maples in the nursery trade.

Acer argutum Maximowicz (1867)

COMMON NAME: Pointed-leaf maple
JAPANESE COMMON NAMES: Asanoha kaede, Miyama momiji

This delightful small tree makes an excellent companion plant in combined landscaping. It has beautiful foliage and forms a well-shaped, compact tree which matures up to 10 m (33 ft.) in height. The small five-lobed leaves are 5–9 cm long and wide, divided about halfway to the leaf base, prominently veined, and covered in fine white hairs beneath. The upper surface is a little rough and uneven to the touch, rather like the primrose leaf. The lobes are broadly triangular-ovate with acuminate tips. The conspicuous, sharp double teeth on the leaf margins give rise to the specific name *argutum*, meaning "sharp-toothed."

Acer argutum is among the most overlooked maples, yet one of the most attractive once you catch sight of the remarkable symmetry of the pretty green leaves with their uniform sharp teeth—highlighted when the foliage turns a clear, even yellow in the fall. This species is confined to Honshu and Shikoku Islands in Japan, growing in the upper temperate to lower subalpine mountain forest zones at elevations from 800 to 2000 m (2640–6600 ft.) above sea level. It grows along moist streamsides and in forests of the lower mountain slopes.

Facing: *Acer sieboldianum,* habit and fall color.
Photo by Peter Gregory

Below: *Acer argutum.*
Photo by Peter Gregory

Acer buergerianum Miquel (1865)

COMMON NAMES: Trident maple,
Three-pronged maple

JAPANESE COMMON NAMES: Hana
zakura, Kakunimo, Sankaku kaede, Te
kaede, Toyama kaede

This beautiful small tree matures in the landscape at about 10 m (33 ft.) in height. Under the most favorable culture conditions it may exceed 12 m (40 ft.). It has been used in many countries for street plantings since it adapts well to dry conditions and to air pollution from traffic, and has good structural strength. It has an upright growth pattern.

The leaves have a glossy, green upper surface with ivylike texture, a glaucous green to blue-gray underside, a narrow angled or rounded base, and usually three forward-pointing lobes—hence the common name. Each leaf is 5–10 cm long and 4–8 cm wide and has a distinctive three-nerved venation, one nerve (or midrib) to the tip of each lobe. When they first emerge the leaves are glossy red to purple-red. The fall color is a spectacular blend of oranges, reds, and purples in interesting and variable combinations. Since the leaves are shiny, the colors are very bril-

Acer buergerianum.
Photo by J. D. Vertrees

liant. The fall color appears late in the season, with the leaves often not falling until late autumn or early winter (late November to early December).

Acer buergerianum is also excellent for and widely used in bonsai. It dwarfs well in container culture, and the leaves become quite small as the plant adapts to the training of bonsai methods.

This maple is full of anomalies. It was named from a tree in Japan, yet is native only to eastern China and Taiwan. It was introduced into cultivation in Japan many centuries ago, liked the conditions, and became "native"—rather like the European sycamore in England. This species is included with the maples from Japan because Japanese horticulturists have developed many interesting cultivars from it. These are usually included in lists of Japanese maples in the trade.

One supposed cultivar, 'Jako kaede', was included in Japanese maple lists for decades as a musk-scented buergerianum and was regarded as a rare form. Thomas Delendick submitted plant material to the noted authority on leaf venation, Toshimasa Tanai of Hokkaido University, who identified it as *Premna japonica*, a member of the family Verbenaceae, and not a maple at all!

Acer buergerianum 'Akebono'

This cultivar is almost identical to *Acer buergerianum* 'Goshiki kaede'. In Western cultivation is usually treated as synonymous with 'Goshiki kaede', because it is almost impossible to tell the difference. It is still grown in Japan as 'Akebono kaede' and occurs in Japanese collections. It is reported to have slightly more white variegation in the foliage, and when the leaves first emerge, they are yellowish with lightly bronzed margins. The name means "daybreak maple."

Acer buergerianum 'Eastwood Cloud'

This pale-colored form has almost pure white spring foliage. During the first few weeks it slowly turns a creamy pink, then progresses to a light green. The green holds well during the summer, turning into the excellent red tones of the typical fall color of the species. The growth rate of this cultivar is noticeably slower than that of the species. It makes a rounded, small tree. The foliage is larger than that of another white-leaved form, *Acer buergerianum* 'Wakō nishiki'. Ron Gordon of Taihape, New Zealand, raised 'Eastwood Cloud' from seed. The original plant was selected in 1949. Peter Cave of Cave's Tree Nursery, Hamilton, New Zealand, propagated and introduced this plant, and registered its name.

Acer buergerianum 'Goshiki kaede'

This variegated cultivar has smaller leaves than the species, ranging from 3 to 5 cm long and wide. Basic leaf color is a rich green. The white variegation varies from totally covering the leaf to covering only half the leaf (the midvein separating the green half from the white half) to appearing as small flecks on the shiny green background. Leaves with large white flecks are often sickle-shaped or distorted. New growth is often pink to rusty pink in the variegations, and later turns to white or cream, sometimes with a yellow sheen. Because leaf color is so variable, this cultivar is called 'Goshiki kaede', literally "five-colored maple." The growth habit is semi-dwarf and it becomes a bushy, shrublike plant. It can be pruned and trained to a single-stemmed, upright, short bush. 'Tōyō nishiki' is possibly a synonym of 'Goshiki kaede'.

Acer buergerianum 'Goshiki kosode'

This selection is thought to originate from a chance seedling hybrid of 'Goshiki kaede' and other *Acer buergerianum* cultivars at Maplewood, and was originally named 'Sue's Surprise'. It was discovered by Suzanne Olsen, then renamed and propagated by Howard Hughes of Montesano, Washington. The name means "multicolored kimono."

'Goshiki kosode' appears to be similar to the species in vigor and in leaf shape and size, but the leaves are variegated. It does not introduce large segments of creamy white as does 'Goshiki kaede', but instead offers mottled areas or a dusted mix of cream and green, not unlike that occurring with *A. palmatum* 'Ukigumo'. This type of variegation has not previously been reported in *A. buergerianum*. The creamy areas of the emerging young leaves are shaded with pink or red tones. 'Goshiki kosode' forms an upright small tree and, like most variegated plants, is sensitive to excessive sun and benefits from some shade, especially in the hottest part of the day.

Acer buergerianum 'Hana chiru sato'

The very heavily variegated foliage is similar to that of the older, better-known *Acer buergerianum* 'Waka momiji', but is said to be more robust. The spring leaves emerge

Acer buergerianum 'Goshiki kaede'.
Photo by J. D. Vertrees

a pale pink with bright pink-red leaf stalks, becoming cream with pink "throats" and slowly changing to creamy white with thin green veins. Fall color is bright red. This cultivar grows into a broad shrub up to about 3 m (10 ft.) in height. It was selected and named by R. Hayashida in 1960 and introduced from Japan into Europe in the 1990s.

Acer buergerianum 'Hana chiru sato'. Photo by Talon Buchholz

Acer buergerianum 'Kōshi miyasami'. Photo by Peter Gregory

Acer buergerianum 'Iwao kaede'

This cultivar, the "rock maple," has leaves slightly larger than those of the species but with a short leaf stalk. The appearance is very broad, since the two lobes extend sharply at right angles. The leaf base is broadly subcordate. All three lobes are triangular, tapering rapidly to a blunt tip. The three main veins are prominent. New foliage is a dark green-red to bright red, depending upon the amount of shade. It later becomes a very shiny, dark green with a leathery texture. This maple has been known under the name 'Iwao nishiki'.

Acer buergerianum 'Kōshi miyasami'

This strong-growing cultivar was imported to the Netherlands from Japan in 1979 and makes a densely branched shrubby tree up to 6 m (20 ft.) tall. The small leathery leaves have rounded leaf bases and short, blunt lobes. The spring leaves are a clear pink-red with a yellow-green main vein down the center of each of the three lobes. The leaves become completely green from the midribs through the summer and turn a fiery red in the fall. The name of this cultivar is derived from the color of the blood-red new shoots.

Acer buergerianum 'Kyūden'

'Kyūden' is a very dwarf form of the species. The internodes on the slender twigs are very close together, forming a dense leaf pattern. The leaves are also small, and usually distorted, so that few leaves are the same. The typical leaf outline is ovate to triangular-ovate, and the leaf base is heart-shaped. Each lobe is small, irregular, and roundish with a blunt tip. One or both side lobes may be absent or very small. The leaf stalks are very short. Leaf color is a very shiny, deep green above and glaucous beneath. Spring leaves are a light, bronzed green, changing gradually to dark green for the summer, and turning glossy yellow and orange for the fall. This rare cultivar is not easily propagated. 'Miyadono' is so like it in size, habit, and leaf that it is often treated as synonymous. 'Kyūden' means "palace."

Acer buergerianum 'Marubatō kaede'

The foliage of this form differs from the species in texture and shape. It is bright green in color, firmer, leathery, and not as deeply lobed. The side lobes are short and blunt and are placed toward the leaf tip. The leaf surface is quite shiny and appears covered with minute, pinpoint impressions. The leaf base is slightly heart-shaped. The three mid-veins are prominent. The leaves are larger than normal with the center lobe dominant and gradually pointed. The leaf stalks are sturdy and short. The fall colors are a brilliant orange-red. This upright-growing, small tree is slow to attain its ultimate height of 9 m (30 ft.). It forms a round-topped tree and is hardy in most locations.

Acer buergerianum 'Mino yatsubusa'

The very odd leaves of this cultivar are most unmaplelike! They are three-lobed, with the center lobe being long and narrow. The side lobes are quite short and extend at right angles to pointing slightly forward. The lobes are divided about a third of the distance or less from the leaf base. The leaf mainly consists of a long, narrow, gradually tapering center lobe which ends in a very sharp point and has irregularly notched margins. The side lobes end in rather blunt points and have mainly plain margins. The sides of all the lobes tend to turn up.

Spring leaves emerge a bronzed green with green veins, the green spreading over the whole leaf for the summer. The summer foliage is a very shiny, rich green. The fall color is a brilliant combination of scarlet and orange. The shiny leaves have the appearance of being lacquered as the fall colors develop.

This dwarf plant makes a dense, rounded, small shrub. Leaf nodes are closely spaced on the shoots. Lateral buds occur at the leaf stalk bases and produce tiny new side shoots or small leaf clusters. 'Mino yat-

Acer buergerianum 'Kyūden'.
Photo by J. D. Vertrees

Acer buergerianum 'Marubatō kaede'.
Photo by J. D. Vertrees

Acer buergerianum 'Mino yatsubusa'.
Photo by J. D. Vertrees

subusa' is hardy, but it is very difficult to propagate (even on *Acer buergerianum* stock) and remains one of the rarer forms in cultivation.

Acer buergerianum 'Mitsubatō kaede'

This form has the leaves placed very close together. The resulting leaf cover is very dense. The foliage is bright green and is a lighter, thinner texture than the species. When grown in the shade, the leaves are quite shiny. The leaf forms a distinctive T-shape. The long center lobe is twice as long as the two side lobes, which extend at right angles to the base. The leaf base is straight, forming a flat "top" to the T. The margins are notched or lobulate. 'Mitsuba kaede nishiki siyou' was imported from Japan in 1975, but cannot be distinguished from 'Mitsubatō kaede', so is treated as a synonym. The latter cultivar has also been misspelled 'Mitsuba kaede'.

Acer buergerianum 'Miyasama'

This delightful form has small, thick, leathery leaves. They are dark green, durable, compact, and glaucous underneath. The leaf base is rounded or shallowly heart-shaped. The side lobes are usually short, rounded, and occasionally indistinct as they form an ovate leaf. The cen-

ter lobe is bluntly pointed. The typical leaf forms a triangular-ovate outline and has smooth margins. The short light green leaf stalks are persistent, thus prolonging the fall color period. Fall colors are pleasing tones of yellow and orange and, because the leaves persist, the fall color period is extended.

This form is not as tall-growing as the species. The leaf nodes are close together on the twigs, resulting in dense foliage. It tends to be a well-rounded, upright shrub, probably not more than about 4 m (13 ft.) in height. The growth habit is stubby. This hardy addition to any landscape is noticeably different. Seed was distributed in the early years to many bonsai nurseries, and there are now many old bonsai specimens of this maple.

This cultivar is from the subspecies *formosanosum*, indigenous to Taiwan. Prior to the 1940s it was called 'Fushima kaede'. One of the oldest specimens was in the garden of Prince Fushimi. Now it is known as 'Miyasama', which means "prince," and is sometimes called 'Miyasama kaede', the "prince's maple."

Acer buergerianum 'Miyasama yatsubusa'

This plant, which is almost identical to 'Miyasama' except for size, is short and stubby and grows only a few centimeters per year. It forms a very dense plant.

The small leaves are very similar to those of 'Miyasama'. Each leaf has three short, broad, triangular-ovate lobes with short tips, and a rounded to shallowly heart-shaped base. The side lobes are prominent, forming right-angles at about the center of the leaf sides. The three midribs are prominent, one in the center of each lobe. The leaf stalks are short and stiff. The leaves are green with bronze-red tips and margins as they develop. As the shiny leaves attain full size, they become a typical bright green.

Acer buergerianum 'Miyasama yatsubusa'.
Photo by J. D. Vertrees

The texture is rather firm, almost leathery. The undersurface is bluish green. Fall colors are yellow-gold with shades of rose.

This delightful dwarf is rather rare in collections and slightly difficult to propagate. It has also been named 'Miyasama kaede yatsubusa'.

Acer buergerianum 'Narutō'

This interesting cultivar is noted for its surprising foliage. Each leaf appears to form a sharp-pointed T. The center lobe is a long triangle, and the side lobes extend at right angles, all being sharply pointed. All three lobes have margins which are strongly incurved, making the lobes appear much narrower. The incurled margins are almost smooth, or very lightly toothed. These rolled margins and sharp points accentuate the T-shape of the leaf. The leaves are almost as broad as long. The leaf stalks are strong and short. The heavy-textured leaves are a deep, rich green. The top surface is shiny, but the undersurface is glaucous, giving a two-toned effect to the foliage. Fall colors are a rich gold, blended with red.

This sturdy shrub grows up to 4 m (13 ft.) tall. It soon forms a rather dense, twiggy plant. It is a little-known but interesting form of the species, also seen under the name 'Narutō kaede'.

Acer buergerianum 'Nusatori yama'

The leaves of this delicate plant are almost entirely white (*ubu fu* variegation). As they first emerge in the spring, they have a strong orange-pink overtone, which soon turns white or cream and green for the summer. Fall colors are yellows to reds.

The foliage varies according to conditions under which this sensitive plant is grown. Leaves are usually 2–3 cm long and wide, but may be twice this size under optimum conditions. The shape of the leaf is triangular, but side lobes are sometimes suppressed into small, rounded portions. Occasionally, the side lobes are entirely lacking, resulting in an ovate leaf. The texture of the leaf is rather thin and delicate. The margins are slightly bluntly toothed to lobulate. The leaf stalks are short and sturdy. This very slow-growing plant reaches about 1 m (3 ft.) tall. All twigs and branches are slender.

'Nusatori yama' is extremely difficult to maintain in cultivation. It is also very difficult to propagate. To grow a new graft into a two- to three-year-old plant takes special care and attention. Since the foliage is almost totally lacking in chlorophyll or food-processing tissue, it is necessary to leave a small amount of the understock,

Acer buergerianum 'Naruto'.
Photo by Peter Gregory

Acer buergerianum 'Nusatori yama'.
Photo by J. D. Vertrees

which should produce the normal green foliage. This, in turn, helps sustain the grafted cultivar through photosynthetic support.

This cultivar is not particularly beautiful or attractive, but it is of considerable interest to the collector of rare plants. It should be grown in shade to prevent leaf scorch from the direct sun. It also seems quite sensitive to mold or fungi.

Acer buergerianum 'Subintegrum'. Photo by Peter Gregory

Acer buergerianum 'Tanchō'. Photo by Harry Olsen

Acer buergerianum 'Subintegrum'

This maple is hardy and grows into a shrubby tree with leathery leaves which are only slightly three-lobed. The leaves are shiny green above and glaucous beneath.

'Subintegrum' is similar to *Acer buergerianum* 'Kōshi miyasami', but with longer and less obviously lobed leaves. It has also been known under the name 'Integrifolium'.

Acer buergerianum 'Tanchō'

This cultivar is much like 'Narutō' in foliage but has much smaller habit. The small leaves are as long as wide, and the slender leaf stalk is almost as long. Each leaf is strongly three-lobed with the lobe margins rolled tightly. The rolled margins are slightly toothed, but this feature is hidden. As the center lobe and the two side lobes are tightly rolled, the leaf appears to be T-shaped. The leaf cups upward from the leaf stalk. The leaves are bronze-red initially, becoming a deep, rich, glossy green above, with the lower surface glaucous. Since both sides show on each leaf because of the curling, the foliage appears two-toned. Fall color is a glossy yellow to orange. The leaves are set closely on the twigs, forming dense foliage.

This dwarf maple may grow 8–12 cm per season. It becomes rather dense and shrubby. It is a most unusual and little-known form of the species which is not easily propagated and which remains rare in collections. It has also been known under the name 'Tanchō kaede'.

Acer buergerianum 'Wakō nishiki'

The tiny variegated leaves of this dwarf cultivar set it apart from all the others. The oblong-ovate leaves rapidly taper to a very sharp tip on the center lobe. The two very small side lobes, which extend almost at right angles, break the ovate outline. The stiff leaf stalk is very short. New leaves emerge a light pink. They may become totally white to cream in some growth, but most are very light green, heavily to almost completely shaded white to cream. The white color is due to the concentration of very tiny dots which merge together and become almost solid. In the leaves with most white, the three main veins are a distinct, contrasting green. Fall colors are oranges to reds.

This very slow-growing, compact shrub is not easy to propagate and requires extra care in cultivation. Nonetheless, it is very popular in Japan.

Acer capillipes Maximowicz (1867)

COMMON NAMES: Hair-foot maple, Red snakebark, Red-shoot maple

JAPANESE COMMON NAMES: Ashiboso urinoki, Hoscoe kaede, O karabana, Urika nishiki

This desirable form of snakebark maple can become a large tree, usually reaching up to 15 m (49 ft.) high, though up to 20 m (66 ft.) in the wild. The attractive bark is green to gray with light, lengthwise stripes. It turns gray-brown with darker stripes and becomes slightly fissured as it ages.

The three- to five-lobed leaves have a characteristic, dominant, broad triangular center lobe with a narrow, pointed tip and small, sometimes inconspicuous, shallow side lobes. The base is heart-shaped to rounded. The leaves vary in size from 8–12 cm long and 5–9 cm wide. The margins are irregularly toothed. The dominant center lobe has numerous hornbeam-like pairs of parallel lateral veins. This, and the curious tiny, light-colored bridges or pegs often seen in the vein axils beneath, make *Acer capillipes* easily recognizable.

The leaves, leaf stalks and young shoots are pink-red to scarlet as they appear in the spring. Although the leaves become a bright green, the bright red persists on the leaf stalks and shoots throughout the growing season. While this tree is endemic to Japan and is distributed throughout the main islands of Honshu and Shikoku, it is concentrated in a fairly small area of central Honshu, in the mountain areas around Tokyo, where it is quite common. It is a

Acer buergerianum 'Wakō nishiki'.
Photo by Cor van Gelderen

Acer capillipes, leaves.
Photo by Hugh Angus

Acer capillipes, bark.
Photo by Peter Gregory

bold, beautiful tree which is useful in overstory plantings in the landscape. Received the RHS Award of Garden Merit.

Acer carpinifolium Siebold & Zuccarini (1845)

COMMON NAME: Hornbeam maple

JAPANESE COMMON NAMES: Arahago, Chidorinoki, Taniasa, Tsubanok, Yamashibe kaede

The characteristic leaves of this most unmaplelike looking species are quite distinct in the genus *Acer* but closely resemble those of *Carpinus*, the hornbeam. They have the same rough-textured surfaces, long, ovate-oblong shape, tail-like tip, heart-shaped base, numerous (12–23 pairs) of conspicuous, lateral veins, and coarse, sharply pointed, double-toothed margins. The pairs of leaves are openly spaced along the shoots, lying horizontally. Each leaf is 8–15 cm long and 3–7 cm wide. The leaf stalks are very short.

This large, multistemmed shrub or small tree matures at 12 m (40 ft.), and forms a wide-spreading, mushroom-domed crown. It is hardy and durable, and makes an outstanding specimen plant for landscaping. It is a native of Japan and is common in temperate, deciduous forests on moist soils in the ravines of Honshu, Shikoku, and Kyushu Islands, at an elevation of 200–1300 m (660–4290 ft) above sea level.

Acer carpinifolium.
Photo by Hugh Angus

Acer carpinifolium 'Esveld Select'.
Photo by Talon Buchholz

Acer carpinifolium 'Esveld Select'

Acer carpinifolium is very uniform in its characteristics, hence this unique cultivar is a surprise. It was selected from a batch of seedlings at Firma C. Esveld, Boskoop, Netherlands in the early 1970s. It is a narrowly fastigiate dwarf form, attaining a height of only 3 m (10 ft.) in 20 years. The small leaves are shaped like those of the species and turn golden yellow in the fall. This very distinctive plant needs some shade and a moist site, and is difficult to propagate.

Acer caudatum subsp. *ukurunduense* (Trautvetteri & Meyer) A. E. Murray (1966)

JAPANESE COMMON NAMES: Arahaga, Arahana, Hozaki kaede, Ogara bana

This variable-growing plant forms a large shrub or small tree up to 10 m (33 ft.) tall. The bark of older trunks is light gray-brown and peels off in small, thin flakes. The bark on young shoots is yellow-brown and pubescent. The leaves are circular and shallowly five-angled. They measure 7–13 cm long and 8–15 cm wide, and have heart-shaped bases. The green leaf has a dull, yellow to brown pubescence underneath. The five lobes are ovate-triangular, acuminate, with margins sharply and coarsely toothed.

The type species is endemic to the Himalayas, northern India, Myanmar, and western China, while the subspecies *ukurunduense* is more widely distributed in Japan, Kurile Islands, Korea, southeastern Siberia, and Manchuria. It is closely related to *Acer spicatum*, the mountain maple of eastern North America. Zones 4–10.

Acer circinatum Pursh (1814)

COMMON NAME: Vine maple

Although *Acer circinatum* is not a Japanese maple, it is included here for comparative purposes because it is a close relative of the Japanese species in the series *Palmata* and due to this relationship is able to hybridize with these species to produce new cultivars. It is a native of the Pacific Northwest of in North America, the only member of the series *Palmata* occurring naturally outside Asia. All the other closely allied members are indigenous to Japan, China, and adjacent areas. This lends credence to the theory that there was once a land bridge connecting Alaska with East Asia, which allowed plants and animals to migrate between the two continents.

The close affinity is further demonstrated by success in cross-hybridizing and interspecific grafting of *Acer circinatum* onto *A. japonicum* and *A. palmatum* understock. It is also possible to make reverse grafts successfully, although *A. circinatum* heals too slowly to be a more desirable understock than *A. palmatum*.

The vine maple can form a small tree up to 8 m (26 ft.) tall or, more often, a wide-spreading, multistemmed shrub. In its native habitat, under an overstory of large conifers, it becomes a tall, viny stemmed, slender tree, winding its way up to the sunlight, ultimately reaching a height of 12 m

Acer caudatum subsp. *ukurunduense.* Photo by Peter Gregory

Acer circinatum growing wild in the Canadian Rockies. Photo by Peter Gregory

Acer circinatum, fall color. Photo by J. D. Vertrees

(40 ft.). This winding, vinelike growth gives rise to the common name.

Vine maple is most appreciated in the Pacific Northwest for its beautiful fall colors—a brilliant scarlet suffused with orange and yellow tones. Plants growing in the rich coastal regions turn a plain yellow color, whereas those growing in the drier, thin-soiled, infertile mountainsides turn to flame. This difference has led to suggestions that these intense colors do not develop where abundant moisture and fertility prevent the plant from being under stress. In the spring the circular leaves are a bright green. They have seven to nine lobes and vary from 7–10 cm long and 5–9 cm wide. The lobes are shallowly toothed to about one third of the way to the leaf base and they taper sharply to the tip. The margins are distinctly toothed.

This maple is an excellent, trouble-free small tree for landscaping as a companion plant for many types of perennials and shrubs. It is a very useful and tolerant plant for any size or shape of garden. It is perfectly hardy and grows in most conditions of soil, sun, shade, dryness or moisture. Zones 5–9.

Acer circinatum 'Burgundy Jewel'

Selected and named by Peacedale Nursery in Oregon, 'Burgundy Jewel' has leaves that are similar in shape and size to the species but different in color. While the species has green leaves, this selection has burgundy red leaves. The color is maintained throughout the summer when the plant is grown in full sun, which it seems to prefer. Foliage turns vivid reds and oranges in the fall.

The leaves have seven shallowly divided, broadly triangular lobes with bluntish tips. Unique characteristics are the ridges running between the lobe junctions and the base, the leaf margins slightly curved downward, both giving a slight concertina effect. The red upper surface has a slight sheen and narrow green midribs. The short stout leaf stalks have a central groove and are slightly hairy. The shoots, buds, and leaf stalks are bright red. 'Burgundy Jewel' grows into a small tree or shrub up to 2 m (6 ft.) tall in 10 years and has proven to be hardy up to –20°F (–29°C).

Acer circinatum 'Del's Dwarf'

The outstanding characteristic of this dwarf cultivar is the attractive copper-colored foliage in the spring and early summer. It greens out in midseason and changes to yellows, oranges and reds in the fall. The seven- to nine-lobed circular leaves are relatively large for a dwarf plant at 6–8 cm in diameter. The broadly ovate lobes, with short, pointed tips, are divided about one quarter of the way to the leaf base and have coarsely toothed margins. Leaf stalks are thick and short. This cultivar forms a compact shrub which grows to about 1 m (3 ft.) tall and a little wider. The original plant was purchased by Del Loucks and propagated and introduced by Del's Japanese Maple Nursery.

Acer circinatum 'Elegant'

This dissected leaf form of the species was introduced by the Dominium Arboretum, Ottawa, Canada, and listed by Brian Mulligan (1958). It is similar to the well-known 'Monroe', but the leaves are not quite as

Acer circinatum
'Burgundy Jewel'.
Photo by Talon Buchholz

finely cut. It is slightly more vigorous, and openly branched. At maturity it attains a height of about 6 m (20 ft.).

Acer circinatum 'Glen-Del'

The narrow, upright habit and lightly variegated five- to seven-lobed leaves distinguish this semidwarf form of vine maple. The leaves are small, 3–4 cm long and 4–5 cm wide. They also vary in shape. Some have broad lobes joining halfway to the leaf base with broadly notched edges. Other leaves, on newer growth, have lobes which are quite narrow, long and do not join until almost at the leaf base, giving a fingerlike appearance. The basic color is light green, but there is a subdued variegation of cream-green as an irregular margin on each lobe. Occasionally, the plant has shoots with leaves which revert to the leaf shape of the species.

This stubby, slow-growing form is fairly balanced but not as dwarf as 'Little Gem'. It was first observed at Del's Lane Country Nursery, propagated, then named and registered in 1984 by Del Loucks.

Acer circinatum 'Little Gem'

This beautiful dwarf has a circular leaf with seven to nine lobes. These are very shallow, divided about one quarter of the way to the leaf base, and are ovate-triangular with lightly toothed margins. On the smallest leaves, the lobes are hardly more than a toothed margin. Many lobes measure only about 1 cm in diameter, while others are 2.5–3.0 cm. The foliage is a light shade of green with the surface very lightly roughened. Fall colors are orange and crimson. The leaf nodes are very close together, forming a dense, compact, rounded shrub up to about 1 m (3 ft.) high and wide. New growth is as little as 2–3 cm long and up to 8 cm.

Alleyne Cook of North Vancouver, British Columbia, sent the original plant to Maple-

Acer circinatum 'Del's Dwarf', habit.
Photo by Talon Buchholz

Acer circinatum 'Del's Dwarf', spring color.
Photo by Talon Buchholz

Acer circinatum 'Glen-Del'.
Photo by Talon Buchholz

wood Nursery. It came from a witches'-broom on *Acer circinatum* in Stanley Park, Vancouver. It is an excellent dwarf form. Zones 5–9.

Acer circinatum 'Monroe'

Acer circinatum 'Little Gem'. Photo by Peter Gregory

Acer circinatum 'Monroe'. Photo by J. D. Vertrees

'Monroe' is the first-known true variant of *Acer circinatum* to be described and named. The leaves range from 6 to 10 cm long and from 7 to 13 cm wide. They have five to seven lobes that are separated entirely to the leaf base. The sides of each lobe are deeply incised almost to the midrib. These sublobes are further incised or toothed, forming very irregular margins. The inner third of the lobe is restricted almost to the width of the midrib. The two basal lobes are usually very small, at times only sublobes, but otherwise completely separate from the other lobes and clasping the leaf stalk.

The leaves are reminiscent of and intermediate between *Acer japonicum* 'Aconitifolium' and *A. palmatum* f. *dissectum*. Spring leaves are light yellow-green, becoming green for the summer, and turning yellow, orange, and scarlet in the fall. This sturdy plant forms an upright bush to 4 m (13 ft.) tall, becoming broad with age.

Warner Monroe, a philosophy professor at Warner Pacific College in Portland, Oregon, discovered this plant. It is fortunate for horticulture that Monroe is an observant and persistent person. While conducting a nature study hike with a group of young people, he noted a plant which "looked different." It was in the deep conifer forests on the headwaters of the McKenzie River, high in the Cascade Mountains. The 10 years following discovery in 1960 were spent in trying to identify this plant. Meanwhile, Monroe layered a side branch *in situ* and successfully moved the resulting plant to his home. In 1965 he successfully layered another side branch, which came to Maplewood Nursery in 1970. The original plant remains in the dense conifer forest, almost smothered under low-growing native plants. Brian Mulligan, Director Emeritus of the University of Washington Arboretum, published the original description in 1974. 'Monroe' was registered the following year. Zones 5–9.

Acer circinatum 'Pacific Fire'

This small multistemmed, shrubby tree, up to 2 m (6 ft.), has bright red stems and shoots which, with the colorful spring and fall foliage, provide year-round color. The small circular leaves emerge orange with purple-red veins in the spring, becoming a light green for the summer, before turning a stunning yellow-gold in the fall.

Acer circinatum 'Sunglow'

This distinctive cultivar has very small circular leaves, especially pretty in the spring when they emerge a peach to light orange-apricot color. The color lasts for four to six weeks in the sun, disappearing more quickly in shade, and becoming a medium green for the summer. In the fall, the color changes to plum red, purple and crimson. The seven-lobed leaves are shallowly divided to less than a quarter of the way to the leaf base and measure only 3.0–3.5 cm long and 4.0–4.5 cm wide. Each lobe is broadly ovate with a short, pointed tip and with an irregularly toothed margin.

This slow-growing, bushy plant forms a small, round ball and reaches a little over 1 m (3 ft.) in 10 years. Like other dwarf cultivars of *Acer circinatum* and many other Japanese dwarfs, it is susceptible to mildew attacks. First discovered by Floyd McMullen of Portland, Oregon, it was propagated and introduced by Buchholz and Buchholz Nursery, Oregon. It is very different from any other *A. circinatum* cultivar and is highly desirable. Zones 5–9.

Acer cissifolium (Siebold & Zuccarini) K. Koch (1864)

COMMON NAME: Vine-leaf maple
JAPANESE COMMON NAMES: Armahogi, Amako kaede, Amakuki, Mitsude kaede, Mitsude momiji

The trifoliate leaves of this species are similar to the leaves of some of the *Cissus* (grape ivy) species, hence the species and common names. The foliage also resembles that of the North American box elder, *Acer negundo*, which has three to five leaflets, occasionally up to nine, and is closely

Acer circinatum 'Pacific Fire', winter bark.
Photo by Talon Buchholz

Acer circinatum 'Pacific Fire', spring color.
Photo by Talon Buchholz

Acer circinatum 'Sunglow'.
Photo by Peter Gregory

Acer cissifolium,
contorted branching
of mature tree.
Photo by Peter Gregory

Acer cissifolium,
fall color.
Photo by Peter Gregory

related. The young leaves emerge a light yellow-green, often pink-tinged to bronzed, before becoming a light to medium green for the summer. In the fall they turn yellow with pink tones, finally becoming a fiery red.

The three leaflets are fairly uniform in shape and size, each leaflet 7–10 cm in length and about half as wide. The individual leaflet is ovate with an acuminate tip, angled base, and coarsely toothed outer margin. The long, slender leaf stalk is a bright red and has a broad, swollen base which completely encloses the bud.

Native to Japan, *Acer cissifolium* grows in moist conditions in the lower mountain forests from southern Hokkaidō through Honshu to central Kyushu in the south. It occurs at elevations of 200–1300 m (660–4290 ft.) above sea level. It is per-

fectly hardy, relatively easy to grow, and enjoys moist situations in cultivation. It forms a small to medium-sized tree with a wide-spreading, mushroom-shaped crown, reaching up to 15 m (49 ft.) tall at maturity and about as wide. There are no known cultivars in Western cultivation, but a yellow-variegated form, 'Gotenba nishiki', is grown in Japan.

Acer crataegifolium Siebold & Zuccarini (1845)

COMMON NAMES: Hawthorn maple, Uri maple

JAPANESE COMMON NAMES: Ao uri, Hana kaede, Hon uri, Meuri noki, Shira hashi noki, Shira kaede, Uri kaede, Yama kaede

An excellent small tree for landscaping and as a companion plant for flowering shrubs and perennials, *Acer crataegifolium* does not become too large, usually up to 8 m (26 ft.), and is not overly aggressive in root competition with other plants. It is hardy, holds its foliage color very well, and stands full sun.

The resemblance of its leaves to those of the hawthorn (*Crataegus*) requires a little imagination. The three-lobed leaves are rather distinct in shape—long triangular-ovate with tapering tips and heart-shaped to rounded bases. The two very small side lobes have blunt to broadly pointed tips and are occasionally absent. The margins are irregularly toothed and slightly undulate. The leaves are 5–7 cm long and 4–5 cm wide, with stiff leaf stalks 1–3 cm long. Leaf color is a pleasing blue-green above, often bronze-purple with purplish margins and purplish green beneath. *Acer crataegifolium* is one of the smallest snakebark maples with an indistinct patterning, especially on older branches and stems. The bark is green with faint white to dark gray striations. Young shoots are purplered to green.

This species grows wild in central and southern Japan on Honshu, Shikoku, and Kyushu Islands, preferring open sunny conditions. Only two variegated cultivars are established in Western cultivation, but several more are grown in Japan.

Acer crataegifolium 'Eiga nishiki'

This slow-growing Japanese shrub has variegation similar to that of *Acer crataegifolium* 'Veitchii', well-known in Western cultivation, but is much smaller, only reaching about 2 m (6 ft.) or so tall. The spring leaves emerge yellow to bright pink. In summer they have a dark green background with a creamy white and pale green splashed variegation. In fall they turn to yellow and red. The shoots and leaf stalks are bright red and very slender. 'Eiga nishiki' was introduced by Ishii Yuga, Japan. 'Meuri-no-ōfu' is a synonym.

Acer crataegifolium 'Meuri ko fuba'

This variegated form has leaves slightly smaller than those of the species. The vigor of the plant affects the leaf size, which ranges from 3 to 5 cm long and from 3 to 4 cm wide. The ovate leaves terminate in slender tips. The two side lobes are small and often rounded, or even entirely lacking.

Acer crataegifolium 'Eiga nishiki'.
Photo by Talon Buchholz

The margins are very lightly toothed, and the base is heart-shaped. The leaf stalks are short. Leaf color is a deep purplish green. Variegation occurs rather sparingly and is not constant, often being completely absent. The markings are usually white, but occasionally include a faint pink. The variegation is of the *haki komi fu* (brushed in) type. In the fall, the white portions become a rich rose tone. The shoots and branches are green with white striations. This shrubby, tall bush or short tree reaches up to 4 m (13 ft.) at maturity. The original stock received at Maplewood Nursery from a large collection in the eastern United States was mislabeled *Acer crataegifolium* 'Beni uri'. A cultivar of *A. rufinerve* is named 'Beni uri'. 'Meuri ko fuba' has also been known under the name 'Meuri kaede-no-fuiri'.

Acer crataegifolium 'Veitchii'

This variegated form is often quite spectacular in the marking of the foliage. The leaves are about the usual size for the species at 5–8 cm long and 3–5 cm wide. They are triangular-ovate, tapering to a slender tip. The two side lobes are small and bluntish, but often suppressed or totally lacking. The margins are toothed and often undulate. The leaf stalks are short and stiff. The base color of the leaf is blue-green. The variegation patterns are complex. The white to cream markings appear as specks, flecks, or "cut-in" sections or occupy the entire leaf. There are often flecks or streaks of pink intermixed with the white. Also, areas of white overshadowed with green occur, giving a light gray-green tone. Some leaves are entirely marked, while others are totally unmarked. In the fall, the white portions become rosy pink to scarlet. This cultivar forms a tall shrub or small tree, reaching 6 m (20 ft.) in height. Synonyms are 'Albovariegatum', 'Foliis albovariegatum', 'Fueri kouri kaede', 'Fuiri kouri kaede', 'Hillieri', and 'Variegatum'.

Acer diabolicum Blume ex K. Koch (1864)

COMMON NAMES: Devil maple, Horned maple

JAPANESE COMMON NAMES: Kaji kaede, Kiriha kaede, Oni momiji

The scientific and common names arise from the curious hornlike stigmas which persist at the inner junction of the fruit nutlets, resembling the horns of the devil. This strong, medium-sized tree is sturdy in appearance and reaches up to 15 m (49 ft.) tall. It tends to grow with a fairly broad, rounded canopy.

Acer crataegifolium 'Meuri ko fuba'.
Photo by J. D. Vertrees

Acer crataegifolium 'Veitchii'.
Photo by J. D. Vertrees

The five-lobed leaves have a thick texture and are rather large, up to 15 cm long and 16 cm wide. The lobes are divided to about halfway to the leaf base and end with short, acuminate tips. The middle three lobes are broadly lanceolate-ovate, while the two basal lobes are short and small. The margins are irregularly, coarsely, and bluntly toothed. The medium to deep green leaves are glabrous above and have numerous short white hairs beneath.

Though one of the least colorful maples in the fall, *Acer diabolicum* can be one of the most spectacular in flower, particularly when the bunches of large, red male flowers appear. A flowering tree has been described as "looking like the smoldering embers of a gigantic bonfire." This maple is endemic to Japan, common in the northern areas, less frequent in the south. It is found in open areas on sunny, lower mountain slopes, from 400 to 1300 m (1320–4290 ft.) above sea level. A yellow-variegated cultivar, 'Nagashima', is grown in Japan.

Acer distylum Siebold & Zuccarini (1845)

COMMON NAME: Lime-leaved Maple
JAPANESE COMMON NAMES: Hitotsuba kaede, Maruba kaede

The unusual, long, heart-shaped foliage makes this a very notable specimen plant. It becomes a medium-sized tree up to 15 m (49 ft.) tall. The lightly furrowed bark is gray to gray-brown. The ovate leaf has a deeply cordate base and a short, acuminate tip; it measures 10–16 cm long and 8–13 cm wide. The margins are very finely toothed, the teeth often crenate. The unlobed leaves, when they emerge in the spring, are an unusually attractive, downy light gray, dusted with a sandy or pinkish hue, becoming semishiny, medium to dark green for the summer. They turn a clear bright yellow in the fall.

Acer distylum is a rare species with very distinctive leaves, hence its common name, "lime-leaved maple." The leaf shape also gives rise to the Japanese name "Maruba kaede," which means "round-leaved maple." The species occurs in the mountains of northern and central Honshu, Japan, growing on moist and moderately fertile soils at elevations of 700–1600 m (2310–5,200 ft.) above sea level. Although it is rare in the wild and in cultivation, its has a beauty that suggests its wider use in landscaping. There are no cultivars of this species in Western

Acer diabolicum.
Photo by Peter Gregory

Acer distylum.
Photo by Peter Gregory

culture, but there is at least one in Japan, 'Angyō-no-sato', with yellow variegation.

Acer japonicum Thunberg ex Murray (1784)

COMMON NAME: Full moon maple
JAPANESE COMMON NAMES: Ha uchiwa kaede, Hobako ha uchiwa, Itaya, Itaya meigetsu, Meigetsu, Meigetsu kaede, Shinano uchiwa

This important species in the series *Palmata* is second only to *Acer palmatum* in contributing to the large number of cultivars in the "Japanese maples" of commercial nurseries. A very important feature is the brilliant fall coloration. All the cultivar and seedling selections display brilliant tones of yellow, orange, and red at the end of the growing season. This feature makes the japonicums worthwhile for landscaping. Most of them are sturdy, strong-growing trees, adaptable to most culture situations.

The rich, green leaves are generally round in outline and usually have 9–11 lobes, sometimes as few as 7 or as many as 13. Each lobe is separated about a third of the way to the leaf base. The lobe end tapers rapidly to a point and the lobe margins are coarsely toothed. The leaves vary from 8 to 11 cm in diameter, occasionally as large as 14 cm. *Acer japonicum* is a desirable small to medium-sized tree. Plants may reach 10 m (33 ft.) in height. Ken Ogata (1965b)

Acer japonicum.
Photo by Andrea Jones, Garden Exposures Photo Library

reports that the species grows to 15 m (49 ft.) in its native forests in Japan.

Two native varieties have been recorded by Jisaburo Ohwi (1965), *Acer japonicum* var. *insulare* and *A. japonicum* var. *kobakoense*. Variety *insulare* (Japanese common names: Shinano ha uchiwa, O meigetsu) occurs on Honshu and is distinct in having the wings of its samaras spreading horizontally. Variety *kobakoense* (Japanese common name: Kobako ha uchiwa) occurs on the island of Hokkaidō. It has lobes with the leaves simply and coarsely toothed. Both varieties are considered synonymous with the species in *Maples of the World* (van Gelderen et al. 1994), which mentions two additional varieties: *A. japonicum* var. *stenolobum* with dense, hairy samaras and *A. japonicum* var. *villosum* with tormentose leaf undersides.

It may be assumed this species is more genetically stable than *Acer palmatum* since fewer cultivars have evolved over the past centuries of cultivation. Trees resulting from open-pollinated seed may show subtle variations from the leaf type of the species, particularly when seed is collected in arboreta, where cross-pollination with other species in the series is possible. In the native forests, some cross-pollination is evident. Likewise, arboreta-collected seed has produced some seedlings which vary greatly from the type.

Among the extraordinary forms of *Acer japonicum* are the delicately dissected, pendulous 'Green Cascade', the fernlike-leaved 'Aconitifolium', the large-leaved 'Ō isami', and the variegated 'Kujaku nishiki'. Most other cultivars are variations from the species in leaf size and lobe shape. The golden-leaved 'Aureum' and similar, small-leaved cultivars used to be included under *A. japonicum*, but chemical and floral evidence resulted in their transfer to *A. shirasawanum*.

Some exceptional forms may result from cross-pollination. In a controlled cross

Acer japonicum, detail.
Photo by Peter Gregory

made at Maplewood Nursery, 'Aconitifolium' and 'Filicifolium' (the latter now considered to be so similar to 'Aconitifolium' it is treated as a synonym) produced a generation of seedlings with great foliage variations. They ranged from small, cascading plants with multidissected leaves, to bold upright trees with exceptionally large, circular foliage. There were all degrees of variation between. There is an opportunity in controlled hybridization to obtain additional, interesting cultivars. It is a time-consuming process, but could be rewarding. Intercultivar crosses within the japonicums should be tried, as well as controlled hybridizing between them and the better cultivars from other, closely allied species of the series *Palmata*.

Acer japonicum 'Aconitifolium'

COMMON NAME: Fern-leaf maple
This cultivar name is so firmly established and is seen in virtually every arboretum, botanic garden, and collection that it has become one of the rare cases where the Western name, 'Aconitifolium', is preferred to the Japanese name, 'Maiku jaku', which means "dancing peacock."

The leaves of this bold form are multi-

divided and deeply cut. They separate into lobes, which divide almost to the leaf base. Each lobe is again divided, on each side, with numerous cuts which extend almost to the midrib. These are irregularly dissected, producing a fernlike appearance, which gave rise to the English common name. The leaf form approaches that of the monkshood genus, *Aconitum*, hence the cultivar name. The points of the dissected segments are not sharp. The inner one third of each lobe narrows almost to the midrib, giving an open form to the center of the leaf. The lobes hold fairly close together as in a half-closed fan. The leaf thus becomes longer than it is wide.

Each leaf usually has 11 lobes, but the number may vary on the same plant from 7 to 13 lobes. The leaves vary from 7 to 17 cm long and from 6 to 14 cm wide. The leaf stalks are sturdy, often curved, up to 7 cm long, and are usually reddish in color. The foliage is deep green. The underside has inconspicuous tufts of minute hairs at some vein junctions. When first unfolding, the leaves show some pubescence on the surface. Leaves of vigorous plants tend to be held horizontally, giving an Asian appearance. The white and maroon blossoms are quite prominent on this cultivar and are more striking than their counterparts on most maples.

An additional, desirable feature of this cultivar is the intense fall coloration. Brilliant scarlet tones develop, shaded with carmine and sometimes into the purple range. The leaves persist on the plant, thus giving a long fall color period. The prominent seeds, held in clusters of samaras and colored maroon-red in the fall, add to the attractiveness.

This strong-structured plant is never weak or willowy. It is upright in habit with sturdy and stiff shoots. It forms a round-topped, small tree that ultimately reaches 6 m (20 ft.) in height, depending upon the site and vigor. It is one of the largest-leaved forms of the species, exceeded only by 'Ō isami' and 'Vitifolium', which are undissected forms. Although its foliage is large, 'Aconitifolium' is not a coarse tree. The dissection of the lobes gives it a lacy appearance. This cultivar is one of the most desirable forms of *Acer japonicum* for any size landscape. Received the RHS Award of Garden Merit.

'Filicifolium' is so similar to 'Aconitifolium' in leaf characteristics, habit, and growth that it is not possible to tell the two apart, and they are treated as synonyms, although references and evidence suggest they were originally separate clones. Other names by which 'Aconitifolium' has been know are 'Fern Leaf', 'Filicifolium', 'Hau hiwa', 'Hey hachii', 'Laciniatum', 'Palmatifidum', 'Parsonii', and 'Veitchii'.

Acer japonicum 'Ao jutan'

This low spreading cultivar was selected by E. Wood and introduced by Buchholz and Buchholz Nursery, Oregon. The large green leaves are very deeply divided to the leaf base, the lobes themselves also deeply divided, similar to those of the *Acer palmatum* Dissectum Group. Like dissectums, it also tends to form a wide-spreading dome with cascading foliage, as indicated by the name which means "green spreading." Fall colors are brilliant golden orange to deep red shades. 'Ao jutan' prefers sun or partial shade and has proven hardy down to −20°F (−29°C).

Acer japonicum 'Attaryi'

This large upright shrub or medium-sized tree to 12 m (40 ft.) tall has large seven- to nine-lobed leaves divided at least three quarters of the way to the leaf base. The leaves are similar to those of 'Aconitifolium' in most respects, except they are larger and not as deeply cut and the lobe bases are not as narrow. *Maples of the World*

(van Gelderen et al. 1994) has an excellent illustration of the foliage and fruits. The nomenclature of this plant has been confused. Plant material labeled *Acer sieboldianum* 'Attaryi' turned out to be identical to that from *A. japonicum* scions received from Maplewood Nursery and provisionally named 'Aconitifolium USA'.

Acer japonicum 'Fairy Lights'

The foliage of this small tree selection from Australia is multidissected. Each leaf measures 8 cm long and 14 cm wide. The lobes radiate outward from the leaf base, each well separated and, in turn, very deeply dis-

Page 304:
Acer japonicum 'Aconitifolium' (center) and *A. palmatum* 'Ornatum' (foreground).
Photo by J. D. Vertrees

Acer japonicum 'Aconitifolium'.
Photo by J. D. Vertrees

This page:
Acer japonicum 'Ao jutan'.
Photo by Talon Buchholz

Acer japonicum 'Fairy Lights'.
Photo by Peter Gregory

sected, giving a total lacelike appearance. The foliage is quite reminiscent of 'Green Cascade', but more finely divided. The plant makes a rather stiff, informal, upright, large bush and grows very slowly, reaching a height and spread of only about 1 m (3 ft.) in seven years. The spring and summer color is light green, varying to deeper shades. The fall colors are quite notable, as they are in many of the japonicums, ranging through a mixture of gold and scarlet and adding a real glow to the quality. Arnold Teese of Yamina Rare Plant Nursery, Victoria, Australia, selected a seedling from an open-pollinated 'Aconitifolium'. It is thought the pollen source could have been *Acer palmatum* f. *dissectum*, but the seedling selection exhibits only *A. japonicum* characteristics. Teese registered this cultivar in 1988, having observed it since 1979. Zones 5–9.

Acer japonicum 'Green Cascade'

This cultivar is one of the excellent japonicums developed in the United States. It was selected, named, and propagated by the late Art Wright, an Oregon nurseryman who registered it in 1973. The original plant was grown from open-pollinated seed collected from 'Aconitifolium' in the late 1950s. This unique selection has a weeping or pendulous habit, almost prostrate. The growth habit is much like that of *Acer palmatum* f. *dissectum*. The parent plant was grown on a raised site where it cascaded down a bank, forming a green mantle. Young plants should be staked to form a center stem from which the limbs can cascade. The individual leaf is a rich green with 9–11 lobes. Each lobe is 8–10 cm long, radiating out from the leaf stalk and separated entirely to the leaf base. The lower end of each lobe is very little wider than the midrib. From this extremely narrow base, which continues upward for one third of the length, the leaf lobe becomes broad, but is deeply dissected into narrow sections so that the entire effect of the double division of the leaf is lacelike. The fall colors are quite brilliant and range through yellow, orange, and crimson. Zones 5–9.

Acer japonicum
'Green Cascade'.
Photo by J. D. Vertrees

Acer japonicum
'Irish Lace'.
Photo by Harold Greer

Acer japonicum 'Irish Lace'

The outstanding feature of this deeply cut-leaf cultivar is the bright pink young foliage, which becomes green with pink then develops bronzed edges and tips. This coloration, added to the pleated and rumpled leaf lobes, gives the plant a charm of its own. Both pink new growth and green older growth continue throughout the growing season. Fall colors are attractive reds and golds. The medium-sized seven-lobed leaves are deeply dissected and little more than the width of the midrib at the lobe junctions. The lobes are also dissected to within 1–3 mm of the midrib, with slender, hooked, sharply pointed teeth along the margins. The stubby lobes often become folded and rumpled, with a "parsley leaf" appearance. The reddish leaf stalks are short and slender. 'Irish Lace' grows into broad cascading mound, up to about 2.5 m (8 ft.) in height.

Acer japonicum 'Itaya'

'Itaya' is one of the large-leaved forms of the species, comparable in leaf size with 'Taki-no-gawa' and 'Vitifolium'. The light green leaves can be 15 cm or more long and wide. The general leaf outline is round. The (7–)9(–11) lobes are broadly ovate, tapering to a point with shallowly toothed margins. The lobes rarely separate more than a third of the way to the leaf base. The strong, short leaf stalks have swollen bases. The leaves have a slightly roughened surface and are often slightly folded upward between radiating main veins. As with most japonicums, the fall color is worth waiting for; bright tones of yellow, orange, and red blend in various combinations. This stocky, sturdy, small tree has short, angular twigs. These form an inner structure, which is picturesque during the winter. The tree is round-headed and up to 6 m (20 ft.) tall.

The name 'Itaya' can be confusing. It is widely used as the cultivar name of *Acer japonicum* as described here. The name has also been used in older Japanese literature for other maples. For instance, "Itaya" or "Itaya meigetsu" is a Japanese name for *A. sieboldianum*, a closely related species. Also, references show *A. pictum* (synonym *A. mono*) and, in some cases, *A. truncatum*, as "Itayo," "Itayi," or "Itaya kaede." It has also been used by some authors to describe *A. pictum* subsp. *mayrii*, as well as one

form of *A. shirasawanum*. Masato Yokoi of Chiba University, Japan, considers "Itaya" and "Itaya meigetsu" as synonyms for *A. japonicum* and *A. shirasawanum* (van Gelderen et al. 1994). Zones 5–9.

Acer japonicum 'Kujaku nishiki'

This very rare form of the species has leaves which are identical in shape and size to those of 'Aconitifolium'. They differ in being variegated. The white variegation of the *haki homi fu* (brushed-in type) occupies a large part of the deeply dissected leaves, often covering half a lobe on one side of the midrib and sometimes the whole lobe. The leaves are otherwise medium to dark green in color. This cultivar is tender and very difficult to propagate. Zones 5–9.

Acer japonicum 'Ō isami'

The large, orbicular leaves measure 12–20 cm or more across, and the 9–11 lobes are elongate-ovate, separating about halfway into the leaf. The tapering ends of the lobes are deeply notched. The short leaf stalks are quite sturdy. The new leaves are light yellow-green, especially the outer ends of the lobes. The older leaves become a rich green, which persists well into the fall

Acer japonicum 'Kujaku nishiki'.
Photo by Cor van Gelderen

Acer japonicum
'Ō isami'.
Photo by Talon Buchholz

Acer japonicum
'Ō taki'.
Photo by Harry Olsen

Acer japonicum
'Vitifolium'.
Photo by Peter Gregory

without sunburning. The upper surface of the newer leaves has a scattered amount of very fine, silvery hair. There is also pubescence on the leaf stalks. The fall coloration is an outstanding combination of reds and yellows, blending with deeper tones of scarlet. This vigorous plant forms a round-topped, medium-sized tree which reaches 8 m (26 ft.) or more tall. 'Taiyō' is a synonym of 'Ō isami'. Zones 5–9.

Acer japonicum 'Oregon Fern'

This cultivar is similar to 'Green Cascade' in leaf shape and to 'Aconitifolium' in growth habit. It differs principally in the fall color, which is a truly sensational ruby red. The deeply dissected leaf has very narrow lobe bases like those of 'Green Cascade', so the lobes spread out like an open fan. 'Oregon Fern' arose from a selection made at Maplewood Nursery. Zones 5–9.

Acer japonicum 'Ō taki'

The circular leaves range from 6 to 8 cm in diameter, but are occasionally larger on vigorous new growth. They have 9–13 lobes. The lobes lie close together but are divided about halfway to the leaf base. The leaf stalks are stiff and relatively short. The lobe margins on the outer end are deeply toothed, giving a feather edge appearance. The leaf surface is sometimes sparingly covered with fine, silvery hairs. Spring and summer color is a deep, rich green, almost a blue-green in partial shade. The fall color is an outstanding feature of this cultivar. The blended red, crimson, gold, and orange colors are brilliant. The shoots and small branches are thick, sturdy and short. This maple forms a small tree up to 4 m (13 ft.) at maturity and enjoys full sun. The name has also been spelled 'O daki'. Zones 5–9.

Acer japonicum 'Vitifolium'

As the name implies, the large leaves of this selection resemble the grape genus, *Vitis*.

They are deep green, have stiff leaf stalks, and measure 10–12 cm long and 12–16 cm wide. The lobes number 9–11. Each lobe is separated almost halfway to the leaf base. The lobe bases are close together, making the outer ends of the lobes appear ovate. They terminate in a sharp point. The margins are toothed and prominent. The main veins show distinctly as a lighter green. The fall colors are magnificent. The golds predominate at first, with strong tones of crimson and scarlet, changing to a vivid scarlet before the leaves drop. This strong-growing tree is upright and becomes broad and round-topped with age. 'Vitifolium' is large for the species, reaching at least 10 m (33 ft.) tall and wide. Received the RHS Award of Garden Merit. Zones 5–9.

Acer maximowiczianum Miquel (1867)

COMMON NAME: Nikko maple
JAPANESE COMMON NAMES:
Chojanoki, Chyojanoki, Kochonoki, Megure, Megusurinoki, Megusyumi kaede, Ōmitsude kaede, Seminoki

This sturdy, medium-sized to large tree has a broad, round crown and matures at up to 20 m (66 ft.) in height. Its most distinctive feature is the stout, dense hairiness of all its parts—shoots, leaves, leaf and flower stalks, and fruits. The leaves are trifoliate with three relatively large, almost stalkless, ovate, irregularly bluntly toothed or wavy edged leaflets. Each leaflet measures 6–12 cm long and 3–6 cm wide and has a short, bluntly pointed tip. The upper surface is a matt, medium to dark green, with an attractive blue-gray to gray underside which is thickly felted with stiff, gray hairs. It is one of the last maples to change color in the fall, beginning with subtle pastel shades of yellow and pink, turning to orange and red, and becoming a deep, flaming red which lasts well into November.

The nutlets are hairy and have very hard, thick seed coats, which makes germination

Acer maximowiczianum.
Photo by Peter Gregory

of this species very difficult. Germination often takes two or more years to occur, even with stratification and other seed treatments. As the common name implies, this species is a native of Japan, with an extensive range from northern Honshu to southern Kyushu, and also extends into China. It grows in the lower mountain forests on moist, well-drained, fertile, valley soils at elevations of 500–1800 m (1600–5940 ft.) above sea level. It is still seen in collections under its synonym *Acer nikoense*.

Acer micranthum Siebold & Zuccarini (1845)

COMMON NAME: Small-flowered maple
JAPANESE COMMON NAME: Ko mine kaede

Acer micranthum is another of the delicate-appearing species of snakebark maples and one of the smallest. It is not fragile, but rather hardy and adaptable. The leaf shape and size and the light, slender limb structure contribute to the attractive appearance. This tree is one of my favorite snakebark maples, along with *A. tschonoskii*.

The foliage and shoots are an enchanting bright red when they first appear in the spring and contrast well with the numerous red and yellow-green flowers. The dainty, small five-lobed leaves with tail-like tips mature to a brighter green, often pink-

Acer micranthum.
Photo by Peter Gregory

flushed. The leaves pass through various shades of orange, pink, and scarlet in the fall to become a fiery red. They measure 5–8 cm long and about as wide. The two basal lobes are very small, and the center lobe dominates the leaf. It is long-ovate, acuminate, and tapers to a long, slender tip. The margins are strongly and coarsely toothed.

The common and specific names aptly describe the flowers, which are some of the smallest among maples. They appear as festoons hanging through the foliage and, in spite of their small size, can be so numerous they occupy a third of the crown. They develop into small, red-tinged fruits. *Acer micranthum* forms a tall shrub or small tree up to 11 m (36 ft.) high.

This Japanese native occurs from northern Honshu to Kyushu Island in the south. It grows in open, sunny areas of the forests of the middle and upper mountain slopes at elevations of 700–2300 m (2310-–7590 ft.). Only one cultivar has been named, 'Candelabrum', which is stronger growing with larger, less delicate leaves than those of the species.

Acer miyabei Maximowicz (1888)

COMMON NAME: Miyabe's maple
JAPANESE COMMON NAMES: Kurobi itaya, Shibata kaede

This medium-sized to large tree reaches 25 m (83 ft.) tall. It is sturdy and strong-branching, forming a broad canopy. The five-lobed leaves are similar to but larger than those of the European field maple, *Acer campestre*, to which it is closely related. The lobes are separated to about halfway, are rectangular-ovate with acuminate, bluntly pointed or rounded tips, and have irregularly lobulate teeth. The leaves are 8–15 cm long and 10–16 cm wide. The leaf stalks are short and contain a milky sap. Young leaves are pubescent on both sides and become a matt olive-green when fully developed. The fall color is a buttercup yellow, but is not outstanding. *Acer miyabei* is endemic to Japan, growing in moist woods along streamsides throughout northern and central Honshu. It is not widely found in cultivation and is considered rather rare. It was name for Kingo Miyabe, a Japanese plant researcher.

Acer morifolium Koidzumi (1914)

COMMON NAME: Yaku maple
JAPANESE COMMON NAMES: Shima uri kaede, Yakushima ogarabana, Yakushima onaga kaede

This small to medium-sized snakebark maple reaches up to 15 m (49 ft.) in height. It is very closely related to the better-known *Acer capillipes* and is a Japanese native, confined to the tiny islands of Yaku and Tanego, off the southernmost tip of Kyushu.

The leaves are sometimes unlobed, usually slightly three- to five-lobed, and measuring 7–10 cm long and 5–7 cm wide. They are ovate with tail-like pointed tips and toothed margins. The foliage is an eye-catching shiny, bronze-green when the leaves first appear. They become a deep green above and paler green below for the summer. In the fall, the color changes to golden yellow with red tones.

The strong shoots are green to purplish green, becoming a darker green with conspicuous, attractive white striations characteristic of the snakebark maples. This very rare maple has given rise to several variegated cultivars which, until recently, had not been heard of outside Japan. Among them are 'Beni yaku nishiki', 'Hime yaku nishiki', 'Waki saka nishiki', and 'Yakushima nishiki'.

Acer nipponicum H. Hara (1938)

COMMON NAME: Nippon maple
JAPANESE COMMON NAMES: Tetsu kaede, Tetsu-no-ki

This tree has large, bold foliage which is shallowly five-lobed. The leaves are roughly hexagonal in shape, 14–18 cm long and 15–20 cm wide, with a heart-shaped base. The lobes are broadly triangular with short pointed tips. The margins are sharply toothed. The upper surface of the leaf is a pleasing green with a roughish, primrose-textured appearance. The lower surface is lighter green with rusty brown hairs, especially along the veins.

The Nippon maple forms a medium-sized, openly branched tree, reaching up to 16 m (52 ft.) tall in cultivation, but may grow up to 20 m (66 ft.) in the wild. An excellent specimen in the Zuiderpark, The Hague, Netherlands, is most impressive when in full bloom. The bold racemes are large and quite beautiful. The long, narrow, cylindrical flower spike, packed with hundreds of small yellow, saucer-shaped flowers, points outward and is slightly curved and pendulous like a swan's neck. The blooms appear in early to mid summer (mid-June or July), later than any other maple.

As its common name implies, the Nippon maple is endemic to Japan on the mountain regions of Honshu, Shikoku, and

Acer miyabei.
Photo by Peter Gregory

Acer morifolium.
Photo by Daniel Otis

Acer nipponicum.
Photo by J. D. Vertrees

Kyushu. It is common in the forests on the lower and middle mountain slopes of central and northern Honshu, at elevations of 500–2000 m (1600–6600 ft.) above sea level, especially on wet sites along streamsides. It is much rarer further south and west.

Acer pictum Murray (1784)

COMMON NAME: Painted maple
JAPANESE COMMON NAMES: Ao kaede, Itagi kaede, Itaya, Itaya kaede, Shiraki kaede, Tokiwa kaede, Tsuta momiji, Yorokko kaede

This very variable species is better known under the name *Acer mono*. The older name of *A. pictum* has now been accepted as legitimate by the International Botani-cal Congress, and so it takes precedence over *A. mono*.

This fast-growing, medium-sized to large tree develops a rounded, spreading canopy and reaches up to about 14 m (42 ft.) high when mature in cultivation, but up to 25 m (83 ft.) in the wild. It is quite hardy and relatively free of insect and disease problems. It is a fine selection for over-story shade in large perennial and shrubbery plantings.

The five- to seven-lobed leaves measure 8–12 cm long and 10–16 cm wide and are usually shallowly divided one quarter to one third of the way to the leaf base. In some forms, leaves may be divided up to three quarters of the way to the leaf base. The lobes are usually short, broad, and triangular-ovate to triangular, with acuminate, sharply pointed tips. The margins are untoothed. The long, green leaf stalks contain a milky sap. Foliage color is a bright to matt green throughout the spring and summer, and resistant to sunburn. In the fall, the leaves change to a brilliant gold with crimson blending and shading through each leaf. This colorful patterning gives rise to the common English name.

Acer pictum has a wide distribution from central and northeastern China and Manchuria, eastern Siberia, Korea, and throughout Japan. There are several sub-species, varieties, and forms, indicating the variation in type, appearance, and leaf shape to be found in different localities throughout the natural range of this species.

Acer pictum 'Dissectum'

The leaves of this form contrast with those of the species by being deeply cut, that is, dissected in the sense of the leaves deeply incised into lobes, not as in the Dissectum Group of *Acer palmatum* where the lobes themselves are also deeply dissected. The five lobes are separated more than halfway

Acer pictum.
Photo by J. D. Vertrees

Acer pictum 'Dissectum'.
Photo by J. D. Vertrees

to the leaf base, with the undulating ends tapering to long, sharp points. Each leaf is about 7–8 cm long and wide and shiny, deep green in color, turning golden in the fall. This tree is not widely planted in Japan and it is reputed to be difficult to propagate. It is usually shorter than the species, reaching up to 12 m (40 ft.) tall. Ogata (1964) pointed out that the leaves of 'Dissectum' (as *A. mono* var. *marmoratum* f. *dissectum*) are the juvenile type of foliage for this species. Synonyms of this cultivar are 'Akikaze kifu' and 'Asahi kaede'.

Acer pictum 'Hoshi yadori'

The remarkable foliage has variegations of both the *hoshi fu* (starlike) type, which consists of tiny scattered flecks or specks, and the *sunago fu* (sand-dusted) type. The white or cream-colored markings boldly cover the deep green basic leaf color in varying amounts. In some leaves, the light tone markings predominate completely, masking the green in some cases, while in other leaves the green is dominant. There are all gradations of patterns, from light dots to bold color slashes. The color varies according to the light intensity. In full shade the markings are almost pure white. In full sun, they are a light yellow to gold, but full exposure to hot sun causes leaf damage. Spring foliage is pinkish red and the fall colors are various shades of yellow and gold.

The leaves have five to seven lobes, with each lobe broadly triangular and not deeply cut into the leaf. Leaf shape varies, depending upon the degree of variegation. A few leaves have only three lobes. In general, the leaves measure up to 9–10 cm in diameter. This cultivar forms a medium-sized shrub up to 5 m (16 ft.) tall. It is rather compact and broadens with age. When it is sited near a path, the unique foliage can be easily seen and appreciated.

Acer pictum 'Hoshi yadori'. Photo by J. D. Vertrees

Acer pictum 'Hoshi zukiyo'

This cultivar is very like *Acer pictum* 'Hoshi yadori', and the literature on the subject indicates it was originally a bud sport of it. The leaf shape, growth habit, and most other characteristics are identical. The variegations are very similar, but usually are more intense in color and cover the leaf more fully; at times, they are so concentrated that the colors coalesce and become solid. It is possible to find all degrees of variations on both cultivars, so descriptions of both overlap. 'Hoshi zukiyo' is not widely propagated because it is not easy to differentiate from 'Hoshi yadori'. It has also been known under the alternative spelling of 'Hoshi tsukiyo'.

Acer pictum 'Tokiwa nishiki'

This cultivar has the typical leaf shape of the species—broad leaves with five to seven lobes. The lobes are very shallow and the ends form short triangles. The leaves are 7–10 cm long and wide, with untoothed margins. The leaf stalks are 5–6 cm long. The new leaves emerge a pinky red, becoming green with pink-cream variegations. Summer color is a strong, green tone. The variegations within the leaf are quite heavy and sometimes occupy the entire area. The markings vary from white to light cream or yellow. Occasionally, the light area fills half the leaf, divided by the center vein, and the other half is green. It is a bolder green and denser variegation than that found in the similarly variegated cultivars 'Hoshi yadori' and 'Hoshi zukiyo'. Fall color is yellow to orange. This hardy, small tree or large shrub, up to 7 m (23 ft.) tall, is a favorite for landscaping in Japan, and it should be better known and more widely used elsewhere.

Acer pictum 'Usugumo'.
Photo by J. D. Vertrees

Acer pycnanthum.
Photo by Daniel Otis

Acer pictum 'Usugumo'

'Usugumo' has a very unusual leaf form that has been likened to a bat's wing. The leaf is more beautiful than this term would indi-

cate. The "fabric" appears to be stretched between the sharp-pointed lobe end and the prominent main vein in each of the 7–9 lobes. The lobes are triangular, but very short, and terminate in sharp points. This results in a large, undivided leaf surface. The tissue extending between each lobe is slightly folded so that the leaf surface is not flat.

The leaves are 8–11 cm long and wide, with a long, slender leaf stalk. The green leaves are thickly speckled with very fine dots of white, usually rather scattered, but occasionally concentrated, making the leaf appear whitish green. A narrow strip, which is almost pure white, runs along both sides of the center vein of each lobe. The vein is a contrasting strong green. When the leaves first appear in the spring, they are an unusually pale pink-yellow before becoming whitish green for the summer, then turning yellow in the fall.

This upright, but not strong-growing maple reaches up to 4 m (13 ft.) in height rather slowly. It is difficult to propagate and not widely known in collections. The name has been misspelled 'Usugumori'. Zones 5–9.

Acer pycnanthum K. Koch (1864)

COMMON NAME: Japanese red maple
JAPANESE COMMON NAMES: Hana kaede, Hana no ki

This species, which is rare even in its small natural range in Japan, is closely related to *Acer rubrum*, which is quite common in its native habitat in eastern North America. The Japanese red maple is restricted to a radius of about 60 km (37 mi) centered on Mount Etna on the main Japanese island of Honshu and in a smaller locality 120 km (75 mi) further north. It grows on the lower mountain slopes in moist, swampy conditions at elevations of 400–500 m (1320–1600 ft.) above sea level.

The leaves are triangular to circular,

usually three-lobed, 5–9 cm long and 4–7 cm wide. The lobes are ovate-triangular, bluntly pointed, often very short and sometimes almost absent. The margins are irregularly and bluntly toothed. The upper surface of the leaf is medium to deep green, the undersurface a glaucous blue to gray, with rusty brown hairs in the vein axils. The foliage turns beautiful shades of yellow to red in the fall. The leaves are on slender leaf stalks, so, like aspen (*Populus tremula*) leaves, they flutter in the wind to expose the gray undersides.

The species flowers in spring before the leaves appear. The red flowers appear in tight, compact balls or bunches at the end of every twig, to outline the crown in a halo of red. Attractive reddish fruits soon replace the flowers. The seeds mature early compared to most other maples. They ripen in mid-May and soon spiral to the ground to germinate almost immediately. This is a survival procedure because, in the swampy conditions, if the seed did not germinate early during the drier season, it would rot. Because the seed is short-lived, it is difficult to store.

This large maple grows to 25 m (83 ft.) at maturity. It is a valuable tree for overstory shade in mixed landscapes. Ken Ogata (1965b) mentioned that several old trees in the wild, and a few in cultivation, were designated "national monuments" by the Japanese government—a rather special kind of tree preservation order. There are no cultivars of this species in Western culture, but two variegated forms grow in Japan—'Asayake nishiki' and 'Kihin nishiki'.

Acer pycnanthum 'Asayake nishiki'

This colorful cultivar, named by Hisao Nakajima in 1990, has splashed and mottled variegation, occasionally occupying the whole leaf. The spring leaves emerge with a deep orange variegation, becoming reddish yellow on a yellowish green base color, changing to creamy yellow and light green variegation on a midgreen base for the summer. The leaf stalks are a contrasting light red. Fall color is a stunning yellow-orange-red. The name means "variegated morning glow." 'Hananoki aka fu' and 'Hananoki nishiki fu' are synonyms.

Acer rufinerve Siebold & Zuccarini (1845)

COMMON NAMES: Red-veined maple, Honshu maple

JAPANESE COMMON NAMES: Ao kaede, Ao momiji, Iizuka, Komori kaede, Koniji noki, Urihada nishiki, Uri noki

This strong-growing, upright tree of medium height reaches up to 15 m (49 ft.) tall. It tends to grow upright at first, then spreads out at the top as the canopy develops. It is one of the snakebark maples and has an unusual and attractive bark, with dark, narrow, lengthwise gray stripes running up the lustrous green surface, which gradually becomes grayer with age. Its most unusual character is the soft bluish gray bloom occurring on the new shoots.

The leaves are of a heavy texture and appear almost rugose. They are three- to five-lobed, with the pair of basal lobes small and the middle three lobes pointing forward. The dominant center lobe is

Acer rufinerve.
Photo by J. D. Vertrees

triangular. Each leaf measures 6–12 cm long and about the same across. The base is shallowly heart-shaped and the margins are toothed. The stiff leaf stalks are green.

The upper surface is medium to dark green, the undersurface a lighter green with dense, rusty brown hairs along the veins when young, hence one of its common name. The leaves become glabrous later in the season, except for tufts of brown hairs in the vein axils beneath. The deep green foliage changes to exceptionally bright color tones in the fall—a rich yellow and gold, heavily and brightly suffused with crimson. Received the RHS Award of Garden Merit.

In Japan, the native stands grow in the middle and upper parts of the mountain forest slopes, up to an elevation of 2000 m (6600 ft.). This species adapts well in gardens, accepting dry and moist situations, although it prefers sunny and moist conditions. It does not tolerate saturated soils.

Acer rufinerve 'Albolimbatum'

The five-lobed leaves are typical of the species in shape. They are rounded to heart-shaped at the base, and the two basal lobes are very short, with the center lobe dominant, so forming an ovate-triangu-

Acer rufinerve 'Albolimbatum'.
Photo by Peter Gregory

lar shape. The leaf size ranges from 7–15 cm long and 5–9 cm wide. The margins are lightly toothed. The amount of white variegation in the deep, green foliage varies greatly. The margins are usually tinged with white, sometimes as a very thin band, but on some leaves the markings are scattered in specks, splashes, and patches and extend over the whole leaf. Some leaves are entirely free of white mottling. High levels of fertility and the resulting rapid growth mask the tendency to variegated marking. As the trees slow in growth rate, the variegation becomes more marked. Fall color ranges from yellow to orange.

This slow-growing, upright tree is smaller than the species, attaining up to 12 m (40 ft.) in height. It is a very old cultivar, cultivated in the West since the mid-nineteenth century. It is found in Japanese collections and nurseries under the name 'Hatsu yuki kaede', and in Japanese literature. Hence, it is probably of Japanese origin. The name 'Albolimbatum' is so firmly entrenched in Western gardens, collections, and the trade that attempts in earlier editions to encourage the use of the Japanese name were not successful.

Other names by which this plant has been known are 'Albomarginatum', 'Argenteum', 'Fuiri urihada kaede', 'Hatsu yuki', 'Marginatum', 'Marmoratum', 'Shufu nishiki', 'Uriha nishiki', and 'Whitedot'.

Acer rufinerve 'Beni uri'

This bright, yellow-variegated cultivar has a larger leaf than the species, measuring 8–14 cm long, and occasionally slightly wider, depending upon the amount of variegation. The leaves are not as triangular as those of the species. This is due to the altered shape, where strong variegations occur in the blade. The three to five lobes are short and triangular and terminate in a sharp point, with the margins toothed.

The basic leaf color is a deep green,

strongly variegated with yellow. It is the *kiri fu* (cut in) type of marking, which sometimes occupies half the lobe, dividing the colors at the main vein. There are other, lesser markings, which form only slender yellow streaks in the green. These are mainly bold and diversified variegations. In the fall the light-colored portions change to a bright crimson, hence the name 'beni' meaning "red."

This plant is not as strong-growing as the species and is rather capricious in cultivation. Because it is difficult to propagate, it is rare in collections. The name 'Beni uri' was used on cultivars of two maple species. In the United States it has been wrongly applied to a variegated form of *Acer crataegifolium*, which should be named 'Veitchii'. *Acer rufinerve* 'Beni uri' has also been known under the name 'Kyo nishiki.'

Acer rufinerve 'Erythrocladum'

This slow-growing, small-leaved form of the species is notable for its unusual light yellow shoots, which become a bright red and orange during the winter, rather similar to the shoots of the *Acer pensylvanicum* cultivar with the same name. It does not have a strong constitution and is difficult to propagate and grow. It needs more care, attention, and shelter.

Acer rufinerve 'Shirayuki'

This variegated form is identical to 'Albolimbatum' in growth, vigor, leaf shape and size, and variegated patterns. It differs only in the color of the variegation, which is yellow rather than white. The more open the situation in which this cultivar is grown, the deeper the yellow of the variegated markings. The cultivar has also been known under the name 'Luteovariegatum'.

Acer rufinerve 'Winter Gold'

This notable addition to the larger trees with interesting bark originated from a chance seedling observed by the late Peter Douwsma, Victoria, Australia, in 1974. Arnold Teese of Yamina Rare Plants, Victoria, evaluated and propagated it for several years, and registered the name in 1988. In the summer the bark is a definite yellow-green. The winter color is a bright golden yellow, which readily attracts attention. The foliage is typical for the species, with the usual triangular lobes. Fall colors are yellow to burnt orange. This cultivar is slightly smaller than the species, but is vigorous. It is quite striking near *Acer palmatum* 'Sango kaku'. Zones 5–10.

Acer rufinerve 'Erythrocladum'.
Photo by Talon Buchholz

Acer rufinerve 'Winter Gold'.
Photo by Robert Jamgochian

Acer shirasawanum Koidzumi (1911)

COMMON NAME: Shirasawa's maple
JAPANESE COMMON NAMES: Ezo meigetsu kaede, Itaya, Itaya meigetsu, O
hauchiwa, O itaya meigetsu

This tree adds a delicate foliage pattern to
mixed plantings. The texture of the leaves
differs from that of other species in series
Palmata. The leaves feel like rather stiff
paper (chartaceous) and are a little thin,
almost translucent. Sunlight through the
foliage dramatizes the difference from
other, closely related species. Though
appearing delicate, the leaves resist sunburn more than most maples.

Acer shirasawanum,
habit.
Photo by Peter Gregory

Acer shirasawanum,
leaves.
Photo by J. D. Vertrees

The light yellow-green young leaves are
covered in soft, white hairs when they first
appear, becoming glabrous and a light tone
of lime-green that sets this species apart.
Fall coloration ranges into the gold tones,
with a blending of crimson. The total effect
of the foliage texture and color makes this
species a desirable choice as a companion
tree for shrubbery plantings.

The small orbicular leaves have (9–)11(–
13) short-ovate lobes, which separate only
a third of the way to the leaf base. The Japanese name "Ezo meigetsu kaede" means
"the maple with small, round leaves." The
leaves, which are characteristically saucer-shaped because of the overlapping
basal lobes and slight "pleating" along the
numerous main veins, are ovate, terminating in short, pointed tips. The margins are
prominently toothed. The new shoots are
bright green and sometimes glaucous.

As the tree matures, the growth is slender and multibranched and forms an interesting scaffold pattern. Very old trees in
the wild reach up to 20 m (66 ft.), but they
have rarely exceeded 10 m (33 ft.) in cultivation so far. This species is native to central and southern Honshu. It is found on
moist, well-drained mountain valley slopes
at elevations ranging from 700 to 1800 m
(2310–5940 ft.) above sea level. *Acer shirasawanum* var. *tenuifolium* extends

the range of this species southward onto Kyushu Island.

Chemical analyses were carried out in the early 1980s following observations by the late Brian Mulligan, then director of the University of Washington Arboretum, that the flowers of 'Microphyllum' were held above the leaves, while those of other *Acer japonicum* plants hung down. These studies resulted in the transfer of 'Microphyllum' to *A. shirasawanum*. Other old, popular, small-leaved cultivars transferred from *A. japonicum* to *A. shirasawanum* for the same reasons include 'Aureum', 'Ezo-no-o momiji', 'Jūnihitoe', and 'Palmatifolium.'

Acer shirasawanum 'Aureum'

COMMON NAME: Golden full moon maple

This spectacular yellow-leaved tree is highly prized in culture. The spring foliage is a bright yellow of a very distinct tone. As the season progresses, the leaves gradually become a yellow-green to medium green. In partial shade, the foliage retains the yellow tones a little longer than in the bright sun, but the color is more subdued. Direct hot sun causes some leaf scorch in hot climates, but this cultivar can tolerate full sun better than most yellow forms. The fall colors are often spectacular, varying from orange through red and occasionally blended with purple tones.

The round leaves form a dense cover on the plant rather than the open pattern found in the species. The leaves have 9–13 sharply pointed lobes. Each lobe separates one third of the way into the leaf. The leaf measures (5–)6–8(–11) cm wide. Young plants can grow quite vigorously for the first few years, but the plant becomes more bushy as it matures. In older plants, the angular branching forms a most attractive scaffold which is striking in the winter when it is exposed. Received the RHS Award of Garden Merit.

The bark on the new shoots is an interesting bluish green, almost glaucous. The fruits form in light bunches of samaras and become a bright red. These generally stick up through the golden foliage and add one or more attractive features to this fine

Acer shirasawanum 'Aureum', habit.
Photo by Peter Gregory

Acer shirasawanum 'Aureum', leaves and samaras.
Photo by J. D. Vertrees

plant. Large trees are not commonly seen. In fact, Jiro Kobayashi (1967) mentions in his nursery catalog descriptions that they do not grow very large and are mostly used as container plants.

The most magnificent example of this cultivar grows in Boskoop, Netherlands, at the home of D. M. van Gelderen. The tree is nearly 150 years old and about 8 m (26 ft.) in height with an even greater spread. It forms a large golden dome at the end of the main path in the nursery of Firma C. Esveld. No records have been found of any trees larger than the *Acer shirasawanum* 'Aureum' at Boskoop. Scions for grafting have been taken from this plant for several generations, so the progeny of this fine specimen are growing in many places around the world.

This popular cultivar has also been known under the names 'Aureum Oblongum', 'Flagelliforme Aureum', 'Golden Moon', 'Kakure gasa', 'Kin kakure', 'Macrophyllum Aureum', 'Ogon itaya', and 'Yellow Moon'. Zones 5–9.

Acer shirasawanum 'Autumn Moon'

This small tree has attractive foliage of an unusual burnt orange color with an underlying base shade of green. These colors are strongest when the plant is in full sun or very high shade. Shaded leaves carry pale yellow-green tones, and the plant shows a complete range of all tones in between those two extremes, depending on the degree of shade. In the fall the leaves turn a rich orange and red.

The leaves are in the shape typical of the species, with 9–11 short lobes which separate only about one third of the distance to the leaf base. The lobes are ovate with a short, sharp tip and with margins which are delicately and finely toothed. The lobes radiate in almost a full circular pattern with prominent midribs of a rusty color on some leaves. This color contrasts with that on many leaves. The leaves range from 5 to 8 cm long and from 7 to 12 cm wide. The strong leaf stalks are short.

This attractive tree with beautiful summer color was selected at Maplewood Nursery in 1978. The original seedling stood out from a mixed population of *Acer shirasawanum* 'Aureum' seedlings with the usual light green to yellowish green leaves. It is best grown where plenty of sunlight develops the colors. The tree seems to stand heat well. It is vigorous, easy to grow, and grows into an upright tree, reaching 6 m (20 ft.) or so in height. Zones 5–9.

Acer shirasawanum 'Ezo-no-o momiji'

The leaves are circular in shape, broken only by the sharp lobe tips. The 11 lobes are divided about one quarter of the way to the leaf base, and each abruptly terminates in a sharp tip. The margins are only slightly toothed. The leaves are variable in size, mostly 6–8 cm wide. The stiff leaf stalks hold the leaves out firmly. Spring color is a light yellow-green with inside foliage a darker green tone. This green is not the same intense tone found in *Acer shirasawanum* 'Aureum', but has a duller appearance due to the rougher surface texture. The green darkens during the summer, but develops the strong blends of golden

This page:
Acer shirasawanum
'Autumn Moon'.
Photo by Peter Gregory

Page 321::
Acer shirasawanum
'Ezo-no-momiji'.
Photo by Cor van Gelderen

Acer shirasawanum
'Johin'.
Photo by Talon Buchholz

Acer shirasawanum
'Jordan'.
Photo by Peter Gregory

red in the fall. This small tree matures up to 6 m (20 ft.) tall. It is medium hardy, rather difficult to grow, and hard to propagate. The pithy scions do not heal rapidly in grafting.

Acer shirasawanum 'Hemelrijk'

This Dutch cultivar differs from the usual yellow- to green-leaved *Acer shirasawanum* cultivars in having red leaves. These are a bright pink-red when they first appear, gradually darkening to a purplish or bronzed red for the summer with green midveins, and turning a very attractive orange-red in the fall. The leaf stalks are bright red and the shoots a darker red. The foliage color is a deeper purple-red in full sun, but tends to become green tinged when shaded. The seven- to nine-lobed leaves are divided to about halfway to the leaf base and have conspicuously toothed margins which curve downward slightly.

Acer shirasawanum 'Johin'

This very attractive medium-sized tree, propagated and named by Buchholz and Buchholz Nursery, Oregon, fully justifies its Japanese name which means "elegant." Originating as a seedling of 'Palmatifolium', 'Johin' has beautiful burnished dark coppery red leaves, with the main veins a contrasting yellow-green which persists for most of the season. The nine-lobed leaves are very similar to those of the well-known 'Trompenburg', with toothed slightly rolled margins, but not as deeply divided.

Acer shirasawanum 'Jordan'

Another outstanding yellow-leaved cultivar, 'Jordan' comes from Fratelli Gilardelli Nursery, Italy. The name is the English translation of Giordano, the first name of one of the owners of the nursery. The nine- to eleven-lobed circular leaf is typical in size and shape for the species. In the spring the leaves emerge a bright yellow with rose-

orange edging, becoming a clear yellow for the summer. The gray bark of the trunk and branches, with its vertical white striping, contrasts well with the yellow foliage. 'Jordan' is a vigorous, upright, small tree suitable for most garden landscapes.

Acer shirasawanum 'Jūnihitoe'

This cultivar is similar to 'Microphyllum' and has the smallest leaves in the species. They measure 4–7 cm long and wide and are circular. Each of the 11 lobes is very short, separating about one third or less toward the leaf base. The lobe ends in a short, rounded tip and is lightly toothed on the margins. The short, stiff leaf stalks hold the leaves out horizontally, in contrast to those of 'Microphyllum', which extend at various angles. The fall color is brilliant orange. The fruits, in tight bunches of samaras, also turn orange and add to the beauty. New bark is gray-green, changing to gray-brown in older wood. This stubby-growing, short tree matures at about 5 m (16 ft.) and 30-year-old trees may only be 3 m (10 ft.) tall. 'Jūnihitoye', an alternative spelling of this cultivar's name, is listed in old catalogs from Japanese nurseries. Henry Hohman of Kingsville Nursery carried it in his early listings. It is also referred to in old literature, where it is given as a Japanese term for the species. Koidzumi in 1911 showed it in his synonym list for the form *typicum*. Zones 5–9.

Acer shirasawanum 'Kawaii'

This unusually hardy dwarf has deep orange-red foliage and was discovered by Jim Baggett and named by Talon Buchholz, Oregon. The small to medium-sized nine-lobed leaves are deeply divided right to the leaf base. The lobes themselves are also divided into sublobes which have coarse hooked teeth around the margins. This feature points to one of the Dissectum Group cultivars of *A. palmatum* as the other parent. The lobes tend to spread; some, with the tips curved sideways, occasionally cross each other. The tree creates a cute appearance, hence the name, which means "cute." 'Kawaii' forms a low, spreading mound, reaching 60 cm (2 ft.) tall and almost 1 m (3 ft.) wide in 10 years.

Acer shirasawanum 'Microphyllum'

The round leaves are slightly cupped at the attachment to the leaf stalk. The 9–11 lobes are short and ovate-triangular, each coming to a sharply pointed tip and each separating only about one third of the way to the leaf base. The margins are shallowly toothed. The leaves are 6–8 cm long and 8–10 cm wide. The basal lobes

overlap and, with the upturn of the leaf, form a shallow cup. The underside of the leaf is semiglossy and a lighter green. The red leaf stalks are sturdy and about 5 cm long. Foliage color is dark green in summer; in the fall it is a very bright blend of reds and yellows. The leaves remain firmly attached into late fall, thus extending the color period. The growth seems less vigorous than that of the species, although the plant forms a small tree up to 6 m (20 ft.) tall. The shoots and branches are sturdy and form an interesting branch structure which adds to the winter beauty. This cultivar appears to be a sturdy and hardy form. It originated from a clone in the Coimbre Botanic Garden, Portugal (van Gelderen et al, 1994). 'Microphyllum' has also been known under the names 'Yezo meigetsu kaede' and *Acer japonicum* 'Microphyllum'. Zones 5–9.

Acer shirasawanum 'Minori-no-tsuki'

This striking seedling from *Acer shirasawanum* 'Aureum' was selected and propagated by Carl Munn and named in 1988. It has proven to be very colorful in the spring when the young cascading leaves emerge a bright pink-red, before turning yellow, then yellow-green contrasting with the deep maroon leaf stalks, before becoming light to mid green for the rest of the summer Fall color is orange to gold. The outstanding characteristics are the striking contrasts between the emerging red, developing yellow, and mature green foliage, plus the cultivar's relative hardiness and resistance to sun scorch. In all other respects—leaf shape, growth habit, and size—it resembles its parent. The name means "harvest moon."

Acer shirasawanum 'Mr Sun'

This unusual form has the normal-sized *Acer shirasawanum* leaves, but there the resemblance ends. The seven- to nine-

lobed leaves, divided to at least to halfway, appear to have long narrow triangular and long pointed lobes, because the margins are rolled under right to the long pointed tips. In addition, the center lobe is often shortened, suggesting that this cultivar originated from a witches'-broom. A third distinction is that everything—the leaves, leaf stalks, shoots, and branches—is bright green. The plant also fruits abundantly.

Acer shirasawanum 'Ogura yama'

'Ogura yama' is one of my favorite medium-sized Japanese maples. Every fall the brilliant display of rich orange blended with scarlet dominates this plant's portion of the garden. Spring foliage is a light yellow-green. The leaves soon change to a purer green with a silvery overcast due to a covering of extremely fine pubescence. In midsummer the pubescence disappears, and the leaves darken further. Fall brings forth the dependable brilliant color.

The circular leaves have mainly 9–11 lobes. These are separated one third of the way to the leaf base. The edges remain adjacent, even overlapping slightly. Only the tapering, sharply pointed tips are separated, with each margin noticeably toothed. The smaller lobes on more mature leaves have a tendency to cup upward. The outer

Acer shirasawanum 'Palmatifolium'.
Photo by Harry Olsen

leaves measure 6–8 cm long. Throughout the inner areas of the tree, smaller leaves of 4–5 cm dominate. The leaf stalks are stiff, short, and hairy.

'Ogura yama' is similar to 'Microphyllum' in appearance and leaf but is slower growing, reaching about 4 m (13 ft.) tall. It makes a sturdy plant and is quite hardy. Although most references, including the Japanese, place this maple as a cultivar of *Acer shirasawanum*, it has been described by some as a cultivar of *A. sieboldianum*. Zones 5–9.

Acer shirasawanum 'Palmatifolium'

This very beautiful selection has distinct foliage which is most attractive in all seasons. The bright green leaves take full sun without burning and have an almost translucent appearance. The fall colors are very spectacular and persist for a long period. The colors are bright blends of yellow and gold which are mottled and shaded with crimson.

The leaf has 11 lobes which are long and ovate with sharp, narrow tips. They separate distinctly over halfway to the leaf base and radiate openly. The margins are prominently toothed and roll slightly downward, making the separation between lobes even more distinct. The veins on the underside stand out prominently. The leaves measure up to 10 cm in diameter.

The bark of the shoots and young branches is a dusty green with prominent white striations. The older wood assumes a darker gray-green. This sturdy, upright small tree forms a rounded canopy and matures at about 8 m (26 ft.) in height. It is hardy and accepts a wide range of culture conditions. Zones 5–9.

Acer shirasawanum 'Sayo shigure'

This cultivar is little known and not particularly outstanding. The foliage is green with a dusty looking sheen. The leaves are nine-lobed with margins lightly toothed. The lobes are ovate with short tail-like tips and divided halfway to the leaf base. The leaves measure 5–7 cm long and wide. The fall colors become gold blended orange. 'Sayo shigure' is a medium-sized tall shrub or small tree. Japanese writers indicate that this cultivar is not planted widely at present.

Acer shirasawanum 'Sensu'

This beautiful selection from the Buchholz and Buchholz Nursery, Oregon, forms a medium-sized tree and is notable for its stunning orange to pink-red fall color. Its seven- to nine-lobed medium-sized deeply divided leaves move in the breeze like a Japanese fan, hence the name which means "a moving fan." The broad arrow-shaped leaf base, with all the lobes pointing forward, also contributes to this effect. As the season moves on, the leaves spread out. Spring leaves are a yellow-green with a strong orange-brown bronzing from the toothed margins. Summer leaves are green with some bronzing persisting and enhanced in full sun.

Acer shirasawanum 'Susanne'

This seedling of *Acer shirasawanum* 'Aureum' was selected by H. J. Drath of Barmstedt, Germany, given to Thiensen Arboretum, and named after the director's daughter. It is a vigorous cultivar, with leaves like its parent in shape and size, but differing in color. The color is between that of 'Aureum' and *A. shirasawanum* 'Microphyllum'. The leaves have (9–)11(–13) lobes and are a light yellow-green throughout the growing season, turning a deep gold in the fall. Like 'Aureum', this cultivar has small, sharp, red-tipped teeth, giving the appearance of a very thin red edge around the lobe margins. The pleating of the leaves is slightly stronger than in 'Aureum'. 'Susanne' forms a strong-growing, upright, small tree which makes a good companion plant in the landscape. The lobe tips, like those of most forms of the species, singe in prolonged hot, sunny conditions.

Acer shirasawanum 'Sensu', spring color.
Photo by Talon Buchholz

Acer shirasawanum 'Sensu', fall color.
Photo by Talon Buchholz

Acer sieboldianum,
habit and fall color.
Photo by Peter Gregory

Acer sieboldianum,
leaf detail.
Photo by J. D. Vertrees

Acer sieboldianum Miquel (1865)

COMMON NAME: Siebold's maple
JAPANESE COMMON NAMES: Aiai gasa,
Itaya meigetsu, Kibana uchiwa kaede,
Ko hau uchiwa kaede

The bright green leaves have (7–)9(–11) lobes. The leaf surface has a minute pubescence when first unfolding, but this is soon lost as the leaf matures. The leaf stalks are also pubescent when young, as well as the main veins on the undersurface of the leaf. The leaves are 5–8 cm long and 6–9 cm wide. They are circular, with ovate-oblong lobes separating about halfway to the leaf base. Each lobe terminates in a sharp point, and the margins are sharply toothed.

The fall color is an outstanding feature of this species. It becomes a brilliant scarlet with some orange leaves. *Acer sieboldianum* is a dependable plant for color in the landscape—more so than *A. circinatum*. The latter usually colors poorly when grown in mixed shrubbery plantings, while *A. sieboldianum* displays color very well under these conditions of moisture and fertility. It forms a tall, multistemmed shrub or small tree up to 10 m (33 ft.) at maturity. It is a very hardy, trouble-free plant for mixed landscapes.

Acer sieboldianum is one of the most common species in the mountain woods and thickets of Japan on the main islands of Honshu, Shikoku, and Kyushu. It is widely used in horticulture and has many popular cultivars.

Acer sieboldianum 'Kasatori yama'

The small circular leaves have 9–11(–13) ovate lobes that separate at least one third of the way into the leaf. The lobe ends taper rapidly to a sharply pointed tip, and the lobe margins are toothed. Foliage color is a pale or yellowish green. Fall color is in strong combinations of yellow and orange-crimson. This stocky tree does not grow as tall as the species, maturing at up to 5 m (16 ft.) in height.

Acer sieboldianum 'Kinugasa yama'

The foliage is a distinct blue-green color and is heavily covered with silvery pubescence. The small hairs are longer and more obvious than those usually found on foliage of other *Acer sieboldianum* cultivars. The leaf stalks are also strongly pubescent. This silky hairiness gives rise to the first part of the cultivar name, "kinu gasa," which means "silk umbrella." The fall colors are blends of brilliant orange and red which vary on different portions of the tree. The leaves range from 4 to 6 cm to as large as 8–10 cm. Each leaf has seven to nine lobes which separate at least halfway to the leaf base. The lobes are broadly ovate with sharp tips, and the margins have prominent teeth. 'Kinugasa yama' is a stocky, small tree which is strongly branched and forms a round-topped plant. It matures at 7 m (23 ft.) high and is not difficult to grow.

Acer sieboldianum 'Mikasa yama'

Kobayashi (1975) gave this cultivar status in *Acer japonicum*. After close study of the bud scales, hairs on the foliage and shoots, and other characteristics, I feel it rightly belongs in *A. sieboldianum*. The outline of the leaf is circular with seven to nine lobes cut halfway to the leaf base. The lobe sides remain close together except for the outer ends, which rapidly taper to a sharp point. The margin of this outer taper is sharply toothed. The new foliage has a pleated appearance and is a pale green with distinctly yellowish margins and short light hairs covering the entire surface. This imparts a silvery sheen to the young leaves. The hairs disappear from the green leaves during the summer. The 2- to 3-cm-long leaf stalks are also covered with minute hairs. Fall colors are golden, occasion-

Acer sieboldianum 'Kinugasa yama'.
Photo by J. D. Vertrees

ally tinged with crimson. The average leaf measures 4–7 cm long and wide, although larger leaves occur. This sturdy, small tree is similar to 'Kinugasa yama', but with smaller leaves, narrower lobes and less coarse toothing. It is not widely known and is not very spectacular.

Acer sieboldianum 'Momiji gasa'

The foliage has a light or whitish green appearance, which is partly due to the dense covering of short silvery hairs over the light green base color. The leaf underside, as well as the leaf stalk, is also covered with short hairs. The fall colors develop brilliant gold tones blended with red. The leaves have nine lobes, which separate deeply into the leaf. The lobes hold close together on the inner half, with the outer half oval in shape and tapering to a long, narrow pointed tip. The margins have coarse teeth. The leaf is 5–7 cm long and 7–8 cm wide, with the leaf stalk 4 cm long. This plant forms an upright shrub or small tree. Like the species, it is hardy. It has been placed under *Acer japonicum* and *A. shirasawanum* in some references. It has also been suggested that this cultivar is possibly a hybrid between *A. shirasawanum* and *A. palmatum*. The name has been misspelled 'Momiji gasane'.

Acer sieboldianum 'Sode-no-uchi'

This dwarf cultivar has the smallest leaves of any form of the species. The foliage is a bright, light green which holds well through the season. The fall colors are predominantly bright yellow with red tones. The leaf size varies from 2.5 to 4.0 cm long and 3–5 cm wide. The seven to nine lobes radiate evenly outward and are separated at least halfway to the leaf base. Each lobe is ovate, terminating in a short, tail-like tip. The margin of the leaf is distinctly toothed. The stiff leaf stalks are only 4 cm long. This

Acer sieboldianum 'Sode-no-uchi', spring color.
Photo by J. D. Vertrees

Acer sieboldianum 'Sode-no-uchi', fall color.
Photo by Peter Gregory

little plant tends to form a rounded bush. The annual growth is only 10–12 cm long on young shoots and much less on older wood. It is an attractive plant, which fits well into many types of planting, particularly in alpine gardens and in containers on patios. It is also popular for bonsai in Japan, forming a tight shape with little pruning. Zones 4–9.

Acer tataricum subsp. aidzuense

(Franchet) de Jong (1994)

JAPANESE COMMON NAME: Karakogi kaede

Although *Acer tataricum* (Tatarian maple) is endemic to southern Europe and western Asia, from Austria through to the Ukraine, two of its subspecies are native to Japan: subsp. *aidzuense* and subsp. *ginnala*. The two subspecies are similar and share the same Japanese common name. In horticulture, subsp. *aidzuense* is not as important as subsp. *ginnala*. The trees and leaves of subsp. *aidzuense* are slightly smaller with almost unlobed leaves, intermediate between the type species and subsp. *ginnala*. Subsp. *aidzuense* is confined to the islands of Honshu, Shikoku, and Kyushu.

Acer tataricum subsp. ginnala

(Maximowicz) Waesmel (1890)

COMMON NAME: Amur maple
JAPANESE COMMON NAME: Karakogi kaede

Amur maple is one of the hardiest small tree species in the genus *Acer*. It forms a multistemmed, dome-shaped, large bush or small tree, reaching 8 m (26 ft.) or so in height. The tree is quite trouble-free and adapts to most cultural conditions. The three-lobed leaves have an oblong-triangular center lobe which is much more prominent and longer than the other two, rather short, side lobes. Each leaf measures 5–8 cm long and 3–5 cm wide. The lobe tips are pointed and the margins are toothed. The leaf stalks are 3–4 cm long. The foliage is a bright green all season and durable, withstanding full sun. The fall color is bright scarlet. Subsp. *ginnala* grows wild in northeastern China, Manchuria, North Korea, and on the Japanese islands of Honshu, Shikoku, and Kyushu.

Acer tataricum subsp. *ginnala* 'Bailey's Compact'

This cultivar has a dense, compact habit and a relatively dwarf form. It was selected and introduced by Bailey Nurseries, Minnesota, and registered in 1979. The leaves are the same as those of its parent in shape, slightly smaller in size, and similar in color and texture. They turn a bright, shiny red in the fall. 'Bailey's Compact' is ideally suited for the small garden or as a container plant. It was originally named 'Compact Amur Maple'.

Acer tataricum subsp. *ginnala* 'Durand Dwarf'

This very shrubby, mound-shaped dwarf form is thought to have originated from a witches'-broom. It is an exceptionally fine plant which fits into almost any landscape. The shrub is very compact because of its branching growth habit. Its seasonal shoot growth is only 10–20 cm. As the tree branches, the terminals shorten. The tree eventually reaches about 2 m (6 ft.) tall. The three-lobed leaves resemble those of the Amur maple in shape, with the elongate center lobe and shortened side lobes, but are smaller at about 4 cm long and 2–3 cm wide. The foliage during the growing season is a shiny, light green, changing to a brilliant crimson in the fall. This color is uniform over the entire plant. 'Durand Dwarf' is indeed a "burning bush" and makes a spectacular accent plant.

Acer tataricum subsp. *ginnala* 'Embers'

This fast-growing broad tree reaches 6 m (20 ft.) tall and spreads 4 m (13 ft.) across. It has clusters of red fruits protruding from the glossy green leaves, and a stunning red fall color. 'Embers' makes a fine specimen or patio tree.

Acer tataricum subsp. *ginnala* 'Emerald Elf'

This dense compact dwarf rarely exceeds 2 m (6 ft.) tall or wide. It has glossy green foliage which turns a vivid burgundy red in the fall. 'Emerald Elf' prefers full sun or light shade and makes an excellent patio or container plant.

Acer tataricum subsp. *ginnala* 'Fire'

This vigorous form was received from Canada by Firma C. Esveld, Netherlands, and was named and propagated there. The dark green three-lobed leaves are the same shape as those of the Amur maple. The fall color is a brilliant scarlet, which lasts for several weeks. 'Fire' forms an upright shrub which is estimated to reach a mature height of up to 8 m (26 ft.). It has a very reliable fall color for a long period.

Acer tataricum subsp. *ginnala* 'Flame'

This medium-sized shrubby tree, which can reach 7 m (23 ft.) in height, has outstanding fall color. The leaves have the typical shape and size of the subspecies. The

Acer tataricum subsp. *ginnala*.
Photo by Bernard Pye

glossy green foliage contrasts with the large clusters of red fruits from early summer onward. Fall color is a fiery red. 'Flame' makes a fine specimen tree among other plants in a shrub border or as a patio tree. Like 'Fire', it originated in Canada and was named and propagated by Firma C. Esveld, Netherlands.

Acer truncatum Bunge (1833)

COMMON NAMES: Purple-blow maple, Shantung maple

JAPANESE COMMON NAMES: Akaji, Akajika itaya, Akaji nishiki, Mansen itaya

This species is very closely related and quite similar to *Acer pictum*. It is a native of northern China, Manchuria, Siberia, North Korea, and the Japanese island of Sakhalin, growing on the plains and lower mountain slopes at elevations of 100–900 m (330–2970 ft.) above sea level. It is included with maples from Japan because of its close relationship with *A. pictum*, its popularity in Japanese horticulture, and because, though its main base is China, it

is native to Sakhalin Island. This desirable maple grows into a large, wide-spreading bush or medium-sized tree up to 15 m (49 ft.) in height. The bark is reputed to be the roughest and most deeply fissured of any maple.

The attractive, deeply divided, glossy ivylike leaves are more deeply divided than those of the typical *Acer pictum*, separating at least two thirds of the way toward the leaf base. The leaves have (3–)5(–7) lobes and are usually broader than long, measuring 8–16 cm wide and 6–13 cm long. Often the leaf base is characteristically straight, hence the specific name *truncatum*. Each lobe is triangular-ovate, with a long, slender, pointed tip. The center lobe may have one or two broad, pointed teeth on the outer shoulder. The emerging leaves, when they first appear, are an eye-catching red to purple shade, soon becoming glossy green for the summer. They turn to yellow-orange-red to purple, which lasts well into late fall. The leaf stalks, like those of *A. pictum*, contain a milky sap. Zones 5–9.

Acer truncatum 'Akikaze nishiki'

The desirable feature of this maple is the white-on-green color pattern of the foliage. The basic color is a rich green, but each leaf is marked differently, ranging from all-white to hardly any flecks of white. The main pattern is white or cream in a portion of the green leaf, a type of variegation known as *kiri fu* (cut). In these leaves the variegated portion is curved or sickle-shaped, usually quite strongly so. Often the green leaf is stippled with tiny specks of white, forming a solid pattern with the green showing through from beneath.

The leaf is usually deeply divided into five lobes, but it can vary from three to seven lobes, depending on the intensity of the variegation. The lobe generally is triangular-ovate, but all lobes with white areas are irregular and curved. Although the size

Acer truncatum.
Photo by Ray Prag

of the leaves can vary greatly on each plant, the average size is 6–8 cm long and 5–6 cm wide. As the new foliage appears, it has a definite pink tone which soon changes and becomes white or cream, marking the variegation.

This cultivar forms a tall shrub, reaching up to 5 m (16 ft.) in height. It is not a rapid grower, especially after the first few years. As with most variegated maples, this one should have some protection from hot afternoon sun which burns the light-colored leaf portions. 'Albovariegatum', 'Albovittatum', 'Shūhū nishiki', 'Tricolor', and 'Variegatum' are synonyms of 'Akikaze nishiki'. Incorrect names for this plant include 'Akaji nishiki' and 'Shuen nishiki'.

Acer tschonoskii Maximowicz (1886)

COMMON NAME: Tschonoski's maple
JAPANESE COMMON NAMES: Hakusan momiji, Hime ogurabana, Mine kaede

The delicacy of its foliage makes this small, graceful snakebark maple a very pleasant choice for mixed landscapes. It forms a shrublike plant or small tree, maturing at up to 7 m (23 ft.) in height, and never looks coarse in mixed plantings.

The circular leaf has five rhombic-ovate lobes, sometimes with long, tapering tips. The pair of basal lobes is often very short. The margins are coarsely double-toothed. The leaves measure 5–8 cm long and slightly wider to 9 cm. They are bright green in color, with a rusty brown pubescence beneath, becoming glabrous except for tufts of brown hairs in the vein axils. The fall colors are yellow to golden, sometimes tinged red. Though it is one of the least sensational Japanese maples in the fall, it has a quiet beauty of its own.

The branching is not coarse, although it is sturdy. The striped patterning on the stems and branches is one of the least

conspicuous of the snakebark maples. Although it is one of the easiest, hardiest, most tolerant (except on alkaline soils), and least invasive maples, Tschonoski's maple is very rare in gardens. With its quiet grace, it deserves a place in the landscape.

This species is a native of northern Japan, occurring as isolated shrubs or in scattered groups in the subalpine higher mountain forest zone, at elevations ranging from 1400 to 2500 m (4620–8250 ft.). *Acer tschonoskii* var. *australe* extends its range into southern Japan, and *A. tschonoskii* subsp. *komarovii* is native to Manchuria and Korea.

Acer truncatum 'Akikaze nishiki'. Photo by J. D. Vertrees

Acer tschonoskii. Photo by Hugh Angus

JAPANESE WORDS and Their Meanings

THE FOLLOWING LIST OF JAPANESE WORDS AND their English equivalents is used in the names of numerous cultivars. In many cases the translations are direct applications of meaning. In others, they are portions or combinations of interpretations which cannot be applied literally. Many cultivar names are only abbreviated references to a more complex meaning, such as in the case of 'Shigitatsu sawa' and 'Tanabata'. The latter is the Festival of the Stars (7 July), but has a delightful "fairy tale" behind the name, as told to me. In the skies of Japan there are two constellations related to the Festival of the Stars. One is called Kengyū (the young boy who cared for the cows), and the other is Syokūjō (the girl who was a weaver at the loom).

Once upon a time there were two diligent young people, Kengyū and Syokūjō. When they met the first time, they fell in love at once. After this happened, they didn't work very hard any more, but spent all their time walking together.

When the gods noticed this, they became very angry and separated the two young people by a great river (the Milky Way). After this the young people could not be together any more. But the gods said that if they worked very hard they could see each other again once a year. So they worked very hard and could see each other once a year on 7 July. Thus, *Tanabata* came to mean "Festival of the Stars" or "Festival of the Weaver."

The terms described in the following list will enable the reader to understand more of the names which have combined terms. 'Beni shidare', for example, comes from *beni* (red) and *shidare* (drooping, cascading) and identifies this maple as "the red, cascading variety." Many Japanese words have several different meanings, hence it is often necessary to know what the Japanese character is before it is possible to interpret the meaning correctly.

aida space, interval
aka red
akane madder plant
akebono daybreak, dawn
aki autumn, the fall
ama fisherman, heaven
ami reticulated
ao blue-green
aoba green leaves
aocha yellow-green
aoyagi a green willow

ara rough
ariake daybreak, dawn
asagi pale yellow
asahi rising sun
asayaki morning glow
azuma east

ba leaves
beni deep red
bushi warrior

cha tea, brown
chi blood
chidori a plover
chiri mottled
chirimen crêpe paper
chishio blood
chitose a thousand years

daidai orange
daimyō feudal lord
dan banded

do way, school of thought
dono feudal lord

Edo old name for Tokyo
eiga splendor, glory
emi smile
ezo picture, painting

fu variegated
fuji unexpected
fuku cover

furi scattered
fuyu winter

gai cliff
gaki fence
gaku flower calyx
Ganjitsu New Year's Day
Garyū the sleeping lion
gasa umbrella
gasane layered, overlapping
gashira lion's mane, lion's head
gasshō ensemble, chorus
gasumi mist, haze
gata bay, beach, lagoon
gawa river
gen dark-colored
go fine
gohon little
goma sesame seed
goshiki multicolored
gōsō splendor
gumo spider
gure cloud

hagoromo angel's dress or cloth
hai gray
hake splashed
haku white
hana flower
hane wing, feather, plumage
haru springtime
hashi bridge
hata flag
hatsu springtime, first
hi bright scarlet, sunlight, fire, day
hibari skylark
higan springtime
hikasa sunshade, parasol
hime princess, pretty, little
hinshu cultivar, variety

hitode starfish
hiyodori thrushlike bird
hōgyoku jewel
hoki broom of twigs, besom
homare glory, fame
hon long
hoshi star
hoso slender

ibo warty
ichi one
ichiyo one leaf
ike pond
inazuma thunder
ine rice-plant
iro colored, hue
ishi rook
iso beach
ito fine string, thread
iwa boulder, reef
iwato rock

ji temple
jiban ground
jirō white
jishi lion
jō supreme, first-class, young lady
jochin lantern
johin elegance
jutow spreading, carpet
juzu rosary beads

kaba hippopotamus
kagami mirror
kagerō gossamer
kaki fence
kaku tower
kakure shade, shelter
kamagata falcate, hooked
Kami God
kan border, edge, rim, cold
kara ancient Chinese

karasu crow, raven
kare dry
karei magnificent
kasa umbrella
kasane layered, overlapping
kashi filament
kashiri lion's mane
kasume mist, haze
kasumi mist, haze
kata beach, lagoon
katsura wig
kawa bark, river
kawai cute
kaze wind, breeze
ke hairy
kenko healthy
ki yellow, plants
kiku chrysanthemum
kin gold
kinu silk
kirei beautiful
kiri mist, misty, silk
kirin giraffe
ko deep (color), child
kō red, swan, tribute, prince
kogane golden
koi thick, dark
komachi beautiful girl, dwarf
komon figure, fine pattern
kosode silk garment, kimono
koto old harp
koya wild, desolate
kū emptiness
kuguri passing under
kujaku peacock
kukuri bundle, bunch
kumo spider, cloud
kuro black, innocent
kurui confused, crazy
kuzu dust
kuzure irregular

kyo beautiful dress, ancient capital
kyo hime fairy tale princess, pretty, little princess
kyūden palace

ma view, viewing, space
machi waiting
mai dance, dancing
maiko dancing girl
mama any which way, doing as one pleases
maru round
masu wooden cup
matsu pine tree, lime tree
me female
meigetsu bright moon
Mejishi mythical female lion
men paper
meo cotton
mi three, remote
midori light green
mikazuki new moon
misho seedling
miyabi elegant, refined
miyama remote high mountain
miyasama prince
mizu water
mochi rice cake
momo peach
momoiro peach-colored
mon gate
mori forest, guard
moyo patterned
mu emptiness, nothingness
mura cluster
murasaki purple
mure flock, group

naka centered
nami wave, billow
ne ridge, origin

nioi fragrance, scent
nishiki brocade, variegated, rough
niwa garden
no of, from
nome cloud
nomura beautiful

ō big, large
o tail, male, husband
obi kimono, waistband
ōgon gold
Ōjishu mythical male lion
oka hill
oku deeply hidden,
  interior
otome maiden, virgin

rin circle, ring
roji dewy ground, tea
  garden
ryoku green
ryū dragon

sa small
sake alcoholic drink,
  salmon
saki point, tip
sakka turning red
saku fence
same rain, leather
sami early summer
samidare early summer
  rain, soft rain
san hill, mountain
sango coral
Saotome rice-planting
  girl
sarasa beautiful figured
  fabric
sato garden

satō sugar
satsuki azalea
sawa marsh, swamp
sazanami small source,
  ripples
sei blue-green, clear
  stream, stature
seki border, rim, edge
semi wing, skin
sensu moving fan
shi gentleman, four,
  poetry, threads
shiba grass
shibumi quiet, somber
shichi seven
shichihenge changeful
shidare cascading,
  willowy
shi en smoke
shigure soft drizzle,
  autumn rain
shika male Japanese deer
shima island, stripe
shime New Year's Day
  decoration
shimo frost, east
shin new, improved
shinto sacred
shio tide
shira brazen it out
shiro white, castle
shishi legendary lion
shōen estate
shōjō red-faced monkey
  of Japanese drama
shū autumn, fall, vermil-
  lion red
shu master, sort (kind)
sode sleeve, wing
sono garden
soto outer

su web
sui worldly, the best
sukashi transparent
sumi charcoal, corner
sumizone dyed black,
  stained with ink
suna sand
sunago dusted, sprinkled

tai thick, big
takane lofty peaks
take bamboo
taki waterfall
tama gem, ball
tamuke tribute, offering
tana shelves, layers
Tanabata Festival of the
  Stars
tatami straw matting
teiboku spreading
tennyo angel
tome distant view
tōme stillness
tono feudal lord
tora tiger
tsū professionalism,
  connoisseur
tsuchi Earth
tsuki artifical, moon
tsuma nail
tsuru stork, crane

uba old woman
ubu albino, innocent
uchi within, pocket
uchiwa fan-leaf
udzu eddy
Ueno a park in Tokyo, famous for its flowering
  cherries and flower
  parties

uki drift, float
ukigumo floating clouds
ukon bright yellow,
  turmeric
umineko seagull
un cloud
usu thin
uzu eddy

wabi subdued taste
wabito hermit, lonely
  person
washi eagle

yae double
yagi beautiful, seat of
  coral
yama high mountain,
  steep hill
yanagi willow
yatsubusa dwarf,
  compact
yō leaf
yoi early evening
yū evening
yu purified, clean or hot
  water
yubi finger
yūbi grace, elegance
yugure sunset, twilight
yuki snow

zakura cherry
zan mountain
zō elephant
zono garden
zu head
zuma thunder
zuru swan

THIS GUIDE TO JAPANESE MAPLE USES AND CHARACTERISTICS is provided to assist in the selection of plants for individual situations, taking into consideration their ultimate size, habit, color, and special cultural needs and conditions. Before making selections from the guide, the reader is urged to turn back to the cultivar description to double-check the suitability of a specific cultivar in terms of the particular location or use the reader has in mind. The classifications are not rigid criteria but are designed to suggest the qualities and uses of the plants described. Each classification must be interpreted for the reader's specific needs and locality. The symbols used and an explanation of the categories are as follows:

HEIGHT OF MATURE PLANT
In meters

FORM OF MATURE PLANT
mound mound-shaped shrub or tree
round round-shaped shrub or tree
up upright shrub or tree
wide wide-spreading shrub or tree

COLOR OF FOLIAGE
green green to yellow summer leaves, may have reddish edging
red red to bronze-green summer leaves
var variegated leaves

GROUP
amoe (amoenum) leaves divided up to two-thirds to leaf base
diss (dissectum) leaves deeply dissected; laceleaf
dwarf cultivar normally less than 2 m (6 ft.) in height
linear (linearilobum) leaf lobes narrow and straplike
matsu (matsumurae) leaves divided more than three-fourths to leaf base

palma (palmatum) leaves divided two-thirds to three-fourths to leaf base
other cultivar not fitting into any of the above groups

EFFECTS IN THE GARDEN
drama (dramatic) plant notable for dramatic or unusual foliage, bark, or growth
fall plant notable for outstanding fall foliage color
gen (general) plant suitable for general garden use
spring plant notable for the color of the spring foliage

CONTAINER
yes plant suitable for a container on a patio. Nonetheless, note that all cultivars will adapt to container culture.

BONSAI
yes plant popular for bonsai culture due to the nature of the cultivar. Nonetheless, note that most cultivars will adapt to bonsai training.

ROCKERY
yes plant appropriate for rockery and alpine gardens

COMPANION
yes plant fits in very well with most other shrubbery, perennial and mixed plantings. These cultivars are not overly aggressive and keep their shape well.

LIGHT REQUIREMENTS
any plant tolerates any light conditions from partial shade to full sun.
shade plant benefits from partial shade. These cultivars are not necessarily restricted to shade but rather grow better in it and are less likely to suffer sun scorch and exposure damage.
sun plant benefits from full sun. These cultivars grow well in full sun though some leaf tips may burn in extreme conditions.

CULTIVAR NAME	HEIGHT	FORM	COLOR	GROUP	EFFECTS	CONTAINER	BONSAI	ROCKERY	COMPANION	LIGHT
'Abigail Rose'	2 m	round	var	dwarf	spring	yes	–	yes	yes	shade
'Aka kawa hime'	2–3 m	up	green	palma	drama	yes	–	–	–	any
'Akane'	2–3 m	wide	green	palma	spring	yes	–	–	yes	any
'Akegarasu'	5–6 m	up	red	matsu	gen	–	–	–	yes	any
'Akita yatsubusa'	1–2 m	round	green	dwarf	gen	yes	yes	–	–	any
'Alpenweiss'	3 m	up	var	palma	spring	yes	–	yes	yes	shade
'Amagi shigure'	2–3 m	wide	green	matsu	gen	yes	–	–	–	sun
'Amber Ghost'	3 m	wide	var	matsu	spring	–	–	–	yes	shade
'Aoba jō'	<1 m	mound	green	dwarf	gen	yes	yes	yes	yes	sun
'Aoba nishiki'	3 m	up	var	amoe	gen	–	–	–	–	any
'Ao kanzashi'	4 m	up	var	palma	gen	–	–	–	yes	any
'Ao shidare'	5 m	mound	green	diss	gen	yes	–	–	yes	any
'Ao shime-no-uchi shidare'	2–3 m	up	green	linear	gen	yes	–	–	–	any
'Aoyagi'	8 m	up	green	palma	drama	–	–	–	yes	any
'Arakawa'	8 m	up	green	palma	drama	yes	yes	–	–	any
'Aratama'	1–2 m	mound	red	dwarf	drama	yes	yes	yes	yes	sun
'Ariadne'	3 m	wide	var	matsu	spring	yes	—	—	yes	shade
'Ariake nomura'	6–12 m	up	red	amoe	gen	–	–	–	–	any
'Asahi zuru'	8 m	up	var	palma	gen	–	–	–	yes	shade
'Atrolineare'	2–4 m	up	red	amoe	gen	–	–	–	yes	any
'Atropurpureum'	6–12 m	up	red	amoe	gen	–	–	–	–	any
'Atsu gama'	5 m	wide	green	amoe	fall	–	–	–	yes	any
'Attraction'	6–12 m	up	red	palma	gen	–	–	–	yes	any
'Aureovariegatum'	4–8 m	up	var	matsu	gen	–	–	–	–	shade
'Aureum'	6–8 m	up	green	palma	fall	yes	–	–	–	shade
'Autumn Fire'	2–4 m	wide	green	diss	fall	yes	yes	–	yes	any
'Autumn Flame'	6–8 m	up	green	palma	fall	–	–	–	yes	any
'Autumn Glory'	4–6 m	up	green	matsu	fall	–	–	–	–	any
'Autumn Red'	4–6 m	up	green	matsu	fall	–	–	–	yes	sun
'Azuma murasaki'	4–6 m	up	red	matsu	gen	–	–	–	yes	any
'Baby Lace'	1–2 m	round	green	dwarf	gen	yes	yes	yes	–	any
'Baldsmith'	2–4 m	mound	red	diss	gen	–	–	–	yes	any
'Beni chidori'	3 m	up	green	palma	spring	yes	yes	yes	–	any
'Beni fushigi'	3 m	up	red	palma	gen	–	–	–	yes	any
'Beni gasa'	4 m	round	red	matsu	fall	yes	–	–	yes	any

CULTIVAR NAME	HEIGHT	FORM	COLOR	GROUP	EFFECTS	CONTAINER	BONSAI	ROCKERY	COMPANION	LIGHT
'Beni hime'	<1 m	mound	red	dwarf	spring	yes	yes	yes	yes	sun
'Beni hoshi'	1–2 m	round	green	dwarf	spring	yes	yes	–	–	any
'Beni kagami'	4–8 m	wide	red	matsu	gen	–	–	–	yes	any
'Beni kawa'	4–6 m	up	green	palma	drama	–	–	–	yes	any
'Beni komachi'	2–3 m	round	red	palma	spring	yes	yes	yes	–	shade
'Beni kumo-no-su'	2–3 m	mound	red	diss	gen	yes	–	yes	–	any
'Beni maiko'	2–3 m	up	red	palma	spring	yes	–	–	–	any
'Beni ōtake'	4–8 m	up	red	linear	gen	–	–	–	yes	any
'Beni shichihenge'	4–6 m	up	var	palma	spring	yes	–	–	yes	any
'Beni shidare'	2–6 m	mound	red	diss	gen	yes	–	–	yes	any
'Beni shi en'	4–6 m	up	var	palma	gen	–	–	–	yes	any
'Beni shigitatsu sawa'	3–4 m	up	var	matsu	spring	yes	yes	–	yes	shade
'Beni tsukasa'	3–5 m	up	red	palma	spring	yes	yes	–	yes	any
'Beni yatsubusa'	2–4 m	mound	green	palma	fall	yes	–	–	yes	any
'Beni yubi gohon'	3 m	wide	red	linear	gen	yes	yes	–	–	sun
'Beni zuru'	3 m	round	green	palma	spring	yes	yes	yes	–	any
'Berrima Bridge'	4 m	mound	green	diss	gen	–	–	–	yes	any
'Berry Dwarf'	1–2 m	wide	green	dwarf	gen	yes	yes	–	–	any
'Bewley's Red'	3 m	wide	red	diss	gen	–	–	–	yes	sun
'Bi hō'	4 m	up	green	palma	drama	–	–	–	yes	any
'Bloodgood'	10 m	up	red	amoe	gen	–	–	–	yes	sun
'Boskoop Glory'	6–8 m	up	red	amoe	gen	–	–	–	yes	sun
'Brandt's Dwarf'	<1 m	round	red	dwarf	gen	yes	yes	yes	–	any
'Brocade'	2–4 m	mound	red	diss	gen	yes	yes	–	yes	any
'Bronzewing'	3 m	mound	red	diss	gen	–	–	–	yes	any
'Burgundy Lace'	4–6 m	wide	red	matsu	gen	–	–	–	yes	shade
'Butterfly'	6 m	up	var	palma	drama	yes	yes	–	yes	any
'Calico'	3 m	up	green	palma	spring	yes	–	–	yes	any
'Caperci Dwarf'	1–2 m	round	green	dwarf	gen	yes	yes	yes	–	any
'Carlis Corner'	2 m	round	red	dwarf	gen	yes	–	–	–	any
'Chantilly Lace'	3 m	mound	green	diss	gen	–	–	–	yes	any
'Chikumano'	3–5 m	wide	red	amoe	gen	–	–	–	yes	any
'Chirimen nishiki'	2–4 m	up	var	palma	spring	yes	yes	–	yes	sun
'Chishio'	2–4 m	wide	green	palma	spring	yes	yes	–	–	any
'Chitose yama'	2–4 m	mound	red	matsu	spring	yes	yes	–	–	any

CULTIVAR NAME	HEIGHT	FORM	COLOR	GROUP	EFFECTS	CONTAINER	BONSAI	ROCKERY	COMPANION	LIGHT
'Coonara Pygmy'	1–2 m	round	green	dwarf	fall	–	yes	yes	–	any
'Corallinum'	2–4 m	up	green	palma	spring	yes	–	–	yes	any
'Coral Pink'	1–2 m	up	green	dwarf	spring	–	–	–	–	shade
'Crimson Carol'	5 m	up	red	matsu	gen	–	–	–	yes	sun
'Crimson Queen'	2–4 m	mound	red	diss	gen	yes	–	–	yes	any
'Curtis Strapleaf'	3–4 m	up	red	linear	gen	–	–	–	yes	any
'Demi Sec'	3 m	round	green	diss	gen	–	–	–	–	any
'Deshōjō'	2–4 m	up	red	palma	spring	–	yes	–	yes	sun
'Deshōjō nishiki'	3 m	up	var	palma	spring	yes	–	yes	yes	any
'Diana'	2 m	round	green	dwarf	fall	–	yes	yes	–	any
'Dissectum Nigrum'	3–5 m	mound	red	diss	spring	–	–	–	yes	sun
'Dr Tilt'	6 m	up	green	palma	gen	–	–	–	yes	sun
'Eagle's Claw'	3 m	mound	green	diss	fall	yes	yes	yes	–	any
'Eddisbury'	3–4 m	up	green	palma	drama	–	–	–	yes	sun
'Edna Bergman'	6 m	up	red	matsu	gen	–	–	–	–	any
'Eimini'	2 m	round	green	dwarf	gen	–	yes	–	–	any
'Elegans'	3–4 m	wide	green	matsu	gen	–	–	–	yes	any
'Elizabeth'	1–2 m	up	red	dwarf	gen	–	yes	yes	–	any
'Ellen'	1 m	wide	green	diss	gen	–	–	–	yes	any
'Emerald Lace'	2–4 m	wide	green	diss	gen	–	yes	–	yes	any
'Emi'	3 m	up	var	palma	gen	yes	–	–	–	shade
'Emma'	3 m	mound	red	diss	gen	–	–	–	–	any
'Emperor 1'	6–8 m	up	red	amoe	gen	–	–	–	yes	sun
'Englishtown'	<1 m	up	red	dwarf	gen	–	yes	yes	–	any
'Enkan'	2–4 m	up	red	linear	gen	–	yes	–	yes	any
'Ever Autumn'	4–6 m	up	green	palma	fall	–	–	–	–	any
'Fairy Hair'	3 m	round	green	linear	gen	yes	–	yes	–	any
'Fall's Fire'	6 m	up	green	palma	fall	–	–	–	yes	any
'Fascination'	8 m	up	green	matsu	gen	–	–	–	yes	any
'Felice'	3–4 m	wide	red	diss	gen	–	–	–	yes	any
'Filigree'	2–4 m	mound	var	diss	gen	yes	–	–	yes	any
'Filigree Rouge'	3 m	mound	red	diss	gen	–	–	–	–	any
'Fior d'Arancio'	4–6 m	up	red	matsu	gen	yes	–	–	–	any
'Fireglow'	4–5 m	up	red	amoe	gen	yes	–	–	yes	sun
'First Ghost'	4 m	wide	var	matsu	spring	–	–	–	yes	shade

CULTIVAR NAME	HEIGHT	FORM	COLOR	GROUP	EFFECTS	CONTAINER	BONSAI	ROCKERY	COMPANION	LIGHT
'Fjellheim'	3–5 m	up	green	palma	drama	yes	–	–	yes	any
'Flavescens'	2–4 m	mound	green	diss	spring	yes	–	–	yes	any
'Fujinami nishiki'	5 m	up	var	matsu	gen	–	–	–	yes	any
'Garnet'	4–5 m	mound	red	diss	gen	yes	–	–	yes	sun
'Garyū'	1–2 m	mound	green	dwarf	drama	yes	yes	yes	–	any
'Gasshō'	5 m	wide	green	amoe	gen	–	–	–	–	any
'Geisha'	1–2 m	round	var	dwarf	gen	yes	–	yes	–	shade
'Geisha Gone Wild'	2 m	up	var	palma	gen	–	–	–	yes	any
'Germaine's Gyration'	3–5 m	mound	green	diss	gen	–	–	–	yes	any
'Globosum'	1–2 m	round	green	dwarf	gen	yes	–	–	–	any
'Glowing Embers'	3 m	up	red	palma	gen	–	–	–	yes	sun
'Golden Pond'	3 m	wide	green	amoe	fall	–	–	–	yes	any
'Goshiki kotohime'	<1 m	round	var	dwarf	drama	yes	yes	yes	yes	any
'Grandma Ghost'	3 m	wide	var	matsu	gen	–	–	–	yes	shade
'Green Globe'	4–6 m	round	green	diss	gen	–	–	–	yes	any
'Green Hornet'	3 m	mound	green	diss	gen	–	–	–	–	any
'Green Lace'	3–4 m	mound	green	diss	fall	yes	–	–	yes	any
'Green Mist'	3 m	mound	green	diss	gen	–	–	–	yes	any
'Green Star'	8 m	up	green	amoe	fall	–	–	–	yes	any
'Green Trompenburg'	6–12 m	up	green	matsu	drama	–	–	–	yes	sun
'Groundcover'	<1 m	wide	green	dwarf	gen	–	–	yes	–	any
'Hagoromo'	6 m	up	green	other	drama	–	–	–	yes	sun
'Hama otome'	2–4 m	up	green	amoe	gen	–	–	–	yes	shade
'Hanami nishiki'	1–2 m	round	green	dwarf	spring	yes	yes	yes	yes	any
'Hanazono nishiki'	1–2 m	round	var	palma	gen	–	–	–	–	shade
'Harusame'	2–4 m	up	green	palma	fall	–	–	–	yes	any
'Hazeroino'	2–3 m	up	var	other	gen	yes	–	–	–	shade
'Heartbeat'	4–6 m	mound	red	diss	gen	–	–	–	–	any
'Helena'	3 m	up	green	palma	fall	yes	–	–	yes	any
'Heptalobum Rubrum'	6 m	up	red	amoe	fall	–	–	–	yes	any
'Herbstfeuer'	4–6 m	up	green	palma	fall	–	–	–	yes	any
'Hessei'	4–6 m	wide	red	matsu	gen	yes	–	–	yes	any
'Hikasa yama'	6–9 m	up	var	palma	drama	yes	yes	–	yes	any
'Hinata yama'	8–12 m	up	red	amoe	gen	–	–	–	–	any
'Hiryū'	4 m	up	var	palma	gen	yes	–	–	–	any

CULTIVAR NAME	HEIGHT	FORM	COLOR	GROUP	EFFECTS	CONTAINER	BONSAI	ROCKERY	COMPANION	LIGHT
'Hōgyoku'	4–6 m	up	green	amoe	fall	–	–	–	yes	any
'Hondoshi'	10 m	wide	green	amoe	gen	–	–	–	–	any
'Hoshi kuzu'	<1 m	up	var	dwarf	gen	yes	yes	yes	yes	any
'Hupp's Dwarf'	<1 m	up	green	dwarf	gen	–	yes	yes	–	any
'Ibo nishiki'	4–6 m	up	green	palma	drama	–	–	–	yes	any
'Ichigyō ji'	6–10 m	up	green	amoe	fall	–	–	–	yes	any
'Iijima sunago'	6–10 m	up	var	matsu	gen	–	–	–	yes	any
'Inaba shidare'	3–5 m	mound	red	diss	gen	–	–	–	yes	any
'Inazuma'	8–12 m	up	red	matsu	fall	–	–	–	yes	any
'Iso chidori'	1–2 m	round	green	dwarf	gen	–	yes	yes	–	any
'Issai nishiki momiji'	1–2 m	up	green	dwarf	gen	–	–	yes	yes	any
'Italy Red'	3–4 m	up	red	amoe	gen	yes	–	–	–	any
'Japanese Princess'	2 m	round	green	dwarf	gen	yes	–	yes	–	any
'Japanese Sunrise'	5–7 m	up	green	palma	drama	–	–	–	yes	sun
'Jerre Schwartz'	2 m	up	red	dwarf	gen	–	–	–	yes	any
'Jirō shidare'	2–4 m	wide	green	palma	fall	–	–	yes	yes	any
'Johnnie's Pink'	3 m	round	red	palma	gen	yes	–	yes	yes	any
'Kaba'	2 m	up	green	dwarf	gen	yes	–	–	yes	any
'Kagerō'	3–5 m	up	var	amoe	drama	–	–	–	yes	shade
'Kagiri nishiki'	6–12 m	up	var	palma	gen	–	yes	–	yes	any
'Kamagata'	1–2 m	round	green	dwarf	drama	yes	–	yes	–	any
'Kandy Kitchen'	1–2 m	round	red	dwarf	gen	yes	yes	yes	–	any
'Kara ori nishiki'	2–4 m	up	var	palma	gen	–	–	–	–	shade
'Karasu gawa'	3–5 m	up	var	palma	spring	–	–	–	–	shade
'Kasagi yama'	6–10 m	up	var	matsu	spring	–	–	–	yes	any
'Kasen nishiki'	4–6 m	up	var	palma	gen	–	–	–	yes	shade
'Kashima'	1–2 m	round	green	dwarf	gen	yes	yes	–	yes	any
'Katja'	4 m	up	green	palma	gen	–	–	–	–	any
'Katsura'	4–6 m	up	green	palma	spring	yes	yes	–	–	any
'Keiser'	4 m	up	red	linear	gen	–	–	–	yes	any
'Ki hachijō'	4–6 m	up	green	matsu	fall	–	–	–	yes	any
'Killarney'	5 m	up	green	matsu	fall	–	–	–	yes	any
'Kingsville Red'	6–12 m	up	red	palma	gen	yes	–	–	yes	any
'Kingsville Variegated'	6–10 m	up	var	palma	drama	–	–	–	yes	shade
'Kinky Krinkle'	4 m	up	green	palma	gen	yes	–	–	–	any

CULTIVAR NAME	HEIGHT	FORM	COLOR	GROUP	EFFECTS	CONTAINER	BONSAI	ROCKERY	COMPANION	LIGHT
'Kinran'	3–5 m	round	red	matsu	fall	yes	yes	–	–	any
'Kinshi'	2–4 m	up	green	linear	fall	yes	–	–	–	any
'Kiri nishiki'	2–4 m	mound	green	diss	fall	–	–	–	yes	sun
'Kiyohime'	1–2 m	up	green	dwarf	spring	yes	yes	–	yes	any
'Koba shōjō'	4 m	mound	red	matsu	gen	yes	yes	–	–	any
'Kogane nishiki'	10–14 m	up	green	palma	fall	–	–	–	yes	sun
'Kogane sakae'	10–14 m	up	green	amoe	drama	yes	–	–	–	any
'Koko'	5 m	up	red	matsu	gen	–	–	–	yes	any
'Kokobunji nishiki'	2 m	round	var	dwarf	gen	yes	–	–	–	shade
'Kokyo'	9 m	up	green	amoe	fall	–	–	–	yes	any
'Komachi hime'	2 m	up	green	dwarf	gen	yes	–	yes	–	any
'Komon nishiki'	2–4 m	up	var	palma	gen	yes	yes	yes	yes	any
'Ko murasaki'	3–5 m	up	red	matsu	gen	–	–	–	yes	any
'Korean Gem'	6–10 m	up	green	amoe	fall	yes	–	–	yes	any
'Koriba'	5 m	up	green	palma	fall	–	–	–	–	any
'Koshibori nishiki'	2–4 m	wide	var	palma	gen	yes	–	–	yes	any
'Koshimino'	6–8 m	up	green	other	drama	yes	–	–	–	any
'Kotohime'	1–2 m	up	green	dwarf	gen	–	yes	yes	yes	any
'Koto ito komachi'	1–2 m	round	green	dwarf	gen	yes	–	yes	–	any
'Koto maru'	1–2 m	wide	green	dwarf	gen	–	yes	yes	–	any
'Koto-no-ito'	2–4 m	up	green	linear	gen	–	–	–	yes	any
'Kōya san'	2 m	mound	green	dwarf	gen	–	–	yes	–	any
'Kurabu yama'	2–4 m	up	green	matsu	fall	yes	–	–	yes	any
'Kuro hime'	2 m	round	green	dwarf	spring	yes	–	yes	yes	any
'Kurui jishi'	1–2 m	up	green	dwarf	gen	–	–	yes	–	any
'Lemon Lime Lace'	2–4 m	mound	green	diss	gen	–	–	–	yes	any
'Lionheart'	2–4 m	up	red	diss	gen	yes	–	–	yes	any
'Long Man'	4 m	up	red	matsu	gen	–	–	–	–	any
'Lozita'	5 m	up	red	palma	drama	yes	–	–	yes	any
'Lutescens'	6–12 m	up	green	amoe	fall	–	–	–	yes	any
'Maiko'	2–4 m	up	green	palma	drama	yes	–	–	yes	any
'Mai mori'	3–5 m	up	var	palma	gen	–	–	–	–	shade
'Mama'	2–4 m	up	green	palma	gen	yes	–	–	–	any
'Manyō-no-sato	4–6 m	up	var	palma	fall	–	–	–	–	any
'Mapi-no-machi hime'	2–4 m	round	green	dwarf	spring	yes	yes	yes	–	any

342

CULTIVAR NAME	HEIGHT	FORM	COLOR	GROUP	EFFECTS	CONTAINER	BONSAI	ROCKERY	COMPANION	LIGHT
'Marakumo'	4–6 m	up	red	matsu	gen	–	–	–	yes	shade
'Margaret Bee'	4–6 m	up	red	amoe	gen	–	–	–	yes	sun
'Marjan'	4 m	up	red	matsu	gen	–	–	–	–	any
'Masu kagami'	2–4 m	up	var	palma	gen	–	–	–	yes	shade
'Masu murasaki'	6–12 m	up	red	matsu	gen	–	–	–	yes	sun
'Matsugae'	3–5 m	up	var	palma	gen	–	–	–	yes	sun
'Matsu kaze'	2–4 m	mound	green	matsu	gen	–	–	–	yes	any
'Matsuyoi'	2–4 m	wide	green	amoe	gen	–	yes	–	yes	any
'Matthew'	1 m	round	green	dwarf	gen	yes	–	yes	–	any
'Mei hō'	4 m	up	var	amoe	gen	–	–	–	–	any
'Midori-no-teiboku'	1–2 m	wide	green	dwarf	gen	yes	–	yes	yes	shade
'Mikawa yatsubusa'	<1 m	round	green	dwarf	gen	–	yes	yes	–	any
'Mikazuki'	4 m	up	var	matsu	gen	–	–	–	yes	shade
'Mini Mondo'	2–4 m	up	green	palma	gen	yes	–	yes	–	any
'Mirte'	6–12 m	up	green	matsu	gen	–	–	–	yes	any
'Miyagino'	2–4 m	wide	green	matsu	fall	–	–	–	yes	any
'Mizuho beni'	4–6 m	up	green	palma	spring	–	–	–	yes	shade
'Mizū kiguri'	2–4 m	wide	green	amoe	spring	–	–	–	–	any
'Momenshide'	3–4 m	up	green	other	gen	yes	–	yes	–	any
'Momiji gawa'	5 m	wide	red	matsu	gen	–	–	–	–	any
'Momoiro kōya san'	2 m	round	green	dwarf	drama	yes	yes	–	–	shade
'Mon Papa'	4 m	wide	red	matsu	gen	–	–	–	yes	any
'Mon zukushi'	4–6 m	up	green	amoe	gen	–	–	–	yes	any
'Moonfire'	6–12 m	up	red	matsu	fall	–	yes	–	yes	any
'Murakumo'	6–8 m	up	red	matsu	gen	–	–	–	yes	any
'Murasaki hime'	1–2 m	round	red	dwarf	gen	–	–	yes	–	any
'Murasaki kiyohime'	1–2 m	up	green	dwarf	gen	yes	yes	yes	–	any
'Mure hibari'	4–6 m	up	green	matsu	gen	–	–	–	yes	any
'Muro gawa'	2–4 m	round	red	amoe	gen	–	–	–	yes	any
'Musashino'	8–12 m	up	red	matsu	gen	–	–	–	yes	any
'Nanase gawa'	2–4 m	wide	green	amoe	spring	yes	–	–	–	any
'Naruo nishiki'	2–4 m	up	var	palma	gen	yes	–	–	–	shade
'Nicholsonii'	4–6 m	up	green	matsu	fall	–	–	–	yes	any
'Nigrum'	4–6 m	up	red	amoe	gen	–	–	–	yes	any
'Nishiki gasane'	2–4 m	up	var	palma	gen	yes	–	–	–	shade

CULTIVAR NAME	HEIGHT	FORM	COLOR	GROUP	EFFECTS	CONTAINER	BONSAI	ROCKERY	COMPANION	LIGHT
'Nishiki gawa'	4–6 m	up	green	palma	drama	–	yes	–	–	any
'Nishiki momiji'	4–6 m	up	green	palma	fall	yes	–	–	yes	any
'Novum'	6–12 m	up	red	amoe	gen	–	–	–	yes	any
'Nuresagi'	4–6 m	up	red	matsu	drama	–	–	–	yes	any
'Octopus'	2–4 m	mound	red	diss	gen	–	–	–	yes	any
'Ogi nagashi'	6–10 m	up	var	palma	gen	–	–	–	–	shade
'Ogi-no-nagare'	4–6 m	up	var	palma	gen	–	–	–	yes	any
'Ōgon sarasa'	4–6 m	up	red	amoe	gen	–	–	–	yes	any
'Ō jishi'	1–2 m	round	green	dwarf	gen	–	yes	yes	–	any
'Ō kagami'	4–6 m	up	red	palma	gen	yes	–	–	yes	any
'Okukuji nishiki'	5–8 m	up	var	palma	gen	–	–	–	yes	any
'Okushimo'	6–8 m	up	green	palma	drama	–	yes	–	yes	any
'Omato'	6–10 m	up	green	amoe	gen	–	–	–	yes	any
'Omure yama'	4–6 m	up	green	matsu	fall	yes	–	–	yes	any
'Orange Dream'	2–4 m	up	green	palma	spring	yes	–	–	yes	shade
'Orangeola'	2–3 m	mound	red	diss	spring	–	–	–	yes	any
'Oregon Sunset'	4–6 m	round	red	matsu	fall	yes	–	–	yes	any
'Oridono nishiki'	4–6 m	up	var	palma	spring	yes	yes	–	yes	shade
'Ornatum'	2–4 m	mound	red	diss	spring	–	–	–	yes	any
'Ō sakazuki'	6–12 m	up	green	amoe	fall	–	–	–	yes	any
'Oshio beni'	6–10 m	up	red	amoe	gen	–	yes	–	yes	any
'Oshū beni'	4 m	round	red	matsu	gen	yes	–	–	–	any
'Oshū shidare'	4–6 m	wide	red	matsu	gen	yes	–	–	yes	sun
'Oto hime'	<1 m	wide	green	dwarf	gen	–	yes	yes	–	any
'Otome zakura'	2–4 m	up	red	palma	spring	yes	–	–	–	sun
'Palmatifidum'	2–4 m	mound	green	diss	gen	–	–	–	yes	any
'Peaches and Cream'	2–4 m	round	var	matsu	spring	yes	–	–	yes	shade
'Pendulum Julian'	2–4 m	mound	red	diss	gen	–	–	–	yes	sun
'Phoenix'	5 m	wide	green	palma	spring	yes	–	–	yes	any
'Pink Ballerina'	3 m	round	var	diss	gen	–	–	–	yes	shade
'Pink Filigree'	2–4 m	mound	red	diss	spring	–	–	–	yes	sun
'Pixie'	1–2 m	round	red	dwarf	gen	yes	yes	yes	–	any
'Purple Ghost'	4 m	round	var	matsu	gen	–	–	–	yes	shade
'Purple Mask'	2–4 m	up	green	linear	gen	–	–	–	yes	any
'Purpureum'	6–8 m	up	red	palma	gen	–	–	–	yes	any

CULTIVAR NAME	HEIGHT	FORM	COLOR	GROUP	EFFECTS	CONTAINER	BONSAI	ROCKERY	COMPANION	LIGHT
'Raraflora'	3 m	mound	green	diss	gen	–	–	–	–	any
'Red Autumn Lace'	3–5 m	mound	green	diss	gen	–	–	–	yes	any
'Red Baron'	5 m	up	red	amoe	gen	–	–	–	yes	any
'Red Cloud'	4 m	round	red	linear	gen	–	–	–	–	any
'Red Dragon'	2–3 m	mound	red	diss	fall	yes	yes	yes	–	any
'Red Elf'	<1 m	round	red	dwarf	gen	–	yes	yes	–	any
'Red Filigree Lace'	2–4 m	mound	red	diss	drama	–	yes	–	yes	sun
'Red Flash'	3–5 m	up	red	amoe	gen	–	–	–	yes	sun
'Red Pygmy'	2–4 m	round	red	linear	gen	–	–	–	yes	any
'Red Spider'	3–6 m	up	red	linear	gen	–	–	–	yes	any
'Red Spray'	12 m	up	red	amoe	gen	–	–	–	–	any
'Red Wood'	4 m	up	green	palma	drama	yes	–	–	yes	any
'Reticulatum Como'	5 m	up	var	matsu	spring	–	–	–	yes	shade
'Rokugatsu en nishiki'	4 m	up	var	palma	gen	–	–	–	yes	shade
'Royle'	2 m	round	red	dwarf	gen	yes	–	–	yes	any
'Rubrifolium'	2–4 m	mound	red	diss	gen	–	–	–	yes	any
'Rubrum'	2–4 m	up	red	amoe	gen	–	–	–	yes	any
'Ruby Ridge'	4 m	up	red	matsu	gen	–	–	–	–	any
'Rufescens'	2–4 m	up	red	palma	gen	–	–	–	–	any
'Rugose'	2–4 m	up	green	matsu	fall	–	–	–	yes	any
'Ryoku ryū'	3 m	up	green	palma	gen	yes	–	–	–	any
'Ryūmon nishiki'	2–4 m	up	var	palma	gen	yes	–	–	–	shade
'Ryū sei'	3 m	mound	green	palma	drama	–	–	–	yes	any
'Ryūzu'	2–4 m	round	green	dwarf	gen	–	yes	yes	–	any
'Samidare'	4–6 m	up	green	amoe	gen	–	–	–	yes	sun
'Sandra'	1 m	round	green	dwarf	gen	–	yes	yes	–	any
'Sango kaku'	6–10 m	up	green	palma	drama	–	–	–	yes	any
'Saoshika'	2–4 m	wide	green	amoe	fall	–	–	–	yes	any
'Saotome'	2–4 m	round	green	palma	gen	yes	–	–	–	any
'Satsuki beni'	6–12 m	up	green	amoe	fall	–	–	–	yes	any
'Sawa chidori'	3 m	wide	var	matsu	gen	–	–	–	yes	shade
'Sazanami'	4–6 m	up	green	matsu	drama	–	–	–	yes	any
'Seigai'	3–6 m	up	red	matsu	spring	yes	yes	–	–	any
'Seigen'	1–2 m	round	green	dwarf	spring	–	yes	–	–	any
'Seiryū'	4–6 m	up	green	diss	fall	yes	–	–	yes	any

345

CULTIVAR NAME	HEIGHT	FORM	COLOR	GROUP	EFFECTS	CONTAINER	BONSAI	ROCKERY	COMPANION	LIGHT
'Seiun kaku'	3 m	up	green	palma	gen	–	–	yes	yes	any
'Sekimori'	2–4 m	mound	green	diss	gen	–	yes	–	yes	any
'Sekka yatsubusa'	2–4 m	round	green	palma	gen	–	yes	yes	–	sun
'Semi-no-hane'	6–8 m	up	red	matsu	gen	–	–	–	–	any
'Shaina'	2–4 m	up	red	palma	gen	yes	–	yes	yes	sun
'Sharp's Pygmy'	3 m	wide	green	palma	gen	–	yes	yes	–	any
'Sherwood Flame'	4–6 m	round	red	matsu	gen	–	–	–	yes	any
'Shichihenge'	4–6 m	up	red	palma	gen	–	–	–	yes	any
'Shidava Gold'	1–2 m	up	green	dwarf	gen	–	yes	yes	–	any
'Shigarami'	2–4 m	up	green	palma	gen	yes	–	–	yes	any
'Shigi-no-hoshi'	4–6 m	up	var	matsu	gen	–	–	–	–	any
'Shigitatsu sawa'	4–6 m	up	var	amoe	drama	–	–	–	yes	shade
'Shigure bato'	2–4 m	up	green	matsu	gen	–	–	–	–	any
'Shigure zome'	2–4 m	up	red	matsu	gen	–	–	–	–	sun
'Shikage ori nishiki'	4–6 m	wide	red	palma	gen	–	–	–	yes	sun
'Shime-no-uchi'	2–4 m	round	green	linear	gen	–	–	–	yes	any
'Shin chishio'	2–4 m	up	green	palma	spring	yes	yes	–	–	any
'Shin deshōjō'	2–4 m	round	green	palma	spring	yes	yes	–	–	any
'Shinobuga oka'	4–6 m	up	green	linear	gen	yes	yes	–	–	any
'Shinonome'	2–4 m	up	red	matsu	spring	yes	–	–	yes	any
'Shiraname'	2–4 m	up	green	matsu	gen	–	–	–	–	any
'Shirazz'	4 m	wide	var	palma	gen	–	–	–	yes	shade
'Shishigashira'	4–6 m	up	green	palma	drama	yes	yes	–	yes	any
'Shishio hime'	1–2 m	wide	green	dwarf	gen	yes	yes	—	–	any
'Shōjō'	2–4 m	up	red	amoe	gen	–	–	–	yes	sun
'Shōjō-no-mai'	2–4 m	up	var	palma	spring	yes	–	–	–	shade
'Shōjō nomura'	2–4 m	up	red	amoe	gen	–	–	–	–	any
'Shōjō shidare'	2–4 m	mound	red	diss	gen	–	–	–	yes	sun
'Shū shidare'	3 m	mound	green	diss	gen	–	–	–	yes	any
'Sister Ghost'	4 m	wide	var	matsu	gen	–	–	–	yes	shade
'Skeeter's Broom'	1–2 m	up	red	dwarf	gen	yes	yes	yes	–	any
'Sode nishiki'	3 m	up	green	palma	spring	yes	–	–	yes	any
'Spring Delight'	2–4 m	mound	green	diss	drama	–	–	–	yes	shade
'Squitty'	2 m	up	var	dwarf	drama	yes	–	yes	–	shade
'Stella Rossa'	2–4 m	mound	red	diss	gen	–	–	–	yes	sun

CULTIVAR NAME	HEIGHT	FORM	COLOR	GROUP	EFFECTS	CONTAINER	BONSAI	ROCKERY	COMPANION	LIGHT
'Sumi nagashi'	4–6 m	up	red	matsu	gen	–	–	–	yes	shade
'Summer Gold'	4 m	up	green	palma	spring	yes	–	–	yes	sun
'Sunset'	2–4 m	mound	green	diss	gen	–	–	–	yes	sun
'Sunshine'	4 m	up	green	palma	spring	yes	–	–	yes	any
'Taimin'	10 m	up	red	amoe	gen	–	–	–	–	any
'Taimin nishiki'	4–6 m	up	var	amoe	gen	–	–	–	–	shade
'Taiyō nishiki'	3 m	up	var	palma	gen	–	–	–	–	any
'Takao'	6–10 m	up	green	palma	fall	–	–	–	yes	any
'Taki-no-gawa'	4–6 m	mound	green	matsu	gen	–	–	–	yes	sun
'Tama hime'	1–2 m	up	green	dwarf	fall	–	yes	–	–	any
'Tama nishiki'	2–4 m	up	var	palma	gen	yes	–	–	–	shade
'Tamaori nishiki'	3–5 m	up	var	palma	gen	–	–	–	yes	shade
'Tamuke yama'	2–4 m	mound	red	diss	gen	–	–	–	yes	any
'Tana'	4–6 m	up	green	amoe	drama	yes	–	–	yes	any
'Tanabata'	4–6 m	up	red	matsu	gen	–	–	–	yes	any
'Taro yama'	2 m	round	green	dwarf	gen	–	yes	yes	–	any
'Tatsuta gawa'	2–4 m	mound	green	amoe	fall	yes	–	–	–	any
'Tattoo'	2 m	round	green	dwarf	gen	–	–	yes	–	any
'Taylor'	3 m	wide	var	palma	drama	yes	–	–	yes	shade
'Tendō'	4 m	round	green	palma	gen	–	–	–	–	any
'Tennyo-no-hoshi'	4–6 m	up	var	palma	gen	–	–	–	yes	sun
'Teri ha'	4 m	up	red	matsu	gen	yes	—	–	yes	any
'The Bishop'	4–6 m	up	red	amoe	gen	–	–	–	yes	any
'Tiger Rose'	3 m	mound	var	matsu	gen	–	–	–	yes	shade
'Tiny Leaf'	1 m	round	green	dwarf	gen	yes	yes	yes	–	any
'Tobiosho'	4–6 m	up	green	palma	fall	–	–	–	yes	any
'Toyama'	3–5 m	mound	red	diss	gen	–	–	–	yes	any
'Toyama nishiki'	2–3 m	mound	var	diss	gen	yes	–	–	–	shade
'Trompenburg'	6–12 m	up	red	matsu	drama	–	–	–	yes	sun
'Tsuchigumo'	2–4 m	up	green	palma	drama	yes	yes	–	–	any
'Tsukomo'	1–2 m	up	green	dwarf	drama	–	–	yes	–	any
'Tsukubane'	6–12 m	up	green	amoe	gen	–	–	–	yes	any
'Tsukushi gata'	4–6 m	wide	red	amoe	drama	–	–	–	yes	any
'Tsuma beni'	2–4 m	round	green	amoe	spring	–	–	–	yes	any
'Tsuma gaki'	2–4 m	round	green	amoe	spring	–	–	–	yes	any

CULTIVAR NAME	HEIGHT	FORM	COLOR	GROUP	EFFECTS	CONTAINER	BONSAI	ROCKERY	COMPANION	LIGHT
'Tsuri nishiki'	4–6 m	up	green	matsu	gen	–	–	–	yes	any
'Twisted Spider'	2–4 m	up	green	palma	drama	yes	–	–	–	any
'Ueno homare'	4–6 m	up	green	palma	gen	–	–	–	yes	any
'Ukigumo'	2–4 m	up	var	palma	drama	yes	–	–	–	shade
'Umegae'	2–4 m	up	red	amoe	gen	–	–	–	yes	any
'Uncle Ghost'	3 m	up	var	matsu	gen	–	–	–	yes	shade
'Utsu semi'	2–4 m	wide	green	amoe	gen	–	–	–	yes	any
'Vandermoss Red'	4–6 m	up	red	matsu	gen	–	–	–	yes	sun
'Variegatum'	4–6 m	up	red	amoe	gen	–	–	–	–	shade
'Versicolor'	6–12 m	up	var	palma	gen	–	–	–	yes	shade
'Vic Pink'	2–4 m	mound	green	diss	fall	–	–	–	–	any
'Villa Taranto'	2–4 m	mound	green	linear	drama	yes	–	–	yes	sun
'Viridis'	3–5 m	mound	green	diss	gen	yes	–	–	yes	any
'Volubile'	4–6 m	up	green	palma	fall	–	–	–	yes	any
'Wabi bito'	2–3 m	up	green	palma	gen	–	–	–	yes	any
'Waka momiji'	6–10 m	up	var	palma	gen	–	–	–	yes	any
'Wakehurst Pink'	4–6 m	up	var	matsu	gen	–	–	–	yes	any
'Waterfall'	2–4 m	mound	green	diss	gen	yes	–	–	yes	sun
'Watnong'	3 m	mound	red	diss	gen	–	–	–	yes	sun
'Wendy'	3 m	wide	green	palma	drama	yes	–	–	yes	any
'Westonbirt Orange'	4 m	up	green	amoe	fall	–	–	–	yes	any
'Westonbirt Red'	4 m	wide	green	matsu	fall	–	–	–	yes	any
'Whitney Red'	6–10 m	up	red	amoe	gen	–	–	–	yes	any
'Wild Goose'	4 m	up	green	palma	gen	–	–	–	yes	any
'Willow Leaf'	3–5 m	up	red	linear	gen	–	–	–	yes	any
'Wilson's Pink Dwarf'	1–2 m	up	green	dwarf	spring	yes	–	yes	–	any
'Winter Flame'	2–4 m	up	green	palma	drama	yes	–	–	yes	any
'Wou nishiki'	2–4 m	up	green	matsu	gen	–	–	–	yes	any
'Yasemin'	6–12 m	up	red	matsu	drama	–	–	–	yes	any
'Yatsubusa'	1–2 m	round	green	dwarf	gen	–	yes	yes	–	any
'Yezo nishiki'	6–10 m	up	red	amoe	drama	–	–	–	yes	sun
'Yūbae'	4–6 m	up	var	matsu	gen	–	–	–	yes	any
'Yūgure'	4–6 m	up	red	matsu	gen	–	–	–	yes	any
'Yuri hime'	<1 m	round	green	dwarf	gen	–	yes	yes	–	any

C CULTIVARS Not Yet Assessed

The cultivars briefly described here have yet to be assessed for stability and worthiness. Additional data is needed for these new maples, some of which appear to be very promising. Unless otherwise stated, they are cultivars of *Acer palmatum*.

'Adrian's Compact'
DWARF
RED

A medium-sized upright growing shrub with bright pink-red new leaves, in summer becoming burgundy red for the summer, then turning bright orange and red in the fall.

'Alpine Surprise'
MATSUMURAE GROUP
RED

A medium-sized tree with purple-red five- to seven-lobed leaves, deeply divided almost to the base. The long narrow lobes have irregular coarsely toothed margins. Fall color is a bright crimson.

'Ao yagi gawa'
LINEARILOBUM GROUP
GREEN

This Japanese strapleaf is distinct in that most leaves have very narrow untoothed lobes but a fair proportion, although still in the strapleaf category, are broader and have clearly toothed margins. Most leaves are five-lobed, but a scattering of the broader lobed leaves have only three lobes. The spring leaves are a light green, becoming midgreen for the summer, then turning a fiery orange red in the fall.

'Ara kawa ukon'
MATSUMURAE GROUP
GREEN

This rough-barked maple from Japan is similar to 'Nishiki gawa', but with yellow fall color, not red. The corky bark begins to appear in the second year.

'Banda hime'
PALMATUM GROUP
VARIEGATED

This slower growing form is otherwise very like 'Beni shichihenge' in leaf shape, variegation and coloring. The variegation is tinged deep pink in the spring, becoming flushed brownish pink during the summer.

'Adrian's Compact'. Photo by Peter Gregory

'Alpine Surprise'. Photo by Peter Gregory

'Ao yagi gawa'. Photo by Peter Gregory

'Barrie Bergman'
DISSECTUM GROUP
RED

This maple is similar to 'Ornatum', but slow growing and with rusty red summer color, turning orange-red in the fall. It has been known under the name 'Dissectum Barrie Bergman'.

'Beni komachi Sport'
PALMATUM GROUP
GREEN

This vigorous sport from the well known 'Beni komachi' has a more normal palmatum-type leaf shape, similar to 'Shin deshōjō'—hence, possibly, a reversion. The blood-red spring leaves become green with red edging. The name is illegitimate because it includes both Japanese and English words. This plant has been sold under the abbreviated name 'Beni K Sport'.

'Beni otome'
PALMATUM GROUP
GREEN

This Japanese cultivar is very similar to 'Beni tsukasa' but with a deeper spring coloring—deep pink edging on orange-yellow leaves. It is a very promising plant.

'Beni tsukasa shidare'
DISSECTUM GROUP
RED

This bronze-brown dissectum from Japan has dark red leaves in the spring, changing to a rich orange in the fall.

'Birthday Wishes'
DISSECTUM GROUP
GREEN

The lacy leaves emerge a soft orange with rosy overtones, becoming green for the summer, before turning to rosy red in the fall. This cultivar was named and introduced by Miyama Asian Maple Nursery, California. Originally named 'Birthday Dissectum'.

'Bonnie Bergman'
AMOENUM GROUP
GREEN

A fast growing cultivar, Raised and named by F. W. Bergman. The spring leaves are a light yellow-green with reddish margins and tips, becoming midgreen for summer, often with a bronzed flush. Fall color is orange-red to scarlet. It is an upright fast growing tree up to 5 m (16 ft.) tall. Zones 5–9.

'Captain McEacham'
PALMATUM GROUP
GREEN

This maple is one of the bright pink-red spring color group of cultivars similar to 'Corallinum'. It originated from a tree growing in the Villa Taranto in Italy, and is named after the villa's former owner.

'Chishio Sanguineum'
PALMATUM GROUP
GREEN

This small form of 'Chishio' has vivid orange-red spring foliage and excellent fall colors. It originates from Australia, but has an illegitimate name with a mixture of Japanese and Latin words.

'Collingwood Ingram'
PALMATUM GROUP
GREEN

This European cultivar has regular, mainly seven-lobed palmatum-type leaves divided to about halfway to the leaf base. New leaves are a light green with bronze-red tips, becoming midgreen for the summer, and turning a bright yellow-orange to fiery red for the fall. The leaf stalks and young shoots are pink-red. 'Collingwood Ingram' develops into an upright tree up to about 4 m (13 ft.) tall.

'Crimson Prince'
PALMATUM GROUP
RED

This cultivar is very similar in color to 'Bloodgood', but is said to retain its deep purple-red color longer into late summer. Spring leaves are bright red, and fall color is scarlet. It forms an upright tree, reaching 6 m (20 ft.) in height.

'Crinkle Leaf'
MATSUMURAE GROUP
GREEN

The leaves of this strange cultivar have five coarse, broad, distorted lobes that narrow sharply to the leaf base. The margins have coarse, irregular, stubby teeth. The lobes overlap and are crinkled and distorted to varying degrees. The cultivar originated from a chance seedling at Johnnie's Pleasure Plants Nursery in Tallassee, Alabama.

'Crippsii'
PALMATUM GROUP
GREEN

This small shrub has small five-lobed leaves with rolled-up margins, very like the leaves of 'Okushimo' and

'Bonnie Bergman'. Photo by Peter Gregory

'Collingwood Ingram'. Photo by Peter Gregory

'Kurui jishi'. It was named and introduced by Hillier's Nursery in Hampshire, England.

'Daniel'
DWARF GROUP
GREEN

This witches'-broom on a 100-year-old tree was found by Bill Schwartz of Green Mansions Nursery, Pennsylvania, and named by him. It is similar to 'Coonara Pygmy' and has yellow fall color. It differs from most witches'-brooms in not having shortened central lobes on the leaves, and in producing viable seed.

'Dezome irizome'
PALMATUM GROUP
GREEN

This Japanese cultivar has large five- to seven-lobed green deeply divided leaves. Young leaves are a lovely clear yellow-green on short red leaf stalks when they first emerge. The leaf margins are distinctly and regularly, but not deeply, toothed.

'Diana Verkade'
PALMATUM GROUP
VARIEGATED

This American cultivar has bright pink variegation in the spring and semipendulous branches. It is like a weeping form of 'Oridono nishiki', but with a broader crown, becoming as wide as tall.

'Dōnzuru bo'
MATSUMURAE GROUP
RED

Masayoshi Yano (2003) mentions that this Japanese cultivar arose as a seedling from 'Tsukuma no'. The spring color is a bright bronze-green, becoming purple-red for the summer, then turning a vivid red in the fall. The mainly seven-lobed leaves are divided almost to the base, each lobe narrowly ovate with a long tail-like tip and clearly toothed margin.

'Dragon's Fire'
DISSECTUM GROUP
RED

One of the more normal-sized mushroom-shaped dissectums, 'Dragon's Fire' has bright red emerging leaves which darken during the summer and turn yellow-orange and crimson in the fall.

'Dr Baker'
DISSECTUM GROUP
RED

A vigorous, hardy, American cultivar whose foliage turns scarlet in the fall.

'Dr Brown'
DISSECTUM
GREEN

A small spreading tree with unusual light brown-red new leaves, turning green with brown-red margins for the summer. Fall color is an outstanding yellow to orange. The leaves have seven finely cut narrow lobes which curve downwards to form a dome, and are divided right to the leaf base.

'Dr Seuss'
LINEARILOBUM
VARIEGATED

A small rounded shrub with relatively small straplike leaves. It was introduced by Buchholz & Buchholz Nursery, Oregon. New leaves are bronze-green, becoming medium green with subtle yellow variegation for the summer. Fall color is yellow to orange.

'Ebony'
DISSECTUM GROUP
RED

A delightful, moderately slow-growing weeping cultivar. The red summer leaves are a persistent red, turning bright orange and scarlet in the fall.

'Ed's Red'
MATSUMURAE GROUP
RED

This upright-growing cultivar is similar in habit and color to 'Nuresagi'.

'Dr Baker'. Photo by Peter Gregory

'Crippsii'. Photo by Peter Gregory

'Dōnzuru bo'. Photo by Peter Gregory

'Dr Brown'. Photo by Peter Gregory

It has deep purple-red leaves which change to an attractive orange-red in the fall.

'Emery's Dwarf'

DWARF GROUP
VARIEGATED

This dense bushy Australian dwarf is from a seedling of 'Filigree'. It has the same variegated dissected foliage but the leaves are much smaller, only up to one inch (2.5 cm) long. The red leaf stalks and shoots contrast well with the yellow-green leaves.

'Erena'

MATSUMURAE GROUP
VARIEGATED

This Japanese introduction belongs in the 'Shigitatsu sawa' variegated group. The deeply divided leaves have long, narrow lobes and tail-like tips, and are medium to deep green with whitish tones between the veins.

'Fireball'

DWARF GROUP
RED

A witches'-broom found by David Verkade, New Jersey. It has small five-lobed, deeply divided red leaves, often with the central lobe shortened and rounded.

'Flushing'

PALMATUM GROUP
RED

This vigorous, upright cultivar is very like 'Bloodgood' in leaf shape and color. The leaves are deep, purple-red.

'Fude gaki'

MATSUMURAE GROUP
GREEN

This rare maple has medium to large seven-lobed leaves which are very deeply divided almost to the base. The lobes are long-ovate, becoming very narrow toward the lobe junctions, and have irregular toothed margins.

'Fūjin'

PALMATUM GROUP
VARIEGATED

The variegated leaves of this Japanese cultivar are similar to those of 'Tennyo-no-hoshi', but are more regular and open. They are green with a narrow band of creamy, white edging on the leaves.

'Furu kawa'

MATSUMURAE GROUP
GREEN

The large leaves are very deeply divided into seven lobes. The lobes are long-ovate with regular sharply toothed margins. The leaves are a light almost yellow green with contrasting bright red leaf stalks and young shoots.

'Gekkō nishiki'

PALMATUM GROUP
GREEN

This neat, small plant from Japan has bright yellow spring leaves with pink-red outer edges and tips. The leaves turn green for the summer but the red tones persist near the leaf tips, making the plant look like a larger version of 'Kamagata', with flatter leaves. New light colored leaves, appearing through the summer, make an attractive contrast to the darker older foliage. The small leaves have five fairly deeply divided lobes. The name means "moonlight brocade," and although the name includes the word "nishiki," there is no variegation.

'Ginja'

PALMATUM GROUP
VARIEGATED

An interesting sport from 'Taiyo nishiki', this cultivar was introduced by John Emery, Raraflora Nursery, Australia. It is similar to the well known 'Tennyo-no-hoshi', but with the variegation reversed, the yellow-green leaves having irregular mid-green margins. Fall color is yellow-orange. It has contrasting bright red leaf stalks and shoots. Like most variegates, it is best to avoid full sun.

'Girard's Dwarf'

DISSECTUM GROUP
GREEN

A very unusual dissectum, named by Girard's Nursery, Ohio, with exceptionally large, coarse, dissected leaves with only a few, very coarse teeth.

'Hamano maru'

DWARF GROUP
GREEN

This Japanese cultivar, from a witches'-broom, has a leaf shape and size similar to 'Koto maru'. The small five-lobed green leaves have yellow midribs and pink-red toothed edges. The center lobe is often shortened.

'Hana matoi'

DISSECTUM GROUP
VARIEGATED

This rare Japanese cultivar has lovely deep red, pink, yellow-green and cream variegation in sections along

'Fude gaki'. Photo by Peter Gregory

'Furu kawa'. Photo by Peter Gregory

the lobe edges and sometimes covering the entire lobe. The base color is green. The medium-sized leaves are seven-lobed and divided right to the leaf base. Each lobe has very finely divided and toothed sub-lobes, giving a lacy effect. 'Hana matoi' is considered by Guy Maillot, France, to be one of the finest of the variegate dissectums, although difficult to propagate.

'Hanzell'
DISSECTUM GROUP
RED

A hardy, vigorous dissectum with finely cut leaves that turn bright orange in the fall. Reputed to be versatile enough to grow in full sun or deep shade. Its finely cut seven-lobed leaves are bluish red in the spring, becoming purple-red in full sun, but greening up easily in shade to become bluish green. It forms the normal mushroom-shaped mound, wider than tall.

'Hatsukoi'
PALMATUM GROUP
VARIEGATED

This Japanese cultivar is one of the bright, pink-red variegated spring color group of cultivars, similar to 'Beni shichihenge'. The spring coloring of the variegated lobe margins is between the bright pink of 'Beni shichihenge' and the slight pink-flushed cream of 'Butterfly', but unlike 'Butterfly' it holds its pink through the summer. The small, deeply divided leaves have mainly five lobes, but the variegation in strips and blotches along the lobe margins causes considerable distortion of the leaves. The leaf stalks and young shoots are a contrasting red.

'Hatsu shigure'
DISSECTUM GROUP
RED

The lacy leaves of this dissectum are similar in shape to the leaves of 'Garnet', but the new foliage is a vivid red becoming dark purple. This cultivar has been known under the illegal name 'Pendulum Hatsu shigure'.

'Heisei nishiki'
PALMATUM GROUP
VARIEGATED

This cream and green variegated cultivar from Japan has young leaves which emerge orange and red, becoming green with occasional patches of cream of varying size. The cream patch may occupy up to half the leaf lobe, causing the lobe to curve. The five- to seven-lobed leaves are divided up to three quarters of the way to the leaf base. The lobes are broad ovate with tail-like tips. With its deeply cut leaves and finely toothed margins, 'Heisei nishiki' is borderline between the Matsumurae and Amoenum Groups.

'Hime yatsubusa'
DWARF GROUP
GREEN

This attractive dwarf from Japan is similar to 'Ryūzu', with small, star-shaped, five-lobed leaves. The leaves emerge yellow with reddish tips and upper margins before turning green with bronzed tips.

'Hinode nishiki'
MATSUMURAE GROUP
VARIEGATED

This delightful multicolored Japanese variegate has very deeply divided, mainly seven-lobed leaves. New leaves appearing in the spring and throughout the summer, emerge a bright yellow to yellow-green with pink blushing, changing to purple-red with pink and some green variegation. The variegation is mottled and in patches of varying sizes. Fall colors are yellow, orange and red. 'Hinode nishiki' was discovered, propagated and named by T. Tanmura, Japan.

'Hino tori nishiki'
PALMATUM GROUP
GREEN

One of the bright, pink-red, spring-flowering palmatums, this newer, colorful cultivar is similar in shape and growth to the well-known 'Deshōjō', but the leaves are much more deeply divided and the leaf is triangular in shape with long, tail-like tips. The summer color is green with pink persisting on the margins

'Hanzell'. Photo by Peter Gregory

'Hatsukoi'. Photo by Peter Gregory

'Hino tori nish'. Photo by Peter Gregory

and lobes, turning yellow-orange and red in the fall. It was selected and named by Dick van der Maat, Netherlands.

'Hisae nishiki'
PALMATUM GROUP
VARIEGATED

This Japanese cultivar has butter-yellow to cream variegation which is similar to that of 'Karasu gawa' and 'Oridono nishiki'. The leaf shape and size are also like those of 'Karasu gawa'. 'Kyu ei nishiki' is a synonym of this cultivar.

'Hitode'
AMOENUM
GREEN

A small upright tree with green starfish-shaped leaves divided to halfway into nine lobes. The edges of the lobes curl down and are colored purple. This cultivar was introduced and named by Buchholz & Buchholz Nursery, Oregon. The name means "starfish."

'Hondo ji'
MATSUMURAE GROUP
GREEN

This Japanese cultivar has leaves with five to seven lobes divided almost to the base and with finely toothed margins, hence is borderline between the matsumurae and amoenum groups. It has very attractive salmon-pink spring foliage, becoming light to medium green in summer, then turning orange and red in the fall. 'Shūzan ko' is a synonym of this cultivar.

'Hupp's Red Willow'
LINEARILOBUM
RED

This vigorous, red, strap-leaved maple is similar to 'Beni ōtake', but with larger, deeper burgundy red leaves. The bright pink young growth makes an attractive contrast. The large leaves have coarse, linear lobes. This cultivar was introduced and named by the Red Maple Nursery in 1992. The name has been misspelled 'Hubb's Red Willow'. It has also been labeled just 'Red Willow'.

'Hyōtei'
MATSUMURAE GROUP
RED

This Japanese cultivar has long, ovate lobes which narrow toward the lobe junctions leaving clear gaps between the lobes. The young leaves emerge a pink-bronze before becoming a light maroon for the summer.

'Ide-no-sato'
MATSUMURAE GROUP
GREEN

This newer Japanese import with seven-lobed, bronze-green leaves is somewhat like a green form of 'Kin-ran'. The leaves turn to gold and orange in the fall.

'Isobel'
PALMATUM GROUP
GREEN

Another bright pink-red spring-flowering cultivar, named and selected by Dick van der Maat, and similar in shape and size to the well-known

'Deshōjō'. It differs in the variable-shaped leaves which can be small and crinkly with narrow lobes to large and very broadly lobed. The leaves slowly become green with bronzed margins for the summer, turning orange-red in the fall.

'Itami nishiki'
PALMATUM GROUP
VARIEGATED

This Japanese import in the 'Butterfly' group has green leaves and cream-variegated margins tinged orange-pink.

'Jane'
PALMATUM GROUP
GREEN

A small to medium-sized cultivar selected by Dick van der Maat, Netherlands, for its beautiful long-lasting fall color. The small, mainly seven-lobed, moderately deeply divided green leaves turn a brilliant bright yellow-orange in the fall. The leaf stalks and shoots are red. It forms a wide-crowned shrub or tree up to 3 m (10 ft.) tall.

'Isobel'. Photo by Peter Gregory

'Hitode'. Photo by Peter Gregory

'Hupp's Red Willow'. Photo by Peter Gregory

'Itami nishiki'. Photo by Harry Olsen

'Japanese Sunset'
PALMATUM GROUP
GREEN

This cultivar is almost identical to 'Japanese Sunrise', but the bark coloring of the shoots and branches is in reverse (that is, red on the shaded side and yellow on the exposed side). Otherwise, both maples are very similar to 'Sango kaku'.

'Johnnie's Surprise'
PALMATUM GROUP
GREEN

The green, twisted leaves are similar in color and shape to those of 'Twisted Spider', but do not grow in clusters as on the latter. The foliage turns orange in the fall. This cultivar is vigorous, reaching about 3 m (10 ft.) tall and 2 m (6 ft.) wide in six years. It was selected and named by Harold Johnston of Johnnie's Pleasure Plants Nursery.

'Julian'
DISSECTUM GROUP
GREEN

This cultivar has soft green foliage, changing to a soft yellow in the fall. It forms a pendulous mound about as wide as tall.

'Kasane jishi'
PALMATUM GROUP
VARIEGATED

This exciting cultivar from Japan has five- to seven-lobed green leaves, with a fairly uniform, narrow, butter-yellow edging around the margins. As the leaves first emerge, the var-iegation appears as an orange-pink-bronze edging before turning butter-yellow. The leaf shape and size are similar to those of 'Nishiki gasane'.

'Katsura hime'
PALMATUM GROUP
GREEN

This smaller form of 'Katsura' has orange-yellow young leaves in the spring, edged with deep orange-red.

'Katsura nishiki'
PALMATUM GROUP
VARIEGATED

This variegated form of 'Katsura' has white to cream edging on the leaves and pink toning on the outer half of the lobes.

'Kenzan'
MATSUMURAE GROUP
GREEN

A wide spreading smallish tree up to about 3 m (10 ft.) tall, with medium to large, mainly seven-lobed, very deeply divided leaves. The lobes are ovate with long triangular, pointed tips.

'Kibune'
MATSUMURAE GROUP
GREEN

The medium to large, seven-lobed leaves are divided at least three quarters of the way to the leaf base. The lobes are broad ovate with clearly toothed margins. The spring leaves are a light green, becoming mid-green for the summer before turning orange-red in the fall. The leaf stalks and young shoots are bright red.

'Kippō nishiki'
MATSUMURAE GROUP
VARIEGATED

This Japanese cultivar has mottled, pink-cream variegation on the five-lobed, deeply divided green leaves.

'Ki shūzan'
MATSUMURAE GROUP
GREEN

This promising import from Korea has deeply divided and coarsely toothed, seven- to nine-lobed, feathery leaves. The lobe tips tend to curve downward. The dark green leaves turn to a bright yellow-orange

'Julian'. Photo by Peter Gregory

'Kibune'. Photo by Peter Gregory

'Jane'. Photo by Peter Gregory

'Kenzan'. Photo by Peter Gregory

'Ki shūzan'. Photo by Peter Gregory

in the fall. Spring leaves are light green, becoming mid to dark green often with brown tips for the summer, then turning yellow to red in the fall. The name has been misspelled as 'Kishousan'.

'Ko chidori'
PALMATUM GROUP
GREEN

The small five-lobed leaves of 'Ko chidori' are divided at least three quarters of the way to the leaf base. The lobes are long-ovate, mostly broadest in the middle, with toothed margins which are not as conspicuous as in the typical palmatum leaf. The young leaves are light green with bronze-red lobe tips, becoming midgreen with contrasting red leaf stalks and young shoots for the summer. Fall color is orange-red.

'Kuchi beni nishiki'
PALMATUM GROUP
VARIEGATED

This Japanese variegate of the 'Beni shichihenge' group has pretty bright pink-red variegated margins on the small five-lobed leaves. The lobes are broader with a daintier appearance than the lobes of most cultivars in this group.

'Kurenai'
PALMATUM GROUP
GREEN

This Japanese cultivar in the spring color group has seven-lobed leaves,

'Ko chidori'. Photo by Peter Gregory

with the lobe tips pointing forward. The leaves are a bright orange-red when they first appear, becoming green with bronzed tips for the summer. This cultivar has been known under the name 'Kureha'.

'Kyōgoku shidare'
MATSUMURAE GROUP
GREEN

A seedling from 'Inaba shidare', this Japanese selection forms a spreading cascading tree or shrub. Its medium to large, mainly seven-lobed leaves are divided almost to the base and are very coarsely toothed to give a feathery effect. The midgreen leaves turn a bright red in the fall.

'Kyōryū'
DWARF GROUP
GREEN

This slow-growing Japanese dwarf was imported to the Netherlands and is similar to 'Sekka yatsubusa'. An interesting characteristic of this cultivar is the flattened, fasciated shoots which often appear. The young leaves are a bronze-green, becoming green for the summer, before turning yellow in the fall.

'Leather Leaf'
PALMATUM GROUP
GREEN

This cultivar is aptly named after the larger-than-usual palmatum-type olive to dark green leaves which are fairly thick, semishiny and leathery to the touch. It grows to more than 4 m (13 ft.) tall.

'Lemon Chiffon'
DISSECTUM GROUP
GREEN

This mushroom-shaped cultivar has bright yellow-green spring foliage which becomes light green for the summer, then turns yellow to orange with red flushes in the fall. It needs protection from the hot afternoon sun.

'Lockington Gem'
DWARF GROUP
GREEN

This cultivar was selected and registered in 1992 by Donald Dosser, Australia, because of its very dwarf, slow-growing habit and tiny leaves which are one third the size of those of 'Coonara Pygmy' and 'Goshiki kotohime'. Fall color is red. It forms a small dense shrub, no more than about 1 m (3 ft.) tall and 60 cm (2 ft.) wide.

'Lucky Star'
MATSUMURAE GROUP
GREEN

This is a medium-sized upright cultivar with outstanding orange to

'Lemon Chiffon', spring color.
Photo by Peter Gregory

'Lemon Chiffon', fall color.
Photo by Bill Schwartz

orange-red fall color. The spring leaves are light yellow-green with pink-red lobe tips, becoming light to medium green for the summer. The large mainly seven-lobed leaves have ovate lobes very deeply divided almost to the leaf base, and with conspicuous slightly crinkled teeth around the margins.

'Lydia'
PALMATUM GROUP
GREEN

'Lydia' is another palmatum selected for its glorious autumn color by Dick van der Maat, Netherlands. The five-lobed leaves vary in size and, to some extent, shape. They emerge a light yellow-green with orange-brown margins, becoming a shiny medium to dark green and are somewhat crumpled for the summer. They turn a very bright orange in the fall. It is estimated it will form a small upright

'Lucky Star'. Photo by Peter Gregory

'Lydia'. Photo by Peter Gregory

tree, reaching at least 3 m (10 ft.) in height.

'Malon'
PALMATUM GROUP
GREEN

The unusual summer color of this strong-growing cultivar catches the eye. It is a deep yellow-green with broad bronze-red or purple margins and tips, turning orange-red in the fall. The medium-sized leaves have five to seven ovate lobes and are moderately deeply divided. It forms an upright tree, estimated to reach up to 5 m (16 ft.) in height.

'Margaret'
PALMATUM GROUP
GREEN

This Dutch cultivar, named by Dick van der Maat, was selected for its outstanding bright yellow fall color. The small five- to seven-lobed leaves emerge a light pink with yellow-green centers which gradually changes to light green for the summer. It forms an upright tree, estimated to reach 3 m (10 ft.) in height.

'Mary Katherine'
DWARF GROUP
RED

Another witches'-broom, with the five- to seven-lobed deeply divided red leaves of the Matsumurae Group. The lobes are narrowly ovate, often with a shortened central lobe.

'Margaret'. Photo by Peter Gregory

'Mei hō nishiki'
AMOENUM GROUP
VARIEGATED

This relatively large-leaved Japanese variegate has green leaves with yellow patches and blotches as they emerge, occasionally covering the whole leaf. This changes to creamy white on green for the summer, then turning bright red in the fall. The leaves are very deeply divided into seven ovate lobes with tail-like tips and finely toothed margins. The shoots become green with fine gray stripes.

'Melanie'
PALMATUM GROUP
GREEN

A rare small tree with small mainly five-lobed typical palmatum-type leaves, divided to about halfway to the leaf base. The lobes are broad ovate with toothed margins. Spring leaves emerge a shiny pink-red, changing to bronze-red then shiny green for the summer, often tinged bronze.

'Meoto'
PALMATUM GROUP
GREEN

Characteristic of this Japanese cultivar is that the basal lobes of the small palmate leaves tend to overlap and the margins have relatively large conspicuous teeth. The seven lobes are fairly deeply divided. Spring

'Melanie'. Photo by Peter Gregory

leaves are light green with bronze-red margins and tips, becoming mid-green for the summer, then turning yellow-orange in the fall.

'Mioun'

DISSECTUM GROUP
RED

This cultivar has bronze-red foliage, turning to yellow-orange in the fall. It is hardy, but prefers light shade. 'Mioun' has also been known as 'Dissectum Mioun'.

'Miss Piggy'

PALMATUM GROUP
GREEN

Another selection from Dick van der Maat's Dutch Nursery. Its shape and leaves are similar to the better known 'Sharp's Pygmy', but it is much more vigorous, reaching up to 3 m (10 ft.) in height. The leaves have much coarser teeth on the margins and the center lobe is not as long pointed and dominant. Also, the outer sides of the leaves are bowed

'Meoto'. Photo by Peter Gregory

'Miss Piggy'. Photo by Peter Gregory

upward like an upturned shallow bowl.

'Miyabi nishiki'

PALMATUM GROUP
VARIEGATED

This Japanese cultivar has leaf shape, color and variegation similar to that of 'Asahi zuru'. In the fall the variegation turns a bright gold-orange.

'Murasaki shikibu'

PALMATUM GROUP
VARIEGATED

This Japanese variegate is similar in size and leaf to the popular 'Asahi zuru' but is more upright. The new leaves emerge bright pink becoming green with creamy white blotches and mottled variegation. Fall color is red. The young shoots have pink streaks along them. The five- to seven-lobed leaves have conspicuous toothed margins. The lobes are irregular ovate and often hooked with the pointed lobe tips in all directions because of the irregular amount of variegation.

'Nathan'

MATSUMURAE GROUP
RED

This Dutch cultivar, selected by Cor van Gelderen and named after his son, has bright pinky red leaves in the spring, becoming purple-red for the summer, and turning a bright orange-scarlet in the fall. The seven-

'Nathan'. Photo by Peter Gregory

lobed medium-sized leaves are fairly deeply divided with ovate lobes and long triangular, pointed tips. It forms a relatively small upright tree to about 3 m (10 ft.) tall and 2 m (6 ft.) wide.

'Nomura kōyō'

MATSUMURAE GROUP
RED

This Japanese cultivar is similar to 'Musashino' and 'Nomura ōba'. It has slightly narrower lobes and an even lighter red color. The name is synonymous with 'Nomura ōjō' and 'Nomura ōrō'.

'Nomura ōba'

MATSUMURAE GROUP
RED

This Japanese cultivar is very similar to 'Musashino', but with more numerous, sharper-pointed teeth and a lighter red color. The young leaves are a bright pink-red.

'Nose gawa'

PALMATUM GROUP
RED

This Japanese cultivar has bright, fresh, light green leaves on short, green leaf stalks, causing the leaves to bunch into clusters on the shoots. The leaves are long-triangular and widest near the base.

'Ō izu'. Photo by Peter Gregory

'Ō izu'

MATSUMURAE GROUP
GREEN

A Japanese introduction whose leaves have a distinct feathery appearance. They are medium-sized, light green, seven-lobed and moderately deeply divided. The lobes are ovate with long pointed tips, and with distinct deeply and regularly toothed feathery margins. Fall color is yellow-orange.

'Okina'

DWARF GROUP
GREEN

This cultivar is similar in appearance to 'Kamagata', but the five lobes, divided almost to the base, are very narrow and hold stiffly in a star shape. The leaves emerge a bright pink, changing to green with red tingeing round the crinkled leaf edges. This very promising dwarf has been misspelled 'Okimo' and 'Okino'.

'Oranges & Lemons'

PALMATUM GROUP
GREEN

Named after the bright yellow-orange spring foliage, which changes to dark green for the summer, then to deep orange in the fall. It forms a medium-sized open shrub or tree.

'Orion'

DWARF GROUP
GREEN

Richard P. Wolff of Red Maple Nursery, Pennsylvania, discovered this curious dwarf on a witches'-broom. The leaves have deeply divided lobes with "feathery" toothed margins.

'Paul's Variegate'

PALMATUM GROUP
VARIEGATED

This, distinctly different, variegate has medium-sized palmate leaves and broad lobes. The basic color is a dark green with splashes of creamy white variegation. Howard Hughes of Montesano, Washington, introduced this cultivar.

'Peve Dave'

LINEARILOBUM GROUP
RED

This strapleaf is similar to the green 'Kinshi' in habit and size, but has slightly broader lobed leaves which are not quite divided to the base. It was selected and named by D. Vergeldt, Netherlands.

'Peve Multicolor'

MATSUMURAE GROUP
VARIEGATED

This attractive Dutch cultivar, selected and named by D. Vergeldt, is a welcome addition to the 'Shigitatsu sawa' group of variegates. Its spring leaves emerge a bright yellow with pink margins and tips, gradually becoming creamy white to light cream-green with a midgreen network of veins for the summer. It is reasonably vigorous and will reach up to 4 m (13 ft.) tall.

'Pung kil'

LINEARILOBUM GROUP
RED

This Korean cultivar is similar to 'Red Pygmy' but with longer, narrower, straplike lobes. The young leaves are light red, becoming dark red for the summer and holding their color well. 'Pung kil' originated from a seedling of *A. palmatum* f. *atropurpureum*. The name has been misspelled 'Pung kill'.

'Pygmy'

DWARF GROUP
GREEN

This pretty very slow-growing dwarf has palmatum-type leaves with a dominant center lobe. It grows very slowly, forming a low spreading bush, reaching a height of about 1 m (3 ft.) and spreading a little wider.

'Red Jonas'

MATSUMURAE GROUP
RED

A promising Dutch cultivar, named by J. der Netherlandser, whose leaves have five to seven very deeply divided ovate lobes with fairly regular finely toothed margins. The violet-red leaves turn orange to crimson in the fall. It is a vigorous grower and forms an upright tree to at least 3 m (10 ft.) in height.

'Red Strata'

DWARF GROUP
RED

This dwarf dissectum hugs the ground like a red disc, hence its name. The spring foliage is reddish pink, becoming pink-green. Full sun retains the pink-red color best and this cultivar greens easily in the shade.

'Peve Dave'. Photo by Peter Gregory

'Red Jonas'. Photo by Peter Gregory

'Renjaku maru'
DWARF GROUP
GREEN

This delightful, small-leaved, Japanese dwarf is similar to 'Kiyohime'. The leaves are green with reddish edging and tips, and the center lobe is often truncate, indicating its witches'-broom origins.

'Rhode Island Red'
PALMATUM
RED

A small upright rounded tree with medium-sized deep red leaves. The five- to seven-lobed leaves are deeply divided and have conspicuously toothed margins. The two small basal lobes are angled backwards toward the red leaf stalks.

'Rilas Red'
DISSECTUM GROUP
RED

A mushroom-shaped dissectum with very finely dissected leaves of glowing red, especially in the fall.

'Rhode Island Red'. Photo by Peter Gregory

'Rilas Red'. Photo by Peter Gregory

'Roseum Ornatum'
DISSECTUM GROUP
RED

Bronze-red spring foliage with glowing red-pink new growth during summer. The leaves turn orange to red in the fall.

'Ruben'
PALMATUM GROUP
GREEN

One of the red spring-flowering members of the Palmatum Group, similar to the popular 'Deshōjō' in leaf and color. The leaves tend to be slightly crinkled with the lobe tips curved sideways or downward.

'Ruth's Red'
PALMATUM GROUP
RED

This plant is a seedling, possibly from 'Bloodgood', introduced by Greg Gulden of Suncrest Gardens, Pennsylvania, and named after his mother. It has large, deep purple-red, seven-lobed leaves. The lobes are broadly ovate with tapering tips. The margins are very evenly and finely toothed, the teeth with sharp-pointed tips.

'Saint Jean'
MATSUMURAE GROUP
RED

This attractive cultivar from Arboretum Kalmthout in Belgium is similar to 'Shinonome'. The seven-lobed, deeply divided leaves emerge a bright pink-red, changing to bronze-red,

'Ruben'. Photo by Peter Gregory

then to pink on green later in the summer.

'Sakura hime'
PALMATUM GROUP
VARIEGATED

This interesting cultivar was imported from Japan in 1991 by Firma C. Esveld, Boskoop, Netherlands. The creamy white variegation forms a broad band around the margins and often encroaches on the irregular green centers of the lobes, occasionally occupying the whole lobe or leaf. 'Izu-no-odoriko' is a synonym of this cultivar.

'Sharon'
MATSUMURAE GROUP
RED

This upright small tree, reaching 4 m (13 ft.) tall, has large seven-lobed moderately deeply divided leaves. The lobes are ovate with variably toothed margins. Spring leaves are a bright pink-red becoming purple-red for the summer, then turning orange-scarlet in the fall.

'Saint Jean'. Photo by Peter Gregory

'Sharon'. Photo by Peter Gregory

'Sir Happy'
DWARF GROUP
GREEN

This cute cultivar from Crispin's Creation Nursery, Oregon, resembles 'Hupp's Dwarf' but is much smaller, and could be the smallest dwarf on the market. The leaves are of the palmatum type.

'Suisei'
DISSECTUM GROUP
VARIEGATED

This slow-growing dissectum was imported into the Netherlands from Japan and is similar in leaf and variegation to 'Filigree'. The basic color is green with conspicuous speckling of white on young leaves, which, like 'Filigree', gradually fades to green as the leaf ages.

'Susan'
DWARF GROUP
GREEN

This Dutch dwarf from the Dick van der Maat Nursery, has very small light green palmatum-type leaves in the spring, becoming a shiny mid-green for the summer, and turning yellow in the fall. It forms a dense round bush up to 1 m (3 ft.) or so in height. Because of the small leaves, plant size and shape, it is well suited for bonsai culture.

'Suzu maru'
DWARF GROUP
GREEN

This Japanese cultivar is similar to 'Kotohime', with bunched-up leaf clusters and pink-flushed young leaves on a light green background of older leaves.

'Tiny Tim'
DWARF GROUP
GREEN

This hardy, dense, round, green dwarf is very similar to 'Coonara Pygmy'. The small, fresh green leaves are on reddish leaf stalks and turn yellow and red in the fall. 'Tiny Tim' originated from a witches'-broom, found and named by Richard P. Wolff of Red Maple Nursery, Media, Pennsylvania. Zones 6–10.

'Tsukuma no'
OTHER GROUP
GREEN

This Japanese import into the Netherlands has stalkless, five-lobed leaves, similar to those of 'Hagoromo' and 'Koshimino'. Bark, shoots and leaves are green, and the lower midribs, like those of 'Hagoromo', are tinged pink-red. The leaves are divided to the leaf base, with the narrow lobes only the width of the midrib in the lower third. The name has been misspelled 'Tsuka mano'.

'Unebi'
MATSUMURAE GROUP
GREEN

This cultivar has large five- to seven-lobed moderately deeply divided leaves, with distinctly and regularly toothed margins. Occasionally, the central lobe is shortened with rounded tip, suggesting it may have arisen from a witches'-broom. Spring leaves are a shiny bronzed green, becoming medium green for the summer, then turning an attractive yellow-orange in the fall.

'Usu midori'
PALMATUM
GREEN

A small hardy tree with colorful spring foliage, similar to 'Katsura'. The young leaves emerge a light reddish pink, becoming yellow-orange with pink margins, then yellow-green before turning light green for the summer. Fall color is orange-red.

'Van den Akker'
MATSUMURAE GROUP
GREEN

A large-leaved cultivar with excellent orange autumn color. The moderately deeply divided green leaves have seven ovate lobes with long

'Suisei'. Photo by Peter Gregory

'Susan'. Photo by Peter Gregory

'Unebi'. Phto by Peter Gregory

'Usu midori'. Photo by Peter Gregory

pointed tips and regular sharply toothed, almost feathery margins.

'Ven's Red'
DWARF GROUP
RED

Unlike most red-leaved dwarf cultivars, 'Ven's Red' tends to be upright rather than spreading. The spring leaves are bright crimson, becoming ribbed with green during the summer, and turning yellow-orange-red in the fall. Its height at maturity is about 1.5 m (5 ft.).

'Victoria'
DWARF GROUP
RED

This rounded dwarf has frequent, truncated center leaf lobes, showing its witches'-broom origins. The bright red of spring fades to a rusty green later in summer, before turning a vivid crimson in the fall.

'Warburton Pygmy'
DWARF GROUP
GREEN

This cultivar was selected and registered in 1992 by Donald Dosser, Australia, because of its dwarf, flat-topped habit. It has only reached 30 cm (12 in.) high and wide after 10 years and will not grow long shoots, even after heavy feeding and grafting.

'William S. Campbell'
PALMATUM GROUP
GREEN

A cultivar with small to medium-sized, mainly seven-lobed typical palmatum type leaves. The lobes are divided to about halfway to the leaf base, and are broadly ovate with distinctly toothed margins. The leaf stalks and young shoots are conspicuously red.

'Wolff's Broom'
DWARF GROUP
RED

This dwarf originated from a witches'-broom on *Acer palmatum* f. *atropurpureum*. It was found and named by Bill Schwartz of Green Mansions Nursery, Pennsylvania, after the late Richard P. Wolff of Red Maple Nursery, Media, Pennsylvania. The leaves emerge a bright red, becoming a rusty green by late July and changing to orange-red in the fall. Like most maple cultivars from witches'-brooms, it forms a well rounded, compact small shrub.

Acer buergerianum 'Inazuma nishiki'
This cultivar has a *shimo furi* (frost-scattered) type of yellow variegation.

Acer buergerianum 'Jōroku aka me'
This medium-sized bush has shiny green leaves that have three forward-pointing lobes, the center lobe dominant. Attractive orange-red to bronze-red young leaves appear throughout the summer.

Acer buergerianum 'Kifu nishiki'
This dwarf variegate was imported into the Netherlands from Japan by Firma C. Esveld, Boskoop. The small, dense shrub reaches a little over 1 m (3 ft.) in height. The small, stubby, almost unlobed leaves have a creamy variegation on the lower half of the leaf.

'Van den Akker'. Photo by Peter Gregory

'William S. Campbell'. Photo by Peter Gregory

'Wolff's Broom'. Photo by Billie Schwartz

Acer buergerianum 'Musashi'

The leaves of this Japanese cultivar are similar in shape to those of *Acer buergerianum* 'Mino yatsubusa'—a dominant long-ovate central lobe, about twice as long as the obliquely pointed side lobes. The young leaves emerge an attractive, shiny, bronze-red. 'Hime kaede' is a synonym of this cultivar.

Acer buergerianum 'Nokori bi'

This cultivar has large, very shiny, dark green leaves which are a beautiful bronze-red when first emerging. The leaves have three forward-pointing lobes in the outer third of each leaf. They are slightly wavy and bunched, with occasional teeth on the margin.

Acer buergerianum 'Shirley Debacq'

The green leaves of this upright, fastigiate cultivar are divided to about halfway to the leaf base.

Acer circinatum 'Hidden Valley'

This vine maple cultivar has a round, bright green leaf with pink to red fall colors. It grows into a neat shrub to a height of 3.5 m (11 ft.) when in full sun. 'Hidden Valley was named and introduced by Miyama Asian Maple Nursery, Laytonville, California.

Acer circinatum 'Pacific Sprite'

A dwarf tree with small deep green crinkly leaves turning orange-red in the fall. The irregular crumpled leaves are deeply divided into five to seven very broad oval lobes and have unusually coarsely toothed margins.

Acer circinatum 'Sunny Sister'

New from Talon Buchholz, 'Sunny Sister' has yellow-gold leaves in spring with pink tinges, later turning green with pink tinges. As the name suggests, this vine maple thrives in a site in sun.

Acer japonicum 'Aka omote'

The seven-lobed, medium-sized leaves are shallowly divided only one third of the way to the leaf base. The lobes are short and fat. The leaves are green with light bronzing, especially when first appearing, contrasting with the light green at the leaf junction with the leaf stalks.

Acer japonicum 'Gossamer'

A cross between *A. japonicum* and a green *A. palmatum* f. *dissectum*, this cultivar has the hardiness of its female parent and the deeply dissected leaves of its male parent. The fall color is orange-gold. 'Gossamer' is reputed to be one of the slowest-growing of the *A. japonicum* cultivars.

Acer pictum 'Asagiri nishiki'

This Japanese cultivar has five-lobed, deeply divided leaves, similar to those of *A. pictum* 'Dissectum', but variegated with a network of light variegation following the finely reticulate veins of the green leaves. The variegation is rather like that on the leaves of *A. palmatum* 'Shigitatsu sawa'. The name has been misspelled 'Asagira'.

Acer pictum 'Marmoratum'

This shrub to 8 m (26 ft.) tall, with slightly white-dotted variegation on the leaves, is similar to *Acer pictum* 'Hoshi yadori', but not as worthwhile.

Acer pictum 'Naguri nishiki'

The variegation of this Japanese cultivar is almost a cross between 'Hoshi yadori' and 'Usugumo'—a mixture of heavily concentrated white dots and specks of varying sizes and intensities.

Acer pictum 'Nikkōense'

This Japanese cultivar has laciniate lobes and pubescent veins.

Acer pictum 'Satsuki beni'

This shallowly lobed variegate growing in Japan, has a bewildering mixture of variegation patterns from dusting to splashes, from totally white leaves to totally green and all stages between.

Acer shirasawanum 'Diana'

This variegated form has nine- to eleven-lobed leaves with irregular splashes of white variegation on the medium green base color.

Acer shirasawanum 'Gloria'

The nine- to eleven-lobed, deeply divided leaves, with coarsely toothed

Acer circinatum 'Pacific Sprite'.
Photo by Peter Gregory

Acer circinatum 'Sunny Sister'.
Photo by Peter Gregory

Acer shirasawanum 'Gloria'.
Photo by Peter Gregory

margins are similar to those of *A. palmatum* 'Yasemin'. Both would seem to be hybrids between *A. shirasawanum* and *A. palmatum*. The young leaves emerge a bright red in the spring, becoming bronze-green, then turning a vivid red in the fall.

Acer shirasawanum 'Kakure gasa'

This cultivar is better known in Western cultivation as *A. shirasawanum* 'Ogon itaya', and earlier thought to be an *A. japonicum* cultivar. Previously, it was regarded as a synonym of *A. shirasawanum* 'Aureum', but Japanese records indicate 'Kakure gasa' is a very old cultivar in its own right, and was first recorded in 1782. 'Kin kakure' is a relatively recent synonym of 'Kakure gasa'.

Acer shirasawanum 'Little Green Star'

This interesting new cultivar differs from other *A. shirasawanum* cultivars in that the small, mainly nine-lobed leaves are relatively deeply divided with the lobes spread outward and the conspicuously toothed margins slightly curved downward like upside down troughs.

Acer sieboldianum 'Albiflorum'

This form is like the type species in growth, habit and leaves but, as the name implies, has white flowers instead of the normal yellow.

Acer sieboldianum 'Mikasa yama nishiki'

This variegated form has deeply cut lobes and a network variegation similar to that of *A. palmatum* 'Shigitatsu sawa'.

Acer shirasawanum 'Kakure gasa'.
Photo by Peter Gregory

Acer shirasawanum 'Little Green Star'.
Photo by Peter Gregory

Acer sieboldianum 'Sayo ginu'

This form has very small leaves which turn a vivid red in the fall.

Acer sieboldianum 'Tortuosum'

This unusual cultivar has contorted shoots and branches.

Acer tataricum 'Aureovariegatum'

This, more delicate form of the Amur maple has yellow-variegated leaves which are prone to scorching in full sun or cold winds, so need a sheltered position, shaded from direct sun.

Acer tataricum 'Coccineum'

The fruits are an outstanding red, even brighter than those of the type species.

Acer tataricum 'Mondy'

This large, multistemmed shrub was raised by Monrovia Nurseries of California and given the trademark name Red Rhapsody™. The fall colors are yellow and orange, becoming bright scarlet.

Acer truncatum 'Asahi nishiki'

This deeply divided variegate from Japan has a *sunago fu* (sand-dusted) type of variegation, often in large, bold splashes occupying half the lobe or more.

'Acutum' (*A. palmatum*)

'Afterglow' (*A. palmatum*)

'Aiai gasa' (*A. sieboldianum*)

'Aizumi nishiki' (*A. palmatum*)

'Akaba' (*A. palmatum*)

'Akagi san nishiki' (*A. rufinerve*)

'Akahada yama' (*A. palmatum*)

'Akaha nishiki' (*A. palmatum*)

'Aka hosada' (*A. palmatum*)

'Aka itaya nishiki' (*A. pictum*)

'Akaji-no-nishiki' (*A. palmatum*)

'Akame hagoromo' (*A. palmatum*)

'Akame hauchiwa' (*A. japonicum*)

'Akame itaya meigetsu' (*A. sieboldianum*)

'Aka moyo (*A. palmatum*)

'Akane hagoromo' (*A. palmatum*)

'Akane zome' (*A. palmatum*)

'Akebono nishiki' (*A. buergerianum*)

'Akikaze' (*A. pictum*)

'Aki kogane' (*A. palmatum*)

'Aki-no-iro' (*A. palmatum*)

'Aki-no-utage' (*A. palmatum*)

'Aki-no-yūgure' (*A. palmatum*)

'Akishino' (*A. palmatum*)

'Akishino nishiki' (*A. palmatum*)

'Aki tsuma beni' (*A. palmatum*)

'Akitsu shima' (*A. palmatum*)

'Akitsu shū' (*A. palmatum*)

'Akitsu su' (*A. palmatum*)

'Akitsuta' (*A. palmatum*)

'Aki zome midare' (*A. palmatum*)

'Alleyne Cook' (*A. circunatum*)

'Alloys' (*A. palmatum*)

'Amagatsuji' (*A. palmatum*)

'Amagi' (*A. palmatum*)

'Ama kumo' (*A. palmatum*)

'Andreanum' (*A. palmatum*)

'Annick' (*A. palmatum*)

'Ansung' (*A. palmatum*)

'Ao gaki yama' (*A. palmatum*)

'Ao ha' (*A. palmatum*)

'Ao shidare kōyō' (*A. palmatum*)

'Aotya nishiki' (*A. palmatum*)

'Arakawa momiji' (*A. palmatum*)

'Arakawa tokaede' (*A. buergerianum*)

'Arano' (*A. palmatum*)

'Arano araya' (*A. palmatum*)

'Arashi yama' (*A. palmatum*)

'Arima yama' (*A. palmatum*)

'Arlene' (*A. palmatum*)

'Arto' (*A. palmatum*)

'Asagi nishiki' (*A. palmatum*)

'Asahi zuru shiro fu' (*A. palmatum*)

'Asa-no-ha' (*A. palmatum*)

'Asa-no-hoshi' (*A. palmatum*)

'Asashi yama' (*A. palmatum*)

'Asatsuyu' (*A. palmatum*)

'Asa zakura' (*A. palmatum*)

'Asa zuma' (*A. palmatum*)

'Ascendens' (*A. japonicum*)

'Ashi-no-ha' (*A. palmatum*)

'Ashi-no-sato' (*A. palmatum*)

'Ashurst Wood' (*A. palmatum*)

'Asuka' (*A. palmatum*)

'Asuka gawa nishiki' (*A. palmatum*)

'Asuka kawa' (*A. palmatum*)

'Asuka yama' (*A. palmatum*)

'Aureum' (*A. pictum*)

'Autumn Dream' (*A. palmatum*)

'Autumn Glow' (*A. palmatum*)

'Autumn Showers' (*A. palmatum*)

'Awa uri nishiki' (*A. crataegifolium*)

'Awa yuki' (*A. tataricum*)

'Aya hatori' (*A. palmatum*)

'Ayai gasa' (*A. sieboldianum*)

'Azuma nishiki' (*A. palmatum*)

'Baby Dragon' (*A. truncatum*)

'Baby Ghost' (*A. palmatum*)

'Balcombe Green' (*A. palmatum*)

'Barbara' (*A. palmatum*)

'Beethoven' (*A. tataricum*)

'Beni bato' (*A. palmatum*)

'Beni goromo' (*A. palmatum*)

'Beni hauchiwa' (*A. japonicum*)

'Beni homare' (*A. palmatum*)

'Beni kaede' (*A. palmatum*)

'Beni kagami nishiki' (*A. palmatum*)

'Beni ko hime' (*A. palmatum*)

'Beni kosode' (*A. palmatum*)

'Beni michinoku' (*A. palmatum*)

'Beni mikawa' (*A. palmatum*)

'Beni murasaki gawa' (*A. palmatum*)

'Beni musume' (*A. palmatum*)

'Beni-no-nami' (*A. palmatum*)

'Beni ōgi' (*A. palmatum*)

'Beni ori zuru' (*A. palmatum*)

'Beni sazanami' (*A. palmatum*)

'Beni sen' (*A. palmatum*)

'Beni sengoku' (*A. palmatum*)

'Beni shōjō shidare' (*A. palmatum*)

'Beni suzume' (*A. palmatum*)

'Beni zashi' (*A. palmatum*)

'Beni zome shizuku' (*A. palmatum*)

'Beni zukashi' (*A. palmatum*)

'Ben's Broom' (*A. palmatum*)

'Bergiana' (*A. tataricum*)

'Bicolor' (*A. palmatum*)

'Bill Dale's Red' (*A. palmatum*)

'Bob's Big Green' (*A. palmatum*)

'Bō jō' (*A. palmatum*)

'Bradley's Broom' (*A. palmatum*)

'Brevilobum' (*A. palmatum*)

'Brian' (*A. palmatum*)

'Bronson's Crinkle' (*A. palmatum*)

'Bujō ji' (*A. palmatum*)

'Bultinck' (*A. palmatum*)

'Burgundy' (*A. tataricum*)

'Burgundy Flame' (*A. palmatum*)

'Byakugō ji' (*A. palmatum*)

'Camille' (*A. palmatum*)

'Candy Stripe' (*A. capillipes*)

'Carolyn Wolff' (*A. palmatum*)

'Caudatum' (*A. palmatum*)

'Charlotte' (*A. palmatum*)

'Chichibu hime' (*A. palmatum*)

'Chi otome' (*A. palmatum*)

'Chiri hime' (*A. palmatum*)

'Chi sato' (*A. palmatum*)

'Chishio-no-ito' (*A. palmatum*)

'Chitori' (*A. palmatum*)

'Chitose nishiki' (*A. palmatum*)

'Chitose no' (*A. palmatum*)

'Chōkei ji' (*A. palmatum*)

'Chōkyū ji' (*A. palmatum*)

'Chō-no-mai' (*A. palmatum*)

'Chouguraji' (*A. palmatum*)

'Chūgū ji' (*A. palmatum*)

'Chuzen ji' (*A. palmatum*)

'Cindy' (*A. palmatum*)

'Circumlobatum' (*A. palmatum*)

'Claire' (*A. palmatum*)

'Como' (*A. palmatum*)

'Compactum' (*A. palmatum*)

'Coral Magic' (*A. palmatum*)

'Cordifolium' (*A. tataricum*)

'Crassifolium' (*A. japonicum*)

'Crimson King' (*A. palmatum*)

'Crispatum' (*A. tataricum*)

'Crispifolium' (*A. palmatum?*)

'Cultriforme' (*A. tataricum*)

'Cuneatum' (*A. palmatum*)

'Curiel's Gold' (*A. tataricum*)

'Cuspidatum' (*A. tataricum*)

'Cynthia' (*A. palmatum*)

'Cynthia's Crown Jewel' (*A. palmatum*)

'Dad's Best' (*A. palmatum*)

'Dai' (*A. palmatum*)

'Daiji sen' (*A. palmatum*)

'Dainty Dotty' (*A. palmatum*)

'Daiō' (*A. palmatum*)

'Dalton' (*A. palmatum*)

'Darwin nishiki' (*A. palmatum*)

'Dawy' (*A. nipponicum*)

'Dentelle de Binche' (*A. palmatum*)

'Dezome hatsu yuki' (*A. rufinerve*)

'Diane's Dissectum' (*A. palmatum*)

'Doai guchi' (*A. palmatum*)

'Don' (*A. palmatum*)

'Dōsen bō' (*A. palmatum*)

'Drew' (*A. cissifolium*)

'Durone ' (*A. tataricum*)

'Earthfire' (*A. palmatum*)

'Echigo' (*A. palmatum*)

'Eda murasaki' (*A. palmatum*)

'Ed Carmin' (*A. palmatum*)

'Ed Wood' (*A. japonicum*)

'Elmwood' (*A. palmatum*)

'Emmit's Pumpkins' (*A. japonicum*)

'Ena san' (*A. pycnanthum*)

'Enkō nishiki' (*A. pictum*)

'Enshōji' (*A. palmatum*)

'Eono momiji' (*A. palmatum*)

'Erythrocarpum' (*A. tataricum*)

'Ezo itaya nishiki' (*A. pictum*)

'Ezo ō momiji' (*A. shirasawanum*)

'Fall Delight' (*A. palmatum*)

'Fire Engine' (*A. palmatum*)

'Fubuki' (*A. rufinerve*)

'Fudikage' (*A. palmatum*)

'Fugen bō' (*A. palmatum*)

'Fuji domoe' (*A. palmatum*)

'Fujinami' (*A. palmatum*)

'Fuji nishiki' (*A. diabolicum*)

'Fuji-no-takane' (*A. palmatum*)

'Fuji-no-yama' (*A. rufinerve*)

'Fujiyama' (*A. palmatum*)

'Fukaya' (*A. palmatum?*)

'Fukaya gawa' (*A. palmatum*)

'Fukin agashi' (*A. palmatum*)

'Fukui' (*A. palmatum*)

'Full Moon' (*A. shirasawanum*)

'Fumoto dera' (*A. palmatum*)

'Furi tsuzumi' (*A. shirasawanum*)

'Furu kuro' (*A. palmatum*)

'Furu sato' (*A. palmatum*)

'Fusui' (*A. palmatum*)

'Futa omote' (*A. palmatum*)

'Futago yama' (*A. pictum*)

'Futai ji' (*A. palmatum*)

'Gaki-no-sugi' (*A. palmatum*)

'Gangō ji' (*A. palmatum*)

'Garden Glory' (*A. shirasawanum*)

'Garnet Bond' (*A. palmatum*)

'Garnet Tower' (*A. palmatum*)

'Genji yama' (*A. palmatum*)

'Genshi yama momiji' (*A. palmatum*)

'Gentaku' (*A. palmatum*)

'Giant Moon' (*A. japonicum*)

'Gibbons' (*A. palmatum*)

'Gibbsii' (*A. palmatum*)

'Gimborn' (*A. capillipes*)

'Gion-no-nishiki' (*A. palmatum*)

'Goblin' (*A. sieboldianum*)

'Golden Dragon' (*A. truncatum*)

'Golden Flame' (*A. palmatum*)

'Gold Splash' (*A. rufinerve*)

'Gold Spring' (*A. shirasawanum*)

'Goshiki suzumaru' (*A. palmatum*)

'Gosho zome' (*A. palmatum*)

'Goten nomura' (*A. palmatum*)

'Grace' (*A. palmatum*)

'Green Elf' (*A. palmatum*)

'Green Fingers' (*A. palmatum*)

'Green Flag' (*A. palmatum*)

'Green Snowflake' (*A. palmatum*)

'Groenendael' (*A. rufinerve*)

'Hachiman yama' (*A. palmatum*)

'Hadare yuki' (*A. rufinerve*)

'Hagoromo kaede' (*A. palmatum*)

'Haha so' (*A. palmatum*)

'Haibara' (*A. palmatum*)

'Haibara beni' (*A. palmatum*)

'Hakkan shikin' (*A. crataegifolium*)

'Hakodate yama' (*A. palmatum*)

'Hakuhō' (*A. palmatum*)

'Hanabi' (*A. rufinerve*)

'Hanabi-no-mai' (*A. palmatum*)

'Hana fubuki' (*A. palmatum*)

'Hana gata' (*A. palmatum*)

'Hananoki ki fu' (*A. pycnanthum*)

'Hananoko' (*A. pycnanthum*)

'Hananoko-no-sazanami' (*A. pycnanthum*)

'Hana tsukasa' (*A. palmatum*)

'Hana yamato' (*A. palmatum*)

'Hanaze' (*A. palmatum*)

'Hanbi-no-mai' (*A. palmatum*)

'Han sen' (*A. palmatum*)

'Harriet Waldman' (*A. palmatum*)

'Haru biyō' (*A. palmatum*)

'Haru iro' (*A. palmatum*)

'Haru-no-akebono' (*A. palmatum*)

'Haru sake' (*A. palmatum*)

'Haru sazanami' (*A. palmatum*)

'Haru yama' (*A. palmatum*)

'Harvest Red' (*A. palmatum*)

'Hashio' (*A. palmatum*)

'Hatamono-no-oto' (*A. palmatum*)

'Hatsu hana' (*A. palmatum*)

'Hatsu momichi' (*A. palmatum*)

'Hatsu momiji' (*A. palmatum*)

'Hatsuse' (*A. palmatum*)

'Hatsuse yama' (*A. palmatum*)

'Hatsu shimo' (*A. palmatum*)

'Hatsu yuki beni fukurin' (*A. rufinerve*)

'Heathcoat-Amory' (*A. palmatum*)

'Heavy Seed' (*A. palmatum*)

'Hefner's R ed' (*A. palmatum*)

'Heguri' (*A. palmatum*)

'Heijō sazanami' (*A. palmatum*)

'Heiwa' (*A. palmatum*)

'Helena' (*A. shirasawanum*)

'Hess Broom' (*A. palmatum*)

'Hibari' (*A. palmatum*)

'Hibari yama' (*A. palmatum*)

'Hida hanabi' (*A. palmatum*)

'Hikaru genji' (*A. palmatum*?)

'Hikaru genji momiji' (*A. palmatum*)

'Hima ha uchiwa' (*A. palmatum*?)

'Hime chidori' (*A. palmatum*)

'Hime jishi' (*A. palmatum*)

'Hime nishiki' (*A. buergerianum*)

'Hime shōjō' (*A. palmatum*)

'Hime tōyō nishiki' (*A. buergerianum*)

'Hime tsuma gaki' (*A. palmatum*)

'Hime yama' (*A. palmatum*)

'Hina some' (*A. palmatum*)

'Hina zuru' (*A. palmatum*)

'Hi-no-tsukasa' (*A. palmatum*)

'Hirai gawa' (*A. palmatum*)

'Hiroha koshimino' (*A. palmatum*)

'Hiroha yama momiji' (*A. palmatum*?)

'Hiro tai shaku' (*A. palmatum*)

'Hisen nishiki' (*A. palmatum*)

'Hito koto beni' (*A. palmatum*)

'Hitoshio' (*A. palmatum*)

'Hitosome' (*A. palmatum*)

'Hiyoku ba' (*A. palmatum*)

'Hiyoku nishiki' (*A. palmatum*)

'Hō beni' (*A. palmatum*)

'Hoerner' (*A. tataricum*)

'Hoki momiji' (*A. palmatum*)

'Hokotate gawa' (*A. palmatum*)

'Hokuwa' (*A. palmatum*)

'Honami gawa' (*A. palmatum*)

'Honeydew' (*A. capillipes*)

'Hōno gawa' (*A. palmatum*)

'Hōno o' (*A. palmatum*)

'Hō ō beni' (*A. palmatum*)

'Hō ō murakumo' (*A. palmatum*)

'Hō ō nishiki' (*A. palmatum*)

'Hō ō shidare' (*A. palmatum*)

'Hōrai nishiki' (*A. palmatum*)

'Hōrai nishiki' (*A. diabolicum*)

'Hōraku nishiki' (*A. rufinerve*)

'Hōren beni' (*A. palmatum*)

'Hōren hatsu yuki' (*A. rufinerve*)

'Horizontalis' (*A. palmatum*?)

'Hosada' (*A. palmatum*?)

'Hoshi miyasama' (*A. pictum*)

'Hoshi nishiki' (*A. palmatum*)

'Hoshi-no-yama' (*A. palmatum*)

'Hosoba beni' (*A. palmatum*)

'Hosoba koshimino' (*A. palmatum*)

'Hosoba ō momiji' (*A. palmatum*)

'Hototokiso' (*A. palmatum*)

'Huru gawa' (*A. palmatum*)

'Ibo juhi' (*A. palmatum*)

'Ichigyō in' (*A. palmatum*)

'Ichigyōji nishiki' (*A. palmatum*)

'Ichi-no-moto' (*A. palmatum*)

'Ifuku gō' (*A. palmatum*?)

'Ikaruga' (*A. palmatum*)

'Ikoma' (*A. palmatum*)

'Iku aki' (*A. palmatum*)

'Iku shio' (*A. palmatum*)

'Ilarian' (*A. palmatum*)

'Illustre' (*A. palmatum*)

'Ima kumano' (*A. palmatum*)

'Imose gawa' (*A. palmatum*)

'Imo yama' (*A. palmatum*)

'Inado' (*A. palmatum*)

'Inasa yama' (*A. palmatum*)

'Iro iro' (*A. palmatum*)

'Iro-no-seki' (*A. palmatum*)

'Iseji beni' (*A. palmatum*)

'Isis' (*A. sieboldianum*)

'Iso-no-nami' (*A. pictum*)

'Iso shibuki' (*A. palmatum*)

'Issun bōshi' (*A. buergerianum*)

'Italy Lace' (*A. palmatum*)

'Itaya momiji' (*A. japonicum*)

'Ito momiji' (*A. palmatum*)

'Ito nishiki' (*A. palmatum*)

'Itsu maku tane' (*A. palmatum*)

'Ittai san nishiki' (*A. crataegifolium*)

'Iwahashi-no-sato' (*A. palmatum*?)

'Iwahata' (*A. palmatum*)

'Iwai gojūsan' (*A. palmatum*)

'Iwao' (*A. buergerianum*)

'Iwashita' (*A. palmatum*)

'Iwate yama' (*A. palmatum*?)

'Iwato kagami' (*A. palmatum*)

'Iza shidare' (*A. palmatum*)

'Izayoi' (*A. japonicum*)

'Izu-no-sato' (*A. palmatum*)

'Jane Platt' (*A. palmatum*)

'Jim Baggett' (*A. palmatum*)

'Jingo ji' (*A. palmatum*)

'Jōdo' (*A. palmatum*)

'Jucundo' (*A. japonicum*)

'Jūga ya' (*A. shirasawanum*)

'Julia' (*A. palmatum*?)

'Jun nishiki' (*A. palmatum*)

'Kabata' (*A. palmatum*)

'Kaempferi' (*A. japonicum*)

'Kaga beni' (*A. palmatum*)

'Kaga kogane' (*A. palmatum*)

'Kaga kujaku' (*A. palmatum*)

'Kaga ō beni' (*A. palmatum*)

'Kaga ō tamagawa' (*A. palmatum*)

'Kaga sudare' (*A. palmatum*)

'Kaga tamagawa' (*A. palmatum*)

'Kaga zome' (*A. palmatum*)

'Kageori men' (*A. palmatum*)

'Kageshiki men' (*A. palmatum*)

'Kagi nishiki' (*A. palmatum*)

'Kaki kaede' (*A. palmatum*)

'Kaki momiji' (*A. palmatum*)

'Kaki shidare' (*A. palmatum*)

'Kaki shitare' (*A. palmatum*)

'Kalmthout' (*A. shirasawanum*)

'Kamega yatsu' (*A. palmatum*)

'Kami kase' (*A. palmatum*)

'Kamina tsuki' (*A. palmatum*)

'Kamina zuki' (*A. palmatum*)

'Kami-no-nusa' (*A. palmatum*)

'Kamisaka nishiki' (*A. pictum*)

'Kan nondaira' (*A. sieboldianum*)

'Kantan' (*A. palmatum*)

'Kara fu' (*A. buergerianum*)

'Karakogi kaede ki fuiri' (*A. tataricum*)

'Kara koromo' (*A. palmatum*)

'Kara kurenai' (*A. palmatum*)

'Kara nishiki' (*A. palmatum*)

'Kariba beni' (*A. palmatum*)

'Karu kaya' (*A. palmatum*)

'Kasado' (*A. japonicum*)

'Kasama gawa' (*A. palmatum*)

'Kasa nui' (*A. palmatum*)

'Kasasaki' (*A. palmatum*)

'Kasen dono' (*A. palmatum*)

'Kasen nishiki fugawari' (*A. palmatum*)

'Kase odori' (*A. palmatum*)

'Kashihara' (*A. palmatum*)

'Kashiwa mori' (*A. palmatum*)

'Kasuga' (*A. palmatum*)

'Kasugano' (*A. palmatum*)

'Kasugano nishiki' (*A. palmatum*)

'Kasuga yama' (*A. palmatum*)

'Kasumi goromo' (*A. rufinerve*)

'Katsuragi' (*A. sieboldianum*)

'Katsuragi san' (*A. sieboldianum*)

'Katsurani' (*A. palmatum*)

'Kawa hara-no-midori' (*A. palmatum*?)

'Kawa hime' (*A. palmatum*)

'Kawa kaze' (*A. palmatum*)

'Kegon' (*A. palmatum*)

'Keikan zan' (*A. shirasawanum*)

'Ken bu' (*A. palmatum*)

'Kenkō nishiki' (*A. palmatum*)

'Kiev nishiki' (*A. buergerianum*)

'Kihachi gire' (*A. palmatum*)

'Kihou nishiki' (*A. palmatum*)

'Kikko sho momiji' (*A. palmatum*)

'Kim' (*A. palmatum*)

'Kin pai' (*A. palmatum*?)

'Kinshi jima' (*A. palmatum*?)

'Kinshō' (*A. palmatum*)

'Kinshōjō' (*A. palmatum*)

'Kin yo' (*A. palmatum*)

'Ki oridono-no-nishiki' (*A. palmatum*?)

'Kiri kagami' (*A. palmatum*)

'Kisodani nishiki' (*A. rufinerve*)

'Kitsu shidorie' (*A. palmatum*)

'Kiyohime akame' (*A. palmatum*)

'Kiyo taki' (*A. palmatum*)

'Koba nomura' (*A. palmatum*)

'Ko beni nishiki' (*A. palmatum*)

'Kobuchizawa nishiki' (*A. rufinerve*)

'Kodono' (*A. palmatum*)

'Kofuji nishiki' (*A. crataegifolium*)

'Kohaku iro no' (*A. palmatum*)

'Ko hauchiwa shidare' (*A. sieboldianum*)

'Kōi' (*A. palmatum*)

'Kōi kiyohime' (*A. palmatum*?)

'Koide' (*A. palmatum*)

'Koizumi' (*A. palmatum*)

'Kōkan shikin' (*A. crataegifolium*)

'Ko kibune' (*A. palmatum*)

'Ko kinran' (*A. palmatum*)

'Kokono e' (*A. shirasawanum*)

'Koma gaeri' (*A. palmatum*)

'Koma gaeri beni' (*A. palmatum*)

'Koma nishiki' (*A. palmatum*)

'Koma todomi' (*A. palmatum*)

'Komachi beni' (*A. palmatum*)

'Komadome' (*A. palmatum*)

'Komyo ji' (*A. palmatum*)

'Konbu in' (*A. palmatum*)

'Kongō nishiki' (*A. rufinerve*)

'Kōrai momiji' (*A. palmatum*)

'Kōrin' (*A. palmatum*)

'Kōryō' (*A. palmatum*)

'Kosame-no-nishiki' (*A. palmatum*)

'Koshima' (*A. palmatum*)

'Koshimino nishiki' (*A. palmatum*)

'Kosui-no-tsuki' (*A. palmatum*)

'Kotobuki' (*A. palmatum*)

'Kotobuki hime' (*A. palmatum*)

'Koto ito yatsubusa' (*A. palmatum*)

'Kotoji nishiki' (*A. palmatum*)

'Koto kubunji' (*A. palmatum*)

'Kōyamadani nishiki' (*A. palmatum*)

'Kōyō ao shidare' (*A. palmatum*)

'Kōzuhara nishiki' (*A. sieboldianum*)

'Kōzui gawa' (*A. palmatum*)

'Kuchi ba' (*A. pictum*)

'Kuchibeni zukashi' (*A. palmatum*)

'Kuchiheni' (*A. palmatum*)

'Kujaku bato' (*A. japonicum*)

'Kujaku myo o' (*A. japonicum*)

'Kujaku nishiki akame' (*A. japonicum*)

'Kumoi nishiki' (*A. sieboldianum*)

'Kuni-no-sato' (*A. palmatum*)

'Kurenai jishi' (*A. palmatum*)

'Kurenai-no-ho' (*A. palmatum*)

'Kure yama' (*A. palmatum*)

'Kurokami yama' (*A. palmatum*)

'Kuro kogo beni' (*A. rufinerve*)

'Kuro koma' (*A. palmatum*)

'Kuro wu yama' (*A. palmatum*)

'Kusa momiji' (*A. palmatum*)

'Kyō kibune' (*A. palmatum*)

'Kyokiuzu' (*A. palmatum*)

'Kyō-no-aki' (*A. palmatum*)

'Kyra' (*A. palmatum*)

'Lady's Choice' (*A. palmatum*)

'Lana' (*A. cissifolium*)

'Laura's Love' (*A. palmatum*)

'Lazy Leaf' (*A. palmatum*)

'Lin-ling' (*A. palmatum*)

'Little Heart' (*A. palmatum*)

'Little Joe' (*A. circinatum*)

'Little Little Gem' (*A. circinatum*)

'Lobatum' (*A. palmatum*)

'Macranthum' (*A. japonicum*)

'Macrocarpum' (*A. japonicum*)

'Macrophyllum' (*A. japonicum*)

'Magnificum' (*A. japonicum*)

'Maki tatsu yama' (*A. palmatum*)

'Makimuku' (*A. palmatum*)

'Maki-no-ha' (*A. palmatum*)

'Mallet' (*A. palmatum*)

'Mama nishiki' (*A. palmatum*)

'Mardi Gras' (*A. palmatum*)

'Marlo' (*A. palmatum*)

'Martha's Ghost' (*A. palmatum*?)

'Mary Eddinglow' (*A. palmatum*)

'Masago' (*A. crataegifolium*)

'Masa yoshi' (*A. palmatum*)

'Matoi nishiki' (*A. palmatum*)

'Matsu kubo' (*A. palmatum*)

'Matsu-no-tsuki' (*A. palmatum*)

'Matsuo' (*A. palmatum*)

'Matu kase' (*A. palmatum*)

'Meckelii' (*A. japonicum*)

'Meguri ai' (*A. rufinerve*)

'Meiō nishiki' (*A. palmatum*)

'Metallic Gold' (*A. maximowiczianum*)

'Meuri ōmadora' (*A. crataegifolium*)

'Michi shiruhe' (*A. palmatum*)

'Michi zome' (*A. palmatum*)

'Midore mure hibari' (*A. palmatum?*)

'Midori seigai' (*A. palmatum*)

'Mikage nishiki' (*A. crataegifolium*)

'Mikaki mori' (*A. palmatum*)

'Mikata nishiki' (*A. palmatum*)

'Mikawa hachijūkyū' (*A. palmatum*)

'Mikawa nishiki' (*A. palmatum*)

'Mikita nishiki' (*A. palmatum*)

'Mikomo nishiki' (*A. palmatum*)

'Milton Park Broom' (*A. palmatum*)

'Mima' (*A. palmatum*)

'Mimaye' (*A. palmatum*)

'Mimi nashi' (*A. palmatum*)

'Mimuro' (*A. palmatum*)

'Mimuro yama' (*A. palmatum*)

'Minare zao' (*A. palmatum*)

'Minnesota Red' (*A. tataricum*)

'Minobe gawa' (*A. palmatum*)

'Mino kasa' (*A. palmatum?*)

'Mino kasa yama' (*A. palmatum*)

'Mino o' (*A. palmatum*)

'Minowa' (*A. palmatum*)

'Mischa' (*A. palmatum*)

'Misty Moon' (*A. palmatum?*)

'Misu-no-uchi' (*A. palmatum*)

'Mitchii' (*A. palmatum*)

'Mitsu cha' (*A. palmatum*)

'Mitsude kaede kifu' (*A. cissifolium*)

'Mitsu kagami' (*A. palmatum*)

'Mitsu kukri' (*A. palmatum*)

'Mitsu shika' (*A. palmatum*)

'Miwa' (*A. palmatum*)

'Miyabi' (*A. rufinerve*)

'Miyagi yana' (*A. palmatum*)

'Miyaki no' (*A. palmatum*)

'Miyako kaeri' (*A. palmatum*)

'Miyako-no-hana' (*A. palmatum*)

'Miyama' (*A. palmatum*)

'Miyasama nishiki' (*A. buergerianum*)

'Miya taki' (*A. palmatum*)

'Mizū kagami' (*A. palmatum*)

'Mizū kukuri' (*A. palmatum*)

'Mizū moyo' (*A. palmatum*)

'Mizū nami nishiki' (*A. rufinerve*)

'Mocha Rose' (*A. maximowiczianum*)

'Moji suru' (*A. palmatum*)

'Mokuji' (*A. palmatum*)

'Momichi kasane' (*A. rufinerve*)

'Momiji gai' (*A. pictum*)

'Momiju yama' (*A. palmatum*)

'Momi-no-nami' (*A. palmatum*)

'Mon dukushi' (*A. palmatum*)

'Monju in' (*A. palmatum*)

'Mon nishiki' (*A. palmatum*)

'Mono zi gawa' (*A. palmatum*)

'Mo-no-nishiki' (*A. palmatum*)

'Mon tsuki' (*A. palmatum*)

'Mon tsukushi' (*A. palmatum*)

'Moon Shadow' (*A. palmatum*)

'Mori-no-miya' (*A. palmatum*)

'Morogi' (*A. palmatum*)

'Morogino' (*A. palmatum*)

'Morogino gawa' (*A. palmatum*)

'Morton' (*A. miyabei*)

'Moto koto-no-ito' (*A. palmatum*)

'Mozart' (*A. tataricum*)

'Mufura' (*A. palmatum*)

'Mugiwara nishiki' (*A. palmatum*)

'Muka' (*A. palmatum*)

'Mukō buchi' (*A. palmatum*)

'Mukō gasa' (*A. palmatum*)

'Multifidum' (*A. palmatum*)

'Mume gae' (*A. palmatum*)

'Muncaster' (*A. palmatum*)

'Murakumo shidare' (*A. palmatum*)

'Murasaki daka' (*A. palmatum*)

'Murasaki iroha' (*A. palmatum*)

'Murasaki-no-ne' (*A. palmatum*)

'Murasaki taka' (*A. palmatum*)

'Murasame' (*A. shirasawanum*)

'Mure sora suzume' (*A. palmatum*)

'Mure suzume' (*A. palmatum*)

'Mure uzura' (*A. palmatum*)

'Muro kogane' (*A. palmatum*)

'Muro obene' (*A. palmatum*)

'Musashi nishiki' (*A. buergerianum*)

'Musatori yama' (*A. palmatum*)

'Mushiro momichi' (*A. palmatum*)

'Mutsu beni' (*A. palmatum*)

'Mutsu beni shidare' (*A. palmatum*)

'Mutsu-no-kane' (*A. palmatum*)

'Myagino' (*A. palmatum*)

'Myogi san' (*A. palmatum*)

'Naga ito' (*A. palmatum*)

'Nagatsuka' (*A. palmatum*)

'Nagisa hime' (*A. palmatum?*)

'Nakahara beni' (*A. palmatum*)

'Naka-no-go' (*A. palmatum*)

'Nakaoku gawa' (*A. palmatum*)

'Nakatsu gawa nishiki' (*A. palmatum*)

'Nana komachi' (*A. palmatum*)

'Nanase kawa' (*A. palmatum*)

'Nanatsu boshi' (*A. palmatum*)

'Naniwa beni' (*A. palmatum*)

'Nanjō' (*A. palmatum*)

'Nankin momiji' (*A. shirasawanum*)

'Nanum' (*A. tataricum*)

'Nara yama' (*A. palmatum*)

'Nari hari beni' (*A. palmatum*)

'Narihira' (*A. palmatum*)

'Naruo kata' (*A. palmatum*)

'Nasu nishiki' (*A. palmatum*)

'Natori kawa' (*A. palmatum*)

'Natsumi gawa' (*A. palmatum*)

'Ne zami' (*A. palmatum*)

'Nichi rin' (*A. palmatum*)

'Nihon beni' (*A. palmatum*)

'Nihon tō' (*A. tataricum*)

'Nikaido' (*A. palmatum*)

'Nikkō' (*A. palmatum*)

'Nimura' (*A. palmatum*)

'Nino kami yama' (*A. palmatum*)

'Nisaka gawa' (*A. palmatum*)

'Nishiki gi' (*A. palmatum*)

'Nishiki kaede' (*A. buergerianum*)

'Nishiki-no-murasaki' (*A. palmatum*)

'Nishiki tatsugawa' (*A. palmatum*)

'Nishiki yamato' (*A. palmatum*)

'Nishiki zuru' (*A. palmatum*)

'Nishitani gawa' (*A. palmatum*)

'Nobu hime' (*A. palmatum*)

'Noki bata' (*A. palmatum*)

'Nomura momiji' (*A. palmatum*)

'Noto' (*A. palmatum*)

'Nukai dake' (*A. palmatum*)

'Nukata' (*A. palmatum*)

'Nukata-no-ōkimi' (*A. palmatum*)

'Nuke botoke' (*A. palmatum*)

'Nunomi gawa' (*A. palmatum*)

'Nure garasu' (*A. palmatum*)

'Nyaku ōji' (*A. palmatum*)

'Obadani gawa' (*A. palmatum*)

'Oba hachijō' (*A. palmatum*)

'Oba iroha momiji' (*A. palmatum*)

'Obata' (*A. palmatum*)

'Oba uri nishiki' (*A. crataegifolium*)

'Oboku' (*A. palmatum*)

'Oboro zuki' (*A. palmatum*)

'Obtusum' (*A. palmatum*)

'Ochikochibito' (*A. palmatum*)

'Oda nishiki' (*A. palmatum*)

'Ogi-no-sen' (*A. japonicum*)

'Ogi-no-zu' (*A. palmatum*)

'Ogi tsuma gaki' (*A. palmatum*?)

'Ogon' (*A. palmatum*)

'Ogon itaya kaede' (*A. palmatum*)

'Ogon kunshi' (*A. palmatum*)

'Ogon shidare' (*A. palmatum*)

'Ogon shidare sekka' (*A. palmatum*)

'Ogon sunago' (*A. palmatum*)

'Ogotoi' (*A. palmatum*)

'Ohara yama' (*A. palmatum*)

'Oiso nishiki' (*A. palmatum*)

'Oitaya meigetsu atozae' (*A. shirasawanum*)

'Oki kasane' (*A. palmatum*)

'Oki-no-nami' (*A. palmatum*)

'Oki tsu fune' (*A. palmatum*)

'Oki tsu nami' (*A. palmatum*)

'Olga' (*A. palmatum*)

'Olsen's Frosted Strawberry' (*A. palmatum*)

'Omata shidare' (*A. palmatum*)

'Omi nishiki' (*A. palmatum*)

'Ominato' (*A. palmatum*)

'Omogo nishiki' (*A. pictum*)

'Omona' (*A. palmatum*)

'Omur H.' (*A. palmatum*)

'Oni itayi fuiri' (*A. pictum*)

'Oni itayi kifu' (*A. pictum*)

'Oni sudare' (*A. pictum*)

'Oo momiji' (*A. palmatum*)

'O ran' (*A. palmatum*)

'Oregon' (*A. palmatum*)

'Oregon Cascade' (*A. palmatum*)

'Oridono-no-nishiki' (*A. palmatum*)

'Oriental Lace' (*A. palmatum*)

'Oriental Mystery' (*A. palmatum*)

'Original Peaches' (*A. palmatum*)

'Ori hime' (*A. palmatum*)

'Orika nishiki' (*A. palmatum*)

'Ori san' (*A. sieboldianum*)

'Ori zuru' (*A. palmatum*)

'Ori zuru momofu' (*A. palmatum*)

'O sakai' (*A. palmatum*)

'Osaka yama' (*A. palmatum*)

'O sakazuki akame' (*A. palmatum*)

'O sakazuki-no-akame' (*A. palmatum*)

'O sakazuki o' (*A. palmatum*)

'O sayo shiki' (*A. palmatum*)

'Oshin kuzu' (*A. palmatum*)

'Oshuzan' (*A. palmatum*)

'Osiris' (*A. sieboldianum*)

'Otafuku' (*A. palmatum*)

'Ōtaishaku' (*A. palmatum*)

'Otto's Dissectum' (*A. palmatum*)

'Ōuda beni' (*A. palmatum*)

'Ō urihada' (*A. palmatum*)

'Owugon shidare' (*A. palmatum*)

'Owuri yama' (*A. palmatum*)

'Pattern Perfect' (*A. tataricum*)

'Pendulum' (*A. palmatum*)

'Peve Limbo' (*A. palmatum*)

'Peve Pond' (*A. palmatum*)

'Philsm' (*A. palmatum*)

'Pink Lace' (*A. palmatum*)

'Platanifolium' (*A. japonicum*)

'Princeps' (*A. japonicum*)

'Pulchrum' (*A. palmatum*?)

'Pulverulentum' (*A. palmatum*)

'Pulverulentum' (*A. tataricum*)

'Purple Glory' (*A. palmatum*)

'Purple Splendor' (*A. palmatum*)

'Raigō ji' (*A. palmatum*)

'Rainbow' (*A. palmatum*)

'Rakushisha' (*A. palmatum*)

'Red Blush' (*A. palmatum*)

'Red Crusader' (*A. palmatum*)

'Red Dawn' (*A. shirasawanum*)

'Red Falcon' (*A. palmatum*)

'Red Feathers' (*A. palmatum*)

'Red Ribbon Leaf' (*A. palmatum*)

'Red Rocket' (*A. palmatum*)

'Red Star' (*A. palmatum*)

'Red Wing' (*A. tataricum*)

'Red Wonder' (*A. palmatum*)

'Renjaku' (*A. palmatum*)

'Reticulatum Purple' (*A. palmatum*)

'Reticulatum Rubrum' (*A. palmatum*)

'Rhodoneurum' (*A. palmatum*)

'Rin Ka' (*A. palmatum*)

'Rising Sun' (*A. palmatum*)

'Rokka on' (*A. palmatum*)

'Rokumonji' (*A. palmatum*)

'Rubricaule' (*A. palmatum*)

'Rubrinerve' (*A. palmatum*)

'Rubrum' (*A. tataricum*)

'Rubrum Kaiser' (*A. palmatum*)

'Ruby Lace' (*A. tataricum*)

'Rugose Select' (*A. palmatum*)

'Ruslyn-in-the-Pink' (*A. palmatum*)

'Ruth Murray' (*A. palmatum*)

'Ryokka meuri' (*A. crataegifolium*)

'Ryokurin' zan' (*A. palmatum*)

'Ryū gan' (*A. palmatum*)

'Ryū gu' (*A. palmatum*)

'Ryūgan nishiki' (*A. palmatum*)

'Ryūku u' (*A. palmatum*)

'Ryūsen' (*A. palmatum*)

'Ryūsho in' (*A. palmatum*)

'Ryūto' (*A. palmatum*)

'Ryū un kaku' (*A. palmatum*)

'Sagami' (*A. palmatum*)

'Sagamihara nishiki' (*A. buergerianum*)

'Saihō' (*A. palmatum*)

'Sainan in yukon' (*A. palmatum*)

'Saka meuri' (*A. crataegifolium*)

'Sakura' (*A. palmatum*)

'Sakura ga e' (*A. palmatum*)

'Sakura-no-sato' (*A. palmatum*)

'Samurai Sword' (*A. palmatum*)

'Sa mushiro' (*A. palmatum*)

'Sango asahi zuru' (*A. palmatum*)

'Sango nishiki' (*A. palmatum*)

'Sango tsu' (*A. palmatum*)

'Sanuki hime' (*A. palmatum*)

'Sao hime' (*A. palmatum*)

'Sao yama' (*A. palmatum*)

'Sasa nami' (*A. palmatum*)
'Satoaki shidare' (*A. palmatum*)
'Satō kaede' (*A. rufinerve*)
'Satō-no-ha' (*A. palmatum*)
'Satō shidare' (*A. palmatum?*)
'Satō shigure' (*A. palmatum*)
'Sa utome' (*A. palmatum*)
'Sawa gani' (*A. palmatum*)
'Sawa ibuki' (*A. palmatum*)
'Sawa-no-kani' (*A. palmatum*)
'Sayo chidori' (*A. palmatum*)
'Sayo goromo' (*A. palmatum*)
'Sayu yama' (*A. palmatum*)
'Sazame koto' (*A. palmatum*)
'Scarlet Wonder' (*A. palmatum*)
'Schmidt' (*A. palmatum*)
'Scotum Roseum' (*A. palmatum*)
'Searle's Variegated' (*A. palmatum*)
'Seido hokori' (*A. palmatum*)
'Sei fu' (*A. palmatum*)
'Sei hime' (*A. palmatum*)
'Seijaku' (*A. palmatum*)
'Seiren ji gawa' (*A. palmatum*)
'Seiryū nishiki' (*A. palmatum*)
'Sei sunouchi' (*A. palmatum*)
'Seki sho' (*A. palmatum*)
'Senski' (*A. palmatum*)
'Sensu agasi' (*A. palmatum*)
'Seuss's Sister' (*A. palmatum*)
'Seuss's Son' (*A. palmatum*)
'Shadow Selection' (*A. palmatum?*)
'Shakudo' (*A. palmatum*)
'Sheila' (*A. cissifolium*)
'Sherwood Elfin' (*A. palmatum*)
'Shichi goni' (*A. palmatum*)
'Shichmenzan' (*A. sieboldianum*)
'Shidare' (*A. sieboldianum*)
'Shidare kaede' (*A. palmatum*)
'Shidare momichi' (*A. palmatum*)
'Shien' (*A. palmatum*)
'Shigi' (*A. palmatum*)
'Shigi-no-mai' (*A. palmatum*)
'Shigure-no-hato' (*A. palmatum*)
'Shigure yama' (*A. palmatum*)
'Shikai nami' (*A. palmatum*)
'Shika momiji' (*A. palmatum*)
'Shikarami' (*A. palmatum*)
'Shikishima' (*A. palmatum*)
'Shikure yama' (*A. palmatum*)

'Shima kakure' (*A. palmatum*)
'Shima momichi' (*A. palmatum*)
'Shimauri kaede' (*A. morifolium*)
'Shime-no-aka' (*A. morifolium*)
'Shime-no-ao' (*A. morifolium*)
'Shime nomura' (*A. palmatum*)
'Shimo furi nishiki' (*A. palmatum*)
'Shimon nishiki' (*A. palmatum*)
'Shina kawa' (*A. palmatum*)
'Shinamata' (*A. palmatum*)
'Shin aocha nishiki' (*A. palmatum*)
'Shin hikasa' (*A. palmatum*)
'Shin hoshi zukiyo' (*A. pictum*)
'Shinju' (*A. palmatum*)
'Shinjuku shidare' (*A. palmatum*)
'Shin koba shōjō' (*A. palmatum*)
'Shin kotohime' (*A. palmatum*)
'Shinobu' (*A. palmatum*)
'Shinobu nishiki' (*A. palmatum*)
'Shinofu' (*A. palmatum*)
'Shin ogi' (*A. palmatum*)
'Shin seyu' (*A. palmatum*)
'Shin taimin' (*A. palmatum*)
'Shin toyama' (*A. palmatum*)
'Shin tōyō nishiki' (*A. buergerianum*)
'Shin tsuzure nishiki' (*A. palmatum*)
'Shio-no-name' (*A. palmatum*)
'Shirakami nishiki' (*A. palmatum*)
'Shira kumo' (*A. palmatum*)
'Shira Lace' (*A. palmatum*)
'Shira Red' (*A. shirasawanum*)
'Shira tama' (*A. palmatum*)
'Shirayuki hime' (*A. rufinerve*)
'Shirofu nishiki' (*A. palmatum*)
'Shirofu uriha nishiki' (*A. rufinerve*)
'Shiro nishiki' (*A. palmatum*)
'Shiro tai' (*A. palmatum*)
'Shi ryu' (*A. palmatum*)
'Shishigashira-no-yatsubusa' (*A. palmatum*)
'Shishimen zan' (*A. palmatum*)
'Shi taka' (*A. palmatum*)
'Shiyuka' (*A. palmatum*)
'Sho chiku bai' (*A. palmatum*)
'Shohrei kiji' (*A. palmatum*)
'Shōjō momichi' (*A. palmatum*)
'Shōjō nishiki' (*A. palmatum*)
'Shoku-no-nishiki' (*A. palmatum*)
'Shōnan nishiki' (*A. palmatum?*)

'Shorty's Red' (*A. palmatum*)
'Shōryaku ji' (*A. palmatum*)
'Shōryū-no-tsume' (*A. sieboldianum*)
'Shouman nishiki' (*A. palmatum*)
'Shōwa-no-mai' (*A. palmatum*)
'Shūfuki nishiki' (*A. palmatum*)
'Shū ka' (*A. palmatum*)
'Shūzan ko hondoshi' (*A. palmatum*)
'Shuzen ji' (*A. palmatum*)
'Snow Goose' (*A. buergerianum*)
'Sode gakure' (*A. shirasawanum*)
'Sode-no-nami' (*A. palmatum*)
'Sode shigarami' (*A. palmatum*)
'Soma-no-kawa' (*A. palmatum*)
'Soma yama' (*A. palmatum*)
'Some ito' (*A. palmatum*)
'Someno' (*A. palmatum*)
'Some tono' (*A. palmatum*)
'Soni' (*A. palmatum*)
'Sono hara' (*A. palmatum*)
'Sonya Marie' (*A. shirasawanum*)
'Spider' (*A. palmatum*)
'Sport' (*A. palmatum*)
'Spring Festival' (*A. buergerianum*)
'Spring Surprise' (*A. palmatum*)
'Sugawara' (*A. palmatum?*)
'Sumi shidare' (*A. palmatum*)
'Summer Splendour' (*A. tataricum*)
'Summer Sunset' (*A. palmatum*)
'Sunaga sawa' (*A. palmatum?*)
'Suncrest Broom' (*A. palmatum*)
'Super Red' (*A. palmatum*)
'Super Ruby' (*A. palmatum*)
'Suruga nishiki' (*A. palmatum*)
'Suru sumi' (*A. palmatum*)
'Suzaku mon' (*A. palmatum*)
'Suzu kaze' (*A. palmatum*)
'Syoku-no-nishiki' (*A. palmatum*)
'Syonan nishiki' (*A. palmatum*)
'Taima' (*A. palmatum*)
'Taima beni' (*A. palmatum*)
'Taimei' (*A. palmatum*)
'Taimei nishiki' (*A. palmatum*)
'Taimin nomura' (*A. palmatum*)
'Taishaku ten' (*A. pictum*)
'Tai sokai' (*A. rufinerve*)
'Taiyō nishiki kawahira' (*A. palmatum*)
'Taiyū' (*A. sieboldianum*)

'Takagi yama' (*A. palmatum*)
'Takamado yama' (*A. palmatum*)
'Takami yama' (*A. palmatum*)
'Takao beni' (*A. palmatum*)
'Takao nomura' (*A. palmatum*)
'Takao san' (*A. palmatum*)
'Takao zome' (*A. palmatum*)
'Takara-no-kuni' (*A. palmatum*)
'Takara yama' (*A. palmatum*)
'Takasago' (*A. palmatum*)
'Taka tame' (*A. palmatum*)
'Takatori' (*A. palmatum*)
'Takigo' (*A. palmatum*)
'Taki-no-o' (*A. pictum*)
'Takitani gawa' (*A. japonicum*)
'Tama-no-awayuki' (*A. palmatum*)
'Tama-no-nishiki' (*A. palmatum*)
'Tama-no-o' (*A. palmatum*)
'Tama sudare' (*A. palmatum*)
'Tama wata' (*A. palmatum*)
'Tamoto-no-nishiki' (*A. palmatum*)
'Tamoto tsuta' (*A. palmatum*)
'Tana hata' (*A. palmatum*)
'Tanigawa dake' (*A. palmatum*)
'Tanise' (*A. palmatum*)
'Tansyanno nishiki' (*A. palmatum*)
'Tate ito' (*A. palmatum*)
'Tate nami' (*A. palmatum*)
'Tate zukushi' (*A. palmatum*)
'Tatsuta gire' (*A. palmatum*)
'Tawara moto' (*A. palmatum*)
'Tayome nishiki' (*A. palmatum*)
'Tedori gawa' (*A. palmatum*)
'Teika' (*A. palmatum*)
'Tennō ji' (*A. palmatum*)
'Tenri' (*A. palmatum*)
'Tensyanno nishiki' (*A. tataricum*)
'Tenzan nishiki' (*A. tataricum*)
'Tequila Sunset' (*A. palmatum*)
'Teutcheri' (*A. palmatum*)
'Tezome-no-ito' (*A. palmatum*)
'Thomas Akao' (*A. palmatum*)
'Tobi hino' (*A. palmatum*)
'Tobi hino nishiki' (*A. palmatum*)
'Tōdai ji' (*A. palmatum*)
'Tōgen kyo' (*A. palmatum*)
'Tōhoku shichihenge' (*A. palmatum*)
'Tōjō gawa' (*A. palmatum*)
'Tōkai nishiki' (*A. pycnanthum*)

'Tōkamachi' (*A. palmatum*)
'Tōkin' (*A. palmatum*)
'Tokiwa' (*A. pictum*)
'Tokiwa-no-nishiki' (*A. pictum*)
'Tokonatsu' (*A. palmatum*)
'Toma yakata' (*A. palmatum*)
'Tomio' (*A. palmatum*)
'Tō-no-mine' (*A. palmatum*)
'Torimi yama' (*A. palmatum*)
'Tori-no-o' (*A. palmatum*)
'Tō shidare' (*A. buergerianum*)
'Tō shinobu' (*A. palmatum*)
'Toune mine' (*A. palmatum?*)
'Toyama-no-nishiki' (*A. palmatum*)
'Toyora dera' (*A. palmatum*)
'Tricolor' (*A. pictum*)
'Trompenson' (*A. palmatum*)
'Tsia nishiki' (*A. palmatum*)
'Tsubame kaeshi' (*A. palmatum*)
'Tsūden' (*A. palmatum*)
'Tsugara fubuki' (*A. pictum*)
'Tsuge' (*A. palmatum*)
'Tsukasa nishiki' (*A. palmatum*)
'Tsukasa Silhouette' (*A. palmatum*)
'Tsukasa yatsubusa' (*A. palmatum*)
'Tsuki ga se' (*A. palmatum*)
'Tsukuha ne' (*A. palmatum*)
'Tsuma goto' (*A. palmatum*)
'Tsuma zome' (*A. palmatum*)
'Tsumma jio' (*A. palmatum*)
'Tsuno moji' (*A. palmatum*)
'Tsuru' (*A. palmatum*)
'Tsuru nishiki' (*A. palmatum*)
'Tsuru-no-mai' (*A. palmatum*)
'Tsuta katsura' (*A. palmatum*)
'Tsuta-no-ha' (*A. palmatum*)
'Tsuten' (*A. palmatum*)
'Tsutsui' (*A. palmatum*)
'Tsuyu-no-tama' (*A. palmatum*)
'Tsuzure nishiki' (*A. palmatum*)
'Twombley's Red Sentinel' (*A. palmatum*)
'Uchimaki gawa' (*A. palmatum*)
'Uchiwa nagashi' (*A. palmatum*)
'Uchi yukashi' (*A. palmatum*)
'Uda' (*A. palmatum*)
'Uda gawa' (*A. palmatum*)
'Uda hatsu yuki' (*A. rufinerve*)
'Uda kinsen' (*A. palmatum*)

'Uda kogane' (*A. palmatum*)
'Uda matsukaze' (*A. palmatum*)
'Uda mure hibari' (*A. palmatum*)
'Uda shinku' (*A. palmatum*)
'Ueno yatsubusa' (*A. palmatum*)
'Ueshima momiji' (*A. palmatum*)
'Ugashi gawa' (*A. palmatum*)
'Ukashi-no-sato' (*A. palmatum*)
'Uki gumo kawariba' (*A. palmatum*)
'Uki kogane' (*A. sieboldianum*)
'Uncle Red' (*A. palmatum*)
'Unka' (*A. palmatum*)
'Uno gawa' (*A. palmatum*)
'Ura beni' (*A. palmatum*)
'Ura heni' (*A. palmatum*)
'Urajiro itaya kifu' (*A. pictum*)
'Urajiro itaya shirofu' (*A. pictum*)
'Uranihon' (*A. pictum*)
'Ura-no-tomaya' (*A. palmatum*)
'Urika nishiki' (*A. palmatum*)
'Ushi-no-tsume' (*A. palmatum*)
'Us murasaki' (*A. palmatum*)
'Usu beni shidare' (*A. palmatum*)
'Usu goromo' (*A. palmatum*)
'Usu kaki' (*A. palmatum*)
'Uta fuku' (*A. palmatum*)
'Uta hime' (*A. palmatum*)
'Utakata' (*A. palmatum*)
'Utano' (*A. palmatum*)
'Utano hatsu yuki' (*A. rufinerve*)
'Utano homare' (*A. palmatum*)
'Utano koshimino' (*A. palmatum*)
'Utano-no-sato' (*A. palmatum*)
'Utano shinku' (*A. palmatum*)
'Uta yama' (*A. palmatum*)
'Utsura-no-ha' (*A. palmatum*)
'Utsuri beni' (*A. palmatum*)
'Uzen nishiki' (*A. palmatum*)
'Van der Maat' (*A. palmatum*)
'Vanhouttei' (*A. palmatum*)
'Vens Broom' (*A. palmatum*)
'Verkades Broom' (*A. palmatum*)
'Vic Broom' (*A. palmatum*)
'Victoria' (*A. circinatum*)
'Viride' (*A. japonicum*)
'Waasland Dwarf' (*A. tataricum*)
'Waga tatsu soma' (*A. palmatum*)
'Wajima' (*A. palmatum*)
'Wajima suo' (*A. palmatum*)

'Waka kusa' (*A. palmatum*)

'Wakakusa yama' (*A. palmatum*)

'Waka midori' (*A. palmatum*)

'Waka murasaki' (*A. palmatum*)

'Waka tsuki' (*A. palmatum*)

'Wani' (*A. palmatum*)

'Washi-no-o shidare' (*A. palmatum*)

'Wasure ji' (*A. palmatum*)

'Wasure katami' (*A. palmatum*)

'Wasuri yuki' (*A. rufinerve*)

'W.B.Hoyt' (*A. circinatum*)

'Werner's Dwarf' (*A. palmatum*)

'Werner's Little Leaf' (*A. palmatum*)

'Werner's Pagoda' (*A. palmatum*)

'Westonbirt Spreading Star' (*A. palmatum*)

'Wetumpka Red' (*A. palmatum*)

'White Butterfly' (*A. palmatum*)

'Whitney Maple' (*A. palmatum*)

'Will's Devine' (*A. palmatum*)

'Winkworth' (*A. palmatum*)

'Wjimasuo' (*A. palmatum*)

'Wuta hime' (*A. palmatum*)

'Yadawara' (*A. palmatum*)

'Yaguruma (*A. palmatum*)

'Yagyū-no-sato' (*A. palmatum*)

'Yakushima nishiki' (*A. rufinerve*)

'Yakushima o nishiki' (*A. morifolium*)

'Yakusimi nishiki' (*A. capillipes*)

'Yamashiro' (*A. palmatum*)

'Yamato' (*A. morifolium*)

'Yana gawa' (*A. palmatum*)

'Yasaka' (*A. palmatum*)

'Yase gawa' (*A. palmatum*)

'Yashio' (*A. palmatum*)

'Yashio beni' (*A. palmatum*)

'Yashio miyagi' (*A. palmatum*)

'Yata yama' (*A. palmatum*)

'Yatsubusa hikasa yama' (*A. palmatum*)

'Yatsubusa keishima' (*A. palmatum*)

'Yellow Bird' (*A. palmatum*)

'Yellow Variegated' (*A. palmatum*)

'Yodo gawa' (*A. palmatum*)

'Yodo nishiki' (*A. palmatum*)

'Yogo gawa' (*A. palmatum*)

'Yoimiya' (*A. palmatum*)

'Yō kihi' (*A. palmatum*)

'Yokisan' (*A. palmatum*)

'Yonabari' (*A. palmatum*)

'Yōraku momiji' (*A. palmatum*)

'Yori ito' (*A. palmatum*)

'Yoshimine ji' (*A. palmatum*)

'Yoshimizu' (*A. palmatum*)

'Yoshino gawa' (*A. palmatum*)

'Yū fuji' (*A. palmatum*)

'Yū giri' (*A. palmatum*)

'Yū hi' (*A. palmatum*)

'Yuki-no-katsura' (*A. palmatum*)

'Yū kiri' (*A. palmatum*)

'Yume dono' (*A. palmatum*)

'Yuri hime Sport' (*A. palmatum*)

'Yū shigure' (*A. palmatum*)

'Yū shihen' (*A. palmatum*)

'Yū shikure' (*A. palmatum*)

'Yūyake nishiki' (*A. palmatum*)

'Yūzen momiji' (*A. palmatum*)

'Yūzuki' (*A. palmatum*)

'Zaaling' (*A. palmatum*)

'Zan getu' (*A. japonicum*)

'Zan su' (*A. palmatum*)

'Zu jeddelo' (*A. palmatum*)

THE MAPLE SOCIETY

J. D. VERTREES WAS A VICE-PRESIDENT AND ACTIVE supporter of the Maple Society since its formation in 1989. Its current president is the popular plantsman, broadcaster, and author, Roy Lancaster. The society was formed to cater for and foster interest in this delightful genus. Its objects are to encourage the cultivation of maples, to enable members (gardeners, professionals, and researchers) to learn from each other about their propagation, cultivation, introduction, and identification, and to facilitate the study of the botany, uses, and cultural needs of maples.

The Maple Society invites anyone interested to join and find out more about this fascinating group of plants which offers variety every month of the year. Fall is the highlight of the maple season, with the brilliant colors of the Japanese maples in particular, but there are maples for all seasons. Even in winter, the snakebark and paperbark maples are eyecatching, with others revealing graceful and unusual crown and branch patterns. Late winter sees the bright red bursts of the red and silver maple flowers, followed in early spring by the yellow clusters of Norway and Greek maples and by red flowers and fruits of the Japanese maples. Then come the delicate yellow flower chains of the snakebarks, culminating in early summer with the beautiful, conspicuous, red blooms of the devil's maple. Summer sees the maple leaf in all its varieties of shape, size, and texture, with colors ranging through green, yellow, red, purple, gold, and variegated, leading to the color explosion in the fall.

Since the 1970s, maples have become increasingly popular, with more and more people planting them in their gardens. There are more than 120 species growing wild throughout Europe, North Africa, Asia, and North America, of which more than 80 thrive in cultivation, plus about 2000 cultivars. What other tree genus can offer gardeners, horticulturists, and landscapers the variety and scope for large or small gardens, patio or container planting that can be found among the numerous maple species and cultivars? Selections for size, form, bark, foliage, flowers, leaves, or spring and autumn color are abundant. There are species for wet or dry soils, acid or alkaline soils, full sun or shade, and exposed or sheltered conditions.

The Maple Society publishes a quarterly journal containing information on maples in cultivation and in the wild, and to which members are welcome to contribute articles of interest, news, views, and so forth. Two or three outings to major collections and gardens are organized each year, and members can send in their maple problems for advice. The annual seed distrbution program is organized so that members can acquire and exchange seed.

Currently there is a branch of the society in North America and discussions are in progress about forming a branch in Japan. For a brochure and more information, please write to one of the following:

Membership Secretary
The Maple Society
12 Rustens Manor Road
Wymondham, Norfolk
England NR18 0NH

Membership Secretary
NABTMS
217 N. Eighth Street
River Fall, WI 54022, USA

NURSERY SOURCES

This is a partial list of nurseries that specialize in Japanese maples and in maples from Japan. Many of them offer hard-to-find plants. Catalogs or lists are available from most. No endorsement is intended, nor is criticism implied of sources not mentioned. Most good local garden centers usually stock a wide selection of cultivars.

Belgium
CECE Choteau
Avenue Leopold 3, no. 22
B7130 Bray (Binche)
32 (0) 64 33 82 15
www.cece-choteau.be/fr/
    index.php

Canada
Grey Cat Farm Nursery
4610 Simmons Road
Chilliwack, British Columbia V2R 4R7
(604) 823-4780

Mosterman Plants
43583 Adams Road
Chilliwack, British Columbia V2R 4L1
(604) 823-4713
wholesale only

France
Pépinière Maillot Bonsaï
Le Boix Frazy
01990 Relevant
33 (0) 4 74 55 23 48
www.maillot-bonsai.com

Italy
Fratelli Gilardelli Nursery
1-20041 Agrate Brianza
Via le delle Industrie, 21
    Milan
44 (0) 39 653 216
www.gilardelli.it/index.
    html

Zuliani Vivai Piante
via Palazzina 2
37134 Verona
39 (0) 45 505 128
www.zulianivivai.it

Netherlands
Dick van der Maat
Japanese Maple Nursery
Laag Boskoop 92
2771 GZ Boskoop
31 (0) 172 218 337
www.dvandermaat.com

Firma C. Esveld
Rijneveld 72
2771 XS Boskoop
31 (0) 172 213 289
www.esveld.nl

Planten Tuin Oirsprong
Eindhovensedijk 34b
5688GN Oirschot
31 (0) 40 262 1021
www.oirsprong.nl

United Kingdom
Bodwen Nursery
Pothole, St. Austell
Cornwall PL26 7DW
England
44 (0) 1726 883 855
www.bodwen.com

Burncoose Nurseries
Gwennap, Redruth
Cornwall TR16 6BJ
England
44 (0) 1209 860 316
www.burncoose.co.uk

Choice Ornamental Plant
    Nursery
Hill Side, Mill Lane
Aldington, Ashford
Kent TN25 7AL
England
44 (0) 1233 720 218

Credale Nursery
Upper Hill, Leominster
Herefordshire HR6 0JZ
England
44 (0) 1568 720 476
www.credale.co.uk

Goscote Nurseries
Syston Road, Cossington
Leicestershire LE7 4UZ
England
44 (0) 1509 812 121
www.goscote.co.uk

Hergest Croft Gardens
Ridgebourne, Kington
Herefordshire HR5 3EG
England
44 (0) 1544 230 160
www.hergest.co.uk

Hippopottering Nursery
Orchard House
East Lound, Haxey
Doncaster DN9 2LR
England
44 (0) 7979 764 677
www.hippopotteringma
    ples.co.uk/index.asp

Mallet Court Nursery
Curry Mallet, Taunton
Somerset TA3 6SY
England
44 (0) 1823 481 493
www.malletcourt.co.uk

M.G.H. Nurseries
50 Tullyhenon Road
Banbridge, County Down
  BT32 4EY
Northern Ireland
44 (0) 2840 622 795

Otter Nurseries
Gosford Road
Ottery St. Mary, Devon
  EX11 1LZ
England
44 (0) 1404 815815
www.otternurseries.co.uk

Perryhill Nurseries
Edenbridge Road
Hartfield, East Sussex TN7
  4JP
England
44 (0) 1892 770 377
www.perryhillnurseries.
  co.uk

P.M.A. Plant Specialities
Junker's Nursery
Lower Mead, West Hatch
Taunton, Somerset TA3
  5RN
England
44 (0) 1823 480 774
www.junker.co.uk

Westonbirt Arboretum
  Plant Centre
Westonbirt, Tetbury
Gloucestershire GL8 8QS
England
44 (0) 1666 880 554
www.westonbirtarbore
  tum.com

United States

Acer Acres
P.O. Box 122
Montpelier, Virginia 23192
(804) 883 8765
wholesale only

Arbutus Garden Arts
24639 NW Gerrish Valley
  Road
Yamhill, Oregon 97148
(503) 662 3704
www.arbutusgarden.com

Artful Maples Nursery
31941 Hamilton Creek
  School Road
Lebanon, Oregon 97355
(541) 258 3892

Blackhawk Nursery
41106 Bushman Road
Quincy, California 95971
(530) 283 4769
www.blackhawknursery.
  com

Bloom River Gardens
39744 Deerhorn Road
Springfield, Oregon 97478
(541) 726 8997
www.bloomriver.com

Brotzman's Nursery
6899 Chapel Road
Madison, Ohio 44057
(440) 428 3361
www.brotzmansnursery.
  com
wholesale only

J. Carlson Growers
8938 Newburg Road
Rockford, Illinois 61108
(815) 332 5610

Cloud Mountain Farm
6906 Goodwin Road
Everson, Washington
  98247
(360) 966 5859
www.cloudmountainfarm.
  com

Del's Japanese Maples
30050 Heather Oak Drive
Junction City, Oregon
  97448
(541) 688 5587

Dragon Cloud Japanese
  Maples
5750 Keller Court
Rocklin, California 95677
(916) 847 9075

Eastfork Nursery
P.O. Box 435
La Center, Washington
  98629
(360) 263 2662
www.eastforknursery.com

Eastwoods Nurseries
634 Long Mountain Road
Washington, Virginia
  22747
(540) 675 1234
www.japanesemaples.com

Fantastic Plants
5865 Steeplechase
Bartlett, Tennessee 38134
(901) 438 1912
www.fantasticplants.com

Forest Farm Nursery
990 Tetherow Road
Williams, Oregon 97544
(541) 846 7269
www.forestfarm.com

Greer Gardens
1280 Goodpasture Island
  Road
Eugene, Oregon 97401
(541) 686 8266
www.greergardens.com

Heritage Seedlings
4194 71st Avenue SE
Salem, Oregon 97301
(503) 585 9835
www.heritageseedlings.
  com
wholesale only

Highland Creek Nursery
269 Drake Farm Road
Fletcher, North Carolina
  28732
(828) 687 7653
www.highlandcreeknurs
  ery.com
wholesale only

Iseli Nursery
30590 SE Kelso Road
Boring, Oregon 97009
(800) 777 6202
www.iselinursery.com
wholesale only

Johnnie's Pleasure Plants
  Nursery
31 Ware Road
Tallassee, Alabama 36078
(334) 567-7049

Kellygreen Nursery
P.O. Box 1130
Drain, Oregon 97435
(800) 447 5676

Lake's Nursery
8435 Crater Hill Road
Newcastle, California
  95658
(530) 885 1027
www.lakesnursery.com

Living Art Nursery
97 Bartell Road
Rockford, Illinois 61108
(360) 482 3037

Maples By Design
18197 Apple Colony Road
Tuolumne, California
    95379
(209) 928 3991
www.maplesbydesign.com

Marca Dickie Nursery
P.O. Box 1270
Boyes Hot Spring, Califor-
    nia 95460
(707) 996 0364

Mendocino Maples
    Nursery
41569 Lilttle Lake Road
Mendocino, California
    95460
(707) 937 1189
www.mendocinomaples.
    com

Metro Maples
4890 S. Dick Price Road
Fort Worth, Texas 76140
(817) 797 3419
www.metromaples.com

Miyama Asian Maples
P.O. Box 1719
Laytonville, California
    95454
(707) 984 8314
www.miyamaasianmaples.
    com

Momiji Nursery
2765 Stony Point Road
Santa Rosa, California
    95407
(707) 528 2917
www.momijinursery.com

Mountain Maples Nusery
P.O. Box 1329
Laytonville, California
    95454
(888) 707 6522
www.mountainmaples.
    com

Oakland Bay Nursery
5960 Highway 3
Shelton, Washington
    98584
(360) 427 7172

Rarefind Nursery
957 Patterson Road
Jackson, New Jersey 08527
(732) 833 0613
www.rarefindnursery.com

Surry Gardens
Route 172, P.O. Box 145
Surry, Maine 04684
(207) 667 4493
www.surrygardens.com

Topiary Gardens
1840 Stump Road
Marcellus, New York 13108
(315) 374 8125
www.topiary-gardens.com

Wells Medina Nursery
8300 NE 24th Street
Medina, Washington
    98039
(425) 454 1853
www.wellsmedinanursery.
    com

Whitney Gardens &
    Nursery
P.O. Box 170
306264 Highway 101
Brinnon, Washington
    98320
(360) 796 4411
www.whitneygardens.com

Wildwood Farm
10300 Sonoma Highway
Kenwood, California
    95452
(707) 833 1161
www.wildwoodmaples.
    com

GLOSSARY

acuminate narrowing gradually to a point

bud stick a twig or branch section with several mature buds. Budsticks are usually taken from the current season's growth and are grafted onto a rootstock.

chartaceous papery

chimera any living organism or tissue with abnormal cells growing adjacent to normal cells, as occurs with some forms of leaf variegation

cordate heart-shaped

crenate scalloped

cultivar a plant maintained solely by cultivation, a cultivated variety

cuneate wedge-shaped

dendrologist a person who studies trees, especially their taxonomy

dentate toothed

dieback a condition or disease, often caused by fungi, which kills a plant, starting from the tips of twigs and branches and moving backward through the plant

falcate sickle-shaped

fastigiate having a growth habit where branches grow at acute angles to the stems, tending to form a narrow, erect tree or shrub

glabrous smooth and hairless

glaucous coated with a waxy, white to blue-gray covering

involute rolled inward at the edges

lanceolate lancelike; narrow and tapering at both ends as in some leaves

leaf stalk petiole

lenticular lens-shaped

lobulate having small lobes

lobule a small lobe

midrib the central vein (mid vein) in a leaf or leaf lobe

nomenclature the system of naming plants

obtuse blunt

orbicular round and flat

ovate egg-shaped

palmate shaped like a hand, with fingers (lobes) spread outward

patch bud a square-shaped piece of budding material for a graft, often used for certain species or for special uses on larger material

pendulous bending downward, hanging

pilose covered with short fine hairs

pinna a division of a compound leaf

pinnate having a featherlike arrangement, with leaves on both sides of a common axis

pinnatifid deeply cut to the midrib

propagation increasing the number of plants, usually by seed, cuttings, grafting, or layering

prostrate lying flat on the ground

pubescent covered with short hairs

raceme a main flower stem with flowers on small stalks that bloom from bottom to top

reticulated having a conspicuous network of fine veins

rhombic diamond-shaped

rootstock the lower part of a graft; an understock

rugose wrinkled or ridged

samara the single-seeded, winged fruit of the maple

scion a short piece of a shoot which is inserted in an understock to form a graft

sessiliform without a leaf stalk, attached directly to the stem

serrate having sawlike teeth (on the leaf margins)

sinus the space between two lobes

spike a stem with stalkless flowers attached directly to it

sport a mutation or abnormal growth

stigma the (female) part of a flower that receives pollen

stratification the process of preserving (stratifying) seed by layering it in moist sand or peat moss and keeping it in cold storage until planting time

subcordate shallowly heart-shaped

sublobulate small-lobed

taxonomy the science of classification

T-budding a method of grafting which involves inserting the grafting material into a T-shaped cut on the understock

tomentose covered with dense, soft hairs

trifoliate three-leaved

truncate cut straight across, as when the leaf base is at right angles to the leaf stalk

type species the single specimen on which the description and the name of the species are based

understock the lower part of a graft, a rootstock

undulate having a wavy surface

variegate a plant with variegated leaves, that is, leaves of two or more colors

veneer grafting a method of grafting which involves inserting the grafting material in the side of an understock to retain the understock top above the graft for additional growth. Also known as side grafting, side-veneer, or side-wedge.

witches'-broom an abnormal growth of closely bunched, usually dwarfed, twigs on a branch or stem

BIBLIOGRAPHY

Adams, P. 2006. *Bonsai with Japanese Maples*. Portland, Oregon: Timber Press.

Angyo Maple Nursery. 1930. Catalog. Tokyo.

Anonymous. 1891. *Kaede Rui Ziko* (Maples with illustrations). 3 vols. Japan.

Anstey, J. M. 1969. "Acers from Cuttings." *International Plant Propagators' Society Proceedings* 19: 211.

Baker, K. F., ed. 1957. *The University of California System for Producing Healthy Container-grown Plants*. University of California Divisions of Agricultural Sciences, Manual 23. Berkeley, California.

Barrett, R. 2004. *Maples*. New York: Firefly Books.

Bean, W. J. 1978. *Trees and Shrubs Hardy in the British Isles*. 8th ed. London: John Murray.

Carey, D. P. 1974. "Production of Japanese Maples by Cuttings." *International Plant Propagators' Society Proceedings* 24: 137.

Carville, L. L. 1975. "Propagation of *Acer palmatum* Cultivars from Hardwood Cuttings." *International Plant Propagators' Proceedings* 25: 39.

Chang, C.-S. 1989. *A Systematic Study of the Genus Acer L., Section Palmata Pax, Series Palmata (Aceraceae)*. Ph.D. thesis, University of Georgia.

Chugai Shokobutsu Yen. 1931–1932, 1938–1939, 1940–1941. Nursery catalogs. Yamamoto, Kawabegun, Japan.

Coggeshall, R. G. 1957. "Asiatic Maples: Their Propagation from Softwood Cuttings." *Arnoldia* 17 (July): 45–55.

Curtis, W. J. 1969. "Seed Germination and the Culture of *Acer palmatum*." *International Plant Propagators' Society Proceedings* 19: 142.

Delendick, T. J. 1981. *A Systematic Review of the Aceraceae*. Ph.D. thesis, City University of New York.

Delendick, T. J. 1984. "Reconsideration of Two Intraspecific Taxa of the Fullmoon Maple, *Acer japonicum* (Aceraceae)." *Brittonia* 36: 49–58.

Essig, E. O. 1929. *Insects of Western North America*. New York: MacMillan.

Fang, W. P. 1939. "A Monograph of Chinese Aceraceae." *Contribution from the Biological Laboratory of the Science Society of China* 11. Nanking, China.

Fordham, A. J. 1969. "*Acer griseum* and Its Propagation." *International Plant Propagators' Society Proceedings* 19: 346.

Galle, F. C. 1987. *Azaleas*. Rev. ed. Portland, Oregon: Timber Press.

Garner, R. J. 1967. *The Grafter's Handbook*. 3rd ed. East Mailing Research Station, Oxford University Press.

Gregory, P., and H. Angus. 2008. *World Checklist of Maple Cultivar Names*. Tetbury, Gloucestershire: Forestry Commission of Great Britain, National Arboretum, Westonbirt.

Hanado, S.-N. 1695. *Kadan Chikinshō*. 6 vols. Tokyo.

Hara, H. 1938. "Observations ad plantas Asiae Orientalis 15." *Journal of Japanese Botany* 14: 50–51.

Harris, D. C. 1976. "Propagation of Japanese Maples by Graftings." *International Plant Propagators' Society Proceedings* 26: 169.

Harris, J. G. S. 1973. "Propagation of Acers." *International Dendrology Society Yearbook*.

Harris, J. G. S. 1975. "Maples from Japan." *Journal of the Royal Horticultural Society* 99: 394–399.

Harris, J. G. S. 1976. "Growing Maples from Seed." *The Garden* (October).

Harris, J. G. S. 1983. "An Account of Maples in Cultivation." *The Plantsman* 5: 35–58.

Hartmann, H. T., D. E. Kester, F. E. Davies Jr., and R. L. Geneve. 2001. *Hartmann and Kester's Plant Propagation: Principles and Practices*. 7th ed. Englewood Cliffs, New Jersey: Prentice-Hall.

Hillier, H. G. 1973. *Hillier's Manual of Trees and Shrubs*. 3rd ed. Winchester, England.

Hitchcock, C. L. and A. Cronquist. 1973. *Flora of the Pacific Northwest: An Illustrated Manual*. Seattle: University of Washington Press

Hobson, J. 2007. *Niwaki: Pruning, Training, and Shaping Trees the Japanese Way*. Portland, Oregon: Timber Press.

Hohman, H. J. 1968. *List of Plants in Collection*. Kingsville, Maryland.

Hutchinson, P. A. 1971. "Propagation of Acers from Seed." *Internationa Plant Propagators' Society Proceedings* 21: 233.

Iconographia Cormophytorum Sinicorum. 1972. Botanical Institute of the University of Peking, China.

International Code of Botanical Nomenclature. 2000. Königstein, Germany: Koeltz Scientific Books.

International Code of Nomenclature for Cultivated Plants. 2004. Leuven, Belgium: International Society for Horticultural Science.

Ishii, Y. 1932. *Gen Shoku Engei Shokobutsu Zukan*. Vol. 4. Sebundo, Tokyo.

Itō, I. 1710. *Zōho Chikinshō* (Revised, enlarged Chikinshō). 8 vols. Japan.

Itō, I. 1719. *Kōeki Chikinshō* (Publicly useful Chikinshō). 8 vols. Japan.

Itō, I. 1733. *Chikinshō Furoku* (Chikinshō supplement). 3 vols. Japan.

Itoh, J. 1911. *Momiji*. Tokyo: Geichikudo.

Jong, P. C. de. 1976. "Flowering and Sex Expression in *Acer* L. A Biosystematic Study." *Mededelingen Landbouwhogeschool Wageningen* 76 (2): 1–201.

Kim, P.-K. 1996. *Check List of Maple Species and Cultivars*. Milim Botanical Garden, Kyonggi, South Korea.

Kobayashi, J. 1967. Nursery catalog. Angyō, Japan.

Kobayashi, J. 1975. *Maples for Beginners*. Tokyo: Nihon-Bungei Sha.

Koidzumi, G. 1911. "Revisio Aceracearum Japonicarum." *Journal of the College of Science, Imperial University of Tokyo* 32.

Krüssman, G. 1984. *Manual of Cultivated Broad-leaved Trees and Shrubs*. Vol. 1. Portland, Oregon: Timber Press.

Kurata, S., ed. 1968. *Illustrated Important Forest Trees of Japan*. Vol. 2. Tokyo: Japan Forestry Technical Association.

Lamb, J. G. D. 1972. "Vegetative Propagation of Japanese Maples at Kinsealy, Eire." *International Plant Propagators' Society Proceedings* 22: 240.

Lamble, G. 1997. *The Cultivation of Japanese Maples*.

Lancaster, R. 1974. *Trees for Your Garden*. New York: Scribner.

Lancaster, R. 1976. "Maples of the Himalaya." *The Garden* (December).

Lancaster, R. 1991. "Maple Magic in Japan." *Country Life* (7 November).

Matsumura, Y. 1954. "Maples of Japan." *University of Washington Arboretum Bulletin* 17. Seattle.

McMinn, H. E., and E. Maino. 1967. *Illustrated Manual of Pacific Coast Trees*. Berkeley, California: University of California Press.

Mulligan, B. O. 1958. *Maples Cultivated in the United States and Canada*. Lancaster, Pennsylvania: American Association of Botanical Gardens and Arboretums.

Mulligan, B. O. 1974. "*Acer circinatum* 'Monroe'." *Baileya* 19.

Mulloy, M. S. 1976. "Variability in Japanese Maples." *American Rock Garden Society Bulletin* 24.

Murray, A. E., Jr. 1969, 1970. "*Acer* Notes." *Kalmia* 1 and 2.

Murray, A. E., Jr. 1970. *A Monograph of the* Aceraceae. Ph.D. thesis, Pennsylvania State University.

Nakamura T., et al. 1974. *Momiji & Kaede*. Tokyo: Seibundo Shinkosha.

Ogata, K. 1964. "On the Varieties of *Acer mono* found in Japan." *Journal of Geobotany* 12. Tokyo.

Ogata, K. 1965a. "A Dendrological Study of the Japanese Aceraceae, with Special Reference to Geographical Distribution." *Bulletin of the Tokyo University Forests* 60.

Ogata, K. 1965b. "On *Acer pycnanthum*." *Journal of Geobotany* 13. Tokyo.

Ogata, K. 1967. "A Systematic Study of the Genus *Acer*." *Bulletin of the Tokyo University Forests* 63.

Ohwi, J. 1965. *Flora of Japan*. Washington, D.C.: Smithsonian Institute.

Oka, S., I. Itō, and J. Itō. 1882. *Kaede Binran* (Maple list). Japan.

Pax, F. 1902. "Aceraceae." In A. Engler, *Das Pflanzreich*. Leipzig: Verlag von Wilhelm Englemann. 4: 163.

Pringle, J. S. 1973. "The Concept of the Cultivar." *Bulletin of the Royal Botanical Gardens, Hamilton, Ontario* 27 (3): 13–27.

Rapley, B. A. 1974. "Grafting Maples from Imported Scions." *International Plant Propagators' Society Proceedings* 24: 303.

Rehder, A. 1929. *Manual of Cultivated Trees and Shrubs*. New York.

Rehder, A.1938. "New Species, Varieties . . . of the Arnold Arboretum." *Journal of the Arnold Arboretum* 19.

Satake, Y. 1991. *Wild Flowers of Japan: Woody Plants*. 2 vols. Tokyo: Heibonsha.

Savella, L.1971. "Top Grafting of Japanese Maples and Dogwood." *International Plant Propagators' Society Proceedings* 21: 395.

Shurtleff, M. C. 1966. *Plant Diseases in Home and Garden*. Ames, Iowa: Iowa State University Press.

Tominari and Hayashi. 1971. *Nihon no ka boku* (Ornamental trees and shrubs of Japan.) Tokyo: Kodansha.

Townsend, M. A., and W. K. Hock. 1973. "Tolerance of Half-sib Families of Red Maple to *Verticillium* Wilt." *Phytopathology* 63.

Uehara, K. 1961. *Iyuboku Daiju Setsu*. 3 vols. Tokyo: Ariake Shobū, Bunkyo-ku.

U.S. Department of Agriculture, Forest Service. 1948. *Woody Plant Seed Manual.* Miscellaneous Publication 654. Washington, D.C.: Government Printing Office.

van Gelderen, C. J., and D. M. van Gelderen. 1999. *Maples for Gardens.* Portland, Oregon: Timber Press.

van Gelderen, D. M. 1969. "Japanese Maples." *Dendroflora* 6: 19–36.

van Gelderen, D. M., P. C. de Jong, H. J. Oterdoom, and J. R. P. van Hoey-Smith. 1994. *Maples of the World.* Portland, Oregon: Timber Press.

Van Klaveren, R. 1969. "Growing *Acer palmatum* from Cuttings." *International Plant Propagators' Society Proceedings* 19: 144.

Vertrees, J. D. 1972. "Observations on the Propagation of Asiatic Maples." *International Plant Propagators' Society Proceedings* 22: 192.

Vertrees, J. D. 1973. "Maples of Japan." *American Horticulturist* 52 (2)..

Vertrees, J. D. 1974. "Maples." *American Horticulturist* 53 (3).

Vertrees, J. D. 1975. "Japanese Maples Gain Recognition." *American Nurseryman* 142 (2).

Vertrees, J. D., and P. A. Gregory. 2007. *Timber Press Pocket Guide to Maples.* Portland, Oregon: Timber Press.

Vrugtman, F. 1970. *Notes on the Acer Collection of the Botanical Gardens and the Belmonte Arboretum.* Miscellaneous Paper 6, Landbouw University, Wageningen, Netherlands.

Wada, K. 1938. Hakoneya nursery catalog. Numazu, Shizuoka, Japan.

Weaver, R. E., Jr. 1976. "Selected Maples for Shade and Ornamental Planting." *Arnoldia* 36 (4).

Wells, J. S. 1968. *Plant Propagation Practices.* 3rd ed. New York: Macmillan.

Wolff, R. P. 1973. "Success and Failure in Grafting Japanese Maples." *International Plant Propagators' Society Proceedings* 23: 339.

Yano, M. 2003. *Book for Maples.* Ukashi Utano-ku, Udashi, Nara, Japan: Japan Maple Publishing Group.

Yokohama Nursery. 1898. Catalog. Kanagawa, Japan.

GENERAL INDEX

Abies atlantica 'Glauca', 63
Acacia, 164
Aconitum, 304
adaptability of maples, 39, 51
Aiai gasa, 326
air circulation, 54, 60, 61, 65, 71, 99
air layering, 78–79
Akaji, 330
Akajika itaya, 330
Akaji nishiki, 330
Akashi Bay, 221
Amako kaede, 297
Amakuki, 297
Amoenum Group, 82, 83
Amur maple, 328, 364
Angyo Maple Nursery, 26
anthracnose, 61
Ao kaede, 312, 315
Ao momiji, 315
Ao uri, 299
Aphididae (family), 56
aphids, 54, 56–57, 67
Arahaga, 292
Arahago, 292
Arahana, 292
Arboretum Kalmthout, 96, 117, 360
Arguta (series), 30
Armahogi, 297
Asanoha kaede, 283
Ashiboso urinoki, 291
aspen, 315
atropurpureum, definition of, 269

backlighting, 40, 132, 227
Baggett, Jim, 322
Bailey Nurseries, 329
ball-and-burlap maples, 44

Baltzer Nursery, 85
bare-rooted maples, 44, 74
bark beetles, 67–68
bark color, 23, 42
    red, 41, 101, 178
bark structure, 72
bark texture, 42, 43, 151
    corky, 41, 89, 197, 349
    rough, 89, 90, 151, 154, 197, 330, 349
Bartel, Andreas, 146
Belder, Jelena de, 117
Belder, Robert de, 96
bench graft, 75
Bergman, Fred W., 123, 350
Berrima Bridge Nursery, 107
Bewley's Nursery, 108
Bloodgood Nursery, 109
bonsai culture, 22, 43, 98
botanical names, 35
Botrytis, 60, 67, 99
box elder, 297
Brachyrhinus, 58
Buchholz, Talon, 322, 363
    Amoenum Group plants, 170
    Dwarf Group plants, 154, 247
    Linearilobum Group plants, 128, 215
    Matsumurae Group plants, 133, 187
    Palmatum Group plants, 165, 219
Buchholz and Buchholz Nursery, 297, 305, 321, 325
    Amoenum Group plants, 354
    Flora Wonder Collection, 136

Ghost Series, 133, 139, 213, 246
    Linearilobum Group plants, 351
    Matsumurae Group plants, 222
bud grafts, 76–77
bud sport, 190
bud sticks, 76
Bump, Dr. and Mrs., 258

Calocedrus decurrens, 40
cambium, 72–73
cankers, 63
cankerworm, fall, 57
Caperci, Jim, 113
Carpinus, 292
Cascade Mountains, 296
Cascio, 121
caterpillars, 57, 67
Caudata (series), 30
Cave, Peter, 285
Cave's Tree Nursery, 285
Cedrus atlantica 'Glauca', 63
chance seedling, 123, 125, 130, 218, 247, 264
Chidorinoki, 292
chimera, 23
chip budding, 76
chlorophyll and leaf variegation, 23, 289
chlorosis, 62
Chojanoki, 309
Chyojanoki, 309
Cissifolia (series), 30
Cissus, 297
classification system, 30–31
cleft graft, 74

Coimbre Botanic Garden, 323
collector's maple, 131, 151, 170, 217, 290
commercial production of maples, 65, 134–135
companion plants, 22, 40, 41, 42, 43
container-grown Japanese maples, 51–56
    pests and diseases of, 54–55
    planting of, 53
    watering of, 48
containerized stock, 44, 45
containers, 53, 55
Cook, Alleyne, 295
Corbin, Dr. 186
Crataegus, 299
Crispin's Creation Nursery, 361
cross-hybridizing, 293
cross-pollination, 35
cultivar, definition of, 25–26, 35
cultivar names, 35
Curtis, William, 118, 218, 235
cuttings, 77–78, 109

damping-off, 60, 63, 67
Delaware Valley Agricultural School, 97
Del's Japanese Maple Nursery, 95, 99, 102, 125, 294
Del's Lane Country Nursery, 295
der Netherlandser, J., 359
devil maple, 300
dieback, 59–60

diseases of maples, 59–63, 67

Dissectum Group, 40–41, 50, 83, 269
  leaf shape, 69, 305
  grafting of, 71, 75
  habit of, 42, 121, 305
  in the landscape, 22
  mature height of, 39
  twiggy growth of, 49

Distyla (series), 30

Dominium Arboretum, 294

Dosser, Donald, 356, 362

Douwsma, Peter, 317

drainage, 46, 61

Drath, H. J. 325

drought tolerance, 46

Duncan and Davies Nursery, 95, 135, 178, 216, 242, 276

Dwarf Group, 22, 37, 39, 43, 83

Ebbinge and Groos, 110

Edo era, 26

Eisenhut, Otto, 124

Emery, John, 236, 352

Ezo meigetsu kaede, 318

fern-leaf maple, 303

fertilizing maples, 48

festival of fans, 200

Festival of the Stars, 255, 333

Festival of the Weaver, 333

field-grown maples, 44

field maple, 310

Firma C. Esveld, 292, 320, 329, 330, 362
  Amoenum Group plants, 138, 273
  Dissectum Group plants, 119, 125, 127, 130
  Dwarf Group plants, 117, 156
  Linearilobum Group plants, 128, 219, 269

Matsumurae Group plants, 90, 142, 169, 188, 260, 272, 275, 277
  Palmatum Group plants, 84, 146, 360

fogging technique, 65

Fratelli Gilardelli Nursery, 321
  Amoenum Group plants, 132, 218
  Dissectum Group plants, 139, 140, 212, 215, 248
  Matsumurae Group plants, 96, 132
  Palmatum Group plants, 204, 249

freezing temperatures, 45

frost damage, 54, 62

fu, 24–25

fukurin fu, 24, 112, 184

fukurin kuzure, 24, 103, 184

full moon maple, 302

fungi, soil-borne, 60, 63

Fusarium, 60

Galle, Fred, 68

Genroku era, 237

Ghost Series, 86, 132, 139, 213, 229, 246, 266

Gibbons, John, 256

Ginnala (section), 31

Girard's Nursery, 352

Glabra (section), 30

Goddard, William, 218

golden full moon maple, 319

goma fu, 24, 265

Gordon, Ron, 285

Gosaburō Itō, 27

grafting, 70–77
  and cambium union, 72–73
  and wilt, 59
  old Japanese method of, 71–72
  scions for, 72
  timing of, 70
  understock for, 65, 71–72, 293

grafting compatibility, 29

grafting techniques, 73–77

grape, 308

grape ivy, 297

Green Mansions Nursery, 155, 225, 351, 362

green-striped maple worm, 57

Greer Gardens, 205

Grisea (series), 31

Guldemond, 134

Gulden, Greg, 360

hair-foot maple, 291

haki homi fu, 25, 197, 300, 307

Hakusan momiji, 331

Hanado, San-nojō, 27

Hana kaede, 299

Hana no ki, 314

Hana zakura, 284

hardening off grafts, 77

hardiness of maples, 43

Ha uchiwa kaede, 302

hawthorn, 156, 299

hawthorn maple, 299

Hayashida, R., 286

Heims, Dan, 128

Hepburn system of transliteration, 36

Heterorhabditis megidis, 58

Hillier, Sir Harold 117

Hillier Gardens and Arboretum, 117, 172, 196

Hillier's Nursery, 351

Hime ogurabana, 331

Hippopoterring Nursery, 156

historical literature on maples, 27, 32

history of Japanese cultivars, 25–27

Hitotsuba kaede, 301

Hobako ha uchiwa, 302

Hohman, Henry, 164, 165, 211, 258, 272, 322

Honshu maple, 315

Hon uri, 299

hornbeam maple, 292

horned maple, 300

horse chestnut scales, 58

Hoscoe kaede, 291

hoshi fu, 25, 313

hoso fu, 25

hoso fukurin fu, 25, 184

Hozaki kaede, 292

Hughes, Howard, 285, 359

Hupp, Barbara, 150

hybridizing, 69–70, 303

Iizuka, 315

Indivisa (section), 30

insect pests, 56–58, 67

intensifying fall foliage color, 21

International Botanical Congress, 312

International Code of Botanical Nomenclature, 35, 172

International Code of Nomenclature for Cultivated Plants, 35, 68, 240

International Cultivar Registration Authority for Maples, 36, 70

iroha momiji, 81

Iseli, Germaine, 137

Iseli Nursery, 218, 259

Itagi kaede, 312

Itaya, 302, 307, 312, 318

Itaya kaede, 307, 312

Itaya meigetsu, 302, 307, 318, 326

Itayi, 307

Itayo, 307

Itō, Ibei, 26, 27

Itō, Isaburō, 27

ito fukurin fu, 25

iwato beni, 81

Japanese emperor's garden, 170

Japanese maples, 20–21, 39
  characteristics of, 20–23

Japanese maples [*continued*]
  classification of, 29–31
  definition of, 19
  number of cultivars, 26, 27
  old specimens of, 39, 97, 104
  sizes of, 21–22
Japanese names, 32, 33, 36, 262, 264
Japanese red maple, 314
Johnnie's Pleasure Plants Nursery, 105, 264, 350, 355
Johnston, Harold, 83, 121, 156, 214, 216, 247, 264, 355
Jong, P.C. de, 29
judging seedling quality, 51

Kadan Chikinshō, 27
kaede, 20
Kaede Binran, 26
kaede noki, 81
Kaede Rui Zuko, 27
Kaji kaede, 300
Kakunimo, 284
kanji, 33, 207
Karakogi kaede, 328
Kibana uchiwa kaede, 326
Kingsville Nursery, 322
kiri fu, 25, 144, 317, 330
Kiriha kaede, 300
Kobako ha uchiwa, 303
Kobayashi, Nursery, 225, 268
Kochonoki, 309
Kōeki Chikinshō, 27
Ko hau uchiwa kaede, 326
Koidzumi, Gen'ichi, 239
Ko mine kaede, 309
Komori kaede, 315
Koniji noki, 315
Kristoff, Stephen, 127
Kurobi itaya, 310

laceleaf, 40
Latinized cultivar names, 35, 93, 172, 220, 350
Latin plant names, 34–35

layering, 78–79, 296
leaf blights, 61
leaf cutter bees, 56
leaf hoppers, 56
leaf miner flies, 56
leaf scorch, 47, 62
legginess of maples, 46
Lemaire, Charles, 227
Lepidoptera (order), 57
light requirements of maples, 39–40
limb structure, 41, 42, 50
lime-leaved maple, 301
Linearilobum Group, 22, 51, 83, 83, 88
Linnaeus, Carl, 34
lion, mythical, 201, 242
Lithocarpa (section), 31
Lithocarpa (series), 31
locations, 39–40
Loucks, Del, 84, 125, 177, 294, 295

Macrantha (section), 30
Maillot, Guy, 109, 353
Mansen itaya, 330
mapleleaf cutter, 57
maples of Japan, definition of, 19
Maplewood Nursery, 82, 93, 154, 159
  frost damage at, 60
  grafting at, 71
  growing Amoenum Group plants, 42, 87, 149, 154, 267
  growing Dissectum Group plants, 40, 254
  growing Dwarf Group plants, 150–151, 159, 209
  growing Matsumurae Group plants, 223, 279
  growing Other Group plants, 142
  growing Palmatum Group plants, 93, 94, 240, 257
  growing seedlings at, 67, 69, 150, 159, 174

growing species and cultivars at, 285, 295, 296, 300, 305
hybridization at, 69, 174, 303
layering at, 78
propagating plants at, 142
pruning at, 48, 49
registering cultivars at, 69, 159, 174, 257, 279
seed germination at, 66
selecting plants at, 308, 320
maple worm, green-striped, 57
Maruba kaede, 301
mass plantings, 42–43
Matsumurae Group, 83, 83, 116
McKenzie River, 296
McMullen, Floyd, 297
Megure, 309
Megusurinoki, 309
Megusyumi kaede, 309
Meigetsu, 302
Meigetsu kaede, 302
Meuri noki, 299
microclimates, 46, 58
micronutrients, 62
midges, 57
Milim Botanic Garden, 149
Mine kaede, 331
Miquel, Friedrich A. W., 222
misting, 76
mites, 57, 67
Mitsch, John, 218
Mitsude kaede, 297
Mitsude momiji, 297
Miyabe, Kingo, 310
Miyabe's maple, 310
Miyama Asian Maple Nursery, 350, 363
Miyama momiji, 283
moisture and fall color, 21
moisture requirements of maples, 47–48
momiji, 20, 81

monkshood, 304
Monroe, Warner, 296
Monrovia Nurseries, 364
Morrey and Son Nursery, F., 123
Mossman, Frank, 129
moth, leaf-roller, 57
Mountain Maples Nursery, 154, 224
Mount Etna, 314
Mount Omure, 204
Mount Taro, 255
Mount Tsukuba, 262
mulch, 45–46
Mulligan, Brian, 294, 296, 319
Munn, Carl, 323
Muro river, 194
mutant, 35

Nakai, Takenoshin, 171
Nakajima, Hisao, 27, 315
naming difficulties, 32, 33, 180
naming of cultivars, 35–36, 51, 68–69
naming of seedlings, 68
naming of wild plants, 34–35
Nanase river, 195
Nectria, 63
Negundo (section), 30
nematodes, beneficial, 58
New Zealand, 95
Nikko maple, 309
Nippon maple, 311
nitrogen in soil, 48, 51, 62
Noh plays, 185
nomenclature of Japanese maples, 32–34, 153

Ogara bana, 292
O hauchiwa, 318
O itaya meigetsu, 318
Oka, Seigorō, 26, 27, 154
O karabana, 291
old Japanese cultivars, 85, 89, 189, 191, 194, 208, 210, 259, 322

from the 1600s, 195, 239, 251

from the 1700s, 160, 203, 230, 237, 238, 242, 250, 254, 255, 271, 280, 364

from the 1800s, 208, 267

Olsen, Suzanne, 285

Ōmitsude kaede, 309

Ō momiji, 81

Oni momiji, 300

Other Group (of *A. palmatum* cultivars), 83

Otiorhynchus, 58

Oyodo, Michakaze, 237

Pacific Northwest, 164, 237, 294, 393

painted maple, 312

Palmata (section), 30

Palmata (series), 19–20, 29, 30, 70, 293, 302, 318

Palmatum Group, 82, 83

Parviflora (section), 30

Parviflora (series), 30

patch budding, 76

patents, 70

Pax, Ferdinand, 222

Peacedale Nursery, 294

Pentaphylla (section), 31

Phytophthora, 63

pine, Japanese black, 197

pine bark maple, 197

Pinus thunbergii, 197

plant appearance and cultural conditions, 50–51

planting hole, 44

planting method, 44–45

planting stock, 44

Platanoidea (section), 31

pointed-leaf maple, 283

popcorn foliage, 20, 83

Populus tremula, 315

post-graft care, 77

powdery mildew, 62

Premna japonica, 284

pricking out seedlings, 67

Prince Fushimi, 288

propagation, 29, 65–79, 168

pruning maples, 48–50

Pulvinaria, 58

purple-blow maple, 330

Pseudomonas, 60

Pythium, 60

Queen Otohime, 209

Raraflora Nursery (Australia), 108, 235, 236, 352

Raraflora Nursery (Pennsylvania), 97, 124, 246

Red Maple Nursery, 127, 141, 234, 354, 359, 361, 362

red-shoot maple, 291

red snakebark, 291

red-veined maple, 315

registering cultivars, 60

repotting, 55

reticulated foliage, 160, 363

Rey, Rick, 97

RHS (Royal Horticultural Society) Award of Garden Merit, 292, 305, 309, 316, 319

Amoenum Group plants, 110, 197, 207

Dissectum Group plants, 118, 135, 153, 231

Linearilobum Group plants, 219

Matsumurae Group plants, 112, 116, 261

Palmatum Group plants, 163, 226

Roberts, Graham, 216

Rodd, Edward, 97, 124, 246

root rots, 60–61

roots of Japanese maples, 43, 44

root weevils, 58, 67

rough bark maple, 89

Rubra (section), 31

Russell, Jim, 181

Sabo, David, 125

saddle graft, 74

Sagama-Ōiso, 237

salt spray damage, 46, 62

Sankaku kaede, 284

Savill Gardens, 175

scales, 58

Schwartz, William, 114, 155, 164, 185, 221, 225, 256, 351, 362

Schwerin, Fritz K. A. von, 196

scions, 24, 72

Scolytidae (family), 57

seed germination, 66

seedling mass production, 63, 65

seed sowing, 66–68

Sekihin Binran, 97, 115, 145, 152, 186, 190

Seminoki, 309

sequoia, giant, 42

Sequoiadendron giganteum, 42

Shantung maple, 330

Sharp, Jimmy, 234

Sheffield Park Garden, 38

Shibata kaede, 310

Shima uri kaede, 310

shimo furi fu, 25, 362

Shinano uchiwa, 302

shin fukurin fu, 25, 148, 362

Shira hashi noki, 299

Shira kaede, 299

Shiraki kaede, 312

Shirasawa's maple, 318

shoot dieback, 59–60

side graft technique, 73-74

Siebold's maple, 326

Siesmayer, J. A., 223

slugs, 67

small-flowered maple, 309

smooth Japanese maple, 81

snakebark maple, 291, 299, 309, 311, 315

soft-tip condition, 67

soil conditions, 46–47

soil pH, 24, 46, 62

sooty molds on maples, 56

Sorenson, Ilo, 133

Spingarn, Joel, 131

sport, 35, 120, 212, 214, 216, 251

spring foliage of maples, 20

Stanley Park, 296

stick budding, 218

stooling, 79

stratification, 66

strawberry root weevil, 56, 58

Stupka, Joseph, 159, 221

summer cuttings, 77–78

summer grafting, 75–76

sunago fu, 25, 144, 152, 171, 172, 252, 313, 364

sunago fukurin, 25

sunburn, 39

Suncrest Gardens, 360

sunlight, 39–40, 50

Suzuki, Hideo, 174

tako kaede, 81

Tanai, Toshimasa, 284

Taniasa, 292

Tanmura, T., 353

Taranto, Villa, 124, 169, 269, 350

Tatarian maple, 328

tattered appearance, 271

taxonomy of *Acer palmatum*, 31

taxonomy of maples, 29–31

T-budding, 76

T.C. Plants company, 85, 103

Te kaede, 284

Teese, Arnold, 116, 211, 306, 317

Terra Nova Nurseries, 128

Tetranychidae (family), 57

Tetsu kaede, 311

Tetsu-no-ki, 311

The Ford, 39

Thiensen Arboretum, 325

three-pronged maple, 284

thrips, 56
Tilt, Ken, 121
tissue culture, 65
Tobie, Milt, 259
Tokiwa kaede, 312
Toshu Gu shrine, 235
Toyama district, 260
Toyama kaede, 284
trace elements, 62
transplanting maples, 44
Trident maple, 284
Trifida (series), 31
Trifoliata (section), 31
Trompenburg Arboretum, 210, 260
Tschonoski's maple, 331
Tsubanok, 292
Tsukushi gata bay, 262
tsuma fukurin fu, 25, 262
Tsuta momiji, 312
twig dieback, 59–60

ubu fu, 25, 289
uniform water supply, 47
University of Washington Arboretum, 296, 329
upright-growing maples, 41–42
Urihada nishiki, 315
Uri kaede, 299
Urika nishiki, 291
Uri maple, 299
Uri noki, 315
using maples in the garden, 40–43, 46, 59, 62

van der Horst, Fritz, 126
van der Maat, Dick
    Dissectum Group plants, 212
    Dwarf Group plants, 120, 176, 191, 226, 361
    Matsumurae Group plants, 178, 183
    Palmatum Group plants, 126, 146, 163, 250, 273, 275, 354, 357, 358
Vandermoss, Bob, 137
van Gelderen, Cor, 117, 119, 128, 278, 358
van Gelderen, D. M., 91, 188, 320
van Hoey-Smith, J. R. P., 260
variability of *Acer palmatum*, 31
variegation of foliage, 23–24, 51, 180, 279
vegetative propagation, 24
veneer graft technique, 73–74
Vergeldt, D., 359
Verkade, David, 352
Verticillium wilt, 59–60
vine-leaf maple, 297
vine maple, 293
vine weevil, 56, 58
viridis, definition of, 269
viruses, 24
Vitis, 308

Wakehurst Place Gardens, 272
wall, effect on maples, 46
Warner Pacific College, 296
waterlogged soil, 46, 53
Wattez, Constant, 93
weaning of grafts, 77
weevils, 58, 63, 71
Westonbirt Arboretum, 63, 64, 70, 82, 273, 274
Wezelenburg and Son, K., 137
Whitney Gardens, 275
Wil-Chris Acres, 118
Willowwood Arboretum, 272
Wilson, James, 276
wilt. See *Verticillium* wilt.
wind sensitivity, 46, 97
winter cuttings, 78
winter grafting, 75
winter protection of container plants, 52
witches'-broom, 97, 296, 324, 329, 351
    as source of dwarf cultivars, 35, 91, 113, 116, 124, 185, 352, 359, 361
    center lobe flattened, 91, 108, 127, 155, 175, 357, 360, 362
    on *A. palmatum* cultivars, 90, 133, 188, 213, 235, 246, 259
    on *A. palmatum* f. atro-

purpureum, 105, 110, 159, 221, 234
Wolff, Richard P., 127, 188, 192, 215, 234, 259, 359, 361, 362
Wood, Edward, 103, 219, 305
woolly scales, 58
World War II, 32, 110, 261
worms, 56, 57
Wright, Art, 164, 306
Wright's Nursery, 110

Yaku maple, 310
Yakushima ogarabana, 310
Yakushima onaga kaede, 310
Yama kaede, 299
yama momiji, 81
Yamashibe kaede, 292
Yamina Rare Plant Nursery, 306, 317
Yano, Masayoshi, 27, 210
yatsubusa, definition of, 278
Yokohama Nursery, 27, 208, 211
Yokoi, Masato, 307
Yorokko kaede, 312
Yoshimichi, Hirose, 134
Yuga, Ishii, 299

Zōho Chikinshō, 26, 27, 230
Zuiderpark, 311

INDEX OF JAPANESE MAPLES

Boldface indicates main entry pages. *Italic bold-face* indicates a photo page when an illustration appears apart from its main entry.

'Abigail Rose', **83**, 247, 337
Acer (genus), 30–31, 328
Acer acuminatum, 30
Acer amoenum, 31
Acer argutum, 30, **283**
Acer barbinerve, 30
Acer buergerianum, 19, 31, **284**, 288
　subsp. *formosanosum*, 288
Acer campestre, 31, 310
Acer capillipes, 30, **291–292**, 310
Acer cappadocicum, 31
Acer carpinifolium, 30, **292**
Acer caudatifolium, 30
Acer caudatum, 30
　subsp. *ukurunduense*, **292–293**
Acer ceriferum, 30
Acer circinatum, 19, 20, 29, 30, 25, 95, 146, **293–294**, 326
Acer cissifolium, 30, **297–299**
Acer crataegifolium, 19, 30, **299**, 317
Acer davidii, 30
Acer diabolicum, 31, **300–301**
Acer dissectum, 31
Acer distylum, 30, **301–302**
Acer duplicato-serratum, 19, 30

Acer fabri, 55
Acer griseum, 31
Acer henryi, 30
Acer japonicum, 19–22, 30, 32, *69*, 77, 293, **302–309**, 319, 327
　var. *insulare*, 303
　var. *kobakoense*, 303
　var. *stenolobum*, 303
　var. *villosum*, 303
Acer longipes, 31
Acer mandshuricum, 31
Acer maximowiczianum, 31, **309**
Acer micranthum, 30, **309–310**
Acer miyabei, 31, **310**
Acer mono, 307, 312
　var. *marmoratum* f. *dissectum*, 313
Acer morifolium, 30, **310–311**
Acer nambuana, 31
Acer negundo, 297
Acer nikoense, 309
Acer nipponicum, 30, **311–312**
Acer ornatum, 31
Acer palmatum, 19–22, 25–26, *27*, *28*, 30, 31–32, 39, *63*, **81–83**, 293
　subsp. *amoenum*, 31, **81**
　f. *atropurpureum*, 31, 65, 93, 110, 227, 234. Also see 'Atropurpureum'
　var. *coreanum*, 171. See 'Korean Gem'
　subvar. *crispum*, 203
　f. *dissectum*, 40, *41*, 296, 306, 363

f. *dissectum rubrifolium*, 222
　subvar. *eupalmatum* f. *crispum*, 33
　subsp. *genuinum* subvar. *crispum*, 33
　var. *heptalobum*, 31
　var. *koreanum*, 171. See 'Korean Gem'
　forma *linearilobum*, 31
　subsp. *matsumurae*, 31, 32, 68, **81–82**
　subsp. *matsumurae* f. *roseomarginatum*, 33
　subsp. *palmatum*, 21, 31, **81**, 86, 172
　f. *purpureum*, 227
Acer pauciflorum, 20, 30
Acer pectinatum, 30
Acer pensylvanicum, 30, 317
Acer pentaphyllum, 30
Acer pictum, 19, 31, 32, 307, **312**, 330
　subsp. *mayrii*, 307
Acer platanoides, 29, 31
Acer polymorphum, 31
Acer pseudoplatanus, 30
Acer pseudosieboldianum, 19, 30
Acer pubipalmatum, 20, 30
Acer pycnanthum, 31, **314–315**
Acer robustum, 20, 30
Acer rubescens, 30
Acer rubrum, 30, 31, 314
Acer rufinerve, 19, 29, 30, 33, **315–316**
Acer saccharinum, 30, 31
Acer sanguineum, 31
Acer septemlobum, 31

Acer shirasawanum, 19–20, 30, 32, 70, 277, 303, 307, **318–319**, 327
　var. *tenuifolium*, 318
Acer sieboldianum, 19, 20, 30, 32, 70, *282*, 307, 324, **326**
Acer sinopurpurascens, 31
Acer spicatum, 30, 293
Acer stachyophyllum, 30
Acer sterculiaceum, 31
Acer tataricum, 31, 328
　subsp. *aidzuense*, **328**
　subsp. *ginnala*, **328–329**
Acer tegmentosum, 30
Acer tenellum, 31
Acer triflorum, 31
Acer truncatum, 19, 31, 32, 307, **330**
Acer tschonoskii, 30, 309, **331**
　var. *australe*, 331
　subsp. *komarovii*, 331
'Aconitifolium' (*A. japonicum*), 20, 21, 129, 278, 296, **303–305**, 306, 307, 308
'Aconitifolium USA' (*A. japonicum*), 305
'Acutum', 365
'Adlerschwanz', 221. See 'Rubrifolium'
'Adrian's Compact', 349
'Afterglow', 365
'Aiai gasa' (*A. sieboldianum*), 365
'Aizumi nishiki', 365
'Akaba', 365
'Akagi san nishiki' (*A. rufinerve*), 365
'Akaha nishiki', 365

'Akahada yama', 365
'Aka hosada', 365
'Aka itaya nishiki' (*A. pictum*), 365
'Akaji nishiki' (*A. palmatum*), 230. See 'Seigai'
'Akaji nishiki' (*A. truncatum*), 331
'Akaji-no-nishiki', 365
'Aka kawa hime', **84**, 337
'Akame hagoromo', 365
'Akame hauchiwa', 365
'Akame itaya meigetsu' (*A. sieboldianum*), 365
'Aka moyo, 365
'Akane', **84**, 107, 337
'Akane hagoromo', 365
'Akane zome', 365
'Aka-no-hichi gosan', 92. See 'Atrolineare'
'Aka-no-hichi goshi', 239. See 'Shime-no-uchi'
'Aka-no-shichi gosan', 239. See 'Shime-no-uchi'
'Aka omote' (*A. japonicum*), 363
'Aka shidare', 254. See 'Tamuke yama'
'Akashigata', 221. See 'Rubrifolium'
'Aka shigitatsu sawa', 33, 106. See 'Beni shigitatsu sawa'
'Aka washi-ni-o', 207. See 'Ornatum'
'Akebono' (*A. buergerianum*), **284**
'Akebono kaede' (*A. buergerianum*), 284
'Akebono nishiki' (*A. buergerianum*), 365
'Akegarasu', **85**, 337
'Akikaze' (*A. pictum*), 365
'Akikaze kifu' (*A. pictum*), 313
'Akikaze nishiki' (*A. truncatum*), 25, 230, **330–331**
'Aki kogane', 365
'Aki-no-iro', 365
'Aki-no-utage', 365

'Aki-no-yūgure', 365
'Akishino', 365
'Akishino nishiki', 365
'Akita yatsubusa', **85**, 337
'Aki tsuma beni', 365
'Akitsu shima', 365
'Akitsu shū', 365
'Akitsu su', 365
'Akitsuta', 365
'Aki zome midare', 365
'Albiflorum' (*A. sieboldianum*), 364
'Albolimbatum' (*A. rufinerve*), **316**, 317
'Albomarginatum' (*A. palmatum*), 184. See 'Matsugae'
'Albomarginatum' (*A. rufinerve*), 316
'Albovariegatum' (*A. crataegifolium*), 300
'Albovariegatum' (*A. palmatum*), 268. See 'Versicolor'
'Albovariegatum' (*A. truncatum*), 331
'Albovittatum' (*A. truncatum*), 331
'Alleyne Cook' (*A. circinatum*), 365
'Alloys', 365
'Alpenweiss', **85–86**, 337
'Alpine Surprise', 349
'Amagatsuji', 365
'Amagi', 365
'Amagi shigure', **86**, 337
'Ama kumo', 365
'Ama-no-hagoromo', 145. See 'Hazeroino'
'Amatum', 207
'Amber Ghost', **86**, 337
'Amelopsifolium', 264
'Amine nishiki', 154. See 'Issai nishiki momiji'
'Anaba shidare', 153. See 'Inaba shidare'
'Andreanum', 365
'Angustilobum', 92
'Angustilobum Purpureum', 92

'Angyō-no-sato' (*A. distylum*), 302
'Annick', 365
'Ansung', 365
'Aoba bo', 87. See 'Aoba jō'
'Aoba cho', 87. See 'Aoba jō'
'Aoba fue', 270. See 'Volubile'
'Aoba fuke', 270. See 'Volubile'
'Aoba jō', **86–87**, 337
'Aoba nishiki', **87**, 337
'Aoba-no-fue', 270. See 'Volubile'
'Aoba-no-fuye', 270. See 'Volubile'
'Aoba shidare', 88. See 'Ao shidare'
'Aocha nishiki', 87. See 'Aoba nishiki'
'Ao gaki', 89. See 'Aoyagi'
'Ao gaki yama', 365
'Ao ha', 365
'Ao jutan' (*A. japonicum*), **305**
'Ao kanzashi', **87–88**, 257, 337
'Aokii', 268. See 'Versicolor'
'Aome-no-uchi', 241. See 'Shinobuga oka'
'Ao meshime-no-uchi', 241. See 'Shinobuga oka'
'Ao-no-hichi gosan', 241. See 'Shinobuga oka'
'Ao-no-shichi gosan', 241. See 'Shinobuga oka'
'Ao shichi gosan', 239. See 'Shime-no-uchi'
'Ao shidare', **88**, 337
'Ao shidare kōyō', 365
'Ao shimen-no-uchi', 239, 241. See 'Shime-no-uchi'
'Ao shime-no-uchi shidare', **88**, 337
'Ao shime-no-uchi', 241. See 'Shinobuga oka'
'Aotya nishiki', 365
'Aoyagi', **88–89**, 270, 337
  bark color of, 41, 42, 49

growth habit of, 236
in the landscape, 109, 141, 226
'Ao yagi gawa', 349
'Arakawa', 41, **89–90**, 198, 337
'Arakawa momiji', 365
'Arakawa tokaede' (*A. buergerianum*), 365
'Ara kawa ukon', 349
'Arano', 365
'Arano araya', 365
'Arashi yama', 365
'Aratama', *71*, **90**, 337
'Argenteomaculatum', 268. See 'Versicolor'
'Argenteomarginatum', 184. See 'Matsugae'
'Argenteum' (*A. palmatum*), 268. See 'Versicolor'
'Argenteum' (*A. rufinerve*), 316
'Ariadne', 35, **90–91**, 337
'Ariake nomura', **91**, 337
'Arima yama', 365
'Arlene', 365
'Arto', 365
'Asagi nishiki', 365
'Asagira' (*A. pictum*), 363. See 'Asagiri nishiki' (*A. pictum*)
'Asagiri nishiki' (*A. pictum*), 363
'Asahi beni zuru', 92. See 'Asahi zuru'
'Asahi juru', 92. See 'Asahi zuru'
'Asahi kaede' (*A. palmatum*), 92. See 'Asahi zuru'
'Asahi kaede' (*A. pictum*), 313
'Asahi nishiki' (*A. truncatum*), 364
'Asahi nomura', 92. See 'Asahi zuru'
'Asahi zuru', **91–92**, 251, 337
  bark color of, 206, 220, 358

in the landscape, 41
leaf variegation of, 20, 87,
160, 220, 358
'Asahi zuru shiro fu', 365
'Asaji', 92. See 'Asahi zuru'
'Asa-no-ha', 365
'Asa-no-hoshi', 365
'Asashi yama', 365
'Asatsuyu', 365
'Asayake nishiki' (*A. pyc-
nanthum*), **315**
'Asa zakura', 365
'Asa zuma', 365
'Ascendens' (*A. japonicum*),
365
'Ashi-no-ha', 365
'Ashi-no-sato', 365
'Ashitaka nishiki', 220. See
'Rokugatsu en nishiki'
'Ashurst Wood', 365
'Asuka', 365
'Asuka gawa nishiki', 365
'Asuka kawa', 365
'Asuka yama', 365
'Atrodissectum', 196. See
'Nicholsonii'
'Atrolineare', **92–93**, 119,
164, 218, 337
'Atropurpureum', **93**, 178,
182, 270, 337
'Atropurpureum Lacinia-
tum', 147. See 'Hessei'
'Atropurpureum Novum',
198. See 'Novum'
'Atropurpureum Super-
bum', 93. See
'Attraction'
'Atropurpureum Variega-
tum', 267
'Atsu gama', **93**, 337
'Attaryi' (*A. japonicum*), **305**
'Attaryi' (*A. sieboldianum*),
305
'Attraction', **93–94**, 337
'Aureomaculatum', 94. See
'Aureovariegatum'
'Aureovariegatum' (*A. pal-
matum*), **94**, 171, 337
'Aureovariegatum' (*A.
tataricum*), 364

'Aureum' (*A. palmatum*),
50, **94–95**, 250, 337
'Aureum' (*A. pictum*), 365
'Aureum' (*A. shiras-
awanum*), 21, 95, 303,
319–320, 323, 325,
364
'Aureum Oblongum' (*A.
shirasawanum*), 320
'Aureumvariegatum', 94.
See 'Aureovariegatum'
'Autumn Dream', 365
'Autumn Fire' (green-
leaved), **95**, 337
'Autumn Fire' (red-leaved),
96. See 'Autumn
Flame'
'Autumn Flame', 35, 70,
95–96, 337
'Autumn Glory', 41, **96**, 337
'Autumn Glow', 365
'Autumn Moon' (*A. shiras-
awanum*), **320**
'Autumn Red', **96**, 337
'Autumn Showers', 365
'Awa uri nishiki' (*A. cratae-
gifolium*), 365
'Awa yuki' (*A. tataricum*),
365
'Aya hatori', 365
'Ayai gasa' (*A. sieboldi-
anum*), 365
'Azuma murasaki', **96–97**,
258, 337
'Azuma nishiki', 365

'Baby Dragon' (*A. trunca-
tum*), 365
'Baby Ghost', 365
'Baby Lace', 43, **97**, 337
'Bailey's Compact' (*A.
tataricum*), **329**
'Balcombe Green', 365
'Baldsmith', **97–98**, 273,
337
'Baltzer-Hig', 86. See
'Alpenweiss'
'Banda hime', 349
'Barbara', 365
'Barrie Bergman', 350

'Beethoven' (*A. tataricum*),
365
'Beni bato', 365
'Beni chidori', **98**, 337
'Beni fushigi', **98**, 212, 337
'Beni gasa', **98–99**, 337
'Beni goromo', 365
'Beni hagoromo', 251. See
'Tamuke yama'
'Beni hauchiwa' (*A. japoni-
cum*), 365
'Beni hime', 60, *61*, **99**, 175,
338
'Beni homare', 365
'Beni hoshi', **99–100**, 338
'Beni kaede', 365
'Beni kagami', **100**, 338
'Beni kagami nishiki', 365
'Beni kawa', *37*, **100–101**, 338
'Beni ko hime', 365
'Beni komachi', 20, 98,
101–102, 210, 338,
350. Also see 'Otome
zakura'
'Beni komachi Sport', 350
'Beni komo-no-su', 102. See
'Beni kumo-no-su'
'Beni kosode', 365
'Beni K Sport', 350. See
'Beni komachi Sport'
'Beni kumo-no-su', **102**, 338
'Beni maiko', **102–103**, 338
'Beni michinoku', 365
'Beni mikawa', 365
'Beni murasaki gawa', 365
'Beni musume', 365
'Beni-no-nami', 365
'Beni-no-tsukasa', 106. See
'Beni tsukasa'
'Beni ōgi', 365
'Beni ori zuru', 365
'Beni ōtake', **103**, 216, 338
'Beni otome', 350
'Beni saihō shidare', 217.
See 'Red Filigree Lace'
'Beni sazanami', 365
'Beni schishihenge', 104.
See 'Beni shichihenge'
'Beni seigen', 117. See
'Corallinum'

'Beni sen', 365
'Beni sengoku', 365
'Beni shichihenge', 24, **103–
104**, 113, 244, 245, 338,
353, 356
'Beni shidare', **104**, 333, 338
'Beni shidare Tricolor', 260
'Beni shidare Variegated',
260
'Beni shi en', **104–105**, 181,
214, 242, 338
'Beni shigitatsu sawa', 33,
105–106, 133, 211, 266,
338
'Beni shishihenge', 104. See
'Beni shichihenge'
'Beni shōjō shidare', 365
'Beni suzume', 365
'Beni tsukasa shidare', 350
'Beni tsukasa', 98, **106**, 338,
350
'Beni tsuma', 33
'Beni tsuri', 107. See 'Beni
zuru'
'Beni ubi gohon', 107. See
'Beni yubi gohon'
'Beni ubi ocha', 107. See
'Beni yubi gohon'
'Beni uri' (*A. crataegifo-
lium*), 300, 317
'Beni uri' (*A. rufinerve*), 33,
300, **316–317**
'Beni yaku nishiki' (*A.
morifolium*), 311
'Beni yatsubusa', **106**, 338
'Beni yubi gohon', **106–107**,
338
'Beni zashi', 366
'Beni zome shizuku', 366
'Beni zukashi', 366
'Beni zuru', **107**, 338
'Ben's Broom', 366
'Bergiana' (*A. tataricum*),
366
'Berrima Bridge', **107**, 338
'Berry Dwarf', **108**, 338
'Bewley's Red', **108**, 338
'Bicolor', 366
'Bi hō', 41, **109**, 338
'Bill Dale's Red', 366

'Birthday Dissectum', 350.
    See 'Birthday Wishes'
'Birthday Wishes', 350
'Bloodgood, **109–110**, 127,
    182, 338
    cuttings of, 77
    growth habit of, 132, 154,
        192, 197, 198, 208, 219,
        275
    in the landscape, 41, 42
    leaf color of, 93, 94, 219,
        267, 278, 350, 352
    seedlings of, 68, 360
    witches'-brooms on, 213,
        246
'Blood Leaf', 93. See
    'Atropurpureum'
'Blood Vein', 92. See
    'Atrolineare'
'Bob's Big Green', 366
'Bō jō', 366
'Bonfire', 230. See 'Seigai'
'Bonnie Bergman', 350
'Boskoop Glory', **110**, 338
'Bradley's Broom', 366
'Brandt's Dwarf', **110–111**,
    338
'Brevilobum', 366
'Brian', 366
'Brocade', **111**, 338
'Bronson's Crinkle', 366
'Bronzewing', **111**, 338
'Bujō ji', 366
'Bultinck', 366
'Burgundy' (*A. tataricum*),
    366
'Burgundy Flame', 366
'Burgundy Jewel' (*A. circi-
    natum*), **294**, 338
'Burgundy Lace', **111–112**,
    235, 338
'Butterfly', 24, **112–113**, 338,
    354
    growth habit of, 88, 158,
        184, 202
    in the landscape, 41
    leaf color of, 86, 103, 180,
        353
    seedlings of, 165, 360
'Byakugō ji', 366

'Calico', 113, 338
'Camille', 366
'Candelabrum' (*A. micran-
    thum*), 310
'Candy Stripe' (*A. capil-
    lipes*), 366
'Caperci Dwarf', **113**, 338
'Capersian Dwarf', 113. See
    'Caperci Dwarf'
'Capersi Dwarf', 113. See
    'Caperci Dwarf'
'Captain McEacham', 350
'Carlis Corner', **113–114**,
    338
'Carmineum', 117, 231. See
    'Corallinum'; 'Seigen'
'Carolyn Wolff', 366
'Caudatum', 366
'Chantilly Lace', **114**, 273,
    338
'Charlotte', 366
'Chiba', 162. See 'Kashima'
'Chiba yatsubusa', 162. See
    'Kashima'
'Chichibu', 174. See
    'Kotohime'
'Chichibu hime', 366
'Chichibu yatsubusa', 174.
    See 'Kotohime'
'Chikumano', **114**, 338
'Chikushi gata', 32, 262
'Chi otome', 366
'Chiri hime', 366
'Chirimen', 202, 203. See
    'Okukuji nishiki';
    'Okushimo'
'Chirimen kaede', 254. See
    'Tamuke yama'
'Chirimen momiji', 254.
    See 'Tamuke yama'
'Chirimen nishiki', **115**, 338
'Chi sato', 366
'Chishio', 20, 32, **115**, 239,
    240, 338, 350
'Chishio hime', 244. See
    'Shishio hime'
'Chishio Improved', 240.
    See 'Shin chishio'
'Chishio-no-ito', 366
'Chishio Sanguineum', 350

'Chishio yatsubusa', 99. See
    'Beni hime'
'Chisio', 115, 230. See
    'Chishio'; 'Seigai'
'Chitori', 366
'Chitose nishiki', 366
'Chitose no', 366
'Chitose yama', **115–116**,
    168, 338
'Chiyo hime', 181
'Cho cho', 113. See
    'Butterfly'
'Choco-no-mai', 113. See
    'Butterfly'
'Chōkei ji', 366
'Chōkyū ji', 366
'Chō-no-mai', 366
'Chouguraji', 366
'Christy Ann', 266. See
    'Vandermoss Red'
'Chūgū ji', 366
'Chuzen ji', 366
'Cindy', 366
'Cinnabarinum', 226. See
    'Sango kaku'
'Cinnabar Wood Maple',
    226. See 'Sango kaku'
'Circumlobatum', 366
'Claire', 366
'Coccineum' (*A. tataricum*),
    364
'Collingwood Ingram', 350
'Como', 366
'Compact Amur Maple', 329
'Compactum', 366
'Coonara Pygmy', **116**, 186,
    259, 339, 351, 356, 361
'Coral Bark Maple', 226.
    See 'Sango kaku'
'Corallinum' (green-leaved),
    113, 115, **116–117**, 230,
    339, 350
'Corallinum' (red-leaved),
    20, 98. Also see 'Seigai'
'Coral Magic', 366
'Coral Pink', **117**, 276, 339
'Cordifolium' (*A. tatari-
    cum*), 366
'Coreanum', 172. See
    'Korean Gem'

'Crassifolium' (*A. japoni-
    cum*), 366
'Crested', 203. See
    'Okushimo'
'Crimson Carol', **117–118**,
    339
'Crimson King', 366
'Crimson Prince', 350
'Crimson Queen', *47*, **118**,
    121, 253, 339
    growth habit of, 216
    in the landscape, 41
    leaf color of, 98, 104, 111,
        178, 206
'Crinkle Leaf', 350
'Crippsii', 350–351
'Crispa', 33, 34, 203, 230.
    See 'Okushimo';
    'Seigai'
'Crispatum' (*A. tataricum*),
    366
'Crispifolium', 366
'Crispum', 33, 203, 230. See
    'Okushimo'; 'Seigai'
'Cristata', 33, 203, 230. See
    'Okushimo'; 'Seigai'
'Cristatum', 203, 230, 243.
    See 'Okushimo'; 'Sei-
    gai'; 'Shishigashira'
'Cristatum Variegatum', 33.
    See 'Hikasa yama'
'Crumple Leaf', 223. See
    'Ruby Ridge'
'Cultriforme' (*A. tatari-
    cum*), 366
'Cuneatum', 366
'Curiel's Gold' (*A. tatari-
    cum*), 366
'Curtis Strapleaf', **118–119**,
    339
'Cuspidatum' (*A. tatari-
    cum*), 366
'Cynthia', 366
'Cynthia's Crown Jewel',
    366

'Dad's Best', 366
'Dai', 366
'Daiji sen', 366
'Daimyō', 250. See 'Taimin'

'Daimyō nishiki', 33, 250
'Dainty Dotty', 366
'Daiō, 366
'Dalton', 366
'Daniel', 351
'Darwin nishiki', 366
'Dawy' (*A. nipponicum*), 366
'Decomposition', 143, 173. See 'Hagoromo'; 'Koshimino'
'Del's Dwarf' (*A. circinatum*), **294**
'Demi Sec', **119**, 339
'Dentelle de Binche', 366
'Deshōjō', 43, **119–120**, 240, 339, 353, 354, 360
'Deshōjō nishiki', **120**, 339
'Desyōjō', 120. See 'Deshōjō'
'Dezome hatsu yuki' (*A. rufinerve*), 366
'Dezome irizome', 351
'Diana' (*A. palmatum*), 43, **120**, 339
'Diana' (*A. shirasawanum*), 363
'Diana Verkade', 351
'Diane's Dissectum', 366
'Digitatum Atropurpureum', 196. See 'Nicholsonii'
'Discolor Versicolor', 268. See 'Versicolor'
'Dissectum' (*A. palmatum*), 270
'Dissectum' (*A. pictum*), **312–313**, 363
'Dissectum Atropurpureum', 104, 207. See 'Beni shidare'; 'Ornatum'
'Dissectum Atrosanguineum', 121. See 'Dissectum Nigrum'
'Dissectum Aureum', 134. See 'Flavescens'
'Dissectum Barrie Bergman', 350. See 'Barrie Bergman'
'Dissectum Ever Red',

121. See 'Dissectum Nigrum'
'Dissectum Flavescens', 134. See 'Flavescens'
'Dissectum Garnet', 135. See 'Garnet'
'Dissectum Inazuma', 153. See 'Inazuma'
'Dissectum Matsu kaze', 185. See 'Matsu kaze'
'Dissectum Mioun', 358. See 'Mioun'
'Dissectum Nigrum', 33, 98, 111, **120–121**, 206, 216, 248, 253, 339
'Dissectum Ornatum', 207. See 'Ornatum'
'Dissectum Palmatifidum', 210. See 'Palmatifidum'
'Dissectum Paucum'. 210. See 'Palmatifidum'
'Dissectum Pendulum Julian', 211. See 'Pendulum Julian'
'Dissectum Rubellum', 221. See 'Rubrifolium'
'Dissectum Rubrifolium', 222. See 'Rubrifolium'
'Dissectum Sessilifolium', 143, 254. See 'Hagoromo'
'Dissectum Tamuke yama', 254. See 'Tamuke yama'
'Dissectum Tinctum', 221. See 'Rubrifolium'
'Dissectum Unicolor', 134. See 'Flavescens'
'Dissectum Waterfall', 272. See 'Waterfall'
'Doai guchi', 366
'Don', 366
'Dōnzuru bo', 351
'Dōsen bō', 366
'Dragon's Fire', 351
'Dr Baker', 351
'Dr Brown', 351
'Drew' (*A. cissifolium*), 366
'Dr Seuss', 351
'Dr Tilt', **121–122**, 339

'Durand Dwarf' (*A. tataricum*), **329**
'Durone' (*A. tataricum*), 366

'Eagle's Claw', **122**, 339
'Earthfire', 366
'Eastwood Cloud' (*A. buergerianum*), **285**
'Ebi nishiki', 265. See 'Ueno homare'
'Ebi-no-hige', 225. See 'Sango kaku'
'Ebo nishiki', 150. See 'Ibo nishiki'
'Ebony', 351
'Echigo', 366
'Eda murasaki', 366
'Ed Carmin', 366
'Eddisbury', 8, 35, **122–123**, 339
'Edna Bergman', **123–123**, 339
'Ed's Red', 351–352
'Ed Wood' (*A. japonicum*), 366
'Effigi', 132. See 'Fireglow'
'Effigy', 132. See 'Fireglow'
'Eiga nishiki' (*A. crataegifolium*), **299**
'Eimini', **124**, 339
'Elegans', **124**, 339
'Elegans Atropurpureum', 147. See 'Hessei'
'Elegans Purpureum', 147. See 'Hessei'
'Elegant' (*A. circinatum*), **294–295**
'Elizabeth', **124–125**, 159, 339
'Ellen', 41, **125**, 339
'Elmwood', 366
'Embers' (*A. tataricum*), **329**
'Emerald Elf' (*A. tataricum*), **329**
'Emerald Lace', 41, **125–126**, 339
'Emery's Dwarf', 352
'Emi', **126**, 339

'Emma', **126–127**, 339
'Emmit's Pumpkins' (*A. japonicum*), 366
'Emperor 1', 41, **127**, 339
'Ena san' (*A. pycnanthum*), 366
'Englishtown', **127**, 339
'Enkan', **128**, 339
'Enkō nishiki' (*A. pictum*), 366
'Enshōji', 366
'Eono momiji', 366
'Erena', 352
'Erythrocarpum' (*A. tataricum*), 366
'Erythrocladum' (*A. rufinerve*), **317**
'Esveld Select' (*A. carpinifolium*), **292**
'Ever Autumn', **128**, 339
'Ever Red', 33, 121. See 'Dissectum Nigrum'
'Ezo itaya nishiki' (*A. pictum*), 366
'Ezo-nishiki', 279. See 'Yezo nishiki'
'Ezo-no-o momiji' (*A. shirasawanum*), 319, **320–321**
'Ezo ō momiji' (*A. shirasawanum*), 366

'Fairy Hair', **128–129**, 339
'Fairy Lights' (*A. japonicum*), **305–306**
'Fall Delight', 366
'Fall's Fire', 26, **129**, 339
'Fascination', **129–130**, 339
'Felice', **130**, 339
'Fern Leaf' (*A. japonicum*), 305
'FG1', 132. See 'Fireglow'
'Fichtenast', 184. See 'Matsugae'
'Filicifolium' (*A. japonicum*), 303, 305
'Filigree', 41, **130–131**, 339, 352, 361
'Filigree Rouge', **131**, 339

'Filifera Purpureum', 92.
See 'Atrolineare'
'Fingerlobe', 241. See 'Shi-
nobuga oka'
'Fior d'Arancio', 40, **131–
132**, 339
'Fior d'Arangio', 132. See
'Fior d'Arancio'
'Fire' (*A. tataricum*), **329**,
330
'Fireball', 352
'Fire Engine', 366
'Fireglow', **132**, 182, 339
'First Ghost', **132–133**, 339
'Fischergeraete', 143. See
'Hagoromo'
'Fjellheim', **133**, 340
'Flagelliforme Aureum' (*A.
shirasawanum*), 320
'Flame' (*A. tataricum*),
329–330
'Flavescens', **133–134**, 340
'Flushing', 352
'Foliis albovariegatum' (*A.
crataegifolium*), 300
'Frost in der Erste', 203. See
'Okushimo'
'Fubuki' (*A. rufinerve*), 366
'Fude gaki', 352
'Fudikage', 366
'Fueri kouri kaede' (*A. cra-
taegifolium*), 300
'Fugen bō', 366
'Fuiri kouri kaede' (*A. cra-
taegifolium*), 300
'Fuiri urihada kaede' (*A.
rufinerve*), 316
'Fuji domoe', 366
'Fūjin', 352
'Fujinami', 366
'Fujinami nishiki', **134**, 340
'Fuji nishiki' (*A. diaboli-
cum*), 366
'Fuji-no-takane' (*A. palma-
tum*), 366
'Fuji-no-yama' (*A. rufin-
erve*), 366
'Fujiyama', 366
'Fukagire o momiji', 100
'Fukaya', 366

'Fukaya gawa', 366
'Fukin agashi', 366
'Fukui', 366
'Full Moon' (*A. shiras-
awanum*), 366
'Fumoto dera', 366
'Furi tsuzumi' (*A. shiras-
awanum*), 366
'Furu kawa', **352**
'Furu kuro', 366
'Furu nishiki', 264
'Furu sato', 366
'Fushima kaede' (*A. buerge-
rianum*), 288
'Fusui', 366
'Futago yama' (*A. pictum*),
366
'Futai ji', 366
'Futa omote', 366

'Gaki-no-sugi', 366
'Gangō ji', 366
'Ganseki momiji', 89. See
'Arakawa'
'Garden Glory' (*A. shiras-
awanum*), 366
'Garnet', 40, 41, 50, **134–
135**, 340, 353
'Garnet Bond', 366
'Garnet Tower', 366
'Garyū', *43*, **135**, 340
'Gasshō', **135**, 340
'Gassyo', 135. See 'Gasshō'
'Geisha', **135–136**, 340
'Geisha Gone Wild', **136**,
340
'Gekkō nishiki', 352
'Genji yama', 366
'Genshi yama momiji', 366
'Gentaku', 366
'Germaine's Gyration', **137**,
340
'Giant Moon' (*A. japoni-
cum*), 366
'Gibbons', 366
'Gibbsii', 366
'Gimborn' (*A. capillipes*),
366
'Ginja', 352
'Ginshi', 166. See 'Kinshi'

'Gion-no-nishiki', 366
'Girard's Dwarf', 352
'Glen-Del' (*A. circinatum*),
295
'Globosum', **137**, 340
'Gloria' (*A. shirasawanum*),
363–364
'Glowing Embers', 41, **137–
138**, 340
'Goblin' (*A. sieboldianum*),
366
'Golden Dragon' (*A. trun-
catum*), 366
'Golden Flame', 366
'Golden Moon' (*A. shiras-
awanum*), 320
'Golden Pond', **138**, 340
'Gold Splash' (*A. rufinerve*),
366
'Gold Spring' (*A. shiras-
awanum*), 366
'Goshiki kaede' (*A. buerge-
rianum*), 284, **285**
'Goshiki kosode' (*A. buer-
gerianum*), **285**
'Goshiki kotohime', 22,
138–139, 340, 356
'Goshiki shidare', 260
'Goshiki suzumaru', 366
'Gosho zome', 366
'Gossamer' (*A. japonicum*),
363
'Gotenba nishiki' (*A. cissi-
folium*), 299
'Goten nomura', 366
'Grace', 366
'Grandma Ghost', **139**, 340
'Green Cascade' (*A. japoni-
cum*), 35, 303, **306**, 308
'Green Elf', 366
'Greenet', 237. See 'Shigi-
tatsu sawa'
'Green Filigree', 131. See
'Filigree'
'Green Fingers', 366
'Green Flag', 366
'Green Globe', 119, **139–140**,
340
'Green Hornet', **140**, 340
'Green Lace', **140**, 215, 340

'Green Mist', 41, **140–141**,
177, 340
'Green Snowflake', 366
'Green Star', **141**, 340
'Green Trompenburg', **141–
142**, 340
'Groenendael' (*A. rufin-
erve*), 366
'Groene Trompenburg',
142. See 'Green
Trompenburg'
'Groundcover', 43, **142**,
340

'Hachiman yama', 366
'Hadare yuki' (*A. rufinerve*),
366
'Hageriono', 145. See
'Hazeroino'
'Hagoromo', 51, **142–143**,
145, 173, 190, 340, 361
'Hagoromo kaede', 366
'Haha so', 366
'Haibara', 366
'Haibara beni', 366
'Hakkan shikin' (*A. cratae-
gifolium*), 366
'Hakodate yama', 366
'Hakuhō', 366
'Haly Red', 154. See 'Italy
Red'
'Hamano maru', 352
'Hama otome', **143**, 340
'Hanabi' (*A. rufinerve*), 366
'Hanabi-no-mai', 366
'Hana chiru sato' (*A. buer-
gerianum*), **285**
'Hana fubuki', 366
'Hana gata', 366
'Hana izumi nishiki', 162.
See 'Kasen nishiki'
'Hana kanzashi', 220. See
'Rokugatsu en nishiki'
'Hana matoi', 352–353
'Hanami nishiki', **143–144**,
188, 340
'Hananoki aka fu' (*A. pyc-
nanthum*), 315
'Hananoki ki fu' (*A. pyc-
nanthum*), 366

'Hananoki nishiki fu' (*A. pycnanthum*), 315
'Hananoko' (*A. pycnanthum*), 367
'Hananoko-no-sazanami' (*A. pycnanthum*), 367
'Hana otome', 143. See 'Hama otome'
'Hana tsukasa', 367
'Hana yamato', 367
'Hanaze', 367
'Hanazono nishiki', **144**, 340
'Hanbi-no-mai', 367
'Han sen', 367
'Hanzell', 353
'Harriet Waldman', 367
'Haru biyō', 367
'Haru iro', 367
'Haru-no-akebono', 367
'Haru sake', 367
'Harusame', *24*, **144–145**, *332*, 340
'Haru sazanami', 367
'Harusume', 145. See 'Harusame'
'Haru yama', 367
'Harvest Red', 367
'Hashio', 367
'Hatamono-no-oto', 367
'Hatsu hana', 367
'Hatsukoi', 353
'Hatsu momichi', 367
'Hatsu momiji', 367
'Hatsuse', 367
'Hatsuse yama', 367
'Hatsu shigure', 353
'Hatsu shimo', 367
'Hatsu yuki' (*A. rufinerve*), 316
'Hatsu yuki beni fukurin' (*A. rufinerve*), 367
'Hatsu yuki kaede' (*A. rufinerve*), 316
'Hau hiwa' (*A. japonicum*), 305
'Hazeroino', **145**, 340
'Heartbeat', **145**, 340
'Heathcoat-Amory', 367
'Heavy Seed', 367

'Hefner's Red', 367
'Heguri', 367
'Heijō sazanami', 367
'Heisei nishiki', 353
'Heiwa', 367
'Helena' (*A. palmatum*), **145–146**, 340
'Helena' (*A. shirasawanum*), 367
'Hemelrijk' (*A. shirasawanum*), **321**
'Heptalobum Elegans', 124, 147. See 'Elegans'; 'Hessei'
'Heptalobum Rubrum', **146**, 340
'Herbstfeuer', **146**, 340
'Hess Broom', 367
'Hessei', **146–147**, 340
'Hey hachii' (*A. japonicum*), 305
'Hibari', 367
'Hibari yama', 367
'Hichihenge', 235. See 'Shichihenge'
'Hida hanabi', 367
'Hidden Valley' (*A. circinatum*), 363
'Higasa yama', *33*, 148. See 'Hikasa yama'
'Higūga yama', 149. See 'Hinata yama'
'Hikaru genji', 367
'Hikaru genji momiji', 367
'Hikasa yama', *69*, **147–148**, 340
    flower quality of foliage buds, 20, *21*, 83, 85
    many names of, 33, 158
    variegation of, 25, 51
'Hillieri' (*A. crataegifolium*), 300
'Hima ha uchiwa', 367
'Hime chidori', 367
'Hime jishi', 367
'Hime kaede' (*A. buergerianum*), 363. See 'Musashi' (*A. buergerianum*)
'Hime nishiki' (*A. buergerianum*), 367

'Hime shōjō', 367
'Hime tōyō nishiki' (*A. buergerianum*), 367
'Hime tsuma gaki', 367
'Hime yaku nishiki' (*A. morifolium*), 311
'Hime yama', 367
'Hime yatsubusa', 278, 353
'Hina some', 367
'Hinata yama', **148–149**, 340
'Hina zuru', 367
'Hinode nishiki', 353
'Hino tori nishiki', 353–354
'Hi-no-tsukasa', 367
'Hirai gawa', 367
'Hiroha koshimino', 367
'Hiroha yama momiji', 367
'Hiro tai shaku', 367
'Hiryū', **149**, 340
'Hisae nishiki', 354
'Hisaga yama', 148. See 'Hikasa yama'
'Hisen nishiki', 367
'Hitode', 354
'Hito koto beni', 367
'Hitoshio', 367
'Hitosome', 367
'Hiūga yama', 149. See 'Hinata yama'
'Hiyoku ba', 367
'Hiyoku nishiki', 367
'Hō beni', 367
'Hoerner' (*A. tataricum*), 367
'Hōgyoku', 34, 42, 138, **149**, 341
'Hōgyuko', 34, 149. See 'Hōgyoku'
'Hohman's Variegated', 165. See 'Kingsville Variegated'
'Hoki momiji', 367
'Hokotate gawa', 367
'Hokuwa', 367
'Holland Select', 153. See 'Inaba shidare'
'Honami gawa', 367
'Hondo ji', 354
'Hondoshi', **149–150**, 341

'Honeydew' (*A. capillipes*), 367
'Hōno gawa', 367
'Hōno o', 367
'Hō ō', 271. See 'Wabi bito'
'Hō ō beni', 367
'Hō ō murakumo', 367
'Hō ō nishiki', 367
'Hō ō shidare', 367
'Hōrai nishiki' (*A. diabolicum*), 367
'Hōrai nishiki' (*A. palmatum*), 367
'Hōraku nishiki' (*A. rufinerve*), 367
'Hōren beni', 367
'Hōren hatsu yuki' (*A. rufinerve*), 367
'Horizontalis', 367
'Hosada', 367
'Hoshi kuzu', **150**, 341
'Hoshi miyasama' (*A. pictum*), 367
'Hoshi nishiki', 367
'Hoshi-no-yama', 367
'Hoshi tsukiyo', 313
'Hoshi yadori' (*A. pictum*), 25, **313**, 314, 363
'Hoshi zukiyo' (*A. pictum*), **313**, 314
'Hosoba beni', 367
'Hosoba koshimino', 367
'Hosoba ō momiji', 367
'Hototokiso', 367
'Hubb's Red Willow', 354. See 'Hupp's Red Willow'
'Hupp's Dwarf', **150–151**, 341, 361
'Hupp's Red Willow', 354
'Huru gawa', 367
'Hyōtei', 354
'Hyuga yama', 149. See 'Hinata yama'

'Ibo juhi', 367
'Ibo nishiki', 41, *42*, **151**, 341
'Ichigyō in', 367
'Ichigyō ji', 42, **151–152**, 207, 341

'Ichigyōji nishiki', 367
'Ichijoji', 152. See 'Ichigyō ji'
'Ichi-no-moto', 367
'Ide-no-sato', 354
'Ifuku gō', 367
'Ighigyoji', 152. See 'Ichigyō ji'
'Iibo nishiki', 151. See 'Ibo nishiki'
'Iijima sunago', 23, **152**, 341
'Ikaruga', 367
'Ikoma', 367
'Iku aki', 367
'Iku shio', 367
'Ilarian', 367
'Illustre', 367
'Ima deshōjō', 120
'Ima kumano', 367
'Imose gawa', 367
'Imo yama', 367
'Inaba shidare', 41, **152–153**, 206, 216, 341, 356
'Inabe shidare', 153. See 'Inaba shidare'
'Inado', 367
'Inasa yama', 367
'Inazuma', **153**, 341
'Inazuma nishiki' (*A. buergerianum*), 25, 362
'Integrifolium' (*A. buergerianum*), 290
'Involutum', 203. See 'Okushimo'
'Irish Lace' (*A. japonicum*), **306–307**
'Iro iro', 367
'Iro-no-seki', 367
'Iseji beni', 367
'Isis' (*A. sieboldianum*), 367
'Isobel', 354
'Iso chidori', **153–154**, 341
'Iso-no-nami' (*A. pictum*), 367
'Iso shibuki', 367
'Issai nishiki', 154. See 'Issai nishiki momiji'
'Issai nishiki momiji', **154**, 341
'Issun bōshi' (*A. buergerianum*), 367

'Italy Lace', 367
'Italy Red', **154**, 341
'Itami nishiki', 354
'Itaya' (*A. japonicum*), 32, **307**
'Itaya momiji' (*A. japonicum*), 367
'Ito momiji', 367
'Ito nishiki', 367
'Itsu maku tane', 367
'Ittai san nishiki' (*A. crataegifolium*), 367
'Iwahashi-no-sato', 367
'Iwahata', 367
'Iwai gojūsan', 367
'Iwao' (*A. buergerianum*), 367
'Iwao kaede' (*A. buergerianum*), 286
'Iwao nishiki' (*A. buergerianum*), 286
'Iwashita', 367
'Iwate yama', 367
'Iwato kagami', 367
'Iza shidare', 367
'Izayoi' (*A. japonicum*), 367
'Izu-no-odoriko', 360. See 'Sakura hime'
'Izu-no-sato', 367

'Jako kaede' (*A. buergerianum*), 284
'Jane', 354
'Jane Platt', 367
'Japanese Princess', 43, **154–155**, 341
'Japanese Sunrise', **155**, 341, 355
'Japanese Sunset', 355
'Jedo nishiki', 279. See 'Yezo nishiki'
'Jerre Schwartz', **155–156**, 341
'Jim Baggett', 367
'Jingo ji', 367
'Jirō shidare', **156**, 225, 341
'Jōdo', 367
'Johin' (*A. shirasawanum*), **321**
'Johnnie's Pink', **156**, 341

'Johnnie's Surprise', 355
'Jordan' (*A. shirasawanum*), **321–322**
'Jōroku aka me' (*A. buergerianum*), 362
'Jucundo' (*A. japonicum*), 367
'Jūga ya' (*A. shirasawanum*), 367
'Julia', 367
'Julian', 355
'Julian shidare', 211. See 'Pendulum Julian'
'Jūnihitoe' (*A. shirasawanum*), 319, **322**
'Jun nishiki', 367

'Kaba', **156–157**, 341
'Kabata', 367
'Kaempferi' (*A. japonicum*), 367
'Kaga beni', 367
'Kaga kogane', 367
'Kaga kujaku', 367
'Kaga ō beni', 367
'Kaga ō tamagawa', 367
'Kagari nishiki', 158. See 'Kagiri nishiki'
'Kaga sudare', 367
'Kaga tamagawa', 367
'Kaga zome', 367
'Kageori men', 367
'Kageori nishiki', 157, 239. See 'Shikage ori nishiki'
'Kagerō', **157**, 341
'Kageshiki men', 367
'Kagi nishiki', 367
'Kagiri', 158. See 'Kagiri nishiki'
'Kagiri nishiki', 33, 103, 113, 147, **157–158**, 165, 184, 341
'Kagon nishiki', 160. See 'Karasu gawa'
'Kaki kaede', 368
'Kaki momiji', 368
'Kaki shidare', 368
'Kaki shitare', 368
'Kakure gasa' (*A. shirasawanum*), 320, 364

'Kakure mino', 143. See 'Hagoromo'
'Kalmthout' (*A. shirasawanum*), 368
'Kamagata', 69, 150, **158–159**, 341, 352, 359
'Kamega yatsu', 368
'Kami kase', 368
'Kamina tsuki', 368
'Kamina zuki', 368
'Kami-no-nusa', 368
'Kamisaka nishiki' (*A. pictum*), 368
'Kandy Kitchen', 124, **159**, 341
'Kan nondaira' (*A. sieboldianum*), 368
'Kantan', 368
'Kara fu' (*A. buergerianum*), 368
'Karakogi kaede ki fuiri' (*A. tataricum*), 368
'Kara koromo', 368
'Kara kurenai', 368
'Kara nishiki', 368
'Kara ori', 160. See 'Kara ori nishiki'
'Kara ori nishiki', **160**, 341
'Karasu gawa', 20, 23, 144, **160**, 341, 354
'Kariba beni', 368
'Karu kaya', 368
'Kasado' (*A. japonicum*), 368
'Kasagi yama', **160–161**, 214, 341
'Kasama gawa', 368
'Kasane jishi', 355
'Kasa nui', 368
'Kasasaki', 368
'Kasatori yama' (*A. sieboldianum*), **326–327**
'Kasen dono', 368
'Kasen nishiki', 20, 23, **162**, 341
'Kasen nishiki fugawari', 368
'Kase odori', 368
'Kashihara', 368
'Kashima', **162**, 341

'Kashima yatubusa', 162.
    See 'Kashima'
'Kashiwa mori', 368
'Kasuga', 368
'Kasugano', 368
'Kasugano nishiki', 368
'Kasuga yama', 368
'Kasumi goromo' (*A. rufin-erve*), 368
'Katja', **163**, 341
'Katsura', **163**, 204, 205
    growth habit of, 22, 189, 355
    in the landscape, 41, 42
    leaf color of, 84, 189, 247, 341, 361
'Katsuragi' (*A. sieboldianum*), 368
'Katsuragi san' (*A. sieboldianum*), 368
'Katsura hime', 355
'Katsurani', 368
'Katsura nishiki', 355
'Katsura yatsubusa', 163.
    See 'Katsura'
'Kawa hara-no-midori', 368
'Kawa hime', 368
'Kawaii' (*A. shirasawanum*), **322**
'Kawa kaze', 368
'Kegon', 368
'Keikan zan' (*A. shirasawanum*), 368
'Keiser', **164**, 341
ìKeiser-Wanabee,î 164. See 'Keiser'
'Ken bu', 368
'Kenkō nishiki', 368
'Kenzan', 355
'Kibune', 355
'Kiev nishiki' (*A. buergerianum*), 368
'Kifu nishiki' (*A. buergerianum*), 362
'Kihachi gire', 368
'Ki hachijō', **73**, **164**, 341
'Kihatsijo', 164. See 'Ki hachijō'
'Kihin nishiki' (*A. pycnanthum*), 315

'Kihou nishiki', 368
'Kikko sho momiji', 368
'Killarney', **164**, 341
'Kim', 368
'Kingsville Red', **164–165**, 341
'Kingsville Variegated', **165**, 341
'Kin kakure' (*A. shirasawanum*), 320, 364
'Kinky Krinkle', **165–166**, 341
'Kin pai', 368
'Kinran', 99, **166**, 169, 342
'Kinshi', **166**, 342, 359
'Kinshi jima', 368
'Kinshō', 368
'Kinshōjō', 368
'Kinugasa yama' (*A. sieboldianum*), **327**
'Kin yo', 368
'Ki oridono-no-nishiki', 368
'Kippō nishiki', 355
'Kiri kagami', 368
'Kiri nishiki', 88, **166–167**, 342
'Kishousan', 356. See 'Ki shūzan'
'Ki shūzan', 355–356
'Kisodani nishiki' (*A. rufin-erve*), 368
'Kitsu shidorie', 368
'Kiyohime', 62, **167–168**, 181, 209, 231, 342, 360
'Kiyohime akame', 368
'Kiyohime yatsubusa', 168.
    See 'Kiyohime'
'Kiyo taki', 368
'Koba nomura', 368
'Koba shōjō', **168**, 342
'Ko beni nishiki', 368
'Kobuchizawa nishiki' (*A. rufinerve*), 368
'Ko chidori', 356
'Kochō nishiki', 113, 115.
    See 'Butterfly'; 'Chiri-men nishiki'
'Kochō-no-mai', 113. See 'Butterfly'
'Kodono', 368

'Kofuji nishiki' (*A. crataegifolium*), 368
'Kogane nishiki', **168**, 342
'Kogane sakae', 42, **168–169**, 342
'Kogane sunago', 168. See 'Kogane nishiki'
'Kohaku iro no', 368
'Ko hauchiwa shidare' (*A. sieboldianum*), 368
'Kōi', 368
'Koide', 368
'Kōi kiyohime', 368
'Koi murasaki', 171. See 'Ko murasaki'
'Koizumi', 368
'Kōkan shikin' (*A. crataegifolium*), 368
'Ko kibune', 368
'Ko kinran', 368
'Kokko', 169. See 'Koko
'Koko', **169**, 342
'Kokobunji nishiki', **169–170**, 342
'Kokono e' (*A. shirasawanum*), 368
'Kokyo', **170**, 342
'Komachi beni', 368
'Komachi hime', **170**, 342
'Komadome', 368
'Koma gaeri', 368
'Koma gaeri beni', 368
'Koma nishiki', 368
'Koma todomi', 368
'Komon nishiki', 94, **170–171**, 342
'Ko murasaki', 90, **171**, 342
'Komyo ji', 368
'Konbu in', 368
'Konde shōjō', 119
'Kongō nishiki' (*A. rufin-erve*), 368
'Kōrai momiji', 368
'Korean Gem', **171–172**, 342
'Koreanum'. 171. See 'Korean Gem'
'Koriba', **172**, 342
'Kōrin', 368
'Korui jishi', 177. See 'Kurui juishi'

'Kōryō', 368
'Kosame-no-nishiki', 368
'Koshibori nishiki', **172–173**, 342
'Koshima', 368
'Koshimino', 143, 145, **173**, 342, 361. Also see 'Hagoromo'
'Koshimino nishiki', 368
'Kōshi miyasami' (*A. buergerianum*), **286**, 290
'Kosui-no-tsuki', 368
'Kotobuki', 368
'Kotobuki hime', 368
'Kotohime', 22, 138, 139, 150, 170, **173–174**, 342, 361
'Kotohime yatsubusa', 174.
    See 'Kotohime'
'Koto ito komachi', 22, 69, 129, **174–175**, 342
'Koto ito yatsubusa', 368
'Kotoji nishiki', 368
'Koto kubunji', 368
'Koto maru', **175**, 342, 352
'Koto mura', 175. See 'Koto maru'
'Koto-no-ito', 128, **175–176**, 216, 342
'Kōyamadani nishiki', 368
'Kōya san', **176**, 342
'Kōyō ao shidare', 368
'Kōzuhara nishiki' (*A. sieboldianum*), 368
'Kōzui gawa', 368
'Kuchi ba' (*A. pictum*), 368
'Kuchibeni', 236. See 'Shigarami'
'Kuchi beni nishiki', 356
'Kuchibeni zukashi', 368
'Kuchiheni', 368
'Kujaku bato' (*A. japonicum*), 368
'Kujaku myo o' (*A. japonicum*), 368
'Kujaku nishiki' (*A. japonicum*), 303, **307**
'Kujaku nishiki akame' (*A. japonicum*), 368
'Kumoi nishiki' (*A. sieboldianum*), 368

'Kuni-no-sato', 368
'Kurabeyama', 176. See 'Kurabu yama'
'Kurabu yama', **176**, 342
'Kureha', 356. See 'Kurenai'
'Kurenai', 356
'Kurenai jishi', 368
'Kurenai-no-ho', 368
'Kure yama', 368
'Kuro hime', **176**, 342
'Kurokami yama', 368
'Kuro kogo beni' (*A. rufinerve*), 368
'Kuro koma', 368
'Kuro wu yama', 368
'Kurui jishi', **177**, 342, 351
'Kusa momiji', 368
'Kyōgoku shidare', 356
'Kyō kibune', 368
'Kyokiuzu', 368
'Kyo nishiki' (*A. rufinerve*), 317
'Kyō-no-aki', 368
'Kyōryū', 356
'Kyra', 368
'Kyūden' (*Acer buergerianum*), **286**
'Kyu ei nishiki', 354. See 'Hisae nishiki'

'Laciniatum' (*A. japonicum*), 305
'Laciniatum Purpureum', 147. See 'Hessei'
'Lady's Choice', 368
'Lana' (*A. cissifolium*), 368
'Latifolium Purpureum', 147, 227. See 'Sanguineum'
'Latilobatum', 176. See 'Koto-no-ito'
'Laura's Love', 368
'Lazy Leaf', 368
'Leather Leaf', 356
'Lemon Chiffon', 356
'Lemon Lime Lace', **177–178**, 342
'Lineare', 241. See 'Shinobuga oka'
'Linearifolium', 241. See

'Shinobuga oka'
'Linearilobum', 241. See 'Shinobuga oka'
'Linearilobum Purpureum', 92. See 'Atrolineare'
'Linearilobum Rubrum', 92. See 'Atrolineare'
'Lin-ling', 368
'Lionheart', **178**, 342
'Lion's Heart', 178. See 'Lionheart'
'Little Gem' (*A. circinatum*), **295–296**
'Little Green Star' (*A. shirasawanum*), 364
'Little Heart', 368
'Little Joe' (*A. circinatum*), 368
'Littleleaf', 188
'Little Little Gem' (*A. circinatum*), 368
'Little Princess', 181. See 'Chiyo hime'; 'Kiyohime'; 'Mapi-no-machi hime'
'Lobatum', 368
'Lockington Gem', 356
'Long Man', **178**, 342
'Lozita', **179**, 342
'Lucky Star', 356–357
'Luteovariegatum' (*A. rufinerve*), 317
'Lutescens', **179**, 342
'Luteum', 179. See 'Lutescens'
'Lydia', 357

'Machi kaze', 185. See 'Matsu kaze'
'Machiyou', 185. See 'Matsuyoi'
'Macranthum' (*A. japonicum*), 368
'Macrocarpum' (*A. japonicum*), 368
'Macrophyllum' (*A. japonicum*), 368
'Macrophyllum Aureum' (*A. shirasawanum*), 320

'Magnificum' (*A. japonicum*), 368
'Maiko', **179–180**, 342
'Maiku jaku' (*A. japonicum*), 303
'Mai mori', **180**, 342
'Maioka', 180. See 'Maiko'
'Maki tatsu yama', 368
'Makimuku', 368
'Maki-no-ha', 368
'Mallet', 368
'Malon', 357
'Mama', **180–181**, 342
'Mama nishiki', 368
'Manyō-no-sato', **181**, 342
'Maoka', 180. See 'Maiko'
'Mapi-no-machi hime', **181**, 342
'Maragumo', 182. See 'Marakumo'
'Marakumo', **182**, 343
'Mardi Gras', 368
'Margaret', 357
'Margaret B', 182. See 'Margaret Bee'
'Margaret Bee', **182**, 343
'Marginatum' (*A. palmatum*), 237. See 'Shigitatsu sawa'
'Marginatum' (*A. rufinerve*), 316
'Marjan', **182–183**, 343
'Marlo', 368
'Marmoratum' (*A. palmatum*), 237. See 'Shigitatsu sawa'
'Marmoratum' (*A. pictum*), 363
'Marmoratum' (*A. rufinerve*), 316
'Martha's Ghost', 368
'Marubatō kaede' (*A. buergerianum*), **287**
'Marusame', 145. See 'Harusame'
'Mary Eddinglow', 368
'Mary Katherine', 357
'Masago' (*A. crataegifolium*), 368
'Masa yoshi', 368

'Masu kagami', **183**, 343
'Masu murasaki', **183–184**, 343
'Matoi nishiki', 369
'Matsugae', 20, 25, **184**, 343
'Matsu kase', 185. See 'Matsu kaze'
'Matsu kaze', **184–185**, 343
'Matsu kubo', 369
'Matsumura saki', 184. See 'Masu murasaki'
'Matsu-no-tsuki', 369
'Matsuo', 369
'Matsuyoi', **185**, 343
'Matthew', **185–186**, 343
'Matu kase', 369
'Meckelii' (*A. japonicum*), 369
'Meguri ai' (*A. rufinerve*), 369
'Mei hō', **186**, 343
'Mei hō nishiki', 357
'Meiō nishiki', 369
'Mejishi', 201, 242
'Melanie', 357
'Meoto', 357–358
'Meshime-no-uchi shidare', 88. See 'Ao shime-no-uchi shidare'
'Metallic Gold' (*A. maximowiczianum*), 369
'Meuri kaede-no-fuiri' (*A. crataegifolium*), 300
'Meuri ko fuba' (*A. crataegifolium*), **299–300**
'Meuri-no-ōfu' (*A. crataegifolium*), 299
'Meuri ōmadora' (*A. crataegifolium*), 369
'Michi shiruhe', 369
'Michi zome', 369
'Microphyllum' (*A. shirasawanum*), 319, **322–323**, 324, 325
'Midore mure hibari', 369
'Midori-no-teiboku', **186**, 343
'Midori seigai', 369
'Mikage nishiki' (*A. crataegifolium*), 369

'Mikaki mori', 369
'Mikasa yama' (*A. sieboldianum*), **327**
'Mikasa yama nishiki' (*A. sieboldianum*), 364
'Mikata nishiki', 369
'Mikawa hachijūkyū', 369
'Mikawa kotohime', 187
'Mikawa nishiki', 369
'Mikawa yatsubusa', 150, 154, **187**, 231, 256, 343
'Mikazuki', **187–188**, 343
'Mikita nishiki', 369
'Mikomo nishiki', 369
'Milton Park Broom', 369
'Mima', 369
'Mimaye', 369
'Mimi nashi', 369
'Mimuro', 369
'Mimuro yama', 369
'Minare zao', 369
'Mini Mondo', **188**, 343
'Minnesota Red' (*A. tataricum*), 369
'Minobe gawa', 369
'Mino kasa', 369
'Mino kasa yama', 369
'Mino o', 369
'Minori-no-tsuki' (*A. shirasawanum*), **323**
'Minowa', 369
'Mino yatsubusa' (*A. buergerianum*), **287–288**, 363
'Minus', 243. See 'Shishigashira'
'Mioun', 358
'Mirte', **188**, 343
'Mischa', 369
'Miss Piggy', 358
'Misty Moon', 369
'Misu-no-uchi', 369
'Mitchii', 369
'Mitsuba kaede' (*A. buergerianum*), **288**
'Mitsuba kaede nishiki siyou' (*A. bergerianum*), 288
'Mitsubatō kaede' (*A. buergerianum*), **288**

'Mitsu cha', 369
'Mitsude kaede kifu' (*A. cissifolium*), 369
'Mitsuho beni', 189. See 'Mizuho beni'
'Mitsu kagami', 369
'Mitsu kukri', 369
'Mitsu shika', 369
'Miwa', 369
'Miyabi' (*A. rufinerve*), 369
'Miyabi nishiki', 358
'Miyadono' (*A. buergerianum*), 286
'Miyagino', **189**, 343
'Miyagi yana', 369
'Miyaki no', 369
'Miyako kaeri', 369
'Miyako-no-hana', 369
'Miyama', 369
'Miyasama' (*A. buergerianum*), **288**
'Miyasama kaede' (*A. buergerianum*), 288
'Miyasama kaede yatsubusa' (*A. buergerianum*), 289
'Miyasama nishiki' (*A. buergerianum*), 369
'Miyasama yatsubusa' (*A. buergerianum*), **288–289**
'Miya taki', 369
'Mizuho beni', **189**, 343
'Mizū kagami', 369
'Mizū kiguri', **189–190**, 343
'Mizū kukuri', 369
'Mizū moyo', 369
'Mizū nami nishiki' (*A. rufinerve*), 369
'Mocha Rose' (*A. maximowiczianum*), 369
'Moji suru', 369
'Mokuji', 369
'Momenshide', **190**, 343
'Momichi kasane' (*A. rufinerve*), 369
'Momiji gai' (*A. pictum*), 369
'Momiji gasa' (*A. sieboldianum*), **327–328**
'Momiji gasane' (*A. sieboldianum*), 328

'Momiji gawa', **190**, 343
'Momiju yama', 369
'Momi-no-nami', 369
'Momoiro kōya san', **191**, 343
'Mon dukushi', 369
'Mondy' (*A. tataricum*), 364
'Monju in', 369
'Mon nishiki', 369
'Mo-no-nishiki', 369
'Mono zi gawa', 369
'Mon Papa', **191**, 343
'Monroe' (*A. circinatum*), 294
'Mon tsuki', 369
'Mon tsukushi', 369
'Mon zukushi', **191–192**, 343
'Moonfire', 93, **192**, 208, 343
'Moon Shadow', 369
'Mori-no-miya', 369
'Morogi', 369
'Morogino', 369
'Morogino gawa', 369
'Morton' (*A. miyabei*), 369
'Moto koto-no-ito', 369
'Mozart' (*A. tataricum*), 369
'Mr Sun' (*A. shirasawanum*), **323–324**
'Mufura', 369
'Mugiwara nishiki', 369
'Muka', 369
'Mukō buchi', 369
'Mukō gasa', 369
'Multifidum', 369
'Mume gae', 369
'Muncaster', 369
'Muraguma', 193. See 'Murakumo'
'Muragumo', 193. See 'Murakumo'
'Murakama', 193. See 'Murakumo'
'Murakuma', 193. See 'Murakumo'
'Murakumo', **192–193**, 343
'Murakumo shidare', 369

'Murasaka hime', 193. See 'Murasaki hime'
'Murasaki daka', 369
'Murasaki hime', **193**, 343
'Murasaki iroha', 369
'Murasaki kiyohime', **193–194**, 243, 343
'Murasaki-no-ne', 369
'Murasaki shikibu', 358
'Murasaki taka', 369
'Murasame' (*A. shirasawanum*), 369
'Mure hibari', **194**, 343
'Mure sora suzume', 369
'Mure suzume', 369
'Mure uzura', 369
'Muro gawa', **194**, 343
'Muro kogane', 369
'Muro obene', 369
'Musakaga', 184. See 'Masu kagami'
'Musa kagami', 184. See 'Masu kagami'
'Musa murasaki', 184. See 'Masu murasaki'
'Musashi' (*A. buergerianum*), 363
'Musashi nishiki' (*A. buergerianum*), 369
'Musashino', 91, 134, 148, **194–195**, 235, 343, 358
'Musatori yama', 369
'Mushiro momichi', 369
'Mutsu beni', 369
'Mutsu beni shidare', 369
'Mutsu-no-kane', 369
'Myagino', 369
'Myogi san', 369
'Myoi', 185. See 'Matsuyoi'

'Naga ito', 369
'Nagashima' (*A. diabolicum*), 301
'Nagatsuka', 369
'Nagisa hime', 369
'Naguri nishiki' (*A. pictum*), 363
'Nakahara beni', 369
'Naka-no-go', 369
'Nakaoku gawa', 369

'Nakatsu gawa nishiki', 369
'Nana komachi', 369
'Nanase gawa', **195**, 343
'Nanase kawa', 369
'Nanatsu boshi', 369
'Naniwa beni', 369
'Nanjō', 369
'Nankin momiji' (*A. shirasawanum*), 369
'Nanum' (*A. tataricum*), 369
'Nara yama', 369
'Nari hari beni', 369
'Narihira', 369
'Naruo kata', 369
'Naruo nishiki', **195–196**, 343
'Narutō' (*A. buergerianum*), **289**, 290
'Narutō kaede' (*A. buergerianum*), 289
'Narvo nishiki', 196. See 'Naruo nishiki'
'Nasu nishiki', 369
'Nathan', 358
'Natori kawa', 369
'Natsumi gawa', 369
'Ne zami', 369
'Nichi rin', 369
'Nicholsonii', 191, **196**, 272, 343
'Nigrum' (Amoenum Group), **196–197**, 343
'Nigrum' (Dissectum Group), 121. See 'Dissectum Nigrum'
'Nigrum Dissectum', 121. See 'Dissectum Nigrum'
'Nigrum Select', 212
'Nihon beni', 369
'Nihon tō' (*A. tataricum*), 369
'Nikaido', 369
'Nikkō', 369
'Nikkōense' (*A. pictum*), 363
'Nikko shichihenge', 235. See 'Shichihenge'

'Nimura', 369
'Nino kami yama', 369
'Nisaka gawa', 369
'Nishiki gasane', 25, 39, **197**, 343, 355
'Nishiki gawa', 42, 89, 154, **197–198**, 344, 349
'Nishiki gi', 369
'Nishiki kaede' (*A. buergerianum*), 369
'Nishiki momiji', **198**, 344
'Nishiki-no-murasaki', 369
'Nishiki sho', 89. See 'Arakawa'
'Nishiki tatsugawa', 369
'Nishiki yamato', 369
'Nishiki zuru', 369
'Nishitani gawa', 369
'Nobu hime', 369
'Noki bata', 369
'Nokori bi' (*A. buergerianum*), 363
'Nomura', 195. See 'Musashino'
'Nomura kaede', 195. See 'Musashino'
'Nomura kōyō', 358
'Nomura momiji', 369
'Nomura nishiki', 195. See 'Musashino'
'Nomura ōba', 358
'Nomura ōjō', 358. See 'Nomura kōyō'
'Nomura ōrō', 358. See 'Nomura kōyō'
'Nomura shidare', 245. See 'Shōjō shidare'
'Nose gawa', 358
'Noshi', 171. See 'Ko murasaki'
'Noto', 369
'Nou nishiki', 277. See 'Wou nishiki'
'Novum', **198**, 344
'Nukai dake', 370
'Nukata', 370
'Nukata-no-ōkimi', 370
'Nuke botoke', 370
'Nunomi gawa', 370

'Nure garasu', 370
'Nuresagi', *73*, 93, 192, 196, 198, **199**, 208, 344, 351
'Nusatori yama' (*A. buergerianum*), 23, 25, **289–290**
'Nyaku ōji', 370

'Oa hanzashi', 88. See 'Ao kanzashi'
'Obadani gawa', 370
'Oba hachijō', 370
'Oba iroha momiji', 370
'Obata', 370
'Oba uri nishiki' (*A. crataegifolium*), 370
'Oboku', 370
'Oboro zuki', 370
'Obtusum', 370
'Ochikochibito', 370
'Octopus', **199**, 344
'O daki' (*A. japonicum*), 308
'Oda nishiki', 370
'Ogashika', 228. See 'Saoshika'
'Ogi nagashi', 188, **200**, 344
'Ogi-no-nagare', **200**, 344
'Ogi-no-sen' (*A. japonicum*), 370
'Ogi-no-zu', 370
'Ogi tsuma gaki', 370
'Ogon', 370
'Ōgona sarasa', 201. See 'Ōgon sarasa'
'Ogon itaya' (*A. shirasawanum*), 320, 364
'Ogon itaya kaede', 370
'Ogon kunshi', 370
'Ōgon sarasa', **200–201**, 344
'Ogon shidare', 370
'Ogon shidare sekka', 370
'Ogon sunago', 370
'Ogotoi', 370
'Ogura yama' (*A. shirasawanum*), **324**
'Ohara yama', 370
'Oh momiji', 251. See 'Takao'
'Ō isami' (*A. japonicum*), 41, 303, 305, **307–308**

'Oiso nishiki', 370
'Oitaya meigetsu atozae' (*A. shirasawanum*), 370
'Ō izu', 359
'Ō jishi', 137, **201**, 243, 344
'Ō kagami', 190, **201**, 344
'Oki kasane', 370
'Okikoji nishiki', 202. See 'Okukuji nishiki'
'Okimo', 359. See 'Okina'
'Okina', 359
'Okino', 359. See 'Okina'
'Oki-no-nami', 370
'Okishima', 203. See 'Okushimo'
'Oki tsu fune', 370
'Oki tsu nami', 370
'Okukuji nishiki', **202**, 344
'Okushimo', *69*, 115, 177, **202–203**, 344, 350. Also see 'Seigai'
'Okustanea', 203. See 'Okushimo'
'Olga', 370
'Olsen's Frosted Strawberry', 370
'Omara yama', 204. See 'Omure yama'
'Omata shidare', 370
'Omato', **203**, 344
'Ominato', 370
'Omi nishiki', 370
'Omogo nishiki' (*A. pictum*), 370
'Omona', 370
'Omura yama', 204. See 'Omure yama'
'Omure yama', 128, 129, **203–204**, 208, 258, 344
'Omur H', 370
'Oni itayi fuiri' (*A. pictum*), 370
'Oni itayi kifu' (*A. pictum*), 370
'O nishiki', 277. See 'Wou nishiki'
'Oni sudare' (*A. pictum*), 370

'Oo momiji', 370

'O ran', 370

'Orange Dream', 42, **204–205**, 249, 344

'Orangeola', **205**, 344

'Oranges & Lemons', 359

'Oregon', 370

'Oregon Cascade', 370

'Oregon Fern' (*A. japonicum*), **308**

'Oregon Sunset', **205**, 344

'Oridono nishiki', **206**, 268, 344

    bark color of, 23, 92

    growth habit of, 351

    in the landscape, 20

    leaf variegation of, 160, 162, 271, 354

'Oridono-no-nishiki', 370

'Oriental Lace', 370

'Oriental Mystery', 370

'Original Peaches', 370

'Ori hime', 370

'Orika nishiki', 370

'Orion', 359

'Ori san' (*A. sieboldianum*), 370

'Ori zuru', 370

'Ori zuru momofu', 370

'Ornatum', 111, 126, **206–207**, 212, 213, 259, 344, 350

'Ornatum Purpureum', 207. See 'Ornatum'

'O sakai', 370

'Osaka yama', 370

'Ō sakazuki', 21, 33, 42, 141, 151, 203, **207**, 275, 344

'O sakazuki akame', 370

'Ō sakazuki midorime', 207. See 'Ō sakazuki'

'O sakazuki-no-akame', 370

'O sakazuki o', 370

'O sayo shiki', 370

'Ō shidare', 193. See 'Murakumo'

'Oshin kuzu', 370

'Oshio beni', 170, **207–208**, 344

'Oshiu beni', 208. See 'Oshū beni'

'Oshiu shidare', 208. See 'Oshū shidare'

'Oshū beni', **208**, 344

'Oshū shidare' (Dissectum Group), 209

'Oshū shidare' (Matsumurae Group), **208–209**, 344

'Oshuzan', 370

'Oshyu beni', 208. See 'Oshū beni'

'Osiris' (*A. sieboldianum*), 370

'Ō siu shidare', 209. See 'Oshū shidare'

'Ō syu beni', 208. See 'Oshū beni'

'Ō syu shidare', 209. See 'Oshū shidare'

'Otafuku', 370

'Ōtaishaku', 370

'Ō taki' (*A. japonicum*), **308**

'Oto hime', *37*, **209**, 344

'Otome zakura', **209–210**, 344

'Otome zakure', 210. See 'Otome zakura'

'Otto's Dissectum', 370

'Ōuda beni', 370

'Ō urihada', 370

'Owugon shidare', 370

'Owuri yama', 370

'Pacific Fire' (*A. circinatum*), **296–297**

'Pacific Sprite' (*A. circinatum*), 363

'Palmatifidium', 210. See 'Palmatifidum' (*A. palmatum*)

'Palmatifidum' (*A. japonicum*), 305

'Palmatifidum' (*A. palmatum*), 122, 153, 206, **210**, 231, 232, 238, 268, 344

'Palmatifolium' (*A. shira-sawanum*), 319, 321, **324**

'Parsonii' (*A. japonicum*), 305

'Pattern Perfect' (*A. tataricum*), 370

'Paucum', 210. See 'Palmatifidum'

'Paul's Variegate', 359

'Peaches and Cream', **210–211**, 344

'Pendulum', 370

'Pendulum Angustilobum Atropurpureum', 92. See 'Atrolineare'

'Pendulum Atropurpureum', 92. See 'Atrolineare'

'Pendulum Hatsu shigure', 353. See 'Hatsu shigure'

'Pendulum Inazuma', 153. See 'Inazuma'

'Pendulum Julian', *45*, **211**, 344

'Pendulum Matsu kazi', 185. See 'Matsu kaze'

'Pendulum Nigrum', 121. See 'Dissectum Nigrum'

'Pendulum Omure yama', 204. See 'Omure yama'

'Peve Dave', 359

'Peve Limbo', 370

'Peve Multicolor', 359

'Peve Pond', 370

'Philsm', 370

'Phoenix', **211–212**, 344

'Pink Ballerina', **212**, 344

'Pinkedge', 158. See 'Kagiri nishiki'

'Pink Filigree', **212–213**, 344

'Pink Lace', 370

'Pinnatum', 124. See 'Elegans'

'Pixie', 43, 127, **213**, 344

'Platanifolium' (*A. japonicum*), 370

'Princeps' (*A. japonicum*), 370

'Pulchrum', 370

'Pulverulentum' (*A. palmatum*), 370

'Pulverulentum' (*A. tataricum*), 370

'Pung kil', 359

'Pung kill', 359. See 'Pung kil'

'Purple Ghost', **213–214**, 344

'Purple Glory', 370

'Purple Mask', 214, 344

'Purple Splendor', 370

'Purpureum', 214, 344

'Purpureum Angustilobum', 92. See 'Atrolineare'

'Purpureum Superbum', 214. See 'Purpureum'

'Pygmy', 359

'Raigō ji', 370

'Rainbow', 370

'Rakushisha', 370

'Raraflora', **214–215**, 345

'Red Autumn Lace', **215**, 345

'Red Baron', **215**, 345

'Red Blush', 370

'Red Cloud', **215–216**, 345

'Red Crusader', 370

'Red Dawn' (*A. shirasawanum*), 370

'Red Dragon', 27, **216**, 345

'Red Elf', **216–217**, 345

'Red Emperor', 127. See 'Emperor 1'

'Red Falcon', 370

'Red Feathers', 370

'Red Filigree Lace', 35, **217–218**, 345

'Red Flash', **218**, 345

'Red Jonas', 359

'Red Lace', 218. See 'Red Filigree Lace'

'Red Pygmy', **22**, *69*, **218–219**, 345, 359

    growth habit of, 22, 92, 216, 269, 276

    leaf color of, 128, 276

'Red Ribbon Leaf', 370
Red Rhapsody™ (*A. tataricum*), 364. See 'Mondy' (*A. tataricum*)
'Red Rocket', 370
'Red Select', 153. See 'Inaba shidare'
'Red Spider', **219**, 345
'Red Spray', **219**, 345
'Red Star', 370
'Red Strata', 359
'Red Willow', 354. See 'Hupp's Red Willow'
'Red Wing' (*A. tataricum*), 370
'Red Wonder', 370
'Red Wood', 42, **219–220**, 345
'Renjaku', 370
'Renjaku maru', 360
'Reticulatum', 237. See 'Shigitatsu sawa'
'Reticulatum Como', *36*, **220**, 345
'Reticulatum Purple', 370
'Reticulatum Rubrum', 370
'Rhode Island Red', 360
'Rhodoneurum', 370
'Ribescifolium', 243. See 'Shishigashira'
'Ribesifolium', 243. See 'Shishigashira'
'Rilas Red', 260
'Rin Ka', 370
'Rising Sun', 370
'Rokka on', 370
'Rokugatsu en nishiki', **220**, 345
'Rokumonji', 370
'Rosamarginalis', 158. See 'Kagiri nishiki'
'Rosavariegata', 158. See 'Kagiri nishiki'
'Roscoe Red', 198. See 'Novum'
'Roseomaculatum', 268. See 'Versicolor'
'Roseomarginatum', 148, 158. See 'Hikasa yama'; 'Kagiri nishiki'

'Roseopictum', 158. See 'Kagiri nishiki'
'Roseotricolor', 158. See 'Kagiri nishiki'
'Roseovariegata', 158. See 'Kagiri nishiki'
'Roseovariegatum', 268. See 'Versicolor'
'Roseum', 268. See 'Versicolor'
'Roseum Ornatum', 360
'Royal', 221. See 'Royle'
'Royale', 221. See 'Royle'
'Royle', **221**, 345
'Rubellum', 222. See 'Rubrifolium'
'Ruben', 360
'Rubricaule', 370
'Rubrifolium', **221–222**, 345
'Rubrinerve', 370
'Rubrolatifolium', 227. See 'Sanguineum'
'Rubrum' (*A. palmatum*), **222**, 345
'Rubrum' (*A. tataricum*), 370
'Rubrum Kaiser', 370
'Ruby Lace' (*A. palmatum*), 217. See 'Red Filigree Lace'
'Ruby Lace' (*A. tataricum*), 370
'Ruby Ridge', **222–223**, 345
'Ruby Star', 100
'Rufescens', **223**, 345
'Rugosa', 224. See 'Rugose'
'Rugose', **223–224**, 345
'Rugose Select', 370
'Ruslyn-in-the-Pink', 370
'Ruth Murray', 370
'Ruth's Red', 360
'Ryokka meuri' (*A. crataegifolium*), 370
'Ryokurin' zan', 370
'Ryoku ryū', **224**, 345
'Ryū gan', 370
'Ryūgan nishiki', 370
'Ryū gu', 370
'Ryūku u', 370
'Ryūmon nishiki', **224–225**, 345

'Ryū sei', **225**, 345
'Ryūsen', 370
'Ryūsho in', 370
'Ryūto', 370
'Ryū un kaku', 370
'Ryūzu', **225**, 255, 345, 353

'Sagami', 370
'Sagamihara nishiki' (*A. buergerianum*), 370
'Sagara nishiki', 197. See 'Nishiki gasane'
'Saihō', 370
'Sainan in yukon', 370
'Saint Jean', 360
'Saintpaulianum', 197. See 'Nishiki gasane'
'Saka meuri' (*A. crataegifolium*), 370
'Saku', 236. See 'Shigarami'
'Sakura', 370
'Sakura ga e', 370
'Sakura hime', 360
'Sakura-no-sato', 370
'Samari', 106. See 'Beni shigitatsu sawa'
'Samidare', **225–226**, 345
'Samurai', 106. See 'Beni shigitatsu sawa'
'Samurai Sword', 370
'Sa mushiro', 370
'Sandra', **226**, 345
'Sango asahi zuru', 370
'Sango kaku', 101, 117, **226–227**, 276, 345, 355
   bark color of, 41, 49, 100, 219, 277
   growth habit of, 122
   in the landscape, 42, 89, 109, 317
   leaf color of, 84, 155, 277
   witches'-brooms on, 133
'Sango kaku Dwarf', 133. See 'Fjellheim'
'Sango nishiki', 370
'Sango tsu', 370
'Sanguineum', 222, **227**
'Sanguineum Chishio', 115. See 'Chishio'

'Sanguineum Seigai', 230. See 'Seigai'
'Sanuki hime', 370
'Sao hime', 370
'Saoshika', **227–228**, 345
'Saotome', **228**, 345
'Sao yama', 370
'Sasa nami', 371
'Satoaki shidare', 371
'Satō kaede' (*A. rufinerve*), 371
'Satō-no-ha', 371
'Satō shidare', 371
'Satō shigure', 371
'Satsuki beni' (*A. palmatum*), **228–229**, 345
'Satsuki beni' (*A. pictum*), 363
'Satzuki beni' (*A. pictum*), 363. See 'Satsuki beni' (*A. pictum*)
'Sa utome', 371
'Sawa chidori', **229**, 345
'Sawa gani', 371
'Sawa ibuki', 371
'Sawa-no-kani', 371
'Sayo chidori', 371
'Sayo ginu' (*A. sieboldianum*), 364
'Sayo goromo', 371
'Sayo shigure' (*A. shirasawanum*), **324–325**
'Sayu yama', 371
'Sazame koto', 371
'Sazanami', **229**, 345
'Scarlet Wonder', 371
'Schichigosan', 239. See 'Shime-no-uchi'
'Schichihenge', 235. See 'Shichihenge'
'Schmidt', 371
'Scolopendrifolium', 128, 215, 241. See 'Shinobuga oka'
'Scolopendrifolium Purpureum', 92. See 'Atrolineare'
'Scolopendrifolium Rubrum', 92. See 'Atrolineare'

'Scolopendrifolium Viride', 241. See 'Shinobuga oka'
'Scotum Roseum', 371
'Searle's Variegated', 371
'Seido hokori', 371
'Sei fu', 371
'Seigai', 20, 42, 103, **230**, 345
'Seigaiha', 230. See 'Seigai'
'Seigen', **230–231**, 345
'Sei hime', 371
'Seijaku', 371
'Seika ha', 231. See 'Seigen'
'Seika nishiki', 87. See 'Aoba nishiki'
'Seiren ji gawa', 371
'Seiryū', 178, **231**, 345
'Seiryū nishiki', 371
'Sei sunouchi', 371
'Seiun kaku', **231–232**, 346
'Seiwen kaku', 232. See 'Seiun kaku'
'Sekaiha', 230. See 'Seigai'
'Sekimori', 88, **232**, 346
'Seki sho', 371
'Sekka yatsubusa', **232–233**, 346, 356
'Select Red', 153. See 'Inaba shidare'
'Seme-no-hane', 233. See 'Semi-no-hane'
'Semi-no-hane', **233**, 346
'Senkaki', 227. See 'Sango kaku'
'Senski', 371
'Sensu' (*A. shirasawanum*), **325**
'Sensu agasi', 371
'Septemlobum Elegans', 124. See 'Elegans'
'Septemlobum Rubrum', 222. See 'Rubrum' (*A. palmatum*)
'Septemlobum Sakazuki', 207. See 'Ō sakazuki'
'Septemlobum Sanguineum', 227. See 'Sanguineum'
'Seuss's Sister', 371

'Seuss's Son', 371
'Shadow Selection', 371
'Shaina', 35, 127, **233–234**, 346
'Shakudo', 371
'Sharon', 360
'Sharp's Pygmy', 35, 85, **234**, 346, 358
'Sheerwater Flame', 235. See 'Sherwood Flame'
'Sheila' (*A. cissifolium*), 371
'Sherwood Elfin', 371
'Sherwood Flame', **234–235**, 346
'Shichi goni', 371
'Shichihenge', **235**, 346
'Shichmenzan' (*A. sieboldianum*), 371
'Shidaba Gold', 236. See 'Shidava Gold'
'Shidare' (*A. sieboldianum*), 371
'Shidare kaede', 371
'Shidare momichi', 371
'Shidava Gold', 43, **235–236**, 346
'Shien', 371
'Shigarami', **236**, 254, 346
'Shigi', 371
'Shigi-no-hoshi', **236–237**, 346
'Shigi-no-mai', 371
'Shigitatsu', 237. See 'Shigitatsu sawa'
'Shigitatsu sawa', 105, **237**, 346
   growth habit of, 236
   leaf color of, 90, 220, 352
   reticulated veins of, 229, 359, 363, 364
   seedlings of, 24, 211, 214
'Shigure bato', 165, **237–238**, 346
'Shigure-no-hato', 371
'Shigure yama', 371
'Shigure zome', **238**, 346
'Shigure zono', 238. See 'Shigure zome'
'Shikage ori nishiki', **238–239**, 346

'Shikai nami', 371
'Shika momiji', 371
'Shikarami', 371
'Shikishima', 371
'Shikure yama', 371
'Shima kakure', 371
'Shima momichi', 371
'Shimauri kaede' (*A. morifolium*), 371
'Shime-no-aka, 371
'Shime-no-ao' (*A. morifolium*), 371
'Shime nomura', 371
'Shime-no-uchi', **239**, 346
'Shimo furi nishiki', 371
'Shimon nishiki', 371
'Shina kawa', 371
'Shinamata', 371
'Shin aocha nishiki', 371
'Shin chishio', **239–240**, 346
'Shin deshōjō', 119, 212, **240**, 346, 350
   in the landscape, 20, 42
   leaf color of, 102, 103, 115, 239
'Shin hikasa', 371
'Shin hoshi zukiyo' (*A. pictum*), 371
'Shinideshiojo', 240. See 'Shin deshōjō'
'Shinju', 371
'Shinjuku shidare', 371
'Shin koba shōjō', 371
'Shin kotohime', 371
ìShinn's #2,î 148
'Shinobu', 371
'Shinobuga oka', **69**, 88, **241**, 346
'Shinobu nishiki', 371
'Shinofu', 371
'Shin ogi', 371
'Shinonome', **241–242**, 346, 360
'Shin seyu', 371
'Shin taimin', 371
'Shin toyama', 371
'Shin tōyō nishiki' (*A. buergerianum*), 371
'Shin tsuzure nishiki', 371

'Shioname', 242. See 'Shinonome'
'Shio-no-name', 371
'Shirakami nishiki', 371
'Shira kumo', 371
'Shira Lace', 371
'Shiraname', **242**, 346
'Shiranami', 242. See 'Shiraname'
'Shira Red' (*A. shirasawanum*), 371
'Shira tama', 371
'Shirayuki' (*A. rufinerve*), **317**
'Shirayuki hime' (*A. rufinerve*), 371
'Shirazz', 136, **242**, 346
'Shirley Debacq' (*A. buergerianum*), 363
'Shirofu nishiki', 371
'Shirofu uriha nishiki' (*A. rufinerve*), 371
'Shiro nishiki', 371
'Shiro tai', 371
'Shi ryu', 371
'Shishigashira', 22, *34*, 201, **242–243**, 261, 346
'Shishigashira-no-yatsubusa', 371
'Shishi hime', 244. See 'Shishio hime'
'Shishimen zan', 371
'Shishio', 115. See 'Chishio'
'Shishio hime', **243–244**, 346
'Shishio Improved', 240. See 'Shin chishio'
'Shishi yatsubusa', 187. See 'Mikawa yatsubusa'
'Shi taka', 371
'Shiyuka', 371
'Sho chiku bai', 371
'Shohrei kiji', 371
'Shōjō', 93, 119, **244**, 346
'Shōjō momichi', 371
'Shōjō nishiki', 371
'Shōjō-no-mai', **244–245**, 346
'Shōjō nomura', 215, **245**, 346

'Shōjō shidare', **245**, 346
'Shoku-no-nishiki', 371
'Shōnan nishiki', 371
'Shorty's Red', 371
'Shōryaku ji', 371
'Shōryū-no-tsume' (*A. sieboldianum*), 371
'Shouman nishiki', 371
'Shōwa-no-mai', 371
'Shuen nishiki' (*A. truncatum*), 331
'Shūfuki nishiki', 371
'Shufu nishiki' (*A. rufinerve*), 316
'Shūhū nishiki' (*A. truncatum*), 331
'Shū ka', 371
'Shū shidare', **245–246**, 346
'Shūzan ko', 354. See 'Hondo ji'
'Shūzan ko hondoshi', 371
'Shuzen ji', 371
'Siecha', 87. See 'Aoba nishiki'
'Siecha nishiki', 87. See 'Aoba nishiki'
'Silver Lace', 131. See 'Filigree'
'Sinobuga oka', 241. See 'Shinobuga oka'
'Sinuatum', 279. See 'Yezo nishiki'
'Sioiou nomura', 245. See 'Shōjō nomura'
'Sir Happy', 361
'Sister Ghost', **246**, 346
'Skeeter's Broom', 216, **246–247**, 346
'Snow Goose' (*A. buergerianum*), 371
'Sode gakure' (*A. shirasawanum*), 371
'Sode nishiki', **247**, 346
'Sode-no-nami', 371
'Sode-no-uchi' (*A. sieboldianum*), **328**
'Sode shigarami', 371
'Soiou nomura', 245. See 'Shōjō nomura'

'Soma-no-kawa', 371
'Soma yama', 371
'Some ito', 371
'Someno', 371
'Some tono', 371
'Soni', 371
'Sono hara', 371
'Sonya Marie' (*A. shirasawanum*), 371
'Spider', 371
'Spiderleaf', 207. See 'Ornatum'
'Sport', 371
'Spring Delight', **247**, 346
'Spring Festival' (*A. buergerianum*), 371
'Spring Fire', 117. See 'Corallinum'
'Spring Surprise', 371
'Squitty', **247**, 346
'Stella Rossa', 212, **248**, 346
'Striatum', 237. See 'Shigitatsu sawa'
'Subintegrum' (*A. buergerianum*), **290**
'Sue's Surprise' (*A. buergerianum*), 285
'Sugawara', 371
'Suisei', 361
'Sulphureum', 134. See 'Flavescens'
'Sumi nagashi', **248–249**, 347
'Sumi shidare', 371
'Summer Gold', 41, **249**, 347
'Summer Splendour' (*A. tataricum*), 371
'Summer Sunset', 371
'Sunaga sawa', 371
'Suncrest Broom', 371
'Sunglow' (*A. circinatum*), **297**
'Sunny Sister' (*A. circinatum*), 363
'Sunrise', 95. See 'Aureum' (*A. palmatum*)
'Sunset', **249–250**, 347
'Sunshine', **250**, 347

'Superbum', 94. See 'Attraction'
'Super Red', 371
'Super Ruby', 371
'Suruga nishiki', 371
'Suru sumi', 371
'Susan', 361
'Susanne' (*A. shirasawanum*), **325**
'Suzaku mon', 371
'Suzu kaze', 371
'Suzu maru', 361
'Syoiou', 244. See 'Shōjō'
'Syoiou noumura', 245. See 'Shōjō nomura'
'Syojo', 244. See 'Shōjō'
'Syojo shidare', 245. See 'Shōjō shidare'
'Syoku-no-nishiki', 371
'Syonan nishiki', 371

'Taihai', 207. See 'Ō sakazuki'
'Taima', 371
'Taima beni', 371
'Taimei', 371
'Taimei nishiki', 371
'Taimin', **250**, 347
'Taimin nishiki', 33, **250–251**, 347
'Taimin nomura', 371
'Taishaku ten' (*A. pictum*), 371
'Tai sokai' (*A. rufinerve*), 371
'Taiyō' (*A. japonicum*), 308
'Taiyō nishiki', **251**, 347
'Taiyō nishiki kawahira', 371
'Taiyū' (*A. sieboldianum*), 371
'Takagi yama', 372
'Takamado yama', 372
'Takami yama', 372
'Takao', **251**, 347
'Takao beni', 372
'Takao nomura', 372
'Takao san', 372
'Takao zome', 372

'Takara-no-kuni', 372
'Takara yama', 372
'Takasago', 372
'Taka tame', 372
'Takatori', 372
'Takawo momiji', 251. See 'Takao'
'Takigo', 372
'Takiniyama', 254. See 'Tamuke yama'
'Taki-no-gawa', **252**, 307, 347
'Taki-no-o' (*A. pictum*), 372
'Takitani gawa' (*A. japonicum*), 372
'Tama hime', 231, **252**, 347
'Tama nishiki', 25, **252**, 347
'Tama-no-awayuki', 372
'Tama-no-nishiki', 372
'Tama-no-o', 372
'Tamaori nishiki', **252–253**, 347
'Tama sudare', 372
'Tama wata', 372
'Tamoto-no-nishiki', 372
'Tamoto tsuta', 372
'Tamuke yama', **67**, 216, **253–254**, 347
'Tana', 236, **254**, 255, 347
'Tanabata', **254–255**, 333
'Tana hata', 372
'Tanchō' (*A. buergerianum*), **290**, 347
'Tancho kaede' (*A. buergerianum*), 290
'Tanigawa dake', 372
'Tanise', 372
'Tansyanno nishiki', 372
'Taro yama', 43, **255**, 347
'Tate ito', 372
'Tate nami', 372
'Tate zukushi', 372
'Tatsuta gawa', **255–256**, 347
'Tatsuta gire', 372
'Tattoo', **256**, 347
'Tawara moto', 372
'Taylor', **256**, 347
'Tayome nishiki', 372

'Tedori gawa', 372
'Teika', 372
'Tendō, 257, 347
'Tennō ji', 372
'Tennyo-no-hoshi', 87, 251, **257**, 347, 352
'Tenri', 372
'Tensyanno nishiki' (*A. tataricum*), 372
'Tenzan nishiki' (*A. tataricum*), 372
'Tequila Sunset', 372
'Teri ha, **257–258**, 347
'Teutcheri', 372
'Tezome-no-ito', 372
'The Bishop', **258**, 347
'Thomas Akao', 372
'Tiger Rose', **258–259**, 347
'Tiny Leaf', 43, 188, **259**, 347. See 'Mini Mondo'; 'Ogi nagashi'
'Tiny Tim', 113, 361
'Tobi hino', 372
'Tobi hino nishiki', 372
'Tobiosho', **259**, 347
'Tōdai ji', 372
'Tōgen kyo', 372
'Tōhoku shichihenge', 372
'Tōjō gawa', 372
'Tōkai nishiki' (*A. pycnanthum*), 372
'Tōkamachi', 372
'Tokao', 251. See 'Takao'
'Tōkin', 372
'Tokiwa' (*A. pictum*), 372
'Tokiwa nishiki' (*A. pictum*), **313–314**
'Tokiwa-no-nishiki' (*A. pictum*), 372
'Tokonatsu', 372
'Tokyo yatsubusa', 174. See 'Kotohime'
'Toma yakata', 372
'Tomio', 372
'Tō-no-mine', 372
'Torimi yama', 372
'Tori-no-o', 372
'Tortuosum' (*A. sieboldianum*), 364

'Toshi', 97. See 'Azuma murasaki'
'Tō shidare' (*A. buergerianum*), 372
'Tō shinobu', 372
'Toune mine', 372
'Toyama', 39, **259**, 347
'Toyama nishiki', **259–260**, 347
'Toyama-no-nishiki', 372
'Toyo nishiki' (*A. buergerianum*), 285
'Toyora dera', 372
'Tricolor' (*A. pictum*), 372
'Tricolor' (*A. truncatum*), 331
'Trompenburg', 41, **69**, 141, 142, **260–261**, 277, 278, 321, 347
'Trompenson', 372
'Tsia nishiki', 372
'Tsubame kaeshi', 372
'Tsuchigumo', 22, 165, **261**, 347
'Tsūden', 372
'Tsugara fubuki' (*A. pictum*), 372
'Tsuge', 372
'Tsukasa nishiki', 372
'Tsukasa Silhouette', 372
'Tsukasa yatsubusa', 372
'Tsuki ga se', 372
'Tsukomo', **37**, 150, **261**, 347
'Tsukubane', **262**, 347
'Tsukuha ne', 372
'Tsukuma no', 351, 361
'Tsuka mano', 361. See 'Tsukuma no'
'Tsukushi gata', **262**, 347
'Tsuma beni', 25, **262–263**, 347
'Tsuma gaki', 20, **263**, 347
'Tsuma goto', 372
'Tsuma zome', 372
'Tsumma jio', 372
'Tsuno moji', 372
'Tsuri nishiki', **263–264**, 348
'Tsuru', 372

'Tsuru nishiki', 372
'Tsuru-no-mai', 372
'Tsuta katsura', 372
'Tsuta-no-ha', 372
'Tsuten', 372
'Tsutsui', 372
'Tsuyu-no-tama', 372
'Tsuzure nishiki', 372
'Twisted Spider', **264**, 348, 355
'Twombley's Red Sentinel', 372

'Uchimaki gawa', 372
'Uchiwa nagashi', 372
'Uchi yukashi', 372
'Uda', 372
'Uda gawa', 372
'Uda hatsu yuki' (*A. rufinerve*), 372
'Uda kinsen', 372
'Uda kogane', 372
'Uda matsukaze', 372
'Uda mure hibari', 372
'Uda shinku', 372
'Ueno homare', 42, **264–265**, 348
'Ueno-no-homare', 265. See 'Ueno homare'
'Ueno yama', 265. See 'Ueno homare'
'Ueno yatsubusa', 372
'Ueshima momiji', 372
'Ugashi gawa', 372
'Ukashi-no-sato', 372
'Ukigumo', 24, **265**, 285, 348
'Uki gumo kawariba', 372
'Uki kogane' (*A. sieboldianum*), 372
'Ukigumo nishiki', 265. See 'Ukigumo'
'Ukon', 89. See 'Aoyagi'
'Ukon nishiki', 89. See 'Aoyagi'
'Umegae', **265–266**, 348
'Umegai', 266. See 'Umegae'
'Uncle Ghost', 41, **266**, 348
'Uncle Red', 372

'Unebi', 361
'Unka', 372
'Uno gawa', 372
'Ura beni', 372
'Ura heni', 372
'Urajiro itaya kifu' (*A. pictum*), 372
'Urajiro itaya shirofu' (*A. pictum*), 372
'Uranihon' (*A. pictum*), 372
'Ura-no-tomaya', 372
'Uriha nishiki' (*A. rufinerve*), 316
'Urika nishiki', 372
'Ushi-no-tsume', 372
'Us murasaki', 372
'Usu beni shidare', 372
'Usu goromo', 372
'Usugumo' (*A. pictum*), **314**, 363
'Usugumori' (*A. pictum*), 314
'Usu kaki', 372
'Usu midori', 361
'Uta fuku', 372
'Uta hime', 372
'Utakata', 372
'Utano', 372
'Utano hatsu yuki' (*A. rufinerve*), 372
'Utano homare', 372
'Utano koshimino', 372
'Utano-no-sato', 372
'Utano shinku', 372
'Uta yama', 372
'Utsura-no-ha', 372
'Utsuri beni', 372
'Utsu semi', **266**, 348
'Uzen nishiki', 372

'Van den Akker', 361–362
'Van der Maat', 372
'Vandermoss Red', **266–267**, 348
'Vanhouttei', 372
'Variegatum' (*A. crataegifolium*), 300
'Variegatum' (*A. palmatum*), 267, 348